Textbook of
Psychoanalysis

Textbook of Psychoanalysis

Edited by

Edward Nersessian, M.D.
Training and Supervising Analyst,
New York Psychoanalytic Institute;
Clinical Associate Professor of Psychiatry,
New York Hospital–Cornell Medical Center
New York, New York

Richard G. Kopff, Jr., M.D.
Faculty, New York Psychoanalytic Institute;
Clinical Assistant Professor of Psychiatry,
New York Hospital–Cornell Medical Center
New York, New York

Washington, DC
London, England

Note: The authors have worked to ensure that all information in this book concerning drug dosages, schedules, and routes of administration is accurate as of the time of publication and consistent with standards set by the U.S. Food and Drug Administration and the general medical community. As medical research and practice advance, however, therapeutic standards may change. For this reason and because human and mechanical errors sometimes occur, we recommend that readers follow the advice of a physician who is directly involved in their care or the care of a member of their family.

Copyright © 1996 American Psychiatric Press, Inc.
ALL RIGHTS RESERVED
Manufactured in the United States of America on acid-free paper
99   98   97   96   4   3   2   1
First Edition

American Psychiatric Press, Inc.
1400 K Street, N.W., Washington, DC   20005

Library of Congress Cataloging-in-Publication Data
   Textbook of Psychoanalysis /   edited by Edward Nersessian, Richard
   G. Kopff, Jr.
       p.   cm.
   Includes bibliographical references and index.
   ISBN 0-88048-507-8
   1. Psychoanalysis. 2. Psychoanalytic interpretation. I. Nersessian,
   Edward. II. Kopff, Richard G.
   [DNLM: 1. Psychoanalysis. 2. Freudian Theory. WM 460 T355 1995]
   RC504.T44 1995
   616.89'17—dc20
   DNLM/DLC
   for Library of Congress   95-8218
                                                                          CIP

British Library Cataloguing in Publication Data
A CIP record is available from the British Library.

Contents

Section II
Psychoanalytic Theory of Psychopathology

Section V
Current Topics of Special
Interest to Psychoanalysts

Contributors

Jacob A. Arlow, M.D.
Training and Supervising Analyst, New York Psychoanalytic Institute; Clinical Professor of Psychiatry, New York University, New York, New York

Charles Brenner, M.D.
Training and Supervising Analyst, New York Psychoanalytic Institute, New York, New York; Clinical Professor of Psychiatry, State University of New York—Brooklyn, Brooklyn, New York

Stanley J. Coen, M.D.
Training and Supervising Analyst, Columbia University Center for Psychoanalytic Training and Research; Clinical Professor of Psychiatry, Columbia University College of Physicians and Surgeons, New York, New York

Paul A. Dewald, M.D.
Training and Supervising Analyst, St. Louis Psychoanalytic Institute; Clinical Professor of Psychiatry, St. Louis University School of Medicine, St. Louis, Missouri

James S. Grotstein, M.D.
Training and Supervising Analyst, Los Angeles Psychoanalytic Institute and the Psychoanalytic Center of California, Los Angeles; Clinical Professor of Psychiatry, University of California—Los Angeles School of Medicine, Los Angeles, California

Judy L. Kantrowitz, Ph.D.
Training and Supervising Analyst, Boston Psychoanalytic Institute; Adjunct Associate Professor, Graduate School of Clinical Psychology, Boston University; Assistant Clinical Professor, Department of Psychiatry, Harvard Medical School, Boston, Massachusetts

Richard G. Kopff, Jr., M.D.
Faculty, New York Psychoanalytic Institute; Clinical Assistant Professor of Psychiatry, New York Hospital–Cornell Medical Center, New York, New York

Robert J. Leider, M.D.
Training and Supervising Analyst, The Institute for Psychoanalysis of Chicago; Assistant Professor of Psychiatry, Northwestern University Medical School, Evanston, Illinois

Carol C. Nadelson, M.D.
Professor of Psychiatry, Harvard Medical School, Boston, Massachusetts; Editor-in-Chief, American Psychiatric Press, Inc., Washington, D.C.; Member, Boston Psychoanalytic Society, Boston, Massachusetts

Edward Nersessian, M.D.
Training and Supervising Analyst, New York Psychoanalytic Institute; Clinical Associate Professor of Psychiatry, New York Hospital–Cornell Medical Center, New York, New York

John M. Oldham, M.D.
Director, New York Psychiatric Institute; Professor and Associate Chairman, Department of Psychiatry, Columbia University College of Physicians and Surgeons; Training and Supervising Analyst, Columbia University Center for Psychoanalytic Training and Research, New York, New York

Ethel Spector Person, M.D.
Training and Supervising Analyst, Columbia University Center for Psychoanalytic Training and Research; Professor of Clinical Psychiatry, Columbia University College of Physicians and Surgeons, New York, New York

Michael S. Porder, M.D.
Training and Supervising Analyst, New York Psychoanalytic Institute; Associate Clinical Professor of Psychiatry, Mt. Sinai School of Medicine, New York, New York

Leo Rangell, M.D.
Training and Supervising Analyst, Los Angeles Psychoanalytic Institute; Clinical Professor of Psychiatry, University of California—Los Angeles, Los Angeles, California; Clinical Professor of Psychiatry (Psychoanalysis), University of California—San Francisco, San Francisco, California

Morton F. Reiser, M.D.
Training and Supervising Analyst, Western New England Institute for Psychoanalysis; Albert E. Kent Professor of Psychiatry (Emeritus), Yale University School of Medicine, New Haven, Connecticut

Owen Renik, M.D.
Training and Supervising Analyst, San Francisco Psychoanalytic Institute; Associate Clinical Professor of Psychiatry, University of California—San Francisco, San Francisco, California; Editor-in-Chief, *Psychoanalytic Quarterly*

Steven P. Roose, M.D.
Faculty, Columbia University Center for Psychoanalytic Training and Research; Associate Professor, Columbia University College of Physicians and Surgeons, New York, New York

Howard Shevrin, Ph.D.
Professor of Psychology, Department of Psychiatry, University of Michigan Medical Center, Ann Arbor, Michigan; Member, Michigan Psychoanalytic Society

Martin A. Silverman, M.D.
Training and Supervising Analyst, The Psychoanalytic Institute, New York University Medical Center; Clinical Professor of Psychiatry, New York University, New York, New York; Associate Editor, *Psychoanalytic Quarterly*

Troy L. Thompson II, M.D.
Faculty, Philadelphia Psychoanalytic Institute; Daniel Lieberman Professor and Chair of Psychiatry, Jefferson Medical College, Philadelphia, Pennsylvania

Phyllis Tyson, Ph.D.
Training and Supervising Analyst and Child Supervisor, San Diego Psychoanalytic Institute; Associate Clinical Professor, Department of Psychiatry, University of California—San Diego, La Jolla, California

Robert S. Wallerstein, M.D.
Training and Supervising Analyst, San Francisco Psychoanalytic Institute; Formerly Chairman of Psychiatry, University of California—San Francisco School of Medicine; Formerly Director, Langley Porter Psychiatric Institute, San Francisco, California

Edward M. Weinshel, M.D.
Training and Supervising Analyst, San Francisco Psychoanalytic Institute; Clinical Professor of Psychiatry, University of California Medical Center, San Francisco, California

Martin S. Willick, M.D.
Training and Supervising Analyst, New York Psychoanalytic Institute; Lecturer in Psychiatry, Columbia University College of Physicians and Surgeons, New York, New York

Thomas Wolman, M.D.
Faculty, Philadelphia Psychoanalytic Institute; Assistant Clinical Professor of Psychiatry, University of Pennsylvania; Lecturer in Psychiatry, Jefferson Medical College, Philadelphia, Pennsylvania

Introduction

Richard G. Kopff, Jr., M.D.
Edward Nersessian, M.D.

Psychoanalysis is only 100 years old. As such, it is a very young science, although interest in mental functioning, both normal and pathological, is as old as mankind. Today, with the explosion of knowledge in the neurosciences, renewed attention is being given to the understanding of mental processes, so much so that the United States Congress has proclaimed the 1990s as the "Decade of the Brain." Because psychoanalysis is that science whose focus is on the main product of the brain—namely, the mind—it seems especially timely to offer to the scientific community a book surveying current psychoanalytic thinking. In this textbook we endeavor to present what psychoanalysis has discovered so far about the mind and the ways in which it works.

As is true with all sciences, the current state of our knowledge is both imperfect and incomplete, and much remains to be discovered about the structure, organization, processes, and components of the mind. Like the neurosciences, psychoanalysis has experienced a recent ferment of activity and exploration, resulting in a profusion of new information, much of which has yet to be properly evaluated. In deciding what to include in this volume, we attempted to give the reader an understanding of the basic tenets of psychoanalysis while at the same time providing an up-to-date picture of the field. We have necessarily omitted some topics of interest, but we hope both the seasoned practitioner and the neophyte student will find the chapters contemporary, valuable, and useful.

One of the difficulties inherent in organizing and editing a textbook such as this derives from the very nature of the way ideas in the field have developed and evolved. Freud, of course, was the first psychoanalyst and laid the foundations for studying the mind through the method of psychoanalysis. He was an active and avid student of mental processes, and his ongoing researches led him to continuously refine and change his theories, as dictated by his clinical data. Psychoanalysts after Freud have continued this process of refinement and revision, incorporating and changing many of Freud's ideas, while remaining close to his general theory. Abraham, Fenichel, Hartmann, and Brenner are all good examples of such theorists.

On the other hand, other theorists in psychoanalysis have diverged more fundamentally from Freud's ideas. Some, such as Adler and Jung, have done so to such an extent as to be outside the mainstream of contemporary psychoanalysis. Others have diverged less markedly and can still be considered integral to present-day psychoanalysis; this latter group includes the Kleinians, the members of the object relations school, the self psychologists, and the developmentalists. Although the proponents of these various schools agree in important ways with classical Freudian psychoanalysts, their views are sufficiently different to evoke strongly expressed disagreements and debate. The divergences between these groups and the classical Freudians have created a tension that has been a stimulus for scientific discussion and exploration, inexorably leading to the enrichment of psychoanalytic theory.

Another challenge in organizing this volume is also related to the history of the evolution of ideas in psychoanalysis. As with all sciences, new ideas in the field have met with varying degrees of enthusiasm, skepticism, mistrust, and outright rejection. Over time, some have been retained and assimilated into the main body of theory, and others have been discarded; older findings have been superseded by new ones, and still others have been proven to be erroneous. At times, ideas that had been considered wrong or of limited usefulness have been rediscovered and then readapted to current ways of thinking and conceptualizing. Wilhelm Reich's theory of character armor and Karl Abraham's direct linking of complex behavior to specific levels of libidinal development, as well as Freud's early view that transference should be interpreted only when it is a resistance, all fall into the category of ideas that have been abandoned or supplanted. In contrast, some of Karen Horney's ideas about female sexual development that fell into disuse years ago have recently been revived.

This book could have been written from an exclusively Kleinian or object relations perspective or from an exclusively Kohutian/self psychology perspective; alternatively, it could have been organized along historical lines, giving an important place to each of the early theorists and to their subsequent followers. Instead, we have opted for a primarily Freudian perspective and have focused on creating a modern, up-to-date textbook that will enable the reader to appreciate psychoanalysis as it is understood, taught, and practiced by classical analysts today. Most of the chapters are written from this perspective, although the reader will be able to detect influences from other theoretical vantage points. We have included a chapter on object relations and one on self psychology to give the reader a general idea about the other main schools of psychoanalytic thought that are currently prevalent.

We want to emphasize that this is a textbook intended to provide an overview of psychoanalysis and that it is in no way an exhaustive review of the vast amount of knowledge accumulated in the field. We hope the reader will come to appreciate the complexities of the human mind and will be stimulated to learn more, both by further reading and through his or her own clinical experience and researches.

Section I

Psychoanalytic Theories of the Mind

Introduction to Section I

Richard G. Kopff, Jr., M.D.
Edward Nersessian, M.D.

This first section begins with a description, in Chapter 1 by Leo Rangell, of the inception of psychoanalysis and Freud's development of the first psychoanalytic theory of the functioning of the mind, called the topographical theory. In what follows, the reader is introduced to certain select psychoanalytic theories of the mind that are arguably the most widely accepted and prevalent today. It must be noted, however, that there are other important schools of thought and that within these schools—as within the so-called Freudian school—there are divisions and dissensions. The French analyst Jacques Lacan, whose widely read and debated work is not included in this volume, is an example of a psychoanalytic theorist whose ideas are in many ways strongly anchored in Freud's but who, nevertheless, has taken a direction widely divergent from that of the more "classical" analysts.

As the reader progresses through Jacob Arlow's presentation of the structural theory in Chapter 2, James Grotstein's description of object relations theory in Chapter 3, and Robert Leider's elucidation of self psychology in Chapter 4, he or she will immediately become aware of the diversity in current theorizing about operations of the mind. Some attempts have been made to establish a basis for converging these disparate theoretical elements, most notably by Robert Wallerstein, who has proposed what he terms a "common ground" for psychoanalysis. Unfortunately, however, convergence seems far from being a reality, but perhaps one day analysts' efforts in that direction will prove fruitful.

There are, nevertheless, some basic concepts that are part of all psychoanalytic theories of the mind. First, there is the very important idea that unconscious mentation has a determining influence on behavior, thinking, and emotions. Of similar import is the belief that dreams have meaning and that unraveling them is very useful in elucidating issues of psychological significance to the patient. Likewise, as Wallerstein points out, the concept of transference is utilized in all schools, no matter what the theoretical bias. On the other hand, the theory of drives (sexual and aggressive), so central to classical Freudian theory and to what is called "ego psychology" in this country, is not universally accepted. Both Freudian and non-Freudian schools are in agreement, however, that ideation with sexual and aggressive content has an impact on psychological development, although the relative emphasis that each school places on this perspective differs.

Ferment and controversy are not new to psychoanalysis; since its beginning, psychoanalytic theory has undergone continuous revisions and reassessments. On a number of occasions, Freud himself took stock of his findings and changed those theories that did not fit his data, sometimes radically altering his views. His "seduction theory" affords a good example of just such a shift. Originally, Freud believed that actual sexual seduction was a causative factor in neurosis; later, he recognized that a fantasy of having been seduced could form the basis for a neurosis, and he revised his theory accordingly. It should be noted that Freud did *not* negate or minimize the harmful effects of actual sexual seduction on a child; rather, he was surprised by the preponderance of such ideas in the associations of his patients and concluded that in many cases there were only fantasies of seductions, not actual seductions.

Another major shift in Freud's thinking and one that has had a major influence on psychoanalytic thought for the last 70 years is his elaboration of *the structural theory.* Prior to 1923, as Leo Rangell explicates in Chapter 1, the overarching hypothesis of mental organization was *the topographical theory,* whereby the mind was seen as divided into three parts. These divisions, known as the "Conscious," the "Preconscious," and the "Unconscious," defined the degree to which an idea and its associations were within awareness.

In 1923, however, Freud decided that a different tripartite division better explained his findings and so, according to this new theory, separated the functions of the mind into the "Id" (as a mental representation of the drives), the "Ego" (as the executive agent of the mind), and the "Super-Ego" (which is the agency that evaluates the person and functions as the conscience).

Reassessment and revision continue to be crucial to the growth and development of psychoanalytic theory and occur both within and between schools of psychoanalysis. In classical theory, important revisions have come about through Hartmann's modifications, which initiated the era of *ego psychology*, and, more recently, through the revisions of Brenner, which have put conflict and compromise formation in the center of analytic discourse.

Although most of the chapters in this volume were written from a classical Freudian perspective, it is hoped that the inclusion in the first section of discussions of two other major schools of thought will orient the reader to the fertile soil of today's psychoanalytic thinking and theorizing.

1

The Origins and First Phase of Psychoanalytic Theory

Leo Rangell, M.D.

Psychoanalysis is a branch of psychology, with an interface with biology, that constitutes a theory of mental functioning. Psychoanalysis was created by a physician, psychiatrist, neurologist, and neuropathologist in Vienna, Sigmund Freud, who conceived and began to develop this new discipline in the 1890s, at about the age of 40. From then until his death in 1939 in London at the age of 85, Freud expanded, modified, and reshaped central aspects of what by then had become an evolving theoretical system of thought known and utilized throughout the scientific and intellectual world. At Freud's death, his theory was left to others to reassess and extend. By then, Freud's name had become part of language: "Freudian" came to mean "to have unconscious psychological meaning."

The development of psychoanalysis from its beginnings followed two paths, variably related to each other. One line of development consisted of the process by which the new theoretical structure was added to, altered, and refined as it was shaped into what came to be considered the main body of psychoanalytic theory. The early discoveries of Freud were elaborated and supplemented by a creative group of early adherents looked upon as the "pioneers" in the new field. Among these investigators, as the movement spread outside of Vienna, were Karl Abraham in Berlin, Ernest Jones in London, and Sandor Ferenczi in Budapest. Later, as Freud's work continued and the field spread worldwide, a burgeoning group of workers and contributors to the science took up and extended the work in depth, scope, and applicability.

The other line of development, from early on, consisted of contributions and opinions of colleagues who had joined Freud in promulgating the new science but soon objected to some of his basic formulations and developed new theories or directions of thinking that split the small group of original contributors into competing factions. These colleagues included, among the best known, Carl Jung, Alfred Adler, and Otto Rank, each of whom stressed some aspect of the new psychology at variance from the main body of thought at the expense of other central aspects. These changes were at first debated and discussed but ultimately led to the establishment of alternative theoretical systems. Whether the split-off groups continued to be forms of the same science still to be considered psychoanalysis became increasingly both an organizational question and a theoretical subject of division and debate. While Freud was still alive, the steady output of his own evolving contributions and the elaborations of his ideas by others were generally taken to be the accepted or main, if not the only, theory of psychoanalysis. Jungian and Adlerian psychologies were less universally recognized as the theory and method of psychoanalysis proper.

Later in the development of psychoanalysis, when psychoanalysis no longer was confronted by active, hostile opposition from the prevailing scientific intellectual world, divisions of thought that were perhaps equally as alien as those that split the original group of contributors and that continued to be considered the mainstream began to be accommodated within the borders of the field. Although this accommodation made for more inclusiveness and organizational cohesion, the debates about "alternative" versus "traditional," "classical," or "main" theories were no less intense or divisive, and psychoanalysis became divided within itself rather than split into separate, competing entities.

Freud himself continued to develop psychoanalytic theory throughout his life and to apply its insights at many levels, from problems of individual behavior to group psychology, to the discontents of civilization itself. While maintaining the main trunk, having to do with unconscious conflict, Freud, about halfway through his 40-year scientific career, effected a major shift in scientific orientation with respect to central aspects of his theory, especially the theory of anxiety and the structure and composition of psychic conflict. With that shift as a reference point, "Freudian" psychoanalytic theory can be said to be divided into two phases, an early theory, developed up to about 1920, and a more final, "structural" psychoanalytic theory, developed from 1920 until Freud's death in 1939. Since Freud's time, modern, or current, psychoanalytic theory, building on this second phase of psychoanalytic theory, further developed and expanded the main direction and offered a series of complex major as well as minor revisions.

In this chapter I describe the origins of Freud's early psychoanalytic theory and its development by gradual increments and discoveries. Whereas some psychoanalysts today are opposed to teaching or learning psychoanalysis by retracing Freud's original steps, others contend that the recounting of the original sequence of discoveries retains heuristic as well as scientific value. Each initiate in the field may retrace the sequence of discoveries that, taken as a whole, constitute psychoanalysis, much as ontogeny recapitulates phylogeny. In a certain sense, the training of every psychoanalyst, as well as the treatment of every patient by psychoanalysis, entails a similar journey of gradual discovery. Acquisition of the new knowledge may involve a specific, and perhaps even necessary, process of not only cognitively understanding but also affectively absorbing the building blocks that make up the newly acquired theoretical structure. Discoverer, student, or patient all experience in a similar way the overcoming of the resistances to knowledge, a crucial step in the discovery and appreciation of unconscious processes.

Freud's breakthrough has been compared to those of Copernicus and Darwin, each of whom overcame an emotionally held prejudice or resistance of humankind: in Copernicus's case, that the earth was the center of the universe, and in Darwin's, that a human being was a living creature sui generis, unrelated to all other species. Both Copernicus and Darwin countered external myths directed toward explaining the human surround. Freud, however, overcame an inner resistance to relinquishing the conviction that humans are the master of their thoughts, feelings, decisions, and actions. Each of these three explorers had to overcome a resistance based on humankind's narcissism, to promote knowledge that would reduce humans' stature. The resistance overcome by Freud functioned between a human being and his or her inner life. In overcoming this internal barrier, Freud not only scaled the resistance but studied it and came to understand its nature. Resistance was a datum, not to be bypassed, but to be included in humankind's knowledge. To study a complication or obstacle to knowledge as a phenomenon to be understood in itself was another achievement of Freud's in his odyssey of discoveries. Resistance came to be seen as part of, and intrinsic to, human unconscious psychic conflict.[1]

Not only do Freud's discoveries constitute an immense leap forward in humankind's mastery of self, but the history of their development is a tale of human interest comparable to Leeuwenhoek's discovery of the microscope (or, on the biological side, the advances by Koch, Pasteur, and the microbe hunters). The new analytic method is the microscope that focuses on human behavior.

Origins of Psychoanalytic Theory

Freud's Early Years and Training

A study of the chronological sequence of Freud's intellectual development and discoveries will help us understand the significance of these early experiences for the first phase of theory as well as for its future development.

---

[1]Resistance, narcissism, unconscious, intrapsychic, conflict—all are words that came to acquire new meanings following their incorporation into the evolving psychoanalytic vocabulary. The concepts that these words embodied all became essential ingredients in the new armamentarium of understanding.

Freud as a boy already seems to have had a sense of his own destiny. In one of a group of his earliest known letters, written at age 16 to a friend in Pribor, Czechoslovakia, upon Freud's return to Vienna after visiting his place of birth in Pribor, which he had left when he was 3 years old, Freud demonstrates a prophetic and rather poignant insight into his feelings and excitement: "I enjoy tracing the closely-knit web of connecting threads which chance and fate have woven around us" (Freud 1969, p. 421). He then counsels his young friend to preserve Freud's letters: "Guard them well—you never know" (p. 425).

An interest in science—natural science, the science of nature and particularly human nature—came early. After some vacillation about career choice, Freud, at 17, confided his decision to his friend in Pribor: "I have decided to be a Natural Scientist . . . I shall gain insight into . . . nature, perhaps even eavesdrop on her eternal processes" (Freud 1969, p. 424). The study of medicine, which he appears to have resisted, was not his first love or intention. His medical school education at the University of Vienna took 3 years longer than the standard time for completion, as the young medical student attended a wide array of ancillary courses—in biology, physics, zoology, Darwinism—beyond those for medical students, and lectures in philosophy, including Aristotle, and the physiology of plants.

Pursuing his interest in training for advanced research, Freud attended lectures of the eminent scientists of the period and worked assiduously in the laboratories of the preclinical scientific faculty, dividing his time between these activities and his more official medical studies. His strongest mentor during these student years was the neurophysiologist Ernst Brucke, who had come to Vienna from Berlin, where he had been part of a small group of influential scientists under the leadership of Helmholtz, whose physical and physiological philosophy influenced all of European scientific thought. Promulgating a theoretical orientation that was to exert a strong influence on Freud during his entire search for meaning and understanding, these philosophical scientists imbued their followers, who in turn dominated the thinking of their own students, with the conviction that all nature—including organisms, humans included—could be explained by physical-chemical forces and understood by the methods of physics and mathematics.

The teachings that filtered down to Freud from Brucke and Helmholtz had a strong impact on him. Although his life work was to direct him to the world of aims, goals, intentions, purpose, and motives—which his respected mentors had no use for—Freud struggled throughout his life to fuse these teleological forces, or at least to make them compatible, with the physical forces of determinism in nature. Freud entered and grappled with the world of teleology but had no motive to separate this human stream of motivation from deterministic forces that were thought to apply to all of nature. During these formative scientific years, Freud, in his first research study, assigned to him by the comparative anatomist Carl Claus, identified the gonad of the male eel, which had never been identified before (an auspicious beginning for one who was to discover the role of unconscious sexuality in human affairs!). Among other studies undertaken by the young researcher and experimenter, mainly under Brucke but also stemming from others' instigations, were the histology of the spinal ganglion cells of the petromyzon (a genus of fish belonging to the Cyclostomatae), and of the nerve cells of the crayfish, demonstrating the composition of the axis cylinders, and the relation of these findings to the understanding of what was soon to be called the "neurone." Although the nervous system, then known as the seat of action, was becoming the main focus in the scientific ambience of the time, these issues and discoveries of the role of nerve cells were to have significance for questions of religion, evolution, and the nature and philosophy of man.

From Neuropathology to Psychopathology

In the immediate years following his graduation from the medical school of the University of Vienna in 1881, Freud did not enter practice at once but immersed himself in a career of combined clinical work and continuing research in neuroanatomy and neurophysiology. His interest in science and investigative work and his zeal to extract "the secrets of nature" were always stronger than his interest in medicine, which had been a circuitously reached, secondary, and practical choice. He continued to work in Brucke's laboratory for over a year, when, in 1883, because of a blockage of advancement in Brucke's Institute of Physiology, he joined The Psychiatric Clinic, headed by Theodor Meynert, a distinguished psychiatrist who was also the greatest brain anatomist of his time (a form of amentia bears his name). For a period that stretched into 3 years, Freud worked in the General Hospital of Vienna, first under Meynert and then others, combining research with clinical experience. A continuous conflict between scientific research and clinical practice posed a dilemma for Freud, the resolution of which was influenced by his becoming engaged and needing to think with increasing pressure of making a living.

Freud quickly began to achieve unusual notice for a young man. He studied the anatomy, histology, and histopathology of the spinal cord, the medulla and brain stem, and the acoustic and other cranial nerves, establishing neural pathways from the periphery to their central subcortical and cortical ramifications. Based upon original work—from experimentally tracing neuronal pathways evolutionarily from fish to humans, to conducting definitive clinical studies of cerebral diplegia in children and other organic neurological syndromes in pediatric and adult neurology—Freud was establishing himself as a researcher, lecturer, teacher, and clinician who was becoming increasingly visible in the austere scientific community of his day. His neurological studies, after a series of scientific papers, culminated in 1891 in his first published book, *On Aphasia*, considered a major treatise on the subject in which older ideas were refuted. In this book, the content of which is still valid today, Freud disputed theories of Wernicke and also of Meynert, pioneers in this field at the time. Substituting for their anatomical, topographic views of localization a dynamic formulation and functional theory of speech and language, Freud, even at this early stage, introduced a psychological component to a mechanistic understanding of the development of speech and reading.

Freud's interest, even during this early, productive organic phase of his studies, had already begun to be deflected from neuropathology to psychopathology, both because of the prevalence of hysteria and neuroses in the patient population of that time and because of his own inner proclivities and scientific curiosity. Concomitant with Freud's medical training, an eminent physician, as well as man of science, in Vienna, Josef Breuer, 14 years Freud's senior, who had befriended Freud at the Institute of Physiology during Freud's medical school days, had been discussing with Freud, in mutually animated conversations, a patient he was treating (between 1880 and 1882) in whom the telling of painful events and experiences was accompanied by the alleviation of her "hysterical" symptoms. The patient, Anna O., a young woman of 21, exhibited a repertoire of nonorganic symptoms that at that time were considered to constitute "hysteria" but that today might be thought of by many as in the "more disturbed" range of psychopathology. Stimulated by Breuer's sympathetic listening to her complaints, the patient would of her own accord enter a state of autohypnosis during which her symptoms were found to be connected to various disturbing events around the death of her father. With each such recountal, the symptoms in question would disappear. Following this observation, Breuer began to apply hypnosis on a daily basis to actively facilitate these somnambulistic states and their associated revelations. Freud followed the events of this case with great interest.

As an addendum to this experience and a harbinger of insights and discoveries to come, over the course of this unusual attention and treatment, which persisted for over a year, Breuer's wife became increasingly morose and distressed by her husband's immersion in his case, an immersion that was certainly unusual in a medical practice of the times. Responding to his wife's unexpressed jealousy and his own confused state, Breuer suddenly announced to the patient, who by now was much improved, an abrupt termination of the treatment. That same evening, however, he had to return to see the patient when she entered a regressed, excited state, with her symptoms having returned as severely as ever. Noting now that the patient had developed a pseudocyesis, Breuer departed, according to Ernest Jones (1953, pp. 224–225), Freud's biographer, "in a cold sweat," after which he and his wife left for Venice for a second honeymoon. Transference and countertransference, concepts and terms to be introduced much later, were operative but far yet from being recognized or understood.

A nodal point of Freud's historic turn from the study of organic processes to his emergent interest in hysteria and the neuroses was his sabbatical fellowship of 4½ months in the laboratory of Charcot at the Salpêtrière in Paris from October 1885 to February 1886. Freud had already been sensitized to introspection and internal psychic processes, not only by his discussions with Breuer but by his nature and constitution and by living and struggling in fin de siècle Vienna, with its mores, culture, courtliness, music, antisemitism, charm, hypocrisy, and sex. He came to observe and absorb the teachings and performance of the great master-clinician-teacher Charcot, who, in most timely fashion, was thrusting upon the scientific world and making respectable the phenomena of hysteria and hypnosis. Surrounded by Babinski, Marie, Tooth, Gilles de la Tourette, and the pantheon of scientific neurological names of France, Freud watched and absorbed the concept and conviction that ideas introduced into the mind of a patient can produce disease and that their removal can eventually result in the patient's condition being cured. Charcot, with the force of his prestige and authority, rescued hypnosis from the realm of skepticism and fraud and established that mental illness, heretofore in the domain of infectious or degenerative disease of the nervous system (or the general paresis of syphilis when nothing else could be demonstrated), could be caused by an abnormal fate of dissociated thought.

Following his return from Paris, Freud set up a private practice in neurology and psychiatry in Vienna. In the procession of patients over the next 10 to 15 years coming to him, one of the "nerve specialists" of those days, Freud, imbued with his thoughts and excitement about what he had absorbed and was thinking about from Charcot and Breuer, eschewed the current treatments of the day—the electrical stimulation, massages, or hydrotherapy prescribed for hysteria—and began to urge his patients to talk. He listened to their stories, which gradually, by incremental steps of conviction and courage, became their case histories. During this time, Freud (1886, 1892–1894), continuing to work through his Paris experience, translated Charcot's famous *Leons de Mardi* [*Tuesday*

Lectures] into German, an assignment Charcot had agreed to at Freud's suggestion. What emerged now from Freud's close observational data and his developing clinical method was a method of treatment. By successive steps, Freud changed his technique from hypnosis to suggestion (i.e., urging, asking questions), and then to the method of free association, the patient being asked to say everything that came to mind.

In this period of his life, Freud collected data and concomitantly attempted to create an explanatory theory to fit the observations. The original goal was treatment, but what also emerged was the creation of a theory of the mind. Gradually, the evolving procedure became simultaneously a method of treatment, a means of investigation (or a research method), and a theory of the workings of the mind. The three functions could hardly be separated. During the laborious and steady collecting of observational data, Freud noted the following:

1. Sexual factors were frequent—and Freud finally felt he could say ubiquitous—in the histories of neuroses.
2. The further patients were willing (or more accurately enabled) to talk and free-associate, the more these sexual conflicts and "traumata" were seen to have occurred in childhood.
3. During the "treatment," and what he came to see as part of the therapeutic procedure, Freud became aware of the unwillingness of the patients to disclose painful or unwelcome memories. This unwillingness Freud termed *resistance,* which he connected with *repression,* the process by which certain memories are kept outside of consciousness. These memories, Freud theorized, were replaced by symptoms, both psychological and somatic.
4. During this early period, when a patient (Frau Emmy; see Breuer and Freud 1893–1895) suddenly threw her arms around him, Freud conceived this as a *transference,* which he considered a problem of scientific interest. Alongside the accumulation of positive discoveries, clinical experiences that might have been discouraging and might have led to the abandonment of his research were consistently seen, instead, as data, that is, as findings in themselves. All of these early discoveries—resistance,

repression, transference, unconscious processes, sexual conflicts, free associations—were to become hallmarks of psychoanalysis.

The First Phase of Psychoanalytic Theory

Studies in Hysteria

In the midst of this creative period, in 1895, Breuer and Freud published *Studies on Hysteria*, considered to be the first book of psychoanalysis. This joint work consisted of presentation and discussion of Breuer's original case of Anna O. and four cases treated by Freud, as well as a theoretical chapter by Breuer and a chapter on the psychotherapy of hysteria by Freud. By now, Freud had moved from using Breuer's hypnotic, "chimney sweep" method to what he called his intermediate "concentration technique," and finally to what he called "psychical analysis." The name "psychoanalysis" was not introduced by Freud until a year later, in his paper "Further Remarks on the Neuro-Psychoses of Defence" (Freud 1896b). In these studies, although Freud recognized transference as a scientific issue in the Frau Emmy case, he had not yet formulated its precise composition, noting only the erotic basis of the patient-doctor relationship. Psychopathology was seen as being due to repression of incompatible (i.e., conflictual) ideas. The displacement of these repressed ideas, generally thought of as memories of traumatic sexual events, led to overt hysterical states or to somatic conversion. "Psychical analysis" consisted of the patient's and the analyst's coming to know, or the analyst's conveying to the patient, the contents of the repressed ideas and the pathogenic sequence of events.

Although Breuer was a full collaborator in this work, and Freud even generously credited him as being the father of psychoanalysis, Breuer came as far as he could with this work. The final personal incident during the treatment of Anna O. years before had had a severe influence in restricting Breuer's future openness to this continuing path of interest. His traumatic experience with the unrecognized transference and his near panic at his threatening countertransference remained as severe impediments to any continued objectivity in these investigations. The persistence, enthusiasm, and continuing productivity of his younger colleague, however, for a time kept Breuer further involved, but ambivalently so. In spite of Freud's efforts and encouragement for Breuer to continue in the research and writing, Breuer felt an increasing antipathy to the concept of the ubiquity of the sexual etiology of the neuroses, probably particularly the involvement of childhood sexuality. Freud, who was receiving a cool and hostile reception from the medical and scientific community, felt that Charcot, as well as Breuer, had ceased to approve of the direction of his conclusions about the extent of sexual etiology. Breuer's and Freud's collaborative book, *Studies on Hysteria* (1893–1895), was their last mutual effort. The relationship between Freud and Breuer grew increasingly cool and distant, becoming finally even a bitter one.

Wilhelm Fliess

Two years before the break with Breuer, Freud began a correspondence with a Dr. Wilhelm Fliess, an ear, nose, and throat specialist in Berlin, 2 years Freud's junior, who had come to Vienna for a postgraduate course of study where he had met Breuer, who advised him to attend some lectures of Freud. A friendship developed that grew in intensity and that served for Freud as a private sounding board for his developing ideas. Fliess, not Breuer, came to represent for Freud what later came to be known as a transference figure. From 1887 until 1902, Freud confided his developing scientific ideas to Fliess. As their friendship developed, in a voluminous correspondence, Freud pursued his earlier investigations and produced many of his original findings. Later to become a record of their creative origins (Freud 1887–1902), this exchange preserved, to some extent, the course of Freud's mental processes in the form of speculative descriptions, preliminary drafts of papers, and thoughts and reflections contained within the letters themselves.

Most important, and a milestone of scientific advance, was Freud's performance of his own self-analysis under the stimulation and externalization made possible by these intimate letters. It was during his exploration of this inner process in himself that Freud discovered and achieved conviction about a nodal point in normal mental development, the *Oedipus complex*—that is, the child's erotic attraction to the parent of the opposite sex and his or her hostility and concomitant jealousy toward the parent of the same sex. Although he had been analyzing his individual dreams since about 1895, Freud began his self-analysis in earnest and on a regular basis under the impact of the death of his father in October 1896. His analysis, which began in July 1897, continued with decreasing intensity and external descriptions until the end of the Fliess relationship in 1902, although Jones (1953) states that Freud continued to devote the last half-hour of each day to that purpose on a regular basis for the rest of his life.

The "Project"

At the same time as he was embarking on the road toward a scientific conception of psychopathology, Freud did not lose sight of an earlier ambition: to traverse the path from neurophysiology to psychopathology and establish the connections between the two. In 1895, just after writing the last chapter of *Studies on Hysteria*, Freud wrote a long essay that he called "Psychology for Neurologists," later to become known as the "Project for a Scientific Psychology" (Freud 1950[1895]). Written in a few weeks in what Jones (1953) characterized as a feverish burst of intense activity, the "Project" contains an elaborate set of propositions, arrived at by Freud, partly still in collaboration with Breuer, describing anatomical and physiological characteristics of "neurones" in the central nervous system that flow over in their functioning into psychological outcomes. Freud's aim was to secure the place of psychology firmly within natural science. Psychical processes, Freud posited, are determined by "Quantity," the sum of excitations in material neurones. Two types of neurones, permeable and less permeable neurones, serve functions of perception and memory, respectively. The nervous system endeavors to keep constant the sum of excitations. A third set of neurones transforms Quantity into "Quality" and, Freud hypothesized, is responsible for the quality of consciousness. The concept of physical breaking of barriers by stimuli, from the outer world as well as from the inner body, was to evolve later into the concepts of psychic trauma and the signal function of anxiety.

One crucial theme introduced in the "Project" was the distinction between primary and secondary processes, reflecting differences in the flow from excitation to discharge. Primary process, under the pressure of a wish's demand for satisfaction, evokes a hallucination of the satisfying object that is unrealistic. Secondary process, on the other hand, through the inhibiting powers of the ego, enables the perception and recognition of the reality of the absence of satisfaction, thus leading to the establishment of the *reality principle.* Although an ego appears here, it is not the ego of the later structural view, but instead can be considered consonant with the whole nervous system. Yet, it is a concept upon which the later system "ego" is built.

Following a brief but intense effort, during which he alternately expressed both hope and discouragement, many times to the points of euphoria and despair, Freud gave up or put aside his attempt at a somatopsychic bridge via the "Project" and from then on adopted a view of psychophysical parallelism. Contrary to the opinions of many, the ideas that Freud developed in the "Project" were never eliminated, but remained or returned in many forms. Some psychological insights deriving from his psychophysical speculations became central to future formulations. The basic hope of a unified theory was not considered unattainable but was left for others to fulfill in the future. Some authors relegate the "Project" to oblivion along with other of Freud's early formulations, such as Freud's first theory of anxiety (i.e., of direct toxic transformation); other scientists today, however, are impressed with the remarkable confluence of the Helmholtzian contents of the "Project" (i.e., the physical-chemical and mathematical explanation of all nature, including humankind) and modern electrochemical neurophysiology. Freud ceased actively working on the "Project," however, toward the end of 1895, the same year he had begun the work. From that point on, Freud's researches and activities were directed exclusively toward psychological investigations and expansions.

Early Nosology, Etiology, and the First Theory of Anxiety

In the 1890s, before and during the Fliess period, a central thrust of Freud's research and formulations had to do with the phenomenology, classification, and theoretical understanding of the psychoneuroses as known at that time. In a series of clinical and theoretical papers, Freud (1894, 1895a[1894], 1895b[1894], 1896a, 1896b, 1896c, 1898) dissected out and organized the symptomatology and etiological backgrounds drawn from work with his patients into several discrete nosological entities: neurasthenia, hysteria, and anxiety-neurosis, as well as shorter references to obsessional states and paranoia. In understanding these entities, Freud at first continued to hew to the line of his previous interest, attempting to do justice to both the body and the mind and to understand the relationships and borders between the two.

Although Freud had established sexual factors as being related to all of the presenting syndromes, he conceived the fates and modes of action of the various sexual dysfunctions as being different in the separate entities. In an overall way, Freud at this stage classified the neuroses into two major divisions, the psychoneuroses and the "actual neuroses," within which Freud's first theory of anxiety came to be embedded. Whereas psychoneuroses were thought to result from psychic conflict, actual neuroses were explained in purely physiological terms. Neurasthenia, the major "actual neurosis," along with such general symptoms as fatigue and irritability, was considered by Freud to be the most purely physical result of sexual disturbances. Because of inadequate relief of sexual tension, mostly from some form of masturbation, the tension in this syndrome was considered, in Freud's formulation of that time, to be expressed mainly and directly in physical terms. In hysteria, on the other hand, which at that time, along with obsessive-compulsive neurosis, constituted the psychoneuroses, sexual trauma has occurred but has been repressed. It is the memory of the repudiated event that finds its way into the hysterical attack or the obsessive symptom, or other derivative symptomatic effects, which may be expressed in either psychic or physical disturbances.

In a separate paper, Freud (1895a[1894]) identified anxiety-neurosis and established it as a separate neurosis from neurasthenia, but considered both to be "actual neuroses." With this paper, Freud was on the trail of the presence of anxiety in neuroses but was far from his later formulation of anxiety as having a central and universal role. At this phase of Freud's investigations, Freud attributed the anxiety he noted within the actual neuroses to a failure of discharge of sexual excitation, occurring from such practices as abstinence or coitus interruptus. In these cases, as in the direct symptoms of neurasthenia, unrelieved sexual pressure was postulated as being converted directly into anxiety, with no psychic intervention taking place and the anxiety having no psychological meaning. Freud considered this anxiety "actual" (i.e., current [not from the past] and real [physical, with no mental meaning]). This view of the genesis of anxiety—direct somatic transformation of repressed, undischarged sexual libido into anxiety—was the essence of Freud's first and long-lasting theory of anxiety. Although the presence of anxiety in neuroses was observed and appreciated, the explanation of its role was partial, rooted in the physiological; the teleological and universal role of anxiety was not yet understood.

Discharge of excitation into the somatic field occurs in both actual neuroses and psychoneuroses; in actual neuroses somatic excitation is discharged directly, whereas in the psychoneuroses psychological stimulation resulting from repression of psychic conflict is manifested as symptoms. The direct discharge of somatic excitation is a matter of mounting tension—that is, of quantity and degree—and spells out the psychoeconomic condition of neurosis. The psychoneuroses involve psychodynamics, the qualitative issue of the nature of the wishes. In hysteria and obsessive-compulsive psychoneuroses, repression of sexual impulses because of the unacceptability of sexual wishes results in psychical excitation that is then transformed into symptoms, either in the psychic or somatic sphere. In the actual neuroses, physical tension does not enter the psychical field but remains in a physical path. These differentiating descriptions and criteria, Freud's first attempts at formulating nosological order into the neuroses that presented themselves to the practitioners of the day, were to be largely supplanted by a more logical and unified theoretical system in his later phases of theory formation.

A crucial nodal point in Freud's theoretical development, shifting significantly the center of gravity of his explanatory system, is evident in Freud's letter to Fliess on September 21, 1897. Disappointed that continuing experience did not confirm the presence of the sexual traumas of which his patients had informed him, Freud came to the altered view that part of his findings had to do with a sexually prepared soil within the patients themselves, prepared especially in their childhood years. This new understanding resulted in the much discussed shift by Freud from his theory of external seduction as the sole source of symptoms to the theory of unconscious internal fantasies as another, equally important etiological source. Here, too, Freud avoided a deflection of the researcher that may have been the lot of a more easily discouraged explorer. A profound expansion of understanding was the result. Reality does not consist solely of external events. There is a psychic reality that needs to be taken into account equally alongside of external reality. Instinctual wishes, the source of the symptoms of hysteria, also produce as intermediate products unconscious fantasies, which then operate as foci to fuel and determine the variety of neurotic outcomes. Freud effected a major shift in the understanding of the genesis of neuroses, a conceptual shift that was to become a locus of increased understanding as well as of misinterpretation and controversy.

Dreams

During the 1890s—a formative decade for Freud, with its simmering acme of creativity—there was another area of human behavior and experience that was quietly cumulating in Freud's growing data bank. In addition to hearing the free associations of his patients and accounts of their symptoms, Freud was regularly hearing accounts of their dreams. Looking into himself as well, before and during his self-analysis, Freud did not overlook his own dreams, and they came to be of special interest. Freud had been interested in his dreams even as a boy (Jones 1953), but in the 1880s, with his developed scientific mind observing and speculating, he began to collect and look into his dreams with serious and studied purpose.

Among the most creative of Freud's crucial breakthrough recognitions was his realization of the ways in which dreams were similar to symptoms—that both sets of phenomena were of the same composition and that both had the same origins and derived from the same motivations. Along with trying to understand dreams, in keeping with his therapeutic quest, Freud began to "interpret" them to his patients and to himself. Dreams served, as often as did the presenting symptom, as definitive markers in reconstructing the past. But although symptoms led to the understanding of psychopathology, the dream led equally to understanding these normal if puzzling experiences of everyday life.

An original and major thrust of understanding the work of the dream came with the solid establishment of the method of *free association*, which Freud was able to apply from work with his patients to his self-analysis and the analysis of dreams. The remembered dream, referred to as the "manifest dream," is the manifest portion of the full dream, the visible tip of the iceberg, just as the symptom is the observable manifestation of general psychopathology. Knowledge of the full dream—the deeper latent contents and their meanings—comes from the patient's associating freely to each element of the manifest dream. The hidden aspects, which here too are unconscious, are always more relevant and more voluminous than the conscious part. The dream is always triggered by a psychological event of the preceding day, usually an unattended element, a trivial thought or incident, or unfinished intention—all seemingly indifferent material of the preceding day. This content, termed the "day residue," usually starts the train of associations to the dream. The complex, unconscious weblike substrate of the dream constitutes the significant background of its origins, motives, and meanings. The day residue connects with an unconscious mental network containing elements of varying types and intensities that can be tapped during sleep.

Every dream, Freud contended, is a wish fulfillment. The basic and universal wish is the wish to sleep, and the dream protects sleep by discharging psychic excitations that would otherwise disturb the dreamer's sleep. The wish fulfilled by a specific dream consists of impulses that have been repressed but continue to strive for discharge. Freud takes up directly the problem of dreams that appear to be unpleasurable and that seem to contradict the formulation of dreams as wish fulfillments. Disturbing dreams, from the mildly disturbing dream to the traumatic nightmare, are seen to be consistent with Freud's overall theory of dreams in a number of ways. From these seemingly contradictory observations, Freud postulated that disturbing dreams fulfill a need for punishment, the gratification of masochistic impulses, or the wish to prove Freud wrong (to the extent that transference was operative and already recognized). Another explanation of an anxiety dream, including a nightmare that awakes the dreamer, is that the dream has failed in its purpose, being unable therefore to maintain the state of sleep.

Freud believed that in dreams, as in the neuroses, the repressed contents consist of forbidden sexual wishes and that further associations will lead to sexual conflicts and concerns of the childhood years. In dreams, as in neuroses, the anxiety builds up as a result of the failure of release of sexual tensions, and the "dammed-up libido" is directly transformed into "actual anxiety." These conceptualizations constitute Freud's first theory of anxiety as derived from and applied to the dream. With respect to the data uncovered by the free associations to the dream and the nature of the repressed memories and wishes that emerge after the lifting of repression, Freud found the same layerings of psychic contents in the dream as he did in hysteria and the entire range of psychoneuroses. Centrally exposed throughout this definitive book on the universal phenomenon of human dreams, as it was similarly from clinical material, was the Oedipus complex. Freud saw in dreams too a combination of derivative psychic outcomes—those resulting from psychic conflict and those that are direct transformations from repressed libido.

Along with the wish and its repression, Freud postulated the function of the censor, which requires distortion of the forbidden repressed wishes sufficiently to allow them conscious discharge in the dream. Censorship, a concept from dream theory that is a forerunner of the superego in Freud's later, structural theory, makes the disguises necessary. The specific distortions, or disguises, are carried out through the process of the "dream work" (which, in his later, structural theory, Freud also included as a function of the "ego"). The dream work, in which the latent contents are altered into forms that allow these contents to appear in the manifest dream, determines the substance and contents of the remembered dream. The censor is responsible for the forgetting of dreams as well as for the distortions within them. The analysis of a dream includes an understanding of how it is forgotten as well as of what it is made of and how it is remembered.

The dream work has a number of dream mechanisms at its disposal, among them condensation, displacement, symbolism, reversal into the opposite, and conversion of conceptual to visual images. In *condensation,* a whole train of thought is compressed and may then be concentrated on a single ideational element. This mechanism results in dreams being brief, meager, and laconic in comparison with the range and wealth of the underlying dream thoughts. In *displacement,* an idea or affect is moved from one object or incident to another, thereby throwing off the meaning or intensity of the significant psychic element. The *symbolization* that occurs in dreams is the same as that which is commonly evident in folklore, myths, proverbial wisdom, and current jokes. Symbols can represent an object, a person, or an event. In his characteristically succinct summary of a vast amount of human experience in dreams, Freud noted that symbolic representation of latent dream thoughts refers to a relatively narrow range of underlying subjects: the human body, parents, children, brothers, sisters, birth, death, nakedness, and sexual life. Dream thoughts that lend themselves to *transposition from conceptual to visual representation* are preferred for utilization in the manifest dream contents, because the latter consist mostly of pictorial representations.

Dreams, as symptoms, are compromises between the wish and the censorship. Because in sleep, however, access to motility is diminished and guarded, it is safe for the ego to allow more regression to primary process thinking than is the case during the day. The contents of a dream, with its hallucinatory wish fulfillment, would be considered a psychosis if entertained during the day. Yet, the dream can appear as normal because there is no danger that these contents would be acted out in the environment during sleep.

The Topographic Model

A densely written Chapter 7 of the *The Interpretation of Dreams* (Freud 1900) contains Freud's theory of the mind as he had developed it up to that point. Freud's conception of the unconscious mind and, within this conception, the libido theory of the pressures of repressed sexuality are central to this theory. Although the concept of repression was indispensable and ubiquitous, the precise theoretical position of this mechanism in the sequence of intrapsychic events was more difficult to work out and awaited a later elaboration and clarification of anxiety theory. In Freud's early theory, anxiety is the result of the failure of repression, whereas in his later theory, it is seen as the cause of (i.e., motive for) repression. There is, however, a special connection between repression and sexuality. More important, or at least equally important, in the future for determining the topographic dividing line between conscious and unconscious is whether a psychic element belongs to the primary or the secondary process. This distinction is a forerunner of the later advance from the topographic to the structural point of view.[2]

Freud's psychology of dream processes, like his conception of the mental processes involved in the formation of neuroses, is based on his *topographic* model: the stratification of psychic contents into the systems of conscious, preconscious, and unconscious mentation. *Unconscious* thought processes operate under the principle of primary process (i.e., nonrational thinking with no concern for logic or consistency), whereas *conscious* mental processes are characterized by secondary process thinking (i.e., thinking dominated by rationality and ordinary logic). Preconscious contents can be called up into consciousness by an act of will or of conscious direction, whereas unconscious contents can be accessed only by first overcoming a defense barrier that is opposed to the direction toward the conscious.

The completion of Freud's book on the dream and the progress of his self-analysis occurred under the impact and psychological

---

[2]Some theorists see this move as a replacement of the topographic by the structural view, whereas others see it as an addition of the structural to the topographic view.

stimulation of the death of Freud's father in 1896, which Freud described, in the preface to the second edition of *The Interpretation of Dreams,* as "the most important event, the most poignant loss, to happen in a man's life" (Freud 1900, p. xxvi). Freud's persistent self-analysis following this event resulted in the insight and conviction that enabled him to unequivocally formulate the power and universality of the Greek-named Oedipus complex, the erotic love of the boy for his mother and his jealousy and hostility toward his father. With the death of Freud's father and the continuation of Freud's self-analysis, the concentrated effort required to bring *The Interpretation of Dreams* to conclusion liberated Freud from the normal defenses, enabling this universal and momentous discovery of the Oedipus complex to be added to man's armamentarium of scientific knowledge. In this work, and later in "Totem and Taboo" (1913b[1912–1913]), Freud traced the operation of this complex throughout cultural history and, drawing on social anthropology, explored its origins. With his analysis of *Hamlet,* Freud provided a specific example in intellectual history of the pathognomonic significance of the Oedipus complex.

Many speculations that survived from Freud's incompleted "Project" appear in the psychological formulations in *The Interpretation of Dreams.* In the "Project," the mind was divided topographically into unconscious, preconscious, and conscious. "Sums of excitations" from the "Project" became the economic point of view, relating to force, energy, intensities of stimuli, and displaceability of affects. A neurone filled with Quantity as "an electric charge over the memory traces of an idea" became, in *The Interpretation of Dreams,* affective cathexis, and the increase and decrease of the levels of Quantity became the pleasure-unpleasure principle.

In a much-quoted formulation from *The Interpretation of Dreams,* Freud stated his position on the role of the dream in the therapeutic quest: "The interpretation of dreams is the royal road [the *via regia*] to a knowledge of the unconscious activities of the mind" (Freud 1900, p. 608). Yet, Freud had doubts and misgivings about this major work, some of which he confided to Fliess. Freud had doubts not about his theories and his growing convictions about them, but about the reception of these theories and the effects they would have. He pursued the subject of the dream in spurts and frequently pulled back, wondering, as he put it later, what would be thought and said "about one 'who disturbed the sleep of the world'" (Freud 1914b, p. 21).

About this, Freud was prophetic. *The Interpretation of Dreams,* which Freud came to consider his most outstanding work, was finished in 1896 but was not published until 1900. Although its reception was slow (only 351 copies were sold in the first 6 years), Freud always looked back upon this book as his major opus. Whenever he had doubts about the validity of his work, thinking back on the dream, he wrote later, would restore his spirits. Years after *The Interpretation of Dreams* first appeared, in the preface to the third (revised) English edition in 1931, Freud wrote, "Insights such as this fall to one's lot but once in a lifetime" (Freud 1900, p. xxxii).

Toward a General Psychology

Although Freud delayed publication of *The Interpretation of Dreams,* allowing it to gestate for several years, it was the publisher who finally held it another year to make the date of the publication 1900. This was an auspicious end to one century and an introduction to another. Having started with the clinical and proceeded to the normal, Freud's work from this point on moved equally between psychopathology and normal psychological phenomena. A strong characteristic of Freud's, in fact, was his seeing in all his observations the bridge and continuity between psychopathology and normal psychological phenomena. Having established the presence of infantile sexuality behind neurosis, Freud followed this by demonstrating, shockingly to the world, expression of the same conflicts in normal sleep and dreams.

After the appearance of the dream book, Freud, around 1905, published three books, each in its way connected to and a continuation of his work on dreams and on the neuroses. These studies, like that on the dream, carried the new discoveries more completely into normal psychological life and toward a theory of general psychology. Each, however, stressed the pathognomonic addition to general knowledge that comes from the new discipline of psychoanalysis—that is, the source and origin of human behavior in the unconscious system of mental life.

Three Essays on the Theory of Sexuality

One of these three books, much smaller than his book on dreams, was *Three Essays on the Theory of Sexuality* (1905c). In this work Freud organized and considerably amplified all that he had discovered in his work on the sexual instinct in psychoneuroses and dreams. Just as psychoneuroses and dreams, as noted by Freud, have complex substructures, sexuality is also not what it seems on the surface: sexuality is not a uniform activity leading to one restricted outcome; it consists of multiple components and variations.

Defining an instinct as having a source, aim, and object, Freud examined transgressions and aberrations with respect to both the aims and the object of human sexuality. With regard to "deviations" in the sexual object, Freud started with the inference of widespread homosexuality, either exclusively or under external circumstances that restrict heterosexual choice. Freud regarded this aberration as "inversion," that is, a transgression of the sexual object from the usual heterosexual drive choice to the object of the same sex. Examining the many variations in sexual life as seen in psychoanalytic investigation, Freud concluded that bisexuality exists universally in the unconscious of both genders.[3] Referring to bisexuality and homosexual practices not only in modern life but in ancient civilizations and primitive people, Freud pointed out that the object of the instinct varies not only in its sex but in its age (children, or immature adolescents or young adults, may be the object choices), in its specific characteristics or requirements, and even in species (animals, under certain conditions, being substituted for humans as an object choice).

The aims toward which the sexual instinct strives can also vary, lingering or stopping at preliminary stages normally quickly passed over on the path toward genital union. Intermediary aims of the

---

[3] On this point, he draws on and agrees with views held and communicated to him by Fliess.

sexual act, such as touching or looking, that are utilized and traversed during foreplay can become exaggerated and exist as goals in themselves to supplant the genital aim. Many sources of sexual stimulation, involving bodily regions other than the genital, such as mouth, anus, skin, or other specific areas, or even bits of clothing, such as women's underwear in fetishism, can come to take the place of genital organs as the aim of the sexual drive.

Freud related these deviations to the history of infantile sexuality and, from observations derived from psychoanalyses, constructed a developmental view of the course of sexuality throughout life. Applying sexuality in a broader sense than to genitality and reproduction, Freud emphasized that sexuality does not begin at puberty but at birth. Certain aspects of mother-infant interaction are described, from breast-feeding to related thumb sucking; also described are autoeroticism and infantile masturbation. Libido is the force through which the sexual instinct expresses itself in the more general sense. Freud traced the developmental history of the sexual instinct through various stages, defining oral and anal-sadistic phases that precede the 4- to 5-year-old's oedipal phase, which had been pointed to so much in his previous writings. A period of latency, or relative quiescence, with respect to sexual development then follows, until the onset of puberty.[4]

Ontogenetically, a preliminary stage of the process of development can, either through regression or fixation, be accentuated and can come to substitute for the entire action in sexual performance. Looking, being looked at, touching, smelling, hurting, being hurt—each can be accentuated to lead to various pathological sexual manifestations, such as scopophilia, exhibitionism, or sadomasochism. An important contribution in this work is the insight that many "deviations" can function in a mild form in normal life. Many of the early components or primitive developmental phases of sexual instincts find a function in adult life in the preliminary pleasure or

---

[4]Cumulative experience later speaks against this view. Latency turns out not to be so devoid of sexual content; further research and writings have filled in many gaps that existed in this earlier theory.

forepleasure of normal sex. What makes them pathological and "perversions" are their hypertrophy, their exclusivity, and their imperative nature.

In the psychoneuroses, the repressed sexual impulses are not typically of a normal kind but more often consist of repressed "partial" or "component" instincts, as Freud calls these impulses, emanating from erogenous zones that succeed each other developmentally en route to genitality. The findings of these repressed impulses in the neuroses, along with their overtness and excessiveness in the sexual aberrations, led to a formula of Freud's that "neuroses are . . . the negative of perversions" (Freud 1905c, p. 165). This formulation, although less visible and less quoted in recent years, has more recently been revived by the author (Rangell 1991) as still currently operative and useful, as it had been considered in the past.

Factors determining the outcomes of inversion or any of the forms of the perversions span from congenital to acquired. These factors operate in a complementary series, a concept that was to have a strong explanatory influence and wide applicability to many other polarities or dualities in mental functioning. With a strong input from one side, the other etiological factor would need to be mild, and vice versa, to produce the same final effect. Strong constitutional determinants need little psychological input, whereas intense psychological experiences or traumas can result in pathological outcomes with mild or absent biological factors. The factor of bisexuality, which was stressed by Freud, is operative in the entire gamut of the deviations or perversions.

The sexual theories of children arise from their own sexual constitution, their incomplete knowledge and observations, and their sexual fantasies. In spite of their errors and individualistic theories, children show more understanding than they are given credit for. Infantile sexuality, oedipal and other, is given up under the impact of the castration complex. Derivatives of infantile theories and early sexuality survive in later character traits, filtered and distorted by defense mechanisms such as reaction formation and sublimation. Throughout this clinical, observational, and theoretical work is the insight by Freud that there is reciprocity between the oedipal and preoedipal. Pregenital conflicts cause fixations (i.e., developmental lags or arrests) at earlier stages that affect the future oedipal phase, whereas unresolved oedipal conflicts bring about regressions (i.e., returns to previous points of pregenital fixations).

Freud ends *Three Essays on the Theory of Sexuality* by noting the opposition between civilization and the freedom of sexual development, a reflection that would be amplified by others in succeeding years, which indicates a wide and global applicability of his theories.

Slips and Jokes

The Psychopathology of Everyday Life.   Another of the books that appeared in close succession was *The Psychopathology of Everyday Life* (Freud 1901). Connected in subject matter and spirit to the phenomena of dreams, and also relating to normal phenomena rather than to psychopathology, the data pointed to and studied in this book involved forgetting, slips of the tongue, slips of the pen, and unexpected and inexplicable errors, trivial or serious, usually attributed to accident or chance. These "parapraxes," as they came to be known, were shown by Freud to be of the same order of unconscious motivation as dreams, symptoms, and other psychic outcomes. With these phenomena, copiously collected and intriguingly described, Freud demonstrated further his overriding thesis of psychic determinism, which was partly derived from and strongly maintained by his Helmholtzian influence.

The numerous examples provided from Freud's own life, from his clinical experiences, and from common events and observations demonstrate the same mechanism as is involved in the formation of neurotic symptoms—that is, final psychic outcomes that consist of compromise formations between repressed ideas and the repressing tendencies. Moreover, that which is repressed is the same infantile material that is repressed in dreams and neuroses, and sexual conflicts and anxieties play a universally prominent part. Although the concepts and mechanisms contained in *The Psychopathology of Everyday Life* are as complicated as, and qualitatively related to, the ideas underlying Freud's views on dreams and neuroses, they were easier for the public to absorb, so that this book and its contents became the most popular of Freud's writings and the most quickly integrated into public acceptance. The "Freudian slip," having a specific meaning (i.e., an "error," whether in speech or in writing, based on the irruption of a repressed impulse), became part of everyday language and communication.

Jokes and Their Relation to the Unconscious.   At about the same time, and in the same vein—this was a period in Freud's life of prolific creativity and converging insights—Freud (1905b) published *Jokes and Their Relation to the Unconscious.* This book, like the works on slips and errors, stemmed in part from the plays on words, which occur in dreams as well as in analytic and in common everyday experiences, and which frequently merge into slips, jokes, or curious expressions difficult to define. The sources and origins of these plays on words often go back to childhood, when there was a type of playing with words before the establishment of secondary-process logic and reality. Although the observations in these works on dreams, jokes, sexuality, and errors began in the late 1890s, these books were developed and written concurrently and were published in close succession from 1900 to 1905.

This serious book on wit and jokes demonstrates that the psychology of humor shares mechanisms in common with the methods, composition, and meaning of dreams. Condensation, displacements from essential to trivial ideas, symbolism, and superficial illogic in trains of thought are all present in humor, and their meaning and logic can be ascertained only from understanding the composition of the compromise formations from which they were formed. All stem equally from repression of unacceptable wishes and impulses from the unconscious. With respect to object relations, jokes need an audience to respond with laughter, to fulfill a social function of gain and pleasure.

The Case Histories

Freud's (and Breuer's) previous case reports had been numerous but relatively brief. In the period following 1900, however, Freud published a series of much more detailed clinical reports that came to be known as "the great case histories." These case histories are clinical experiences, pursued over variable periods of time, that have had a profound effect on both scientific and literary readerships. These histories read like novels but contain scientific data and observations from which groundbreaking theoretical advances in understanding can be claimed. Together with all other previous observations by Freud and, later, by other analysts, these clinical reports constitute the evidential base from which psychoanalytic theory is derived. Taken as a whole, these data add to the recognition that psychic reality, no less than physical reality, has a role in the causation of human behavior, both pathological and normal.

Dora

The first of the great case histories was that of Dora, an 18-year-old "hysterical" young woman whose treatment revolved around the analysis and interpretation of two dreams (see Freud 1905a [1901]). A complicated unconscious, repressed sexual history, past and ongoing, was brought to the surface, leading eventually to the removal of symptoms. The patient was caught in a complex web of sexual feelings, aroused and threatening, involving her father; a Herr K., a close friend of her father; and the wife of Herr K., the couple being close friends of both of Dora's parents. Although the treatment dealt with the adolescent patient's aroused sexual impulses and their repression, the patient's transference reactions to Freud were not exposed and interpreted adequately in this analysis, and consequently the treatment was prematurely terminated by the patient after 3 months. Transference in this case was recognized but not analyzed. In a postscript to the written account of the case, Freud defined transference, in a way that is enduring in spite of later modifications in its meaning, as new editions of impulses and fantasies aroused and made conscious during the analysis, displaced from earlier significant objects to the person of the analyst.

Little Hans

The second of Freud's great case histories concerned the analysis of a phobia of horses in a 5-year-old boy, Little Hans (Freud 1909a). This treatment was not conducted by Freud but by the patient's father under the guidance of Freud; both parents had been early adherents of Freud's. In view of the prominent presence of anxiety—the patient was afraid to leave the house for fear of being bitten by a horse—Freud considered the case as one of anxiety hysteria.

The illness began at age 3, when Hans began to have an excessive interest in and concern about his "widdler" (i.e., penis), comparing it with the "widdler" of his father and noting the lack of a "widdler" in his mother. A sister was born when the child was 3½ years old. The presence or absence of the "widdler" differentiated for Little Hans the animate from the inanimate as well as the boy from the girl. The analysis revolved around phallic conflicts, ignorance and anxiety about the anatomical differences between the sexes, masturbation, castration anxiety, and the Oedipus complex. Little Hans had a fantasy of a big giraffe (father), with a long neck (penis), and a smaller crumpled giraffe, which related to the boy's concept of parental intercourse (as from behind, as children see in animals). Hans had taken close notice of his mother's pregnancy and, associated with his own developed anal eroticism, had entertained a fantasy and concept of anal birth. In Hans's fantasy, his little sister was a "lumf" that came out of the behind of the crumpled giraffe.

Interpretations of the little boy's unconscious anxieties, especially his fear of castration, his infantile theories of sexuality and childbirth, and his unconscious fantasies, were presented to the patient by his father under the guidance and with the advice of Freud. From the many insights gained in the treatment, the patient recovered, and his case was much quoted in the history of psychoanalysis.

Although this case later had the distinction of being thought of as the first child analysis, Freud himself was at that time more aware of the limitations than of the possibility of child analysis in general.

It was also, however, the first instance in which Freud's retrospective reconstructions from adult analyses, such as those involving the Oedipus complex and castration anxiety, were confirmed by direct observations of the developing child.

The Rat Man

Another of the great case histories of Freud's was the analysis of an obsessional neurosis in a patient who came to be known as the "Rat Man" (Freud 1909b). The name came from the patient's symptom of an obsessive fear that some rats would burrow up the anus of a lady friend and also the anus of his father (who was deceased). A complicated story was traced involving the payment of money to a particular person, in a particular way, with many peculiar obstructing circumstances, necessitating numerous obsessive thoughts and compulsive acts. The treatment brought out much material about guilt, scopophilia, death wishes against the father, and early punishment for masturbation.

Anal concerns and anal erotism were prominent, and fixation and psychopathology focused on the anal-sadistic phase of development. Symbolism, as in the dream, was strongly utilized in the understanding of the symptoms, along with a play on words and thoughts. The rat was equated with feces, and with the penis and with money. The equation feces = money, which was brought out here, was to become a common formula in analyses from that time on. Character traits around repressed anality, first described in detail in this clinical report, were later amplified by Freud and others and extended to widely seen phenomena in life. These amplifications would form the nucleus of many future contributions on character pathology, much as would the concept that neurotic symptoms stem from other specific points of fixation or regression. The preoedipal and oedipal are interrelated, the clinical material being confirmatory of Freud's thesis of the reciprocity between the two levels of conflict as expressed in his *Three Essays on the Theory of Sexuality.*

In obsessional cases, unlike in cases of hysteria, trauma is remembered but is dealt with by denial and isolation rather than by repression. Typically, the idea is dissociated from its accompanying affect. Obsessive-compulsive patients have a strong penchant for doubt and uncertainty, to mitigate and keep at bay forbidden death wishes. Doubting and compulsion fortify each other, and each makes the other necessary. There is a pronounced ambivalence—love and hate—to self and others. The patient has violent impulses of self-destruction, as well as hostile wishes toward close objects. Because of these impulses, for defensive purposes, thought takes the place of action. There is also a feeling of omnipotence of thought, so that, to the patient, to think hostile thoughts about someone also places that person in realistic danger. Secondary obsessions and compulsions follow, in agonizing succession and profusion, to undo the first series of symptoms. Intrinsic to this unconscious sequence of thought processes is a strong unconscious belief in magical thinking, superstition, and prophecy, all of which the patient in Freud's case demonstrated despite a high intelligence.

Freud's patient underwent a marked cure of these severe symptoms and an improvement in his personality over the course of his 1-year analysis.

Schreber

Yet another of the great case histories reported by Freud (1911b) concerned observations and insights on paranoia, an emphasis that is surprising for early psychoanalysis, given that up to that time it had primarily focused on the neuroses. Like the case of Little Hans, who had been treated by his father, this case also did not come from Freud's direct clinical treatment of a patient, but was an analysis by Freud of the published memoirs of a Dr. Schreber, a successful, intelligent jurist, concerning his own paranoid illness. Contrary to the opinion of many critics that "Freudian" psychoanalysis is rigid and narrowly focused, psychoanalysis, as Freud did, derives data from any source and finds applications to all fields.

A number of important subjects and mechanisms alluded to in and derived from this study were subsequently elaborated upon in future theoretical developments. Projection is the primary defense mechanism in paranoia, as repression is the primary defense mechanism in hysteria. Hypochondriasis is a baseline to paranoia as anxiety is to neurosis.[5] The patient's central delusion of being persecuted by his doctor was related to unconscious, passive homosexual wishes that were repressed and turned into the delusion of being persecuted by the man, father, God, doctor. Schreber had a central fantasy that he would transform and redeem the world, for which he first had to be made into a female and to be submissive to and joined with God. Castration fear, related to the repressed homosexual impulse, was converted to its opposite, Schreber's wish to be transformed into a woman. Freud had traced the sexual instincts developmentally from autoerotism through narcissism to alloerotism; in paranoia, however, as Freud noted, regression occurs in the reverse direction, with the ego moving from object love through passive homosexuality to autoerotism. In the megalomania found in paranoid patients, the sexual instinct invests the subject or the subject's ego with its own libido. The subject of narcissism pointed to here introduced a confusing and disturbing subject for future development.

In a concluding section on the "mechanisms of paranoia," Freud described the various forms taken by paranoid delusions as consisting of all the possible variants by which the underlying proposition "I, a man, love him, a man" can be denied and contradicted. The fate of this wish-impulse leads, by various distortions, to 1) delusions of persecution ("I do not love him, I hate him, and [by projection] he hates me"); 2) erotomania ("I do not love him, I love her, and [by projection] she loves me"); and 3) delusions of jealousy ("I do not love him, she loves him"). A special delusional relation of Schreber's to the sun led Freud to an understanding of myth formation and to the equation in this case of the sun with the father.

The Wolf Man

The last of the detailed great case histories (Freud 1918[1914]), published in 1917–1918, involved probably the most famous patient of

---

[5]This formulation, unlike others derived from this case, did not survive in the same way as did others, because anxiety came to be conceptualized as an important component in all psychopathology.

psychoanalysis, the Wolf Man, who began his treatment in 1910. The patient was followed by various psychoanalysts until his death in 1979 at the age of 92.

The patient, a young man of an aristocratic Russian family, was in a severely helpless mental state and had sought conventional treatment from the most authoritative psychiatrists on the continent, including Kraepelin in Munich, before seeing Freud. By today's standards, the patient would be considered to have a borderline personality or a condition closer to psychosis. His first analytic treatment by Freud lasted 4 years and was ended by an unusual method: by Freud's setting a fixed date for termination to break an impenetrable resistance. This maneuver, which introduced an active analytic role that would be much discussed in later years, resulted at the time in what was considered a successful therapeutic outcome. However, 5 years later, the patient underwent a subsequent period of analysis with Freud for 4 months. Sixteen years later the patient was analyzed again, by Ruth Mack Brunswick, to whom Freud had referred him, for a paranoid psychosis.

The patient's first treatment was mainly an analysis of a childhood neurosis occurring from about ages 3 to 10 years as analyzed retrospectively 15 years later. This treatment, like that with several previous patients, revolved largely around the analysis of a dream, the now-famous childhood dream of this patient, in which six or seven white wolves were sitting silently in a tree outside his opened bedroom window. Interpretations of this dream went on for a few years. From the memories and associations around this period, the infantile life of the patient was reconstructed, weaving together a marked early oral fixation, an anal-sadistic phase, and a complicated Oedipus complex. The analysis revealed a strong bisexuality, latent passive homosexual wishes toward the father, castration anxiety and defenses against these wishes, and an identification with the castrated wolf-mother.

The patient's illness began with a fear of wolves and was followed by a severe obsessional neurosis centering around religious themes. Based on converging clinical data, and not on an actual memory of the patient's, Freud reconstructed the etiology of the neurosis, pointing strongly to an incident involving the patient's witnessing as a child an act of parental intercourse, the associations to which were described in vivid, idiosyncratic detail. (It was from that time on that this event, when observed by a child, was called "the primal scene.") Based on Freud's analysis of the patient's dreams and associative data, the patient, at the age of 18 months, supposedly saw his parents copulating, with the father behind the mother, who was in a crouched position like an animal (cf. Little Hans's fantasy of the big and the crumpled giraffes). The question of whether this event was memory or fantasy was discussed in detail by Freud. His conclusion—that the results would be the same in either case—elevated the role of fantasy to that of actual trauma in the etiology of neuroses, a conceptual shift that would have far-reaching significance for psychoanalytic theory.

Seductions of the patient by his sister (who was 2 years older than the patient and who, since the time the patient was $3\frac{1}{4}$ years old, had played with his penis); sexual excitement from seeing the maid's buttocks, which were inadvertently exposed while she was scrubbing the floor; and castration threats from both of these females—all served as future nuclei for the boy's castration terror. The obsessional neurosis that followed the phobia was rooted in anal erotism and the anal-sadistic phase. In this patient there again emerged the equation money = feces, as in the case of the so-called Rat Man. In addition to deriving much from this case about psychoanalytic theory and technique, Freud used the observed data in this clinical report to counter the theories of Adler and Jung, who both had split from him previously over the issue of childhood sexuality.[6]

[6]After the analysis, the patient spent his subsequent life in Vienna and lived under the aura of having been Freud's famous patient. In addition to undergoing treatment with Ruth Mack Brunswick, as alluded to earlier in this chapter, he was befriended and for many years until his death helped both emotionally and materially by Muriel Gardiner. Although the ex-patient was laudatory and grateful to "the Professor" during many of these postanalytic years, before he died in 1979 he became derogatory toward and accusatory of Freud, as reported in a book by an Austrian journalist (Obholzer 1982) based on interviews with him during the 1970s.

The unusual quality of Freud's style in presenting these case histories was a distinct departure from that usually employed in a scientific discipline. In presenting clinical reports, as well as in delivering lectures, Freud demonstrated a manner both matter-of-fact and nondefensive, anticipating the likely resistances of an average listener or reader. The method and manner may also be viewed in connection with the contents being conveyed. One may extrapolate from Freud's writing and speaking style how his delivery and influence must have been experienced by the listening patient, particularly since the interpretations and understanding Freud was then imparting were totally new, and thus unfamiliar, and capable of arousing shock and disbelief.

All of these major case histories of Freud's provide evidence supporting the theory of the sexual etiology of the spectrum of psychoneuroses and are consistent with and confirmatory of Freud's descriptions in his *Three Essays on the Theory of Sexuality*. All show the span of causative agents from preoedipal to oedipal foci, with fixations at and regressions to all childhood developmental levels, however more prominent one phase may be in a particular neurosis than in another. This is to counteract some misunderstandings and misrepresentations in later years about the sole emphasis on oedipal pathology in early Freudian clinical cases, to the exclusion of preoedipal causative or predisposing factors. These cases also demonstrate how all theory stems from clinical observations, however much the establishment of theory also then guides the clinical analyst in observing and understanding further data. The clinical and theoretical are reciprocal.

The Technique of Psychoanalysis

Considering the complexity and individuality of psychoanalysis as a technical procedure, Freud wrote much less on technique than he did on theory and understanding. However, although his papers on technique are considered relatively meager, scientific and didactic papers by Freud on the technical aspects of psychoanalysis are not completely lacking. Although the therapeutic path of an analysis can proceed only if the analyst himself or herself is free of barriers to listening and resonating to the unconscious of his or her patients, Freud nevertheless did lay down a number of principles and guidelines for his technical method. Besides the sections of his clinical case reports that cast light on technique, in 1911 to 1915 Freud published six papers specifically on technique, on such subjects as dream interpretation (Freud 1911a); the dynamics of transference (Freud 1912a); recommendations to physicians practicing psychoanalysis (Freud 1912b); the beginning of treatment (Freud 1913a); remembering, repeating, and working-through (Freud 1914c); and the analyst's attitude toward transference love (Freud 1915[1914]). Although many aspects of Freud's original recommendations for technique have been caricatured and falsely attacked, such as the popular understanding (or misunderstanding) of analytic neutrality, the essence of the analytic attitude and Freud's explanations of its role and desirability as described in these papers have withstood the test of time.

Narcissism

In 1914, coming near the end of the first phase of psychoanalytic theory formation, Freud now dealt with in some detail a subject that had been alluded to previously in clinical data but had not been considered before as an issue in itself and in its implications for theory. The subject was narcissism, from the Greek myth of Narcissus, the boy who, Freud wrote, was in love with his own body. Narcissism as a trait, as an attitude toward one's own body usually reserved for the body of the sexual object, was described by Freud in an array of observed phenomena, from its connection with the megalomania within the paranoid symptoms of the Schreber case, to its function as a normal intermediate stage in erotic development.

Finding narcissistic phenomena in conditions as diverse as schizophrenia and dementia praecox, in primitive people (Freud always regarded phylogeny as casting light on individual ontogenetic development), and in normal childhood prompted Freud (1914a) to try to incorporate the concept of primary and normal narcissism into his libido and instinct theory. In turning to this subject at this time in a theoretical way, Freud was aiming to incorporate into his general theory narcissistic phenomena that posed problems to instinct theory and at the same time to counter divisive formulations of Jung and Adler that stressed self interests and nonsexual motives while rejecting Freud's libido theory. The result, however, was a complicated and at times tortuous line of reasoning that never reached a satisfactory unified view and that led to amplifications in later years that in many respects were further divisive rather than clarifying.

Writing on narcissism, Freud differentiated object libido and ego libido. As he had defined previously, in the *Three Essays on the Theory of Sexuality, ego libido* is the psychic representative of a quantum of sexual psychic energy contained within, and directed toward, the self. *Object libido* is psychic energy directed toward sexual objects.[7] In development, and throughout life, this reservoir of libidinal energy moves from the self (or the ego) to the object, or, under certain conditions, in the reverse direction (i.e., it can be withdrawn from the object and revert back to the ego). Among various such conditions noted, the path from primary narcissism to object love, from self-absorption to the love of others, is subject to regression, such as during sleep, during painful illness, in some instances of being in love, and in hypochondriasis.

The concept of the *ego-ideal*, introduced by Freud in "On Narcissism: An Introduction" (Freud 1914a), has proved relatively stable and has remained connected to many subsequent discussions and debates about narcissism. Originating from the internalization of cultural and ethical values, the ego-ideal comprises a cluster of guidelines of behavior and is a forerunner of the superego, or actually a formation between and overlapping ego and superego. It is this formation that comes into conflict with instinctual impulses, causing repression.

---

[7]It is important to keep in mind that at this stage Freud uses "ego" to connote the self, or the individual; only later does ego become a psychic system, one of several. For a definition of the "object," see discussion of Freud's five papers on metapsychology later in this chapter.

Status of Psychoanalytic Theory:
The Five Papers on Metapsychology

The development of psychoanalytic theory could, for heuristic purposes, be thought of as occurring in two phases, with the first phase ending near the midpoint of World War I. Toward the end of this first phase of Freud's cumulating theoretical system, he began to introduce new, and what he felt were necessary, concepts and engaged in several summarizing formulations. His confronting the puzzling subject of narcissism was one such undertaking at this time.

In a mood varying between resignation and gradually feeling on the brink of new discoveries, Freud was motivated to sum up his theoretical life work to this point in a proposed book on "metapsychology," a term he used to describe an overall synthesizing view of his evolved theory.[8] By metapsychology, Freud now meant a comprehensive description of any mental process that approaches the subject from the converging directions of all the points of view thus far developed—that is, the dynamic, topographic, economic, and genetic. Twelve papers were the plan for Freud's book on metapsychology, of which five survived and were published and seven were lost (presumably, it is thought, destroyed by Freud). All of those published were written in a period of 7 weeks in the spring of 1915. Ernest Jones, Freud's biographer, surmised that as Freud became increasingly aware of new thoughts that were crowding in on him and that would significantly alter what he had described to that point, he destroyed the seven still unpublished manuscripts.

In the first of the five papers published, "Instincts and Their Vicissitudes" (1915a), Freud, attending again to this original discovery, viewed instincts as on the frontier between the psychic and the somatic; Freud retained his orientation in biology but faced the somatic from his stance within the psychological side of the border. Instincts are the psychic representatives of stimuli originating from within the organism (i.e., from the sources of the instincts). The pressure of an instinct is, in Freud's view, the force of the demand

---

[8]The only other comparable summary of his total theoretical view that he had written to that time was Chapter 7 of *The Interpretation of Dreams*.

for work that the instinct represents. As stated previously, instincts have a source, an aim, and an object. The *source* is the somatic process in an organ or part of the body whose stimulus is represented in mental life by the instinct. The *aim* is satisfaction, which can only be obtained by removing the state of stimulation at its source. The *object* of the instinct is the thing (or person) through which the instinct is able to achieve its aim.

As to how many and which instincts there are, Freud at this phase proposed two primary instincts: an ego, or self-preservative, instinct and a sexual instinct. The first is in the service of preserving the individual, the second in preserving and perpetuating the race. Freud regarded this as a temporary hypothesis to be discarded whenever further knowledge would make its abandonment desirable or necessary. At this point in psychoanalytic theory, the two instincts were conceptualized as being in conflict with each other. The sexual instincts, the main ones studied by psychoanalysis thus far, can follow four paths: repression, sublimation, reversal into the opposite, and being turned back from the object upon the subject.

In the four other papers in this connected group, Freud takes up in greater detail than before, in formulations that have become classic and are much utilized clinically, the following issues: 1) the mechanism of repression (Freud 1915b); 2) the psychology and characteristics of the unconscious (1915d) and the topographical point of view of which it is a central part; 3) a metapsychological supplement to the theory of dreams (1917a[1915]), which adds to the psychology of dreams the effects of the characteristics of sleep itself (i.e., the narcissistic withdrawal that takes place then) on all of the psychic systems; and 4) a bridge between the normal process of mourning over a loss and the pathological depression, even to the point of psychosis, of melancholia.

In "Mourning and Melancholia" (Freud 1917b[1915]), following up on the paper on narcissism written a few years earlier, Freud further developed the critical ego-ideal described in the earlier paper into the construct of the "super-ego," with its role in producing a sense of guilt. The mechanism of identification is stressed in the choice of an object, which is prepared in advance by a wish to incorporate that object into the self. In melancholia, in contrast to mourning, the cathexis or interest in the object is again replaced by an identification with it. The aggression against the self and the self-reviling that take place in melancholia are, according to Freud, due to a turning upon the self of the aggressive wishes that had been directed unconsciously toward the lost object. Freud noted that there is a tendency for psychotic depression to change to a manic phase when the work of melancholia is finished, with the energy that was freed from narcissistic preoccupation being used in a wild and energetic re-cathexis of external objects and the world.

Applied Theory, War, and Death

The Great War was in progress and colored the development of Freud's ideas in his correspondence with European colleagues who were on both sides of the developing conflict. Two of Freud's sons, the eldest and the youngest, were conscripted into the German army. Freud's thoughts during the war turned to the subjects of aggression and death.

In his essay "Thoughts for the Times on War and Death," Freud (1915c) noted the loss of the mental achievements of humanity and civilization, a loss that causes a debasement of highly achieved goals and values and an uncovering of primal man in each individual. The low morality shown by states that pose as the guardians of moral standards, and the brutality shown by individuals who are participants in the highest human civilization, arouse a general sense of disillusionment. The role of death in psychic life and the psychological attitudes toward death are accentuated by the common experience of mortality and death in large numbers during a time of war. Death, which has been denied and repressed, can no longer be defensively distanced. The unconscious denies the fact of our own death and of our murderous wishes toward strangers. War strips away the accretions of civilization and lays bare the primitive man or woman in each of us.

In this essay, Freud not only is looking at current events and reflecting on them from a psychological perspective but is on the brink of certain major theoretical reformulations. Instincts will be reclassified, with an aggressive or even a death instinct added, and the two previously separate instincts—sexual and self-preservative— fused into one. The role of the superego in human life will be given a full place alongside of the instincts and the ego. The theoretical conceptions of the topographic system will yield to, or move aside to include, a view of three nodal clusters of functions taking the form of interacting psychic structures constituting new psychic systems. With these new concepts, the nature of intrapsychic conflict will change. Central to these changes, the theory of anxiety will also change and advance, from the nature of the formation of anxiety to its function and meaning. Anxiety will become an unconscious signal of impending danger.

Another achievement near the end of the first phase of Freud's psychoanalytic theoretical developments is a publication that apparently represents Freud's stocktaking of psychoanalytic theory. In 1916 and 1917, Freud compiled and published his latest university lectures as the *Introductory Lectures on Psycho-Analysis* (Freud 1916[1915], 1916[1915–1916], 1917[1916–1917]). In chapters that could be as valuable to a beginning reader as to the most experienced practicing psychoanalyst, Freud summarized the various subjects, and the relevant concepts, that had been developed, including parapraxes, dreams, and the general theory of the neuroses. The last of these, an overview to that time of Freud's almost entire clinical-theoretical point of view, includes detailed summaries of psychic trauma, resistance and repression, the sexual life, symptom formation, the problem of anxiety, the libido theory, narcissism,[9] transference, and analytic therapy. There are also, at the end of the lectures, lists and indexes of parapraxes, dreams, and symbols.

The war will be coming to an end, psychoanalysis will be reassessed, and the second phase in the development of psychoanalytic theory will proceed rapidly.

---

[9]Energies directed toward the objects of sexual desires are libidinal; those directed toward self-preservation are ego interests; egoism is the nonsexual self-preservation; narcissism is the libidinal component added to egoism.

Summary

The following is a summary of the status of psychoanalytic theory following its first phase of development, from the 1890s to the end of World War I.

1. Psychoanalysis, as it had gradually evolved, is simultaneously a means of treatment, a method of investigation, and a theory of the mind.
2. Psychoanalysis is a psychological theory with biological roots.
3. The interface and interconnecting links between the neurophysiological and the psychological could not at that time be satisfactorily delineated.
4. Human instincts are on the frontier between the somatic and the psychic.
5. Instincts can be classified, as was done during this first phase, as either sexual or self-preservative instincts.
6. Symptoms, dreams, parapraxes, jokes, and all other final psychic outcomes derive from the same unconscious compromise formations between instinctual impulses and defensive forces.
7. Defenses against instincts described during this stage are repression, projection, introjection, sublimation, identification, and, from dreams, reversal into the opposite and turning impulses directed toward the object back upon the subject.
8. Anxiety, as described during this period, is a neurophysiological process that results from direct transformation of repressed libidinal instincts into a somatic and psychic response.
9. A metapsychological, or total converging, psychoanalytic view, as had developed during this phase, includes the dynamic, topographic, economic, and genetic-developmental points of view.

At the end of World War I, Freud is in a synthesizing mood and is about to venture into a major, overall modification of theory. In the process of inner reflection and about to be formulated are the merging of the self-preservative and libidinal instincts, the addition of an aggressive and/or death instinct to the sexual instinct, and a shift in the understanding of anxiety from its physiological method of formation to its hermeneutic role as a signal of danger.

In metapsychology, the structural will be added to the other points of view, and the superego to the id and ego, to now compose three structural systems. Psychic conflict will come to be described in terms of structural components (id, ego, superego) instead of topographic components (Cs, UCs). A more comprehensive understanding will accrue of clinical and other observable phenomena of negative and self-defeating human behavior "beyond the pleasure principle." These additions, which at the end of the first phase of development of psychoanalytic theory are just beginning to take shape, will make for major and significant changes in the understanding of human behavioral outcomes.

Addendum and Postscript

In the 1990s, 100 years later, there is a rather strong disagreement among analysts about the value and practical usefulness of the recountal of this history of the origins of psychoanalysis. Some feel that it is only of historical and academic interest, and of little relevance to modern understanding and practice. Others, such as this author, believe that absorption of this historical progression is an integral part of the knowledge and appreciation of the psychoanalytic experience.

As a heuristic justification for repeating Freud's journey, from a pragmatic point of view, Freud's sequence of discoveries is recapitulated in the steplike increments with which self-discovery takes place in psychoanalysis to this day. A process similar to that which applies to every patient in analysis can be said to apply to every student of psychoanalysis. In both cases, one discovers and comes to acquire conscious knowledge of the unconscious, the sexual instincts and their manifestations in various forms, and a force of resistance against these, operative at every stage, opposing the process of uncovering and insight. These elements, slowly and irregularly accumulated, are gradually appreciated and understood. Some are easily accepted and conveyed, whereas others are resisted, opposed, denied, defended against, and come to have a variety of ultimate fates.

Impulses, thoughts, affects, and distortions are discovered to be present, such as aggression or, conversely, the fear of it, a problem of passivity. Whereas the person generally feels quite normally in control at the beginning of the psychoanalytic quest (as a student or patient, combined in the training analysand), the latent and eventually overt presence of anxiety is discovered and acknowledged, along with other affects, guilt, shame, and depression, which the person had thought were more under control than they turn out to be. Throughout the process there is a struggle between furtherance of insight by the psychoanalyst and resistance against such furtherance of insight by the patient—an interplay or dialectic that becomes a central feature of the process and discipline.

This typical and unique "research" procedure that is ubiquitously experienced by a seeker of psychoanalytic insight, both patient and analyst, in a sense recapitulates the struggle of the first psychoanalyst in coming to the stages of insight attained laboriously and with irregular flashes of progress. Hence, this historical review that opens this book acquires practical importance. The basic psychoanalytic method—that of obtaining observations and data and building theory based on these—though elaborated and refined, remains necessary and enduring.

References

Breuer J, Freud S: Studies on hysteria (1893–1895), in Standard Edition of the Complete Psychological Works of Sigmund Freud, Vol 2. Translated and edited by Strachey J. London, Hogarth Press, 1955, pp 1–319

Freud S: The Origins of Psycho-Analysis. Letters to Wilhelm Fliess, Drafts and Notes (1887–1902). Translated by Mosbacher E, Strachey J. Edited by Bonaparte M, Freud A, Kris E. New York, Basic Books, 1954

Freud S: Preface to the translation of Charcot's Lectures on the Diseases of the Nervous System (1886), in Standard Edition of the Complete Psychological Works of Sigmund Freud, Vol 1. Translated and edited by Strachey J. London, Hogarth Press, 1966, pp 17–22

Freud S: Preface and footnotes to the translation of Charcot's Tuesday Lectures (1892–1894), in Standard Edition of the Complete Psychological Works of Sigmund Freud, Vol 1. Translated and edited by Strachey J. London, Hogarth Press, 1966, pp 129–143

Freud S: The neuro-psychoses of defence (1894), in Standard Edition of the Complete Psychological Works of Sigmund Freud, Vol 3. Translated and edited by Strachey J. London, Hogarth Press, 1962, pp 41–68

Freud S: On the grounds for detaching a particular syndrome from neurasthenia under the description 'anxiety neurosis' (1895a[1894]), in Standard Edition of the Complete Psychological Works of Sigmund Freud, Vol 3. Translated and edited by Strachey J. London, Hogarth Press, 1962, pp 85–117

Freud S: Obsessions and phobias: their psychical mechanism and their aetiology (1895b[1894]), in Standard Edition of the Complete Psychological Works of Sigmund Freud, Vol 3. Translated and edited by Strachey J. London, Hogarth Press, 1962, pp 69–84

Freud S: The aetiology of hysteria (1896a), in Standard Edition of the Complete Psychological Works of Sigmund Freud, Vol 3. Translated and edited by Strachey J. London, Hogarth Press, 1962, pp 187–221

Freud S: Further remarks on the neuro-psychoses of defence (1896b), in Standard Edition of the Complete Psychological Works of Sigmund Freud, Vol 3. Translated and edited by Strachey J. London, Hogarth Press, 1962, pp 157–185

Freud S: Heredity and the aetiology of the neuroses (1896c), in Standard Edition of the Complete Psychological Works of Sigmund Freud, Vol 3. Translated and edited by Strachey J. London, Hogarth Press, 1962, pp 141–156

Freud S: Sexuality in the aetiology of the neuroses (1898), in Standard Edition of the Complete Psychological Works of Sigmund Freud, Vol 3. Translated and edited by Strachey J. London, Hogarth Press, 1962, pp 259–285

Freud S: The interpretation of dreams (1900), in Standard Edition of the Complete Psychological Works of Sigmund Freud, Vols 4 and 5. Translated and edited by Strachey J. London, Hogarth Press, 1953

Freud S: The psychopathology of everyday life (1901), in Standard Edition of the Complete Psychological Works of Sigmund Freud, Vol 6. Translated and edited by Strachey J. London, Hogarth Press, 1960

Freud S: Fragment of an analysis of a case of hysteria (1905a[1901]), in Standard Edition of the Complete Psychological Works of Sigmund Freud, Vol 7. Translated and edited by Strachey J. London, Hogarth Press, 1953, pp 1–122

Freud S: Jokes and their relation to the unconscious (1905b), in Standard Edition of the Complete Psychological Works of Sigmund Freud, Vol 8. Translated and edited by Strachey J. London, Hogarth Press, 1960

Freud S: Three essays on the theory of sexuality, I: the sexual aberrations (1905c), in Standard Edition of the Complete Psychological Works of Sigmund Freud, Vol 7. Translated and edited by Strachey J. London, Hogarth Press, 1953, pp 135–172

Freud S: Analysis of a phobia in a five-year-old boy (1909a), in Standard Edition of the Complete Psychological Works of Sigmund Freud, Vol 10. Translated and edited by Strachey J. London, Hogarth Press, 1955, pp 1–149

Freud S: Notes upon a case of obsessional neurosis (1909b), in Standard Edition of the Complete Psychological Works of Sigmund Freud, Vol 10. Translated and edited by Strachey J. London, Hogarth Press, 1955, pp 151–318

Freud S: The handling of dream-interpretation in psycho-analysis (1911a), in Standard Edition of the Complete Psychological Works of Sigmund Freud, Vol 12. Translated and edited by Strachey J. London, Hogarth Press, 1958, pp 89–96

Freud S: Psycho-analytic notes on an autobiographical account of a case of paranoia (dementia paranoides) (1911b), in Standard Edition of the Complete Psychological Works of Sigmund Freud, Vol 12. Translated and edited by Strachey J. London, Hogarth Press, 1958, pp 1–82

Freud S: The dynamics of transference (1912a), in Standard Edition of the Complete Psychological Works of Sigmund Freud, Vol 12. Translated and edited by Strachey J. London, Hogarth Press, 1958, pp 97–108

Freud S: Recommendations to physicians practising psycho-analysis (1912b), in Standard Edition of the Complete Psychological Works of Sigmund Freud, Vol 12. Translated and edited by Strachey J. London, Hogarth Press, 1958, pp 109–120

Freud S: On beginning the treatment (further recommendations on the technique of psycho-analysis I) (1913a), in Standard Edition of the Complete Psychological Works of Sigmund Freud, Vol 12. Translated and edited by Strachey J. London, Hogarth Press, 1958, pp 121–144

Freud S: Totem and taboo: some points of agreement between the mental lives of savages and neurotics (1913b[1912–1913]), in Standard Edition of the Complete Psychological Works of Sigmund Freud, Vol 13. Translated and edited by Strachey J. London, Hogarth Press, 1953, pp vii–xv, 1–162

Freud S: On narcissism: an introduction (1914a), in Standard Edition of the Complete Psychological Works of Sigmund Freud, Vol 14. Translated and edited by Strachey J. London, Hogarth Press, 1957, pp 67–102

Freud S: On the history of the psycho-analytic movement (1914b), in Standard Edition of the Complete Psychological Works of Sigmund Freud, Vol 14. Translated and edited by Strachey J. London, Hogarth Press, 1957, pp 3–66

Freud S: Remembering, repeating and working-through (further recommendations on the technique of psycho-analysis II) (1914c), in Standard Edition of the Complete Psychological Works of Sigmund Freud, Vol 12. Translated and edited by Strachey J. London, Hogarth Press, 1958, pp 145–156

Freud S: Observations on transference-love (further recommendations on the technique of psycho-analysis III) (1915[1914]), in Standard Edition of the Complete Psychological Works of Sigmund Freud, Vol 12. Translated and edited by Strachey J. London, Hogarth Press, 1958, pp 157–173

Freud S: Instincts and their vicissitudes (1915a), in Standard Edition of the Complete Psychological Works of Sigmund Freud, Vol 14. Translated and edited by Strachey J. London, Hogarth Press, 1957, pp 109–140

Freud S: Repression (1915b), in Standard Edition of the Complete Psychological Works of Sigmund Freud, Vol 14. Translated and edited by Strachey J. London, Hogarth Press, 1957, pp 141–158

Freud S: Thoughts for the times on war and death (1915c), in Standard Edition of the Complete Psychological Works of Sigmund Freud, Vol 14. Translated and edited by Strachey J. London, Hogarth Press, 1957, pp 273–302

Freud S: The unconscious (1915d), in Standard Edition of the Complete Psychological Works of Sigmund Freud, Vol 14. Translated and edited by Strachey J. London, Hogarth Press, 1957, pp 159–215

Freud S: Introductory lectures on psycho-analysis, Part I: parapraxes (1916[1915]), in Standard Edition of the Complete Psychological Works of Sigmund Freud, Vol 15. Translated and edited by Strachey J. London, Hogarth Press, 1961, pp 13–79

Freud S: Introductory lectures on psycho-analysis, Part II: dreams (1916[1915–1916]), in Standard Edition of the Complete Psychological Works of Sigmund Freud, Vol 15. Translated and edited by Strachey J. London, Hogarth Press, 1961, pp 81–239

Freud S: Introductory lectures on psycho-analysis, Part III: general theory of the neuroses (1917[1916–1917]), in Standard Edition of the Complete Psychological Works of Sigmund Freud, Vol 16. Translated and edited by Strachey J. London, Hogarth Press, 1963, pp 241–463

Freud S: A metapsychological supplement to the theory of dreams (1917a[1915]), in Standard Edition of the Complete Psychological Works of Sigmund Freud, Vol 14. Translated and edited by Strachey J. London, Hogarth Press, 1957, pp 217–235

Freud S: Mourning and melancholia (1917b[1915]), in Standard Edition of the Complete Psychological Works of Sigmund Freud, Vol 14. Translated and edited by Strachey J. London, Hogarth Press, 1957, pp 237–260

Freud S: From the history of an infantile neurosis (1918[1914]), in Standard Edition of the Complete Psychological Works of Sigmund Freud, Vol 17. Translated and edited by Strachey J. London, Hogarth Press, 1955, pp 1–123

Freud S: Project for a scientific psychology (1950[1895]), in Standard Edition of the Complete Psychological Works of Sigmund Freud, Vol 1. Translated and edited by Strachey J. London, Hogarth Press, 1966, pp 281–397

Freud S: Some early unpublished letters of Freud. Int J Psychoanal 50:419–427, 1969

Jones E: The Life and Work of Sigmund Freud, Vol 1. New York, Basic Books, 1953

Obholzer K: The Wolf-Man: Conversations With Freud's Patient—Sixty Years Later. Translated by Shaw M. New York, Continuum, 1982

Rangell L: Castration. J Am Psychoanal Assoc 39:3–23, 1991

2

The Structural Model

Jacob A. Arlow, M.D.

Freud's formulation of the topographic theory derived mainly from two sources: from his experience of treating patients who suffered from hysteria and from the analysis of dreams. In conceptualizing the psychological nature of dreams and hysterical symptoms, Freud relied heavily on the ideas of Darwin and Hughlings Jackson, among others. Fundamentally a biologist, Freud thought in terms of the dynamic effect on the mind of the primitive, the instinctual, and the sexual. To this he added the neurological concepts of layering of functional structures—that is, of how later, "more civilizing" cortical developments served to moderate and even subdue entirely the primitive, subcortical, archaic biological pressures for immediate and total gratification. The division of mental activity into what is primitive, instinctual, and repressed and what is rational, realistic, and conscious or preconscious seemed to furnish in one broad stroke a theory that was all-encompassing as well as impressively illuminating. Each mental content is characterized by the degree to which it is accessible to consciousness (i.e., Is the element conscious or does its existence have to be inferred from derivative conscious representations?).

Difficulties With the Topographic Theory

As Freud continued his clinical investigations, however, he came upon many psychological phenomena that did not conform to the postulates of the topographic theory. To wit, he noticed that not all the mental processes that occurred outside of consciousness were necessarily instinctual (i.e., sexual in nature). For example, Freud found that patients regularly were quite unaware of the various means they used to fend off derivatives of the instinctual drives. Also, he discovered that, for the most part, the mechanisms of the mind, later referred to as the mechanisms of defense, regularly function outside the scope of awareness.

In addition, in his topographic theory, Freud had hypothesized that the moral forces of the mind that opposed drive derivatives were components of the system Preconscious (Pcs) or system Conscious (Cs). A number of striking clinical observations clearly contradicted this assumption. Freud found that there are persons who commit crimes in order to be punished; they are criminals out of an unconscious sense of guilt. Freud also discovered this unconscious guilt and need for punishment in, for example, patients who had been wrecked by success. In these patients, depression and neurotic illness appeared as a consequence of some victory or success. Because victory signified, unconsciously, one's having ousted or killed one's competitor, any success carried with it a burden of guilt and a need for self-punishment. An unconscious need for self-punishment lies at the base of many cases of depression, moral masochism, and the negative therapeutic reaction. All of these clinical entities are examples of aggression directed against the self in which the effect of a persistent, *unconscious* self-punitive dynamism is evident. These clinical entities are examples of aggression directed against the self. Freud's consideration of this self-punitive dynamism at this point in his study of the psychic apparatus reflected his concurrent interest in aggression as an independent drive coequal with libido.

In 1915, in his paper "The Unconscious," Freud was already keenly aware of the shortcomings of the topographic theory. According to that theory, the system Unconscious (Ucs) is composed exclusively of highly mobile sexual drive cathexes, pressing for immediate and total discharge. The system Ucs was not thought to contain any specific mental elements or organized object representations. Nonetheless, as Freud noted,

> among the derivatives of the Ucs, instinctual impulses of the sort we have described, there are some which unite in themselves characters of an opposite kind. On the one hand, they are highly organized, free from self-contradiction, have made use of every acquisition of the system Cs and would hardly be distinguished in our judgment from the formations of that system. On the other hand, they are unconscious and are incapable of becoming conscious. Thus, *qualitatively,* they belong to the system Pcs but *factually* to the Ucs . . . of such a nature are those fantasies of normal people, as well as of neurotics, which we have recognized as preliminary stages in the formation both of dreams and of symptoms, and which, in spite of their high degree of organization, remain repressed and therefore cannot become conscious. (Freud 1915, pp. 190–191)

Taking into account these problems, Freud concluded, "The reason for all these difficulties is to be found in the circumstance that the attribute of being conscious, which is the only characteristic of psychical processes that is directly presented to us, is in no way suited to serve as a criterion for the differentiation of systems" (Freud 1915, p. 192).

One further issue—the role of anxiety in mental conflict—must be noted in any discussion of the considerations that led Freud to abandon the topographic theory in favor of the structural theory. In its earlier formulations, Freud's theory of anxiety was a quantitative one. Freud held that anxiety appears as a consequence of accumulated, undischarged libidinal cathexes, a situation brought about by the repression of the instinctual drive derivatives. Closer examination of clinical data suggested to Freud the need to modify his cumulative, or "automatic," concept of anxiety. Freud, around 1925, suggested that anxiety serves as a warning signal of threatening catastrophe brought on by the conflict of forces in the individual's mind. This form of anxiety, which Freud called "signal anxiety," is of much greater significance in the psychoanalytic theory of psychopathology and in psychoanalytic therapy than the cumulative, or "automatic," anxiety he had described earlier.

The Structural Model as a Functional Model

Freud took note of these considerations in the epoch-making "The Ego and the Id" (Freud 1923), in which he reformulated his theory of the mind in terms of a structural organization. He proposed the grouping of mental activities into three major *functional* centers: the mental representation of the drives, which he called the *id*; the mental representations of self-judgment, self-punishment, and ideal aspirations, which he called the *superego*; and an executant agency of the mind, which he called *ego*, that reconciled and integrated the conflicting demands of the other structures and served as their executant, taking into account the need for adaptation and realistic problem solving. This view has since been referred to as the *structural model* of the psychic apparatus.

It must be emphasized, however, that ego, id, and superego represent groupings of mental forces. They are operational concepts rather than rigidly demarcated compartments. In this connection, the term "structure," although etymologically correct, can be misleading, insofar as the term may be taken to suggest a fixed, rigid, compartmentalized organization of the psychic apparatus. It is a mistake to think of these systems of the mind as having sharply defined boundary lines. Clinical data demonstrate with what regularity the functions of the several systems of the mind—ego, id, and superego—overlap. Intrapsychic conflict is the situation par excellence that lays bare the differentiation of these functional centers of the mind (A. Freud 1936/1946). In a very general way, one can say, for example, that in the hysterias, the ego must deal with a sharp conflict between the wishes of the id for forbidden gratifications and the countervailing condemnation of the superego. In severe depressions, the id and the superego impulses join forces in a murderous assault upon the self. In certain forms of psychopathy, an alliance is made between the id and the ego. In asceticism, superego and ego combine to counter the pleasure-seeking impulses of the id. To be sure, these formulations represent extreme simplifications, but they serve to illustrate the clinical conceptualization of intrapsychic conflict within the structural theory.

To repeat, in structural theory, every mental element is considered in the light of the role it plays in intrapsychic conflict, and, in keeping with this criterion, each element becomes functionally identified with one or the other of the structures of the mind—ego, id, or superego.

Functional Components of the Structural Model of the Mind

Ego

The ego represents those functions that collectively orient the individual toward the external world; receives, interprets, and organizes stimuli from whatever source, internal or external; and acts as the executant for the drives and correlates and integrates the demands of the drives with proper regard for moral considerations and the practical consequences of behavior. Broadly stated, the ego is the mediator between the internal and the external world, between the world of thoughts and feelings on the one hand and the world of perception and objects on the other. It is through a study of the activities of the ego that knowledge of the other two psychic agencies may be obtained.

In keeping with the pleasure principle, the ego tends to function in a manner that will maximize pleasure and minimize pain or unpleasure. All the functions of the ego are available in pursuit of this goal. The ego, in fact, is defined by its functions, which include thought, memory, language, motor action, sense perception, reality testing, defense, problem solving, and, above all, adaptation. The ego has at its disposal many mental mechanisms, which will be discussed later, that it may use in resolving conflicts. In addition, the ego has the capacity to inhibit or to suspend the operation of its functions and to regress to more primitive levels of functioning.

Identification and Ego Development

In addition to the individual's native endowment, such as intelligence and so forth, the capacity of the ego to discharge its various responsibilities develops and is enriched by the individual's interaction with the important people in his or her immediate world. From them the individual acquires a wide catalog of methods for coping with difficult situations—preferred solutions to conflicts, skills to master, ideals to aspire to, and so forth. These acquisitions result from an identification that the individual effects with these important "objects." The individual remodels himself or herself in many ways after the object and assumes some aspect of the personality and characteristic traits of others. Through the process of identification, one learns how to master and gratify the demands of the id and superego.

Identification, it should be remembered, is never complete. No person is a psychological clone of another, nor is it possible to predict with what particular aspect of a person an individual will identify. Affective considerations play an important role in this process. Nor is it essential for one to have direct experience with a person in order to identify with him or her. Fantasy objects, such as individuals from literature, history, or religious teachings, may become models from whom the individual acquires modes of thinking and acting. Although the personality and ego structure of the individual are shaped greatly by the identifications effected with primary objects during childhood, it is a fact that identifications are also possible later in life, especially during adolescence. In many instances, such late identifications help to give the final stamp of character upon the personality.

Id

The second component of the structural model of the mind, the id, constitutes the mental representations of the instinctual drives, erotic and aggressive. The wishes emanating from the erotic and aggressive drives are largely biologically determined and shaped by the early interaction of the child with his or her mother and subsequent caregivers. These wishes operate as continuous stimuli to the mind and give rise to manifold, repetitive, relatively predictable patterns of mental representations. Collectively, these wishes and their derivative manifestations constitute that structure of the mind designated as the id. The term "id" derives from the German word for "it," and the choice of the term reflects how alien and unacceptable some of its derivative manifestations are when presented to consciousness.

In summary, the id is the vast reservoir of motivational dynamic that consists of sexual and aggressive wishes that are primitive in nature, self-centered, and often antisocial. Rather than being a seething cauldron of formless, free-floating, instinctual cathexes (as Freud characterized both the system Ucs and the id), the id must be accorded some degree of organization. The broad instinctual drive demands of the mind become clinically manifest in a set of persistent unconscious fantasies that are typical for each individual. Unconscious fantasies serve as the vehicles for the persistent drive demands of the id. In clinical practice, it is through the reconstruction of the unconscious fantasies from their derivative expressions that the nature of the specific id influences becomes known to us. The dynamic potential of the drive wish persists in the mind of the individual, but the specific form it takes varies with time as the individual grows and matures. Throughout one's life, there is a tendency to live out the derivative expressions of a particular set of unconscious fantasy wishes. This tendency is easier to observe in the psychoanalytic treatment situation, where the patient attempts to foist upon the analyst some role in a preconceived, unconscious scenario, one derived from the persistent unconscious fantasy. We call this phenomenon *transference*.

Origin of the Drives

Concerning the origin and the nature of the drives that form the basis for the id, there is much controversy. Freud, as might be expected, emphasized the biological nature and the maturational unfolding of instinctual demands. To be sure, he also took into account developmental vicissitudes—that is, those specific interactions between the child and the adults that tend to encourage or discourage the so-called normal unfolding of the manifestations of the drives, or skew the process in the direction of pathology. Whereas it was relatively easy to demonstrate the biological substrate of the libidinal drives, no such facile parallelism appears to hold for aggressive drives. Thus, although it is inescapable that the fundamental dynamic functioning of the mind must be linked to the activities of the brain and the rest of the body, it seems most consistent at the present time to posit the existence of two fundamental drives—libido and aggression—primarily on the basis of psychological evidence (Brenner 1971). Whether under libido and aggression one can subsume manifestations of other potentiating forces in the mind (e.g., a drive for mastery) remains an open question.

The Oral-Phase Drives

Recent developments in psychoanalytic observations of neonates and very young children have posed many perplexing questions concerning Freud's early views of the sequential unfolding of the instinctual drives. There can be no doubt that the capacity for pleasure is biologically rooted and is related to the physiology of the body. Under ordinary circumstances, the sources of pleasure and the capacity to enjoy experience seem to follow a consistent course of maturation and development. In the earliest months of life, the pleasurable sensations connected with feeding seem to be the most important ones. What is involved in this experience transcends the alleviation of hunger and includes as well all the concomitant sensations associated with the feeding experience—namely, the body contact, the warmth, the mother's gaze, her smell, the sound of her voice, and so forth. The fundamental elements of the child's experience are defined by the central need to be nourished, and the mother is the object that satisfies the need.

Given the long period of biological immaturity, during which the infant is totally dependent upon the mother for its very physical survival and emotional comfort, it is not difficult to understand why the image of the mother plays so important a role in human psychic development. Recent studies have shown how the interaction between infant and mother is more complicated and far-reaching than was originally suspected. Clearly, there is a certain preadaptiveness of the child to the human environment into which he or she is born. Communication at a nonverbal level with other humans, through a reciprocal interplay of sensory signals, is part of the human biological inheritance. The mouth, it should be recalled, is more than a passive, receptive organ for food; it is also an instrument through which the child explores the world about him or her.

During this period, however, the child's mental capacities are far from developed. A notion of the self as distinct from objects is lacking. The ego functions are rudimentary, and the child is incapable of speech, with all the tremendous implications for memory, symbolization, and abstraction that speech presupposes. As a result, it is very hard to know exactly what is going on in the child's mind, and the temptation to project adultomorphic concepts onto the child's mental functioning is very great. Nevertheless, certain persistent wishes—drive manifestations deriving from this early period of life—may be delineated. Among these are the wish to be free from the pangs of hunger and the wish for the gratification that comes with satiety. In addition, one observes attempts to master the external world through the use of the mouth, incorporating what is pleasant and what is desired, and, conversely, expelling what is unpleasant or destroying it by biting or chewing. Patients' fantasies of devouring the object, of being devoured by the object, and of fusion with the object in the experience of sleep have been described by Lewin (1950).

In any event, libidinal and aggressive wishes of an oral nature persist throughout life, more powerfully in some individuals than in others, and, depending upon the vicissitudes of experience, occasionally constitute the starting point for severe intrapsychic conflicts leading to psychopathology. The various components of the libidinal aspects of the oral drives are easy to delineate. The mouth, however, also constitutes an organ of aggression. This becomes more understandable after the appearance of teeth makes biting and incorporation possible. With the development of speech and language, the ability to use the mouth to discharge aggressive wishes expands enormously.

The Anal-Phase Drives

In the second and third years of life, certain interests and activities indicate the influence of drives other than the oral ones. The activities of the digestive and excretory functions now become significant sources of id demands upon the psychic apparatus for discharge. Because of the nature of these id demands, this phase of the individual's development is often referred to as the *anal phase.* Such a characterization, however, is misleading for two reasons. First, oral wishes have not disappeared during this phase; they have not become inactive or inconsequential. Oral drive derivatives persist throughout life and take on greater or lesser significance at different phases in the life of the individual, depending upon his or her experience. Second, referring to this crucial period of development, ages 2 to 4 years, in terms of its dominant drive representation does not do justice to the many other acquisitions and transformations taking place at the time—specifically, the progressive development of the ego and its concurrent influence on the drives. The new drive developments become prominent as the child takes an important step toward socialization, namely, the beginning of toilet training. The way in which the child relates to the adults in his or her world has now become extremely complex and capable of the most subtle variations.

During this period, tremendous changes have been taking place both in the ego and in the id. The child is no longer the passive recipient of adult care. Having achieved the upright position and having learned to walk, the child can separate himself or herself for greater or lesser periods of time from his or her mother or other caregivers. The child begins to consolidate his or her sense of self as an entity independent of other persons. He or she begins to appreciate his or her growing mastery over his or her body and its contents and becomes fascinated by what goes into his or her body and what comes out of it. The adults now begin to accentuate the significance of anal activities; they smile approval at effective execution of excretory functions. On the other hand, the child experiences disapproval, punishment, and loss of love for untoward behavior and mishaps.

The child's notion of what is happening to his or her body and its contents is quite different from that of the adults, who have long since repressed and forgotten the unrealistic, fantastic notions they had about these activities when they were children. For example, the child who has been urged to eat because the food she takes in will make her grow may erroneously conclude that everything she ingests becomes part of her and that she will acquire the characteristics of what she has eaten. Children at this stage of development often consider the freshly passed stool as continuations of themselves, and accordingly they endow it with the unique and special importance they attach to their own persons. That others should have a different view of the matter comes as a disillusioning blow. Accordingly, contradictory attitudes may survive in the mind of the child. The child may at different times conclude that he or she and his or her products are special and valuable, or, conversely, that he or she is an inferior entity and that his or her products deserve to be discarded as worthless waste. The struggle for control and mastery is typical for this period, not merely as a derivative of bowel training, but also as part of the process of separation from the caregiver and the consolidation of the individual's identity. Progressive development depends upon the interplay between the transformation of the drives and the development of the ego, especially as influenced by object relations. This must be borne in mind to avoid the erroneous impression that development hinges exclusively on the transformation of the drives.

In later life, many of the erotic and aggressive drives of the id constitute mental representations of the gratification originally derived from retaining or expelling body contents and of the fantasies associated with such activities. Retaining the stool exemplifies childish concepts of its intrinsic value, and the ability to do so represents an exercise of power. Clinical experience demonstrates how certain subsequent character formations, such as stubbornness, contrariness, the hoarding of possessions, the relationship to money, and so forth, may in part represent a metaphoric transformation of such notions. On the other hand, as the stool comes to represent something worthless and even offensive, it can be used in fantasy as an instrument of hostility—a means of offending, besmirching, destroying, and eliminating what is repugnant and what is hated. Mental representations of drive derivatives originating from this period of development assume a wide variety of forms and, like the oral drives, constitute a persistent pressure upon the ego for gratification throughout life.

The Oedipal-Phase Drives

By the time the child reaches the age of 4 years, he or she has begun to confront some of the existential problems facing all human beings. The issues every child must face are the same, no matter what part of the world the child inhabits, what level of culture or civilization he or she has been born into, or what position his or her parents occupy in the community. The child ponders, "Why am I small and helpless while everyone about me is tall and powerful? Why do I have such trouble controlling my bodily functions while the adults seem to have no difficulty at all? Why are there people with two kinds of genitals? Why aren't they all the same? Where did I come from? Where do babies come from? What was it like when I was inside my mother's body? Why must everyone die?" and so forth. The explanation that adults give—that this is in the nature of things—is no answer at all to the question of "Why?" In fact, there are no satisfactory answers to these questions.

The child then begins to satisfy his or her epistemological needs with the limited intellectual means at his or her disposal, but with rich resources of fantasy and magical, wishful thinking. It is from this set of conditions that the impetus toward religion and mythology develops. From what they have been told but do not quite understand, from what they have observed but do not quite comprehend, from what they feel and wish, children fashion fantasy solutions to these basic, universal problems. It is on the basis of universally shared fantasy solutions to the fundamental questions of existence that a commonality of fantasy formations among individuals and cultures emerges. The specific form that the fantasied or mythic solution eventually assumes may vary from individual to individual and from culture to culture, but the essence of the fantastic solutions to the problems is fundamentally similar the world over. This fact not only accounts for the universal nature of certain themes from mythology and religion, but, perhaps even more important, in large part makes possible empathic identification, not only between individuals of the same culture but even between individuals from other cultures.

The role of the phallus.   The aforementioned issues are those confronting the child during what is perhaps the most crucial period of development in his or her life. Many, if not most, of the unresolved conflicts of childhood so significant in clinical work originate in the period between the ages of roughly 2½–3 and 5½–6 years. During this period the child is intensely preoccupied with the activity of the genitals and their potential for pleasure. Sexual and competitive urges become manifest in speech, in play, in fantasies, and in dreams. The drive representations of this period build upon and continue some of the characteristic features of the earlier phases of drive development. The anatomical difference between the two sexes becomes a crucial issue at this time. In both young boys and young girls, fantasied illusions of magical power attach to the phallus, especially as the child learns of its role in the creation of life. Typically, young boys feel pride in their possession of the phallus, and young girls feel a sense of inferiority and mortification, considering themselves less favorably endowed. Precisely how awareness of anatomical differences will affect the young girl's sense of identity will be influenced decisively by how she is treated interpersonally and by the nature of the prevailing cultural attitudes. Furthermore, the phallus may come to serve as an instrument of the aggressive drives and may appear in fantasies metaphorically transformed into knives, weapons, machinery, and so forth. The activities of the phallus may represent at one and the same time derivative manifestations of both erotic and aggressive impulses. For example, the act of urinating may represent in the mind of the little boy a wish to impregnate and/or a wish to destroy.

Love for and competition with the parents dominate much of the child's thinking at this stage. Classically, the male child aspires to take his father's role in relation to his mother, to possess her and to give her a child. The child fears that he will be punished for these wishes and that the punishment will take the form of bodily mutilation, specifically the loss of his most prized possession, the penis. The danger of castration is the major source of anxiety associated with these id wishes. In keeping with his wishes to assume the father's role in all matters of authority and sex, the young boy begins to imitate his father, to take on his traits and attributes. In a word, he *identifies* with his father. What is crucial in this process is the issue of the sexual identity. Because the central themes of this period involve the importance of the phallus and the wish to possess the mother, this stage of development is called the *phallic-oedipal period.*

Inevitably, the young child's aspirations are doomed to fail. He is not really capable of fulfilling the father's role, and the father, in the child's mind, is too powerful and too threatening. In addition, the mother has certain loyalties and responsibilities to the father that take precedence over the child's wishes. The oedipal defeat constitutes a crushing blow for the boy; how he manages the conflicts aroused in him is crucial for his subsequent development. Whether the individual develops normally or suffers from some form of psychopathology depends largely on how well the ego is able to effect some compromise resolution of the id wishes that originate in this context.

The situation of the young girl passing through the phallic-oedipal period is quite different from that of the young boy. The feeling of phallic inferiority gives rise to a sense of disillusionment and anger that is difficult to overcome. There are many ways these feelings are faced. Some women never get over their anger. They harbor unconscious resentment against the mother for not having equipped them properly for life. They become hostile and vengeful toward men and frequently unconsciously wish to rob the man of his prized possession and to bring him down to what they unconsciously feel to be their presumably inferior level. Other women manage the situation quite differently; they deny the anatomical reality by harboring an unconscious fantasy that they do possess a phallus that is hidden somewhere in the body. They try to live out this illusion by emulating, one way or another, the social and professional activities supposedly typical of men.

Many young girls never overcome the feeling of being inferior and angry because they have no penis. Many young boys feel insecure and frightened when they observe that young girls have no penis. Freud observed that this situation brings about a subtle but persistent sense of antagonism and fear between the sexes. These irrational childhood anxieties and prejudices become institutionalized and consolidated in social custom and practice, thereby continuing the subordination of women and the antagonism between the sexes. And finally, there are those young girls who presumably "accept" their role and find gratification in their hope that the father will give them a child to take the place of the phallus they lack. As in the case of the young boy, these wishes must also end in disappointment, but in this instance, the young girl may hope to fulfill her aspirations in a child from some other male substituting for the father. The oedipal-phallic conflicts of women are just as turbulent as those of men. Antagonism toward the mother is particularly prominent among the psychological residua of this period of id development.

Resolution of oedipal conflicts.   The conflicts of the oedipal phase are never completely mastered. How well the ego can integrate the disappointment, anger, fear, and persistent wishes inevitably depends upon many factors of experience. Prominent among these is the question of traumatization, the kind of stimulation or frustration to which the child has been exposed, and the effect of specific experiences, such as witnessing of parents' intercourse, the arrival of a younger sibling, intercurrent illness, accidents, or loss of a parent. The list could be extended indefinitely; it is composed of the fabric of human existence. In the normal course of events, Freud felt, the effects of these inexorable conflicts of childhood are overcome by the child's fashioning his or her identity after the parent of the same sex, that is, by the child's adopting the sexual, social, and moral identity of the parent. Even as he wrote it, Freud knew that this was hardly ever the case. To begin with, the evidence is clear that identification with the qualities of both parents takes place in every individual. Psychoanalytic investigation demonstrates repeatedly how some derivative representations of the drive wishes and conflicts of this early period of the individual's life appear in the associations of every patient. If it were possible to talk in quantitative terms, one could say that persistent wishes of the phallic-oedipal period constitute the major component of the id.

Before leaving discussion of the phallic-oedipal components of the id, it is of utmost importance to note that the evolution of the oedipal phase presented above is an incredibly simplified model of what actually takes place in any individual case. The wishful constellations of this phase assume an almost infinite number of forms in the mind. It must be stressed that at the time they enter the oedipal phase, persons do not necessarily have the same developmental background. Furthermore, as mentioned above, the actual experience during this phase differs from individual to individual and takes on a special cast depending upon the individual's actual situation. All these conditions serve to determine the specific kind of demands for discharge that the wishes of the id subsequently make upon the ego.

The Superego

The ego also has to take into account those wishes that stem from that structure of the mind that Freud called the superego. This group of functions represents the moral and behavioral imperatives, the judgment of what is right and wrong, as well as the ideal aspirations of the individual. Freud referred to this group of relatively stable functions as the superego not only because they presumably develop later in the life of the mind but also because they act as observer and critic. In this capacity, the superego seemingly stands above and beyond the self, passing judgment upon it, and tends to prohibit certain activities and to enhance the pursuit of others, as well as attempting to wreak punishment on the individual for thoughts, feelings, and behavior that fail to meet its standards.

Freud thought that the superego, as a group of moral imperatives, came into being as a consequence of the attempted resolution of conflicts of the oedipal period. Recognizing his inevitable defeat and fearing punishment, the young boy renounces his competitive wishes toward his father, abandons his quest for exclusive possession of the mother, and instead effects an identification with the father by making as his own what he conceived to be the moral code, the ethical representations of the father's authority. As noted above, however, individuals invariably show evidence of qualities indicating an identification with the mother as well. This fact proved a stumbling block to this simple formulation concerning the origin of the moral sense that Freud had proposed. Freud tried to resolve this dilemma by noting that during the oedipal phase, the male child yearns for and fears both mother and father, and the same is true for the female. Freud's introduction of the concept of both a negative and a positive Oedipus complex failed to resolve the problem. Also, because young girls do not have the same compelling fear of the father, since they are not as much concerned with castration as a form of punishment, Freud concluded that moral scruples are not as important to women as they are to men. This conclusion, dubious at best, failed to stand up against the facts of clinical observation.

More recent observations lead to the conclusion that the sources of superego activity for moral imperatives lie much earlier in psychic development than Freud indicated. In the period preceding the oedipal phase, the child tends to experience whatever the mother or the caregiver approves of as right and good; what she disapproves of is wrong and bad. The fear of losing the mother or the mother's love becomes the moral arbiter in the protomorality of the young child. In addition, as the child develops a sense of himself or herself as an independent entity and an appreciation of other persons as separate selves, he or she becomes capable of forming a compassionate identification with the other. In addition to the fear of retaliation, a sense of compassionate identification acts as a further force inhibiting the doing of what is "bad." On the basis of this protomorality, the child is prepared to accept and integrate the standards of right and wrong articulated by the parents and reinforced by education, religion, and culture in general. As the oedipal phase recedes, the individual enters a new world of experience. He or she becomes educable and is a candidate for acculturation and civilization.

The superego is more than a reflection of the moral demands of the father, and it is *not* simply an internalized replication of the standards and demands of the culture in which the individual is being raised. These elements, although important in shaping the individual's superego, are only part of the history of its evolution. It should be recalled that there is no inherent morality. A moral code is a social acquisition. It represents the received wisdom of what a society can and should expect of the behavior of its individual members. The specific child-rearing practices, the influence of the family, and the nature of the educational and religious institutions of the society all play a role. Psychologically, the role of pedagogy is to mold the character structure of members of the emerging generation so that their traits will be consonant with the ideals and values of their society (A. Freud 1935). Nonetheless, it is wrong to assume that the moral values that dominate the superego functioning of any particular individual are in all respects identical to the traditional moral code of his or her community. The nature of the superego is exquisitely individual. For each person, there is a vast number of possible choices, where individual conflict between moral values and self-seeking, lustful, aggressive, vengeful, materialistic, and narcissistic tendencies abounds. Furthermore, there are special situations in which the moral code of a particular family or of a subgroup in the society articulates behavioral principles at odds with those of the surrounding culture. Criminal groups and criminal subcultures have imperative considerations of what is right and wrong that are not quite consonant with widely accepted morality.

Early clinical observations emphasized how deep-seated and powerful were the antisocial, immoral forces of the mind. Nevertheless, as Freud (1923) pointed out, man is at the same time powerfully moralistic. Since the time of Freud's work, much has been learned about the development of the moral sense. The superego stems from roots that go back far into the early history of the individual. A human being's biological nature predisposes him or her to seek morality as a necessary condition of his or her existence. This is due to the fact that the human infant at birth is unable to sustain itself independently for a considerable period of time. Without the protective, loving care of a mothering object, the infant would soon perish. This factor alone raises to the highest degree the significance of the role of the "other" in the life of the individual. In time, other persons come to play roles of significance for the child. As a result of humankind's very biological nature, a human is not solitary but is inherently a communal animal. It is this interdependence, this connectedness with others, that places the stamp of humanity on an individual.

What serves to strengthen the inherent bond to the caregiver is the fact that the caregiver's life-sustaining activities are subjectively experienced by the infant as pleasurable. Physiological need tension is experienced as painful, and gratification as pleasurable. The pleasure-unpleasure principle, which dominates mental life, clearly must have been of survival value in the course of evolution. Noxious elements, for the most part, were painful, ultimately life-threatening, and therefore to be avoided. On the other hand, life-sustaining activities tended to be experienced as pleasurable, to be sought after repetitively, and to be reexperienced and enjoyed. In a biological sense, what is pleasurable becomes associated with the idea of what is good and what is to be sought after, therefore, and repeated. On the other hand, what is unpleasurable is bad and therefore is to be shunned and avoided. Because gratification and frustration are directly connected with the mother's ministrations, the mother then becomes the arbiter of what is pleasurable and good or of what is unpleasurable and bad.

The mother's pleasure in nurturing her child is enhanced by the child's favorable response to her ministrations. The mother expresses her satisfaction in many ways, which the child is quick to perceive. This is the primordial experience of approval, of feeling good, which soon becomes transformed in the sense of doing the right thing. In this sense, the child is constantly experiencing judgment, although as yet no moral issues are involved. But for the child this judgment is most important in relation to the child's internal emotional state. We may consider this stage of experiencing judgment as a precursor to morality, not true morality, and may tentatively designate this stage as that of *protomorality*. The gradual and progressive understanding of the meaning of the spoken word serves to consolidate the developing protomorality. The child begins to connect his or her pleasurable perception of the mother's positive reactions to the spoken words she customarily exclaims under those circumstances (e.g., "Good boy," "Good girl," as the case may be). Every act, no matter how neutral morally from the adult point of view, becomes for the child fraught with a sense of judgment, of approval or disapproval.

With the acquisition of language, developmental achievements or failures become suffused with implications of right and wrong. If the child takes a meal easily or overcomes some simple obstacle, the child perceives a smiling face and hears a soft voice saying, "Good baby." If he extricates himself from some difficulty, he learns that he has done "the right thing." If he persists in his attempts to put a square peg into a round hole in the playbench, he hears an exasperated voice saying, "No, that's wrong." If he is clumsy and hurts himself, or even falls ill, he perceives in his mother's face an expression that to him represents unpleasure, disapproval, and condemnation. He has been judged "bad." Often many children later on experience guilt when they hurt themselves or fall ill. They feel shame and humiliation when they discover, in attempting to solve some problem, they have done "the wrong thing." Thus, concepts of right and wrong, good and bad, have their origin in an affect-laden set of very early object relations that have only the most distant connection to morality. What is right or good, what brings pleasure and should be pursued, is what mother approves of. What is wrong and bad, what brings pain and should be avoided, is what she disapproves of.

The culmination of the process of separation-individuation (Mahler 1971) in the emergence of a sense of self and an appreciation of the "other" constitutes the next major step on the path of developing a sense of morality. The emergence of a sense of self and other is a gradual process, and until the crystallization of the concept of the self is relatively complete, it is really not possible to speak of the internalization of the caregiver's norms of behavior. Take, for example, the experience of the 15- to 18-month-old child who stands in front of the bookshelf, vigorously and joyfully emptying its contents onto the floor, all the time saying, "No, no, mustn't." She is repeating the memory of a prohibition but has not yet made the prohibition her own, and in her behavior she plays out without distinctions the roles of both mother and child. Somewhat later, in a similar situation, the actual or potential presence of the mother or caregiver ceases to be a necessary condition while the child resolves conflicts of the do's and don't's that have been put before her. It is sufficient for a *mental representation* of the adult authority love object to appear in the individual's mind at the appropriate time of conflict. It is at this level of functioning that one can speak with some degree of accuracy about the internalization of parental demands. The individual desists from doing something because *she* thinks it is wrong. She stops herself. The ease with which one can regress from this level to earlier stages of protomorality is exemplified by the ease with which individuals commit wrongdoing when they feel that they will not be seen or caught, which represents a regression from true internalization of norms of behavior to the level of the need for external control.

A major turning point in the transformation of protomorality toward true morality takes place after the consolidation of object constancy, when the child begins to take into account the pain, physical and psychological, that his or her behavior and wishes may occasion in others. This process has both conscious and unconscious components and is related to a transient identification in conscious and/or unconscious fantasy with the "other," a combination of both empathy and sympathy. This mechanism might be referred to as a compassionate identification. The individual puts himself or herself in the position of the potential victim and anticipates the pain that he or she could cause by imagining the pain he or she would feel in the same situation. This step represents a major advance in object relations, one that is fundamental for the development of morality. It is expressed experientially in the capacity to feel remorse (Furer 1967).

Another step in the development of the superego involves the internalization of the ideals and standards of significant others. These standards now become demands that the individual makes on himself or herself. The original need for approval by others, if satisfied, is now experienced as self-approbation, self-satisfaction, and a heightening of self-worth. This process of internalization of ideals and standards of significant others is gradual and continues throughout the individual's life. The individual identifies with certain ideal qualities that he or she finds in models in daily life and from religion, literature, and mythology. Adolescence is a particularly important period for superego development. During this time the individual has to consolidate his or her sexual, professional, social, and moral identity. The events during this critical period in the individual's life play a critical role in determining the final form of the superego.

Because so much of superego functioning operates at an unconscious level, one has to recognize that conscious morality constitutes only a minor part of the structure of this psychic system. In the demands that the superego makes upon the ego for consideration and action, one recognizes evidence of the primitive aspects of childhood protomorality. There is an urge to pronouce harsh, irrational judgment upon others as well as upon oneself. In childish terms, the superego may demand retribution in the form of talion punishment, that is, literally an eye for an eye and a tooth for a tooth. The punishment must take a form identical to that of the original crime. Like the id, the superego is fraught with contradictions and internal inconsistencies. Abstract principles of justice do not apply.

Irrational distinctions and contradictory demands are the rule rather than the exception. Accordingly, it is inconsistent to think of certain individuals having "lacunae" in their superego, that is, certain defects of morality in what is otherwise a well-developed, "mature" superego. Such a view renders too much honor to the superego as a rational, realistic set of demands toward oneself or others. Generally, the demands emanating from the superego upon the ego are in conflict with those emanating from the id, but this is not always the case. There are instances in which the two unite in common purpose. One example is the phenomenon of moral masochism, in which moral castigation from the superego is enlisted in the service of erotic, masochistic wishes emanating from the id. Another example is the act of religious persecution, in which the persecutors believe that, in the name of moral right and doctrine, it is appropriate, even obligatory, to exercise the harshest forms of aggression, even murder, against unbelievers, whose souls must be saved. Yet another example involves the obsessional neuroses, in which pangs of conscience frequently serve as an outlet for aggressive wishes against one's self. Scrupulosity, in general, may be used as a form of self-torture but also as a means of inflicting pain upon others (i.e., when the scrupulous person makes others comply with rituals to satisfy his or her own self-demands).

Certain persistent, irrational, unconscious wishes from childhood influence the ego in its attempt to reconcile and integrate the wishes of the id with the demands of the superego and considerations of realistic consequences. These wishes originate in connection with typical childhood catastrophes. Their reappearance threatens the possible emergence of painful affective states, such as depression, anxiety, and possibly panic (Freud 1926). The earliest danger resides in the possible loss of the nurturing adult, upon whom the child's life literally depends. Organismic distress resulting from unfulfilled needs can, in the mind of a child, assume devastating proportions. The different manifestations of this potential catastrophe fuse into the child's fear of abandonment. The appearance of a mother's face signals impending relief. When the child is separated from the mother or the mother fails to reappear, a sense of abandonment denotes impending disaster, suggesting the evolution of intense unpleasure and pain. At a somewhat later stage, as the child begins to appreciate the mother as an independent object upon whose good will and loving responses the child depends, fear of losing the mother's love becomes the preeminent danger. Sensing that the mother has turned her love from him or her, the child experiences both anxiety and depression. With this experience comes a lowering of self-esteem. The child seeks to avoid or to overcome this painful state by a process of reconciliation. This mode of interacting with the mother becomes a model later on, with the various maneuvers the individual may use to reconcile himself or herself with his or her superego.

Fear of punishment becomes especially significant during the oedipal phase. The child's fears are misconstrued in terms of his or her own aggressive impulses, and he or she imagines being punished according to the talion principle. Accordingly, an upsurge of drive wishes may represent a danger that a catastrophic situation may develop. As one wishes to kill, one fears being killed; as one wishes to castrate, one fears being castrated. To be sure, such fantastic fears of punishment combine with the earlier dangers of being abandoned by and of losing the love of the protecting object.

With the consolidation of the structure of the superego, additional considerations come into play. The individual now fears not the potential pain that he or she may suffer at the hands of others, but the condemnation of his or her own superego and its exacting demands for retribution and punishment. The superego can become a force as threatening to the inner harmony and equilibrium of the individual, as serious as the dangers posed by the emergence of the imperious, primitive drive wishes of the id.

This is the context in which intrapsychic conflict develops. Intrapsychic conflict should be understood in terms of its components. One component is the wish for instinctual gratification, which tends to give rise to some degree of unpleasure when it raises the possibility of several of the catastrophic situations of childhood. In clinical practice, the commonly identified forms of unpleasure have been described as anxiety and depressive affect. The response of the ego is to institute the process of *defense,* another component of intrapsychic conflict. Almost any mental mechanism may be enlisted to lessen the possibility that overwhelming anxiety or depressive affect may supervene. Modes of ego activity serve purposes other than defense. Identification, repression, displacement, reaction formation, and rationalization, to name just a few, may contribute to achieving the goal of adaptation and also serve to enhance and enrich the ego's capacities. When these mechanisms are mobilized to eliminate or to minimize the danger of impending psychic pain, they properly earn the designation of "defense mechanisms." In the final mental product that the ego arranges, all the elements of conflict achieve some degree of representation.

Not all the components of intrapsychic conflict, however, are equally represented in the final compromise formation, nor is every compromise formation that is effected by the ego a successful one in the sense that it eliminates pain or unpleasure, anxiety or depression. Also, the compromise formation may be a failure in the sense that the final product is fraught with a greater or lesser component of pain and inhibition, or else brings the individual into conflict with his or her environment, raising the possibility of actual danger to his or her person. The function of the ego is an endless exercise in adaptation, reconciliation, and integration. Each individual develops his or her own set of compromise formations to the inner and external pressures that bear down upon his or her ego.

The specific forms that the compromise formations take may best be understood as derivatives of persistent unconscious fantasies (Arlow 1969a, 1969b). Originating as imagined representations of wishes fulfilled in the face of the threatened danger of unpleasure, these fantasies are modified into more acceptable versions by the ego. Although those fantasies are forgotten (i.e., repressed), the persistent dynamic thrust embodied in unconscious fantasies determines how sensory stimuli are perceived, interpreted, and responded to. Whereas the basic wish of the unconscious fantasies remains constant, the derivative manifestations evolve and are transformed over time, in keeping with the advance of the individual's cognitive capabilities, with the appreciation of the real environment, and with the consolidation of moral values. Borrowing an analogy from literature, one might say that the basic plot remains the same but the characters and situations change in time. There is good evidence to support the view that unconscious fantasying goes on all the time we are awake and a good deal of the time we are asleep. Every individual harbors a set of unconscious fantasies typical for him or her. These fantasies represent the special way that the individual integrated the major experiences and relationships, the important traumas, and the drive conflicts of his or her childhood years. Specific events in daily life may resonate with elements of the individual's set of unconscious fantasies and evoke conscious representations of the wishes these fantasies represent. The derivative representations of the unconsious fantasies consist of compromise formations that may be adaptive or maladaptive. The inability of the ego to institute adaptive compromise formations marks the beginning of the process of pathogenesis.

Clinical Presentations

To appreciate fully the significance of the foregoing considerations would require extensive presentation of data stemming from within the psychoanalytic situation during treatment. Nevertheless, in the clinical presentations that follow, one may appreciate how the principles of the structural model illuminate the understanding of mental phenomena.

The first example is a dream of a young woman patient being treated for hysterical symptoms. This dream is typical of a certain category of dreams that depict very sharply the separate contributions of the major components of the structural model. In the course of her treatment, this patient was gradually becoming aware of a perverse erotic wish to be assaulted and raped. The dream occurred one night after the patient had suppressed an impulse to masturbate to the fantasy of being forced to do menial work for several men at one time. During her adolescence, this patient used to serve as her father's model in demonstrating dental techniques to his students.

In the dream it was late at night and the patient was walking along a dark street, heading toward a stairway she intended to ascend. She felt threatened by a gruff man who had been following her and was now coming closer just as she reached the foot of the stairway. At the top of the stairway, at the upper level of the street, was a policeman and, on the other side, an elderly woman who reminded her of her mother. Fearing that she was about to be attacked, the patient tried to cry out for help, but no sound issued from her throat. The policeman did not notice; he kept looking the other way. At the same time the motherly figure seemed to be nodding her head, as if to say, "Serves you right."

In dramatic representation this dream portrays the forces in conflict in the patient's mind, and each actor in the dream articulates the role of one of the psychic structures—ego, id, superego. The gruff and threatening man indicates the dynamism of the id impulse, the wish to be assaulted and raped. The behavior of the patient in the dream indicates the dilemma of the ego. The patient wishes to ward off the danger of assault by summoning her conscience to resist the temptation to yield to an impulse to masturbate to fantasies of a severely masochistic nature. Her efforts to stop herself by appealing to the superego, however, are ineffectual. The policeman looks away, and the patient (the ego) is terrified by the awareness of her inability to control her impulses. Her self-judgment, projected onto the image of the elderly woman, concludes that "you get just what you deserve." Each of the structural systems has contributed to the experience of this frightening dream.

The principles that pertain to the understanding of the structure of the dream apply equally to the structure of symptoms. Symptoms are compromise formations that combine wish fulfillments of the id with considerations of the superego demands, in keeping with the several responsibilities of the ego. Certain patients suffering from compulsion neurosis feel compelled to return to check the gas jets innumerable times. They have to make sure that, through their inadvertence, they will not cause the death of someone. The id impulse to kill by letting gas loose is in this symptom countered by the superego injunction against murder. In the structure of the typical compulsion, the dynamisms of the id and the superego seem equally powerful. The ego, as it were, is caught in the middle. It cannot succeed in integrating the conflicting impulses nor subordinating one to the other. Having failed to effect an appropriate, tension-free compromise formation, the ego has been forced, as it were, to surrender some of its autonomy and independent functioning. Instead of mastering the demands of the id and the superego, it has become subordinate to them.

In the case of compulsion neurosis, hysteria, and phobia, the compromise formations of the ego do not succeed in eliminating the conscious experiencing of unpleasant affect. The situation in the perversions is somewhat different. To illustrate this point, let us examine in a simplified way the structure of a typical fetishistic perversion. At some point in his childhood, the fetishistic person saw the female genital for the first time. To him, this constituted a traumatically frightening experience because it confirmed that the danger of castration was a real one. He had assumed previously that all people had penises. After seeing the female genital, he interpreted the absence of a penis as evidence that castration had taken place and that the same could happen to him. The fetishistic person responds to this traumatic confrontation, first, by denying the reality of what he has observed (i.e., a genital without a penis) and, second, by turning his attention to some concomitant perception that can be used to buttress this denial. He concentrates on other attributes of the woman—her breast, her garter belt, her heel—which he endows with the attributes of a phallus. In other words, to circumvent the castration anxiety generated by the perception of a being without a phallus, the fetishistic person entertains an unconscious fantasy of a woman with a phallus. He gains security and is accordingly able to engage in sexual intercourse by concentrating on a derivative (i.e., symbolic) representation of a female phallus. Under such conditions he is enabled to secure sexual pleasure without experiencing fear or other unpleasant affect.

In the following case it will be possible to trace the ego's transforming of the typical oedipal conflicts arising from the wish to kill the father, take his place with the mother, and have a child with her. The patient, whom we shall call Morris, was the son of deeply religious Chasidic Jews. He was brought to treatment at the age of 4½ because of a tic in one eye, difficulty falling asleep, nightmares, and enuresis. He was afraid of dying and expressed concern over the intactness of his penis. He also feared that if he did anything with his thumb, blood would flow from there. His parents were upset by the fact that he was fascinated by weapons, particularly knives and guns.

In his early fantasies and dreams, he imagined himself as Dracula, killing men and sucking blood from the necks of beautiful women. He had some awareness of the sexual significance of Dracula's activity. The people he killed with his guns and his knives in his fantasy play were men, who were not identified. Thus, even at the beginning phase of treatment, the classic oedipal wishes had been displaced from their primary objects, the mother and father, onto other individuals, but the patient himself remained identified with the killer and the seducer.

In the course of treatment, Morris stopped identifying himself with Dracula but remained intensely interested in stories about Dracula and in watching Dracula on television. That is to say, he dissociated himself from the hostile, aggressive impulses of the id but enjoyed these wishes vicariously through unconscious identification with the monster.

Somewhat later Dracula became the enemy, from whom Morris rescued the beautiful women. In its defensive activities, the ego had substituted rescuing for the more direct sexual representation of sucking blood from the woman's neck.

Further difficulties ensued over the choice of schooling for Morris. He was enrolled in a religious school his father had chosen. His mother, a more liberal minded person, had wanted her son to have a more American education. Morris resisted going to school. He was hyperactive and disobedient, the ringleader of all the mischief. Morris now began to wage war against his teachers. He would draw cartoons of the rabbis, depicting them as devils peeping over the top of the tablets of the Ten Commandments. The hostile impulses formerly directed against the father were now directed against the rabbis as he assaulted them and the prohibitions they represented.

In his dreams he continued the warfare he was waging with authority figures. He would see himself with a water pistol, shooting down enemy planes, and as he did so, he would wet the bed. In a fantasy that was unconscious, he equated the penis with a weapon and the stream of urine with dangerous projectiles. In the dream, however, it was no longer the father or the teachers who were the enemy, but some vague, unidentified opponent.

The same trend continued for the next few years but on a more sophisticated level. Morris now focused on the recent events of world history. He would imagine himself as the British commanding officer at the prison camp in *The Bridge Over the River Kwai,* whom he saw as a warrior but also a decent man devoted to his soldiers, willing to risk his life in order to protect them. Morris felt he would like to be a general. By combining the image of the warrior with the image of the rescuer, Morris rationalized away the aggressive implications of his interest in warfare. The effectiveness of this rationalization proved to be short-lived. From his religious studies, Morris learned that the biblical figure of Aaron, the brother of Moses, was the one to emulate. Aaron was described as a man who loved peace and pursued peace. An ego-ideal of a man who was professionally engaged in killing was no longer acceptable. At this point Morris lost his interest in knives and began to make peace with his teachers. In other words, as a result of a more advanced set of superego demands, the ego was able to effect a more adaptive outlet for this boy's instinctual drives of the id. Morris now began to direct his energies, stemming from both aggressive and erotic impulses, to his studies, and he discovered, to his surprise, that he could be an excellent student.

The theme of rescuing now began to dominate Morris's fantasy life. Morris's fantasies centered around the figures of Abraham Lincoln and Moses, both of whom Morris thought of as liberators and fathers of their people. The fact that Morris's Hebrew name was indeed Moses did not escape him. Thus, the theme of saving life and creating life reemerged in a more adaptive form, vastly changed from the original primitive notion of killing the monster and sucking the blood of the beautiful woman. By way of identification with the new ego-ideals, Lincoln and Moses, the dynamic charge of what was originally an incestuous wish was now put in the service of socially useful adaptive goals. Accordingly, when Morris discovered that he was unusually proficient in mathematics, he began to think of being like Einstein, someone who used his intellect as an extension of power, but power turned to the advancement of science and the betterment of mankind. Thus, through a series of progressively adaptive compromise formations, the terror-fraught fantasies of childhood ultimately eventuated in a well-integrated, satisfying set of compromise formations whose derivative expressions became evident in fantasy, behavior, educational goals, character traits, and so forth. In reviewing this brief clinical excerpt, it is possible to identify many of the typical mental mechanisms the ego employs for defense and other functions. In the material one can recognize the operation of identification, displacement, sublimation, reaction formation, rationalization, isolation, and denial.

No clinical excerpt can render adequately the rich complexities of mental functioning. In the case of the patient who dreamed she was about to be assaulted, the figure of the old woman at the top of the stairway reminded her not only of her mother but of a teacher she admired, a camp counselor she detested, and several other women, all of whom had in common the fact that at some time they had admonished the patient for an injudicious bit of behavior. The image of the old woman in the dream represents a combination of many different experiences of the patient's past. In other words, many determinants entered into the casting of the older woman for her role in the dream. In the same way, many different wishes of the id, sometimes of a contradictory nature, may find expression, as a result of the ego's activity, in a single mental representation. In assembling workable compromises, the ego tries to resolve many conflicts at the same time. Progress results from the way in which successful solutions to earlier conflicts are incorporated into the solution to later conflicts. The process signifies how, in the human mind, the past is embedded in the present. In clinical work, one observes how a symptom, a dream, a character trait, a hobby, a choice of someone to love—and almost every mental phenomenon—can have different meanings in different contexts and can at the same time serve many different functions in relation to reality or to the different parts of the psychic structure. Waelder (1930) called this tendency the "principle of multiple function."

It is primarily in addressing clinical data in the treatment situation that one can appreciate the aptness of the structural model. Essentially, Freud devised the psychoanalytic situation and employed the technique of free association in order to facilitate the study of the representations of the various forces in conflict in the mind. The ebb and flow of instinctual wishes, the initiation of defense, and the influence of moral condemnation or approval constitute the living, dynamic, current record of how a particular person's mind works. The elucidation of mental functioning is the ultimate purpose of the structural model.

References

Arlow JA: Fantasy, memory, and reality testing. Psychoanal Q 38:28–51, 1969a

Arlow JA: Unconscious fantasy and disturbances of conscious experience. Psychoanal Q 38:1–27, 1969b

Brenner C: The psychoanalytic concept of aggression. Int J Psychoanal 52:137–144, 1971

Freud A: Psychoanalysis and the training of the young child. Psychoanal Q 4:15–24, 1935

Freud A: The Ego and the Mechanisms of Defence (1936). New York, International Universities Press, 1946

Freud S: The unconscious (1915), in Standard Edition of the Complete Psychological Works of Sigmund Freud, Vol 14. Translated and edited by Strachey J. London, Hogarth Press, 1957, pp 159–215

Freud S: The ego and the id (1923), in Standard Edition of the Complete Psychological Works of Sigmund Freud, Vol 19. Translated and edited by Strachey J. London, Hogarth Press, 1961, pp 1–66

Freud S: Inhibitions, symptoms and anxiety (1926), in Standard Edition of the Complete Psychological Works of Sigmund Freud, Vol 20. Translated and edited by Strachey J. London, Hogarth Press, 1959, pp 75–175

Furer M: Some developmental aspects of the superego. Int J Psychoanal 48:277–280, 1967

Lewin BD: The Psychoanalysis of Elation. New York, WW Norton, 1950

Mahler MS: The study of the separation-individuation process and its possible application to borderline phenomena in the psychoanalytic situation. Psychoanal Study Child 26:403–424, 1971

Waelder R: The principle of multiple function: observations on overdetermination (1930), in Psychoanalysis: Observation, Theory, Application: Selected Papers of Robert Waelder. Edited by Guttman SA. New York, International Universities Press, 1976, pp 68–83

3

Object Relations Theory

James S. Grotstein, M.D.

W inston Churchill once stated, "The United States and Great Britain are two great democracies divided by a common language." This aphorism may apply generally to variations in the use of psychoanalytic terms worldwide, but it is especially true of the differences between the concepts of "object relations" in the United States and in Britain (where the term has at least two different meanings). As will be discussed in detail later, among the British, both Kleinians' and Independents' conception of the "object," particularly the "internal object" or "internalized object," is not equivalent to ego psychologists' conception of "object representation." Moreover, the British schools' concept of the "internal world" differs significantly from ego psychologists' concept of the "representational world."

When one is attempting to define object relations, there are other important distinctions. Not only must one differentiate the Kleinian, Independent, and American versions of object relations theory, but also one must discriminate between *object relations theory* as a totality and *relational theory*, as it is termed by Jay Greenberg and Stephen Mitchell (Mitchell 1988; Greenberg and Mitchell 1983).

Relational theory derives from and extends the work of Harry Stack Sullivan (1953), in particular the concepts embodied in his term "interpersonal relations," and to some extent the work of Harry Guntrip (1969, 1971), in particular his concept of "personology." In turn, all of these theories must be distinguished from Heinz Kohut's (1971, 1977, 1984) theory of "selfobjects," which are to be distinguished from their forebears, "part-objects." Although not all contributors strictly observe these distinctions, there does seem to be a consensus that object relations theory presupposes an *internal world of objects* that cast their shadows on external objects, and vice versa. That assumption is not necessarily true for relational and self psychological theory.

W. R. D. Fairbairn would most strictly distinguish between "interpersonal relations" and "object relations" (Grotstein 1994a, 1994b). It was his position that "object relations" are, strictly speaking, internal endopsychic structures whose very existence bespeaks relational failures. He believed that satisfying objects do not need to be introjected because they can be relied upon to provide nurturance without the infant's having to internalize them in order to control them.

Yet another prefatory note is in order in reference to what use is to be made of the object. Hegel (1887/1977) observed that man does not desire an object; he desires the object's *desire*! This point was lost to psychoanalytic theory until Lacan. The object (or part-object) in psychoanalytic theory has generally been seen varyingly as facilitating drive discharge and supplying instinctual functions to the satisfaction of bonding, attachment, and love.

Freud's Contributions

The term "object" has a long and complicated history in psychoanalysis. It was first used by Sigmund Freud (1905) to refer to the caretaking parent—and then sexual partner—who facilitated the discharge of drive tension. As such it belonged to the troika of drive characteristics: source, aim, and object. Because the libidinal instinctual drive was the centerpiece of early psychoanalytic theory and technique, the use of the term "object" tended to diminish the importance of human individuals in the external environment and stressed the power of instinctual wishes that, because of superego demands, contribute to intrapsychic conflict and are subjected to repression and other defense mechanisms. In other words, actual human beings were less important in their own right than they were as inhibiting or facilitating (or even exciting) factors in the infant's and child's instinctual life. This line of thought constituted Freud's second theory of psychoanalysis,[1] by which he corrected his first (i.e., traumatic seduction) theory, which emphasized the reality, and therefore the importance, of the role of parents and other key figures in the child's life.

Freud extended the development of the idea of internal objects in a series of papers, which include "Three Essays on the Theory of Sexuality" (1905), "Family Romances" (1909[1908]), "On Narcissism: An Introduction" (1914), "Mourning and Melancholia" (1917[1915]), "'A Child Is Being Beaten'" (1919), and "The Ego and the Id" (1923). His clinical thinking seems to have bifurcated; although he remained more loyal to his libido theory, especially to its emphasis on infantile sexuality, his appreciation of the role of the object in its own right was demonstrated in his conception of the ego-ideal, the superego, and of the Oedipus complex itself. In these contributions, Freud conceived of the object as being incorporated into the psychic structure. (For example, Freud noted how the father is incorporated by the young boy into his conscience.)

Freud's next major contribution to what would later become object relations theory was "On Narcissism: An Introduction" (1914). In that work he accounted for the formation of the ego-ideal, which was to have a separate existence as an *internal object*, that is, "a gradient in the ego." He also discussed the relationship of libido to object relations, reminding us that the first object of libido is the caretaker (the breast). Autoerotism develops after the breast is

---

[1]Freud's second theory of psychoanalysis referred to here differs from that described in Chapter 2 by Jacob Arlow, who refers to the structural model that superseded the topographic model.

withdrawn, and this is then followed by either an anaclitic attachment to the object or a narcissistic object choice.[2]

Freud penetrated most deeply into internal object theory in "Mourning and Melancholia" (1917[1915]) when he discussed mourning and melancholia as alternative results of object loss. The critical factor that was implicated was the individual's ability to tolerate the loss. If the individual was able to tolerate the loss, mourning would result; if the individual was narcissistically unable to tolerate the loss, melancholia would ensue. The normally grieving person can tolerate the loss of the object, mourn it, and reconstitute it as an identification in the ego. (Kleinians would say that the loss is reconstituted as a "good object," whereas classical analysts would say that an "object representation" has become a "self representation.") The narcissistic person, on the other hand, cannot grieve the loss of a separate object because separation from the object has not been experienced; therefore, the loss of an object is felt as the loss of a part of the self. As a result, the narcissistic person denies the loss that he or she, because of his or her immaturity, cannot bear by splitting the image of the object and then internalizing each part in a different way; one part is assigned to the ego-ideal (later the superego) and the other to the ego proper.

Narcissistic rage (protest over object loss) against the departed object is also internalized because the object is believed to belong to the self and therefore has no "right" to depart on its own life agenda. The narcissistic person's sadism (rage) is also projectively attributed to the object, which then becomes identified with (incorporated into) the narcissistic person's ego-ideal ("gradient in the ego," superego) as a sadistic superego, and the rage attributed to the object is then directed toward the ego. The ego is identified with (i.e., becomes like) the object against whom the narcissistic person directs his or her rage. Thus, there are four internal entities—the

---

[2]Narcissistic identifications were to have a far-reaching influence on the Kleinian and Independent Schools as well as on the American School. The first two schools have come to embrace the concept of "dependency," whereas the American School has developed more fully the concept of "identity," particularly "ego-identity" and then "self-identity."

attacking self, the attacking object, the attacked self, and the attacked object—that devolve into two agencies, one sadistic (the superego) and the other masochistic (the ego). This process is exemplified by the following case:

> A 29-year-old female patient announced one day that her boyfriend had just left her and that she felt suicidal. After obtaining the details of the breakup, the analyst suggested interventions that would address her grief over her loss. She rejected them all and plaintively stated, "I haven't lost just a boyfriend! I've lost my ego!" Not only did this event arouse her awareness of having been an adoptee at birth, but it also brought up feelings and phantasies[3] of being so entangled or confused with her lover that she felt "ripped apart," with parts of her going with him as he left her. Her anger at him for leaving had been projectively identified into her image of him—that is, she began to feel that he had become angry with her. He then became installed in her ego-ideal/superego as a critical object who was justified in leaving a worthless her. The latter self-image also contained some elements of him, whose image also was made worthless by her, however. Further associations revealed how angry she was with him and how worthless she thought he was.

Abraham's Contributions

Klein, Fairbairn, and Edith Jacobson developed metapsychological formulations of object relations whose ancestry springs principally from Freud's 1905 and 1917 contributions and from those of Karl Abraham. Abraham (1924/1948) established a virtual lexicon of objects, both external and internal, in his paper on the development of libido. After describing the passive and active phases of the pregenital autoerotic stages (orality and anality), he enumerated objects (external) appropriate to these respective stages and pointed out that these objects were subsequently internalized. For example, the

---

[3]The term *phantasy* is distinguished from *fantasy* topographically. The former connotes imaginative mental life that is totally unconscious, whereas the latter designates preconscious imaginative mental life. "Phantasy" is customarily used by the Kleinian School, whereas "fantasy" is used by classical Freudians.

infant's autoerotism may express itself in the oral stage as passive sucking (incorporating) or active cannibalism (sucking and biting) toward the object, the breast. Abraham meant that in the oral stage the infant experiences phantasies of taking the mother inside by mouth. Abraham posited that in the anal stage there is an analogous dialectic between expulsive sadistic impulses and passive retentive impulses, which, in Abraham's view, the infant expresses toward an object (e.g., the mother). Moreover, Abraham postulated that the infant seeks actively to reincorporate the defecated object, which, following its original incorporation and before its defecation, was considered by the infant to be a part of itself. It is important to realize that Abraham had a profound impact on his patients, Melanie Klein and Edith Jacobson, and on Fairbairn, who, unlike them, continued to employ Abraham's schema uniquely in his own metapsychology.

Abraham posited that the early oral stage is characterized by sucking and is *preambivalent,* in contrast to the later oral stage, biting, which is the beginning of all successive *ambivalent* phases of development. Klein rejected totally the notion of preambivalence, but Fairbairn retained it and made it the centerpiece for his theory of the origin of schizoid personality disorder.

The Hungarian School

The contributions of the Hungarian School to object relations theory had not been sufficiently appreciated until John Bowlby brought them to the attention of the mental health public in a series of works (Bowlby 1969, 1973, 1980). Bowlby demonstrated that the British school of object relations owed its origins, in part, to the British maverick Ian Suttie (1935/1952) and, in part, to the Hungarians, particularly Sandor Ferenczi, Imre Hermann, and Michael and Alice Balint. Although Ferenczi made a number of contributions to the subject, his seminal ones, according to Bowlby, were his concept of the need for "passive love" and his postulation that the infant experiences, along with oral craving, a craving to return to the prenatal state of unity with mother in her womb (Ferenczi 1913/1950).

Hermann (1933, 1936), anticipating the experiments of H. F. Harlow (1959) on primates, observed how infant monkeys cling to their mothers' bodies and how this was also true in human infants. He therefore postulated that infants possess a primary component, the instinct to cling, although, according to Michael Balint (1937/1949) and John Bowlby (1969), he did not go so far as to assign this clinging to an object relations principle per se. Instinctual clinging became the centerpiece for Bowlby's theory of attachment and bonding.

Michael Balint (1937/1949) and Alice Balint (1939/1949), in developing further the theories of Ferenczi and Hermann, repudiated the concept of primary narcissism, with its implication that the infant becomes related to objects only gradually. They postulated that the infant is active from the beginning and experiences itself as separate from the mother and dependent on her relating to it. A. Balint believed that there was a primitive egoistic (narcissistic) instinct, related to clinging, that trivializes the mother's importance as a person and that treats her as an object to support the infant's feeling of omnipotence. She and M. Balint regarded this "instinct" as the basis for "primary object love." Their emphasis on the non-oral components of early infant life became the forerunner of Bowlby's rejection of the concept of orality in favor of attachment behavior. Consequently, psychoanalysts now disagree as to whether "instinct" ("innate behavior coordinators" [Spitz 1946]) or "drive" is more important in infantile mental life. "Drives," as conceived of by Freud, are the mental representations of somatic urges, whereas "instincts" are self-contained biological structures with maps of preset programs of behavior released by experience that enable the individual to deal with reality situations that these structures have been "programmed" to anticipate.

After emigrating to London, M. Balint became a member of the British object relations group and subsequently published a series of papers and books. The most noteworthy underlying theme was his concept of the "basic fault," by which he meant a fundamental breach in the ego that developed during the preoedipal phase. He equated the formation of the basic fault with the loss of the "primary object":

Thus the technique I found usually profitable with patients who regressed to the level of the basic fault or of creation, was to bear with their regression for the time being, without any forceful attempt at intervening with an interpretation. . . . From another angle, the technical problem is how to offer "something" to the patient which might function as a primary object, or at any rate as a suitable substitute for it, or in still other words, onto which he can project his primary love. (qtd. in Bowlby 1969, pp. 277–279)

Thus, Balint suggested that the therapist treating patients who have "basic faults" must offer them the nonverbal opportunity to redevelop "primary love" for the "primary object." One can readily see similarities between this approach and those of Donald Winnicott (the "holding environment") and Harold Searles ("symbiotic relatedness").[4]

When its members' contributions are taken as a whole, the Hungarian School is to be credited for the increased interest in the humanization and personalization of psychoanalytic theory and practice and for the shift of emphasis from the "father complex" to the "mother complex," to infancy rather than childhood, and to infantile dependency rather than infantile sexuality.

The British Schools of Object Relations

The British psychoanalytic experience has been complex and characterized by more diversity than has the American experience (Grotstein 1991a, 1991b, 1991c). The British schools of object relations include the Kleinian and the Independent Groups.[5] It must be remembered that at the time these schools of thought developed, drive theory and the concepts of infantile sexuality and aggression were a central focus of orthodox psychoanalysis. The focus then

---

[4]For a review of the contributions of the Hungarian School to object relations theory, see M. Balint (1968) and Bowlby (1969).

[5]The Independents are also known as the British Middle Group—that is, occupying a middle ground between the Kleinians and the Anna Freud Group (whose ideas resemble those of the American school of ego psychology).

shifted to the study of the ego (conflict, defenses, adaptation, multiple functions, synthetic functions, organizing functions, etc.). The British Kleinians and Independents (Suttie, Fairbairn, Winnicott, Bowlby, and their Hungarian intellectual forebears) began eschewing, to one degree or another, the concept of infantile *autoerotic* sexuality and substituted *infantile dependency on the breast-object* instead. They switched from the concept of drive to that of nurture that had been implicit in Freud's (1910, 1914) life-preservative (ego) instincts that he had abandoned in his paper on narcissism (Freud 1914).

Thus, Kleinians and Independents placed more emphasis on the image of an inchoate infant who needed the breast than did orthodox and classical psychoanalysts, who, because they considered the preoedipal infant to be in a state of primary narcissism and much less invested in objects, emphasized the concept of the oedipal phase. The British and Hungarian analysts disagreed with the concept of primary narcissism, believing that the infant was psychologically separate (though not individuated[6]) from the beginning. They differed among themselves in the importance placed on the external object. Originally, many analysts disagreed with them, and none more than the Americans. Today, however, many of their ideas are taken for granted to one degree or another.[7]

It must also be remembered that the British psychoanalytic experience differed from the American psychoanalytic experience in several ways. First, the ongoing disagreement and dispute between Melanie Klein and Anna Freud created a number of political divisions. Second, there were in Britain many talented nonmedical psychoanalysts, a phenomenon that was not generally tolerated in the United States. Third, and perhaps most important, the British courageously and effectively tackled the psychoanalysis of persons with

---

[6]The reader is referred to the book edited by Moore and Fine (1990) for definitions of "separation" and "individuation."

[7]For an overall summary of the contributions of the Independent School, see Grotstein (1982–1983a, 1991a, 1991b, 1991c), Greenberg and Mitchell (1983), Kohon (1986), Bacal and Newman (1990), and Rayner (1991).

psychotic, borderline, and other primitive mental disorders; most classical analysts in the United States at that time strongly discouraged treatment of these patients with psychoanalysis and recommended their referral to treatment with other modalities.

Nevertheless, there has always been a small group of American classical analysts—including Harold Searles, Peter Giovacchini, Arnold Modell, Alfred Flarsheim, Donald Rinsley, Simon Grolnick, Leonard Barkin, and Kenneth Newman—who allied themselves with the ideas of the British, and this number is rapidly increasing and now includes Thomas Ogden, L. Bryce Boyer, David Feinsilver, M. Gerald Fromm, Bruce Smith, Michael Eigen, James Grotstein, and many others

The Kleinian School of Internal Objects

Melanie Klein, an analysand of both Ferenczi and Abraham, became interested in the analysis of young children (she founded child analysis). She theorized from her analytic findings that in normal development, the infant, rather than existing in a state of primary narcissism and autoerotism until it enters mental life in the Oedipus complex, has been psychologically separate and object-seeking since the very beginning of life.[8] Further, she postulated that the

---

[8]It must be remembered that although Freud acknowledged that the infant chooses mother's breast as its first object (see first footnote to this chapter), this object choice is constrained by the life-preservative (ego), not the libidinal, instincts. Autoerotism is the first infantile *sexual* organization. Even though objects are involved, they are discharge-facilitating objects rather than attachment objects in their own right. More precisely, part-objects are the putative objects of the autoerotic instincts, but they are not whole objects (relationships) per se. "Whole object" attachments begin in the narcissistic stage and develop in the stage of anaclitic object choice. Freud never fully integrated his stages of autoerotism–narcissism–anaclitic object choice with those of primary narcissism and the Oedipus complex. Classical psychoanalytic authors seem to believe that the first stages of object relations occur with the onset of the Oedipus complex and that the object relations of the pregenital stages are regressive elaborations of this complex (see Fenichel 1945). Mahler's (1968) protocol, however, allows for object relations that begin in an earlier stage of development, a tendency that started with Spitz (1957, 1965).

infant experiences a primitive configuration or state of anxiety, which she termed "persecutory anxiety," at approximately 3 weeks of age. This anxiety is the result of schizoid mechanisms (splitting, projective identification, idealization, and magic omnipotent denial). She called the infant's cluster of anxieties in this very early period of development the "paranoid-schizoid position."

At 3 to 4 months of age the infant experiences concern for its object's welfare and desires to restore and repair the object (from the damage it believes it caused the object in phantasy) and to recall its lost projections of self from the object. Klein (1940/1952) termed this state the "depressive position." It occurs at the time when the infant begins to realize that the breast part-object is constituted as a mother whole object, a person with a separate individuality and subjectivity (no longer an object in the narcissistic sense). Although Klein's positions differ from classical stages and phases,[9] the paranoid-schizoid position roughly corresponds to Mahler's symbiosis and the depressive position to her four stages of separation-individuation and especially to object constancy. According to Mahler and colleagues (1975), however, these four stages occur later than the Kleinian positions (Klein 1932/1959, 1940/1952, 1946/1952, 1948, 1952, 1957, 1961; Klein et al. 1952; Mahler et al. 1975).

One can readily observe the Kleinian positions clinically in terms of whether patients predominantly blame external objects for their distress and consequently feel persecuted (paranoid-schizoid position)—that is, feel that others hate or disapprove of them—or feel guilt, remorse, and concern for the object (depressive position). If, for instance, the analyst interprets to the patient that the patient has attacked the analyst (in unconscious phantasy) because of his or her envy of the analyst and his or her having to be so dependent on such an understanding person, and that the patient hates the humiliation of this dependency, the patient may incorporate the inter-

---

[9]Klein's positions are permanent and dialectical—that is, there is a continuing oscillation between the paranoid-schizoid and depressive positions throughout life. Bion (1962), Grotstein (1980–1981a, 1980–1981b), and Ogden (1989) view these positions as being constantly interactive with each other and as having simultaneous origins.

pretation, feel relief, and then become more introspective. The patient may then associate to internal feelings, impulses, and so forth, and their consequences. In so doing, the patient has emerged from the paranoid-schizoid position to the depressive position.

Klein and the Death Instinct

Whereas Freud emphasized the libidinal instinct, with its derivatives and vicissitudes, and only half-heartedly proffered the notion of a death instinct, Klein—without actually so stating—gave weight to both the life-preservative and the death instincts. In fact, the death instinct came to be the centerpiece of her metapsychology. She believed, even more than did Freud, that the infant is born with a sense of inherent destructiveness that must be attenuated by the nursing mother. Klein believed that envy (of the goodness of the breast) was a manifestation of the operation of the death instinct and was to be distinguished from external frustration. This envy, according to Klein, sabotages the goodness of relationships and interdicts the internalizations of good-object experiences that contribute to growth. Gratitude for the goodness of the object helps to mitigate the effects of the envy.

Projective Identification

Klein's rediscovery of the mechanism of projective identification, a mechanism that was first alluded to by Freud (1911a, 1911b) and addressed by Tausk (1919/1933), opened primitive mental thought for psychoanalytic exploration. It helped to account for how the infant explores the world with extensions of or attributions from itself. Projective identification functions as a form of primitive communication between mother and infant and between patient and therapist. It is the mechanism behind empathy. As a defensive mechanism, it can be understood to begin with a splitting-off of unwanted or dangerous feelings, impulses, and images of the self and/or of internal objects and so forth. The infant or patient then experiences these split-off feelings, impulses, and images as being part of the mother or therapist (projection). The reidentification in the mother or therapist of the unwanted feelings leaves the infant or patient empty and confused (with there being an absence of parts of the self and and a state of confusion of self with object).

Perhaps a better way of looking at this process would be that the infant (or patient) shrinks from the outline of a former self that contained the split-off attributes or feelings, which have now become associated with the object. Meanwhile, the infant (or patient) feels persecuted by the projections (the part of the self that is partially lost through projection) because the "disidentification" or disowning of these projected feelings, thoughts, and so forth is never fully successful. Thus, persecutory anxiety follows projective identification. This mechanism was implemented to avert a feeling of danger, but the person still feels the danger. The projectively identified self (now confused with the object) seems to want to return to the self—and may do so. Reintrojection, however, causes a new round of reprojective identification in the object, and as this takes place, the entire process becomes more complex.

The Kleinian object is always fashioned and transformed from elements whose origins lie in the infant; that is, the infant personifies the objects of the external and internal world with elements of its own self (affects, impulses, body experiences, etc.), thereby making the strange into the familiar. What is subsequently introjected is an already projectively altered object.[10] Although Klein postulated that the infant has experienced itself as separate from the object from the very beginning, she did not consider the infant to be sufficiently individuated until the onset of the depressive position. Therefore, the infant's representation of its object is unstable. The infant may then seek to ward off its separation anxiety by a manic defense, that is, by reacting to its experience of being dependent by denying the value of the needed object through a sense of triumph, contempt, and control over feelings, the self, and the object. One of the biggest hurdles the infant experiences, according to Klein, is that

---

[10]According to Kleinian theory, the infant introjects the image of the external object. What distinguishes Kleinian theory from classical psychoanalytic theory is the emphasis given in the former to the initial modification of the image of the object by projective identification. What is then taken in by introjection (the reverse of projection) is an altered object.

of feeling envy of the goodness of the object upon which the infant is dependent. This envy leads to feelings of rivalry that anticipate later oedipal rivalry.

The infant experiences feelings of greed, inchoate destructiveness, and envy (the latter two being manifestations of its inherent death instinct) and splits these feelings off, projects them into objects, and then reinternalizes them as internalized objects. Thus, the infant ultimately experiences an internal and external war between its good and bad objects because of its identifications with each. The nature of the projectively transformed object is of great importance. First, the transformed object is alien and yet indescribably familiar ("déjà vu"). Thus, there is a sense of persecution when the object is experienced as bad. *A feeling of persecution at this stage of development is always due to the return of an alienated part of the self; this feeling is in contrast to the feelings associated with intimidation by an enemy, who has never been part of the self.* Second, the object never seems entirely separate from the self because of the immaturity (i.e., the lack of individuation and the narcissistic orientation) of the self.

The object is always conceived of as being a part of the self and yet, at the same time, separate. This paradox can best be represented by the figure of "Siamese twins"—two heads and one body—where the body can be conceived of, in turn, as a paradoxically discontinuously continuous Möbius strip (Grotstein 1990). The internal object is *not* a representation (more precisely, not a symbolic representation to the psyche) as it will be after the development of evocative memory and object constancy. Symbolic representation, as Klein conceptualized it, does not occur until the onset of the depressive position when the infant experiences it as separate and whole and *accepts* its separateness from the object (i.e., the object has become a *subject* in its own right and no longer the infant's *object*). The object's final transformation most resembles the ego psychological concept of a *representation* when the object attains the status of a symbol instead of being, as it was originally experienced, originally concrete and phantasmal.

The term "object" is unfortunate. The concept of object, especially as used by the Kleinians and by Fairbairn, runs the gamut from the human to the nonhuman, from the person to the chimera (as in the case of the sphinx). The object is invariably alien and may be fragmented or primitive. It may be a transformation not only of the image of the external object but also of parts of the self (e.g., eyes [sight], ears [hearing], mouth [tasting, swallowing, biting], penis, anus, vagina, skin, mind, etc.). Internal objects more resemble "phantoms," "demons," "witches," "warlocks," "angels," "chimeras," "ogres," "furies," and so forth.[11] Thomas Ogden (1983) noted also that the infant identifies with the object in two separate ways: as the "self" aspect of the object and as the object itself. In other words, the object is experienced as being bimodal, or "janus"-like; one aspect of the object is an alien aspect of the self that initiated the projection and that became translocated into the object; the other aspect is identified as a stranger, one who is other than self from the start. When the two aspects are confused, then an eerie déjà vu experience occurs in which one feels persecuted—that is, haunted—by the strangely familiar. This formulation is especially important in clarifying internal object relationships in which one aspect of the self identified within the object acts against another aspect of the object whose nature is known only through one's identification with it—because, as Ogden (1983) observes, objects themselves do not have a psychology when they are internal; they have only the psychology we impute to them through projective identification.[12]

Bion

Kleinian psychology, which is mainly internal object–oriented, has been criticized for its apparent neglect of the importance of the

---

[11]In returning to the more naturalistic origins of that which, later, logical positivism rendered into "objects," I should not neglect to mention C. G. Jung's (1934/1968) "archetypes," those "ready-made," invariant universal mythic structures that have sadly been neglected in the classical, Kleinian, and Independent literature. Unfortunately, space limitations do not allow a proper discussion of this worthy topic.

[12]For an overall view of the Kleinian perspective, see Segal (1973), Grotstein (1980–1981a, 1980–1981b, 1982–1983a, 1982–1983b), Spillius (1988a, 1988b), and Hinshelwood (1989).

external object. Wilfred Bion (1962, 1963), one of Klein's foremost followers, sought to correct this impression in his conception of "the container and the contained." By this he meant that the infant needs (and has a right to expect) a mother who is able to contain the infant's projective identifications ("fears of dying," according to Bion) in a state of "reverie," a state of tolerant receptivity and devotion to the task of sustaining her infant's distress, absorbing it, and then translating it into appropriate actions (interpretations). "Containment" involves sustaining the impact of the projective identifications "without desire" (i.e., unselfishly), translating them into meaningful signifiers of affect and/or need, and properly acting upon them with the infant. This process can be demonstrated in the mother's intuition about her infant's needs in the form of naming them (i.e., hunger, loneliness, anxiety, need to be held, need for the diaper to be changed, etc.) and then acting upon them.

Bion's theory was the first *adaptive* modification of Kleinian theory and paralleled the concept of adaptation proffered by Heinz Hartmann (1939/1958). In developing his theory, Bion not only modified the Kleinian definition of projective identification from pathological to normal but also changed the Kleinian emphasis from a single-person theory to the intersubjective dyad.[13] He is also noted for his application of Kleinian object relations theory to the theory of the group (Bion 1959/1967, 1970).[14]

Case Vignette (demonstrating Kleinian and Bionian principles)

M.G. is a 33-year-old married salesman and entrepreneur who has frequent, compulsive affairs with women. He entered analysis when he felt threatened by a destabilization of his life owing to his having fallen in love with his latest mistress, who was leaving her husband in order to marry M.G. His past history included his having been very upset upon the birth of his brother when he was

---

[13]For a further development of Bion's concepts on projective identification, see discussions by Grotstein (1981) and Ogden (1982).

[14]The reader is referred to Pines (1985), Ashbach and Schermer (1987), and Alford (1989).

2 years old and having felt abandoned by his mother—and his father. He described his mother as a powerful, demanding person who did not offer unconditional love to him but levied expectations of high accomplishment on him, as did his father. Moreover, his mother and father did not get along very well, and M.G. served as his mother's confidant. M.G. did not get along with his wife and complained often to his girlfriends about, in particular, her passivity and extreme dependency on him.

The first analytic intervention consisted of telling him that he experienced his wife and girlfriends as two split objects; his girlfriend represented an exciting breast and his wife represented a disappointing, used-up, spoiled one. I then interpreted that the disappointing breast also represented another aspect of himself that he projected (through projective identification) into his wife—a self that he always longed to be, a passive, dependent, and totally and unconditionally cared-for self that he associated to (and identified with) his envied younger brother. His numerous affairs were unconscious attempts to reactivate this phantasy, that is, of being passively cared for and adored by devoted, exciting mother substitutes. They were also attempts to offset the persecutory anxiety he had developed over the years because of feelings he had projected into his wife, which, when internalized by him from his image of her, caused him enormous anxiety. He felt persecuted internally by what he believed he had done to her. Put another way, because he believed that he had damaged his wife (his image of her) by these affairs and because he projectively assigned his ill-thought-of passive and dependently needy self into her, he experienced her as damaged and therefore persecutory toward him. The archaic him, still being in the paranoid-schizoid (narcissistic) position, could not yet experience empathy—and therefore guilt—toward an object on which he was dependent; the persecutory danger that he experienced in association with the object was in proportion to the degree to which he believed he had damaged it. "As ye sow, so shall ye reap!" says Scripture. His wife then became not only a damaged object within him but also a critical superego object that persecuted (prosecuted) him. Because he was confused with her internally (due to projective identification), he could not leave her or be happy staying with her.

These mechanisms represent the operations of splitting, idealization (of the girlfriends), magic omnipotent denial (of his dependency and humanness), and projective identification (into wife, brother, and girlfriend). Involved in his relations with both wife and girlfriend were ample quantities of greed (he wanted to have it all) and envy (he hated his dependency feelings and the object of his dependency and sought to triumph over it [the manic defense]).

The transference was apparent at the beginning of treatment. He immediately called me by my first name and usurped the footstool that stood between our two chairs (before he went to the couch). In a Monday morning session following a long weekend break, he addressed me as "Jim," then expressed his impatience with the analysis, and then described feelings of suffocation and claustrophobia he had had on the airplane returning home. I interpreted to him that he had experienced the pain of separation from the analysis over the long break and hated me for (paradoxically) abandoning the infant him, following which he had a phantasy of rushing into me to merge so as not to be separate (calling me "Jim") and then felt stuck inside me (claustrophobic anxiety in the airplane). Then he projected his disclaimed dependent self into me disparagingly (manic defense), after which he felt that I, like his wife, was no longer useful or helpful and took too long besides.

Following this interpretation (which actually took place in parts over the course of the entire session), he felt surprised and then greatly relieved. Afterward, he spoke about how he has always needed to be in control and how he has needed to help others and to avoid receiving help because the latter makes him feel too vulnerable. At that instant he entered the depressive position.

The Independent School

Fairbairn's Object Relations and Endopsychic Structures

W. R. D. Fairbairn was perhaps the first to challenge Freud's concept of the dominance of the pleasure principle and to substitute the concept that the infant is object-seeking from the beginning and that the presence of autoerotism indicates a breakdown in the infant's relationship to its mother (and father) (Fairbairn 1952). This shift in emphasis has many far-reaching implications that have not as yet been fully realized. Fairbairn was stating in effect that the infant is born "non-demonic" and "non-hedonic" and is also born "innocent" rather than guilty of the "original sin" of its drive legacy. He did away with the id altogether and transformed it into a "libidinal ego." Although he anticipated the work of Winnicott and Kohut, he was not, until recently, accorded the recognition he deserved (see Bacal 1990; Bacal and Newman 1990; Grotstein 1991a; Robbins 1980).

According to Klein's conceptualization, the infant constructs its view of the object from its own projections and only slowly retransforms them to reality in the depressive position. In her view, the importance of the external object lies in its capacity to *release* destructive and/or constructive forces selectively in the infant. By contrast, Fairbairn believed that the infant has been both separate and in a state of primary identification (primary narcissism) since birth. Further, he conceived that the infant internalizes only bad (unsatisfying) objects as a way of coping with them; good objects, being trustworthy, do not need to be internalized to be controlled. In Fairbairn's view, the infant internalizes the badness of the object because the object is needed and because there is more hope if the infant is bad than if the needed parent is bad (i.e., the moral defense of the superego). In his conception of the moral defense, Fairbairn elaborated the well-known but not sufficiently understood phenomenon of an infant's taking over the parent's badness and identifying with it at the infant's own expense in order to preserve hope and faith in the goodness of the needed parent. The process amounts to a splitting and isolation of the two factors (i.e., a good and a bad parent and a good and a bad self identified with them, respectively). Fairbairn's conception is more elaborate, precise, and helpful than Anna Freud's (1936/1946) concept of "identification with the aggressor."

Thus, because all parents are varyingly satisfying and unsatisfying, the infant experiences a split within its original (primary) object (OO) and its original ego (OE) relating to this object (primary identification), yielding two separate objects (one satisfying and one unsatisfying) and two separate egos (one libidinal [i.e., seeking satisfaction] and one antilibidinal [i.e., rejecting satisfaction]). The satisfying parts of the OE and the OO become the remaining psychic structure of central ego (CE)—or self and ideal object (IO), or ego-ideal—whereas the split-off portion of the object, the unsatisfying object, becomes internalized along with that portion of the split-off ego identified with it. This structure then splits again into a rejecting object (RO) in relation to and identified with a split-off ego known as the antilibidinal ego (AE) (or "internal saboteur"), and an exciting object (EO) linked to the split-off needy libidinal ego (LE). Thus, three dynamic systems result: 1) the central ego linked to the ideal object, 2) the antilibidinal ego in relation to the rejecting object, and 3) the libidinal ego connected with the exciting object.

The six endopsychic structures composing these dynamic systems have a complex relationship with one another, the most basic of which is the repression by the central ego and ideal object of the other two structures (four components). In turn, the rejecting object and the antilibidinal ego, serving as an archaic superego, repress the libidinal ego and the exciting object even further. Whereas guilt and castration anxiety seem to be the mainstay of classical analysis, and persecutory and depressive anxiety that of the Kleinians, shame and terror of the return of the bad internal objects (and egos) to awareness are the mainstay of Fairbairn's psychology. Thus, in Fairbairn's view, the content of the repressed is not the drives but the badness of the objects one was compelled to internalize (i.e., repress) in order to survive. Ogden's (1983) bimodal theory of identifications with internal objects makes considerable sense out of Fairbairn's endopsychic suborganizations. With Ogden's differentiation in mind, one could hypothesize that the endopsychic structures of the internal world consist of three self-object structures. This process is demonstrated in the psychology of children who have been subjected to abuse and molestation and who, consequently, have had to adapt to their environment as "false selves" by internalizing that environment and "correcting" it within.

Fairbairn also emphasized the importance of the schizoid position, which significantly differs from Klein's paranoid-schizoid position. Klein founded her whole metapsychology on the infant's fear of its inherent destructiveness. Fairbairn, while agreeing with Klein on the importance of destructiveness in his concept of the depressive position, proffered a radically different idea in his concept of the schizoid position. His belief was that the infant becomes schizoid in proportion to the extent to which its objects fail to treat it as a person in its own right and fail to accept its *love* as a valid gift. Thus, Fairbairn was perhaps the first existentialist psychoanalyst and started a trend that, after decades of delay, is now becoming established, thanks to infant development research and other changes in psychoanalytic emphasis. The concepts of *attunement, mutuality,* and *reciprocity,* although never named as such, suffuse his work.[15]

Winnicott

Winnicott is perhaps the best known member of the British object relations school, but, until recently, he was known in the United States largely for his concepts of the "transitional object" (Winnicott 1951/1958) and the "holding environment" (Winnicott 1960/1965).[16] His language is paradoxically clear and precise (especially when he addressed parents) and yet circumspect in terms of analytic theory.

---

[15]For an overall view of Fairbairn, see Sutherland (1989), Hughes (1989), and Grotstein and Rinsley (1994).

[16]Winnicott posited that after a few months of life, when the infant confronts its fear of its awareness of separation from its mother, it seems to discover the *transitional object,* a nonhuman item, such as a blanket, teddy bear, and so forth, whose softness resembles that of its mother and therefore becomes a signifier of her. The transitional object is conjured by the infant and offers solace. It is intermediate between infant and mother, a bridge of transition over the chasm of separation, and represents an element of thirdness, that is, an element that is neither infant nor mother and yet conjures a connection between the two. Thus, the concept of the transitional object is paradoxical, as are so many of Winnicott's conceptions. When the infant—now child—is finished with it, the child discards it and does not mourn it.

The *holding environment* is Winnicott's unique way of describing that aspect of mothering that can be conceived of as a background support that supplies environmental provisions to foster the infant's maturation. The holding environment differs from the instinctually needed object mother who is the focus of need. The former, though of consummate importance, is believed by the infant to be unimportant (until absent), whereas the instinctually needed object is known always to be important. That mother—and her breasts—are always in the foreground, whereas the holding environment mother is in the background.

It is now becoming apparent that he was a major clinician and theorist whose ideas will continue to have a profound effect on psychoanalytic thinking and on child rearing (Winnicott 1958, 1965, 1971).

To briefly summarize his work, Winnicott believed that the "good enough mother" was well enough equipped to raise her infant properly, beginning with total immersion ("primary maternal preoccupation") in its being. (As Winnicott [1960/1965, p. 39] noted, "There is no such thing as an infant. There is only the infant and its mother.") Gradually, the mother releases her infant into potential (transitional) space, where it "experiments" with its ruthlessness toward her and with its creativity. The mother must also facilitate the emergence of such "spontaneous gestures" and allow the infant to discover its own originality uncontaminated by parental impingement. The infant plays (*alone,* but in mother's presence as sentinel) in illusory "potential space" where the infant "creates" the object at the same time that mother provides it (i.e., benign omnipotent magic). Only subsequently does mother "err" in her timing and ministrations, thereby affording normal, necessary "me"/"not-me" experiences for differentiation and separation. The transitional object temporarily allows for continuation of the sensory experience of at-one-ment with an absent mother. Severe maternal (and paternal) neglect produces a sense of privation, whereas more moderate neglect or impingement produces deprivation. The psychopathic person enacts rage against the original providers to restore his or her lost entitlement. Extreme failures of care produce annihilation anxiety with a "failure to go-on-being" (infantile catastrophe or psychosis) (Winnicott 1962/1965, p. 66).

Following his formulation of the "true-self" and "false-self" (necessitated by the need of the infant to survive in a dangerous home atmosphere), Winnicott then developed the notion of their normal antecedents in terms of the passive "being self" (female self in either sex) and the active "doing self" (male self). He also postulated two separate mothering functions associated with each. The being self is associated with a "facilitating" or "holding environment" unrelated to instinctual demands, whereas the doing self relates to an object mother who is to be used to satisfy instinctual demands. There is no communication between the environmental mother and the being self because no communication is necessary. The being self is the state of deepest regression of the true self and is associated with unconditional love and acceptance. Further, the being self seeks privacy and needs never to be found, and yet hopes that mother knows that it is hidden and needs to be found (paradox). Ultimately, it is in playing that the infant, discovering its spontaneous gesture—alone—in the presence of mother, develops confidence in a capacity to create itself anew and become progressively more autonomous.[17]

Other Contributors to the Independent School

Others who have contributed under the banner of the Independent School include John Bowlby, Masud Khan, Neville Symington, Gregorio Kohon, Martin James, Margaret Little, John Padel, John Klauber, Adam Limentani, Charles Rycroft, Patrick Casement, Nina Coltart, Harold Stewart, Jonathan Pedder, William Gillespie, Christopher Bollas, Harry Guntrip, and R. D. Laing. Bowlby in particular has expressed an extreme "Independent" view by disavowing the drives altogether in favor of the supraordinate theory of attachment and bonding, a concept that has captured the imagination of current infant development researchers (Stern 1985).[18]

The American School of Object Relations

The term "American School" defines a separate approach to the study of object relations even though the term is somewhat inaccurate. Many advances in object relations theory that reflect the

---

[17]For a review of Winnicott's work, see Grolnick and Barkin (1978), Davis and Wallbridge (1981), and Grolnick (1990).

[18]The work of the Independent School has been detailed, cataloged, and evaluated by Gregorio Kohon (1986) and Eric Rayner (1991). There are many Americans whose work borrows heavily from the Independent School. These include Harold Searles, L. Bryce Boyer, Peter Giovacchini, Arnold Modell, Thomas Ogden, Jay Greenberg, Stephen Mitchell, Jeffrey Seinfeld, James Grotstein, and others.

American consensus were made in England in Anna Freud's School (Hampstead Clinic), especially the contributions of Sandler and Rosenblatt (1962). The rapprochement between the object relations tenets of the British and the Americans has been attempted with salutary (but incomplete) results by Kernberg and has been furthered by infant development research and by the rise of "self psychology."

The British, both Kleinians and Independents, begin with an infant development theory characterized by the principle of genetic continuity (Isaacs 1952)—that is, development begins with and progresses from birth. In the British analysts' theories, infantile dependency is more important than and different from infantile sexuality (autoerotism). The infant is mindful and psychological from birth. In particular, the British theorists' concept of the object, particularly the internal object, is quite different from its so-called equivalent counterpart in the United States, the object representation.

Internal objects are not representations at first. They correspond more to internalizations of *pre*representations, objects that are "phantasmal" or "demonic" and have been formed by projective identification and personalization of the external object into a familiar/strange entity that, at first, hardly resembles the original self or the object into which it has projectively identified itself. Further, there are some differences in constancy, permanency, and constituency between the internal object and a representation. The internal object is constant only insofar as the bad object, in contrast to the good object, seems to persevere because of the inevitability of frustration—thus the success and addictive hold by bad (perverse) objects. An internal object is the external object's prismatic refraction, as it were, of projections from the subject that are then perceived as alien and yet strangely familiar. An internalized object represents the quintessence of "déjà vu" insofar as the projected aspects of the self are alienated (split off), projected into an object, and then introjected, conveying the experience of a strange and yet familiar aspect of the self inside. Thus, an internal object is always more self than object.

The opposite is true of an object representation. Object representations, like self representations, are always singular; they have only one component, the object or the self, but not both. Internal objects, by contrast, are always plural in their nature (alienated and consisting of parts of the self and of the object). Internal objects begin as part-objects in the projective transformations of the paranoid-schizoid position and become whole objects when, during the depressive position, the infant repairs the object and, in so doing, recalls its projections from the object, thus retransforming the object into a symbolic whole object.

From the American School's point of view, object representations naturally *develop*. From the Kleinian point of view, the development of a symbolic object is an *achievement* of the infant's active, ongoing attempts at reparation; such development does not come naturally. Further, Americans tend to use the term "representation" indiscriminately. Jacobson (1964) and Kernberg (1976), for example, speak of "fused self-object representations." The question arises as to who the representer is, or, to be exact, who the representer is who is separated and individuated enough to re-present the self as its object. This seemingly Talmudic-like point is of no casual significance. Re-presentation presupposes object constancy (Fraiberg 1969). In other words, in order to re-present to the psyche one must be separated enough to be a self, an impossibility under the classical conditions of primary narcissism and/or Mahler's (1968) autism and symbiosis. Re-presentation ("evocative memory") is possible only after the object-constancy phase of separation-individuation has been achieved. The Kleinian concept of phantasy bypasses this stricture by doing away with primary narcissism and allowing for internalizations of transformed object images from the beginning of life. This is a central inconsistency in the American School's view of the formation of objects. It is true that Stern (1985), although agreeing with Klein that the infant experiences itself as separate since the very beginning, strongly disavows the early infant's capacity to form fantasies before verbalization skills begin in the second year of life. However, Stern seems to confuse imagination (phantasy) with symbolic thinking.

Hartmann

It was Heinz Hartmann (1939/1958), according to Rapaport (1959), who brought together the disparate strands of contributions to ego psychology and forged the adaptation revolution, thus proffering the first major object relations modification of the then prevailing id psychology. By drawing attention to the concepts of adaptation, of the "average expectable environment," and of the ego's capacity to regulate (i.e., defuse and neutralize) instinct tensions, Hartmann was able to formulate a new metapsychological perspective that enfranchised the nurturing environment as an important participant in mental life. This enfranchisement had been lacking in earlier id analysis and in Kleinian analysis (until Bion) but had been implicit in the contributions of the Independent Group, most particularly those of Fairbairn and Winnicott.

Jacobson

Edith Jacobson (1953, 1954a, 1954b, 1964) followed in the footsteps of Hartmann and other ego psychologists and, based mostly upon her own creative work, became virtually the "Melanie Klein" of the American School. She launched the American version of the object representational world. She studied the moods and affects of neurotic and melancholic depression, also studied infant development and adolescent psychology, and investigated the phenomenon of identity formation.

One of her most important discoveries was that of the nature of the relationship of self identity to the "stellar constellation" arrangements that the self representation and the object representations form. Jacobson pictured the self representation (within the ego) as related to object representations via a troika of psychic energies (libidinal, aggressive, and neutral). The onset of depressive illness, for instance, may result from a shortage of neutral (neutralizing) energy. Then, as neutralization diminishes, libidinal and/or aggressive energy reciprocally swells up and becomes unbalanced. The self representation then desperately "migrates" (in representational space) toward the object representation to aquire the requisite neutral energy (a process that today we would call *regulation* or *attunement*). As the "migration" or approximation proceeds, the self representation becomes suffused with neutralized energy, resulting in regressive transformations of self and object representations, the latter of which become more repersonified and bizarre. Finally, as the self representation begins to fuse with the object representation, the self (ego) boundaries of reality testing dissolve, and the psychotic state ensues. Jacobson thus followed Hartmann in giving the object representation the task of facilitating the separation and individuation of the nascent self representation from its matrix with its object representation and ensuring the self's adaptive survival through a continuing source of instinctual drive neutralization.

Mahler

Margaret Mahler (1952, 1958, 1968) and colleagues (Mahler et al. 1975) reordered the contributions to ego psychology by Hartmann, Jacobson, and others into a developmental framework that has had an important influence on psychoanalytic thinking. Her ideas of infant development fostered a major shift from the older autoerotic scheme to one that was essentially object-oriented from the very beginning. Her conceptions of the initial phases of normal autism and symbiosis were rooted in the classical notion of primary narcissism but attempted an object orientation *in potentia*. The subphases of separation and of individuation[19] constitute a clear-cut object relations epigenetic pathway for the maturing and developing infant and child to traverse. Stern (1985), based on later infant development observation, disavowed Mahler's first two stages because he found that the infant is separate since the very beginning, as Klein had always stated and as had been assumed by many of the British Independents.

Kernberg

Otto Kernberg (1976, 1980) attempted to bridge the gap between the British Schools and the American School. Trained in South America

---

[19]The terms *separation* and *individuation* are commonly linked by a hyphen to designate their relationship with each other. It would be useful as well to consider presenting these terms without the hyphen in order to emphasize the conceptualization that they are also independent functions that can get out of alignment with each other.

as a Kleinian, Kernberg is well versed in the Kleinian and Independent views. When he arrived at the Menninger Foundation, he helped pilot a longitudinal research project on the treatment of patients with borderline personality organization. He thus introduced American therapists to the legitimacy of the psychoanalytic and psychotherapeutic treatment of this primitive mental disorder and established the legitimacy of primitive object relations. Although Kernberg rarely if ever spoke of Winnicott, Balint, or the other Independents and was critical of many aspects of Klein's and Fairbairn's thinking, he integrated what he found useful in their work with concordant ideas in Jacobson and Mahler and added his own strong accent. He eschewed Klein's positions, opting instead for a more extended Mahlerian phase approach:

> Combining Mahler's and Jacobson's formulations with my own observations, I concluded . . . that the early ego has to accomplish two tasks in rapid succession: it must differentiate self-representations from object representations and must integrate libidinally determined and aggressively determined self- and object-representations. The first task is accomplished in part under the influence of the development of primary autonomy; but it largely fails in the psychoses, because a pathological fusion or refusion of self- and object-representations results in a failure in the differentiation of ego boundaries and, therefore, in the differentiation of self from nonself. In contrast, with the borderline personality organization, differentiation of self- from object-representations has occurred to a sufficient degree to permit the establishment of ego boundaries and a concomitant differentiation of self from others. The second task, however—of integrating self- and object-representations built up under the influence of libidinal drive derivatives and their related affects with their corresponding self- and object-representations built up under the influence of aggressive drive derivatives and their related affects—fails to a great extent in borderline patients, mainly because of the pathological predominance of pregenital aggression. (Kernberg 1980, pp. 11–12)

In the above passage, Kernberg tries to integrate the concepts developed by Jacobson, Mahler, and Hartmann. His ultimate scheme for the development of aggressive self-object representations and libidinal self-object representations as units in themselves is borrowed from Fairbairn's endopsychic structures. Following Klein generally and Rosenfeld (1965) specifically, Kernberg posits that excessive splitting exists between the aggressive (bad) self-object representation and its libidinal (good) counterpart.

Other Contributors to Object Relations Theory

In the space allowed for this chapter it is difficult to do justice to all of the significant contributors to this rapidly developing area of investigation. First, mention should be made of the interpersonal or relational school, which was founded by Harry Stack Sullivan, William Alanson White, and their conceptual descendants, whose leading members today include Arthur Feiner, Jay Greenberg, Stephen Mitchell, Edgar Levenson, Eric Witenberg, Benjamin Wolstein, and many others. They, too, are part of the chain of object relatedness schools but have placed more emphasis on external relationships than on phantasmal (internal) relationships. Their concepts, too, like those of the British Schools, are enjoying a resurgence of interest, thanks in no small measure to the contributions by many of their members, especially Greenberg and Mitchell (Greenberg and Mitchell 1983; Mitchell 1988).

In the classical realm the following have made prominent contributions that are worth more than just mention: Joseph Sandler, Ann-Marie Sandler, B. Rosenblatt, Ernest Bibring, Gertrud and Reuben Blanck, Joseph Lichtenberg, John McDevitt, Calvin Settlage, William Meissner, Robert Schafer, Helm Stierlin, Robert Stolorow, George Atwood, Frank Lachmann, Ernest Wolf, Arnold Goldberg, Michael Basch, Gerald Adler, Sheldon Bach, Joyce McDougall, Reid Meloy, and Jeffrey Seinfeld.

Special attention should be called to the work of Harold Searles, L. Bryce Boyer, and Thomas Ogden, each of whom has steadfastly carried the British message to America. Ogden (1981, 1986, 1989) especially has made noteworthy revisions and integrations.

Further mention should be made of the work of Bertrand Cramer (1982a, 1982b, 1984, 1985, 1986) and Maurice Apprey (1987;

Apprey and Stein 1993), each of whom has conducted longitudinal research on infant outcome correlated with unconscious projective identifications from mothers. Apprey (Apprey and Stein 1993) has extended his research to the study of anorexia nervosa and adolescent drug addiction and has found a strong intergenerational factor to be present, particularly the identified patient's grandmother.

References

Abraham K: A short study of the development of the libido, viewed in the light of mental disorders (1924), in Selected Papers on Psycho-Analysis. Translated by Bryan D, Strachey A. London, Hogarth Press/Institute of Psycho-Analysis, 1948, pp 418–501

Alford CF: Melanie Klein and Critical Social Theory. New Haven, CT, Yale University Press, 1989

Apprey M: Projective identification and maternal misconception in disturbed mothers. British Journal of Psychotherapy 4(1):5–22, 1987

Apprey M, Stein HF: Intersubjectivity, Projective Identification, and Otherness. Pittsburgh, PA, Duquesne University Press, 1993

Ashbach C, Schermer VC: Object Relations, the Self and the Group: A Conceptual Paradigm. London, Routledge & Kegan Paul, 1987

Bacal HA: W.R.D. Fairbairn, in Theories of Object Relations: Bridges to Self Psychology. Edited by Bacal HA, Newman KM. New York, Columbia University Press, 1990, pp 135–157

Bacal HA, Newman KM (eds): Theories of Object Relations: Bridges to Self Psychology. New York, Columbia University Press, 1990

Balint A: Love for the mother and mother-love (1939). Int J Psychoanal 30:251–259, 1949 [This version originally published in Int Z f Psa u Imago 24:33–48, 1939]

Balint M: Early developmental states of the ego. Primary object love (1937). Int J Psychoanal 30:265–273, 1949 [Originally published in Imago 23:270–288, 1937]

Balint M: The Basic Fault. London, Tavistock, 1968

Bion WR: Attacks on linking (1959), in Second Thoughts: Selected Papers on Psycho-Analysis. London, Heinemann, 1967, pp 93–109

Bion WR: Learning From Experience. London, Heinemann, 1962

Bion WR: Elements of Psycho-Analysis. London, Heinemann, 1963

Bion WR: Attention and Interpretation: A Scientific Approach to Insight in Psycho-Analysis and Groups. London, Tavistock, 1970

Bowlby J: Attachment and Loss, Vol I: Attachment. New York, Basic Books, 1969

Bowlby J: Attachment and Loss, Vol II: Separation: Anxiety and Anger. New York, Basic Books, 1973

Bowlby J: Attachment and Loss, Vol III: Loss: Sadness and Depression. New York, Basic Books, 1980

Cramer B: Interaction réele, interaction fantasmatique: réflexions au sujet des thérapies et des observations de nourrissons. Psychothérapies 1:39–47, 1982a

Cramer B: La psychiatrie du bébé: une introduction, in La Dynamique du Nourrisson. 7. Edited by Soulé M. Paris, ESF, 1982b, pp 28–83

Cramer B: Modèles psychoanalytiques, modèles interactifs: recoupment possible? Paper presented at the International Symposium on Psychiatry-Psychoanalysis, Montréal, Canada, September 1984

Cramer B: Thérapies du nourrisson, in Traite de Psychiatrie de L'Enfant et de L'Adolescent II. Edited by Lebovici S, Diatkine R, Soulé M. Paris, Presses Universités de France, 1985

Cramer B: Assessment of parent-infant relationship, in Affective Development in Infancy. Edited by Brazelton TB, Yogman MW. Norwood, NJ, Ablex, 1986

Davis M, Wallbridge D: Boundary and Space: An Introduction to the Work of D. W. Winnicott. New York, Brunner/Mazel, 1981

Fairbairn WRD: Psychoanalytic Studies of the Personality. London, Tavistock, 1952

Fenichel O: The Psychoanalytic Theory of Neurosis. New York, WW Norton, 1945

Ferenczi S: Stages in the development of the sense of reality (1913), in Sex in Psychoanalysis. Translated by Jones E. New York, Basic Books, 1950, pp 213–239

Fraiberg S: Libidinal object constancy and mental representation. Psychoanalytic Study Child 24:9–47, 1969

Freud A: The Ego and Mechanisms of Defence (1936). New York, International Universities Press, 1946

Freud S: Three essays on the theory of sexuality (1905), in Standard Edition of the Complete Psychological Works of Sigmund Freud, Vol 7. Translated and edited by Strachey J. London, Hogarth Press, 1953, pp 135–241

Freud S: Family romances (1909[1908]), in Standard Edition of the Complete Psychological Works of Sigmund Freud, Vol 9. Translated and edited by Strachey J. London, Hogarth Press, 1959, pp 235–241

Freud S: The psycho-analytic view of psychogenic disturbance of vision (1910), in Standard Edition of the Complete Psychological Works of Sigmund Freud, Vol 11. Translated and edited by Strachey J. London, Hogarth Press, 1957, pp 209–218

Freud S: Formulations on the two principles of mental functioning (1911a), in Standard Edition of the Complete Psychological Works of Sigmund Freud, Vol 12. Translated and edited by Strachey J. London, Hogarth Press, 1958, pp 213–226

Freud S: Psycho-analytic notes on an autobiographical account of a case of paranoia (dementia paranoides) (1911b), in Standard Edition of the Complete Psychological Works of Sigmund Freud, Vol 12. Translated and edited by Strachey J. London, Hogarth Press, 1958, pp 1–82

Freud S: On narcissism: an introduction (1914), in Standard Edition of the Complete Psychological Works of Sigmund Freud, Vol 14. Translated and edited by Strachey J. London, Hogarth Press, 1957, pp 67–102

Freud S: Mourning and melancholia (1917[1915]), in Standard Edition of the Complete Psychological Works of Sigmund Freud, Vol 14. Translated and edited by Strachey J. London, Hogarth Press, 1957, pp 237–260

Freud S: 'A child is being beaten': a contribution to the study of the origin of sexual perversions (1919), in Standard Edition of the Complete Psychological Works of Sigmund Freud, Vol 17. Translated and edited by Strachey J. London, Hogarth Press, 1955, pp 175–204

Freud S: The ego and the id (1923), in Standard Edition of the Complete Psychological Works of Sigmund Freud, Vol 19. Translated and edited by Strachey J. London, Hogarth Press, 1961, pp 1–66

Greenberg JR, Mitchell SA: Object Relations in Psychoanalytic Theory. Cambridge, MA, Harvard University Press, 1983

Grolnick S: The Work and Play of Winnicott. Northvale, NJ, Jason Aronson, 1990

Grolnick S, Barkin L (eds): Between Reality and Fantasy: Transitional Objects and Phenomena. New York, Jason Aronson, 1978

Grotstein J: The significance of Kleinian contributions to psychoanalysis, I: Kleinian instinct theory. International Journal of Psychoanalytic Psychotherapy 8:375–392, 1980–1981a

Grotstein J: The significance of Kleinian contributions to psychoanalysis, II: Freudian and Kleinian conceptions of early mental development. International Journal of Psychoanalytic Psychotherapy 8:393–428, 1980–1981b

Grotstein J: Splitting and Protective Identification. New York, Jason Aronson, 1981

Grotstein JS: The significance of Kleinian contributions to psychoanalysis, III: the Kleinian theory of ego psychology and object relations. International Journal of Psychoanalytic Psychotherapy 9:487–510, 1982–1983a

Grotstein JS: The significance of Kleinian contributions to psychoanalysis, IV: critiques of Klein. International Journal of Psychoanalytic Psychotherapy 9:511–536, 1982–1983b

Grotstein JS: Of human bonding and of human bondage: the role of friendship in intimacy. Contemporary Psychotherapy Review 5(1):5–32, 1990

Grotstein JS: An American view of the British psychoanalytic experience, Part I: introduction: the Americanization of psychoanalysis. Melanie Klein and Object Relations 9(2):1–15, 1991a

Grotstein JS: An American view of the British psychoanalytic experience, Part II: the Kleinian school. Melanie Klein and Object Relations 9(2):16–33, 1991b

Grotstein JS: An American view of the British psychoanalytic experience, Part III: the British object relations school. Melanie Klein and Object Relations 9(2):34–62, 1991c

Grotstein JS: II. Endopsychic structure and the cartography of the internal world: six endopsychic characters in search of an author, in Fairbairn and the Origins of Object Relations. Edited by Grotstein JS, Rinsley D. London, Free Association Books/New York, Guilford, 1994a, pp 174–194

Grotstein JS: I. Notes on Fairbairn's metapsychology, in Fairbairn and the Origins of Object Relations. Edited by Grotstein JS, Rinsley D. London, Free Association Books, 1994b, pp 112–150

Guntrip H: Schizoid Phenomena, Object Relations, and the Self. New York, International Universities Press, 1969

Guntrip H: Psychoanalytic Theory, Therapy, and the Self. New York, Basic Books, 1971

Harlow HF: Love in infant monkeys. Sci Am 200:68–74, 1959

Hartmann H: Ego Psychology and the Problem of Adaptation (1939). Translated by Rapaport D. New York, International Universities Press, 1958

Hegel GWF: The Phenomenology of Spirit (1887). Translated by Miller AV. London, Oxford University Press, 1977

Hermann I: Zum Triebleben der Primaten. Imago 19:113, 1933

Hermann I: Sich-Anklammern-Auf-Suche-Gehen. International Zeitschrift Psychoanalyse 22:349–370, 1936

Hinshelwood RD: A Dictionary of Kleinian Thought. London, Free Association Books, 1989

Hughes JM: Reshaping the Psychoanalytic Domain: The Work of Melanie Klein, W.R.D. Fairbairn, and D. W. Winnicott. Berkeley, CA, University of California Press, 1989

Isaacs S: The nature and function of phantasy, in Developments in Psycho-Analysis [by Melanie Klein, Paula Heimann, Susan Isaacs, and Joan Riviere]. Edited by Joan Riviere. London, Hogarth/Institute of Psycho-Analysis, 1952, pp 67–121

Jacobson E: Contribution to the metapsychology of cyclothymic depression, in Affective Disorders. Edited by Greenacre P. New York, International Universities Press, 1953, pp 49–83

Jacobson E: Contribution to the metapsychology of psychotic identifications. J Am Psychoanal Assoc 2:239–262, 1954a

Jacobson E: The self and the object world: vicissitudes of their infantile cathexes and their influence on ideational and affective development. Psychoanal Study Child 9:75–127, 1954b

Jacobson E: The Self and the Object World. New York, International Universities Press, 1964

Jung CG: Archetypes and the collective unconscious (1934), in Collected Works of C. G. Jung, 2nd Edition, Vol 9, Part I. Translated and edited by Hull RFC. New York, Princeton University Press, 1968, pp 3–41

Kernberg OF: Object-Relations Theory and Clinical Psychoanalysis. New York, Jason Aronson, 1976

Kernberg OF: Internal World and External Reality: Object Relations Theory Applied. New York, Jason Aronson, 1980

Klein M: The Psycho-Analysis of Children (1932). Translated by Strachey A. London, Hogarth/Institute of Psycho-Analysis, 1959

Klein M: Contributions to Psycho-Analysis, 1921–1945. London, Hogarth/Institute of Psycho-Analysis, 1948

Klein M: Mourning and its relations to manic-depressive states (1940), in Developments in Psycho-Analysis [by Melanie Klein, Paula Heimann, Susan Isaacs, and Joan Riviere]. Edited by Joan Riviere. London, Hogarth/Institute of Psycho-Analysis, 1952, pp 311–338

Klein M: Notes on some schizoid mechanisms (1946), in Developments in Psycho-Analysis [by Melanie Klein, Paula Heimann, Susan Isaacs, and Joan Riviere]. Edited by Joan Riviere. London, Hogarth/Institute of Psycho-Analysis, 1952, pp 292–320

Klein M: Some theoretical conclusions regarding the emotional life of the infant, in Developments in Psycho-Analysis [by Melanie Klein, Paula Heimann, Susan Isaacs, and Joan Riviere]. Edited by Joan Riviere. London, Hogarth/Institute of Psycho-Analysis, 1952, pp 198–236

Klein M: Ego and Gratitude. New York, Basic Books, 1957

Klein M: Narrative of a Child Analysis: The Conduct of the Psycho-Analysis of Children as Seen in the Treatment of a Ten Year Old Boy. London, Hogarth/Institute of Psycho-Analysis, 1961

Klein M, Heinemann P, Isaacs S, et al: Developments in Psycho-Analysis. Edited by Riviere J. London, Hogarth/Institute of Psycho-Analysis, 1952

Kohon G (ed): The British School of Psychoanalysis: The Independent Tradition. London, Free Association Books, 1986 [Published concurrently by Yale University Press, New Haven, CT, 1986]

Kohut H: The Analysis of the Self: A Systematic Approach to the Psychoanalytic Treatment of Narcissistic Personality Disorders. New York, International Universities Press, 1971

Kohut H: The Restoration of the Self. New York, International Universities Press, 1977

Kohut H: How Does Analysis Cure? Edited by Goldberg A, with the collaboration of Stepansky PE. Chicago, IL, University of Chicago Press, 1984

Mahler MS: On child psychosis and schizophrenia: autistic. Psychoanalytic Study Child 7:286–305, 1952

Mahler MS: Autism and symbiosis: two extreme disturbances of identity. Int J Psychoanal 39:77–83, 1958

Mahler MS: On Human Symbiosis and the Vicissitudes of Individuation. New York, International Universities Press, 1968

Mahler MS, Pine F, Bergman A: The Psychological Birth of the Human Infant. New York, Basic Books, 1975

Mitchell SA: Relational Concepts in Psychoanalysis. Cambridge, MA, Harvard University Press, 1988

Moore B, Fine B (eds): Psychoanalytic Terms & Concepts. New Haven, CT, American Psychoanalytic Association/Yale University Press, 1990

Ogden T: Projective identification in psychiatric hospital treatment. Bull Menninger Clin 45:317–333, 1981

Ogden T: Projective Identification & Psychotherapeutic Technique. New York, Jason Aronson, 1982

Ogden T: The concept of internal object relations. Int J Psychoanal 64:227–241, 1983

Ogden T: The Matrix of the Mind. Northvale, NJ, Jason Aronson, 1986

Ogden T: The Primitive Edge of Experience. Northvale, NJ, Jason Aronson, 1989

Pines M (ed): Bion and Group Psychotherapy. London, Routledge & Kegan Paul, 1985

Rapaport D: A historical survey of psychoanalytic ego psychology: an introduction to Erikson EH: Identity and the Life Cycle. Psychological Issues Monograph, 1. New York, International Universities Press, 1959

Rayner E: The Independent Mind In British Psychoanalysis. Northvale, NJ, Jason Aronson, 1991

Robbins M: Current controversy in object relations theory as outgrowth of schism between Klein and Fairbairn. Int J Psychoanal 61:477–492, 1980

Rosenfeld H: Psychotic States. New York, International Universities Press, 1965

Sandler J, Rosenblatt B: The concept of the representational world. Psychoanal Study Child 17:128–130, 1962

Segal H: Introduction to the Work of Melanie Klein. London, Hogarth/ Institute of Psycho-Analysis, 1973

Spillius EB (ed): Melanie Klein Today, Vol 1: Mainly Theory. London, Routledge/Institute of Psycho-Analysis, 1988a

Spillius EB (ed): Melanie Klein Today, Vol 2: Mainly Practice. London, Routledge/Institute of Psycho-Analysis, 1988b

Spitz RA: Anaclitic depression: an inquiry into the genesis of psychiatric conditions in early childhood. Psychoanalytic Study Child 2:313–342, 1946

Spitz RA: No and Yes: On the Genesis of Human Communication. New York, International Universities Press, 1957

Spitz RA: The First Year of Life. New York, International Universities Press, 1965

Stern D: The Interpersonal World of the Infant. New York, Basic Books, 1985

Sullivan HS: The Interpersonal Theory of Psychiatry. New York, WW Norton, 1953

Sutherland JD: Fairbairn's Journey Into the Interior. London, Free Association Books, 1989

Suttie I: The Origins of Love and Hate (1935). New York, Matrix House, 1952

Tausk V: On the origin of 'influence machine' in schizophrenia (1919). Psychoanal Q 2:519–556, 1933

Winnicott DW: Transitional objects and transitional phenomena (1951), in Collected Papers: Through Paediatrics to Psycho-Analysis. New York, Basic Books, 1958, pp 229–242

Winnicott DW: Collected Papers: Through Paediatrics to Psycho-Analysis. New York, Basic Books, 1958

Winnicott DW: The theory of the parent-infant relationship (1960), in The Maturational Processes and the Facilitating Environment: Studies in the Theory of Emotional Development. New York, International Universities Press, 1965, pp 37–55

Winnicott DW: Ego integration in child development (1962), in The Maturational Processes and the Facilitating Environment: Studies in the Theory of Emotional Development. New York, International Universities Press, 1965

Winnicott DW: The Maturational Processes and the Facilitating Environment: Studies in the Theory of Emotional Development. New York, International Universities Press, 1965

Winnicott DW: Playing and Reality. London, Tavistock, 1971

4

The Psychology of the Self (Self Psychology)

Robert J. Leider, M.D.

In this chapter my intent is to familiarize the reader with the *psychology of the self* (self psychology)—a psychoanalytic theory developed over the past 30 years. I discuss the tripolar self, normal and pathological development, disorders of the self, the selfobject transferences, and the therapeutic process from the vantage point of self psychology. In the course of this discussion I highlight those concepts held in common with traditional psychoanalytic theory and practice, and delineate those that differ.

Background

Self psychology began with the work of Heinz Kohut, a psychoanalyst educated in traditional psychoanalytic theory and guided by it in his clinical practice. However, as he listened and struggled to understand his patients, he gradually recognized that the interpretations he offered did not lead to the changes he expected. Indeed, he observed that when classically based interpretations were made, his patients often felt misunderstood and their symptoms worsened. Kohut investigated these occurrences and, after many attempts to refine and reformulate his interpretations, concluded that the problem lay not with the timing or focus of his interpretations but with the basic theory in which they were grounded. As Freud had done when confronted with new findings, Kohut began to revise the theories that informed his clinical understanding. Starting with those revisions, the psychology of the self gradually evolved.

Several factors contributed to the emergence of this new theory. Some psychoanalysts believe that there may have been an increase in the prevalence of borderline and narcissistic personality disorders (and a decrease in the prevalence of neuroses) so that patients with narcissistic and borderline personality disorders were being seen more frequently than when Freud developed his theories in the early part of the 20th century.[1] In any case, there was increased recognition of patients who appeared to be neurotic and who should have, but did not, respond easily, or at all, to treatment informed by Freud's theories. In treatment, these patients experienced regressions more marked than anticipated or desired. They were vulnerable to alarming feelings of fragmentation and disorganization of psychological functioning. They were subject to frequent and intense affect storms (i.e., sudden violent eruptions of primitive affect), and they were unable to maintain observing ego functions. Therapists found it difficult to establish, and impossible to maintain, a therapeutic alliance with these patients.

As clinical experience accumulated, it became clear that these patients did not have psychotic disorders. But neither were their symptomatology and psychological structure those of neurotic disorders. Various diagnostic labels were coined to describe the syndromes with which these patients presented (pregenital character, as-if character, pseudoneurotic schizophrenia, borderline personality organization, narcissistic personality disorder), and diverse

---

[1]Kohut believed this to be the case and attributed this increase to the changes in social and family organization that occurred in the past century (Kohut 1977, pp. 267–280).

recommendations were made regarding the psychotherapeutic and psychoanalytic treatment of such patients.

Nosological Considerations

Out of this diagnostic chaos, nosological order began to emerge. First, as a result of systematic work by Otto Kernberg (1967, 1975) and others (e.g., Grinker et al. 1968; Gunderson 1984), borderline personality disorder was more clearly recognized, delineated, and differentiated from the neuroses and psychoses. (Kernberg, in his early classification, considered narcissistic personality disorders to be "low-level" borderline personality organizations.)

Kohut (1971), working at the same time as Kernberg, focused attention on the narcissistic personality disorders. In contrast to Kernberg, Kohut considered the narcissistic personality disorder to be distinct from the borderline personality disorder. In Kohut's view, the narcissistic personality disorder represents a more stable configuration than the borderline personality organization as a result of the patient's having reached the developmental stage of *the cohesive self*. In contrast, the pathology of the psychoses and borderline states does not involve stable or cohesive structures because a cohesive self is not present. Developmentally, the stage of the cohesive self was not reached or, if reached, was permanently abandoned as a result of severe regression (Kohut 1971, pp. 29–32).

The distinction that Kohut drew was not based on the presenting symptomatology (which he considered an unreliable guide to the diagnosis of the underlying structural pathology), but rather on the evolution of the transference in the analytic situation. Patients with narcissistic personality disorders were those able, with a proper analytic approach, to form (relatively) stable transference configurations; these patients could therefore be analyzed. Those who could not form stable transferences, and who consequently could not be analyzed, were considered to have a borderline personality organization (Kohut 1971, pp. 2–4).

Over the years Kohut modified this position. In the beginning of his posthumously published book *How Does Analysis Cure?* (Kohut

1984, pp. 8–9), he maintained the position described above. In a later section of that book (p. 184), however, he noted that in a substantial number of cases, patients with a borderline personality organization can form workable transferences and can explore the dynamic and genetic causes of their underlying vulnerability—*if* the analyst is able to maintain an empathic stance when confronted with the taxing affect-laden transferences these patients demonstrate.[2] Kohut described himself as a diagnostic "relativist," in that he believed that the diagnosis of borderline organization is relative to the ability of the analyst to maintain effective emotional contact with the patient.

Kernberg, too, modified his early position. In 1967 he considered narcissistic personality disorder to be a subcategory of the borderline organization, a "low level" character disorder. Later (Kernberg 1975, p. 229), he made a distinction between the two, noting that patients with narcissistic personality disorder are often distinguishable from those with borderline organization on the basis of their relatively good social functioning, better impulse control, "pseudo-sublimatory" potential, and better capacity for consistent work.

The distinction between the borderline personality disorder and the narcissistic personality disorder remains, to this day, vague and uncertain. Kohut and other self psychologists (e.g., Atwood and Stolorow 1984; Stolorow et al. 1987) have, in recent years, blurred the distinction between the two. Kernberg and his colleagues, originally not making a distinction between the two disorders, have increasingly come to do so. Others (Adler 1989) consider the two disorders to be on a continuum.[3]

DSM-IV (American Psychiatric Association 1994) includes both the narcissistic personality disorder and the borderline personality

---

[2] Part of this inconsistency may be attributed to the fact that Kohut did not sharply distinguish the borderline personality organization from the psychotic. In the first passage alluded to, Kohut referred to the borderline states as covert psychotic personality organizations; in the second, he apparently intended the term to refer to nonpsychotic organizations.

[3] For a more complete discussion of the nosological issues, the reader is directed to Meissner 1979, Adler 1989, and Gunderson 1989.

disorder, but the diagnoses are not exclusionary. There is overlap in the diagnostic criteria, but both diagnoses may be coded. Current usage considers the narcissistic personality disorder to be less severe than the borderline personality disorder.

For the purpose of this chapter, Meissner's (1979) characterization will be used:

> Narcissistic personality disorders constitute a group of higher-order character pathologies characterized by stable narcissistic transferences (described by Kohut, 1971) . . . possessing evidences of achieved self cohesion, stable characterological traits, minimal regressive tendency, and a stability of functioning. (p. 199)

At this point the reader may ask, What are these patients really like? How can I recognize them?

Syndromes of the Narcissistic Personality Disorder

The severity of narcissistic personality disorders spans a wide range. Persons whose degree of pathology is mild (those whose psychological injuries occurred at higher developmental levels) are unremarkable in any social gathering, dinner party, or, for that matter, professional meeting. Only those whose injuries occurred early are easily noticed—that is, by quick shifts in affect states, by a propensity to socially disapproved behavior, or by other traits viewed as eccentric or obnoxious.

Although less interested in nosological issues than was Kernberg, Kohut provided a detailed phenomenological description of the narcissistic personality disorders—a description very similar to Kernberg's depiction of that disorder. Kohut observed that his patients complained of vague, transitory, fluctuating, dysphoric states, ranging from periods of lethargy, emptiness, lack of zest or pleasure, and low self-esteem, to states marked by an apparent heightened self-esteem. Various methods were used by these patients to maintain their fragile self-esteem, which was highly dependent upon the response of the environment. Their behavior and attitudes were marked by arrogance, entitlement, and exhibitionistic displays, or by righteous certainty, rigid moral conviction, and intolerance of the views and values of others. Unable to obtain a response, these patients experienced marked disturbances of affect (e.g., rage or depression) and made increasingly archaic attempts to elicit the needed response. They were vulnerable to regression in the level of their psychological organization and might even, occasionally, experience episodes of hypochondriacal worry, depersonalization, or autistic-like thinking (Kohut 1971, pp. 16–23).

The following clinical illustrations may clarify the presenting features of this syndrome. First, Mr. A., a person whose disorder is at the less severe end of the spectrum:

> Mr. A. was a very successful businessman in his late 40s, sociable and well dressed, with graying hair and a trim athletic build. He was highly regarded by his colleagues and was often sought for advice, counsel, and support. He was married; had three children, of whom he was proud; and lived in comfortable surroundings. Though his income was high, he was not given to lavish display or excess. Mr. A. appeared to have everything anyone might desire.
>
> Why would this man consult a psychoanalyst? Basically he was unhappy. He was perplexed. Though he had achieved far more than most, he found little joy in life and had spent years seeking circumstances in which he might finally feel the pleasure and satisfaction that eluded him. As he poignantly told me, he could buy anything he wished, could do anything health or wealth would permit, but he was neither happy nor satisfied.
>
> Superimposed on Mr. A.'s chronic vague unhappiness were acute episodes of painful discomfort. For example, Mr. A. invariably did poorly at the annual tennis competition his corporation hosted for his employees. No matter how he tried, how many lessons he took, and how diligently he practiced, he was a bad tennis player. No matter that he was the chief executive officer, that his income had been in seven figures for years, or that he had founded and built the company entirely by his own efforts and skill. No matter that he was personally well liked. He was mortified and painfully ashamed, and he dreaded the annual outing.

A second patient, whose behavior is readily recognized as aberrant, will illustrate the other end of the spectrum of persons with narcissistic personality disorders, those whose pathology is more severe:

> Mr. B., a student in his late 20s, was referred by one of his instructors because his attitude and demeanor were not fitting for his intended vocation. When I first saw this man, I was struck by his disheveled appearance, which stood in sharp contrast to his arrogant, demeaning behavior. Upon entering my office and moving to the chair I indicated, he remained standing, almost imperceptibly nodded, and imperiously said, "Please be seated." (I later learned that his acquaintances referred to him as "Prince.")
>
> This patient complained of having difficulty with his graduate program. Instructors and fellow students did not think well of Mr. B. professionally and shunned him personally. Mr. B. had few friends; people avoided him. He was mystified as to the cause of his isolation and angry at what he perceived as mistreatment by those around him. He was lonely, subject to vague states of tension and a myriad of physical complaints, and driven to search for anonymous, unsatisfying homosexual contacts.
>
> When offended, which was often, Mr. B. was subject to episodes of poorly controlled rage and had, on occasion, demonstrated his displeasure by upsetting food-laden dishes—once, a full plate of soup—at formal dinner parties.

The depth and extent of the injury to the self of Mr. B. were much greater than in the case of Mr. A. No one could fail to notice the signs of the latter's psychopathology.

Evolution of the Psychology of the Self

Familiarity with the evolution of self psychology from its origins in classical psychoanalytic theory will, I believe, facilitate greater understanding of both theoretical perspectives and provide a basis to appreciate the similarities, and recognize the differences, in the two theories. I shall therefore describe that process and highlight the changes introduced.

Introspection, Empathy, and Psychoanalysis

Kohut's paper "Introspection, Empathy and Psychoanalysis" (Kohut 1959) was the first step in the evolution of self psychology from its origins in classical psychoanalytic theory. It was written entirely within the context of classical drive and ego psychology, and only in retrospect can it be seen to presage later developments. In this paper Kohut asserted that access to psychological depths, to emotions and motives, could be obtained only through specific modes of observation: *introspection* into one's own subjective state, and vicarious introspection into, or *empathy* with, another person's subjective state. In his view, the data of psychoanalysis, or of any true depth psychology, are limited to information collected in this manner, and, further, that reliance on such data is a central, defining characteristic of psychoanalysis.[4] Kohut stressed this point because of the increasing tendency to consider psychological data from an external, so-called scientific, perspective—a perspective that, in his opinion, does not, and cannot, be used to gather meaningful *psychological* information on emotions and motives.

Kohut's next major paper, "Forms and Transformations of Narcissism" (Kohut 1966), was the first clearly directed at exploring the phenomena of narcissism and the first in which Kohut introduced changes in basic psychoanalytic theory.

Forms and Transformations of Narcissism

Freud (1914) considered the stage of primary narcissism (a stage in which all libido is invested in the ego) to be the first *psychological* stage.[5] Investment of objects becomes possible as narcissistic libido is detached from the ego, converted into object libido, and directed outward toward (external) objects. In this process, the quantity of narcissistic libido is diminished as that of object libido increases. In Freud's view, mature development requires object investment—

[4]Kohut, in his position on the centrality of empathy, closely followed Freud (1921, pp. 108, 110, fn. 2) (Basch 1983).

[5]A prior prepsychological state of undifferentiated autoerotism was also postulated by Freud.

that is, the investment of objects with a small proportion of narcissistic libido and a large proportion of object libido.

In "Forms and Transformations of Narcissism," Kohut (1966) suggested a modification of this classical theory. Rather than accepting the formulation that object libido develops from a transformation of narcissistic libido, Kohut suggested that object libido has an independent origin—that it does not evolve by transformation of narcissistic libido. In this view, narcissistic libido and object libido have independent origins and separate developmental lines. Correspondingly, Kohut argued, maturity does not result from a conversion of narcissistic libido into object libido, or narcissistic cathexes into object cathexes, but rather by the maturation of narcissistic structures (the transformations of narcissism) parallel to the maturation of object libido and the development of mature object cathexes.

This first self psychological paper was primarily theoretical and was followed in 1971 by *The Analysis of the Self.*

The Analysis of the Self

The Analysis of the Self (1971) is possibly Kohut's most important work.[6] In this work, Kohut concentrated on clinical phenomena and differentiated the *pathology* that results from distortion or arrest in the development of narcissism (the narcissistic disorders) from the pathology that results from drive fixation and conflict (the neuroses). Further, he differentiated the *transferences* that result from the respective areas of pathology.

Kohut described the narcissistic transferences (later called *selfobject transferences*) in detail. He delineated resistances to the development of these transferences and illustrated how they emerged in the proper analytic atmosphere, how they could be understood, and how they could be addressed by *interpretation*. And finally, he demonstrated that his new perspective provided a rational basis for efficacious treatment of patients with narcissistic personality disorder.

---

[6]Kohut believed recognition of selfobject transferences to be his most important discovery (Kohut 1984, p. 104), and *The Analysis of the Self* contains his first major and most extensive exposition of these ideas.

In tandem with his description of narcissistic pathology and of the therapeutic process, Kohut offered an outline (derived from the psychoanalytic treatment of adults) of the *development* of the self and its component structures. In the course of this discussion, Kohut elaborated the concept of the *selfobject* and defined its role in normal development and in psychopathology.[7]

The next step in the evolution self psychology, a watershed, was reached in 1977 upon publication of Kohut's *The Restoration of the Self.*

The Restoration of the Self

In *The Restoration of the Self* (1977), Kohut declared that a satisfactory understanding of development, psychopathology, and the therapeutic process could not be encompassed within the framework of classical drive theory and the structural model of the mind. He asserted that drives, conflict, and the oedipal period were not the sole, or even the main, factors in psychological development and psychopathology. Kohut suggested, instead, that developmental schemata should be conceptualized and organized about the development of the self, its motivational (selfobject) needs, and the dangers that threaten its organization and "cohesion," rather than around the drives and their vicissitudes. He proposed a new model of the mind, the *bipolar self,* to supplant the tripartite structural model that psychoanalysis had used for 50 years.

This work, with its revolutionary ideas, generated a great deal of comment. Some thought Kohut's ideas to be valuable additions to psychoanalytic knowledge, whereas others did not, believing them to be poorly founded. Kohut was concerned about this reception of his ideas and devoted his last work, *How Does Analysis Cure?*, to clarifying the ideas he had propounded, answering questions, and responding to criticism.

---

[7]The term *selfobject* denotes a psychologically important person (or occasionally a group, or even a philosophical ideal) who supports and reinforces cohesion of the self. The concept is discussed in detail later in this chapter.

SHIP TO: ACHEBE, NGOZI
800 E 9TH AVE
TRUTH CONSQ, NM 879011954

BER	SHIP VIA	ORDER DATE	PAGE
	UPS GR	27-FEB-01	1

BJE

	FORMAT	SUB CLASS	ED	PRICE
APP / 96 /	Cloth	PSY	01	

TOTAL HEALTH PRODUCTS, INC.
11559 ROCK ISLAND CT.
MARYLAND HEIGHTS, MO 63043

ORDER NUMBER	CUSTOMER #	PO NUM
742768*00	THP	01218304

QUANTITY ORDERED	QUANTITY PACKED	ITEM #	AUTHOR	DESCRIPTION/ MANUFACTURER
1	1	0880485078	NERSESSIAN	T/B PSYCHOANALYSIS AmericanPsychiatricP

ORDER NOTES:

TOTAL WEIGHT: 2.52 LBS   TOTAL VOLUME: 0.00 CU FT

How Does Analysis Cure?

Kohut's work came to an end with his death in 1981 and the posthumous publication in 1984 of *How Does Analysis Cure?* In this book, Kohut expanded on issues that he had previously discussed: castration anxiety; the need for selfobjects; empathy; and the roles of "understanding" and "explanation" in the curative process. Compared with earlier works, this work contained few theoretical revisions. The one significant exception regarded the *twinship transference* and the so-called alter-ego needs. This transference, previously considered a subtype of mirror transference, was now considered to be a major transference in its own right, corresponding to the mirror and idealizing transferences that Kohut had previously described. Presumably, the model of the mind was to be modified analogously and said to have three poles—a *tripolar self.*

Subsequent Development

Progress in self psychology did not come to an end with Kohut's death. Since that time, other investigators have concentrated on understanding affect, affect communication, affect attunement, empathy, structure formation, and the therapeutic process. Others have pursued epistemological and methodological issues. And still others have continued exploring the relation between the psychology of the self, conflict theory, and object relations theory.

Having completed this overview of the major steps in the development of the psychology of the self, I now turn to a more detailed explication of the important theoretical concepts.

Metapsychological Considerations

Models of the Mind

Models are abstract constructions designed to provide a description of ordering principles (oftentimes a graphical analogy) intended to represent another abstraction (in this case the mind). They include a system of data, assumption, and inference (often not distinguished from assumption) that functions to organize observation and provides a framework for explanation and prediction.[8]

The Tripartite Model

Freud constructed several successive models of the mind but warned against concretizing them and considered them only as aids to understanding—to be revised as his knowledge expanded or as the focus of his inquiry changed.

Freud's last model, the *tripartite model,* was delineated in *The Ego and the Id* (1923). It consisted of the three systems *id, ego,* and *superego,* and its motive force, its energy, was provided by two basic drives, the aggressive drive and the libidinal drive. (A detailed discussion of the structural model may be found in Chapter 2.)

The Model of the Bipolar (or Tripolar) Self

Kohut (1977) came to believe, as previously described, that the "needs" of the self were more central to human motivation than the "drive" concept central to Freud's theories; as a result of this shift of perspective, he introduced a new model of the mind, the *bipolar self* (later amended by some theorists to a *tripolar self*).

The self. How is the concept "self" understood and defined?[9] That question, so apparently simple, is not easy to answer.[10] However, its usage can be described and its meaning thereby discerned.

The *self* is an abstraction meant to represent a group of functions and features (an enduring psychic configuration or system) that

---

[8]Gedo and Goldberg (1973) present an elegant discussion of the use of models and an excellent discussion of Freud's successive models.

[9]Perhaps Kohut's most succinct delineation of this concept may be found in *The Restoration of the Self* (Kohut 1977, p. 177).

[10]Goldberg (1980, pp. 2–11) presents a scholarly discussion of the concept of the self and the difficulties inherent in defining it.

characterize the basic integration, functioning, and organization of the personality.

Selfobject needs. Central to the concept of the self are specific *selfobject needs* described as being "located" at the "poles" of the self: 1) an exhibitionistic need for admiring, approving (mirroring) responses; 2) a need for closeness, acceptance, contact, and support from an omnipotent idealized other; and 3) a need for the presence of another being felt to be alike or similar, an alter-ego or twin, to oneself. Between the poles of the self is said to exist a *tension arc* of psychological activity directed toward the exercise of inborn talents and the satisfaction of these basic needs and their (mature) transformations.

Regulatory principle. A supraordinate *regulatory principle* (often referred to as a need) aimed at maintaining the integrity and *cohesion* of the self is postulated, as is an associated danger, *fragmentation,* correlated with *disintegration anxiety.* Maintenance of psychic equilibrium is central, and cohesion of the self is supported by experiences in which disruptive affect states are ameliorated by the empathic responses of selfobjects to the needs of the self.

Comment. The reader may recognize that the model of the tripolar self is, in form, analogous to the earlier models of Freud's topographic and structural theories and that it was constructed for the same purpose: to represent the phenomena and structures (groups of functions) central to the theory.

One may fairly ask, is this model superior to the previous structural model? Can it replace it? Does it satisfactorily encompass phenomena, such as conflict and guilt, addressed by the structural model?

Many investigators convinced of the usefulness of self psychology and of the concept of the self do not believe that the *model* of the tripolar self is satisfactory as a general model of the mind. It was intended to represent a new motivational system and a different view of the relation of the self to its objects and selfobjects; it is poorly suited to represent other important aspects of mental functioning, such as the defenses (essential to understanding fixations or arrests in development) and the dynamics of repression, disavowal, and transference.[11]

Some investigators suggest that both models (the structural model and the tripolar self model) and their respective theories be retained and that a shift be made from one to the other depending upon the type of pathology under consideration. They advocate *complementarity* of theories.[12] Others do not consider this a satisfactory solution.

Problems with the model of the tripolar self notwithstanding, the important *ideas* can, and should, be separated from the model and considered in their own right, as is done in the following discussion.

Theories of Motivation/Needs

The introduction of the concept of selfobject needs into our discussion raises an important metapsychological issue: the motivational system(s) considered to underlie mental activity. A cursory review of psychoanalytic writing is sufficient to reveal the difficulties encountered in attempting to categorize and account for the panoply of affect, intention, behavior, and response so characteristic of the human species. Psychoanalysts do not agree as to what motivational factors should be considered basic.

The Instincts and the Id

Freud (1950[1895]) originally attempted to ground his theory on neurophysiological considerations but abandoned this project because of the insufficiency of scientific knowledge in that realm.

---

[11]The reader is referred to Basch's (1984a, 1984b, 1986) erudite consideration of the role of these concepts in the psychology of the self.

[12]Kohut initially took this position (1977, pp. xv, 223) but later abandoned it. Shane and Shane (1988) remain its most consistent proponents. Stolorow (1988; Stolorow et al. 1987) suggests that the transference continually oscillates between selfobject and conflictual dimensions.

Next, he concentrated on psychological data and based his theories on information derived from psychoanalytic inquiry into the internal states of his patients (Freud 1900, 1905, 1914, 1915). Further revisions (Freud 1920, 1923, 1926) followed as he revised his classification of instincts, elaborated more fully on aggression, and revised his model of the psychic apparatus and his theory of symptom formation. In Freud's final structural model, all human motivation, the "energy" or "force" behind mental functioning, is derived from the "instincts," endopsychically represented by the libidinal and aggressive *drives*.[13]

The Needs of the Self

Self psychology takes a view of human motivation that is significantly different from that of Freud. Three basic *needs of the self* (selfobject needs) have been delineated: 1) an exhibitionistic need for admiring, approving (mirroring) responses; 2) a need for closeness, acceptance, contact, and support from an omnipotent (idealized) other; and 3) a need for the presence of others felt to be similar to oneself (twinship).

How are these needs to be understood? They are considered to be basic constitutional givens, with their satisfaction being required for integrated, vigorous, harmonious psychological functioning. If these needs are not satisfied, infants, children, and adults suffer emotional distress, psychological impairment, and a degradation of psychological functioning.

The self is said to have three "poles"—the pole of grandiose-exhibitionistic needs, the pole of needs for an omnipotent idealized figure, and the pole of alter-ego needs—structures that crystallize as a result of the interaction between the needs of the self and the responses of those important persons in the environment who function as selfobjects.

---

[13] Freud occasionally considered other types of instincts, for example, ego-instincts. In his last papers he hinted at the possibility of energies other than those of the sexual and aggressive drives, but he did not elaborate that idea.

The Self and the Drives

In self psychology the desires traditionally referred to as the "drives" (of the dual drive theory) are not ignored, but they are not considered to be the most basic psychological needs.[14] Drives are not accorded a central position in self psychology; they are not thought to lead inexorably to conflict or psychopathology.

Many fantasies and activities traditionally viewed as aspects of normal *libidinal* drive development (e.g., oedipal conflict) are considered to be abnormal restitutive phenomena—that is, pathological attempts to defend against painfully perceived defects in the structure of the self resulting from failures in the self–selfobject bond.[15]

Self psychology differs from classical drive theory even more markedly in its formulations regarding *aggression*. The dual drive theory (Freud 1920, 1923, 1926) holds that aggression is a primary drive whose aim is destruction and disintegration. Self psychology, in contrast, considers that aggression as a normal aspect of human behavior comes into play only when the satisfaction of more primary needs is impeded. Assertiveness and normal aggression are not considered to result from neutralizing transformations of a primitive destructive drive as postulated in classical psychoanalytic theory. Instead, aggression is thought to have a developmental line that begins with primitive forms of nondestructive aggression that gradually develop into more organized mature forms. In this process aggression becomes focused and subordinated to the performance of specific tasks and the pursuit of defined goals. It aims at ensuring satisfaction of the desires and needs of the self for object *and* selfobject response, and it subsides when those goals are reached (Kohut 1977, pp. 118–121; Kohut 1984, pp. 137–138; Tolpin 1971, 1986).[16]

---

[14] Stern (1985, p. 238) and Lichtenberg (1989, p. 3) have come to similar conclusions.

[15] More complete discussions may be found in works by Terman (1975) and Kohut (1977, pp. 220–248; 1984, pp. 13–33).

[16] *Narcissistic rage* is often confused with aggression, but they are different phenomena and should be distinguished. Rage is a *pathological* emotion and is discussed later in this chapter in the section on psychopathology and the abnormal development of the self.

Cohesion and Fragmentation

Basic to Kohut's theory are the concepts of *cohesion of the self* and the opposite process, *fragmentation.*

Kohut (1971, pp. 7, 97) observed that when his patients regressed, their psychological organization deteriorated in a characteristic manner. Some might, in varying degree, experience disturbances in bodily sensation or self-perception, occasionally even extending to trancelike states of depersonalization and derealization. Some experienced a degeneration of language, a concretization of thinking, and a disruption in synthetic and observing ego capacities; others experienced states of hypomanic excitement; and still others were plagued with hypochondriacal preoccupations.

The term *fragmentation* was chosen to signify this degradation (disintegration) of higher-level psychological functioning. Vulnerability to fragmentation varies, and fragmentation fluctuates in a manner correlated with the stress of external events, the response of selfobjects, and the degree to which a cohesive nuclear self has already been firmly established.

Cohesion, on the other hand, is the term chosen to denote that state of the self said to underlie healthy, harmonious, integrated, vigorous psychological functioning. This stage, the cohesive nuclear self, is marked by the smooth interplay of ambitions, ideals, and talents with the opportunities of everyday reality, and by a (relative) resistance to fragmentation when circumstances impede satisfaction of object or selfobject needs.

The terms cohesion and fragmentation are evocative and metaphoric; but taken concretely they become obstacles, rather than aids, to understanding.[17]

Disintegration Anxiety

Kohut (1977, pp. 102–104) advanced the idea that there are two basic classes of anxiety: 1) the anxiety experienced by a person with

---

[17]A clinical vignette illustrating fragmentation and cohesion is presented later in this chapter in the section on psychopathology and the abnormal development of the self.

a (more or less) cohesive self when confronted with one of the danger situations described by Freud (1926); and 2) the anxiety experienced by a person who fears that his or her nuclear self is in danger of disintegration. This latter anxiety, *disintegration anxiety,* is, in Kohut's view, the deepest anxiety man can experience. It is not equivalent to any of the classical dangers described by Freud; it is evoked by an unconscious perception of the precarious state of the self rather than by a fear of drive conflict.

Because disintegration anxiety originates in early preverbal stages of psychological development, it does not easily lend itself to verbal description. It should be considered whenever a patient complains of vague, diffuse, hypochondriacal fears or of amorphous tension and terror (Kohut 1977, pp. 102–104).

With elaboration of the concept of disintegration anxiety, the *need for cohesion*[18] was described as a *supraordinate* need, in many regards analogous to the pleasure and reality principles postulated by Freud.

The Development of the Self

It is believed that the infant, normally, is born into a world in which parental figures view it as a whole being and are ready and eager to assume responsibility for its care and nurture. Although the infant does not have an extensive capacity for mental representations, to the extent that it does, it experiences its rudimentary self as cohesive and whole rather than as an agglomeration of disparate nuclei (Kohut 1974/1978, 1977).[19]

The infant is possessed of an intrinsic grandiosity, believing that all power and perfection reside within itself. But to the extent that the infant is able to recognize caregivers as separate beings, it sees the caregiving other as the ideal embodiment of omniscient wisdom

---

[18]This so-called need is on a higher level of abstraction than that of the selfobject needs previously described.

[19]In his early writings Kohut took the latter position (see Kohut 1971).

and power upon whom its own comfort and cohesion are vitally dependent. The infant, within the limits of its cognitive development, also seeks emotional support from the presence of another being recognized, in some vague way, as similar to itself.

The central developmental problem is this: How can perceived "imperfections" in the grandiose self, in the power of the omnipotent other, or in the presence of a similar other be recognized, acknowledged, encompassed, and integrated while avoiding traumatic tension states and maintaining a psychic balance? It is here that the selfobject becomes crucial and functions to buffer the effect of the inevitable disappointments in self or other.

Selfobjects

Selfobject is a term that denotes a psychologically important person (or occasionally a group, or even a philosophical ideal) who supports cohesion of the self. Selfobjects provide (or reinforce) regulatory functions for a self incapable of mastering the tensions and stresses with which it is confronted.[20]

Although they may be cognitively distinct and may at times be related to as true "objects" (i.e., differentiated targets of instinctual drives), persons when functioning as selfobjects are psychologically undifferentiated from the self. They are responded to as if they were an integral, internal part of the self, and hence the conflated term selfobject. Initially, selfobject functions are provided by the infant's caregivers. Later in childhood, as the child's universe expands, the range of potential selfobjects broadens to include parents, relatives, siblings, friends, pets, and so forth. Still later the range is further expanded and may include 1) spouses, children, clients, subordinates, or others who admire (*mirroring selfobjects*); 2) political, religious, military, and academic leaders, or ethical or religious systems or other abstract ideals that are admired (*idealized selfobjects*); or

---

[20] A clinical vignette illustrating the role of selfobjects is presented later in this chapter in the section on psychopathology and the abnormal development of the self.

3) individuals with whom, or groups with which, one identifies (*alter-ego selfobjects*).

The need for selfobjects does not fade with maturity. Selfobjects are required throughout the entire life cycle. The mature self, however, is less dependent on the immediate, concrete presence of or response from the selfobject.

Transmuting Internalization

Small, nontraumatic "failures" in the self or in the responses of the selfobject lead to mild tension states, minor tendencies toward fragmentation, and (later in development) lowered self-esteem. If the selfobject is able to intervene optimally, tension is reduced, cohesion is restored, and a memory trace of the disappointing failure *and* of the soothing, balancing efforts of the selfobject is laid down. This process, *transmuting internalization,* leads to the accretion of an intrapsychic regulating structure, permits the gradual maturation of infantile narcissistic needs, and facilitates the increasingly comfortable acceptance of the limits of one's own talents, of limits in the perfection of others, and of the limitations imposed by reality.[21]

Compensatory Structures

A further complexity is added to our scheme of normal development by the observation that defects resulting from insufficient

---

[21]The term "transmuting internalization" was coined by Kohut to denote the process by which empathic responses of the selfobject lead to the development of intrapsychic regulatory structures. His description is a generalization of the sequence first described by Freud (1917[1915]) in his explanation of mourning. Freud focused on the vicissitudes of drives, object cathexes, and the structure of the ego. Kohut (1971, pp. 47–51) directed his attention to selfobject needs, selfobject response, development of the self, and maturation of selfobject needs. But the key elements in the sequence of transmuting internalization (i.e., optimal frustration, increased tension, selfobject response, reduced tension, memory trace, development of internal regulating structure) are as applicable to the development of ego structure and the "taming of the drives" as they are to the development of the structure of the self and the maturation of selfobject needs. The reader is referred to Chapter 2 for a description of the development of regulatory function in terms of the structural model.

selfobject responses to the needs of one pole of the self may be compensated by structuralizations resulting from the effective responses of the selfobject to the needs of another pole of the self. For example, an arrest in the development of ambitions (a transformation of the primitive needs of the grandiose-exhibitionistic pole) might be compensated for by an unusual elaboration of ideals (the mature transformation of needs of the idealizing pole).

Although *compensatory structures* evolve in an attempt to surmount developmental difficulties and to repair defects in the structuralization of the self, they are functionally effective and are considered to be a variant of normal development.

Psychopathology: Abnormal Development of the Self

When the developmental process goes awry, various arrests, distortions, and defects result, leading to a vulnerability to regression and to variegated forms of psychopathology.

Repression, Disavowal, and Developmental Arrests

Repeated failure to obtain selfobject response interferes with the normal development of tension-regulating structures and leads to states of acute and chronic tension from which the child must protect himself or herself. In the service of defense, infantile narcissistic needs may then be *repressed* and sequestered beneath a *horizontal split*, where (as similarly described in classical theory) they remain arrested at the developmental level existing when the repression occurred.

For example, repression of grandiose-exhibitionistic wishes leads to low self-esteem, a lack of energy and ambition, and a propensity for hypochondriacal complaints. On the other hand, repression of idealizing needs interferes with the development of tension-regulating structures and leads to a diffuse narcissistic vulnerability, defects in idealized values, and cynicism.

The self uses other defense mechanisms in addition to repression to protect its organization. *Disavowal* may be utilized and a *vertical split* established. Here, too, the selfobject needs remain fixed at immature developmental stages; but in the case of the vertical split, these needs have relatively free access to external behavioral expression in a structural organization similar to that postulated by Freud for perversions. The infantile wishes and needs, although consciously expressed, are split off from the rest of the personality, disavowed, and not acknowledged as an integral part of the self.

When, for example, grandiose-exhibitionistic wishes are disavowed, one observes arrogant attitudes and behavior, raw exhibitionistic display, and imperious demands for response and attention. Disavowal of idealizing needs, on the other hand, leads to a continued search for an admired ideal person, organization, or philosophical system with which to associate in the hope that such association will restore a feeling of vitality, cohesion, and value.

The case of Mr. B., introduced earlier in this chapter, exemplifies many of the phenomena associated with horizontal and vertical splits in the structure of the self. As the reader may recall, Mr. B. was rumpled and disheveled. Although he was deeply humiliated by his appearance and by the fact that people shunned him, Mr. B. was unable to alter his bedraggled mode of dress. This unappealing exterior was a sign of the absence of healthy, modulated exhibitionism and was a result of the *repression* of normal grandiose-exhibitionistic wishes—a *horizontal split* in the structure of the self.[22]

Yet Mr. B. was also overtly arrogant and demanding. He clamored constantly for attention and was, in fact, referred to as "Prince." This raw, irritating, demanding behavior (the conscious derivative of arrested, immature, grandiose wishes) signaled a *vertical split* at the pole of exhibitionistic needs. These wishes, though behaviorally expressed, were not fully recognized and acknowledged by Mr. B., but instead were *disavowed*.

Similarly, Mr. B.'s attitude of depreciation, his cynical complaints about authority figures, resulted from repression of his healthy idealizing wishes—of a horizontal split in the realm of

---

[22]This configuration is structurally identical to that of an "inhibition" as defined by Freud (1926).

ideals. Yet, his continual seeking of strong powerful men with whom he could perform fellatio exemplified the behavioral manifestations of a vertical split—in this case a regressive sexualized attempt to fuse with a powerful, idealized man.

Regression and Fragmentation

Developmental arrests interfere with formation of a cohesive self. In such circumstances, failure to obtain needed selfobject response leads to regression, to relative fragmentation of the self, to disintegration anxiety, and to signs or symptoms of fragmentation.

Fragmentation symptoms are an amalgam of, on the one hand, infantile needs, attitudes, actions, and affects that signal the disintegration of the self and, on the other hand, the desperate efforts to restore cohesion. These symptoms include anxiety and panic, hypochondriacal preoccupations, disturbances of thinking, depersonalization and derealization, and variegated, distorted derivatives of libidinal and aggressive urges.

An episode in the treatment of Mr. B. will serve to illustrate these phenomena. Mr. B. had been in treatment for about 9 months. By this time, there had been a noticeable clinical improvement. Mr. B. was less disheveled, had fewer hypochondriacal worries, and was less prone to the arrogant behavior that had so offended his professors and fellow graduate students. With me, Mr. B. had become less critical, depreciating, and demanding.

This period of relative tranquility, of increased *self cohesion,* was dependent upon the establishment of a covert *idealizing transference* and utilization of the therapist as an idealized selfobject.[23] This relatively tranquil period was abruptly shattered—that is, *fragmented*—when I informed Mr. B. of my plans for a 3-week vacation 2 months hence. He looked shocked, outraged, and angry but said nothing about my plans or his reaction to them.

---

[23]The improvement in self cohesion seen here should not be confused with the more permanent change that results from interpretation and transmuting internalization (see subsection on the interpretive process later in this chapter).

In the following session (3 days later), Mr. B. clearly demonstrated signs and symptoms of fragmentation. He angrily reported a marked upsurge in homosexual fantasies, trouble sleeping, and having "cruised" for hours one night. Mr. B. lapsed into a long, detached silence. When I eventually inquired about his thoughts, he responded by asking if I had ever noticed that my office was in the center of the building. (I had not.) In fact, he observed, the centerline of the building must go right through the chair in which he was sitting. Mr. B. continued for quite some time with an eerie monologue about parabolas and hyperbolas, which go off to infinity, and about ellipses, which do not.

After a period of perplexity and considerable consternation, it occurred to me that this autistic-like thinking might relate to his (unconscious) concern about maintaining the (selfobject) connection with me while I was away. I said, "I think you are concerned about the upcoming interruption, about where I will be when away." To my considerable relief, Mr. B. immediately replied that I was correct. The thoughts about geometric figures vanished (never again to return), and he asked where I was going to be. When I answered his question, Mr. B. was visibly relieved. He was familiar with the area I was planning to visit and took great delight in my ignorance of it. In subsequent sessions he haughtily suggested many things that I might see and do but that he was certain I would not be able to appreciate. Mr. B.'s sleep improved, his tension lessened, his thinking refocused, and his homosexual thoughts and activities returned to their usual level. The symptoms of fragmentation faded. Self cohesion had been (tenuously) restored.

Pathological Drive Derivatives

Distorted derivatives of *libidinal* drive impulses are frequently observed with regression and fragmentation of the self. But these *perversions* of aim and object (for instance, compulsive masturbation, promiscuity, voyeurism, exhibitionism) are not understood from a self psychological perspective as efforts to gratify fixated infantile sexual wishes, but rather as attempts by a fragile self to obtain needed selfobject responses through sexual activity.

Narcissistic rage, previously alluded to in my discussion of aggression, has a similar etiology and is another of the many phenomena that may evolve when cohesion of the self is threatened and disintegration anxiety mobilized. To some degree, narcissistic rage is always present when the needs of the self are not met and fragmentation threatens; but the intensity of this rage varies with the level of development of the self and selfobject needs, the degree of structuralization of tension-regulating mechanisms, and the significance of the specific selfobject disappointment. Recognition and expression of rage are further influenced by the effects of various defenses mobilized against it.

Narcissistic rage serves to discharge tension and, when organized, to compel responses that lead to the reestablishment of narcissistic equilibrium, self-esteem, and self cohesion. This rage varies widely in intensity: it may be mild and fleeting, or overwhelming and chronic. It may be little more than a brief annoyance, or it may be an unrelenting need for revenge. In its most malignant form, chronic narcissistic rage, it may consume the entire personality and lead to merciless persecution of others (viewed as sources of narcissistic injury) or to annihilation of the self in a bitter, angry suicide (Kohut 1972; Terman 1975; Wolf 1988).

The Selfobject Transferences

One consequence of pathological development—of the arrest and fixation of archaic narcissistic needs—is the tendency of archaic needs to escape the restraints of the defenses. This escape, the transfer of infantile wishes across the defensive barrier, is a central mechanism in symptom formation. In the situation of treatment, this mechanism is manifest in the development of transferences to the therapist.

The self–selfobject transferences dramatize and reflect the persistence of archaic selfobject needs. They highlight injuries to the self and illuminate the mechanisms used to compensate for, defend against, or conceal defects in the structure of the self.

Three basic selfobject transference configurations, the *mirror transference,* the *idealizing transference,* and the *alter-ego* or *twinship transference,* have been identified. They correspond to, and result from, mobilization of the basic selfobject needs.

The Mirror Transference

In the mirror transference the therapist is expected to confirm the patient's expanded grandiosity, grandiose fantasies, and exhibitionistic displays by vigorous and enthusiastic admiration. Developmentally early variants of the mirror transference are notable for the lack of discrete (object) representation of the therapist. The therapist, in the patient's inner world, functions solely as a disembodied genie, awaiting, anticipating, and granting every unspoken need. For this reason, a primitive mirror transference may be difficult to recognize and difficult for the therapist to tolerate. Countertransference reactions (e.g., rage, boredom, withdrawal) are stimulated, and the therapist's narcissistic equilibrium may be severely taxed by the patient's grandiosity.

Developmentally later versions of the mirror transference are easier to recognize and tolerate. Often they have an enjoyable tone and evoke feelings akin to those experienced in the presence of a playful, cheerful, proud child.

The Idealizing Transference

The idealizing transference recapitulates the developmental position in which the self is consolidated and strengthened, and cohesion maintained, through association with an other perceived as the embodiment of all beauty, wisdom, power, and virtue. The patient feels good, whole, and comfortable as long as the idealization is maintained; correspondingly, he or she fragments when the idealization crumbles or when the idealized figure distances himself or herself.[24]

Countertransference reactions are also common with this transference paradigm. They occur as the therapist responds to the

---

[24]The reader is referred to the clinical illustration of the case of Mr. B. presented earlier in this chapter in the section on psychopathology and the abnormal development of the self.

stimulation of his or her own exhibitionistic wishes. The therapist may note a tendency to make exhibitionistic comments or to engage in subtle exhibitionistic displays. Or, on the other hand, if anxiety and defense are provoked, the therapist may denigrate himself or herself and react in a manner that deflects and diminishes the patient's idealizations.

The Alter-ego, or Twinship, Transference

The alter-ego, or twinship, transference reinstitutes a situation akin to parallel play, in which the self of a small child is consolidated and strengthened by the happy performance of a task in the presence of a similar other. Countertransference reactions are similar to those observed with a mirror transference, although generally milder.

Recognition of Selfobject Transferences

Various factors may make recognition of the selfobject transferences difficult:

1. Defenses and resistances may interfere with the establishment of a selfobject transference and investment of the therapist as a self-object.
2. The narcissistic vulnerability of the patient may be so great that the transference configurations are fragile, transitory, and subject to regressive disintegration.
3. There may be a shift from one transference configuration to another (i.e., layering) in a manner that parallels childhood developmental vicissitudes and makes the clinical transference more complex.
4. There may be, and often is, an absence of defined, discrete references to the therapist as a structural object, and the therapist may therefore mistakenly conclude that a transference has not been established.
5. Countertransference reactions may interfere with the therapist's empathic perception and may lead to responses by the therapist that disrupt, distort, or prevent the continuing development of a cohesive transference configuration.

Transferences may be taxing and troubling, yet their emergence provides the circumstance in which change can occur. How are the desired changes brought about?

The Therapeutic Process: A Self Psychological Perspective

Self psychology recommends a psychoanalytic approach for the treatment of patients with narcissistic personality disorder. Unfortunately, a full description of the therapeutic practice recommended by self psychology is not possible in the space allotted.[25] My discussion will consequently focus only on the most important aspects of technique: 1) abstinence, ambience, and neutrality; 2) resistance; 3) the process of interpretation; and 4) the factors that lead to structural change.

Some analysts do not consider the therapeutic approach recommended by self psychology to be psychoanalytic; rather, they consider it a form of supportive psychotherapy. Many others, however, disagree with that assessment and believe that self psychology adheres to the basic principles delineated by Freud as defining the psychoanalytic method: the mobilization of the dynamic unconscious and the analysis of transference (Basch 1986).

The differences that do exist derive, in the main, from two factors:

1. The needs considered central to human motivation by self psychology are not the same as those postulated as central by traditional psychoanalytic drive theory. The *content* of interpretations informed by the psychology of the self is, therefore, often different from the content of interpretations informed by traditional theory.
2. The analyst's stance, the analytic atmosphere and ambience, recommended by self psychology is more emotionally responsive than is the attitude recommended as classically correct.

-----

[25]Readers interested in more extensive discussion and description of the therapeutic process are referred to Basch 1980, 1989; Goldberg 1978; Kohut 1971, 1984; and Wolf 1988.

In the following subsections I briefly describe the therapeutic practice advocated by self psychology in order to provide a basis for a comparison of the technical recommendations of self psychology with those of "classical" psychoanalytic technique.

Abstinence, Ambience, and Neutrality

Self psychology believes that the therapeutic remobilization of (pathological) archaic needs is best facilitated by an accepting, friendly attitude and a neutral perspective.

The desired *ambience* requires an atmosphere of emotional liveliness and responsiveness. In the absence of an emotionally responsive therapeutic environment, the patient will strongly defend against the emergence and recognition of his or her needs. And if these needs should emerge, the patient will be retraumatized and will be unable to understand the origin of his or her vulnerabilities, and the desired maturation of selfobject needs will not occur.

Kohut (1977) characterized the requisite stance "as the responsiveness to be expected, on an average, from persons who have devoted their life to helping others" (p. 252). Wolf (1976, 1983) tried to capture it in his discussion of "ambience," and Bacal (1985) addressed it with the idea of "optimal responsiveness." All of these authors agree that the optimal attitude implies emotional liveliness and response, concern and compassion for the patient's suffering, an effort to understand, and the avoidance of criticism, contempt, and condemnation.

This stance contrasts with the detached, cold, abstemious, surgeonlike demeanor recommended by Freud in 1912 and thought by some to be the correct "classical" attitude. Self psychologists do not believe that this attitude properly reflects Freud's overall meaning or his understanding of *abstinence*.[26] Rather, his attitude (Freud 1913,

---

[26]Freud introduced the *rule of abstinence* in a discussion of transference resistance and analytic neutrality. He wrote, "The treatment must be carried out in abstinence. By this I do not mean physical abstinence alone, nor yet the deprivation of everything that the patient desired, for perhaps no sick patient could tolerate this. Instead, I shall state it as a fundamental principle that the patient's need and longing should be allowed to persist in her, in order that they may serve as forces impelling her to do work and to make changes" (Freud 1915[1914], p. 165).

1940[1938]) is thought to have been one of helpful, sympathetic understanding (Leider 1983; Panel 1981).

Neutrality has been defined as follows:

> Central to psychoanalytic neutrality are keeping the counter-transference in check, avoiding the imposition of one's own values upon the patient, and taking the patient's capacities rather than one's own desires as a guide. . . . The concept also defines the recommended emotional attitude of the analyst—one of professional commitment or helpful benign understanding that avoids extremes of detachment and over involvement. (Moore and Fine 1990, p. 127)

This definition will satisfactorily serve to define the attitude of neutrality recommended by most self psychologists.

Resistance

Kohut (1971) observed that when the approach described in the previous subsection is consistently maintained, the patient gradually invests the analyst with selfobject needs. Ultimately, a coherent selfobject transference will be established.

Unfortunately, this does not always occur so easily, for as archaic needs are mobilized in the transference regression, so too are archaic dangers. The patient fears repetition of the traumatic situations—the tension, anxiety, and fragmentation—that he or she experienced in infancy or childhood and invokes defenses to protect against these dangers. These defenses are manifest in treatment by *resistance*.

The resistance (i.e., these defenses) must be approached with understanding rather than confrontation; with maintenance of the analytic attitude described in the previous subsection; and with timely, patient interpretation of the dangers against which the patient defends.

The Interpretive Process

Self psychology considers the interpretative process to have two phases: a phase of *understanding* (sometimes of long duration) and a phase of *explanation* and *interpretation*. Both phases are essential to the therapeutic process (Kohut 1984, pp. 104–108; Goldberg 1985).

As therapy proceeds and a selfobject transference is established, the therapist is unconsciously perceived as a selfobject meeting various selfobject needs. As long as the therapist is considered to do so, the cohesion of the patient's self is enhanced, symptoms are reduced, and all is tranquil. Sooner or later, however, the therapist will be perceived as having "failed" in this function. He or she will not have provided the wished-for or needed selfobject response. The patient fragments, and archaic affect states, and the defenses against them, become manifest. These disruptions are inevitable, unavoidable, and necessary for further development and structural repair.

The phase of *understanding* begins when the therapist empathically recognizes the disruption, communicates his or her appreciation of the dysphoric state to the patient, and describes the event(s) that precipitated the disruption and rupture of the self–selfobject transference. In this process of understanding, the patient's psychic equilibrium is gradually reestablished.

The phase of *explanation* begins when this sequence is later explained (interpreted) to the patient in dynamic and genetic terms. The patient *recollects,* or the therapist *reconstructs,* the circumstances of the patient's childhood in which parental selfobjects were consistently and repetitively unable to meet the child's selfobject needs, analogous disruptions occurred, and the self was permanently injured.

With repetition of the sequence of understanding and explanation, arrests are ameliorated, defects are repaired, new structure is internalized, and development resumes.

Curative Principles

Classical psychoanalytic theory holds that cure occurs as a result of the effects of interpretation, insight, and resultant structural change. The analytic atmosphere—the ambience—is not thought to be relevant to the mechanisms of cure. No curative structural transformations are attributed to corrective effects of a benign supportive emotional experience.

From a self psychological perspective, interpretation is crucial to the cure but insufficient to fully explain or understand the mechanisms involved—not only in those conditions that arise from defects in the basic structure of the self but also in those that result from drive conflict. Lest I be misunderstood, most self psychologists consider *interpretation* to be *essential,* but *not sufficient,* to explain the cure. Let me elucidate the factors considered relevant to the process of cure.

Empathy, Understanding, and Transmuting Internalization

When disruptions in the selfobject bond are empathically recognized, and when the therapist regains understanding sufficiently quickly, the patient feels understood and his or her discomfort subsides. With this sequence there is an accretion of psychic structure—a memory trace of the amalgam of disruption of equilibrium, empathic response, and subsequent restoration of equilibrium. This process of *transmuting internalization* is identical to that of normal development and is a factor, among others, in the therapeutic transformation upon which improvement and maturation depend.

Explanation and Structuralization

Most self psychologists (Basch 1980, 1989; Goldberg 1985; Ornstein and Ornstein 1980) consider an explanatory phase, the interpretations, to be essential to buttress the beneficial effects of empathic understanding and to cement permanent, cohesive self structure. Some, however, believe that emersion in an empathic milieu is the curative factor and that explanation is merely an intellectual epiphenomenon serving only to reduce the therapist's guilt about not being interpretive or analytic. Kohut (1977, 1984) considered this matter many times, and yet his position on the factors relevant to the cure was at times ambiguous or contradictory. His final statement was that empathy alone was not curative and that the therapeutic process *required* that a phase of explanation (interpretation) follow the phase of understanding (Kohut 1984, pp. 104–108).

Frustration and Structuralization

Traditional analytic theory holds that frustration is necessary to the process of structuralization. Kohut agreed with that formulation. In all his writing, he maintained the position that optimal frustration is essential to the process of transmuting internalization and to the development of regulating self structure.

This belief—that frustration is essential for structure formation—has been questioned by Bacal (1985, 1988), Terman (1988), and others on the basis of clinical observation and developmental studies. They doubt that frustration provides the sole stimulus for structure formation and believe, rather, that structuralization occurs with "optimal gratification" and "optimal responsiveness."

Empathy and Transference

Before I end, there is one common misconception I wish to correct. It is frequently thought that self psychologists believe that if a therapist is sufficiently empathic, fragmentation, psychic disequilibrium, and other symptoms of narcissistic pathology will not disrupt the smooth course of treatment. In this mistaken view, disruptions are said to be prima facie evidence that the therapist failed to be sufficiently empathic. The therapist is faulted and often feels guilty. It is said that he or she should have been more empathic!

Self psychology does not take that position, nor is it correct. It is a misunderstanding, a misapprehension, of the effects of empathy and the power of transference. As Kohut (1984) once explained (in a discussion of a patient who confronted him with a barrage of paranoid anger),

> What happens is nothing else but the transference clicking into place. Thus, during the calm before the storm, the analyst and the patient have jointly explored the patient's traumatic past, allied in the shared pursuit of a goal; once the storm breaks loose, however, the analytic situation has *become* the traumatic past and the analyst has *become* the traumatizing selfobject of early life. (pp. 177–178)

Self psychology recognizes the effects of earlier experience and the consequent propensity for transference. It does *not* assert that all of the patient's distress in treatment results from faulty attunement or empathic "failure" of the therapist. The patient's reactions are an amalgam (of varying proportions) of expectations, fears, and vulnerabilities transferred from the past, imbricated with the realities of present-day experience.

Self psychology is directed (as are all psychoanalytic approaches) to understanding the relative contributions of past and present and to fostering psychological development so that past injuries are less likely to be remobilized by the privations of present-day reality (see Wolf 1988, pp. 140–142).

Summary

Self psychological and classical analytic theory and practice are comparable. Both share the essential elements of psychoanalysis: belief in a *dynamic unconscious* and recognition of the phenomena of *transference*. Formulations regarding the mechanisms of unconscious mental processes, of dream work, of transference phenomena, and of symptom formation are identical, as is the interpretive method. Self psychology differs from classical theory in only one area: the selection of motivational forces and dangers around which self psychological theories of development and pathology are organized. Classical theory considers the vicissitudes of libidinal and aggressive drives to be central, whereas self psychology places the aspirations of the self—the exhibitionistic, alter-ego, and idealizing needs—in the central position.

References

Adler G: Uses and limitations of Kohut's self psychology in the treatment of borderline patients. J Am Psychoanal Assoc 37:761–785, 1989

American Psychiatric Association: Diagnostic and Statistical Manual of Mental Disorders, 4th Edition. Washington, DC, American Psychiatric Association, 1994

Atwood G, Stolorow R: Structures of Subjectivity. Hillsdale, NJ, Analytic Press, 1984

Bacal H: Optimal responsiveness and the therapeutic process, in Progress in Self Psychology, Vol 1. Edited by Goldberg A. New York, Guilford, 1985, pp 202–227

Bacal H: Reflections on "optimal frustration," in Progress in Self Psychology, Vol 4. Edited by Goldberg A. New York, Guilford, 1988, pp 122–131

Basch M: Doing Psychotherapy. New York, Basic Books, 1980

Basch M: Empathic understanding: a review of the concept and some theoretical considerations. J Am Psychoanal Assoc 31:101–126, 1983

Basch M: The selfobject theory of motivation and the history of psychoanalysis, in Kohut's Legacy. Edited by Stepansky P, Goldberg A. Hillsdale, NJ, Analytic Press, 1984a, pp 3–17

Basch M: Selfobjects and selfobject transference: theoretetical implications, in Kohut's Legacy. Edited by Stepansky P, Goldberg A. Hillsdale, NJ, Analytic Press, 1984b, pp 21–41

Basch M: How Does Analysis Cure?: an appreciation. Psychoanalytic Inquiry 6:403–428, 1986

Basch M: Understanding Psychotherapy. New York, Basic Books, 1989

Freud S: The interpretation of dreams (1900), in Standard Edition of the Complete Psychological Works of Sigmund Freud, Vols 4 and 5. Translated and edited by Strachey J. London, Hogarth Press, 1953

Freud S: Three essays on the theory of sexuality (1905), in Standard Edition of the Complete Psychological Works of Sigmund Freud, Vol 7. Translated and edited by Strachey J. London, Hogarth Press, 1953, pp 135–241

Freud S: Recommendations to physicians practising psycho-analysis (1912), in Standard Edition of the Complete Psychological Works of Sigmund Freud, Vol 12. Translated and edited by Strachey J. London, Hogarth Press, 1958, pp 109–120

Freud S: On beginning the treatment (1913), in Standard Edition of the Complete Psychological Works of Sigmund Freud, Vol 12. Translated and edited by Strachey J. London, Hogarth Press, 1958, pp 121–144

Freud S: On narcissism: an introduction (1914), in Standard Edition of the Complete Psychological Works of Sigmund Freud, Vol 14. Translated and edited by Strachey J. London, Hogarth Press, 1957, pp 67–102

Freud S: Instincts and their vicissitudes (1915), in Standard Edition of the Complete Psychological Works of Sigmund Freud, Vol 14. Translated and edited by Strachey J. London, Hogarth Press, 1957, pp 109–140

Freud S: Observations on transference-love (further recommendations on the technique of psycho-analysis III) (1915[1914]), in Standard Edition of the Complete Psychological Works of Sigmund Freud, Vol 12. Translated and edited by Strachey J. London, Hogarth Press, 1958, pp 157–173

Freud S: Mourning and melancholia (1917[1915]), in Standard Edition of the Complete Psychological Works of Sigmund Freud, Vol 14. Translated and edited by Strachey J. London, Hogarth Press, 1957, pp 237–260

Freud S: Beyond the pleasure principle (1920), in Standard Edition of the Complete Psychological Works of Sigmund Freud, Vol 18. Translated and edited by Strachey J. London, Hogarth Press, 1955, pp 7–64

Freud S: Group psychology and the analysis of the ego (1921), in Standard Edition of the Complete Psychological Works of Sigmund Freud, Vol 18. Translated and edited by Strachey J. London, Hogarth Press, 1955, pp 65–143

Freud S: The ego and the id (1923), in Standard Edition of the Complete Psychological Works of Sigmund Freud, Vol 19. Translated and edited by Strachey J. London, Hogarth Press, 1961, pp 1–66

Freud S: Inhibitions, symptoms and anxiety (1926), in Standard Edition of the Complete Psychological Works of Sigmund Freud, Vol 20. Translated and edited by Strachey J. London, Hogarth Press, 1959, pp 75–175

Freud S: An outline of psycho-analysis (1940[1938]), in Standard Edition of the Complete Psychological Works of Sigmund Freud, Vol 23. Translated and edited by Strachey J. London, Hogarth Press, 1964, pp 139–207

Freud S: Project for a scientific psychology (1950[1895]), in Standard Edition of the Complete Psychological Works of Sigmund Freud, Vol 1. Translated and edited by Strachey J. London, Hogarth Press, 1966, pp 281–397

Gedo J, Goldberg A: Models of the Mind: A Psychoanalytic Theory. Chicago, IL, University of Chicago Press, 1973

Goldberg A (ed): The Psychology of the Self: A Casebook. New York, International Universities Press, 1978

Goldberg A (ed): Advances in Self Psychology. New York, International Universities Press, 1980

Goldberg A: The definition and role of interpretation, in Progress in Self Psychology, Vol 1. Edited by Goldberg A. New York, Guilford, 1985, pp 62–65

Grinker R Sr, Werble B, Drye R: The Borderline Syndrome. New York, Basic Books, 1968

Gunderson JG: Borderline Personality Disorder. Washington, DC, American Psychiatric Press, 1984

Gunderson JG: Borderline personality disorder, in Comprehensive Text-book of Psychiatry/V, 5th Edition, Vol 2. Edited by Kaplan HI, Sadock BJ. Baltimore, MD, Williams & Wilkins, 1989, pp 1387–1395

Kernberg OF: Borderline personality organization. J Am Psychoanal Assoc 15:641–685, 1967

Kernberg OF: Borderline Conditions and Pathological Narcissism. New York, Jason Aronson, 1975

Kohut H: Introspection, empathy and psychoanalysis: an examination of the relationship between modes of observation and theory. J Am Psycho-anal Assoc 7:459-483, 1959 [Reprinted in Kohut H: The Search for the Self, Vol 1. Edited by Ornstein P. New York, International Universities Press, 1978, pp 205–232]

Kohut H: Forms and transformations of narcissism. J Am Psychoanal Assoc 14:243–272, 1966 [Reprinted in Kohut H: The Search for the Self, Vol 1. Edited by Ornstein P. New York, International Universities Press, 1978, pp 427–460]

Kohut H: The Analysis of the Self: A Systematic Approach to the Psycho-analytic Treatment of Narcissistic Personality Disorders. New York, In-ternational Universities Press, 1971

Kohut H: Thoughts on narcissism and narcissistic rage. Psychoanal Study Child 27:360-400, 1972 [Reprinted in Kohut H: The Search for the Self, Vol 2. Edited by Ornstein P. New York, International Universities Press, 1978, pp 615–658]

Kohut H: Remarks about the formation of the self (1974), in The Search for the Self, Vol 2. Edited by Ornstein P. New York, International Universi-ties Press, 1978, pp 737–770

Kohut H: The Restoration of the Self. New York, International Universities Press, 1977

Kohut H: How Does Analysis Cure? Edited by Goldberg A, Stepansky P. Chicago, IL, University of Chicago Press, 1984

Leider R: Analytic neutrality: a historical review. Psychoanalytic Inquiry 3:665–674, 1983

Lichtenberg J: Psychoanalysis and Motivation. Hillsdale, NJ, Analytic Press, 1989

Meissner W: Narcissistic personalities and borderline conditions: a differ-ential diagnosis. Annual of Psychoanalysis 7:171–202, 1979

Moore B, Fine B (eds): Psychoanalytic Terms and Concepts. New Haven, CT, Yale University Press, 1990

Ornstein P, Ornstein A: Formulating interpretations in clinical psycho-analysis. Int J Psychoanal 61:203–211, 1980

Panel: The neutrality of the analyst in the analytic situation. Reported by Leider R. J Am Psychoanal Assoc 32:573–585, 1981

Shane M, Shane E: Pathways to integration: adding to the self psychology model, in Progress in Self Psychology, Vol 4. Edited by Goldberg A. New York, Guilford, 1988, pp 71–78

Stern D: The Interpersonal World of the Infant. New York, Basic Books, 1985

Stolorow R: Integrating self psychology and classical psychoanalysis: an experience-near approach, in Progress in Self Psychology, Vol 4. Edited by Goldberg A. New York, Guilford, 1988, pp 63–70

Stolorow R, Brandchaft B, Atwood G: Psychoanalytic Treatment: An Inter-subjective Approach. Hillsdale, NJ, Analytic Press, 1987

Terman D: Aggression and narcissistic rage: a clinical elaboration. Annual of Psychoanalysis 3:239–255, 1975

Terman D: Optimal frustration: structuralization and the therapeutic pro-cess, in Progress in Self Psychology, Vol 4. Edited by Goldberg A. New York, Guilford, 1988, pp 113–125

Tolpin M: On the beginnings of a cohesive self. Psychoanal Study Child 26:316–352, 1971

Tolpin M: The self and its selfobject: a different baby, in Progress in Self Psychology, Vol 2. Edited by Goldberg A. New York, Guilford, 1986, pp 202–227

Wolf E: Ambience and abstinence. Annual of Psychoanalysis 4:101–115, 1976

Wolf E: Aspects of neutrality. Psychoanalytic Inquiry 3:675–690, 1983

Wolf E: Treating the Self. New York, Guilford, 1988

Section II

Psychoanalytic Theory of Psychopathology

Introduction to Section II

Richard G. Kopff, Jr., M.D.
Edward Nersessian, M.D.

Psychoanalytic theory provides the most comprehensive theory of psychopathology at the present time. Its concepts apply to a broad range of disorders, including the psychoneuroses, character (or personality) disorders, schizophrenia, major depression, sexual disorders, and disorders at the psychosomatic interface.

Today, one often hears some colleagues express the opinion that psychoanalytic theory has a place only in the understanding of personality disorders. The chapters in this section demonstrate, to the contrary, that psychoanalytic theory has applicability to treatment of a wide range of disorders.

In Chapters 5 (Charles Brenner), 6 (Martin Silverman), and 7 (Richard Kopff, Jr., and Edward Nersessian), the authors present facets of a psychoanalytic theory that, when taken as a whole, enhance the clinician's ability to understand neurotic symptoms and character disorders. In Chapters 8 (Michael Porder), 9 (Steven Roose), 10 (Martin Willick and Steven Roose), and 11 (Stanley Coen), the authors demonstrate how psychoanalytic theory enables one to understand the more severe disorders—borderline disorders, depressive disorders, schizophrenia, and sexual disorders, respectively. In Chapter 12 (Thomas Wolman and Troy Thompson II), the authors present a psychoanalytic approach to the understanding of disorders at the psychosomatic interface.

As stated in the introduction to Section I, psychoanalytic theory continues to develop and change in accordance with clinical and research findings. The psychoanalytic perspectives on and sometimes even the basic assumptions underlying an understanding of psychopathology, as represented in the various chapters of this section, are manifold. This multiplicity of viewpoints is a manifestation of the continuing additions to psychoanalytic findings and of the resultant changes in theoretical ideas that were discussed in Section I. Broad agreement does not exist among all psychoanalytic authors, including those who have contributed to this volume, there being more agreement at the level of clinical psychoanalytic observation than at the level of hypothesis. However, the hypotheses of psychoanalytic theorists are useful building blocks toward the development of theories of broader applicability. For example, Michael Porder, who in Chapter 8 presents a psychoanalytic view of the borderline concept, and Otto Kernberg, another major contributor to the understanding of the borderline concept, disagree on many points, as Dr. Porder describes in his chapter. Nevertheless, they both speak the same psychoanalytic language, and the views of each enrich those of the other as each attempts to come to terms with the other's conceptualizations.

The same applies to many of the other chapters. For example, in Chapter 9, on affective disorders, Steven Roose alludes to the impressive recent advances in the understanding of the biological determinants of affective disorders and their treatment. Yet, it is well known that many varieties of depression respond to psychoanalytic understanding and treatment. Among the large numbers of psychoanalysts who are well aware of the recent advances described by Dr. Roose, many consider, on the basis of their clinical experience, that only certain kinds of depressions are not amenable to psychoanalytically informed therapy, namely, major depression with significant biological types of symptoms, severe constriction of ideation, and a high degree of impairment of self-reflection. In addition, many psychoanalysts believe that a combination of modalities (e.g., medication and psychoanalytic treatment) offers a very successful therapeutic approach in numerous cases. In Section III of this textbook (Chapter 15), John Oldham discusses various indications for such an approach.

Systematic psychiatric investigation has become increasingly successful and impressive; psychoanalytic research methods have been less systematic and impressive but are improving, as will be shown in Section IV of this textbook. Findings from many decades of clinical studies and especially clinical experience provide much support for the assertions made in the chapters in this section. Psychiatric and psychoanalytic research do not contradict each other; nor are they at odds with each other. Rather, they complement each other, and a well-informed clinician should be aware of the findings of both.

In conclusion, psychoanalytic theory is central to a comprehensive understanding and conceptualization of psychopathology. This is true even though there are many different modalities for treating psychological disorders and there are many different views (psychoanalytic as well as biological) of the underlying determinants of these disorders.

5

Psychoanalytic Theory of Symptom Formation and Pathological Character Formation

Charles Brenner, M.D.

C onflict and compromise formation are the key concepts to an understanding of symptom formation and pathological character formation. As soon as Freud gave up hypnosis as a method of treatment and instead began to use what he called "free association," it became apparent to him that although his patients agreed to cooperate with him in his efforts to learn the origins of their symptoms, they wanted at the same time *not* to know what the symptoms' origins and causes were. He learned that his patients had wishes that they themselves vigorously rejected and tried to ignore (S. Freud 1894). It became apparent to Freud, in short, that patients have wishes about which they are in conflict. Nor was it long before it became equally clear that every symptom is a compromise formation in the sense that every symptom is at one and the same time the expression of a wish, a means of warding off that wish, and a punishment for having the wish in the first place (S. Freud 1896). That the same is true for pathological character traits was established some two or three decades later (A. Freud 1936/1946; S. Freud 1920, 1923, 1926). It is now generally accepted that psychogenic symptoms and pathological character traits are compromise formations that result from psychic conflict over wishes a patient has but wants to repudiate or deny.

Components of Psychic Conflict

Our current understanding of psychic conflict is as follows. There are four principal components of every conflict: 1) a drive derivative, 2) unpleasure associated with the drive derivative, 3) defense, and 4) superego functioning (guilt, remorse, self-punishment, and atonement). In the language of the structural theory, the drive derivatives represent the id, unpleasure and defense are aspects of ego functioning, and guilt, remorse, self-punishment, and atonement are aspects of superego functioning.

Drive Derivative

The first component of psychic conflict is the *drive derivative,* which is a wish for libidinal and aggressive gratification. The wishes that are of most importance with respect to conflict are those that are characteristic of the second 3 years of life, that is, of the oedipal phase of development. These wishes persist throughout life as the deepest wellsprings of motivation in each of us.

Every drive derivative is specific to the individual person; no two are ever identical. A.'s wishes (i.e., drive derivatives) are specific for A.; they are never the same as those of B., C., or anyone else. There are, nonetheless, enough similarities to allow one to make the following generalizations:

1. There are both libidinal and aggressive elements in every drive derivative.
2. These wishes derive from the early years of childhood—that is,

the drive derivatives of adulthood are persistent or modified childhood wishes.
3. Libidinal wishes often have to do with pleasurable stimulation of particular parts of the body, known as *erogenous zones*.

The available data suggest that in the first 18 months of life, the leading erogenous zone is the oral one. At about 18 months anal wishes become prominent, and sometime shortly after the age of 3 years wishes for pleasurable genital stimulation take their place in mental life as well. What is of special importance to remember is that wishes connected with the various erogenous zones, once these wishes have appeared, remain important throughout the rest of childhood and later life. Thus, oral and anal wishes continue to be very important in the mental lives of 4- and 5-year-olds, and psychoanalytic data give evidence of the fact that they, as well as phallic wishes, are prominent in the conflicts of older children and adults as well.

The drive derivatives of the second 3 years of life, though they are wishes for pleasurable gratification, inevitably give rise to unpleasure as well. They do so for two reasons. First, children at that age are still physically and emotionally largely dependent on their parents, as well as greatly inferior to them both physically and intellectually. Second, children are still sexually immature at that age as far as their bodies are concerned, and they remain so for many years. Many of the libidinal wishes of that time of life cannot be gratified fully because of the immaturity of the child's sexual apparatus. One might say without exaggeration that psychologically 5-year-olds are sexually nearly mature, but physically they must wait what seems to them forever before they can gratify many of their most urgent wishes.

Unpleasure

The second component of psychic conflict—that which triggers conflict in mental life—is the *unpleasure* associated with childhood drive derivatives. This unpleasure can be conveniently classified as comprising two affects: anxiety and depressive affect. Like all unpleasurable affects, each is a composite of a more or less intense sensation of unpleasure and various thoughts or ideas. In the case of anxiety, if the unpleasure is intense, one speaks of terror or panic, and if the unpleasure is mild, of worry or unease. In the case of depressive affect, if the unpleasure is intense, one speaks of misery or severe depression, and if the unpleasure is mild, of unhappiness or of slight sadness. Those ideas that are part of any form of anxiety involve danger—some calamity that threatens or impends; those that are part of depressive affect involve a calamity that is current and a part of life. For example, a child who fears parental disapproval or reprisal in connection with some drive derivative is, by definition, experiencing anxiety, whether it be mild, moderate, or intense. A child who feels unloved or punished in connection with some drive derivative is, again by definition, experiencing some variety of depressive affect. Clearly, the two are not mutually exclusive. They may, indeed, be indistinguishable at times. More often, however, they are separable, and when such is the case, it is important clinically to make the distinction.

The calamities that either impend or are felt to be facts of life are of four kinds: object loss, loss of love, castration, and punishment (S. Freud 1926). They appear sequentially in the course of development: object loss during the first 18 months, loss of love during the next 18 months, and castration and fear of punishment during the ages 3 to 6 years. What is essential to keep in mind, however, is that once a calamity has appeared, it continues to be important throughout the rest of one's life. Object loss and loss of love are calamities in the minds of 4- or 5-year-olds as well as in the minds of much younger children. All four calamities play major roles in mental life, and all four become inextricably intertwined. A 5-year-old girl who feels inferior because she is not a boy is miserable in part because, in her mind, not being a boy means not being loved as she wishes to be loved by father. The girl may attribute her penisless state to mother's punishment for her rivalrous and murderous jealousy of mother. Correspondingly, a boy of the same age may fear loss of father's love not only because he desires that love for its own sake but as much or more because he interprets such loss to mean that father will punish and castrate him.

To repeat, the second component of psychic conflict, the component that initiates conflict, is unpleasure in the form of anxiety, depressive affect, or both. Anxiety is defined as unpleasure with the ideational content that a calamity is impending. Depressive affect is defined as unpleasure with the ideational content that a calamity is a current reality—that it is a part of life. In any case, the calamity is either object loss, loss of love, castration, or punishment, all of which are eventually inextricably intertwined.

Defense

The third component of psychic conflict is *defense*. Whenever anxiety, depressive affect, or both appear in connection with a drive derivative, the mind responds in such a way as to reduce or eliminate unpleasure. Every such response, every effort to reduce or eliminate unpleasure, is what is called defense.

Superego Functioning

The fourth component of psychic conflict, *superego functioning*, is the aspect of mental functioning that has to do with morality, with ideas of what is right and what is wrong in the moral sense of those words. The major share of superego development takes place during the sixth and seventh years of life—that is, toward the end of the period during which conflict over childhood drive derivatives is at its height. For children of this age the arbiters of right and wrong are their parents. The child believes that what his or her parents consider right or wrong *is* what is right or wrong. An expectation of parental disapproval, a fear of punishment, constitutes one aspect of superego functioning (S. Freud 1923). In such cases the superego initiates defense: a morally objectionable drive derivative is defended against to eliminate or mitigate fear of punishment.

Superego functioning encompasses more than defense against a morally objectionable wish, however. Remorse, atonement through self-punishment, attempts to make amends, and identification with one's parents' moral attitudes, real or fancied, are also ways of winning parental approval and, for that reason, are aspects of superego functioning as well (Brenner 1982). The term *guilt* is inadequate to characterize the affects associated with moral transgression. Self-punishment and self-injury by way of remorse and making amends are aspects of superego functioning that are universal. These aspects themselves entail unpleasure and, for that reason, may be defended against just as drive derivatives are when they entail unpleasure. In addition to initiating defense, superego activity in such cases is defended against. Such individuals have a *need* to punish themselves that they themselves do not recognize. This is often referred to as an unconscious sense of guilt (S. Freud 1923).

Thus, the superego participates in conflict in more than one way. In some instances it participates on the side of defense, whereas in other instances it is defended against.

Consequences of Psychic Conflict

Drive derivative, unpleasure in the form of anxiety and depressive affect, defense, and superego manifestations are the components of psychic conflict. What are the consequences of such conflict?

Interaction among the components of psychic conflict results in a compromise formation in which each component plays a part. The drive derivative is gratified, in however incomplete and disguised a way. The anxiety and depressive affect whose ideational content is one or more of the calamities of childhood are expressed in one way or another. Defenses are operating to reduce unpleasure, and superego demands and prohibitions play their part as well. In every compromise formation the drive derivatives are gratified as much as possible without too much unpleasure being aroused, and, conversely, unpleasure is reduced as much as possible while some drive gratification is still allowed for. What we call compromise formation means getting as much pleasure as possible with as little unpleasure as possible.

A compromise formation may be either normal or pathological (Brenner 1982). If a compromise formation allows a sufficient degree of pleasurable gratification to a drive derivative, if the accompanying anxiety and depressive affect are not too severe, if the inhibition of function resulting from the defenses is not too extreme, if self-punishment and self-injury are not too extensive, and if the need to be in conflict with one's environment (by which is meant principally the persons with whom one is in contact in one's life) is not too great, then the compromise formation is considered normal. By contrast, if there is too little gratification of drive derivatives, if there is too much unpleasure, if there is too much inhibition of function because of defense, if there is too much self-punishment and self-injury, and/or if there is too great a need to be in conflict with the environment, then the compromise formation is considered pathological. Such pathological compromise formations are often labeled neurotic symptoms and/or neurotic (or pathological) compromise formations.

Case Presentations

The following cases are examples of pathological compromise formations that are commonly called neurotic symptoms.

> M., a 31-year-old woman who was competent and successful in her professional work, was in analysis because of a variety of personal problems, chief among which was her inability to find one among her many admirers whom she felt ready to marry. In the course of her analysis she revealed that she was afraid to fly. Whenever possible she avoided airplane travel. When she had to fly, she was tormented throughout the flight by anxiety that the plane might crash, killing all aboard. She continued by adding that what she actually feared was that something would happen to the pilot in the cockpit. If this were to occur, she would be helpless to do anything, because as "just a passenger" she would of course not be allowed into the cockpit. Though, she added with a smile, she didn't know what good it would do if she were to go into the cockpit in such an emergency, since she didn't know anything about flying an airplane anyway. Still, the thought of being excluded was very much a part of her frightening fantasy. She paused for a moment, and then went on to say that she remembered one time when she actually enjoyed flying. That time was in a small private plane, a two-seater. She sat in the cockpit beside

the pilot. The plane had dual controls, and she noted that there was nothing scary about it at all. But the next time there was a question of flying in a regular passenger plane, she was as scared as ever.

My patient was genuinely puzzled by her symptom. She was not a timid person. In fact, she enjoyed the spice of danger in other situations. She was, for example, an enthusiastic horsewoman and had often ridden to hunt in years gone by, a sport in which physical injuries are common and fatal accidents, not rare events. Why should flying in a commercial passenger plane be frightening? And how could it be that she was free from anxiety when flying in a private plane, a type of air travel with a safety record much poorer than that of regularly scheduled passenger flights?

The answer to the question became apparent as she talked more about the experience. She liked having a set of controls for herself, she said, and she used the common slang word "joystick" to describe the control, a term that is a euphemism for a penis. She had her own joystick, and she used it briefly to guide the plane during flight.

The dynamics of her symptom were now much clearer. She enjoyed flying when she had her own (symbolic) penis—when she was just as well equipped as the man beside her who piloted the plane. She did not feel at all frightened. However, when access to the equipment she wished for was denied her—when only the pilot had a joystick in his lap—she was beset by anxiety, by thoughts of the pilot being incapacitated, and by thoughts of her own body being dashed to the ground so that she died as well.

It must be added that there was abundant analytic evidence to support the conclusion that M. was both jealous of men and angry that she herself was a woman, though she hid from herself both the extent of her jealousy and the intensity of her anger. As she gradually became more aware of both her jealousy and her anger in the course of her analysis, it became clear as well why she had tried so hard to be as unaware of them as possible. They were both associated with very unpleasurable emotions: depressive affect arising from the realization that she was "just a woman," and anxiety in connection with her vengeful, castrative, and murderous wishes toward persons who were at the same time dear to her. The wishes and conflicts I have been describing originated in her childhood and could be traced back with considerable assurance at least to her sixth year of life, when her brother was born. Her brother's arrival was greeted with joy by both parents, and he was even given her father's name.

In brief, the thought and/or experience of flying exacerbated my patient's lifelong conflict over her wish to be a boy, her wish for her parents' exclusive love and attention, and her desire for revenge at her having been refused or deprived of the penis that she prized so highly. She strove unconsciously to remain unaware of her wishes and to keep them under tight control, but they broke forth in various disguised forms despite her efforts to ward them off. Her wish to be rid of her brother was expressed in her fantasy that the pilot would become sick and/or die. Her wish to be him instead of "just" herself, to be a boy with a penis instead of "just" a girl, was expressed in her fantasy of taking his place and bringing the plane to safety, a fantasy that at the same time expressed her wish to be the one whom her parents/fellow passengers loved and admired the most.

So much for M.'s drive derivatives. What of the anxiety and depressive affect whose ideational content was one or more of the calamities of childhood? That they also played a role in determining her symptomatic compromise formation is equally clear. Her anxiety was quite conscious and was directly associated with her fantasy of being excluded from the pilot's room (the cockpit), just as when she was a child she had feared that she would be unloved (loss of love) and banished (object loss) because of her wish to be rid of and to emasculate her brother. Castration anxiety in connection with the latter of these wishes likewise appeared as fear of bodily injury and death as a result of the plane's crashing to the ground. Depressive affect was also expressed in her feeling that "of course" she would never be allowed into the cockpit because she was, after all, "just a passenger," as in her childhood she had felt miserable and depressed at being "just a girl."

What of the defenses that contributed to her pathological compromise formations? Prominent among them were repression and avoidance. She avoided flying whenever it was possible to do so; she had an airplane phobia. She had no awareness that childhood wishes and fears were stirred up by the idea or experience of flying. These wishes and fears were unconscious (i.e., repressed). Her concern for the pilot's and passengers' health and safety was also defensive and served the purpose of mitigating her anxiety and depressive affect by helping her to deny the wishes that aroused such unpleasure.

The superego contributions to her symptom were equally apparent. Her fantasy was not simply that others would die and/or be maimed and suffer. She included herself among those who were suffering. She was to be punished for her "bad" wishes, not only by sustaining bodily injuries but by being banished and unloved as well. Her expectation of punishment and her need to make amends by suffering are apparent in nearly every feature of her compromise formation.

The foregoing analysis of M.'s pathological compromise formation is by no means complete or exhaustive. One can suspect that her symptom (i.e., pathological compromise formation) was also determined in part by conflicts over primal scene and pregnancy fantasies, for example. Although incomplete, this analysis is sufficient to show that in the case of M., as in the case that follows, a pathological compromise formation is the consequence of an interaction among drive derivatives, anxiety and depressive affect concerning the calamities of childhood, defenses, and superego demands and prohibitions.

C., a 24-year-old homemaker with two children, had entered analysis because of recurrent bouts of unhappiness whose origins were obscure. One day she reported that the previous day she had had an acute anxiety attack of considerable intensity. She had gone for lunch with a woman friend who was an executive in a bank. The dining room to which her friend led her was below ground level. As she walked into the room, C. suddenly became anxious. She felt as if she were suffocating and feared that the room would somehow close in on her and that she would be unable to get out. She even had the thought that she might die. So intense was her discomfort that she had to excuse herself and leave the building, explaining to her friend that she felt physically unwell and had best go home.

After telling me this story of what had happened the day before, she went on to talk about her sister, who had died at the age of 5 years, before the patient was born. Her sister's photograph, taken shortly before the onset of her sister's fatal illness, was kept always on C.'s bureau. It seemed to C. that when C. was a child, her parents never lost an opportunity to compare her unfavorably with the little girl of the photograph. Whenever C. was naughty or even less than completely charming and brilliant, she was told how good, how bright, and how lovable her sister, who had died so young, had been. "It made me so mad," C. said. "Sometimes I wished I'd never been born."

When I suggested to C. that her attack of anxiety the day before might have been related in some way to thoughts about her dead sister that had been stirred up by being in an underground room, C. told me that she did not see how that could have been, since her sister was not buried under the ground. Her coffin was above ground in the family vault that her grandfather had built. "Of course," the patient went on, "on the way to the dining room we passed the vault of the bank. I remember noticing the sign just before we went into the dining room."

From the material at hand it seems that the following conclusions are justified concerning the dynamics of C.'s anxiety attack. Since childhood, C. had been angry at her parents for, as she felt, loving her less than they did her dead sister. She wanted to hurt and punish them, to make them feel as miserable as they made her feel or even to kill them, to get rid of them altogether. These childhood wishes for love and revenge were associated with fears of retribution and with guilt. To avoid the anxiety and depressive affect these wishes aroused, she repressed them and otherwise defended against them from childhood on. When she passed the sign in the bank that read "VAULT," she was unconsciously reminded of her childhood wishes, and the anxiety associated with them became conscious.

It was as though her conscience said to her, "You wanted to be rid of your sister? You wished you'd been born first instead of her so that you'd never have to hear about how wonderful she was? Alright, *be* her, be dead and buried and see how you like it!"

In C.'s pathological compromise formation, as in M.'s (in the previous case illustration), childhood drive derivatives, unpleasure, defenses, and superego demands and prohibitions all played a part. C.'s drive derivatives included a wish to be loved the best, a wish to eliminate her sister and all mention of her sister from her life, and a wish to turn the tables on her parents. The guilt associated with the drive derivatives led to C.'s having a fantasy of herself as being dead and buried—that is, unloved, banished, and suitably punished. She repressed awareness of her bad wishes at the moment she saw the sign "VAULT" and unconsciously identified with the parents with whom she wished to get even. Despite these defenses, however, she experienced intense anxiety and physical discomfort.

The analysis of this pathological compromise formation, like the analysis of the one in the previous case illustration, is incomplete. Nonetheless, it too serves to illustrate the proposition that every pathological compromise formation results from conflict—that is, from the interaction among drive derivatives, anxiety and/or depressive affect, defenses, and superego manifestations.

The same proposition applies to neurotic character traits, as is illustrated in the following case example:

> W., a man in his 30s, had a number of complaints that brought him to analysis. One among them was clearly indicative of a neurotic character trait. He felt himself obliged always to do what was expected of him. No matter how much he chastised himself for his submissiveness, his need to conform, and his inability to assert himself, he always found it necessary to be submissively obedient. He could not change his behavior even when he tried.
>
> As far back as W. could remember he had always been a good student and had never been in disciplinary trouble. He combed his hair, washed his hands and face, and brushed his teeth without having to be reminded, and was generally a credit to his parents in everyone's eyes. In college, too, he had been exemplary. He belonged to the right clubs; he was on a varsity sports team, for which he had trained conscientiously and where he performed creditably; his grades were quite satisfactory in general and well above average in the courses in which it was important for him to do well; he went out with the "right" girls; and so on. His clothes were always conventionally correct. After college he did well in a good firm, and he even went to church occasionally on Sunday to please his mother.

In the course of W.'s analysis many of his associations and several of his dreams supported the conclusion that the character trait in question expressed his strong wish to please his parents, especially his mother. This wish showed itself in his character as submissive obedience toward everyone and everything his mother held dear.

It also appeared in the course of his analysis that the character trait of which he complained was not as simple as he originally thought it to be. To all the world, as to himself, he seemed to be conforming and submissive, as he complained of having to be, but this was only part of the story. He had always studied conscientiously and gotten good grades, but he would forget everything he learned as soon as he no longer needed to remember it, and he had had no real interest in any of his subjects. He had gone to the right parties with the right girls, but he had never cared for any of them. Beginning in college, he secretly frequented bars and patronized prostitutes. As far as his professional work was concerned, he did barely enough to get by and felt himself to be always on the brink of exposure and dismissal.

Thus, although it is correct to say that this young man's behavior was pathologically submissive and conforming, it must be added that he exhibited at the same time the opposite behavior. He wished to please his mother and be a credit to her and yet at the same time to flout her every wish and to humiliate her by disgracing her. He did the things she wanted, but he cared for none of them, and he did many things that he was sure would cause her great pain if she were to find out about them.

It must be mentioned in this connection that the patient had two sisters, one 1 year older than himself and the other 3½ years his junior. From as far back as he could remember he had been convinced that his mother preferred both sisters to himself and that he had no chance of ever being her favorite simply because he had been born a boy instead of a girl.

On the basis of the data presented it is apparent that this patient's neurotic character trait was quite as much a pathological compromise formation as were M.'s airplane phobia and C.'s anxiety attack. Clearly the childhood drive derivatives (i.e., wishes) to be mother's favorite and to avenge himself on her were represented in his compliant/rebellious behavior and attitude. So, too, were the fear of loss of love and the fear of punishment that made him, on the one hand, appear to conform and, on the other, hide his misdeeds from the world. His defenses were several. For one, his submissiveness served the purpose of defending against awareness of his desire to attack and hurt his mother, a desire that was associated with fear that she would punish him by loving him even less. His rebellious behavior and attitude served the defensive function of mitigating the depressive affect associated with his conviction that she did not love him as he wished, as well as the anxiety associated with his wish to be a girl (i.e., to be without a penis). In addition, he had repressed the connection between, on the one hand, the social and sexual behavior that he hid from the world and, on the other, his thoughts and feelings about his mother. Nor did he ever feel consciously angry at her; that, too, was defended against. As for superego manifestations, one need mention only the patient's unconscious conviction that he would be punished if his vengeful, angry wishes should become known.

As in the earlier case illustrations, the foregoing analysis of the patient's pathological compromise formation is by no means complete; it is, however, complete enough to illustrate what is important for one to understand about the dynamics and genesis of pathological character traits. In every case that can be examined analytically (i.e., with the help of the analytic method), one arrives at the same conclusion as in the illustrations just given: *Every neurotic symptom and pathological character trait is a compromise formation that results from psychic conflict of childhood origin. In every instance what is involved is a pathological compromise formation among drive derivatives; anxiety and depressive affect related to the calamities of childhood; defenses; and superego manifestations.*

In this important respect symptoms and neurotic character traits are alike. None is ever just unpleasure; none is ever just defense; none is ever just a superego manifestation. All are compromise formations among all these components of conflict.

The fact that symptoms and neurotic character traits are identical in this important respect raises two questions that are worth discussing here. First, how can the compromise formations referred to as symptoms and those referred to as pathological character traits be distinguished? And, second, how useful is it to distinguish between the two?

In some cases the distinction seems easy to make. If a patient complains of severe anxiety about, for example, flying and the anxiety is of recent and relatively sudden onset, one has no hesitation about labeling the complaint a neurotic symptom. The same is true if a patient feels compelled to check every faucet, every gas jet, or every electrical outlet carefully before leaving the house. On the other hand, if we learn that a patient is consistently provocative and quarrelsome with superiors at work, we apply the label pathological (or neurotic) character trait with equal promptness and assurance.

Not every case is so simple, however. There are persons who all their lives have avoided traveling by air but who are not aware of any special anxiety at the prospect and who justify their avoidance as a preference that they support with sensible-sounding arguments. It may seem to the observer that such a person is unconsciously just as irrationally anxious about flying as was the hypothetical phobic patient mentioned in the previous paragraph. Yet here one is dealing with behavior that is anchored in character and that is accepted by the person in question as his or her own best judgment. Should one call such behavior a symptom, then, or would it be better to classify the behavior as a character trait?

Or consider the following commonplace situation. A patient was rarely at odds with his superiors at work. Indeed, he was usually on very good terms with them. His hostile, provocative wishes were expressed in a sarcastic, critical attitude toward individuals not personally known to him who were part of the social, economic, and political establishment. On certain occasions, however, notably when he had made a new sexual conquest, he was hostile and provocative toward his immediate superiors. How should one classify the patient's behavior? Is such an episodic compromise formation symptomatic or characterological?

The suggestion has been made that one can distinguish symptom from pathological character trait on the following basis. If a patient accepts a pathological compromise formation as part of his or her own personality, it should be classified as a character trait. If, on the other hand, a patient views a pathological compromise formation as something alien to himself or herself, then it is a symptom. In other words, symptoms are ego-alien and character traits are ego-syntonic.

Unfortunately, however, this distinction proves to be invalid. How can one fail to classify stubbornness, or compliance, or impetuosity, or cautiousness as character traits? Yet one often has to treat patients who wish they could be less stubborn, less impetuous, less compliant, or less cautious, to say nothing of the many patients who complain of moods and mood changes and who wish they could control or be rid of them. These patients often feel as unhappy about the character traits of which they complain and as helpless in the face of them as do patients with phobias or obsessional rituals. Pathological character traits are by no means always ego-syntonic.

In fact, neurotic symptoms and character traits are often indistinguishable dynamically and even descriptively. What can be said about the differences between the two is that any pathological compromise formation that has lasted for many years and that is not strikingly different from modes of thought and behavior that are considered to be normal is usually classified as a character trait. On the other hand, any pathological compromise formation that is of short duration, of recent origin, and/or of relatively sudden onset, and/or that strikes one as strange, bizarre, or outside the realm of normal thought and behavior, is apt to be labeled a symptom.

All these considerations appear to justify the conclusion that it is a fruitless task to try to distinguish sharply between symptom and pathological character trait. The similarities between the two are both more extensive and more significant than are the differences. Whatever criteria one uses, there is so much overlap between the two that it is as often impossible to make a clear distinction as it is possible to do so. Nor is there any "reward" when one is able to do so. The differences have no important clinical significance. Both symptom and pathological character trait are to be analyzed in the same way. Every patient who enters analysis presents with some compromise formations that may reasonably be classified as pathological character traits and others that may be as reasonably called neurotic symptoms. The attempt to label each pathological compromise formation as one or the other is of use neither to the patient nor to the analyst. What is not only useful but essential to understand is that, whatever label one gives them, all symptoms and pathological character traits are compromise formations resulting from psychic conflicts of childhood origin.

References

Brenner C: The Mind in Conflict. Madison, CT, International Universities Press, 1982

Freud A: The Ego and Mechanisms of Defence (1936). New York, International Universities Press, 1946

Freud S: The neuro-psychoses of defence (1894), in Standard Edition of the Complete Psychological Works of Sigmund Freud, Vol 3. Translated and edited by Strachey J. London, Hogarth Press, 1962, pp 41–68

Freud S: Further remarks on the neuro-psychoses of defence (1896), in Standard Edition of the Complete Psychological Works of Sigmund Freud, Vol 3. Translated and edited by Strachey J. London, Hogarth Press, 1962, pp 157–185

Freud S: Beyond the pleasure principle (1920), in Standard Edition of the Complete Psychological Works of Sigmund Freud, Vol 18. Translated and edited by Strachey J. London, Hogarth Press, 1955, pp 7–64

Freud S: The ego and the id (1923), in Standard Edition of the Complete Psychological Works of Sigmund Freud, Vol 19. Translated and edited by Strachey J. London, Hogarth Press, 1961, pp 1–66

Freud S: Inhibitions, symptoms and anxiety (1926), in Standard Edition of the Complete Psychological Works of Sigmund Freud, Vol 20. Translated and edited by Strachey J. London, Hogarth Press, 1959, pp 75–175

6

The Neuroses

Martin A. Silverman, M.D.

A neurosis is a psychological condition that, in its minor forms, is more or less universal among human beings but that, in its more major forms, can seriously interfere with a person's life or even be incapacitating. Our understanding of this condition has evolved considerably over the years. The term *neurosis* originated in the mid-19th-century belief that the symptoms that we now recognize as psychological in nature have their origins in disturbances of the neurological system—that is, that they are attributable to physical causation. The terms *neuropsychosis* and *psychoneurosis* were introduced toward the end of the 19th century to denote the connection between the biological and the psychological that was central in the thinking of physicians of that time. The first of these terms fell quickly into disuse, but the term psychoneurosis still is used interchangeably with the simpler and more popular term neurosis.

Several investigators, such as Herbart and Moebius, recognized that mental rather than neurological operations were involved in generating neurotic manifestations. However, it was Sigmund Freud, a Viennese neuroanatomist and neurologist, who established convincingly that neurosis is a psychological phenomenon.

He, like other neurologists, encountered one patient after another who displayed a combination of somatic symptoms that could not be explained in terms of known physical disease entities and that at times defied the principles of neuroanatomical expression, and other symptoms that in their presentation seemed to be mental or emotional rather than neurological. Patients came to his attention with motor weaknesses; paralysis; areas of sensory anesthesia; pains; gastrointestinal, cardiorespiratory, or genitourological disturbances; and other seemingly physical problems—together with such seemingly psychological phenomena as phobias, obsessive-compulsive symptomatology, depression, anxiety, dissociative states, and paranoid fears. How, Freud wondered, could he conceptualize the relationship among these bafflingly incongruent phenomena in such a way as to make sense of them and to enable him to devise an effective method of investigating and treating his patients' disturbances?

Freud familiarized himself with the careful observations of Emil Kraepelin and Eugen Bleuler, who organized psychopathological phenomenology in new ways. An important avenue for solving the mystery was provided by Hippolyte Bernheim, Ambroise Liebault, and especially Jean-Martin Charcot in France. They demonstrated that the neurological-like symptoms that were part of the picture that Freud and his fellow neurologists were observing could be at least temporarily eliminated through the use of hypnosis. Bernheim and Liebault were at times even able to remove symptoms without hypnosis, by encouraging patients to recall traumatic experiences they had undergone. Freud spent a period of time in Paris attending Charcot's demonstrations and lectures at the Salpêtrière. He also translated Charcot's lectures into German. In Vienna, Freud used hypnosis to investigate "hysterical" symptoms in collaboration with a senior colleague, Josef Breuer, who had also been using hypnosis to remove hysterical symptoms.

Early Investigations Into "Hysteria"

Breuer was working with one patient in particular, with whom he was learning a great deal about the origin and removal of hysterical symptoms. This young woman, whom Breuer and Freud subsequently designated as Fraulein Anna O. in their monograph *Studies in Hysteria* (Breuer and Freud 1893–1895), had presented with a host of debilitating symptoms that included paralyses, contractures, a nervous cough, an inability to walk, an inability to speak her native language, and so forth. When Breuer hypnotized the patient and directed her to trace back the symptoms to their point of origin, the symptoms often disappeared and were replaced by emotionally painful memories of traumatic experiences that apparently had overwhelmed her and the psychological coping mechanisms that were at her disposal at that time. An important step was made when Breuer complied with her request to hold back from suggesting away her symptoms under hypnosis and to allow her instead to talk about the traumatic experiences (a process she called "chimney-sweeping") that, as they had found through hypnosis, were lying behind the symptoms, outside of her awareness. Breuer and Freud found that allowing the patient to express and emotionally work over her painful recollections was even more effective in ridding her of her symptoms than was suggesting them away. At the same time that he was learning so much from Anna O., however, Breuer was also experiencing difficulties in his treatment of her. Her symptoms did not always disappear permanently. At times, they dissolved, only to be replaced by other, equally problematic ones. Her thoughts and recollections at times brought her to matters of such a highly personal and delicate nature that it made both doctor and patient uncomfortable. Finally, it became apparent that his patient had fallen in love with him and had developed the hysterical belief that she was carrying his baby. Breuer subsequently gave up his investigations into the nature of hysterical symptomatology, but Freud pushed on.

Freud, too, found that behind the hysterical symptoms for which he was treating his patients were often to be found buried yearnings and desires of a forbidden, sexual nature that were inadmissible to their own conscious sensibilities and moral attitudes. It became increasingly clear to Breuer and Freud that their patients were split apart within themselves into a kind of "double consciousness" (after a term of Charcot's). A fierce opposition existed between, on the one hand, their internalized, civilized, moral, and moralistic views of what is acceptable and unacceptable behavior, expressed in thoughts and feelings of which they were conscious, and, on the other hand, feelings and urges, often sexual and rival-rously aggressive in nature, of which they were not consciously aware and that they themselves would have violently opposed if they had been aware of them. Breuer was inclined to formulate the intense conflict between irreconcilable conscious, moral attitudes and unconscious, forbidden sexual and aggressive inclinations in terms of a hypothetical, primary "hypnoid state" of the mind in which thoughts and feelings of a problematic or objectionable na-ture could not be processed by the higher mental faculties from which they were removed as a result of the splitting of conscious-ness that had taken place. Breuer's own Victorian sensibilities, and the distress he had experienced in his treatment of Anna O. upon the unforeseen development of an erotic attachment to him on the part of his young woman patient, directed him toward a mechanis-tic explanation and away from the forbidden impulses and feelings that his patients were having such difficulty dealing with. Never-theless, Breuer's speculations about the workings of the mind in hysterical phenomena foreshadowed the emergence of the hy-potheses that eventually were to emerge about the structure of the human mind and its operation.

Freud, in contrast to Breuer, found that he could not dismiss the sensitive matters that their patients were pushing out of awareness and were replacing with the largely pseudoneurological (and there-fore much more acceptable as well as self-punitive) symptoms that brought them to physicians for treatment. The intense resistance the patients regularly exerted against becoming aware of the matters that lay behind their symptomatology, either through hypnosis or through the "psycho-analytic method" with which he began increasingly to replace hypnosis, indicated to him that an active effort was being made to press these contents out of conscious awareness and to keep them out of awareness. Otherwise, so much work would not have had to be done to retrieve them from the unconscious realm into which they had been relegated. Freud increasingly appreciated that his patients were not aware that they were resisting his efforts to elucidate the meaning of their symptoms. This eventually led him to the realization that neurotic defenses are largely carried out by a sector of the mind that operates unconsciously.

Freud was not a very good hypnotist. He discovered, however, not only that some of his patients fell into a trancelike state when they lay down upon the couch without his having to hypnotize them, but also that they did not even have to be hypnotized to get at the unconscious contents that lay behind their overt symptomatology. Like Breuer's patient Anna O., they often objected to Freud's interrupting them as they expressed out loud the trains of thought that occurred to them when they were given the opportunity to speak openly and freely to someone who accepted what they had to say uncritically and with an interest in helping them. Freud eventually abandoned the use of hypnosis altogether in favor of the method of "psycho-analysis," which has continued in use to this day as a prime method of investigating and relieving neurotic disorders. In this method of exploration and treatment, patients were asked to lie down on the couch and give themselves over to free and open verbal expression, to think out loud as it were, to say everything that occurred to them without reservation or censorship, and to follow the trains of association between groups of feelings and ideas, whether what they found themselves saying made sense to them or not.

Just as he had done before, in an earlier, ill-fated attempt to study the effects and possible medical uses of cocaine, Freud subjected himself to the same psychoanalytic method of investigation of the human mind and emotions that he offered to his neurotic patients. He did this partly in the hope of obtaining relief from some phobic and psychosomatic symptoms from which he himself suffered (and whose underlying, unconscious elements he, unlike some of his medical colleagues, was willing to face rather than deny their nature), and partly because, as he reported in *The Psychopathology of Everyday Life* (Freud 1901) and *Jokes and Their Relation to the Unconscious* (Freud 1905), he increasingly recognized that what he was observing in his patients were mental phenomena that were equally observable in relatively asymptomatic, psychologically healthy persons. What was observable in daydreams and especially

nocturnal dreams seemed to be very similar to what he was encoun-
tering in his work with neurotic patients, both in the makeup of the
neuroses and in the processes that seemed to be involved in their
formation, and in the difficulties encountered in delving into them
and gaining understanding of them as a mental activity. He also
found that dreams could serve as a window that provided access to
mental contents that during waking hours were removed from
conscious awareness by active opposition to knowing of their existence. As such, dreams could be a particularly fruitful source of
obtaining a view into that part of mental life that was ordinarily
hidden from view by the mental mechanisms with which people
ordinarily defend themselves against intrusion of unwanted, unconscious contents into the orderly, acceptable realm of conscious
mental life. Dreams, Freud found, played an especially useful and
important role in his own self-analysis, as he reported rather fully
and courageously in his work *The Interpretation of Dreams,* which
was published in 1900.

True to his background as a neuroanatomist who had worked
for many years in Brucke's laboratory within a zeitgeist dominated
by von Helmholtz and others, both within and outside of von
Helmholtz's school, who believed that all disease could be traced to
specific anatomical, pathogenetic localization, Freud attempted at
first to construct a theory of the mind that was neuroanatomical and
neurophysiological. Although the "Project for a Scientific Psychology" (Freud 1950[1895]), which he worked on in 1895, was a brilliant
tour de force, he found that he had to break it off, uncompleted, as
untenable given the state of neurological knowledge at that time.
He completely discarded it, in fact, and it was only after his death in
1939 that it was recovered, for its largely historical value. In the
"Project," Freud drew upon the newly discovered but neurophys-
iologically obscure existence within the central nervous system of
networks of "neurones" to posit the existence of facilitatory and
inhibitory neuronal circuits controlling quantities of internal and
external stimulation (differentiated from each other qualitatively) so
as to maintain optimal levels of stimulation within the central nervous system. After he abandoned the "Project," his focus shifted to
a strictly psychological one.

The Psychological Understanding of the Neuroses

Neurosis, it had become clear to Freud, is a psychological state in which the mind is wracked with conflict between opposing forces, a dialectical opposition that the mind finds itself powerless to resolve. On the one hand, thoughts, feelings, memories, urges, desires, and impulses press for recognition, acceptance, approval, enactment, and reenactment. On the other hand, views, attitudes, and moral principles oppose not only putting into action the urges, impulses, and longings that press for discharge, but even permitting their presence in conscious awareness. These urges, impulses, and longings are treated, in accordance with the views and attitudes that oppose them, as if they do not exist. This is accomplished by their being afforded no recognition in consciousness. They are allowed to exist, insofar as the conscious portion of the mind is concerned, only outside of awareness. Because they possess a strong emotional valence, however, they do not accept being squelched and repressed out of consciousness. They push for expression not only in awareness but in action. It is as if, to something within the mind, consciousness and enactment are equated, or at least closely associated. If these urges, impulses, and longings are to be given recognition in conscious awareness, it seems to be felt somewhere within, a danger would exist of advance to the next step of their being expressed in action, and this latter step is vigorously opposed.

If the individual were able to resolve this conflict one way or the other, there would be no neurosis. Either the urges and impulses, and whatever thoughts, fantasies, and memories with which they might be associated, would be permitted to enter awareness, so that conscious decisions might be made as to whether they should be put into action or not, or they would be rejected and relegated once and for all to the limbo represented by unacceptability in action and unacceptability in consciousness. Things are not always so clear-cut, however. Often—for it is the human condition to be continually in flux among inclinations and tendencies that are not necessarily compatible with one another—the opposing forces are evenly enough balanced and the capacity to weigh and decide on one direction or another is not sufficiently powerful for the person to go in either direction. It is human nature, in other words, to be, to some extent, in perpetual unconscious conflict.

What is the outcome of the struggle that is taking place within the mind and emotions of the person involved? If the struggle cannot be resolved, the only reasonable outcome is for some sort of compromise to be effected. Otherwise, the person would be split apart and at war within himself or herself. Such inner conflict would leave him or her in a greatly weakened condition that would place the person at a great disadvantage with regard to the need to cope effectively with stresses and demands that are imposed upon everyone in daily life. Such is the situation that prevails in the borderline conditions. A patient with a borderline personality disorder effects compromises that are much less effective ways of resolving the storms that rage within him or her than are those effected by a neurotic patient. The former's mental and emotional capacities, and the energies that fuel them, are so embroiled in ongoing, poorly resolved inner conflict that he or she is excessively tied up in emotional turmoil. This leaves too little available for the patient's dealing with the stresses and strains of ongoing life, let alone for effectively pursuing constructive goals and ambitions.

Despite their inner preoccupation with grappling with the forces at war within themselves and holding themselves together, borderline patients tend toward experiencing overwhelming anxiety, as they sense themselves failing to effect peace and security within themselves. They also tend toward experiencing periodic depression, as they feel themselves failing to achieve the successful management of life stresses that is necessary for them to maintain an adequate sense of self-esteem.

> A middle-age man sought consultation because, as he put it, his life was falling apart and he was finding himself unable to manage any of the major sectors of his life. He was riddled with somewhat strange and unusual phobias, was oppressed by obsessive preoccupations and indecisive doubts, was frequently so anxious that he felt like he was going to jump out of his skin, and was intermittently depressed to the point of thinking vaguely of suicide. He was paralyzed in his attempts to carry out the responsibilities of

his business and had all but abdicated in favor of his somewhat younger partner, who was beginning to complain that the patient was not pulling his share of the load. At home, he found himself continually exploding in rage, intermittently sexually impotent, and unable to deal with his teenage children, whose respect he felt he was losing. Lately, he would storm out of the house, feel perplexed and defeated, spend his time obsessing over the diet he was having difficulty maintaining, and preoccupy himself with such mundane decisions as whether to buy new shirts and ties or not. He was avoiding people more and more, out of fear of humiliating himself by exhibiting untoward behavior and verbal outbursts, and was finding himself increasingly distrustful of people.

He asked to enter analysis, but it was evident after the initial interviews that he was failing across the board to deal with the psychological struggles for which no effective solutions had been found and that, consequently, were tearing him apart and draining his energies. Also evident was that he lacked the psychological strength he needed for everyday life, let alone for contending effectively with the rigors of psychoanalysis. He accepted, although at first somewhat reluctantly, a recommendation that he enter twice-weekly psychotherapy. The main focus in the therapy was not that of open-ended exploration, although to some extent this was necessary in order to know more about the inner conflicts with which he had been unsuccessfully struggling. The central goal of treatment was that of shoring up and strengthening the psychological resources that the patient would need to negotiate between the contending forces within him and *then of helping him effect workable neurotic compromises between those forces.*

It became evident as we worked together that the patient was filled with primitive sexual and aggressive urges that he was barely able to keep in check because of failing and, therefore, weak and insufficient capacities for delay, reflection, judgment, and ability to tolerate tension and frustration. He had shaky self-esteem that was further beleaguered by the onslaught of intense self-criticism emanating from an extremely harsh, intolerant, primitively organized conscience. This interpretation was not shared with him, however, any more than was absolutely necessary to enable the patient to make more use of reflective thought to help him control his behavior and effect improved integration within himself.

Over the course of his treatment (i.e., 3½ years), the patient gradually pulled himself together, borrowed strength via identification and internalization of the approaches that were being offered to him so that he could make peace among the various forces warring within him, experienced improvement in his self-esteem, and became increasingly more active and effective in the various aspects of his daily life. He continued to be somewhat phobic and obsessive, but within tolerable bounds, at the time his treatment ended; his anxiety by then had greatly diminished, and his depression had faded away in favor of a mild sadness at his not having accomplished more with his life. He was grateful for the assistance that I had given him, but was angry that he still had some phobias and obsessions (which, now, however, seemed to be much more effective in containing and controlling his unconscious impulses without draining away his energies and resources than they had been when he first came for treatment). He had hoped to be rid of them entirely, he said, and he found himself especially unable to forgive me for not having prevented the emergence of a new phobia during the course of the treatment that had replaced some of his old ones. He now was able once again to engage actively in his business activities. However, when he took part in a business conference in which difficult problems had to be struggled over and resolved with adversaries, he had to seat himself near the door in case he became worked up and anxious. That way he could beat a hasty retreat lest he humiliate himself by exposing his agitated and anxious state.

What did the patient accomplish by constructing this new (and, to his doctor's mind, more effective) neurotic symptom of having to sit next to the door during business meetings? In the past, he had had poor success in controlling and regulating his excited, competitive, aggressive impulses despite a value system that forbade his giving in to them in an uncontrolled, uncivilized, hurtful manner, especially with his family members and his business partner. He had attempted to suppress and repress these impulses but had been increasingly unable to do so. His self-esteem had suffered; he had punished himself increasingly harshly, and he had become increasingly anxious and depressed over his failure to either control his impulses or moderate and contain the increasingly intense self-punitive attacks he was leveling against himself unconsciously and, to a limited but increasing extent, even consciously. He had been tormented with sexual and aggressive thoughts that had made him feel that he was going crazy. He had attempted to control and contain himself and to hold himself together by imposing phobic and obsessive symptoms that were vague, unelaborated, and ineffective. He had begun to become distrustful and suspicious.

During the course of his treatment, he strengthened his inner resources, effected greater integration within himself, developed somewhat more effective although limited understanding of the conflicts within him, softened the harshness of his conscience and made it a more effective ally in bringing about self-control, and became more skillful in effecting compromises between the opposing sides of his inner conflicts. The new phobia he developed is illustrative of these changes. Before treatment he had been oscillating between, on the one hand, emergence of terrifying, primitive aggressive and sexual fantasies and/or their eruption into uncontrolled behavior and, on the other, vicious self-criticism and punishment that sapped his self-esteem and made him feel helpless and demoralized, so that all he could do was avoid interaction with people and deny and project his dangerous impulses and excessively harsh self-punitive tendencies onto others. His treatment had enabled him to construct a neurotic, phobic symptom in which he effected a compromise between, on the one hand, his excited and aggressive inclinations and, on the other, his self-punitive ones. He had developed a mild phobia, which he could easily rationalize and hide from others, in which he consciously was afraid not of exploding in uncontrolled anger but only of embarrassing himself by becoming visibly anxious. The distress and displeasure he felt at still having a phobic symptom after all his efforts in psychotherapy were sufficient to satisfy the punitive demands of his now more tolerant and more humane conscience. He also could deflect some of his anger onto his doctor. It was safe to do so because he felt very positive and grateful toward his doctor for the doctor's having been helpful to him. This was an effective, neurotic compromise indeed.

This clinical case has been presented for two reasons. One is that neurotic disturbances and more serious psychological disturbances are not always easy to distinguish from each other. It is necessary to carefully evaluate the ego structure and the object relations of every patient before deciding what kind of treatment is indicated. Psycho-

analytic treatment, or at times even intensive exploratory psychotherapy, may be too strenuous for some patients with borderline
personality organization. It may therefore make their conditions
worse, even seriously so, rather than better. Also, neurotic conditions do not always occur in pure form. There are largely neurotic
patients whose personality organization contains some borderline
features. Some persons with borderline personality organization are
capable of undergoing psychoanalysis or intensive psychotherapy
so long as the borderline features are relatively mild, are clearly
identified, and are capable of being overcome via appropriate ego-
strengthening techniques (Abend et al. 1983).

In the above case, the patient was *not neurotic enough* at the time
he came for treatment. In other words, he was deficient in the
capacity to effect the kind of neurotic compromise formations that
healthier persons employ to deal with inner conflicts they cannot
readily resolve. If neurotic compromise formations are so valuable,
however, why do neurotic persons seek assistance from psychoanalysts? What impels them to do so? If neurosis is a common feature of
human life, why should someone want to be relieved of it? The
answer resides in the degree to which the neurosis is successful in
alleviating the tensions created by the state of inner conflict and the
degree to which the neurotic solution creates new tensions or imposes restrictions upon or inhibits the person's freedom of action so
as to exact too high a price for the relief from inner tension that is
obtained. What is considered normal or abnormal, healthy or indicative of disease, is subjective as well as objective.

People seek treatment for a neurosis or are directed to treatment
by others who perceive their distress or recognize that something is
interfering with their realizing their potential for one of three reasons.

1. The neurotic solutions are failing to deal adequately with the
   person's inner problems, so that he or she is chronically or intermittently observably anxious or depressed. A person in this situation could be said to be suffering from an anxiety neurosis or a
   neurotic depression.
2. The neurotic solutions that the person is employing are experienced as unpleasant, embarrassing, or intolerably restrictive.

What is being referred to here are the symptom neuroses. These take various forms, the most clearly defined of which are phobic neurosis, obsessive or compulsive neurosis, and conversion reaction. Interferences with or inhibitions of functioning such as inability to achieve orgasm, psychogenic sexual impotence, premature ejaculation, and certain types of so-called sexual perversion also fit in this group.

3. The neurotic mechanisms in operation in effecting solutions are exerting a deleterious influence upon the person's life, either by forcing him or her to play out inner conflicts, over and over, in derived form, without his or her realizing what is powering the decisions and actions being taken, or by so delimiting and restricting the range and freedom of action available to the person that the opportunities in life that might otherwise be available to the person are narrowed. A person in this situation suffers from a character neurosis, which may be phobic, obsessive, hysterical or histrionic, sadomasochistic, or mixed in type. The not uncommon "fate neurosis," in which a person unconsciously consigns himself or herself to repeated failure in punishment for objectionable aims and impulses, also fits in this category.

Human beings are complex, however, and do not often fit into a neat configuration. Anxiety attacks, fits of depression, neurotic symptoms, and characterological expression of neurotic conflicts and neurotic solutions may exist in variable combinations in a single person. Although it is much more common to encounter neurotic constellations in a mixed or impure form, it is nevertheless useful to examine each of the major neurotic configurations.

Major Neurotic Configurations

Anxiety Neurosis

In 1895, Freud introduced the term *anxiety neurosis* to differentiate a nervous syndrome—one that he felt, on clinical grounds, was caused by interference with normal, adequate sexual functioning—

from the clinical picture of *neurasthenia,* a diagnostic entity in popular use at that time. The term neurasthenia had been coined by George M. Beard, an American neurologist, to refer to a combination of generalized nervousness, ennui, weakness, exhaustion, and various somatic-related symptoms such as insomnia, dyspepsia, flatulence, constipation, rashes, headache, shortness of breath, and so on, that had been afflicting members of the upper-middle and upper social classes. He had popularized not only the diagnosis but also the indulgent, palliative cure of a trip to a spa "to take the waters" that still is utilized in Europe to this day.

Freud, again on clinical grounds, concluded that neurasthenia derived from a lifestyle of self-centered, self-indulgent dissipation of emotional energies in which masturbatory removal from mature interaction with people in the world around was a prominent feature. In his efforts to achieve meaningful diagnostic specificity, and in accordance with the limited psychological sophistication of his time, Freud detached from neurasthenia a syndrome that, it seemed to him, had a different significance and a different etiology. He was struck by a group of patients who were irritable, chronically anxious, and frightened that terrible things were about to happen. They were hypochondriacal and had episodes of overwhelming anxiety, accompanied by shortness of breath, palpitations, tremulousness, vertigo, paresthesias, nausea, vomiting, and diarrhea.

Freud at first hypothesized an etiology for this condition that involved lack of outlets for discharging sexual excitement. He observed the frequent occurrence of the above clinical picture in adolescent girls in whom sexual excitement was being aroused without the opportunity for its discharge through sexual activity, in young married women who were anorgasmic, in women whose husbands deprived them of sexual fulfillment because of severe potency problems or premature ejaculation, and in women who had lost their husbands or were menopausal. He observed this clinical picture in men with unconsummated sexual excitement, either during a period of engagement preceding marriage or because of sexual inhibition; in men who practiced coitus interruptus for the purpose of birth control; and in men who were experiencing decreased sexual potency along with increasing libido during senescence. Freud at first conjectured that dammed-up libido had become converted somehow into anxiety, but he quickly realized that the anxiety he was observing was much more likely to be an affective state of fear of the psychological danger situation into which the person was thrust by becoming sexually excited without the possibility of relieving that excitement in a satisfactory way. For a while he conceptualized this in terms of the fear of being overwhelmed by instinctual, sexual excitement. It gradually became apparent to him, however, that anxiety is *actively* generated from deep within the psychological self in response to the realization that the capacity to deal effectively with emotional demands and tensions is being stretched or exceeded. When the anxiety serves as a signal mobilizing effective action, it is highly useful and is so minimal that it might not even draw conscious attention. When effective action cannot be implemented, the level of anxiety increases and, in the absence of an effective response, can become intense and chronic.

Freud and the psychoanalytic investigators who increasingly joined him in his research became increasingly aware that not only sexual conflicts but also aggressive conflicts, conflicts involving self-image and self-esteem, and other life struggles could be involved in the development of recurrent, severe anxiety states. In other words, it gradually came to be understood that chronic or recurrent anxiety states were a result of the failure of defense mechanisms to deal adequately with emotional stress and emotional conflict.

In the case cited earlier of the patient with borderline personality who had experienced deteriorating functioning prior to treatment, the patient's symptoms would more or less fit into the category of anxiety neurosis. A number of the early cases cited by Freud would now be seen as persons with weak or borderline ego structure. The patient who came to be known as the "Man With the Wolves" or the "Wolf-Man" (Freud 1918[1914]), after a childhood dream that was investigated at length during the course of his treatment, exemplifies this observation about these early cases. This patient's functioning was severely impaired in just about all areas of his life when he came to Freud for assistance, after having seen a number of other physicians who had not been able to help him. Although his treatment with Freud led to some remarkable improvements in his functioning, he continued to be extremely self-centered and limited in his ability to overcome the effects of losing the fortune that had protected him from the necessity of making his own way in the world. He settled into a relatively low-level occupation that was far beneath his intellectual abilities and educational background. He was extremely dependent upon the doting care of his wife and upon the largesse of the psychoanalytic community; at one point, when his sense of security was threatened by the discovery of serious illness in Freud, his benefactor, he developed an acute paranoid disorder.

The following is an example of a person with what might well be characterized today as an anxiety neurosis:

A man in his mid-30s came for analysis because of dissatisfaction with the way his life was going. He was chronically anxious and filled with continual dread that something terrible was going to happen to him. He identified himself as a "hypochondriac." Obsessed with his appearance and with his health, he watched vigilantly for signs of possible serious illness. He avoided black cats, maneuvered anxiously through every Friday the 13th on guard against some terrible fate befalling him, and so on. He periodically experienced sudden anxiety attacks. At times they were connected with driving through tunnels (which also was a common dream theme), but at other times they seemed to have no rhyme or reason. He had a number of casual friends but was extremely cautious in his relationships with women. He dreaded either being betrayed and abandoned or being ensnared and trapped. An indefinable sense of danger was associated with the idea of his entering into a long-term commitment to a woman. Despite his preoccupation with his health, he spent many of his evenings in bars, counterphobically drinking far too much and excitedly pursuing women with whom he entered into very short-lived relationships.

In the analysis, oedipal themes and indications of extreme castration anxiety quickly emerged. The patient still lived at home with his mother and could only relate on an ongoing basis with women who were distant and unattainable or whom he disliked or distrusted. In his business activities, he was preoccupied with maintaining equipment in tiptop shape and was unable to tolerate the slightest defects in or malfunctioning of that equipment. His father had died a number of years earlier, after a long illness, and the patient lived in mortal terror of dying of the same affliction. His family medical history did not reassure him in this regard. Behind this terror, however, as it gradually became clear, were a self-centered preoccupation with whether he was being cared for and provided for adequately, shallow object relations, and a hungry but distrustful yearning to be filled with whatever it might take to dispel his pervasive feelings of loneliness and emptiness. He yearned wistfully for an older woman who would take care of him and both tenderly and skillfully meet his needs.

In the analytic sessions, it gradually became apparent that the patient looked to the analyst to perceive, appreciate, and relieve his distress without his having to verbally communicate what he was feeling and thinking. There were long silences, which came across at times like fulfillments of the fantasy of blissful, peaceful union and at other times like peremptory flight from being overwhelmed by the tensions and the strain that were experienced in the course of examining and reflecting upon his inner struggles and conflicts. The degree to which he appeared to use his analyst as an object of oedipal transference was far outweighed by the extent to which he cast the analyst in the role of an idealized, powerful parent who would protect him and take perfect, even magical, care of him. At times, the patient even seemed, during the early years of the analysis, to experience his analyst as an idealized extension of himself rather than as a separate person. An affectionate, idealized father-transference developed, in which the wished-for father seemed to possess the qualities of a "better mother" to a significant extent. The patient's continual worries about not only his own health but also his analyst's made him very cautious, however, about giving up excessive drinking, the decision about which was under his control, in favor of turning to psychoanalytic exploration leading to personal change as a more constructive way of dealing with his needs and solving his problems.

In response to a caring, interested approach on the part of his analyst that focused interpretatively upon the patient's loneliness, sadness, chronic rage, and intense longing for care and nurturance, the patient made significant strides in the various dimensions of his life. He began to limit his alcohol intake, and, for a while, he gave up spending his evenings drinking in bars and instead began to frequent sushi bars. He consumed what he described as endless quantities of delectable, pink, raw fish wrapped delicately around pure white rice that were served proudly and lovingly by the dedicated, devoted craftsmen on the other side of the counter. He associatively connected this new interest with his voracious yearning to "cannibalistically" ingest loving breasts to make them an integral, ever-available care-providing part of him, even though he feared that once inside him they might destroy him. From fragments of early memories, it was possible to reconstruct an erratic, unpredictable childhood in which his mother, who had serious emotional problems of her own, had turned him over to the care of maids, whom he recalled as cold, hard, unreliable, and punitive. His father, an anxious, intermittently explosive, tense, demanding man, had been too preoccupied with his business and his health problems to have been consistently available to his son either as an empathic, loving parent or as a model for how one deals effectively and calmly with the stresses and strains of life.

It became clear that the patient had not had the kind of early, formative experiences that might have helped him build an effective, well-integrated, reasonably content and confident ego core with which to deal with frustration, tension, conflict, disappointment, and all the other myriad stresses that are an expectable part of life. He had not developed a strong, positive, loving sense of his own self, nor had he been enabled to acquire a view of others as exciting, interesting, potentially trustworthy and giving beings toward whom it is worthwhile directing love and risking hate. He had arrived at oedipal, rivalrous configurations that were primitive, distorted, and so fraught with terror of loss, horrendous retaliation, murder, and mayhem, and with such debilitating shame and guilt, that it was impossible not only to resolve oedipal conflicts but even to remain at that level of functioning.

It took a great deal of slow, painstaking psychoanalytic work before the patient was able to enter into more intensive, meaningful, trusting, and risk-taking relationships, especially with women. The hypochondriacal tendencies and the general anxiousness gradually diminished. The anxiety attacks became less and less frequent and increasingly less severe. The patient became increasingly capable of dealing with the external stresses that he encountered in his life and then more and more confident about his capacity to deal with his inner impulses, conflicts, and uncertainties. Oedipal anxieties became more and more accessible to analytic scrutiny, so that he could wrestle with and work at resolving them. Superego functioning became progressively more mature, so that the burden of shame and guilt he carried with him became more reasonable and, therefore, more manageable. In all of this, it was apparent that he was using his psychoanalytic treatment not only to recognize, explore, and resolve his neurotic conflicts but, to an at least equally important extent, to slowly but inexorably build the ego capacities that he had not sufficiently developed during his formative years in childhood but that he needed if he were to become able to grapple with those conflicts. It should be evident that borderline features in this patient's personality organization required close attention in the treatment process.

Phobic Neurosis

The phobic neurosis stands in meaningful contrast to the anxiety neurosis, although at first glance they may resemble each other. A person with a phobic neurosis also complains of anxiety, but the anxiety is more focused, contained, delimited, and attached to specific situations that can be avoided or that contain elements that reduce or control the anxiety. The overall ego strength and level of psychological functioning observable in a person with a phobic neurosis are considerably greater than those that are characteristic of the patient who presents with an anxiety neurosis. The symptoms tend to be more clearly defined and to have been created by a set of interlocking defense mechanisms that together form a unified whole. The amount of emotional energy and psychological work tied up in maintaining the defensive activity may drain the person's resources to such an extent that his or her level of success in life is impaired. The phobic restrictions placed on the person's freedom and range of activity may interfere so much with daily life that too great a price is exacted for the relief from inner turmoil that the phobic maneuvers afford. However, the neurotic picture reflects defensive strength rather than defensive weakness.

The technical problems entailed in the psychoanalytic treatment of a person with a phobic neurosis are very different from those encountered in the treatment of a person with an anxiety neurosis. With the patient with a phobic neurosis, the goals, in addition to symptom relief, are different in that replacement of constrictive and restrictive defensive avoidance by higher, more mature, more reflective forms of dealing with emotional conflict and life problems is of central importance. The psychoanalyst seeks to help a patient who comes for assistance in overcoming a phobic neurosis to do even more than that. The analyst is aware that giving up the phobic mechanisms will enable the patient to free up resources that can then be made available for use in realizing potentials that have not been realizable because the resources needed for attaining them have been tied up elsewhere. In fact, facilitation of emotional growth and development is an even more important goal in working with persons with well-organized neurotic constellations than is removal of symptoms.

The primary defense mechanism in phobic neurosis is *repression,* which shuts offending mental contents off from conscious awareness. It is as though what one does not consciously know does not exist. Because looking away from impulses, urges, desires, and emotional conflicts does not actually make them disappear, and because they continue unconsciously to exert pressure toward actualization, additional mechanisms are brought to bear to maintain and reinforce the repression. The mental contents are projected outward, or *externalized,* and are reconnected to external situations or objects that lend themselves to this purpose via associative or symbolic links that facilitate such substitution. Through this mechanism, known as *displacement,* it now becomes possible not only to keep the troubling mental contents out of awareness but also to keep oneself away from the situations or objects onto which the troubling mental contents have been displaced. One cannot get away from one's own inner thoughts and feelings, but one can stay away from that which has been made to represent those thoughts and feelings in the outer world.

An additional mechanism that is utilized is *regression,* in that developmentally earlier forms and contents frequently are substituted for the oedipal conflicts and issues that usually constitute the main focus of the inner sense of danger that mobilizes the defensive ego activity. Regression is evident in another way as well, in that phobic behavior often renders the phobic person less independent and more reliant upon outside care and assistance. Counterphobic measures may also be employed both as an expression of the existence of countervailing wishes toward what is being avoided in the phobic system and as an expression of one's unwillingness to accept the blow to one's pride that goes with backing off out of fear. These measures are accompanied by denial or negation of the anxiety that is secretly being experienced, and the denial impels some phobic persons toward the very places, things, or activities of which they have become phobic. In instituting these mechanisms, persons may be following their own temperamental inclinations (e.g., some persons are from very early on shy, hesitant, and cautious, whereas others actively seek excitement and stimulation); responding to chance experiences and opportunities; or following models presented to them by parents and other significant persons in their lives. Or they may be guided by a combination of these various factors.

In 1909, Freud reported on a case of a nearly 5-year-old boy who suddenly developed an intense fear of horses that was so great that he could not even leave his home to go out onto the street lest he see one. The boy's father, who had become interested in the new science of psychoanalysis, set out, with consultative assistance from Freud, to help his son figure out where his phobia had come from and to help him free himself from it. Although the brief "psychoanalytic" treatment that was carried out can be faulted for a number of reasons (which, of course, in a sense would be unfair because it was the first child analysis ever conducted and was therefore highly experimental in nature), it not only enabled the boy to overcome the phobia but also revealed so much about the origin of phobic disorders that it was of inestimable heuristic value. What came to light was that Little Hans, as he came to be known, had repressed, denied, projected out of himself, displaced, and reconnected the ambivalent feelings toward his father, his mother, and his baby sister that had been mobilized within him by his mother's recent pregnancy and delivery.

Little Hans loved his mother fiercely and did not want to share her with anyone. He had been feeling sexually aroused and increasingly curious about the sexual goings-on that were connected with the pregnancy. He also was extremely competitive not only with his father for being able to engage in sexual intimacies with his mother and present her with a baby, but also with his mother for being able to grow a baby within her body and give birth to and nurse her, and with his baby sister for all the special attention she received after her birth. He harbored intensely hostile feelings toward all three of them, but because he also loved them, he acquired a moral aversion to the angry, hurtful fantasies he was entertaining and self-punitively feared terrible retaliation in kind for what he felt like doing. He was thrust into intense, unbearable, unresolvable emotional conflict. Unable, at his tender age and stage of life, to resolve his conflict, he repressed and denied his feelings and fantasies and projected them outwardly, attaching them to horses, who themselves had excited his curiosity and envious admiration (especially, in the case of male horses, for the size of their genitals), his sadistic impulses, and his compassion for their being beaten with whips and their falling down and being hurt. He gradually discovered, with the help of his father and Professor Freud, that he had transferred onto the horses what he had been feeling about his parents, baby sister, and the pregnancy. The brief "analysis" cured him of his phobia. The report written up by Freud is still fascinating to read (Freud 1909a).

The understanding gained into Little Hans's phobia, occurring as it did in the very early days of the development of psychoanalysis and thus being necessarily incomplete, is remarkable nevertheless. In addition to the oedipal conflicts that were uncovered in the course of the analytic investigation that was carried out, as we have come to understand, there most probably were additional traumatic and preoedipal factors involved in the generation of the phobic symptomatology. Hans's parents were undergoing severe marital problems, for example, and Hans had just undergone a tonsillectomy. He had been exposed to parental nudity, and his mother had been rather seductive and teasing with him. There were indications too of some probable earlier (in part predisposing?) problems and conflicts involving oral- and sadistic-anal–level matters and of indications of apparent separation-individuation struggles (Silverman 1980). We have learned a great deal, in fact, since the time of the Little Hans case about the ways in which preoedipal developmental issues and conflicts contribute to the disposition to and the form and shape of the later oedipal conflicts that occupy a prominent position in the generation of later, neurotic symptomatology.

A more modern example of a phobic neurosis in an adult is in order:

> A young woman came for psychoanalysis on referral from another psychoanalyst whom she had consulted after developing an acute driving phobia that severely restricted her freedom of travel. She had become angry at a friend who also was a rival of hers in several ways, but had not been able to speak to her about it. The next day, while driving her car with her mother in the passenger seat next to her, she became annoyed at something her mother said. She became anxious and was afraid that she might lose control of the car. A driving phobia quickly developed.
>
> At first, she said, she had been angered by the consulting psychoanalyst's recommendation that she enter analysis. After all, she had developed a phobia, of a different type, a few years earlier and had gotten over it through her own force of will without professional help. A few years before that, she had had yet another phobia that she had overcome on her own. And as a youngster and then as an adolescent, she had had some phobic episodes from which she also had recovered. Then, on reflection, she said that she had realized why the consulting psychoanalyst had recommended psychoanalysis. Something within her was periodically generating phobic reactions, and she would have to do something about it or she probably would continue to be plagued with phobias from time to time.
>
> With this insight she entered into psychoanalysis. An erotic transference developed, which eventually came to be understood as the recapitulation of an oedipal situation she had gone through early in her life. What she experienced in the analysis became increasingly comprehensible in terms of childhood experiences in which she had felt angry at her mother for multiple reasons. She had felt that her mother did not treat her father properly and that, as she ultimately remembered feeling, she would have made a better wife to her father. A key experience had occurred when she was 4 years old. For a period of time, because of an acute housing shortage, she shared a room somewhere with her father while her mother and her newborn baby sister lived elsewhere. She had exciting times with her father there. She remembered his reading her bedtime stories (involving a cowboy hero upon whom she had a girlish crush), after which he would leave to play cards with his friends—or, she thought, was it to go and spend time with her mother? Her feelings about her father's exciting her and leaving

her were reenacted in the transference in the form of anger and jealousy at her having to share her psychoanalyst not only with other patients but even with a wife and children. His house reminded her of the one where she and her father had stayed after the birth of her sister.

Largely through the analysis of transference resistances, in which displacements to other people in her life played a prominent part, she and her psychoanalyst came to see that the patient's life was organized by a complex system of checks and balances through which she sought to maintain control of the people with whom she was involved in significant relationships and, ultimately, of her own highly ambivalent and conflicted feelings toward them. It was when circumstances threatened her ability to feel confident about maintaining self-control that phobic reactions occurred.

With regard to the incident that had taken place when she was 4 years old, the patient and analyst came to understand, through a series of transference enactments that they were able to explore together, that the patient's having as a young child shared a bedroom with her father had heightened her fantasies of replacing her mother as the object of her father's love, although this was a problem because it meant losing her mother. Then it became apparent that she had become enraged at her father, despite her love for him, for heightening her fantasies of taking her mother's place but then leaving her to be with his friends and, what was even more infuriating, to be with her mother. Over the course of the analysis, she came to understand that there had been both realistic and unrealistic determinants both of her excitement and of her rage. Then it emerged that she also had been extremely jealous that her father had given her mother a baby, as a product of their love, while she had only been treated as a little girl. Finally, as she and her psychoanalyst discovered together, she had been extremely hurt and angry that her mother had chosen to be with her baby sister and had sent her off to be with her father.

Her relationship, past and present, with her mother, a dominating, controlling, possessive, and at times even cruel and sadistic person, whom she loved, hated, feared, but also accepted as a protective and direction-giving force, became an important focus. The patient became more independent of her mother, internally as well as externally, and assumed more and more responsibility for her actions, her decisions, and the moral principles by which she led her life. She overcame an inhibition that had been blocking her from pursuing the further education she had long wanted en route to embarking on a career, and eventually went on to establish that career. The analysis not only enabled her to overcome her phobias and her phobic tendencies but also facilitated her development into a more mature, effectively assertive, happy, and productive woman.

Obsessional Neurosis

The patient with an obsessional neurosis, like the patient with a phobic neurosis, is concerned with self-control but uses a different constellation of defense mechanisms. Here, too, repression is a primary feature, but mental conflicts are not necessarily so thoroughly and extensively excluded from consciousness as they are in a phobic neurosis because of two related factors. First, persons who develop an obsessional neurosis use thinking itself in a defensive manner. The power of rational thought is utilized not only in its own right as a source of strength in dealing with the tasks and problems with which they are confronted in life, but also as a means by which unruly, irrational urges and impulses can be studied, understood, contained, rationalized, restrained, and controlled. It is as though the admonition to stop and think in order to control oneself is taken extremely literally and seriously. Rather than being projected outwardly to an external locale that can then be avoided, unwanted impulses and fantasies are kept in the mind, where intellectual powers can be applied in order to ride herd on them and keep them under careful scrutiny. The unwanted impulses and fantasies are localized and compartmentalized through the use of intensely focused attention and concentration; in this way, they are essentially surrounded and cut off from other contents and thus reduced individually to a size and extent that renders them manageable.

Second, thoughts and impulses are isolated not only from one another but, very importantly, from the affective charge that threatens to empower them with the capacity to press for active expression and implementation. It is the affect, the feeling, that is most prominently repressed and suppressed. Repression of the affect provides a sense of control over dangerous sexual and aggressive impulses and urges by drying up and defueling the thoughts that derive from and give them shape and form. Sexual and aggressive impulses and urges are thereby reduced to "seemingly" empty thoughts that exist without a dangerous emotional charge. At times, even very raw and primitive thoughts thus isolated from the emotional investment that would make them too offensive, indelicate, or horrible to be contemplated openly can be allowed by the person with an obsessional neurosis to enter consciousness since they appear to be "only thoughts."

That the thoughts which are permitted to enter into awareness actually do have motive force, despite their seemingly having been stripped of it, is attested to by the intensity with which intellectual energies have to be devoted to keeping them under control. The person with an obsessional neurosis *must* think about certain things, *must* go back over certain mental contents over and over, and *must* dwell seriously, repetitively, and intensely on trains of thought that he or she *cannot* put aside or put out of his or her mind even though he or she may feel plagued or tormented by them. The obsessional mentation not infrequently is associated as well, in fact, by seemingly meaningless, silly, incomprehensible compulsive acts that have to be carried out or else intolerable feelings of guilt or anxiety are experienced. The term "obsessive-compulsive neurosis" is often used interchangeably with the term "obsessional neurosis."

A 16-year-old girl was brought for treatment because her parents were concerned with how serious and how hard on herself she was, always driving herself to be good and to do well in everything she undertook. She was bright, pretty, popular, and a good athlete, but she did not seem to be able to relax and enjoy the life that should have been so wonderful for her. Every time she looked at herself in the mirror, she criticized herself. Her hair was not right or her face was not the way it should have been. There were some slight blemishes on her face from a childhood illness, and she could not forgive herself for having caused them by scratching when she was ill. She said, "I can get very down on myself— meanly." And she would never forgive the boy who had made a critical remark to her about those facial blemishes when she was in the sixth grade. She would never want to hurt anyone, she said, not even him, but she *hated* him. She had always been very sensitive and easily hurt, and he had hurt her terribly. She could not even repeat the words he had said.

She had had a dream once, she said, back when she was 8 or 9 years old, that she still thought about anytime anyone mentioned dreams. In the dream she was in a library and President Kennedy was sitting there. Someone from a television show that she liked to watch (one about a girl in a family that was confronted with hard times during which everyone pulled together and loved one another) came in with guns and told everyone to lie on the floor. Everyone lay down except President Kennedy, and they shot him. "That's the way he died?" she asked, with a puzzled look on her face. Then there was a hill and everyone had to run down it.

She recalled another scary time at night. She was sleeping with a stuffed elephant that she had borrowed from someone, and when she awoke, the elephant looked to her like Darth Vader. She must have imagined it she said—or perhaps she had been dreaming then too. This occurred when she was 7 or 8, not long after she had had the childhood illness that had left those blemishes on her face. She never slept with that elephant again.

One of the things that troubled her was that she had "compulsions." Although she knew that it was "stupid"—"just superstitions"—she said, "There are certain things I have to do and I feel if I don't do them, something bad is going to happen." She had to look under her bed at night and couldn't listen to the radio in the morning. This began when she turned 13. Before that, there had been other compulsions. Back when she was in the third grade or so, she had had to put her finger through a hole in the wicker headboard of her bed every night until she "got it through without touching." Otherwise, she could not go to sleep. Even now, she said, she has to turn the radio on and blink three times at night or she cannot sleep. After her dog died, she "had to" talk to her every night or else she would feel that she was betraying her. Before she could agree to their getting a new dog, she had to obtain a "sign" (lightning during a thunderstorm) that her old dog did not object. Otherwise she would have been tormented with guilt and would not have been able to forgive herself. She was so hard on herself, she explained, in order to keep from doing wrong.

The other major element that regularly takes part in obsessional neurosis is developmental regression. Persons with an obsessional neurosis have an excessively harsh but immature conscience that torments and punishes them via the tormenting, obsessional rituals that at the same time serve to impose control over the impulses these persons are struggling violently to resist. As is illustrated in the obsessive-compulsive symptomatology that plagued the 16-year-old whom I have just described, persons who develop obsessional neuroses have undergone reasonably good ego development and have proceeded in their emotional development to an oedipal level of sexual and aggressive organization, with intact, meaningful object relations that have true depth. Obsessional neurosis represents an extreme, exaggerated form of the regressive retreat from oedipal conflicts to a sadistic-anal organization carried out more or less by all children as they pass into "latency." Obsessional persons regress from oedipal, competitive, rivalrous, masturbatory conflicts into a sadistic-anal organization in which control, self-control, the maintenance of order, the following of rules, punishments and self-punishments, infliction of pain and suffering, the warding off of even worse punishments, and preoccupation with being good and doing the right thing are ruling concerns. Intense ambivalence that is once removed from oedipal ambivalence characterizes this emotional organization. Persons with obsessional neuroses struggle to keep hostile and loving feelings, hurtful and compassionate attitudes, and unacceptably bad and self-esteem–building good feelings and inclinations in balance. They are continually doing and undoing, committing unconscious mental crimes and then either canceling them out or making up for them through compassionate thoughts and acts. They are continually expiating the guilt through self-punishments and acts of penance.

The 16-year-old girl's early compulsive ritual of putting her finger through the hole in her headboard over and over until she could do it "without touching" exemplifies the struggle over masturbatory impulses that torments the person with an obsessional neurosis. The obsessions and compulsive rituals simultaneously represent a masturbatory equivalent, a prohibition against the act of masturbation and the fantasies that accompany it, and self-punishment to atone for it. The 16-year-old girl could not be satisfied with obsessive-compulsive symptoms to control her masturbatory urges.

She extended and generalized them into a characterological preoccupation with controlling herself from being bad and hurtful and with being a good girl who never did anything wrong.

This patient's case also illustrates something else that is frequently encountered in persons with obsessional neuroses. At first, she denied ever having had phobic tendencies, other than the isolated incident of the nocturnal anxiety about the borrowed elephant she had slept with, following which she had returned the elephant and made sure never to borrow it again. It gradually came out, however, that she was indeed phobic in certain ways, although the phobic manifestations did not concern her as much as the obsessive-compulsive ones. She was afraid of needles, for example, and was afraid whenever she walked home from school alone, especially as she neared a spot where she and a girlfriend had once seen a homeless man sitting on a bench and looking at them. The nervousness was associated vaguely with fears of being kidnapped. When a person with an obsessional neurosis begins to feel that the obsessional mechanisms do not suffice to control and contain the dreaded and forbidden impulses and urges they are designed to deal with, and when the regressive flight from oedipal concerns is being undone by developmental (e.g., the advent of puberty in the obsessional teenager referred to above) or by environmental stimulation, the person not infrequently experiences an augmentation of phobic mechanisms. Neurotic constellations are not often encountered in pure form, and the "phobic-obsessional neurosis" is far from rare.

When obsessional neurotic symptomatology is present in adults, it more often expresses itself as obsessional character traits than as frank symptoms.

> A man came for analysis because of a number of complaints involving his relationships with women, toward whom he was controlling, dominating, enslaving, often depriving, and even cruel. Although he needed and wanted relationships with women, he could not commit himself to any one woman. The women who most attracted him were the ones who were hard to get or, especially, the ones who were already involved with someone else. It readily became apparent that he had retreated from oedipal conflicts to a preoedipal interaction with women in which power and

control had become the central surface issues. He was an efficient, organized, intelligent, capable man who applied himself to the analytic work the way he applied himself to tasks in general. Everything seemed to go swimmingly in the analysis. He associated freely and exploratively. He remembered his dreams and used them to look into himself. He developed insights into himself that were impressive. But nothing much happened. The insights were indeed aimed in large measure at impressing the psychoanalyst, just as he had always used his intellectual gifts to impress people and demonstrate his superiority over them.

Despite all the knowledge the patient had been gaining about himself, nothing much changed, because the knowledge was intellectual. He did not *feel* what he was saying. He thought that what the analyst pointed out to him sounded right, but he did not *feel* it. When the transference aspects and resistance aspects of what he was enacting with his psychoanalyst were called to his attention, he gradually began to recognize that, without realizing it, he had been engaging in a power struggle with the analyst. The psychoanalyst could not *make* him do anything—even if he himself wanted to do it. He was able to trace this back to important aspects of his relationship with his mother while he was growing up, oedipally as well as preoedipally; but again this realization had little impact until he and his analyst were able to deal with the isolation of affect by which he divested what he was saying of real meaning. While growing up the patient had *had* to put up with certain things, but he had found that he could prevent them from *really* getting to him by not feeling the impact of what was taking place.

As a child, during his early school years, the patient had had a number of bedtime rituals that he had to carry out each night. He had to get into bed in a certain way, repeat it a certain number of times, turn the lights on and off a prescribed number of times, repeat certain things to himself over and over in his mind, and so on. In the present, he puzzled over what the rituals had been about and over what had happened to whatever had been behind them. It was only after a considerable amount of work that he realized that there was a connection between those childhood symptoms and something that plagued him in the present. He would wake up every morning, for days or weeks at a time, thinking about someone who had wronged or insulted him, or who owed him money and had not yet paid him. He would carry on long, angry arguments with the person or plan out complicated acts of revenge to get even with him or her. Try as he might, he could not stop these trains of obligatory thought; he could not shake these thoughts off. They were irresistible and compulsive, as the bedtime rituals had been back in his childhood. The need to control masturbatory as well as hostile impulses turned out to be involved. They did not seem to occur, for example, during times when his sex life was reasonably satisfactory.

Freud, in 1909, the same year in which he published the case of Little Hans, also published another long case history, about a lawyer in his late 20s who had been suffering from obsessions since childhood (Freud 1909b). The obsessional symptoms had grown worse over the preceding 4 years. Recently, there had arisen a particularly intense and distressing obsession involving a young woman whom he admired and his father, whom he had loved. The obsession was extremely abhorrent, because it involved a worry that rats would bore their way into these persons' anuses. It was even more nonsensical in that his father had been dead for 9 years. The son had not been present when his father died, a fact about which he had not ceased feeling guilty. The guilt turned out to have been connected with a thought he had had at the age of 12 years: that if his father died, he would become rich enough to marry a girl he loved. At the time the lawyer consulted Freud he was once again in a situation in which he was thinking about marrying a girl he loved. He also was now in a position similar to that of his father before his father's own marriage. From the age of 7 years, the patient had felt that his parents could read his thoughts. In addition to the obsessions, he also had a recurrent compulsive impulse: to cut his own throat with a razor. He became confusedly and rather strangely obsessed in the course of the treatment with making a payment of some money he owed someone for a pair of glasses he had ordered.

The analysis with Freud, which lasted nearly a year, freed the young man from his tormenting obsessions sufficiently enough to enable him to go on with his life. Unfortunately, he was killed in the war that broke out a few years later. In the course of the treatment, he and Freud worked out multiple significations of the obsessions that had resided in the patient's unconscious mind. These significations centered on sexual oedipal conflicts that had been regressively reworked into sadistic-anal terms. The patient and his father had had many conflicts involving money, and the patient was intensely conflicted between his longing for the moneyless girl who had captured his heart and, concomitantly, his inclination to carry out his father's wish that he follow his father's own lead by marrying a certain attractive, rich, well-connected young woman toward whom his father had directed him. Freud postulated that early in the patient's life, the patient's father had severely chastised him for masturbating, which had both made him angry at his father and contributed to the feeling that he was not permitted to realize sexual satisfaction. His mother had told him that as a child he had been punished for biting someone. He also had as a child suffered for years with intestinal worms that had caused him continual irritation. There had been allusions at one time to a charge of dishonesty against his father involving money. Unconsciously, rats and money had become associated with each other through the words *Rate,* which is German for "installment payment," and *Rattus,* which is the genus that includes the rat. (Freud apparently overlooked the fact that the patient knew that Freud's first office was not at 19 Berggasse but at 7 Rathausstrasse, with its transferential implications [Weiss 1980].)

We have learned a great deal about obsessional neuroses and about neuroses in general since the time of Freud's treatment of the "Rat Man." However, the account written up by Freud is still intriguing and edifying. Much can, of course, be added to Freud's grasp of the case at the time of his reporting upon it. Freud had a very skimpy understanding of the significance of aggressive inclinations in the developmental process, for example, and we have gained additional knowledge about this patient and his early experiences since then. From some of Freud's working notes that have remained preserved, we learn that the Rat Man had an undescended testicle that never had come down, which troubled him considerably. There are suggestions in the notes that the patient might have experienced periodic retraction of the other testicle up into the inguinal canal, something that is anxiety-provoking to boys, which may have contributed to his obsessive preoccupation with rats going up into people's anuses. It also has come to light that the patient's father had told him when he was a boy about something called the "Nuremberg funnel torture," in which rats were allowed to enter a prisoner's anus, that formed the basis of his obsession of a rat boring into an anus. The patient also had had a number of traumatic experiences as a child, including the death of his older sister when he was between 3 and 4 years of age, years of sleeping in his parents' bedroom, and a number of experiences with seductive young governesses (Weiss 1980).

There remains some uncertainty about the accuracy of Freud's diagnosis of obsessional neurosis in the Rat Man case. Like a number of other early psychoanalytic patients, Freud's patient may have been a borderline individual who, in his case, made desperate use of obsessive mechanisms to establish control over a crumbling mental equilibrium and stave off a threatened psychotic deterioration. It is still incumbent upon the diagnostician to distinguish between true obsessional neurosis, for which psychoanalysis is appropriate, and borderline or ambulatory psychosis in which rigid, at times frantic, obsessive maneuvers are resorted to in order to stave off something worse. There also are indications that some "obsessive-compulsive" persons actually are using those mechanisms to exert control over the organic interferences with motor control that stem from a subacute case of Tourette's disorder or a related neurological disturbance. The differential diagnosis of obsessive-compulsive neurosis is a complex area, in which a difficult diagnostic dilemma may be encountered.

Conversion Neurosis (Conversion Hysteria)

The subject of conversion neurosis has already been covered in the section on early investigations of hysteria with which I opened this chapter. We are not likely at this time to come upon dramatic instances of more or less predominant conversion neurosis like the ones that captured Freud's attention in the late 1890s and early 1900s. This is partly because patients with isolated conversion reactions are still likely to present themselves to neurologists (or to internists) rather than to psychiatrists or psychoanalysts, and partly because conversion reactions tend, most of the time, to coexist with other psychological symptoms and because hysterical phenomena tend more often to express themselves characterologically rather than in the form of symptom neuroses. Nevertheless, we do come upon such instances from time to time:

> A young man sought treatment because of a severe and steadily worsening wry neck. His head was being pulled more and more around to the left by muscles that already were becoming hypertrophied. In a course of treatment that was relatively brief (less than a year), it became possible, via an intermediate set of thoughts involving the biblical story of Lot's wife, who was turned to a pillar of salt for disobeying the injunction not to look back upon the sinful city of Sodom that she had just left, to trace the wry neck to its psychological origins. The patient had left home, very far away, it turned out, because of the need to get away from his very attractive sister. A series of associatively linked thoughts and memories led to a key, unconscious recollection. He and his sister, when they were children, had taken off their clothes in order to examine each other's bodies. Suddenly, their father came in unexpectedly. The patient's father became furious at him and excoriated him for what he and his sister had been doing. "If I ever catch you doing that again," his father said, "I'll . . ." The patient could not remember the rest of his father's words. Inquiry about the patient's father led to the patient's recollection that part of his father's work activities involved the gelding of farm animals. When another memory was retrieved of his father's becoming angry when he caught his son masturbating as a young boy, it became possible to reconstruct his father's having threatened or at least seemingly having threatened to castrate him, as he did so often with animals. With this reconstruction the wry neck cleared up. It is significant that the patient had been thinking of giving up his current job and returning home at the time the symptom developed.

> An equally dramatic instance of a conversion reaction involved the father of a child in treatment. The child had been growing increasingly fond of her therapist and had been glowing more and more over the attention she was receiving and the care she was getting from him. Her father, who had had a very deprived, emotionally impoverished childhood and now was working hard to provide his wife and children with some of what he had not been fortunate enough to receive as a child, was very aware of his little child's

positive reaction to the therapist and to her treatment. One day, the child's doctor received a call from her father, who informed the therapist that he had had an acute, extremely painful flareup of an old ulcer condition that had healed years earlier. He was in the hospital, to be operated on the next morning. The therapist visited him in the hospital, where the therapist learned that, although no clear-cut evidence of an active ulcer had been found radiographically, he had been scheduled for a partial gastric resection. Speaking with him convinced the therapist that he did not have an ulcer, but rather had identified with his child in his jealousy, envy, and longing to receive the kind of care and attention the child was receiving. When this impression was shared with him, he erupted in fury. What right did the therapist have to form such an opinion about him, he asked. His child was the therapist's patient, not he. The therapist had no business meddling in *his* life. He ordered the therapist out of his room. The next morning the therapist was awakened by a call from his patient's father. He had been furious at the therapist the previous evening, he said, but then had thought about what the therapist had told him and had to admit that he, the therapist, had been right. His "ulcer" symptoms had disappeared, and he had just signed himself out of the hospital. "There are a couple of surgeons," he said, "who are very angry at you." The ulcerlike symptoms did not recur at any time during the several years in which the therapist had an opportunity to be in touch with him.

Depressive Neurosis

Patients who come for treatment because of a depressive neurosis form a mixed group. Very many are in significant ways similar to patients with an anxiety neurosis, in that their neurotic coping strategies have been relatively unsuccessful in dealing with the stresses and inner conflicts with which these persons have been struggling. They are discouraged, overwhelmed, down on themselves, in the process of giving up the struggle, and feeling defeated. They tend to be guilt-ridden, masochistic, depleted, and/or greatly diminished and undercut in their self-esteem and self-image. Behind the more obvious proximate causes of this condition are old, unconscious causes that are both primary and, in important ways, predisposing influences that have contributed to these patients' having gotten into their current, difficult life situations.

A 40-year-old woman entered analysis after her marriage had broken up. She not only felt rejected, abandoned, alone, and lonely, but also was concerned that she probably had contributed in an integral way to her husband's having come to the decision to end their marriage. For years, she had criticized him and complained about the way he had taken care of her and her needs. She had periodically raised the possibility of a divorce, but this time he agreed rather than trying to talk her out of it. She had told him repeatedly, "I don't know if I love you." Indeed, she had not felt at the time of their marriage that she loved him, but had married him because he loved her and because he fit the picture her parents had presented to her of the kind of man they thought she should marry.

She had always tried to please her parents, although she rarely felt successful at it. She sadly recalled that, rather than doting on her for marrying the kind of man of whom he approved, her father would dismiss her and spend what seemed like hours talking to her husband in the early years after their marriage. She had never been able to capture her father's attention. He had never seemed to regard women very highly and did not seem to respect them. He was always flirting with other women, and he dominated and at times mistreated her mother, who most often took it without protest. Her mother did fight with him at times about his behavior, however, and once, she left him briefly after a huge and dramatic quarrel.

Her mother seemed to be preoccupied with looking after her father's needs. The patient recalled repeated incidents when her mother played with her when she was a little girl, only to get up and leave, saying "Your father needs me," just as the daughter was becoming exhilarated and excited in the interaction with her mother. Eventually, it was possible to point out to her that her mother apparently had been unable to tolerate her daughter's excitement. She had been unable to tolerate disorder or agitation of any kind, in fact; she had "toilet trained" her daughter when her daughter was only 5 months old. How could such utter domination so prematurely in her life foster a true capacity for self-control? The patient remembered, as a very little girl, playing a cruel game with her grandmother. She would beckon to her grandmother, saying, "C'mere, gamma." When her grandmother would approach her smilingly, she would say, bitingly, "Go 'way, gamma." Maybe that's what she had done with her husband, she wondered. Maybe she had teased him and pushed him away. She did tend to be critical and demeaning toward him. She just couldn't control herself.

Self-control was a problem for the patient in a number of ways, one of which involved letting go and giving up control so as to allow herself to experience orgasm. She had long been aware of ambivalent feelings about being female. She connected this with the belief that her father would have liked her more had she been a boy and with her resentment of her father's attitudes toward women. She was disappointed in her mother for her having given up her career plans to wait on her father as his pretty, painted doll. She complained about her mother's having both blocked access to and pushed her toward her father. Through analysis of the patient's continual complaining that her analyst did not do enough to meet her needs and take care of her as she needed while, at the same time, she repeatedly warded off closeness to him, she and her analyst traced her negative feelings about being female to preoedipal separation-individuation and ambivalence conflicts. She traced her difficulty with being female partly to the wish to be different from her mother and partly to the wish to function independently of her. If she had been born a boy, the patient felt, she would have been able to differentiate herself more readily from her mother. She yearned for maternal care and protection but was impelled to get away from her mother in order to feel free and independent. This had been carried forward into her relationships with men, whom she seductively drew to her, only to become frightened, run away, and then excitedly wish for them to chase after her, sweep her up in their arms, and carry her off to bed. These rape fantasies terrified her. This way of relating first with her mother and then with men was enacted in the transference by the patient's stirring her psychoanalyst's interest via productive work and then dropping the subject, either to bring up humdrum matters or to express doubts about continuing the analysis. The aim appeared to be that of inducing him to chase after her and bring her back to the material she had dropped, which would make her feel excited, guilty, and anxious.

Both her parents, she and her analyst came to realize, had looked to her to aggrandize them through high achievement, but she always fell short of their expectations. Self-esteem issues were of central importance throughout the analysis. The patient was exquisitely sensitive to the slightest hint of rejection or rebuff. Once, at the end of a week in which a back problem had made it painful for her psychoanalyst to sit down in his chair and then again to get up from it at the end of each session, she broke into tears. "You don't like me," she sobbed. When he asked what had led her to think that, she replied, "All week, you've been making a face at the end of the

sessions." During the early part of the analysis, she cried a great
deal during sessions and, for a while, spent the weekends in bed,
depressed and crying. She not infrequently sought to have extra
sessions on the weekends during that period of time. She eventually appreciated the persistent confidence shown by her analyst
that she would be able to get through without having the extra
sessions.

She was extremely down on herself for a long time, and she
complained at times that she was not being adequately taken care
of. She expressed helplessness about ever making things better for
herself, and tried in manifold ways to sabotage the treatment so as
to make this a reality. Only patient, attentive, detailed analysis of
the unconscious determinants of her helpless and hopeless attitude enabled her to keep on trying and keep on going. Ultimately,
she vastly improved her self-image, self-esteem, and self-confidence
and slowly rebuilt her life. She eventually established a new relationship with a man, who very much loved and cared for her,
refused to let her push him away, and contributed in his own
ways to her appreciation of herself. She also held a series of jobs, in
which she steadily overcame the self-doubts that plagued her, and
finally went into business for herself. Still somewhat vulnerable to
loss of confidence and doubts about herself when life dealt her
setbacks, she returned for consultation periodically in the years
that followed the termination of the analysis.

Not all patients with a depressive neurosis feel so utterly defeated and destroyed by the failure of their defensive operations to
maintain the intactness of their self-esteem and the integrity of their
self-images as was the woman whose analysis has just been described.
At times, the issues within the patient and within the patient's
experience that have generated the neurotic depression that brings
him or her to treatment are more self-contained and limited than in
the case just described.

A 7-year-old boy entered analysis because of chronic unhappiness,
accompanied by enuresis, that made it impossible to function at
more than a minimal level in any area of his life. He sat hunched
over at the edge of the couch during his first session, with tears
dripping down his face and falling to the floor beneath him. He
was so unhappy that he could not concentrate on his work in
school and was being threatened with expulsion from the private

school he attended. He had no friends, could not mobilize his energies for sports of any kind, felt too weak and helpless to fight back against the boys at school or against the older and younger sisters at home who made his life a misery, and felt utterly dejected and demoralized.

His father was always away on a business trip, he said. His mother was always away from home doing one thing or another; or when she was at home she either was yelling at him or was busy talking on the phone. "You better not answer the telephone if it rings during our sessions," he said. His parents fought all the time, and he was terrified that they were going to get a divorce. His mother ran to the hospital for one miscarriage after another (for which *he* felt guilty). And he certainly would not talk about the terrifying hospitalizations he himself had had a couple of years earlier. He asked a very unusual question during the first session—whether the psychoanalyst with whom he had begun to work had a pet bat. It did not become understandable until several years later, when the patient finally became able to speak directly about his hospitalizations for acute nephrosis. He had been certain that he would die, if not from the illness then from all the X-rays to which he was subjected, from all the bloodlettings the "vampires" kept performing upon him, or from the surgery to which he was subjected to remove the hydrocele that had been found after his enormous body swelling had gone down.

At the beginning of the analysis, the patient felt utterly helpless and hopeless. He looked to his psychoanalyst to protect and care for him and to give him the strength that he felt he lacked in his efforts to cope with all that life had thrown at him. It was only after he was assisted to summon up the will and courage to wrestle with his own problems, and to explore and understand the *internal* contributions to them, that he settled into an analytic process that ranged far and wide over his preoedipal and especially oedipal conflicts, a process that extended over several years. He came out of it with a magnificent analytic result that empowered him for a very successful childhood, adolescence, and adulthood. (His grateful parents kept the psychoanalyst continually apprised of their son's achievements, accomplishments, successes, and happiness in life.)[1]

---

[1]The early part of this analysis has been described at length elsewhere (Silverman 1985).

It will be noted that both of these cases of depressive neurosis come close to fitting into the category of "character neurosis" mentioned at the beginning of this chapter. The same could be said about the presentations of the patient with the borderline ego structure and the one with the "anxiety neurosis" described at the beginning of this chapter. It has become abundantly clear, in fact, that analyzing the symptom neurosis from which a patient seeks relief is never sufficient. Proper psychoanalytic technique requires that equal attention be paid to the patient's underlying character structure, which is replete with and to a large extent determined by a variety of compromise formations designed to control and minimize anxiety, depression, and disturbances of self-image and self-esteem. Character neuroses or disorders will be considered in depth in Chapter 7.

Conclusions

The case material presented in this chapter, when taken as a whole, reflects the enormous variation encountered by the clinician who works with neurotic patients. First, the various types of neurotic constellations that have been described do not often appear in pure form. Individuals utilize a variable array of defensive maneuvers in a proportion that varies from person to person. What has been presented in this chapter is a categorization that can be useful for the purpose of organizing one's thinking about the clinical picture that each patient presents. The mode or modes of wrestling with internal, emotional conflict and of attempting to effect neurotic compromise in response to heretofore insoluble conflict situations will vary from patient to patient, and a mixed picture is more likely to be encountered than one that is pure in form. It can be useful to think in terms of admixtures and of predominance of one or more central modes. At times it can be useful to think of primary defensive constellations and of secondary supportive or developmentally regressive constellations.

Second, it is extremely useful to think carefully, both initially and in an ongoing way, about the basic or overall ego strength present within each patient, regardless of the particular type of neurotic defensive organization or organizations that predominate. In the treatment of neurotic patients, the strengthening of ego capacities, the expansion of ego resources and potentials, the overcoming of rigidity in favor of flexibility, the improvement both of self-esteem and of relationships with others, the replacement of harsh and primitive superego structures and contents with more humane and mature ones, and so on, are at least as important or even more important than elimination of the presenting symptoms that plague the patient. It is personal emotional growth, not symptom removal, that is the sine qua non of psychoanalytic cure. The latter derives from the former and is not a primary objective. Psychoanalytic treatment aims to facilitate the resolution, by the patient rather than by the psychoanalyst, of previously insoluble neurotic conflict and of the symptomatic expressions of the neurotic mechanisms that the person has been employing in the effort to gain some control over the effects of those unresolvable conflicts. The approach used to facilitate such resolution leads to strengthening of the ego capacities available to the patient so that he or she can deal more effectively with the conflict situations that are inevitable in the course of life.

References

Abend SM, Porder MS, Willick MS: Borderline Patients: Psychoanalytic Perspectives. New York, International Universities Press, 1983

Breuer J, Freud S: Studies on hysteria (1893–1895), in Standard Edition of the Complete Psychological Works of Sigmund Freud, Vol 2. Translated and edited by Strachey J. London, Hogarth Press, 1955, pp 1–319

Freud S: The interpretation of dreams (1900), in Standard Edition of the Complete Psychological Works of Sigmund Freud, Vols 4 and 5. Translated and edited by Strachey J. London, Hogarth Press, 1953

Freud S: The psychopathology of everyday life (1901), in Standard Edition of the Complete Psychological Works of Sigmund Freud, Vol 6. Translated and edited by Strachey J. London, Hogarth Press, 1960, pp 1–289

Freud S: Jokes and their relation to the unconscious (1905), in Standard Edition of the Complete Psychological Works of Sigmund Freud, Vol 8. Translated and edited by Strachey J. London, Hogarth Press, 1960, pp 1–242

Freud S: Analysis of a phobia in a five-year-old boy (1909a), in Standard Edition of the Complete Psychological Works of Sigmund Freud, Vol 10. Translated and edited by Strachey J. London, Hogarth Press, 1955, pp 1–149

Freud S: Notes upon a case of obsessional neurosis (1909b), in Standard Edition of the Complete Psychological Works of Sigmund Freud, Vol 10. Translated and edited by Strachey J. London, Hogarth Press, 1955, pp 151–318

Freud S: From the history of an infantile neurosis (1918[1914]), in Standard Edition of the Complete Psychological Works of Sigmund Freud, Vol 17. Translated and edited by Strachey J. London, Hogarth Press, 1955, pp 1–123

Freud S: Project for a scientific psychology (1950[1895]), in Standard Edition of the Complete Psychological Works of Sigmund Freud, Vol 1. Translated and edited by Strachey J. London, Hogarth Press, 1966, pp 281–397

Silverman MA: A fresh look at the case of Little Hans, in Freud and His Patients. Edited by Kanzer M, Glenn J. New York, Jason Aronson, 1980, pp 95–120

Silverman MA: Progression, regression, and child analytic technique. Psychoanal Q 54:1–19, 1985

Weiss SS: Reflections and speculations on the psychoanalysis of the Rat Man, in Freud and His Patients. Edited by Kanzer M, Glenn J. New York, Jason Aronson, 1980, pp 203–214

7

Character Disorders

Richard G. Kopff, Jr., M.D.
Edward Nersessian, M.D.

The psychoanalytic approach to the conceptualization, under-standing, and treatment of character and character disorders provides us with the most in-depth look at how the mind works and the person behaves. At the present time, no other theory of person-ality allows for as comprehensive an understanding of both normal and pathological behavior and functioning as does psychoanalytic theory. Nevertheless, it is important to keep in mind from the outset that this theory is not fully developed and that much is yet to be learned about the subject. It is hoped that the reader will recognize the areas that present conceptual difficulties as he or she progresses through the chapter, but it is useful to begin by seeing that there is not even a comprehensive definition of character. In fact, although a number of definitions from the existing literature are offered after a brief review section, no single one is endorsed and no new one is proposed. Instead, the various building blocks of character are de-lineated and the processes described in order to show that even in this area of somewhat basic assumptions, much remains to be learned.

Evolution of the Meaning and Mode of Classification of "Personality Disorders"

The meanings of the terms *personality* and *personality disorder*, as used by psychiatrists and other mental health professionals, have evolved considerably in recent decades. During most of the 20th century, the American Psychiatric Association has moved gradually toward the development and progressive improvement of a standardized nomenclature. In 1952, the first *Diagnostic and Statistical Manual of Mental Disorders* (now referred to as DSM-I) was published. Under the heading of "personality disorders" was gathered a heterogeneous collection of problems and presentations among which what were then thought of as disorders of conduct tended to dominate and to divert attention from underlying psychodynamic factors. A strong condemnation and social stigma were attached to many of these "conduct disorders," as they were at that time also called (e.g., drug addiction, alcoholism, and homosexuality). Classifying these so-called disorders in this way gave rise to medicolegal problems. These "personality disorders" included a wide range of cases in which malfunctioning was expressed in inflexible and limited patterns of behavior that were most troublesome when they conflicted with social and cultural norms. Some problems were classified as "personality disorders" but would not be so classified today. For example, many of the problems that would be called "sexual disorders" today (such as exhibitionism and fetishism) were classified in DSM-I as "sexual deviations" under the more general heading of "sociopathic personality disturbance."

In 1968, the American Psychiatric Association published the second edition of the *Diagnostic and Statistical Manual of Mental Disorders* (DSM-II; American Psychiatric Association 1968) in an effort to bring the American diagnostic system closer to that of the World Health Organization. Nevertheless, DSM-II did not improve much on DSM-I with respect to one very frequent problem, namely, that clinicians could not agree on the appropriate diagnoses for each patient. There were no specific guidelines for determining which traits were necessary or sufficient to arrive at a particular diagnosis. Clinicians had to depend on their own subjective criteria. This lack of specific, objective criteria was true for diagnoses of all types of disorders, including personality disorders.

The third edition of the *Diagnostic and Statistical Manual of Mental Disorders* (DSM-III), published by the American Psychiatric Association in 1980 and revised in 1987 (DSM-III-R), included many significant changes from DSM-II. DSM-III-R provided a set of specific criteria for each of the personality disorders and placed the disorders on an axis (i.e., Axis II) separate from the one (i.e., Axis I) employed for what had been known previously as psychoses, affective disorders, psychoneuroses, and certain other conditions. In 1994, DSM-III-R was replaced by DSM-IV (American Psychiatric Association 1994). In the latter, as in the former, a "personality disorder" (coded on Axis II) is diagnosed according to a number of listed criteria. In DSM-IV, six criteria are used to make a diagnosis of a "personality disorder," and additional criteria are used to separate out each one of 10 specific personality disorders grouped in three clusters. Although DSM-IV is, as was DSM-III, a major improvement over the nebulous methods for making psychiatric diagnoses in the earlier period in that it decreases subjectivity to some degree, the material in this chapter will, it is hoped, demonstrate the complexity of the problem and the inherent and, at present, unavoidable inadequacy of any attempt at classification.

Psychoanalytic Contributions

Definitions

Character

A number of definitions of "character" exist in the psychoanalytic literature, all of which have some things in common, including the notion that "character" comprises the sum of a person's "character traits." These definitions stress that character consists of the usual, habitual, consistent, continuous ways that a person meets, resolves, deals with, integrates, and adjusts to the demands and influences of the external world (reality and relationships) and of the internal world (biological factors, the id, and the superego) and of conflicts among these.

Some psychoanalysts have assumed that character is an aspect of functioning of the agency of the mind we call ego. Lampl-de Groot (1963) defined character as "the habitual way . . . in which a person's ego solves conflicts with the internal world (id and superego), conflicts with the environment, and conflicts within its own [internal] organization (between its various functions and capacities)" (p. 8).

Others have disagreed with this assumption because it limits character to an aspect of functioning of the ego. Many say that character traits represent stable compromise formations resulting from conflict involving the id, the ego, and the superego (see Charles Brenner's discussion of this subject in Chapter 5) and that character, comprising a combination of all of a person's character traits, represents the totality of these stable compromise formations.

Some psychoanalysts consider character to be a supraordinate concept, namely, one that represents a higher level of abstraction and integration than can be explained by the functioning of the agencies of the mind as described in the structural theory (i.e., id, ego, and superego). These psychoanalysts think of character as including all of the stable compromise formations of a person plus more, especially the modes of relating to other people, various identifications, and other strategies for dealing with the demands of external reality (Baudry 1989). Some psychoanalysts (e.g., Blos 1968, pp. 249–250), agreeing that character is more than the person's stable compromise formations, emphasize the notion that character is a definitive component of adult psychic structure performing an essential regulatory function (psychosomatic homeostasis, self-esteem regulation, and others) in the psychic organism. According to this view, this regulatory function is performed by something in the mind that is not explainable by utilizing only the concepts that constitute the structural model of the mind. That is, the regulatory function cannot be explained by referring only to the id, the ego, and the superego and to how they relate to each other and to the outside world.

On the other end of the spectrum are those psychoanalysts who think that the concept of character is unhelpful in understanding how the mind works because its use as a supraordinate concept cannot be reconciled with the structural model of the mind and, indeed, that the structural model alone is sufficient to explain the functioning of the mind without the use of the concept of character at all.

Character Trait

There is less disagreement about the concept of character trait, in that it can be more clearly delimited than the concept of character, it can be inferred from ongoing observations of a person's behavior, and it is more useful clinically. One must keep in mind that character is more than the sum of a number of character traits. In clinical discussions, however, when one refers to someone's character, one really means a particular trait (often a very prominent one) constituting part of that person's character (see beginning of section "Classification of Character Disorders" later in this chapter for further discussion).

The term *character trait* describes a kind of behavior, with its accompanying emotions, that is repetitive, stable, consistent, and persistent. At times it is readily observable and at times not. This behavior may or may not be in the person's awareness (usually it is not) and may or may not cause conscious distress (usually it does not). Examples of character traits are stubbornness, combativeness, and generosity.

Some Important Factors in the Development of Character and Character Disorders

One's character (or set of character traits) or character disorder represents the result of a long process of development from early childhood through the end of adolescence. By observing a child, one can see clear changes in the child's character as time passes. These changes may be very marked or may be rather minimal. Once adolescence has been completed, the person's character remains *relatively* stable for the rest of his or her life. (For further information about changes occurring during various postadolescent stages of life, see discussions by Dewald [1980] and Emde [1985].)

To understand the origins and development of character and character disorders, one should consider the following factors, which are akin to building blocks in their development and formation. This approach is more useful than trying to arrive at a comprehensive definition of character.

Physiological Factors

In the psychoanalytic theory of character, special importance is attached to the biological givens with which every individual is born, whether these givens are related to the brain or to other parts of the body. These endowments influence the gradual emergence of the infant's relationship with its environment and with other people and, therefore, contribute to and continuously influence the totality of the personality. Freud used the term "innate" to refer to these factors. His use of this term is often understood in a static way, as referring to relatively fixed biological givens. In present-day thinking, biological factors are understood to influence in an ongoing way the reciprocal mind-brain interaction. Therefore, alterations in the functioning of the brain, whatever the original causes of these alterations, have an effect on behavior. The psychiatric literature is increasingly rich in papers focusing on these biological matters.

Most physiological disorders influence thinking, mood, and behavior. Some, because of their chronicity, have longer-lasting effects, making their distinction from character traits of predominantly psychological origin difficult. The possible existence of a slow-growing brain tumor should always be considered when new behavior occurs or when existing traits become accentuated, as in the following case:

> Mr. A. was 50 years old when he began feeling increasingly despondent and overwhelmed with pessimism about his future. Although very successful, he began to worry about finances and even became concerned about losing his job. He lost his appetite, and his sleep became disturbed. A diagnosis of depression was made, and psychotherapy with antidepressant medication was initiated. However, within a few weeks he began having very severe headaches, and extensive neurological examination revealed a benign, operable tumor of the brain.

The so-called temporal lobe personality is another diagnosis to be considered:

> Mr. B. had a very labile character; he would explode easily into a rage and at times would break things. Along with this, he developed the need to perform certain rituals similar to those seen in patients with obsessive-compulsive disorder. EEG studies revealed a temporal lobe focus, and carbamazepine improved his behavior considerably.

The physiology of organs other than the brain affects mental functioning in profound ways, too. In the course of evaluating a patient's personality or character, the clinician should consider in the differential diagnosis the various intracranial disorders (such as those mentioned above) and the many other physical disorders that might cause behavioral changes that simulate character disorders. For example, endocrine and certain autoimmune disorders may lead to personality changes that are relatively stable for the duration of the condition. Space does not permit the detailing of all the physical diseases that might have this effect, but there are many.

In sum, one must keep in mind that the separation between mind and brain is a product of our ignorance and not a reality. Nevertheless, dealing with them separately here offers a way of avoiding becoming entangled in poorly understood areas.

Psychological Factors

In addition to the biological determinants, the following general psychological factors are important in the formation of character and in understanding it after its formation. It should not be forgotten that intrapsychic conflict is always involved in a person's character and character traits, resulting in some kind of compromise that, in the case of character traits, is rather stable.

Role of identification in character formation. *Identification* (described in a simple way) is a process through which some attribute of another person becomes one's own attribute. In other words, through identification, the subject assimilates a characteristic of the object, which now becomes part of the subject's character. Identification differs from *imitation,* which in infants may be a precursor of identification, in that it is an unconscious process and is fully assimilated. Some identification occurs normally during the development of every infant and child and is part of the reason children resemble their parents. The identifications that arise out of intrapsychic conflict are of special importance to psychoanalysts.

A classic example of identification is one that Freud described in his now-famous case of "Dora" (S. Freud 1905[1901]). In this case report, Freud described how a young girl developed a symptom (i.e., a nervous cough) by means of identifying with someone toward whom she had strong feelings that were very conflicted. Another common example occurs in mourning in which the person mourning identifies with some of the traits of the person he or she has lost.

Why is identification relevant to the study of character? The identifications that take place during early development are an important part of the scaffolding upon which other, later compromise formations are added to give form to the adult person. In addition, identifications that occur during the oedipal phase play a central part in the development of the superego, which in the role of conscience is an integral part of character. This process is more fully explained by Jacob Arlow in Chapter 2 of this textbook (see, especially, the sections on resolution of oedipal conflicts and on the superego).

Finally, during adolescence the identifications that take place with teachers, friends, and other significant people in the person's life contribute to the final shape of character.

Role of unconscious fantasy in character formation. Everyone has a set of fantasies that originate in childhood and remain active in the mind in a way that is largely unconscious. These fantasies are manifested in character traits and express all of the following in a way that represents a complex set of solutions to the inevitable conflicts of childhood: wishes in relation to persons important in one's life; affects associated with those wishes and with their gratification; dangers or unpleasant consequences that the person imagines to be associated with the gratification of those wishes; efforts to ward off the wishes; the residues of rewards and encouragements given and prohibitions made by other people (during childhood and later); the effects of superego prohibitions and self-imposed punishments; and many others.

One illustration of how unconscious fantasy plays a crucial role in the formation of character traits can be found by examining a group of patients who appear to repeatedly seek misery, unhappiness, and trouble, although they are completely unaware of seeking such unpleasant outcomes. In fact, their conscious sense is the opposite—that is, that they are seeking success and happiness but that, for reasons of which they are unaware, they fail repeatedly. These characteristics, along with some other traits that will be described later, add up to what psychoanalysts call the "masochistic character." Often, when patients with this type of character are psychoanalyzed, a repressed fantasy becomes conscious, namely, the fantasy of being physically beaten. Analytic exploration of this fantasy reveals that many of the patient's feelings and much of his or her behavior are manifestations of this fantasy. These manifestations are called *derivatives.* In other words, analysis of patients with a masochistic character shows that many of their repetitive and habitual ways of feeling and behaving are derived from the originally unconscious fantasy of being beaten (Nersessian 1983).

Unconscious fantasies can be conceived of as fixed mental "structures" that lead to or determine certain specific modes of behavior. They can in a general way be divided into two groups. One group consists of what have been called *universal fantasies*— oedipal fantasies, primal scene fantasies, intrauterine fantasies, and family romance fantasies—and, although universal, they nevertheless have the specific imprint of each individual. The second group consists of fantasies that are the result of certain experiences and represent the ways the person has responded to these experiences. These fantasies are therefore more specific and individualized. An example of the latter is a fantasy reported by a young man who had lost his father during childhood; the man fantasized that his father would return one day, calling in the street, and that he would be able to recognize his father out of the crowd.

Importance of childhood memories in understanding the origins and meanings of character traits. Early in the history of psychoanalysis Freud made a momentous discovery, namely, that nearly all memories from childhood are distorted. Writing in German, he used a term that was translated into English as "screen," underlining the fact that these memories screen or hide other memories and fantasies (S. Freud 1899). Today we know that screen memories are amalgams of parts of memories, fantasies, and dreams. Freud and others (particularly Phyllis Greenacre in *Trauma, Growth and Personality* [Greenacre 1949/1952]) described certain specific characteristics that they considered important elements of screen memories. Among them are that the person always sees himself or herself as a child, usually observing the scene; that the scene is often well lit and very bright; and that, upon reflection, the person recognizes that there are many incongruous elements in the scene being described.

> A patient reported that at around age 7 he had walked to the kitchen and saw his father giving his mother an injection. His parents were standing in front of the kitchen window and light was pouring in. Analysis revealed that this screen memory represented the recollection of many childhood occurrences that gradually emerged. An incomplete list includes the patient's mother's postpartum depression when he was 5 years old, during which she had periods of agitation and was visited by a doctor in her bedroom; an incident in which the patient had walked into his parents' bedroom while they were having sex; and a serious childhood illness of his own during which his temperature was often taken rectally.

What the person believes he or she remembers may never have occurred in any form, or, at most, only certain small parts of it may connect to events that really occurred (Kris 1956). This is the descriptive aspect of childhood memories and screen memories. The terms *childhood memories* and *screen memories* are being used interchangeably here and are to be distinguished from memories in children and memories told to one by one's family over and over. These screen memories are the person's only autobiographical recollections of his or her childhood.

Screen memories have represented within them many of the issues contributing to the person's neurotic conflicts and the conflicts that make up his or her character. These complex memories, which are much more than recollections, simultaneously reveal the conflict, are part of the conflict, and contain some element of the psychological history of the conflict, as well as of the attempted resolutions of the conflict. Thus, screen memories can also reveal a lot about the development and history of various character traits. In a way, these memories can be said to be part of the character.

Summary

The foregoing discussion was an effort to describe in a simplified way very complex and theoretically unsettled concepts. Obviously, one cannot refer to clear-cut structures in the mind in the way that one refers to structures in the physical world. What are often seen in clinical work are the derivatives of the fantasies, memories, and identifications that we assume exist unconsciously in some organized form. However, we do not really know how these unconscious memories and fantasies persist in the mind, and we only observe them in a relatively fixed form when they have been made conscious and verbalized. Unconscious fantasies can best be viewed as way stations or intermediate links (Abend 1990) between wish, defense, superego, and reality, on the one hand, and behavior and feeling, on the other hand. Because everyone has such fantasies and because repetitive, habitual behavior results from them, they are an important, universal basis of character.

Development of the Concept of Character in Psychoanalysis

Early Phase

The notions of character and character traits began to assume an important role in psychoanalysis in 1908 when Sigmund Freud's paper "Character and Anal Erotism" was published. It is now known that Freud had alluded to character in earlier works—in

particular, "Three Essays on the Theory of Sexuality" (Freud 1905)—
and in correspondence. However, it is the 1908 paper that represents the cornerstone of Freud's character theory and has had
a major, lasting influence on psychoanalytic thinking on the subject.
Freud took several what we today would call character traits—obstinacy, parsimony, and orderliness—and asserted that they are the
result of defenses against instinctual impulses from the anal phase
of development (see Chapter 2 for a discussion of these impulses) in
persons who have a constitutionally strong anal erotogenicity. Par-
enthetically, we can see here Freud's having noted the role of innate
constitutional factors in later character development and how
strongly biologically grounded Freud's early views were. He proposed that such impulses can persist relatively unaltered, can be
sublimated into various interests, or can be defended against (the
specific defense being reaction formation) and transformed into the
three traits. According to Freud, orderliness represents a defense
against dirtying and messing; obstinacy is a defense against letting
the feces go (i.e., by holding in the feces); and parsimony, avarice,
and an excessive interest in money in adulthood result from a defense against childhood interest in feces.

Freud used the terms "character" and "character-types" in
a 1916 paper entitled "Some Character-Types Met With in Psychoanalytic Work." In this paper, he stated that a psychoanalyst treating a patient's neurosis sometimes observes that the work is
"threatened by resistances set up against him by the patient, and
these resistances . . . may justly count as part of the latter's character" (Freud 1916, p. 311). Freud then described three "character-
types": 1) "The 'Exceptions,'" 2) "Those Wrecked by Success," and
3) "Criminals from a Sense of Guilt." He used the term "character-
types" to describe persons who manifest a series of consistent
behavior patterns leading to the same outcome as a result of unconscious strivings or purposes. For example, some persons unconsciously set out to vitiate the success they have worked so hard to
achieve. Freud related all three of these character types to problems
connected with the Oedipus complex. A success in a man's life may
cause anxiety and guilt connected to fantasies of oedipal triumph
over his father, and he may therefore ruin his success in that or

other areas of his life (e.g., marriage, social relations, etc.) to diminish the painful emotions. On the other hand, a person may commit petty crimes to pay for (i.e., decrease the guilt about) the larger crime of triumph in the context of the oedipal rivalries. As for the "exceptions," Freud proposed that in some of these cases these persons had been subjected to some kind of suffering (including physical deformity or trauma), injustice, or painful experience during childhood, toward which they were helpless and guiltless. Now, as adults, they demand special privileges and see themselves as having rights that are denied others precisely because they suffered unjustly in the past.

Among the many pioneer psychoanalysts, it is Karl Abraham who followed up the basic ideas of Freud's 1908 paper in the most systematic way. Beginning in 1921, Abraham published three papers on the subject of character and applied Freud's general concept to the other phases of psychosexual development (Abraham 1921, 1925, 1926). Thus, in addition to making a further contribution to the theory of anal character, Abraham connected certain traits to the oral phase of development and described character formation at the genital level of development. For example, he stated that an excessive urge to talk, an excessive valuation of thought or speech, and the use of speaking as a form of cruelty and of aggressive behavior and as a way of being demanding are derived from urges originating in the oral phase of infant development. He also thought that optimism and its reverse, pessimism, are derived from oral-phase urges. Abraham considered the genital stage the definitive stage of character formation. He wrote, "We are thus led to the conclusion that the definitive character developed in each individual is dependent upon the history of his Oedipus complex, and particularly on the capacity he has developed for transferring his friendly feelings on to other people or on to his whole environment" (Abraham 1926, p. 216). According to Abraham, and to cite an example, if the person has failed in this, then his sexual impulses will be unaccompanied by affectionate relations and there will be difficulty in a proper contact of feeling with others (Abraham 1926).

While this way of understanding character was progressing, that is, through the study of the various levels of psychosexual development and the defenses against the phase-appropriate instinctual impulses, Freud explored other avenues.

In 1931, Freud, in a published paper entitled "Libidinal Types," built on an earlier work (Freud 1923) in which he had proposed a major revision of his theory by introducing the "structural model" of the workings of the mind. In his work on the libidinal types, Freud used this new model to attempt a classification of character. A significant point made by Freud from the outset on this subject of classification needs to be stressed because it continues to be thought by most psychoanalysts today to be true: any classification should establish a *continuum* between the normal and the pathological.

Freud distinguished three main libidinal types: erotic, obsessional, and narcissistic. For persons who represent the erotic type, the demands of the id are very significant. Loving and being loved are most important for these persons. They are dominated by fears of loss of love and are especially dependent on others who may withhold their love from them. The superego holds sway in persons who represent the obsessional type, and they are more dependent on their own internal standards than on external love objects. Persons who represent the narcissistic type are enamored of power. They are depended on by others; they prefer an active role in love, and their main interest is directed toward self-preservation. Freud then suggested that such pure types are hard to find in the clinical setting and that persons who present for treatment represent what more often appear to be mixed types such as the the erotic-obsessional person, the narcissistic-obsessional person, and the erotic-narcissistic person.

A great deal more can be found and learned from all the works mentioned above, especially in light of the fact that many present-day debates, in both psychoanalysis and psychiatry, can be understood to be echoing concerns that are similar to those in the 1930s.

Freud's work in the area of character did not end here. His papers "'A Child Is Being Beaten'" (Freud 1919) and "On the Economic Problem of Masochism" (Freud 1924) laid the foundation for understanding a particular type of character as well as specific sexual perversions. (In this chapter the focus is on character.) Freud discovered that some patients manifest self-injurious, self-punitive, self-humiliating behavior without any masochistic sexual activity.

He called this "moral masochism." For persons in this group, masochism exists only in the form of character traits and does not apply
to their sexual activity. Today most psychoanalysts refer to such
persons as having a "masochistic character" (Brenner 1959).

Later Phase

In the last 50 to 60 years, the study of character has continued to
evolve, and some relevant work by other psychoanalysts includes
Robert Waelder's work on the principle of multiple function
(Waelder 1936), according to which every psychic act is understood
to reflect the needs of the various structures of the mind and reality;
Heinz Hartmann's ego psychology (Hartmann 1964), wherein the
study of the ego and its functions as well as the perspective of
adaptation has become a central focus of psychoanalytic investigation; and Anna Freud's description of the ego's mechanisms of
defense (A. Freud 1936/1946). Otto Fenichel presented the beginnings of today's thinking about character in his comprehensive
textbook *The Psycho-Analytic Theory of Neurosis* (Fenichel 1945; see
also Fenichel 1954). Fenichel conceived of the character of human
beings as being socially determined:

> The environment enforces specific frustrations, blocks certain
> modes of reaction to these frustrations, and facilitates others; it
> suggests certain ways of dealing with the conflicts between instinc-
> tual demands and fears of further frustrations; it even creates
> desires by setting up and forming specific ideals. Different societies,
> stressing different values and applying different educational mea-
> sures, create different anomalies. (p. 464)

Hartmann had stressed that psychoanalysis is the study of humans in conflict and that character or character traits represent the
solution to these conflicts. Fenichel clarified that character involves
the expression of conflicts among id, ego, superego, and the demands of the environment:

> Character, as the habitual mode of bringing into harmony the tasks
> presented by internal demands and by the external world, is nec-
> essarily a function of the constant, organized, and integrating part

of the personality which is the ego; indeed, ego was defined as that part of the organism that handles the communication between the instinctual demands and the external world. The question of character would thus be the question of when and how the ego acquires the qualities by which it habitually adjusts itself to the demands of instinctual drives and of the external world, and later also of the superego. (p. 467)

The reader might compare Fenichel's ideas with those presented by Charles Brenner in Chapter 5 on the theory of pathological character formation, with the general treatment of object relations theory in Chapter 3 by James Grotstein, and with the self psychology theories described in Chapter 4 by Robert Leider (with the latter relying heavily on theories relating to the development of narcissism and attempting to explain certain character disorders [i.e., narcissistic disorders] in light of this theory). The borderline concept is one special area that has been approached from a variety of theoretical vantage points and is discussed at length in Chapter 8 by Michael Porder.

Peter Blos has made important contributions to the understanding of the development of character, especially its development in adolescence. Blos (1968) noted that one can discern distinct character traits in a child; however, he added that "what appears as character in childhood is mainly a pattern of ego attitudes, stabilized by identifications, which, as we know, can undergo a most radical revision during adolescence" (p. 248). He considered character formation and adolescence to be synonymous.

Blos listed four developmental preconditions without which adolescent character formation cannot take its course:

1. "The second individuation," by which Blos meant that the adolescent disengages his or her libidinal and aggressive attachments from his or her childhood objects. The adolescent effects this, for example, by transforming certain important aspects of the love of a parent into an identification with that parent and by replacing, partially, the love of a parent by the love of the self or its potential perfection (the ego-ideal). Also, the adolescent withdraws physically and emotionally from his or her world of

childhood dependencies and develops new relationships and identifications that lead to a consolidation of his or her character.

2. "Residual trauma," by which Blos meant that during adolescence the residual effects of traumatic conditions that had existed during childhood can be stabilized by means of the development of character.[1] Thus, Blos (1968) conceived of character as being "identical with patterned responses to signal anxiety or, generally, with the conquest of residual trauma: not with its disappearance, nor its avoidance, but with its continuance within an adaptive formation" (p. 255). This "characterological stabilization of residual trauma advances the independence of man from his environment, from which the traumatic injury originally emanated at a time when pain was identical with the outside of the self or with the nonself" (p. 256).

3. "Ego continuity," by which Blos meant that ego maturation gives rise to a subjective sense of wholeness and inviolability during the adolescent years, when the envelope of the family has outlived its usefulness.

4. "Sexual identity," by which Blos meant that, whereas gender identity is established at an early age, sexual identity with definitive boundaries develops only at the time of puberty; before then, sexual identity was much more fluid and shifting than it would be after.

Thus, beginning with Freud's ideas about character traits being "either interchanging perpetuations of original impulses, sublimations of them, or reaction formations against them" (Freud 1908, qtd. in Fenichel 1945, p. 470), we now have a number of competing theories that include the notion of character traits being compromise formations involving the three agencies of the mind (a theory espoused by the authors of this chapter); theories based on the role of relations with important objects; and theories stressing the central role of narcissism in certain cases.

---

[1]This concept was touched on above in a slightly different way in the section on the role of unconscious fantasy in character formation, specifically regarding the way fantasies often result from certain experiences and represent the ways the person has responded to these experiences.

Character Disorders

Everyone has a character, and a dissection of that character will reveal many character traits. However, what constitutes a disorder of character? The problem of normality versus pathology is a very complex one in psychoanalysis, particularly regarding the subject of character. Freud's statement can be repeated here, namely, that there is a continuum between the normal and the pathological. For the purpose of elucidating the difficulty in determining what constitutes a disorder of character, a simple example is offered. A businessman may be very aggressive, miserly, pushy, single-minded, self-centered, self-aggrandizing, and even somewhat dishonest but run a very successful, lucrative business that is the envy of his competitors and because of which he is admired. These same character traits, however, may be responsible for his being unhappily married; his wife's feeling left out, unloved, and hurt; and his children's being estranged, combative, unappreciative, and rather selfish. Clearly, what is in part contributing to his success in one field is a cause of much misery in another area of this imaginary person's life.

Other difficulties are encountered in the assessment of character problems. A very common experience in psychoanalysis and in long-term psychotherapy is that a particular trait does not become evident for some time and that even when it does, it takes more time before its problematic aspects can be understood. Therefore, a certain character trait may not be recognizable for some time and, when eventually recognized, may not be viewed as pathological until a later date. The following case provides a clinical example to illustrate this fact:

> After a few months of treatment, a woman manifested strong optimism, both in her description of the various events of her day-to-day life and in her ways of relating to the psychoanalyst. She dealt with all adversities promptly and had the attitude that life must go on and that she must focus on the positive aspects of things. Clearly, for someone who had endured a major loss early in life, it seemed a useful trait. Much later, and very gradually, a certain recklessness in matters relating to her safety and health emerged, and it became

possible to understand that she experienced a sense of vulnerability of which she was hardly aware, and that she warded off an awareness of it earlier by being optimistic and focusing on the positive aspects of things and later by recklessly disregarding certain important preventive and curative health measures.

Classification of Character Disorders

A character disorder is usually conceived of as a group of maladaptive character traits. Unfortunately, all schemas attempting to classify character disorders are imperfect, partly because no two persons are alike and partly because of the complexity that becomes evident when a person's character is examined in depth. Some theorists think that character is not classifiable at all (e.g., V. Calef in Panel 1983b, p. 215). However, many attempts have been made to classify character traits, and significant problems are evident in all of these classifications. In these attempts, one sees descriptions of characters that are more prototypical than real. In actual practice, the clinician sees an intermingling of various groupings of character traits and neurotic symptoms so that a single, clear-cut diagnosis is not possible. For example, a person with a so-called obsessive-compulsive (or obsessional) character, besides showing the characteristic obsessive-compulsive traits, might also evidence traits not typically listed under that rubric (e.g., narcissistic or exhibitionistic ones), may very well have inhibitions (e.g., difficulty enjoying sex) not necessarily related directly to the obsessive-compulsive character, and may also have psychoneurotic symptoms (e.g., a phobia or a depression).

The American Psychiatric Association has attempted since DSM-III to deal with this very common problem by employing a multiaxial classification that explicitly prompts the clinician to evaluate the multiple factors that should be considered in diagnosing the patient, thereby moving the clinician away from the temptation of applying single diagnostic labels. Nevertheless, in the later editions of DSM there is still the potential that discrete diagnoses will be emphasized at the expense of understanding the patient as a whole. Psychoanalysts and other therapists who work in depth with their patients find that as they come to know each patient in a thorough, profound way, they come to know much more about the patient's symptoms, about the nature of the patient's thinking processes and behavior, and about the nature of the patient's character. In so doing, they find that discrete diagnoses are nearly impossible to make.

Another problem in defining and classifying character types is that the terms employed derive from different levels of abstraction, including 1) the libidinal phase involved (e.g., anal character or oral character), 2) the kinds of defenses that predominate or are related to similar psychoneurotic disorders (e.g., compulsive character), 3) the kind of behavior exhibited (e.g., passive-aggressive character), 4) the kind of affect experienced (e.g., depressive character), or 5) the quality of object relations (e.g., narcissistic character or schizoid personality disorder).

It should be kept in mind that a diagnosis made during the initial evaluation is based on the traits that are most prominent at that time. An in-depth study of character through psychoanalytic exploration inevitably reveals many other aspects that were not recognizable at the outset, and, in fact, some cannot be recognized for a very long period of time. Often an initial diagnosis of a character disorder is likely to be distorted, compared with one made after a thorough psychoanalytic study of the person's character.

In the following subsections, we describe some of the attempts made by psychoanalysts after Freud and Abraham (whose contributions were noted earlier in this chapter) to classify character disorders. Although each of these methods of classification has shortcomings, each has a degree of value, and the description of the disorders has therapeutic usefulness.

Wilhelm Reich

Wilhelm Reich attempted, in his book *Character Analysis* (Reich 1933/1990),[2] to construct a classification of character as well as a the-

---

[2]*Character Analysis* was published first in German in 1933, and then translated into English and published by Orgone Press in 1945, and again into English in 1972 and published by Farrar, Straus, & Giroux in New York. The book has been newly translated into English by Vincent R. Carfagno and published by Noonday Press in 1990.

ory of character and character disorder. He tried to differentiate between the character structure of "neurotic people" and that of "individuals capable of work and love," by which he meant, in essence, to differentiate between neurotic character structure and normal character structure.

Reich described several specific neurotic character types, although his effort did not constitute a complete, exhaustive classification. He noted that

> the character consists in a chronic change of the ego which one might describe as a hardening. This hardening is the actual basis for the becoming chronic of the characteristic mode of reaction; its purpose is to protect the ego from external and internal dangers. As a protective formation that has become chronic, it merits the designation "armoring," for it clearly constitutes a restriction of the psychic mobility of the personality as a whole. (Reich 1933/1990)

Also, he thought that the form of the armoring has specific historical determinants, especially in terms of the characters of the important persons early in the individual's life and the stage of development in which the significant events took place.

Hysterical Character

The hysterical character represents the simplest type of character armoring, according to Reich. Persons with this character type manifest obvious sexual behavior and bodily agility with a definite sexual nuance. In women, coquetry in gait, gaze, and speech is evident. In men, softness, overpoliteness, and feminine facial expression and behavior are apparent. Apprehensiveness is prominent, especially when the goal of the sexual behavior seems close to being attained, at which point the person with a hysterical character retreats or assumes a passive, anxious attitude. The total impression is of easy excitability, in contrast to the self-control of the person with a compulsive character. The person with a hysterical character is very suggestible and exhibits a capacity to form sexual attachments of an infantile nature. The person with this character type is often compliant, but this compliance can be replaced easily by quick depreciation and groundless disparagement of the other person. Somatic symptoms are common.

The hysterical character is determined by a fixation at the genital phase of infantile development. Thus, a person with this character type experiences strong genital impulses along with apprehensiveness. The genital incest wishes are repressed but have retained their full cathexis; they are not replaced by pregenital impulses as is the case with the compulsive character. The person with a hysterical character, unlike the person with a compulsive character, suffers from direct sexual tension.

Reich understood the character armor of the hysterical character to be less solidified and more labile than that of the compulsive character. He viewed it as representing a defense against the genital incestuous urges derived from the oedipal phase of childhood. The man or woman with a hysterical character makes what appear to be sexual overtures but then becomes anxious and backs away without realizing that he or she has behaved in a sexual or sexually stimulating way. Reich thought that the person with a hysterical character has little tendency to sublimation, intellectual achievement, or reaction formation because the libido is neither discharged in sexual gratification, which would reduce the hypersexuality, nor anchored in the character; rather, it is discharged in somatic innervations or in anxiety.

Compulsive Character

Reich posited that there are fluid transitions from compulsive symptoms to the corresponding character attitudes. The latter include a pedantic concern for orderliness; a tendency to circumstantial, ruminative thinking with an inability to concentrate more here and less there; a displacement of unconscious cathexes so that conscious ideas are insignificant and replace those that are important unconsciously; thriftiness; and avarice. All of these derive from anal eroticism, that is, as reaction formations against those impulses that played a major role during the toilet-training phase. Sometimes when the reaction formations do not work, one sees the opposite: sloppiness, an inability to deal with money, and a tendency to collect things. According to Reich, other traits derive from reaction formations to sadistic impulses that are experienced during the same toilet-training period of childhood but do not derive directly from anal impulses (e.g., strong reactions of sympathy and guilt feelings).

In the compulsive character, according to Reich, one sees other important traits with a more complex structure, including indecisiveness, doubt, distrust, and affect-block.

Reich thought he observed two layers of repressions in the compulsive character: more superficially, the sadistic and anal, and more deeply, the phallic.

Phallic-Narcissistic Character

According to Reich, the person with a phallic-narcissistic character is self-confident, arrogant, haughty, vigorous, often impressive, and sometimes either cold and reserved or derisively aggressive or "bristly," and often preempts an expected attack with an attack on his or her own part. In relation to the love object, the person is usually narcissistic and sadistic (with the latter more or less disguised). The person with a phallic-narcissistic character differs from the person with a compulsive character in the absence of reaction formations against his or her openly aggressive and sadistic behavior. Men with a phallic-narcissistic character show a high erective potency, although they are orgastically impotent; usually they are contemptuous of women. The phallic-narcissistic character is, according to Reich, less common in women, and those who do have this character are often homosexual and have increased clitoral sexuality.[3]

Reich's ideas about the genesis of this type of character are very complex and show considerable variability, depending on the particular case. A person with this kind of character usually experiences great pride in his (or her) real (or imagined) penis, along with strong phallic aggression. Unconsciously, the penis of a man with phallic-

[3]At the time that Reich was formulating these ideas, clitoral sexuality was thought by many to be less mature (i.e., less psychologically advanced) than vaginal sexuality.

narcissistic character is not only for the purpose of making love but also for the expression of aggression and vengeance; the man with this type of character is primarily interested in proving to the woman how potent he is, as well as piercing or destroying her or degrading her. For a phallic-narcissistic woman, the leading motive is to take vengeance on the man. Sadism is often a prominent component in phallic-narcissistic patients.

It should be noted that although Reich's descriptions and his efforts at classifying character are somewhat useful, his theory of armoring is considered today to be too concrete and outdated. Jenny Waelder-Hall has commented on the problem with Reich's theory of character and on the implications of this theory for technique (reported by Robert Liebert [1988, p. 51]): "For Wilhelm, resistance (that is, character) was the enemy who was to be smashed in battle . . ."

Otto Fenichel

Otto Fenichel attempted an exhaustive psychoanalytic examination and study of character, character traits, and character disorders. He noted that there is no distinct borderline between "personality" and neurotic "symptom," an idea that, as we have seen, was expressed earlier by Freud and that is still believed by most psychoanalysts today to be true. Fenichel thought at the time he wrote his book *The Psycho-Analytic Theory of Neurosis* (Fenichel 1945) that the kinds of patients who were being seen in psychoanalysts' practices were changing:

> Instead of clearcut neurotics, more and more persons with less defined disorders are seen, sometimes less troublesome for the patients themselves than for their environment. The formula, "in a neurosis that which has been warded off breaks through in an ego-alien form," is no longer valid, since the form often is not ego alien, the elaboration of the defense sometimes being more manifest than its failure. (p. 464)

In attempting to define "character," Fenichel emphasized the complexity of the subject. He showed how "character" entails the ego's habitual manner of responding to instinctual demands coming from the id and of responding similarly to environmental influences in such a way as to permit an expression of the instinctual demands, albeit in a somewhat modified form to conform to the demands of the environment. A little later in development, "character" comes to include, also, the ways the ego habitually adjusts id demands and environmental influences to the demands of the superego as well. Fenichel noted, "Thus the ego's habitual modes of adjustment to the external world, the id, and the superego, and the characteristic types of combining these modes with one another, constitute character" (p. 467). Fenichel underscored how the term "character" stresses the habitual form of a given reaction, that is, its relative constancy. Widely differing stimuli produce similar reactions. He stated that this constancy depends partly on the hereditary constitution of the ego, partly on the nature of the instinctual drives with which the ego must contend, and partly on the special attitude forced on the individual by the external world. The development of the superego is decisive in forming the habitual patterns of character, which is why what a person considers good or bad is characteristic of him or her. In addition, the formation and modification of ideals in later life are important in forming character. The reader should note the differences between this view of character and Reich's view of it as armoring against stimuli from the outer world and against inner instinctual impulses. Reich's view emphasizes the ego's defenses, whereas Fenichel's view takes more account of the compromise formations among the instinctual urges coming from the id, the pressures from the real world, the stresses stemming from the superego, issues relating to hereditary constitution, and the ego's efforts at defense.

Thus, in discussing his classification of character traits, Fenichel noted that character attitudes are compromises between instinctual impulses and forces of the ego that try to direct, organize, postpone, or block those impulses. Character traits are precipitates of instinctual conflicts. Fenichel suggested a distinction between what he called the "sublimation type" and the "reactive type" of character traits. In the sublimation type of trait, after the alteration of aim and object, the original instinctual energy is discharged freely.[4] Here, the ego has succeeded in replacing an original instinctual impulse with one that is less offensive to, as well as compatible with, the ego—one that is organized and inhibited as to aim. The ego forms a channel and not a dam for the instinctual stream. In the reactive type of defense, the original instinctual impulse is contrary to the requirements of the ego and is checked by some countercathectic measure, like a dam blocking the instinctual stream.

Fenichel classified character traits in considerable detail. The following summarizes the essence of his classification:

I.   **Pathological behavior directed toward the id (including defenses against affects such as anxiety).**

   A. *Generally frigid and "pseudo-emotional" types.*

      1. The "generally frigid" person avoids emotions altogether. Such a person has a cold nature and is incapable of sympathy for others, instead, as Helene Deutsch noted, "'fleeing to reality' from . . . [his or her] feared fantasies, but to a dead and lifeless reality" (qtd. in Fenichel 1945, p. 477). Fenichel gave as an example a patient who hated his profession, his friends, and life in general and loved only his hobby, mathematics. For him it was the field in which there were no emotions.

      2. The person with a "pseudo-emotional" type of character has intense, uncontrolled emotions but is hyperagitated and cannot put any distance between himself or herself and his or her feelings. This person finds reality full of representatives of his or her feared instincts and flees to substitutive fantasy. This person is not aware of his or her true emotional reactions; instead, he or she creates something that appears to be his or her true feeling but is actually a pseudofeeling.

---

[4] For elucidation of the meanings of some of these concepts, such as "aim" and "object," see discussion by Leo Rangell in Chapter 1, especially the section on Freud's "Three Essays on the Theory of Sexuality."

B. *Conditionally frigid type.* A person with a conditionally frigid type of character is only occasionally, but not entirely, frigid. He or she can tolerate emotions as long as certain reassuring conditions are present. Consequently, in many cases an emotion can be tolerated only until a certain intensity is reached.

C. *Character defenses against anxiety.* The following are some examples:

1. A tendency to think other people are afraid, rather than oneself.
2. An inclination to engage in counterphobic behavior. A person engaging in such behavior might, for example, develop an interest in an activity that had formerly frightened him or her.
3. A readiness to intimidate others as a way of warding off being anxious (a version of turning passivity into activity).
4. An interest in frequently reassuring others to ward off anxiety.

D. *Rationalization and idealization of instinctual impulses.* Emotional attitudes may become permissible if the person can feel these attitudes are justified as "rational." In this way, the person may avoid becoming aware that he or she is actually driven by an instinctual impulse. Sexual or aggressive behavior can thus be sanctioned if the person can believe it is "reasonable" or "rational." One kind of rationalization is idealization. The realization that an ideal requirement is going to be fulfilled results in an increase in self-esteem.

E. *Isolation of instinctual activities.* A person who isolates instinctual activities may feel love and hatred, respectively, toward different people, as a reaction to having formerly experienced both love and hatred toward the same person. This person separates people into two completely antithetical categories, those he loves and those he hates.

F. *Displacement from the original instinctual aim to behavior patterns of the ego* (see the discussion of Freud's and Abraham's work in these areas): oral, anal, urethral, phallic, and genital character traits derived from those phases of psychosexual development.

II. **Pathological behavior directed toward the superego (including defenses against guilt feelings).**

A. *Character defenses against guilt feelings,* such as in the person with a "counter-guilt character," who might try to prove how innocent he or she is through atonement and punishment or remorse, or by showing how the other person is guilty.

B. *Moral masochism or masochistic character* (see Brenner 1959).

C. *Continual seeking of achievements as a means of undoing previous failures and guilt (the "Don Juan of achievement").* For the person who does this, no achievement succeeds in undoing the unconscious sense of guilt, and so he or she is compelled to run from one achievement to another, never feeling satisfied with himself or herself.

III. **Pathological behavior toward external objects.**

A. *Need fulfillment as basis of object relationship.* The development of love and hate is a long psychological process. Any stage of this development may be retained or revived in pathological cases. Fixations on prestages of love may occur. A few examples among the many that could be chosen follow:

1. A person in this situation cares only about having his or her immediate needs satisfied.
2. Such a person may be so dependent on what others provide as to have no interest other than to fulfill the assumed expectations of others.
3. Such a person may be afraid of the intensity of his or her needs for others.

B. *Persisting ambivalence in object relationships.*

C. *Object relationships governed by jealousy.*

D. *Pseudosexuality.* Some acts appear to be normal sexual acts
but actually function as a defense against other impulses
and/or anxiety or guilt about them.

Fenichel discussed the very great difficulties in classifying character types (1945, pp. 525 ff.). Although he noted that every person
manifests traits of both the sublimation and the reactive types, he
felt that this classification was probably the most useful approach to
distinguish personalities in which the sublimation type prevails
from those in which the reactive type is predominant. He felt that
the reactive character is most satisfactorily subdivided by analogy to
the neuroses because the mechanisms employed in the various
symptom neuroses are likewise employed in the formation of character traits. Fenichel classified character disorders as follows:

1. Phobic and hysterical characters
2. Compulsive characters
3. Cyclic characters (in today's language, perhaps cyclothymic per-
    sonalities)
4. Schizoid characters

Herman Nunberg

In his book *Principles of Psychoanalysis,* published first in German in
1932 and then updated and translated into English and published in
1955, Herman Nunberg noted that some patients are free of neurotic
symptoms but behave pathologically, and he called their disorders
"character neuroses."

Nunberg considered character to be a combination or synthesis
of many traits, habits, and attitudes of the ego. Sometimes one trait
prevails, sometimes another. Although it is tempting to evaluate
someone's character on the basis of a single trait, this does not yield
a true picture. Nunberg emphasized the metapsychological point of
view,[5] namely, that to obtain an accurate idea of someone's
character, one must view it from the descriptive, genetic, structural,

---

[5]For further understanding of the metapsychological point of view, see Chapter 1,
especially the section that deals with Freud's papers on metapsychology.

dynamic, economic, and libidinal angles.[6] The reader should compare Nunberg's view with Reich's and Fenichel's views.

Although Nunberg did not make a systematic effort to classify the various kinds of character disorders, he did offer ideas about some character types.

Ambivalent Character

The ambivalent character involves a conflict between the two groups of instincts (e.g., in the ambivalence of thoughts and feelings). Identification can be ambivalent and result in hate as well as love, either simultaneously or alternately. Frequently, hate and love are hidden behind oscillations and indecisions, not only in relation to the love object but also in relation to the subject's own thinking processes, to work, and to other functions of daily life.

In this context, Nunberg wrote about the active, masculine character and the feminine character. Bisexuality is another source of oscillation and indecision. A boy may identify with his father and strengthen his masculinity. A girl may identify with her mother and strengthen her femininity. A third possibility is that a man may have satisfactory heterosexual relations, may marry, and yet may prefer the company of men as friends. In these situations, homosexual impulses are often sublimated into friendship and social feelings.

Masculine Character

If, through identification with his father, a boy masters his castration fears, he overcomes his castration complex, externalizes his aggression, and develops an active, masculine character. If a girl persists in the illusion of having a penis and does not acquire feminine character traits but becomes hyperactive and tomboyish, and develops masculine traits and masculine goals, she is seen to have a masculine character.

---

[6]Nunberg mentioned "libidinal" here but not "aggressive." To be more accurate, one might substitute "instinctual drive angles" for "libidinal angles."

Feminine Character

If a boy experiences difficulty in identifying with his father and experiences excessive masochism or homosexuality, he may retain his castration complex, feel inferior and passive, and acquire a feminine character. If a girl accepts the fact that she has no penis and substitutes a wish for a child, her aggression changes into passivity and she acquires feminine character traits.

Instinctual or Impulsive Character

Nunberg noted that the superego has certain functions that determine the behavior of the individual and contribute to the final molding of the character. Conscience and self-criticism are functions of the superego. The superego also forms ideals and contributes to reality by sanctioning the reality-testing function of the ego.

If the instincts are excessively strong and invade the ego, the superego loses control over the ego and id. The ego is then at the mercy of the instincts and will not be able to tolerate instinctual tension or postpone instinct gratification. The ego will then be weak in relation to the id demands, and the person will manifest the traits of an instinctual or impulsive character. Nunberg said that one might assume that a person in whom this takes place would have no guilt feelings. Such an assumption might not always be valid. There is, as Nunberg notes,

[an] internal system of communication between the psychic agencies. Through this system the superego is informed of the changes within the id as well as within the ego. When the latter is disobedient to the demands of the superego and carries out the urges of the id, feelings of guilt arise. These feelings are equivalents of moral suffering: the "sinner" then appears to be a "hypermoral" person. He tries to atone for his "sinful" deeds by all possible means; this often ends in self-punishment. However, one gains the impression that the need for self-punishment often precedes the moral transgressions. In such instances, the ego provokes dangerous situations and seeks punishment. (Nunberg 1955, p. 310)

Inhibited Character

In the inhibited character type, a strict, harsh, inflexible superego forces the ego to suppress the urges of the id. In this instance the superego succeeds in subjugating both ego and id. A person with such a character is inclined to an ascetic life and may be frugal, religious, scientific, and/or hardworking. He or she may overcompensate by performing "good" deeds, being interested in charity, helping others, and/or making sacrifices. A hard worker not only may be ambitious and aggressive but also may be driven by a harsh conscience.

Further Remarks

These groupings by Nunberg, like those by Reich, are not very useful, except in a descriptive way. According to present-day understanding, many of Nunberg's ideas are too simplified. Notions such as that of the instincts being excessively strong and invading the ego and weakening the superego seem to be based on an analogy with the hydraulic model in physics in a manner that is too concrete. Female psychology and development are now considered much more complex than Nunberg suggested when he seemed to reduce them to the questions of whether the woman is active or passive or whether she has a fantasy of possessing a penis or not. Nunberg's discussion of the "sinner" and the "hypermoral" person and of the "inhibited character" seems to approach a discussion of what would be understood today as masochism and masochistic character, areas in need of further study and research.

Current Classification of Character Disorders

For reasons spelled out in other portions of this chapter, psychoanalysts today tend to find little use for a classification of character. For purposes of generalizing or, at times, communicating in a loose, inexact way, some groupings are occasionally referred to. Among those, the most common are obsessive (or compulsive) character, hysterical character, phobic (and counterphobic) character, impulsive character, narcissistic character, and "as if" character.

A glossary published by the American Psychoanalytic Association, entitled *Psychoanalytic Terms & Concepts* (Moore and Fine 1990), describes some of these types. This glossary does not attempt a systematic classification of character disorders or character traits. However, it does describe a few specific character types. Although there is widespread divergence of opinion about these character types, there is enough agreement regarding the current usefulness of this loose system of classification of terms for them to be included in this official glossary.

Some of the problems in classifying character types are apparent in *Psychoanalytic Terms & Concepts*, which spells out one system of classification in use, the one that is based on libidinal phases and defenses, which is similar in many ways to those systems described by Reich and Fenichel. The glossary merely lists the names of some other character types without specifying the criteria for selecting those (see below).

Oral character: may exhibit either optimism and self-assurance or depression and hostile dependency, according to whether a gratified or a frustrated oral need is being expressed. Such a person may induce others to take care of him by behaving passively or may exhibit cannibalistic, aggressive voraciousness. This person may be generous, in identifying with the feeding mother, or ungenerous, in identifying with the frustrating mother.

Compulsive (anal) character: exhibits characteristics arising from the anal phase of development and are more readily identified by their defensive pattern, unlike the characteristics of the oral character which are defined by their need-satisfying function. The compulsive character is described in terms of characteristics which result from defensive reaction formations, viz., orderliness, parsimony, and perfectionistic strivings.

Urethral character: exhibits characteristics described as ambitious, competitive, and prone to shame.

Phallic-narcissistic character: manifests characteristics such as a tendency to be reckless (counterphobic), self-assured, and exhibitionistic.

Genital character: a psychoanalytic concept of the ideal level of psychosexual development; a person who has achieved the full primacy of genitality in psychosexual development, has resolved the oedipus complex, and is capable of postambivalent object love.

Another classification describes other kinds of characters not described in the above list of those based on libidinal phases and defenses. This group consists of typological terms that describe pathological constellations. These terms include the as-if, borderline, depressive, histrionic, masochistic, narcissistic, neurotic, paranoid, phobic, psychotic, sadistic, schizotypal, and sociopathic characters.

One final group, described by Freud (and discussed earlier in this chapter), that does not fit into such classifications comprises descriptive terms such as "the exceptions," "those wrecked by success," and the related "fate neuroses."

Summary and Conclusions

Psychoanalysts conceive of character as a group of psychic and behavioral phenomena that are "engraved" psychologically in a way that is highly organized and relatively stable and unchangeable. One's character is unique to that person and includes a number of character traits. It is usually something that is observed in one person by another. Character is a more abstract concept than character trait. A character trait is inferred by listening to someone's thoughts, feelings, wishes, and fears and by observing that person's behavior and actions or by listening to a report of his or her behavior and feelings. The psychoanalyst infers the person's character trait from all these observations and understands that they are all verbal and enacted expressions of the person's conflicts and fantasies (principally unconscious ones). In the analysis, these expressions are some of the important manifestations of the transference.

This is a crucial aspect of the analysis of patients; without these transference manifestations, the analyst would be deprived of a useful way of knowing about the patient's character traits; in fact, frequently the transference is the only route through which certain character traits are recognized. Similarly, it is through the analysis of the transference that an understanding of some of the character traits becomes possible.

Just as character is understood by some to consist of the sum of character traits in a person, character disorder is thought of as the sum of related character traits that are maladaptive or problematic in a person.

Innate and acquired physical and physiological factors play important roles in influencing the development and continuation of character and character traits. The latter represent the compromise formations that result from conflicts involving instinctual drive derivatives, superego functioning, and the ego's relationships with them, with the physical aspects of the inner world, and with people and other realities in the world around the person. Identification is one important function involved in the formation of character, especially during childhood and adolescence. Fantasies (mainly unconscious) represent another important function in the formation and persistence of character traits; upon psychoanalyzing a pathological character trait, one often finds an underlying fantasy (or fantasies) expressing psychic conflict. Childhood memories, also known as screen memories, represent another expression of an intrapsychic conflict, and they are explored in the course of every psychoanalysis so that the origins of the character traits may be understood. Although character is not solely the result of intrapsychic conflict, most psychoanalytic work deals with those traits that are the result of such conflict.

At present, there continues to be much divergence of opinion as to how to conceptualize character. Some psychoanalysts think of character as equated with the ego, namely, the part of the mental apparatus that interacts with and mediates among the instinctual impulses, the superego pressures, and factors from the people around the person. Reich thought of character in this way. He emphasized the "armoring" functions of character, that is, armoring against the stimuli of the outer world and against repressed inner impulses. Lampl-de Groot's definition also conceptualizes character as very much the same as the ego, without emphasizing the "armoring" functions that Reich thought were so important.

Another current view (Baudry, reported by Abend in Panel 1983b, pp. 213–214) is that character is more than just the syntheses of the demands of id, superego, and the real world that are effected by the ego. According to this view, character is best understood as an organization of a different order. In this conceptualization, character includes all of a person's stable functioning, which means that character is an amalgam of ego functions, drive derivatives, and superego expressions: it is "a nonphenomenological inner organization corresponding to the outer facade which we can identify as a structure on a somewhat different plane from that of the ego, id, and superego" (Baudry, reported by Abend in Panel 1983b, p. 213). According to this view, character integrates into the ego elements of instinctual drive derivatives and achieves limited gratification of those that are integrated. Another function of character involves interpersonal relations and adaptation to reality, for example, to develop strategies to deal with the demands of external reality and minimize conflicts with other people (Baudry 1989). Character organization, according to this view, is thought to be complete only after the adolescent phase, when the major ego and superego identifications have been accomplished (Baudry, reported by Abend in Panel 1983b, p. 215).

According to another view, Baudry's notion of character as a supraordinate concept, described in the previous paragraph, cannot be easily integrated with the structural model of the mind. In this conceptualization, "'character structure' has become a vague synonym for psychic structure" (Boesky 1983, p. 229). Adherents of this view believe that to conceive of character as a supraordinate organization (referring to the totality of id, ego, and superego) has no special operational or theoretical significance. They also note that other supraordinate terms have been employed by some psychoanalysts, terms such as "identity" and "self," and that self psychology theorists (see Chapter 4 of this textbook for a discussion of self psychology) contend that the use of the concept of self provides "better explanations of personal, subjective experience, of varieties of narcissistic pathology, and of the psychology of motivation than do structural concepts" (reported by Abend in Panel 1983b, p. 222). Many psychoanalysts find that clinical data are understood and explained better when supraordinate concepts, such as self or character, are not employed. Some of these adherents prefer Lampl-de Groot's view because it considers intrapsychic conflict to be central to any understanding of character, and Freud's structural model accomplishes this task very well. They do not agree that character can integrate into the ego elements of instinctual drive derivatives. Rather, they believe the opposite to be true—namely, that it is the ego that integrates conflicts triggered by drive derivatives through the formation of character traits.

No satisfactory classification of character has been accomplished. We have offered in this chapter some examples of attempts at classifications. *What is far more important than trying to classify character or character disorders is trying to understand the origins and meanings of the person's characteristic ways of behaving, thinking, feeling, and interacting with other people.* In psychoanalyzing a patient, the psychoanalyst strives to understand with the patient as much as possible the origins and unconscious meanings of the patient's repetitive maladaptive ways of behaving and relating and the recurring unhappy feelings connected with them. Often the patient manifests these maladaptive kinds of actions and ways of relating in his or her relationship with the analyst, which is a sine qua non for psychoanalyzing character problems that cause difficulties for the patient. In the course of analyzing a patient with such problems, the analyst usually recognizes that the patient's character traits fall into a kind of pattern that is familiar, and, in a very loose way, the analyst may label the patient's character disorder (or perhaps not). The analyst understands that this label of a certain kind of character disorder is tentative and is subject to many changes as he or she gets to know the patient better in the course of the analysis. Each person has his or her own very distinctive set of character traits whose meanings and origins must be understood in a way that is specific to that patient.

References

Abend SM: Unconscious fantasies, structural theory, and compromise formation. J Am Psychoanal Assoc 38:61-73, 1990

Abraham K: Contribution to the theory of anal character. Int J Psychoanal 4:400–418, 1921

Abraham K: Influence of oral erotism on character formation. Int J Psychoanal 6:247–258, 1925

Abraham K: Character formation on the genital level of libido development. Int J Psychoanal 7:214–222, 1926

American Psychiatric Association: Diagnostic and Statistical Manual: Mental Disorders. Washington, DC, American Psychiatric Association, 1952

American Psychiatric Association: Diagnostic and Statistical Manual of Mental Disorders, 2nd Edition. Washington, DC, American Psychiatric Association, 1968

American Psychiatric Association: Diagnostic and Statistical Manual of Mental Disorders, 3rd Edition. Washington, DC, American Psychiatric Association, 1980

American Psychiatric Association: Diagnostic and Statistical Manual of Mental Disorders, 3rd Edition, Revised. Washington, DC, American Psychiatric Association, 1987

American Psychiatric Association: Diagnostic and Statistical Manual of Mental Disorders, 4th Edition. Washington, DC, American Psychiatric Association, 1994

Baudry F: Character, character type, and character organization. J Am Psychoanal Assoc 37:655–686, 1989

Blos P: Character formation in adolescence. Psychoanal Study Child 23:245–263, 1968

Boesky D: Resistance and character theory: a reconsideration of the concept of character resistance. J Am Psychoanal Assoc 31(suppl):227–246, 1983

Brenner C: The masochistic character: genesis and treatment. J Am Psychoanal Assoc 7:197–226, 1959

Dewald PA: Adult phases of the life cycle, in The Course of Life: Psychoanalytic Contributions Toward Understanding Personality Development, Vol 3: Adulthood and the Aging Process (DHHS Publ No [ADM] 81-1000). Edited by Greenspan SI, Pollock GH. Adelphi, MD, Mental Health Study Center, Alcohol, Drug Abuse, and Mental Health Administration, 1980, pp 35–53

Emde RN: From adolescence to midlife: remodelling the structure of adolescent development. J Am Psychoanal Assoc 33(suppl):59–112, 1985

Fenichel O: The Psychoanalytic Theory of Neurosis. New York, WW Norton, 1945

Fenichel O: Psychoanalytic theory of character, in Collected Papers, Second Series. New York, WW Norton, 1954, pp 198–214

Freud A: The Ego and Mechanisms of Defence (1936). New York, International Universities Press, 1946

Freud S: Screen memories (1899), in Standard Edition of the Complete Psychological Works of Sigmund Freud, Vol 3. Translated and edited by Strachey J. London, Hogarth Press, 1962, pp 299–322

Freud S: Fragment of an analysis of a case of hysteria (1905[1901]), in Standard Edition of the Complete Psychological Works of Sigmund Freud, Vol 7. Translated and edited by Strachey J. London, Hogarth Press, 1953, pp 1–122

Freud S: Three essays on the theory of sexuality, I: the sexual aberrations (1905a), in Standard Edition of the Complete Psychological Works of Sigmund Freud, Vol 7. Translated and edited by Strachey J. London, Hogarth Press, 1953, pp 135–172

Freud S: Three essays on the theory of sexuality, II: infantile sexuality (1905b), in Standard Edition of the Complete Psychological Works of Sigmund Freud, Vol 7. Translated and edited by Strachey J. London, Hogarth Press, 1953, pp 173–206

Freud S: Three essays on the theory of sexuality, III: the transformations of puberty (1905c), in Standard Edition of the Complete Psychological Works of Sigmund Freud, Vol 7. Translated and edited by Strachey J. London, Hogarth Press, 1953, pp 207–230

Freud S: Three essays on the theory of sexuality: summary (1905d), in Standard Edition of the Complete Psychological Works of Sigmund Freud, Vol 7. Translated and edited by Strachey J. London, Hogarth Press, 1953, pp 235–241

Freud S: Character and anal erotism (1908), in Standard Edition of the Complete Psychological Works of Sigmund Freud, Vol 9. Translated and edited by Strachey J. London, Hogarth Press, 1959, pp 167–175

Freud S: Some character-types met with in psycho-analytic work (1916), in Standard Edition of the Complete Psychological Works of Sigmund Freud, Vol 14. Translated and edited by Strachey J. London, Hogarth Press, 1957, pp 309–333

Freud S: 'A child is being beaten': a contribution to the study of the origin of sexual perversions (1919), in Standard Edition of the Complete Psychological Works of Sigmund Freud, Vol 17. Translated and edited by Strachey J. London, Hogarth Press, 1955, pp 175–204

Freud S: The ego and the id (1923), in Standard Edition of the Complete Psychological Works of Sigmund Freud, Vol 19. Translated and edited by Strachey J. London, Hogarth, 1961, pp 1–66

Freud S: The economic problem of masochism (1924), in Standard Edition of the Complete Psychological Works of Sigmund Freud, Vol 19. Translated and edited by Strachey J. London, Hogarth Press, 1961, pp 155–170

Freud S: Libidinal types (1931), in Standard Edition of the Complete Psychological Works of Sigmund Freud, Vol 21. Translated and edited by Strachey J. London, Hogarth Press, 1961, pp 215–220

Greenacre P: A contribution to the study of screen memories (1949), in Trauma, Growth, and Personality. New York, WW Norton, 1952, pp 188–203

Hartmann H: Essays on Ego Psychology: Selected Problems in Psychoanalytic Theory. New York, International Universities Press, 1964

Kris E: The recovery of childhood memories in psychoanalysis. Psychoanal Study Child 11:54–88, 1956

Lampl-de Groot J: Symptom formation and character formation. Int J Psychoanal 44:1–11, 1963

Liebert R: The concept of character: a historical review, in Masochism: Current Psychoanalytic Perspective. Edited by Glick RA, Meyers DJ. Hillsdale, NJ, Analytic Press, 1988, pp 27–42

Moore B, Fine B (eds): Psychoanalytic Terms & Concepts. New Haven, CT, American Psychoanalytic Association/Yale University Press, 1990

Nersessian E: The Kris Study Group on Masochism: a summary of findings. Paper presented to the New York Psychoanalytic Society, New York City, January 1983

Nunberg H: Principles of Psychoanalysis: Their Application to the Neuroses (1932). New York, International Universities Press, 1955

Panel: Clinical aspects of character. Reported by Willick MS. J Am Psychoanal Assoc 31:225–236, 1983a

Panel: Theory of character. Reported by Abend SM. J Am Psychoanal Assoc 31:211–224, 1983b

Panel: Psychoanalytic contributions to psychiatric nosology. Reported by Peltz ML. J Am Psychoanal Assoc 35:693–711, 1987

Reich W: Character Analysis (1933). Translated by Carfagno VR. New York, Noonday Press, 1990

Waelder R: The principle of multiple function: observations on over-determination. Psychoanal Q 5:45–62, 1936

8

The Borderline Concept

Michael S. Porder, M.D.

Early History

A historical review of the psychoanalytic understanding of the more disturbed patient should begin with Freud's ideas about psychosis, which provided the theoretical context from which later hypotheses were developed. Throughout his lifetime Freud held to a clear-cut division of mental illness into *neurosis* and *psychosis*. As early as 1894, in "The Neuro-Psychoses of Defence," he attempted to explain the difference between two psychoneuroses, hysteria and obsessional neurosis, and a psychosis called "hallucinatory confusion" (Freud 1894). The crucial difference, he observed, was that in psychosis there was a *break with reality* that was not present in the two neuroses. Evidence of a break with reality was the first criterion that Freud used to distinguish between neurosis and psychosis.

Freud's second group of criteria involved the *specific defense mechanisms* that were used by neurotic and psychotic patients. Thus, Freud, in 1896, introduced the idea that whereas conversion and displacement were used preferentially in hysteria and obsessional neurosis, projection was used preferentially in paranoia (Freud

1896). Then, in 1911, writing about the psychotic productions of the jurist Daniel Paul Schreber, Freud hypothesized that in the neuroses libido was repressed but was still unconsciously attached to objects, whereas in psychosis libido was totally withdrawn from the object world.[1]

Freud (1911, 1914) then developed a third criterion for differentiating neurotic from psychotic patients, namely, *that individuals representing these two groups related differently to the object world.* This distinction was based not only on the presence of different defense mechanisms but on the degree of libidinal attachment to intrapsychic objects (i.e., mental representations of the objects). Freud proposed a continuum for the stages of the development of the libido: beginning with autoerotism, progressing to narcissism, and then on to object love. In paranoia, inversion (Freud's early term for homosexuality), and hypochondria, Freud theorized, there is a regression from object love to narcissism. Freud speculated that in dementia praecox (i.e., schizophrenia), the regression might proceed even further back to the stage of autoerotism. Autoerotism, he postulated, would exist before there was any interest in objects other than the infant's own body. Thus, he used the term *autoerotic* for that stage and located schizophrenic disorders at this phase of development. Neurotic patients, in contrast, have progressed to the stage of object love.

In the 1920s Freud returned to these ideas in his two papers on neurosis and psychosis (Freud 1924, 1924[1923]). He reemphasized that projection and withdrawal of libido were used in the psychoses and not in the neuroses, and that use of these defenses would result in a break with reality. He developed a simple schema: neurosis is the result of conflict between the ego and the id; depression (or as it

---

[1]Freud believed that in the neuroses, whatever was repressed continues to exert pressure in the unconscious. Thus, components of oral, anal, and oedipal wishes, for example, can be observed via their derivatives. In psychosis, however, the drive wishes were eradicated and there would be no observable derivatives. Thus, Freud posited that withdrawal of libido and repression were two distinct defense mechanisms. Such a total withdrawal of libido as observed in psychosis would result in hypochondria, megalomania, or a delusion of the "end of the world." It would not result in more typical neurotic symptomatology.

was called at that time, melancholia or narcissistic neurosis) is the result of conflict between the ego and the superego; and psychosis is the result of conflict between the ego and reality. However, he began to have misgivings about this overly schematized clinical picture. In his later papers "Fetishism" (Freud 1927) and "Splitting of the Ego in the Process of Defence" (Freud 1940[1938]), he presented clinical evidence that did not fit this schema. The first clinical examples related to men who had a fetish and behaved as if they thought that women had a penis, although intellectually they knew that this was not correct. The second example was based on his observations of two young men, each of whom acted as if his dead father were still alive, although he knew intellectually that his father was dead. Neither of these two young men nor the men with a fetish described were psychotic, although they all demonstrated a break with reality.

Freud attempted to solve this dilemma by postulating a new mechanism of defense, "disavowal," which stood midway between repression and the break with reality. Even this explanation was unsatisfactory to him because he observed that certain aspects of neurotic symptomatology always involved a break with reality, even though it might be a minor one, and that it was unusual for psychotic patients to have a *total* break with reality.

Thus, Freud, at the end of his lifetime, left us with a few clear, although inconsistent, ideas about the differences between neurosis and psychosis based on 1) the degree to which there is a break with reality, 2) the type of defense mechanisms predominantly used, and 3) the predominant mode of relating to objects. However, he had also considered another approach to these issues without ever specifying it as such. As early as the time of his discussion of Schreber's case history, Freud (1911) wrote that "a secondary or induced disturbance of the libidinal processes may result from abnormal changes in the ego" (p. 75). In other words, although he had postulated that Schreber's basic conflict was over his homosexual impulses and his narcissistic regression, Freud could not rule out the possibility that these libidinal conflicts were secondary to changes in the ego. This statement, embedded in the attempt to understand psychopathology within the framework of libidinal development, lay relatively dormant until the publication of "The Ego and the Id"

(Freud 1923) and "Inhibitions, Symptoms and Anxiety" (Freud 1926). The introduction of the structural hypothesis (see Chapter 2), which organized the mental apparatus into id, ego, and superego, provided a new way to investigate degrees of psychopathology. These two articles were followed by Anna Freud's *The Ego and the Mechanisms of Defence* (A. Freud 1936/1946) and Heinz Hartmann's "Ego Psychology and the Problem of Adaptation" (Hartmann 1939/1958). These works, along with the classic works of Hartmann (1952, 1956) and those he wrote with Kris and Loewenstein (Hartmann and Loewenstein 1962; Hartmann et al. 1946), introduced the examination of the ego's capacity to deal with the drives in an adaptive or nonadaptive way. These investigations of the ego and the superego took into account the fine discriminations of the functioning of the ego as a mediator between the id and the external world. No longer did it suffice to describe the instinctual urge, the defense, and the symptom. Now, one had to consider the resistance to regression and the capacity of the ego to find different solutions to the conflicts created by the drives and the superego. The growing awareness that there were degrees of pathological adaptation inevitably led to the conclusion that there might be a third large area of psychopathology, occupying a middle ground between the neuroses and the psychoses.

First Concepts of a Borderline Group

Even before Hartmann, Kris, and Loewenstein wrote their theoretical papers, there were already three seminal articles in the literature that described more severely ill patients, many of whom would now be referred to as having borderline personalities. Tausk, in his paper "On the Origin of the Influencing Machine in Schizophrenia" presented to the Vienna Psychoanalytic Institute in 1918, described how the early ego could build up boundaries between the self and the object during infancy (Tausk 1919/1933). He drew his conclusions from the observations of schizophrenic delusions in which the patient felt internal sensations in various parts of his or her body that were experienced as foreign, or "estranged," or were believed to be completely external to the body. The most extreme example of these feelings was the delusion of the "influencing machine."[2] Tausk used the term "transitivism" to describe his patients' belief that others could know the thoughts inside of their heads, and used the phrase "loss of ego boundaries" to describe the confusion between inside and outside that psychotic patients experience. The latter concept has became crucial not only for our understanding of psychosis but for our understanding of problems in ego development observed throughout the entire sicker end of the psychopathological spectrum.

Deutsch, in her paper "Some Forms of Emotional Disturbance and Their Relation to Schizophrenia," published in German in 1934, described a series of cases "in which the individual's emotional relationship to the outside world and to his own ego appears impoverished or absent" (Deutsch 1934/1942, p. 301). She called these patients "as if" because "the individual's whole relationship to life has something about it which is lacking in genuineness and yet outwardly runs along 'as-if' it were complete" (p. 302). Deutsch was, of course, describing patients with profound disturbances in ego development, in superego development, in their own sense of identity, and in their capacity to form mature object relations. She concluded, "Whether the emotional disturbances described in this paper imply a 'schizophrenic disposition' or constitute rudimentary symptoms of schizophrenia is not clear to me. These patients represent variants in the series of abnormal distorted personalities. They do not belong to the commonly accepted forms of neurosis, and they are too well adjusted to reality to be called psychotic" (p. 320). Here, we have the first clear indication that there may be room for a diagnostic category that is neither neurosis nor psychosis, although Deutsch hedged on that conclusion by invoking these patients' failures in reality testing.

Stern, in his 1938 paper "Psychoanalytic Investigation of and

---

[2]Tausk's example was of a woman patient who imagined a coffin-shaped replica of her body that was controlled by others and that was responsible for various bodily sensations, including sexual ones.

Therapy in the Border Line Group of Neuroses," began, "It is well known that a large group of patients fit frankly neither into the psychotic nor into the psychoneurotic group, and that this border line group of patients is extremely difficult to handle effectively by any psychotherapeutic method" (p. 467). Stern clearly accepted the idea of a third grouping of psychopathology, and he emphasized the failures of early mothering as the probable etiology of the pathological narcissism that he believed was the "soil" in which these "border line" disturbances developed. He also believed that the anxiety experienced by patients with such disturbances was "organic," or "somatic," and derived from an earlier time in development than did the castration anxiety of the neuroses. He emphasized the disturbances in the transference that led to idealization of the analyst, the "gigantic size" of the analyst's imago, and the contrasting childlike view that the patient had of his or her own self-image.[3]

After the contributions of these three early authors, it was Klein who made significant contributions to the understanding of these more disturbed patients, with her conceptualization of the paranoid/schizoid and depressive positions. She and her followers observed and treated analytically psychotic and near-psychotic patients. Although she did not directly address the "borderline" diagnosis, she speculated about the conflicts present in earliest infancy and postulated that the early ego of the infant was overwhelmed by the death instinct or by an excessive aggressive drive. She hypothesized that at this early time there was a predominance of "primitive" defense mechanisms, such as splitting and projective identification, which could cause the early ego to "fall to bits" in times of extreme stress. The infant uses primitive idealization as a defense to protect itself from what Klein postulated was the paranoid world in which the infant lives. This world is filled with the

---

[3]There is a close parallel between Stern's ideas about the gigantic size of the parent/analyst imago and those of Klein on primitive idealization and those of Kohut on the "idealized parent imago," both of which I will discuss later. Although each of these authors would explain the dynamics that underlie the clinical picture quite differently from the other two, they seem to agree on this common element.

projections of aggression and the death instinct in order to keep the infant's ego core all-good, but with the result that the outside world is made all-bad and dangerous. According to Klein, these primitive defenses antedate the defenses used by neurotic patients and were predominant during the earliest times of infantile development.

During the 1940s and continuing through the 1960s in the United States, there was a ferment in the investigation of ego development. Greenacre (1941a/1952, 1941b/1952, 1955) speculated about the importance of the anxiety of birth and the early traumas of the first 2 years of life, which might contribute to the development of early narcissism, faulty body image, and ultimately fetishism or other significant failures in the development of healthy object relations. Bak (1954, 1971) investigated the role of aggression in schizophrenia and perversions and concluded that the object relations in the perversions were more primitive than those in the neuroses, but not as pathologized as those in schizophrenia. Jacobson (1954, 1964) introduced an elaborate schema to account for the development of disturbed and healthy identifications within the ego. In her paper "Contributions to the Metapsychology of Psychotic Identifications" and her monograph *The Self and the Object World,* she expressed her view that early identifications of the very young child were more like imitations. Therefore, she hypothesized that these identifications were "magical" and "total" (i.e., the whole love object would be magically incorporated), and thus these identifications were similar to those described by Deutsch in her descriptions of her "as-if" patients. Healthier identifications, in contrast, would partake of realistic likenesses to the love object and would be examples of partial identifications (i.e., only selected aspects of the love object would be assimilated into the ego). She related her concepts of total, magical identifications to the introjection processes described by Klein, although she had some significant differences with Klein's theoretical postulates about the paranoid-schizoid and depressive positions during early infancy.

L. Stone, in "The Widening Scope of Indications for Psychoanalysis" (1954), addressed the question of whether or not these severely ill patients could be effectively treated by the psychoanalytic method. He observed that these patients, although not clearly psychotic, induced in the analyst the conviction of a grave illness. They often exhibited in interviews and during treatment psychotic fragments, marked narcissistic phenomena, and a multiplicity of symptoms. In addition, there was an immediate primitive transference; the patients felt terror of the analytic situation and often made insatiable, unrealistic demands on the analyst for immediate gratification. Attempts to control the analyst or to be completely submissive were coupled with grandiose fantasies, acting out, or narcissistic retreat. Stone used the term "borderline" to describe these patients' condition and recommended a cautious analytic approach with parameters (modifications) for their treatment, which in many cases could lead to a rewarding therapeutic result if the analyst could be extremely patient.

The Borderline Syndrome

The extensive clinical descriptions and theoretical hypotheses elaborated by the aforementioned authors and others laid the groundwork for the introduction of the borderline diagnosis as distinct from those of neurosis and psychosis. Frosch (1964, 1970) was probably the first to organize much of this data from an analytic point of view. He called this third diagnostic entity "psychotic character," and although this term was never accepted by the analytic community, what he described was significant in the following ways. The psychotic character, according to Frosch, is a fixed stable entity whose pathology is more severe than in the neuroses or the neurotic character but not as severe as in the various psychoses (Frosch 1964). Frosch focused on three areas of pathology that would differentiate patients with psychotic character from patients with neuroses and patients with psychoses. These differences were similar to those that many of the aforementioned authors, including Freud, had emphasized.

1. *The nature of the conflict or danger.* Frosch, like Freud, Stern, and Klein, believed that these patients were not defending solely against instinctual impulses but were dealing with primitive issues of survival and dissolution and disintegration of the self.

2. *The preferred defenses used by these patients.* Frosch, in agreement with Klein, believed that the psychotic character utilized defenses of splitting, projective identification, denial, dedifferentiation, fragmentation, and somatization.
3. *The problems in reality testing.* Frosch described disturbances in these patients' sense of reality, which included altered ego states such as depersonalization and derealization. Although, he believed, these patients maintain the capacity to test reality, their "relation to reality" (i.e., their capacity to function in accordance with social reality) is significantly impaired.

However, it was Kernberg who organized and systematized the data concerning this group of patients in the most complete way. In a series of papers and books (Kernberg 1966, 1967, 1975, 1976, 1984) he elaborated his theory of the entity he called "borderline personality organization." He drew heavily on many of Klein's ideas about primitive defenses and on Erikson's, Jacobson's, and Deutsch's ideas about problems in the formation of a stable identity, which he described as "identity diffusion." Kernberg had specific differences with Klein's formulations, repudiating her ideas about the death instinct and her belief that there were fully formed fantasies in the mind of the young infant. However, he did retain certain basic concepts from her descriptions of the paranoid-schizoid and depressive positions.

Central to Kernberg's thinking was the predominance of primitive defenses, particularly splitting and projective identification. Splitting, he postulated, began in infantile life as a result of the immaturity of the psychic apparatus. According to Kernberg, the early mental apparatus grouped mental representations with an affective charge that would result in images of self and/or object representations that were "all-good" or "all-bad." Beyond the first year of life, the persistence of splitting is indicative of pathology. Splitting persists in those patients who have continuing need to protect the "ego core" and the positive introjects. In his early papers Kernberg held that patients with borderline personality organization were constitutionally endowed with excessive aggressive drive, but later he modified his stance to include the possibility that this excessive aggression could be the result of excessive frustration. He also postulated that, particularly in the area of aggressive conflict, these patients demonstrated weakness of ego boundaries and had strong projective needs, so that much of their aggression was projected "into" the object.[4] His evolving definition of projective identification included the need to control the now-threatening object while continuing to maintain "empathy" with the object. By "empathy," Kernberg meant that the patient understood the feelings of the object "onto" whom the impulses were projected. Kernberg contrasted this feeling with those of psychotic patients, who project their impulses but have only a negative connection to the object who has received the projected impulses. Most recently, Kernberg (1987) has added that a crucial aspect of this defense is the induction of the projected affect into the object, most important, the analyst.

The presence of these primitive defense mechanisms that Kernberg observed in the transference and in these patients' relations to others would lead to the formation of split ego states and the predominance of all-good or all-bad self and object images. "Internalized object relations" is the term Kernberg used to describe these split and projected all-good and all-bad self and object images that are hypothesized by him to be present in earliest infantile life. In his view, these internalized object relations persist in more disturbed patients and are responsible for their severe psychopathology.[5] It is Kernberg's belief that all of these pathological developments precede the use of repression and other higher-level defenses that are used by neurotic patients. In his view, neither oedipal conflicts nor superego conflicts that induce guilt are as important in these pa-

---

[4] Kernberg used the word "into" because the term projective identification was first used by Klein to describe a primitive defense used during the paranoid-schizoid position when the infant was preverbal and pre-object-related in the more traditional Freudian sense.

[5] It is important to note that "internalized object relations" are very different from the "object relations" described by Freud and the early ego psychologists mentioned previously in this chapter. The latter refer more to the mother, father, other important caregivers, and siblings in the child's life. Of course, these psychological images are also distorted by conscious and unconscious fantasies, but they do not have the fixed predetermination from infantile life that the term "internalized object relations" implies.

tients as those preoedipal and primitive superego conflicts that result from the pathology of internalized object relations. Another result of the persistence of internalized object relations is the patient's failure to form mature and healthy identifications. The persistence of these more primitive self and object images results in what Kernberg called "identity diffusion."

The final element in Kernberg's description of borderline personality organization is his contention that patients with this personality organization have either intact reality testing or only a transient loss of reality testing, which distinguishes them from psychotic patients.

Later in his work, Kernberg began to draw parallels between borderline pathology and the developmental observations of Mahler and her co-workers (Mahler 1968, 1971). He modified his time frame for the development of borderline pathology, so that he no longer adhered to the Kleinian schema that linked primitive defenses to the first year of life. He changed his developmental sequence and located the beginnings of the development of borderline pathology in the "rapprochement" subphase of the separation-individuation process, which includes the end of the second year and the beginning of the third year of life. By making this conceptual shift, Kernberg was able to conceive of the developmental sequence of borderline pathology as coinciding with the increasing capacity of the child to use language and imagery and to begin to develop an organized fantasy life. Overall, however, Kernberg adhered to a developmental sequence of psychopathology that places the genesis of psychosis within the first year of life, that of borderline personality organization between 9 months and 3 years of age, and that of neurosis and neurotic character pathology after that time, when the oedipal phase would begin, higher-level defenses would be activated, and mature superego pathology with the sense of internalized guilt would be in place.[6]

---

[6]"Internalized guilt" is a problematic term that refers to an internal standard of morality. This contrasts with sicker patients whose superego is more primitive and who expect extreme punishment and death at the hands of a dangerously perceived external world. However, a continuum exists between these two extremes, and most human beings fear external punishment even if they have a strong internal moral code.

The Developmentalists

The "developmentalists" constitute a heterogeneous group of authors who have in common their accepting the premise that borderline pathology is the result of a defect mainly in the development of very early object relations. For most of these authors this concept refers to the mother-child relationship during the first 2 years of life. Of course, all of the authors whose work has already been described in this chapter, and certainly Klein as well, might fit into this context. However, most of those authors—with Stern clearly being an exception—focused more on dynamic conflicts and less on the failures of early mothering. Many of the "developmentalists" base their ideas on Mahler's work on separation and individuation, whereas others draw heavily on the work of Winnicott and Kohut.[7]

Winnicott (1951/1958, 1960/1965; see Chapter 3 of the present volume) has offered two concepts that have been of considerable importance to many psychoanalysts who have written about the treatment of borderline patients: 1) transitional objects and transitional phenomena, and 2) the holding environment. The concepts of transitional objects and transitional phenomena describe the child's ability to creatively imagine a "me/not me," one form of which is the transitional object. This cognitive developmental leap may be used as a bridging phenomenon in the development of object relations. Many analysts conceptualize their role as similar to that of a transitional object because they see themselves as becoming a soothing and comforting extension of the patient. More recently, Adler (1989) has hypothesized that the patient's ability to use the transference to the analyst as a fantasy repeats this early developmental step, which can be fostered by an empathic analyst or discouraged by an insensitive one. The holding environment, on

---

[7]Winnicott and Kohut have developed their ideas in a way that is clearly applicable to borderline patients, so they will be included in the group of developmentalists. Mahler (1971), on the other hand, only mentioned the possible applicability of her work to borderline patients in one paper, so she will be mentioned mainly as an author on whose work others have built their own hypotheses.

the other hand, describes the safe haven where the infant/patient can be alone or alone in the presence of the other, a protected space such as a good mother would provide. Each of these concepts—transitional objects and transitional phenomena, and the holding environment—describes a setting in which a mothering analyst can allow the patient to make up for the failures of the patient's mother.

Bion (1959, 1967) (see Chapter 3 of the present volume) also has used his theory of object relations to inform his approach to the treatment of borderline patients. In Bion's view, the analyst should function as a "container," a repository for the patient's projected impulses and painful affects. During treatment the analyst must accept these projected impulses and affects for a period of time before they can be reintrojected by the patient in a more modified form. Bion believes that this experience in the transference will undo the mother's failure to offer herself as a "container" for her infant's anxieties and impulses.

Kohut (1971; see Chapter 4 of the present volume) was another "developmentalist" whose theory emphasized that the analyst should function as a "selfobject" so that the patient could undo his or her psychological defects. According to Kohut, a selfobject is an object that becomes an adjunct to the self in order to repair defects in psychological development to ensure the healthy integration of the self. Observing patients whom he described as "narcissistic characters," Kohut postulated that there was a developmental failure in these patients' capacity to form a "cohesive self." Evident in these patients were regressive narcissistic structures that Kohut called the "grandiose self" and the "idealized parent imago." Although Kohut insisted that his patients were not borderline, which they probably were not, the grandiosity of these patients and the idealized image of the analyst in the transference fit beautifully into many of the earlier clinical descriptions of borderline patients. For Kohut, the analyst must offer himself or herself as a selfobject to undo the developmental defects that prevented these patients from forming a cohesive self. Kohut, like other authors, believed that the developmental failure evident in these patients was due to the lack of appropriate empathic responses by the parents, but, unlike most of the other authors, Kohut believed that in many instances this failure could have taken place as late as latency, after the major psychic structures had been relatively well integrated.

Adler and Buie have drawn heavily on Winnicott and Kohut to support their hypothesis that the crucial problems of borderline patients relate to "aloneness," "abandonment," and the incapacity to maintain "evocative recall" of the object (Adler 1985, 1989; Buie 1985; Buie and Adler 1982–1983). They believe that these conflicts that are common to all borderline patients originate in failures of early mothering, so that these patients must use the analyst as a transitional object or a self-object to develop the "self-soothing introjects" necessary for healthier emotional development.

Rinsley and Masterson have a different focus (Masterson 1972; Masterson and Rinsley 1975; Rinsley 1977). They believe that their borderline patients demonstrate clearly that the mothers of these patients reward regressive behavior in their children and strongly disapprove of their children's attempts at separation and indi-viduation. Masterson and Rinsley recommend a therapy geared to reverse this specific dynamic—a kind of corrective emotional expe-rience in which the analyst acts to counteract the pathological ef-fects of the mother's actions.

Other Contributions to the Borderline Concept

In addition to those analysts who saw more severely ill patients in their consulting rooms, there were others who worked in inpatient units of hospitals and residential treatment centers. These analysts saw large numbers of patients who were not clearly psychotic but who were definitely more seriously disturbed than patients with neuroses and the less disturbed character disorders seen in the offices of most practicing analysts. Hoch and Polatin (1949) believed these patients to be schizophrenic but recommended the diagnosis of "pseudoneurotic schizophrenia." Knight (1953) was among the first to label these patients "borderline." However, he believed that unstructured interviews and psychological testing would reveal an underlying psychosis. Grinker et al. (1968) offered a specific clinical description of these patients, emphasizing the failure in these patients to develop a stable sense of self and identity, the formation of anaclitic relationships, the presence of depressive feelings based on loneliness, and the preponderance of expressed aggression. Masterson (1972; Masterson and Rinsley 1975) and Rinsley (1977) worked with borderline adolescents and focused on their patients' pathological regressive ties to their mothers and on their failures at separation and individuation. Gunderson (1977, 1984) attempted not only to delineate a clear descriptive entity, "borderline personality disorder," but also to organize the understanding of patients with this disorder around their relationships with the significant objects in their lives. He described the following in his patients: 1) intense, unstable interpersonal relationships; 2) manipulative suicide attempts; 3) unstable sense of self; 4) predominance of negative affects; 5) ego-dystonic psychotic experiences; 6) impulsivity; and 7) low achievement. The degree of psychopathology observed at any given time was related to whether there was a present and supportive major object, a frustrating or potentially absent major object, or an absent or lacking major object. Many of the ideas of these authors have been integrated into DSM-III (American Psychiatric Association 1980).

Preliminary Conclusion

All of what has been said so far indicates that there is almost complete agreement among the authors cited that borderline pathology evolves at a very early developmental stage and is related to either maternal failure or excessive conflict during the first 2 years of life. Anxiety is extreme, and primitive defenses that protect the integrity of the early ego are activated. Object relationships are immature and/or narcissistic. There is an incapacity to maintain a stable sense of self or identity. Further, the boundaries between inside and outside are blurred to the extent that reality testing can be partially compromised, although neither this ego function nor any of the other maladaptations are as severe as those seen in psychotic patients. Most of the conflict is thus rooted clearly in the preoedipal phase of development, with an absence of oedipal, triangular conflict; of evidence of the use of higher-level defenses; and of more mature superego conflicts centering around internalized guilt.

A very clear statement has been made by all of the aforementioned authors. They believe that there is a definite distinction between patients with neuroses and these borderline patients, and that these two groups are clearly distinguishable from psychotic patients. These borderline patients may be said to have a defect in their development that distorts their later ego maturation. Based on these beliefs, these analysts ascribe a special etiology for borderline pathology that is clearly different from that of the neuroses and that of the psychoses. In addition, all of these authors recommend different treatment approaches based on their own hypotheses, and these approaches will be discussed later in this chapter.

The Kris Study Group

From 1973 to 1977, a Kris Study Group of the New York Psychoanalytic Institute formally reassessed the preliminary conclusions described in the previous section. The Kris Study Groups had been created to utilize the clinical data from psychoanalytic patients to examine psychoanalytic concepts and theory. This particular Kris Study Group initially discussed the clinical material from many psychotherapy and psychoanalytic cases but ultimately focused extensively on four fully analyzed cases. Abend, Willick, and Porder (1983, 1988) rethought and reorganized the conclusions reached by the group. These conclusions were significantly different from those of most of the authors previously discussed. To begin with, they concluded that the term "borderline" should be used only to refer to a diverse group of disorders that reveal a more severe psychopathology than that which is seen in neurotic disorders but that do not warrant the improved specific diagnoses of schizophrenia and manic-depressive psychosis, as defined by DSM-III. These conclusions were closer in some respects to those of Kernberg, in that the term "borderline" was found to encompass a broader range of psychopathology than did the DSM-III diagnosis of "borderline personality disorder." On the other hand, "borderline personality organization" did not prove to be a diagnostic entity with a specific underlying psychopathology. In that respect, our conclusion was closer to Gunderson's view that each character disorder should be defined separately. In the end, it was clear that there is no advantage to the diagnostic use of the term "borderline," although it is likely that this term will remain in common usage to describe a heterogeneous group of patients in whom moderately serious degrees of ego pathology are evident.

Reassessment of the Borderline Concept

The members of the Kris Study Group concluded that the term "borderline" describes a broad and varied group of patients and that there is no convincing evidence that these different kinds of patients have specific, identifiable features in common. Therefore, it is highly unlikely that the category can be used to predict analytic results or to determine, in part, a specific treatment approach. Furthermore, it is premature, in the light of current knowledge, to attribute the etiology of borderline conditions to failures in development that occur during a specific phase of life. Although speculation about early development is an honored psychoanalytic tradition, one of its major pitfalls is the idea that adult psychopathology reflects a direct, unmodified continuation of very early, preverbal developmental stages. Such theorizing contributes to fundamental errors in attributing the etiology of the psychoses to disturbances during the first 6 months of life, borderline conditions to the next 24 or so months, and the neuroses after the age of 3 years when so-called object constancy has been achieved.

Such a simple schema is open to serious question. On the one hand, such a conclusion discounts the role of biological factors, which may well prove to be contributory or even responsible for schizophrenia and manic-depressive illness and which also may be present in a certain number of borderline patients. On the other hand, it discounts the impact on fundamental ego capacities of serious trauma at later stages of development.

All of the other authors whose work was cited in the earlier sections of this chapter stated that preoedipal phases and conflicts may be extremely important in creating the severe degree of psychopathology present in borderline patients. At the present time, however, there is scant evidence to place the etiological determinants for the borderline syndrome in any particular phase of development. It is more likely that all psychopathology reflects major determinants from preoedipal and oedipal conflicts and that superego pathology derives from both earlier and later stages of development.

A corollary topic to phase specificity and etiology is the concept of ego defect. Many analysts believe that borderline patients have ego defects that have been caused by developmental failures in structure formation largely independent of intrapsychic conflict. Others, such as M. H. Stone (1986), believe that biological factors play a role in borderline illnesses. Although the evidence is as yet incomplete, one cannot dismiss this latter possibility. The Kris Study Group concluded that whatever the organic and biochemical factors might be, they will result in a significantly different picture from that envisaged by those theorists who postulate psychogenic structural defects. It is likely that, at our current state of knowledge, all psychogenic ego impairments are inseparable from intrapsychic conflict. If this is so, then the concept of "defect," with its implication of irreversibility by interpretation alone, is a problematic one at best.

Furthermore, the hypothesis that regulatory functions from very early in infantile life are disturbed because of a failure in caregiving independent of psychic conflict does not fit with the observations of many analysts. They observe similar disturbances but prefer to conceptualize them as the outcome of quite complicated interactions between unconscious wishes, defenses, and superego attitudes (Calef and Weinshel 1979). Pine (1988) also presents this point of view when he describes how early trauma becomes intertwined with the conflicts from the later developmental phases of childhood.

Reality Testing[8]

In examining the borderline syndrome, as all authors have stated, attention must be paid to the concept of reality testing. As I have already mentioned, the intactness of reality testing is one of the criteria that most theorists believe differentiates borderline conditions from psychoses. It has been repeatedly stated that borderline patients have intact reality testing or only transient failures in this ego function. The members of the Kris Study Group believe that such a simple formulation is inaccurate for the same reasons that Freud's simple schema for differentiating neurosis and psychosis (Freud 1924[1923]) could not be sustained by the clinical data. Although prolonged psychotic episodes are not a prominent feature of these patients, significantly long periods of failure of reality testing may be present in these patients, particularly around the person of the analyst.

Reality testing is itself an extremely complicated function, one for which assessments such as "intact" or "defective" cannot easily be made (Abend 1982). It may well be that the disturbances in reality testing that do exist in these borderline patients are the result in large measure of the impact of conflict on various ego functions. For example, one patient, when discussing specific sexual fantasies for the first time, suddenly got up from the couch and announced that she had heard the nearby church bells chime the noon hour, the time when her session was to end. The analyst indicated that it was only halfway through the hour and interpreted to her that her anxiety was associated with her discussing sexual material. The patient left the hour convinced that the church bells had chimed, and she returned for her Monday session having spent part of the weekend searching for the church whose bells had chimed incorrectly.

Reality testing may also be compromised by pathological identifications that are the result of the patient's being raised in an ex-

---

[8]The material from this subsection on reality testing and from the subsequent subsections on object relations, reaction to separation and loss, superego conflicts, narcissistic pathology, and defense mechanisms was discussed by the Kris Study Group.

tremely pathological environment that distorts the "socialized reality" (Hartmann 1956) of the patient. Patients raised by psychotic, delusional parents or those exposed to extremes of magical and superstitious thinking would be examples of patients with this type of compromised reality testing.

Object Relations

The Kris Study Group also examined the object relations of our patients. The patients all had disturbed relationships with one or both parents that reflected conflicts from both preoedipal and oedipal eras, and they all had experienced significant object loss. They all had made strong identifications with their very disturbed parents. These identifications frequently served a defensive function, an identification with the aggressor, particularly as they involved taking on the sadistic aspects of their parents' behavior. These patients' sexual lives and their relationships in general were permeated with aggression directed outward, toward the self, or both. The projections of aggression caused these patients to fear objects and led to their need to try to control them. These sadomasochistic features involved oral-, anal-, and phallic-phase issues. We did observe severe ambivalence, but we did not regularly encounter the dramatic and persistent division into "all-good" and "all-bad" self and object images that has been emphasized in the literature.

The extensive use of projection by these patients led to confusions between self and other that disturbed their reality testing in conflict areas. We did not, however, observe the severe, gross psychotic distortions of self-object differentiation that one sees in schizophrenic regression. Projections of aggression, envy, greed, homosexual impulses, heterosexual needs, impulses to control, enslave, and exploit others, and superego condemnations and punishments were present.

Reaction to Separation and Loss

Most important for the understanding of these patients was the severity of their reactions to separation and loss, which has been emphasized by all analysts who write about these more severely ill patients. Our case histories revealed a significant degree of actual object loss in childhood. However, it was clear to us that the day-to-day interactions between the child and his or her caregiver might well have been more important than actual separation experiences. Fears of loss of the object and loss of the object's love were found to be present during each phase of psychosexual development. It was always important to analyze in these patients the specific, unique fantasies that provoked separation fears in order to understand the meaning of these fears and to trace their developmental roots. Separation reactions of our patients were more extreme than those in most, but not all, of our neurotic patients.

Superego Conflicts

In contrast to much of the present literature on borderline patients, we observed intense superego conflicts. It is never easy to distinguish between more mature feelings of "internalized" guilt and those of fear of bodily damage, persecution, or punishment. It is true, as other analysts have noted, that in borderline patients the fear of punishment or damage did play a larger role than in many neurotic patients. It is also true that the projection of greedy, controlling, and exploitative wishes allowed guilt feelings to be avoided until the projection had been modified. Nonetheless, it was clear that these patients had developed strong superego condemnations as well. For example, the patient who had heard the church bells ring before the end of the therapy hour (see subsection "Reality Testing" earlier in this section) was overwhelmed with guilt and fear of punishment for her sexual wishes, just as she was, later, extremely guilty about her hostile and destructive wishes toward her sister. Another patient, whose acting out, alcoholism, and masochism dominated years of the treatment, revealed late in the treatment tremendous guilt over an overt sexual episode with her father in early childhood and her continuing seductive involvement with him into her adolescence.

Narcissistic Pathology

The patients whose cases were reviewed by our group demon-strated a profound degree of narcissism, as has been noted by other analysts. These patients were more than usually concerned with gratifying their own needs or subordinating their own needs to those of others in order to be the center of the others' attention, rather than relating to other people in a more mutual, give-and-take manner. In their analyses, words and interpretations were clearly not sufficient; real gratification was demanded. They also used peo-ple for self-esteem regulation (Reich 1960), and they would react with extreme disappointment, withdrawal, or outbursts of rage when people failed to supply them with libidinal and narcissistic gratifications. They also would be unduly euphoric when praise was given. We did not find it helpful either to view narcissistic problems as necessarily caused by failures of parental empathy or to consider narcissism as having a line of development separate from that of object-related libidinal and aggressive drive maturation. Often we found that narcissistic traits were solutions to conflicts or ways of coping with conflict and were not unrelated to conflict as Kohut and others have suggested. For example:

> A 35-year-old man came for a consultation when accused by his girlfriend of being insensitive and ungiving. He revealed a life history of extreme selfishness and disinterest in the feelings of others, mild imposture, mild psychopathic tendencies that were the result of his feeling that he was an exception to many of the ordinary social conventions, and a long history of sexual esca-pades with women whom he exploited and abandoned. His self-esteem fluctuated widely: he ranged from feeling exceptionally gifted and competent to feeling helpless, anxious, and insecure. Anyone who frustrated him became an enemy and filled him with rage. It was clear that he had extensive narcissistic pathology.
>
> Approaching this patient from a theoretical base of ego psy-chology and the structural theory, I was able to understand many of the determinants of his narcissism. He had a profound identifi-cation with two very selfish and angry parents. In particular, he demonstrated an "identification with the aggressor," his father, who had terrorized him with his temper and had been particularly insensitive to his wife's and his children's needs. Both parents also

demonstrated mild psychopathy and a disregard for many social expectations. The patient's castration anxiety was extreme, both because of his fear of his father and because of his having undergone two surgical procedures on his genitals. Surreptitious sexual play with little girls in his small town made him fear exposure and retaliation from the local authorities. Compulsive masturbation in class and on buses increased his fear, guilt, and sense of being dirty and "lower class." In addition, he was narcissistically wounded by his mother's giving birth to twins when he was 4 years old, undoing his belief that he was the special and the only child his parents wanted. In compensation, he observed and then identified with the wealthy, upper-class members of his town's society in an attempt to undo his degraded image of himself and his parents as well as to decrease his sexual anxiety and guilt.

It is clear from this brief and incomplete vignette that I do not consider narcissistic pathology to be the result of a particular type of conflict derived from any specific era of development. But rather, I consider it to be the result of complex and variable intrapsychic conflicts (see discussion by Robert Leider in Chapter 4 of the present volume).

Defense Mechanisms

The Kris Study Group also reconsidered the concept of primitive mechanisms of defense in general. Sigmund Freud and Anna Freud both thought that a hierarchical developmental view of defense mechanisms might be a helpful theoretical construct. Klein's list of primitive defenses and Kernberg's consolidation of those into splitting, projective identification, denial, primitive idealization, and omnipotence and devaluation created a dichotomy between the primitive defenses utilized by psychotic and borderline patients and those so-called higher-level defenses, such as repression, isolation, displacement, reaction formation, and others, utilized by neurotic patients. This dichotomy was not evident in our patients. Our patients demonstrated many of the classical defense mechanisms in their analytic material, and they used more complex behaviors and psychological reactions for defensive purposes as well.

These findings are consistent with a changing view of defenses, one in which defenses are seen less as stereotypical, fixed responses and more as ubiquitous phenomena in mental life that play a role in adaptation and normal development as well as in psychopathology (Brenner 1982; Willick 1983). According to this hypothesis, all mental activity and behavior may be used to ward off unpleasurable affects. For example, one can use intense activity or symptomatic behavior such as anorexia/bulimia to ward off anxiety or depressive affect. One can use sexual involvement to deny aggressive and sadistic feelings, or, conversely, aggressive and sadistic feelings to deny sexual feelings. If one adheres to this more recent hypothesis, then it is not necessary to postulate either a hierarchy of defenses or levels of higher and lower defenses within a specific defense mechanism (i.e., neurotic denial vs. primitive denial). In this later point of view, one should assess patients' total ego functioning and not just their defense mechanisms when judging their degree of psychopathology. However, even utilizing the older conceptualization, we did observe that projection, denial, acting out, identification with the aggressor, the use of one drive derivative to defend against another, and sadomasochistic libidinal regression were used extensively by our patients.

Finally, on the subject of defenses, I have elsewhere (Porder 1987) offered an alternative hypothesis for what has been called "projective identification." I believe that what is observed clinically can best be understood as a compromise formation that includes as its major component an "identification with the aggressor" or a "turning passive into active." One can observe in the analytic setting a two-tiered transference/countertransference structure. On the surface is the familiar transference/countertransference picture of the analyst as the powerful parent and the patient as the helpless child. On another level, however, the patient enacts the role of the dominant parent and the analyst experiences the feelings that the patient had felt as a child. I believe that it is the enactment of these conflicts within the analytic setting that *produces* both groups of feelings in the analyst and that these feelings in the analyst are not *induced* by the presence of primitive defenses that are used by the patient as a result of early infantile conflicts.

Summary

The borderline concept is a controversial one. Not only is the descriptive diagnosis in dispute (i.e., "borderline personality organization" vs. "borderline personality disorder" or the Kris Study Group view that borderline is only a description of a middle area of psychopathology akin and relative to neurosis and psychosis), but also the entire question of the pathognomonic significance of the separation-individuation phase and the preoedipal era as well. Kernberg remains the strongest proponent of the view that borderline personality organization is a discrete clinical entity with its own distinct psychopathology of internalized object relations dating from a specific era of infantile development. M. Stone (1986) has raised the issues of biological genetic loading and the possible importance of sexual trauma in these patients. Pine (1988) has hypothesized how the failure to develop basic adaptive ego functions predisposes the vulnerable child to difficulty in all future developmental tasks. Abend and colleagues (1983, 1988) believe that these patients' conditions are best described as being on a continuum between neurosis and psychosis and that these patients demonstrate admixtures of conflict from all developmental eras and have suffered chronic trauma in relation to their disturbed parent or parents. There is no current resolution to these dilemmas, but it is my hope that from such controversies future clarification and greater understanding will result.

References

Abend SM: Some observations on reality testing as a clinical concept. Psychoanal Q 51:218–238, 1982

Abend SM, Porder MS, Willick MS: Borderline Patients: Psychoanalytic Perspectives. New York, International Universities Press, 1983

Abend SM, Porder MS, Willick MS: A response. Psychoanalytic Inquiry 8:438–455, 1988

Adler G: Borderline Psychopathology and Its Treatment. New York, Jason Aronson, 1985

Adler G: Transitional phenomena, projective identification, and the essential ambiguity of the psychoanalytic situation. Psychoanal Q 58:81–104, 1989

American Psychiatric Association: Diagnostic and Statistical Manual of Mental Disorders, 3rd Edition. Washington, DC, American Psychiatric Association, 1980

Bak RC: The schizophrenic defence against aggression. Int J Psychoanal 35:129–134, 1954

Bak RC: Object-relationships in schizophrenia and perversion. Int J Psychoanal 52:235–242, 1971

Bion WR: Attacks on linking. Int J Psychoanal 40:308–315, 1959

Bion WR: Second Thoughts: Selected Papers on Psycho-Analysis. London, Heinemann, 1967

Brenner C: The Mind in Conflict. New York, International Universities Press, 1982

Buie DH: Book review of Abend SM, Porder MS, Willick MS: Borderline Patients: Psychoanalytic Perspectives. Int J Psychoanal 66:375–379, 1985

Buie DH, Adler G: Definitive treatment of the borderline personality. International Journal of Psychoanalytic Psychotherapy 9:51–87, 1982–1983

Calef V, Weinshel EM: The new psychoanalysis and psychoanalytic revisionism: book review essay on Kernberg O: Borderline Conditions and Pathological Narcissism. Psychoanal Q 48:470–491, 1979

Deutsch H: Some forms of emotional disturbance and their relation to schizophrenia (1934). Psychoanal Q 11:301–321, 1942

Freud A: The Ego and the Mechanisms of Defence (1936). New York, International Universities Press, 1946

Freud S: The neuro-psychoses of defence (1894), in Standard Edition of the Complete Psychological Works of Sigmund Freud, Vol 3. Translated and edited by Strachey J. London, Hogarth Press, 1962, pp 41–68

Freud S: Further remarks on the neuro-psychoses of defence (1896), in Standard Edition of the Complete Psychological Works of Sigmund Freud, Vol 3. Translated and edited by Strachey J. London, Hogarth Press, 1962, pp 157–185

Freud S: Psycho-analytic notes on an autobiographical account of a case of paranoia (dementia paranoides) (1911), in Standard Edition of the Complete Psychological Works of Sigmund Freud, Vol 12. Translated and edited by Strachey J. London, Hogarth Press, 1958, pp 1–82

Freud S: On narcissism: an introduction (1914), in Standard Edition of the Complete Psychological Works of Sigmund Freud, Vol 14. Translated and edited by Strachey J. London, Hogarth Press, 1957, pp 67–102

Freud S: The ego and the id (1923), in Standard Edition of the Complete Psychological Works of Sigmund Freud, Vol 19. Translated and edited by Strachey J. London, Hogarth Press, 1961, pp 1–66

Freud S: The loss of reality in neurosis and psychosis (1924), in Standard Edition of the Complete Psychological Works of Sigmund Freud, Vol 19. Translated and edited by Strachey J. London, Hogarth Press, 1961, pp 181–187

Freud S: Neurosis and psychosis (1924[1923]), in Standard Edition of the Complete Psychological Works of Sigmund Freud, Vol 19. Translated and edited by Strachey J. London, Hogarth Press, 1961, pp 147–153

Freud S: Inhibitions, symptoms and anxiety (1926), in Standard Edition of the Complete Psychological Works of Sigmund Freud, Vol 20. Translated and edited by Strachey J. London, Hogarth Press, 1959, pp 75–175

Freud S: Fetishism (1927), in Standard Edition of the Complete Psychological Works of Sigmund Freud, Vol 21. Translated and edited by Strachey J. London, Hogarth Press, 1961, pp 147–157

Freud S: Splitting of the ego in the process of defence (1940[1938]), in Standard Edition of the Complete Psychological Works of Sigmund Freud, Vol 23. Translated and edited by Strachey J. London, Hogarth Press, 1964, pp 271–278

Frosch J: The psychotic character: clinical psychiatric considerations. Psychiatr Q 38:81–96, 1964

Frosch J: Psychoanalytic considerations of the psychotic character. J Am Psychoanal Assoc 18:24–50, 1970

Greenacre P: The predisposition to anxiety, Part 1 (1941a), in Trauma, Growth, and Personality. New York, International Universities Press, 1952, pp 27–53

Greenacre P: The predisposition to anxiety, Part 2 (1941b), in Trauma, Growth, and Personality. New York, International Universities Press, 1952, pp 53–82

Greenacre P: Further considerations regarding fetishism. Psychoanal Study Child 10:187–194, 1955

Grinker RR Sr, Werble B, Drye RC: The Borderline Syndrome: A Behavioral Study of Ego-Functions. New York, Basic Books, 1968

Gunderson JG: Characteristics of borderlines, in Borderline Personality Disorders. Edited by Hartocollis P. New York, International Universities Press, 1977, pp 173–192

Gunderson JG: Borderline Personality Disorder. Washington, DC, American Psychiatric Press, 1984

Hartmann H: Ego Psychology and the Problem of Adaptation (1939). Translated by Rapaport D. New York, International Universities Press, 1958

Hartmann H: The mutual influences in the development of ego and id. Psychoanal Study Child 7:9–30, 1952

Hartmann H: Notes on the reality principle. Psychoanal Study Child 11:31–53, 1956

Hartmann H, Loewenstein RM: Notes on the superego. Psychoanal Study Child 17:42–81, 1962

Hartmann H, Kris E, Loewenstein RM: Comments on the formation of psychic structure. Psychoanal Study Child 2:11–38, 1946

Hoch P, Polatin P: Pseudoneurotic forms of schizophrenia. Psychiatr Q 23:248–276, 1949

Jacobson E: Contributions to the metapsychology of psychotic identifications. J Am Psychoanal Assoc 2:239–262, 1954

Jacobson E: The Self and the Object World. New York, International Universities Press, 1964

Kernberg O[F]: Structural derivatives of object relationships. Int J Psychoanal 47:236–253, 1966

Kernberg O[F]: Borderline personality organization. J Am Psychoanal Assoc 15:641–685, 1967

Kernberg OF: Borderline Conditions and Pathological Narcissism. New York, Jason Aronson, 1975

Kernberg OF: Object-Relations Theory and Clinical Psychoanalysis. New York, Jason Aronson, 1976

Kernberg OF: Severe Personality Disorders: Psychotherapeutic Strategies. New Haven, CT, Yale University Press, 1984

Kernberg OF: Projection and projective identification: developmental and clinical aspects. J Am Psychoanal Assoc 35:795–819, 1987

Knight RP: Borderline states. Bull Menninger Clin 17:1–12, 1953

Kohut H: The Analysis of the Self: A Systematic Approach to the Psychoanalytic Treatment of Narcissistic Personality Disorders. New York, International Universities Press, 1971

Mahler MS [in collaboration with Furer M]: On Human Symbiosis and the Vicissitudes of Individuation, Vol 1: Infantile Psychosis. New York, International Universities Press, 1968

Mahler MS: A study of the separation-individuation process and its possible application to borderline phenomena in the psychoanalytic situation. Psychoanal Study Child 26:403–424, 1971

Masterson JF: Treatment of the Borderline Adolescent: A Developmental Approach. New York, Wiley, 1972

Masterson JF, Rinsley DB: The borderline syndrome: the role of the mother in the genesis and psychic structure of the borderline personality. Int J Psychoanal 56:163–177, 1975

Pine F: The four psychologies of psychoanalysis and their place in clinical work. J Am Psychoanal Assoc 36:571–596, 1988

Porder MS: Projective identification: an alternative hypothesis. Psycho-anal Q 56:431–451, 1987

Reich A: Pathological forms of self-esteem regulation. Psychoanal Study Child 15:215–232, 1960

Rinsley DB: An object relations view of borderline personality, in Borderline Personality Disorders. Edited by Hartocollis P. New York, International Universities Press, 1977, pp 47–70

Stern A: Psychoanalytic investigation of and therapy in the border line group of neuroses. Psychoanal Q 7:467–489, 1938

Stone L: The widening scope of indications for psychoanalysis. J Am Psychoanal Assoc 2:567–594, 1954

Stone MH: The borderline syndrome: evolution of the term, genetic aspects, and prognosis, in One Hundred Years at the Border: Essential Papers on Borderline Disorders. Edited by Stone MH. New York, New York University Press, 1986, pp 475–497

Tausk V: On the origin of the "influencing machine" in schizophrenia (1919). Psychoanal Q 2:519–556, 1933

Willick MS: On the concept of primitive defenses. J Am Psychoanal Assoc 31(suppl):175–200, 1983

Winnicott DW: Transitional objects and transitional phenomena (1951), in Collected Papers: Through Paediatrics to Psycho-Analysis. New York, Basic Books, 1958, pp 229–242

Winnicott DW: The theory of the parent-infant relationship (1960), in The Maturational Processes and the Facilitating Environment: Studies in the Theory of Emotional Development. New York, International Universities Press, 1965, pp 37–55

9

Depression

Steven P. Roose, M.D.

Depression was one of the first clinical syndromes for which the then young and expanding discipline of psychoanalysis attempted to provide a comprehensive explanation based on a psychodynamic formulation. Not surprisingly, affects (both anxiety and depression) have played a fundamental role in the clinical and theoretical history of psychoanalysis.

Psychoanalytic theories of depression reflect the spectrum of metapsychology, from drive theory (most specifically, the clinical dimensions of the aggressive drive) to ego psychology, to object relations. And it is not surprising, given the emphasis that psychoanalysis has always placed on the enduring impact of early development, that most psychoanalytic theories posit that the critical predisposition of the adult to depression is formed in childhood, whether as a result of disruption of the normal progression of zones of libidinal discharge, as hypothesized by early writers working exclusively in a drive theory context, or the failure to develop self-esteem regulation and the resultant narcissistic vulnerability, as hypothesized by those influenced by object relations theory and ego psychology.

My purpose in this chapter is to review psychoanalytic theories of depression. However, in tracing any topic through more than 80 years of analytic writings, one can anticipate that a second theme will inevitably emerge—namely, the chronological development of psychoanalytic theory from the early emphasis on the drives and their discharge, through the formation of psychic structures and the emergence of the ego as the "CEO of psychic life," to an emphasis on object relations. In addition, because most American psychoanalysts are initially trained in and maintain a connection with clinical psychiatry, the psychoanalytic perspective has been enhanced by and at times revised according to the increasing knowledge of the neurobiological, pharmacological, and genetic dimensions of melancholia.

Psychoanalytic Theories of Depression

Abraham

The first major psychoanalytic writer to consider the etiology of depression was not Freud, but Karl Abraham. Because the earliest psychoanalytic model of psychopathology was based on drive theory, and particularly the obstacles to or variations in the mode of discharge of libido, it is not surprising that Abraham's early writings were primarily concerned with the zones of libidinal discharge and the process of fixation (see, e.g., Abraham 1916/1960, 1924/1960). He began with the clinical observation that depressed patients seemed preoccupied with "oral issues," specifically that they refused to eat or that they did the opposite—used eating (and specifically the eating of sweets) to relieve depression. Abraham understood these seemingly paradoxical types of preoccupation with food as representing the depressed patient's fixation on oral gratification, which had been a powerful experience in the patient's early childhood and which created a temperamental predisposition to depression in adult life.

It was Abraham's belief that certain infants have a constitutional structure (e.g., more nerve endings in the oral mucosa) that results in a greater than normal amount of oral erotism. Such a situation is a two-edged sword, for though there is greater potential to experience pleasure in the oral zone, there is also greater difficulty achieving satisfaction and the mastery that allows for the normal progression of psychosexual development. Thus, as the zones of discharge for libido naturally evolve from oral to anal, to phallic, and eventually to the genital form of discharge, the constitutionally vulnerable child is left with a diathesis to return to orally influenced modes of behavior to maximize gratification and reestablish a sense of safety at times of stress in adult life. However, Abraham felt that constitutional contributions to orality are not in themselves enough to explain a predisposition to depression, but rather that the oral child must experience critical childhood disappointments. Such disappointments may be a normal developmental stage that the child experiences with greater than normal intensity such as the realization that the child is not the mother's only object of love, or they may involve a pathological disappointment in love, for example, when the mother is not loving. Abraham felt it was critical that such disappointments take place before the resolution of the Oedipus complex, because the successful completion of that developmental task attenuates the libidinal desire for the mother and consequently makes such disappointments with respect to her less powerful. Thus, Abraham concluded that the adult with these predisposing factors is vulnerable to having a depression "triggered" by an experience of disappointment in love.

Subsequent to the publication of Freud's "Mourning and Melancholia" (Freud 1917[1915]), Abraham expanded his exclusive focus on orality and libido to include aggression and hostility within theories of depression (Abraham 1924/1960). In brief, he believed that in the face of a disappointment or rejection the patient will feel unloved, a complex emotional state that includes a reactivation of the childhood fear that unacceptable libidinal and aggressive impulses will drive the object away, thereby threatening the attainment of gratification and safety. It is the anxiety over being loved and loving that triggers regression to the oral phase, where previously the patient had found both gratification and safety. Thus, regression to the oral phase is an attempt by the patient to ward off depression in two ways: 1) by attaining pleasure and 2) by holding on to, through oral incorporation, the lost object, both the object of the present and the fantasied lost object of childhood. Abraham felt he had sufficient data—based on patients' fantasies and dreams—to conclude that oral incorporation is not only to hold on to the object but also to destroy and devour it (i.e., to discharge the patient's sadistic aggression). Thus, paradoxical wishes are manifested in the clinical phenomenology of the depressed patient, namely, the desire to take everything in (the overeating and demandingness of the depressed patient) and the desire to destroy (the defense against which can present as a refusal to take anything "in," e.g., the refusal to eat or drink).

Freud

Clearly, the seminal work in psychoanalysis with respect to depression is Freud's classic "Mourning and Melancholia," published in 1917 (Freud 1917[1915]). Freud himself emphasized that, whatever the correctness of his or other theories on the psychodynamic component of melancholia, contributing psychological factors do not have sufficient explanatory power, but only serve to augment the strong "somatic" factors that he believed to be an intrinsic part of the etiology and phenomenology of the illness. Thus, for Freud it was these somatic factors that explained the presence of symptoms for which there was no psychodynamic explanation (e.g., diurnal variation). Freud started with the observation that the symptoms of the melancholic patient, with some important exceptions, are quite similar to the behaviors and feelings of a person in mourning after the death of a loved one. This naturally led Freud to focus on the experience of loss as a precipitant for depression. But Freud, like Abraham, believed that a loss could trigger a depression only if there existed a psychological predisposition, one rooted in the patient's relationship to the lost object—that it had been a "narcissistic object choice." Perhaps few other terms in psychoanalysis have had so many definitions, but most investigators would agree that at a minimum Freud meant that the object was initially chosen because of similarities to the idealized self or that over time the patient's image of the object had been so infused by characteristics of the self, that object love was really equivalent to self-love. He believed that melancholia could only develop in a patient who had predominantly narcissistic object choices because for him or her the loss of a loved object is really the loss of part of himself or herself. One mourns the loss of another, but one is wounded by, angry at, and ultimately depressed about the loss of part of oneself.

In addition to stressing the importance of orality, as Abraham did, Freud stressed the role of ambivalence and aggression in the development of melancholia as evidenced by the self-hatred and self-torture of the depressed patient. Freud hypothesized a series of psychic mechanisms such that in a patient who is predisposed to depression by virtue of having predominantly narcissistic object choices, the experience of a loss, whether intrapsychic or otherwise, would trigger a withdrawal of libido from external objects back into the self through introjection. Thus, the lost object is taken back into the patient's own ego as described in the haunting phrase "the shadow of the object falls upon the ego" (p. 249). It struck Freud that the depressed patient bitterly and relentlessly condemns himself or herself for misdeeds that were in fact "committed" by the lost object, not the patient. However, because the lost object is now within the patient's own ego, attacks against the object take the form of attacks against the self. Extending this formulation, Freud conceived of suicide as an attempt by the ego to destroy the lost and now hated object; but because that lost object now dwells in the ego, the patient must destroy all of himself or herself even though the intent is to destroy only part. This process has been enthroned in the phrase "depression is anger turned against oneself," a concept that has become an enduring part of our psychodynamic metapsychology.

In summary, Freud maintained that the melancholic patient has, in addition to the necessary somatic diathesis, a psychological predisposition that developed early in childhood as a consequence of primarily narcissistic object choices that resulted in an insoluble ambivalence toward the lost object. As a result of this process, the adult is unable to mourn loss but rather experiences loss as a narcissistic wound that triggers depression. The two fundamental psychoanalytic concepts that emerged from Freud's original work and have transcended a strictly narrow psychoanalytic framework to become part of general psychology are 1) loss triggers depression and 2) depression is a form of aggression turned against oneself.

Rado

The writings of Sandor Rado on depression represent a major departure from the theories of Abraham and Freud. Rado, like Abraham and Freud, thought that there was a psychological predisposition in patients who become depressed; but rather than specifying a narrow causation such as oral fixation or narcissistic object choice, Rado believed that the "predisposition"—the struggle to satisfy constant, intense, and pervasive narcissistic needs—was, in reality, the organizing principle of the patient's entire character structure (Rado 1951, 1927/1956). Although both Freud and Rado used the term "narcissistic" in describing how a patient develops a psychological predisposition to depression, each author had a strikingly different meaning for the word. When talking about melancholia Freud used the word narcissistic to define a mode of libidinal investment, whereas Rado used the term in a broader and less specific way to encompass all that the person requires to experience pleasure and therefore feel gratified.

Thus, for Rado the patient who is vulnerable to becoming depressed is the one who needs a constant and robust external supply of narcissistic gratification (to be fed) to maintain a sense of well-being. Consequently, this person is at risk because a diminution of that supply diminishes the sense of well-being (a narcissistic wound), and the affective response to that event is depression. Once wounded, the patient first protests (i.e., becomes angry). If anger effectively reestablishes the relationship with the supplier of narcissistic gratification, then all is well. If not, then, Rado postulated, the mind evokes a complex set of psychic behaviors in an attempt to reestablish a narcissistic homeostasis; the ego begins to punish itself as a way of begging forgiveness from the lost object (i.e., the narcissistic source). These ego operations produce the clinical symptoms of depression. Rado felt that the ego's response is in some way ironically just, because it is the intense (insatiable) narcissistic demands of the patient's ego that most often drive the object away, and so it is appropriate that the ego essentially "apologize."

There were three major conceptual differences between Rado's theory of the etiology of depression and previous psychoanalytic theories of depression. First, though the experience of loss is still critical, the importance of loss necessary to provoke a depressive response is minimal, especially when compared with Freud's clinical examples. Second, whereas Freud considered the self-accusation of the depressed patient to be displaced aggression, Rado believed that guilt and self-reproach represent the patient's genuine supplication, and, in fact, aggression has no significant role in his theory of depression. Third, Rado shifted from talking about patients with the syndrome of melancholia to describing the psychodynamic configuration of patients who are prone to experience repeatedly transitory depressive affects but who are not suffering from an affective episode. This obvious, but unacknowledged, shift by Rado has had sequelae that cannot be overemphasized. Psychoanalytic writers subsequent to Rado used the term depression to describe both an episode of affective disorder and the universally experienced affect that is transitory and whose presence does not necessarily imply a diagnosable disorder.

Bibring

Edward Bibring, focusing on the universally experienced affect of depression, believed that a psychodynamic explanation for such a general psychological phenomenon cannot be narrow, but rather must be broad enough to explain the presence of depressive affect in a wide range of patients and, indeed, in the psychic life of all human beings (Bibring 1953). This perspective led Bibring to focus on the role of self-esteem. He hypothesized that depression develops in the vulnerable patient when he or she is in a situation that produces a sense of helplessness and powerlessness and, consequently, experiences marked lowering in self-esteem. This experience is a repetition of a childhood trauma that produced an unresolved state of helplessness and powerlessness and thereby rendered the child unable to fulfill the need to reestablish safety.

The child, helpless and powerless, feared that he or she would not be loved, not be fed, and not be able to satisfy the narcissistic desire to be good nor the powerful drive to be strong. The frustration of these goals in the developing child thwarted the emergence of durable self-esteem, thereby predisposing him or her to the affect of depression in adult life. In the context of current diagnostic criteria it has been suggested that the patients for whom Bibring developed a dynamic formulation would now be considered to have dysthymic disorder. Though it may be that what has been called "characterological depression" or "depressive neurosis" is roughly equivalent to dysthymic disorder, Bibring's dynamic formulation was not primarily directed toward explaining chronic, persistent dysphoria, but rather transitory affective experiences that are reactive to external events.

Klein

Among psychoanalytic theoreticians, Melanie Klein is unique in her belief that a type of depression is experienced during very early development. Her developmental scheme prominently includes ego and superego development and fantastic, complex psychic mechanisms, all occurring within the first year of life. Further, her developmental scheme is permeated by her belief in a powerful aggressive drive as a manifestation of the death instinct (Klein 1940/1952). The young infant's interactions with part-objects in the external world lead to both gratifying and frustrating experiences, which form the first internal representations. At some point the infant recognizes that part-objects are, in fact, part of a whole and that both the part-object of hate and the part-object of love are parts of an indivisible one. This leads to the experience of ambivalence—that is, an awareness that one loves and hates the same object and that the desire to destroy must be contained in order to preserve the object of love. These experiences constitute the "depressive position," which is a normal developmental stage (occurring at 6 to 9 months) encompassing the integration of good and bad part representations and the control of sadistic, destructive fantasies.

Normally, a child enters the depressive position with sufficient loving experiences with the mother to have internal representation of security and a trusting relationship with a powerful yet benevolent object. These positive internal representations empower the young ego to resolve the pain of ambivalence. If, however, the child's destructive impulses are so intense, either as a result of inherent aggressive drive or as a result of actual mistreatment by the external object, the child is always in fear that he or she will destroy the hated but needed object. These circumstances lead to inhibition, guilt, and depression.

Both Klein and, later, Jacobson essentially supported the construct that, to a significant degree, the intense guilt and self-loathing of the depressed patient were originally reactions against fantasies of destroying the object. However, according to Klein this aggression is a direct expression of the death instinct, whereas according to Jacobson it represents a complex interaction between the aggressive drive and the relation to the object.

Thus, for Klein it is not the depressive position per se that leads to the affect of depression, but rather the inability to resolve successfully the ambivalence of the depressive position that predisposes one to the experience of depression. Klein extended her original work, which was directed primarily at explaining depressive affect in adulthood, to include an explanation for melancholia, which she felt resulted from the initial failure of positive experiences between mother and child, resulting in insufficient good objects within the ego. The consequence of this was both anger at and suspicion of the outside world as well as an internal sense of pervasive "badness," which was then manifested as the self-hating symptoms of melancholia.

Jacobson

To consider the writings of Edith Jacobson on depression is to enter a new level of psychoanalytic discourse in which complex systems of psychic development that encompass object relations, drives, and the formation of psychic structures offer comprehensive explanations of human behavior and motivation (Jacobson 1971). Jacobson, like Bibring, considered loss of self-esteem to be a central issue in the development of depression, and she devoted considerable time tracing the complex process through which the rudimentary self and object representations are infused with psychic energy (libido or aggression) and the relationship of this process to the emergence of psychic structures. She particularly emphasized the importance of the superego as the regulator of this process that results in positive or negative feelings toward oneself. An adult predisposed to depression has deficits in development that leave the psychic apparatus with overly negative (aggressive) self representations as a consequence, in part, of an inadequate, immature superego. The abundance of aggressive energy in the psychic apparatus of a patient who is vulnerable to depression dictates that when the person experiences a loss or frustration, the first response is anger. If this response fails to rectify the threat, then the anger is directed toward the self and the familiar cascade of self-deprecatory depressive symptomatology ensues.

Although the concept was not originated by her, Jacobson was one of the most ardent proponents of the principle that there is a predictable relationship between the stage at which normal psychological development is disrupted and the form of adult psychopathology. Because of her emphasis on the relationship between early development and adult psychopathology, on the importance of aggression, and on the concept that depression is the result of anger turned against the self, Jacobson's writings most clearly echo Freud's in "Mourning and Melancholia." While preserving all the principles of drive theory, she further incorporates object relations and psychic structures, with particular emphasis on the superego, into her dynamic formulations.

Brenner

Among current psychoanalytic writers, Charles Brenner has written extensively and precisely on affects that he defines as a "sensation or experience of pleasure or unpleasure and an idea or ideas" (Brenner 1991, p. 25). He differentiates the affect of anxiety, which is unpleasure with the anticipation of a calamity, from depression, which is unpleasure coupled with the idea that a calamity has already occurred. Brenner postulates that the fundamental and enduring reality of mental life is psychic conflict and that components of psychological content (e.g., behaviors, symptoms, and affects) are products of the compromise formation that emerges from this conflict. Although the affects of unpleasure (i.e., anxiety and depression) always play a central role in psychic conflict, the degree to which these affects are manifest in the compromise formation is much more variable.

Brenner is forthright in specifying that his theories not only apply to the general experience of depressive affect but also are the foundation for understanding depressive illness. Although it might first appear that Brenner is making a much needed effort to differentiate the arena of psychoanalytic metapsychology from the psychiatric discipline of nosology, in fact the opposite is true, and he concludes that "it is a mistake to base a nosology on the premise that the presence of depression distinguishes a class of mental illness in some fundamentally important way. . . . Presence of depressive affect does not distinguish those patients in any fundamental way from other mentally ill patients" (Brenner 1991, p. 42). Thus, in many ways Brenner reasserts the classic analytic view of affects and symptoms as by-products of psychic conflict, and he further maintains that the proper classification of psychological illness rests on an understanding of the unconscious, not on a categorization of manifest phenomenology.

Mania

In a chapter on psychoanalytic theories of depression, a special note should be made of the psychodynamic formulations for mania that developed pari passu. Many psychoanalytic writers felt a compelling need to have a dynamic explanation for the phenomenology of mania so that their theories of depression would be complete. There were, however, a number of factors that mitigated against this being accomplished in a satisfactory way. For example, as a consequence of not considering manic-depressive illness as an entity distinct from unipolar depression, psychoanalysts were left with the impossible task of explaining not only why some depressed patients became manic but also, and equally important, why the rest did not. In general, psychodynamic formulations of mania have been addendums to a theory of depression and are much less developed.

Abraham (1911/1960) was not only the first to formulate a psychoanalytic theory of depression but also the first to consider the psychodynamics of mania. Not surprisingly, he saw mania and depression as opposite "economic" manifestations of the same conflict derived from the constitutionally intense oral eroticism of the patient. What is rigidly repressed in depression is explosively expressed in mania. Only a severe threat to infantile narcissism could account for the pathological dimensions of both the repression and the expression of the psychic conflict. But Abraham felt that the fact that only some depressed patients become manic could not be explained psychodynamically.

Freud also took up the issue of mania in "Mourning and Melancholia," albeit reluctantly. He concluded that if melancholia is the reaction to the loss of the object, then mania is the consequence of the ego's recovery from the initial loss. The manic phase results when the psychic energy that had once been cathected to the object and that was subsequently taken back into the ego after the loss of the object is now available to seek new objects. Freud noted that the clinical evidence to support this formulation is that one of the characteristic features of mania is the frenzied seeking of new objects. However, when one reads these passages, it is hard to ignore the feeling that Freud felt duty bound to offer such an explanation but was enthusiastic neither about his formulation nor about any other such attempt to understand mania in psychodynamic terms.

Subsequent theorists, notably both Lewin (1949) and Rado (1927/1956), conceptualized mania as an expression of sadism repressed during depression. They believed that the critical pathological deviation from normal psychological development that results in the expression of polar opposites (such as depression and mania) is the failure to integrate the split experiences of love and hate into a mature libidinal attachment to the object. Although sharing the same view, Melanie Klein (1940/1952) felt that mania was not a psychic state in itself but rather represented an extreme defense mechanism provoked by the depressive position; but she was left wanting for an explanation as to why mania was present in some depressed patients but not in others.

Perhaps the most focused effort by psychoanalysts to conceptualize mania was the report by Cohen and colleagues (1954) of the consensus conclusions arrived at by a group of psychoanalysts after considering the psychoanalysis or psychoanalytic psychotherapy of 12 manic-depressive patients. It was determined that all of the patients shared a core family dynamic: the mother tended to be devaluing, and the father was considered to be a failure and was the object of open derision from the mother. All of the families felt they were "outsiders" in the community, and the child who later became manic-depressive possessed some special talent or accomplishment that was used by the parents to gain acceptance. Although in each case the patient held a special place in the family, his or her self-esteem was especially vulnerable because it depended exclusively on external affirmation rather than on an integrated, internally regulated, stable sense of identity. In between the manic or depressive episode the patient may have seemed "normal," but, in fact, like his or her parents, he or she only knew how to manipulate and was unable to genuinely care. Although the patient may have seemed hardworking and helpful, in actuality his or her behaviors were only a reaction formation to intense and chronic feelings of insecurity and dependency and to an insatiable need for love and acceptance.

Cohen and colleagues' study also illuminated a second theme that developed in the analytic literature on manic-depressive illness that is not related to the psychodynamics of the illness but rather to difficulties in treating these patients. A number of analytic writers concurred with the Cohen group in concluding that the interepisode character of the manic-depressive person is dominated by themes of envy, exploitation, self-serving relationships, and the inability to empathize.

It would appear that countertransference often made it difficult for Cohen and colleagues to establish a therapeutic relationship with these patients. Clinically, it appears that many psychoanalysts may have not differentiated narcissism from hypomania, and this may have been an obstacle in trying to develop effective treatment strategies.

Ultimately, perhaps in reaction to increasing biological and genetic data and effective pharmacological treatments, psychoanalytic writers lost interest in mania as a focus of psychological investigation, even more so than with melancholia.

A Critique of Psychoanalytic Concepts of Depression

At some point, clinical descriptive psychiatry, with its emphasis on phenomenology and diagnostic categories, and the psychoanalytic model, with its emphasis on intrapsychic experience and unconscious meaning, began to diverge. Not surprisingly, analytic writers after Freud expanded the term depression to include transitory experiences of depressive affects as well as the syndrome of melancholia. Although understandable, since the psychoanalytic model considered that depressive affects and the depressive syndrome share a fundamental dynamic formulation, this approach proved problematic because clinical psychiatry had made a major point of distinguishing between affect and syndrome and studies on the etiology and treatment of affective disorder were predicated on this distinction. Specifically, DSM-IV (American Psychiatric Association 1994) not only distinguishes between bipolar and unipolar illness (the latter including dysthymic disorder) but defines specifiers describing the most recent episode of illness, notably catatonic features, melancholic features, atypical features, and postpartum onset.

With respect to melancholia, it is illuminating to reconsider the clinical material that was the basis for Freud's theories and conclusions. The observation that mourning and melancholia are phenomenologically similar, with the exception that mourning does not include the self-reproach that is so prominent in melancholia, has been questioned. Recent studies of bereavement emphasize that many of the symptoms prevalent in depression, such as suicidal thoughts and feelings of hopelessness and worthlessness, are uncommon in mourning; in fact, mourning and melancholia are differ-ent in as many important ways as they are similar (Clayton 1979). Furthermore, Freud's conclusion that the cause of the self-condem-nation of the depressed patient is his or her anger at the actions of the lost object that is subsequently turned against oneself is often difficult to support from the clinical data.

These clinical findings naturally raise questions about the neces-sity of a "loss" as a reliable or even frequent precipitant of a depres-sive episode. Although after the onset of a depression it is possible to identify retrospectively a loss (especially when the concept of loss is broadened to include a wide range of external and intrapsychic experiences), this does not establish a cause-and-effect relationship between loss and depression. For example, even if one has identi-fied a significant loss that occurred prior to the onset of depression, the same patient may have previously experienced numerous such losses without having developed depression. Although this may simply mean that the timing of the loss may be a crucial variable with respect to precipitating a depressive episode, it would seem that the relationship between loss and melancholia, if one exists, is complex and often not intuitively obvious.

Summary

With respect to melancholia, psychoanalytic theory has an enduring legacy represented by characterizations of depression as being trig-gered by loss, as reflecting aggression turned against oneself, and as being a reaction to narcissistic injury, and by clinical descriptions (particularly the work of Melanie Klein and Edith Jacobson) that are vivid portraits of the fantasies and psychic experience of depressed patients. However, in general, neither psychoanalytic formulations nor psychoanalytic treatment currently has a major role in the clini-cal management of the patient with melancholia. For these patients both antidepressant medication and electroconvulsive therapy are effective treatments, and in patients with milder forms of nonmel-ancholic depression, cognitive, interpersonal, and psychodynamic psychotherapies have also demonstrated efficacy.

However, although the psychoanalytic perspective may not have significant relevance to the syndrome of melancholia, psychoanalytic theory and psychoanalytically based treatment may be important, if not critical, when one is trying to understand the mechanism of transitory depressive affect states and the relationship of these affect states to the experiences of hurt, the maintenance of self-esteem, and anger. The importance of psychoanalytic theory and technique may also apply to the diagnostic categories of atypical depression and dysthymia, that is, patients with persistently depressed affect that does not occur in the context of an acute episode. In these patients, depressive mood is relatively persistent or separated by periods of normal mood lasting a few days to a few weeks. In addition to experiencing this depressed mood, these patients also feel chronically fatigued and have a decreased sense of pleasure, long-standing feelings of inadequacy, and low self-esteem. The vegetative signs that are prominent in melancholia are most often absent. Over the years these patients have been diagnosed as having characterological depression, depressive neurosis, and currently dysthymic disorder. Regardless of what diagnostic label is used, the depressive affect permeates every part of the patient's life and has widespread and profound effects on object relations, career, parenting, and sense of self. Whatever the "etiology" of the chronic depressive affect, the analyst and the patient often come to believe that the depressed mood can be explained as a consequence of fantasies, conflicts, drives, and transferences. For these patients the depressed affect is a fundamental part of their life narrative.

Again, it is important to emphasize that the "origin" of the depressive affect (i.e., Is it "constitutional"?) is not the crucial issue in terms of impact of the affect on psychological development. By analogy, a significant physical malformation such as a missing limb is clearly not psychological in origin, but just as clearly this defect will be a critical influence, albeit not the only influence, on the child's psychological development. Thus, unlike melancholia, which is an episodic illness that has no demonstrative relationship to character structure or defensive operations and responds to somatic treatments, chronic depressive states are a core part of character structure, sense of self, and object ties. When treating a patient with dysthymia, one must understand the dynamic meaning of the depressive affect. It is not surprising that treatment outcome studies of patients with dysthymia have shown that antidepressant medications are often quite useful but not sufficient in themselves. Psychoanalytic formulations and perhaps psychoanalytically oriented treatment still have significant clinical utility if applied to the appropriate group of depressed patients.

References

Abraham K: Notes on the psycho-analytical investigation and treatment of manic-depressive insanity and allied conditions (1911), in Selected Papers on Psycho-Analysis. Translated by Bryan D, Strachey A. New York, Basic Books, 1960, pp 137–156

Abraham K: The first pregenital stage of the libido (1916), in Selected Papers on Psycho-Analysis. Translated by Bryan D, Strachey A. New York, Basic Books, 1960, pp 248–279

Abraham K: A short study of the development of the libido, viewed in the light of mental disorders (1924), in Selected Papers on Psycho-Analysis. Translated by Bryan D, Strachey A. New York, Basic Books, 1960, pp 418–501

American Psychiatric Association: Diagnostic and Statistical Manual of Mental Disorders, 4th Edition. Washington, DC, American Psychiatric Association, 1994

Bibring E: The mechanism of depression, in Affective Disorders. Edited by Greenacre P. New York, International Universities Press, 1953, pp 13–48

Brenner C: A psychoanalytic perspective on depression. J Am Psychoanal Assoc 39:25–43, 1991

Clayton PJ: The sequelae and nonsequelae of conjugal bereavement. Am J Psychiatry 136:1530–1534, 1979

Cohen MB, Baker G, Cohen RA, et al: An intensive study of twelve cases of manic-depressive psychosis. Psychiatry 17:103–137, 1954

Freud S: Mourning and melancholia (1917[1915]), in Standard Edition of the Complete Psychological Works of Sigmund Freud, Vol 14. Translated and edited by Strachey J. London, Hogarth Press, 1957, pp 237–260

Jacobson E: Depression: Comparative Studies of Normal, Neurotic, and Psychotic Conditions. New York, International Universities Press, 1971

Klein M: Mourning and its relation to manic-depressive states (1940), in Developments in Psycho-Analysis [by Melanie Klein, Paula Heimann, Susan Isaacs, and Joan Riviere]. Edited by Joan Riviere. London, Hogarth/Institute of Psycho-Analysis, 1952, pp 311–338

Lewin BD: Mania and sleep. Psychoanal Q 18:419–433, 1949

Rado S: Psychodynamics of depression from the etiologic point of view. Psychosom Med 13:51–55, 1951

Rado S: The problem of melancholia (1927), in Collected Papers, Vol 1. New York, Grune & Stratton, 1956, pp 47–63

10

Schizophrenia and Paranoid States

Martin S. Willick, M.D.
Steven P. Roose, M.D.

I n this chapter we review the major psychoanalytic concepts of a number of disorders that were formerly grouped under the general heading of "the psychoses." Freud, like the descriptive psychiatrists of his time, maintained the distinction between the two main categories of mental illness—the neuroses and the psychoses— a distinction that has too many limitations to be useful today. Many patients, such as those with serious character or personality disorders, do not fit into either classification. Also, there are patients with severe depression and bipolar (manic-depressive) patients in remission who do not exhibit psychotic features.

In the first section of this chapter we address primarily schizophrenia, an illness that has interested psychoanalysts since Freud published his study of the Schreber case (S. Freud 1911). In this section we also describe psychoanalytic formulations of the various paranoid states that constitute a number of illnesses having paranoid features that are classified separately in current psychiatric nomenclature. In the second section, on affective disorders, we discuss depression and manic-depressive illness, which are currently classified as unipolar and bipolar disorders, respectively.

In addition to outlining the development of the psychoanalytic concepts of both of these major groups of disorders, we point out recent changes and advances in psychiatric classification that help to clarify the nature of these illnesses. Finally, we attempt to show how we might begin to integrate recent advances in neurobiological research in schizophrenia and affective illness with psychoanalytic concepts. It is important to note that most psychoanalysts who treat patients with these disorders are now aware that for many of these patients medication will be a necessary part of the treatment regimen.

Psychoanalytic Concepts of Schizophrenia and Paranoid States

The study of schizophrenia and paranoid states has always occupied a central place in the history of psychoanalysis. The reason for this is that Freud found that the examination of the pathology associated with these illnesses was of importance not only in understanding the specific disease processes involved but also in exploring many aspects of the functioning of the mind and the development of psychic structure in general. It was in 1911 that his famous study of the detailed autobiographical memoir of Daniel Paul Schreber, a German judge who developed a severe psychosis in his early 50s, was published (S. Freud 1911). Since that time, psychoanalysts have proposed a number of ideas about the etiology and pathogenesis of the group of schizophrenic disorders and paranoid conditions.

In this section we present an overview of the psychoanalytic concepts of schizophrenia and paranoid states, tracing the historical development of these concepts up to the present time. We present a critical review of these psychoanalytic concepts and attempt to integrate them with the burgeoning data from the field of neurobiology that are relevant to the current understanding of schizophrenia.

Diagnostic Complexities and Uncertainties

Before we begin our review, however, it would be well to take note of the fact that both clinicians and researchers, whether they are interested in the neurobiological or in the psychodynamic aspects of schizophrenia, agree that we are probably dealing with a hetero-geneous illness, one that may have a number of different etiologies and modes of pathogenesis. In many instances it is not easy to make an accurate diagnosis, and certainly not in the early stages of the illness. It has now been shown, for example, that an acute manic psychosis can manifest the same symptoms as an acute schizo-phrenic one. The distinction can only be made after the course of the illness has been followed over an extended period of time. Moreover, psychiatrists have described what appears to be a consis-tent clinical entity termed "schizoaffective illness" that seems to be closer to bipolar disorder in prognosis and response to lithium medication, but that, at the same time, has many of the features of schizophrenia. We are also, in some cases, hard pressed to clearly distinguish other psychoses such as delusional (paranoid) disorder, atypical psychosis, brief reactive psychosis, and schizophreniform disorder from schizophrenia (see the fourth edition of *Diagnostic and Statistical Manual of Mental Disorders* [DSM-IV; American Psychiatric Association 1994]). In this chapter we have retained the psychoana-lytic term "paranoid states" to designate a number of illnesses with paranoid features classified in DSM-IV by different designations. Therefore, the reader should keep these uncertainties in mind as we proceed with this review of the psychoanalytic concepts of schizo-phrenia and paranoid states.

Historical Overview

Schizophrenia

The early years: 1890–1930. Like other psychiatrists of his time, Freud retained the prevalent view that there were two forms of mental illness, namely, psychoses and neuroses. He believed that the major distinction between them was that in the psychoses there was a "break with reality" (S. Freud 1894). He described a particular kind of psychosis, called "hallucinatory confusion," in which the "ego breaks away from the incompatible idea" so that it has "detached itself wholly or in part from reality" (S. Freud 1894, p. 59). By "incompatible idea," he meant an idea that was overwhelmingly painful or unpleasant. He cited as an example of hallucinatory confusion the case of a young woman who, after being jilted by a man who no longer visited her, believed he was present and hallucinated his voice. Freud contrasted this psychosis with hysteria and obsessional neurosis, in which an incompatible idea and the emotion associated with it are repressed and then either converted into somatic symptoms, as in hysteria, or displaced onto another idea, as in obsessional neurosis.

This formulation foreshadowed his later structural theory (see Chapter 2) in which the ego was seen as opposing an "incompatible idea," an early term that was later conceptualized as being the mental representation of the instinctual drives, or the id. Thus, the psychodynamic concept of conflict between the ego and the id was introduced, including the idea that the ego uses "defenses" to avoid painful affects. A few years later Freud described these defenses in more detail, noting that the defense of projection often leads to the presence of paranoid delusions (S. Freud 1896). He was laying the groundwork for the idea that defenses used in psychoses are different from those used in neuroses.

In the Schreber case (S. Freud 1911) and in later papers (S. Freud 1914, 1915), Freud stated that the mechanism of repression, one of the major defenses, in the psychoses is different from that in the neuroses.[1] In the neuroses, he maintained, libido (his term for the psychic interest or energy associated with the sexual drive) is withdrawn from conscious and preconscious mental representations but remains in the unconscious portion of the mind, still attached to the mental representations of objects in the world. These unconscious impulses and their mental representations are constantly striving for expression and, even though they are opposed by the defenses

---

[1] In these papers, when Freud spoke of "psychoses," he was referring to schizophrenia and paranoia.

used by the ego, occasionally break through, leading to the development of neurotic symptoms and slips of the tongue and other parapraxes, and become apparent in the content of dreams.

Freud believed that in psychoses repression is more extensive, with libido being withdrawn from unconscious mental processes as well, including object representations. Such a libidinal withdrawal would account for the apathy and social withdrawal of the patient with schizophrenia, who seems to have lost all interest in the world around him or her. Freud pointed out, however, that libido is withdrawn from the outside world in other conditions such as severe depression and physical illness. The difference, he believed, is that in schizophrenia the withdrawn libido is then turned back toward the ego or the "self," accounting for the familiar symptoms of hypochondriasis, the overcathexis of one's body,[2] and megalomania, in which the "self" or the ego is overcathected. In addition, Freud said that delusions were the result of the attempt to recathect the mental representations of objects with libido, an effort at restitution from a totally withdrawn and narcissistic state.

Observing the symptoms of megalomania and hypochondriasis and the turning away from the world led Freud to introduce his concept of narcissism and place it in a developmental context. He had already written about the psychosexual phases of libidinal development in terms of the leading erogenous zones: the oral, anal, and phallic-oedipal phases (S. Freud 1905). Now he postulated another kind of libidinal development based on the cathexis of the self or of the object. In the first stage, that of *autoerotism,* in which, according to Freud, the earliest and most primitive form of libidinal cathexis is found, the body is cathected even before the infant has a conception of a "self." In the second stage, that of *narcissism,* the self representation (in contrast to the object representation) is highly cathected (one of the manifestations being megalomania). In the third and most mature stage, that of *"object love,"* the object or the object world (in contrast to the self) is highly cathected.

---

[2] Cathexis is the psychic energy invested in mental representations of the body, the self, and objects.

Freud's ideas represent, in a rudimentary and schematic form, the beginnings of object relations theory. Using the idea of the progression of the distribution of libidinal cathexis between the self and the object and the progression of the source of libidinal cathexis in the psychosexual phases, Freud laid the foundation for the concept of developmental regression and fixation. In other words, there can be fixations at various levels of development as well as regressions back to those phases at times of severe conflict.

Freud believed that in the more severe forms of dementia praecox (schizophrenia) the regression is so complete that the libido returns to the stage of autoerotism but that in paranoia the libido only goes as far back as the stage of narcissism. He was careful to say that the Schreber case, which has been studied primarily as an example of schizophrenia, was really a case of paranoia, with a less severe regression having taken place.

Freud also used the Schreber memoirs to show to a skeptical psychiatric community that what he had discovered about the unconscious mental life of neurotic persons and "normal" persons—namely, the presence of sexual fantasies originating in childhood—was not merely an inference he had made from studying neurotic symptoms. He demonstrated that these sexual fantasies and impulses were present in the conscious mind of psychotic patients. For example, one of Schreber's delusions was that he had been changed into a woman so that God could have intercourse with him in order to repopulate the world. This delusion, said Freud, was an outcome of Schreber's ambivalence toward his father in general and his latent homosexual fantasies in particular. Thus, Freud was pointing out that delusions, in addition to serving to recathect the mental representations of objects, had a dynamic meaning as well and were not meaningless.

Freud expanded upon his view that paranoid delusions involved the defense of projection, that is, the attribution of one's own impulses to another person or thing. He suggested that Schreber's delusions of persecution arose from latent homosexual fantasies that were reversed and projected. The homosexual feeling "I [a man] love him" is reversed into "I do not love him; I hate him." This latter thought/feeling is projected onto the other man, leading to the paranoid idea "He hates (and persecutes) me." At this point in his work, Freud was primarily concentrating on various vicissitudes of the libidinal drive. Later, he was to turn his attention to the importance of the aggressive drive. With this latter focus one can see that in delusions of persecution, that which is being projected often is intense hostility or aggression.

It is now understood that in schizophrenia the mental representations of many unconscious impulses can break through into consciousness.[3] The presence of these representations does not necessarily mean that conflicts arising between the ego and these formerly repressed representations play a primary role in the etiology of the disorder, which involves a breakdown of many functions of the ego.

Although Freud discussed schizophrenia primarily from the vantage point of libidinal theory, he was careful to state that it was possible that it was not libidinal regression that caused the abnormalities of the ego, but that, in fact, the reverse could be true, namely, that "a secondary or induced disturbance of the libidinal processes may result from abnormal changes in the ego" (S. Freud 1911, p. 75). He did not specify what changes in the ego he had in mind, but it can be seen that this statement leaves open the possibility that biological disturbances and/or early defects in development could lead to ego impairments.

One can see that Freud believed that by studying the regressive manifestations found in neurotic and psychotic patients, he could determine at what stage of development significant fixations had taken place. For example, he posited that the fixation points in the neuroses were to be found in the later childhood stages, whereas those in schizophrenia and paranoid psychosis occurred in the most primitive phases of libidinal development (S. Freud 1913). Abraham (1908/1960) made the same distinction when he differentiated schizophrenia from hysteria. In later work based on the structural

---

[3]The breakthrough of previously repressed impulses and thoughts derived from many different phases of psychosexual development was demonstrated in an early psychoanalytic case report by Nunberg (1920/1948).

theory enunciated in the 1920s, Freud wrote that in neuroses there is a conflict between the ego and the id, whereas in psychoses there is a conflict between the ego and the external world (S. Freud 1924[1923]). Still later, however, he professed doubts about this distinction and noted that the complete detachment of the psychotic patient's ego from reality seemed "to happen only rarely or perhaps never" (S. Freud 1940[1938], p. 201).

Tausk (1919/1933), anticipating the focus by later theorists on various aspects of ego functioning, described certain kinds of schizophrenic delusions such as the belief that one's mind is being influenced and controlled by forces inside and outside of the body and the belief that everyone could know one's thoughts. He used the concept of a "loss of ego boundaries" to describe this phenomenon, which in general psychiatry had been called "transitivism." Tausk postulated that very early in life the infant does not distinguish inside from outside, or self from the outside world (a condition similar to the stage of autoerotism proposed by Freud). He believed that there is a gradual building up of ego boundaries during childhood and that these boundaries break down when the schizophrenic illness begins. When this breakdown of boundaries occurs, there is a return to more primitive or archaic states of mind in which there is no distinction between self and other.

The middle years: 1930–1960. Whereas the early psychoanalytic work on both the neuroses and the psychoses focused primarily on various aspects of the vicissitudes of the libidinal drive, Freud's introduction of the structural theory led to a more detailed examination of the ego and its defenses and of the importance of the aggressive drive in pathogenesis (A. Freud 1936/1946; S. Freud 1923, 1926).

Hartmann (1939/1958, 1950/1964, 1953) introduced the idea that many functions of the ego, such as perception, memory, and motility, are primary functions of the ego arising from the basic capacity of the ego and not derived from libidinal and aggressive drive energies, although they could be influenced by conflict early in development. He proposed that in schizophrenia there is a failure in the process of neutralization, an important ego function that enables the drives to be contained and brought under control by the ego. The failure of this function in schizophrenia leads to the eruption of manifestations of both aggressive and libidinal drives, both in behavior and in the conscious expression of previously repressed unconscious impulses and fantasies. Hartmann believed that there may be an inborn primary defect in the capacity for neutralization or that this function could be impaired by faulty development. He felt that this failure leads to an incapacity to erect stable defenses during childhood and that under severe stress the ego of the schizophrenic person breaks down.

Bak (1954, 1971) emphasized the schizophrenic person's failure to deal effectively with aggression. Bak conceived of the withdrawal from the world and the subsequent turning inward as a defense against aggression and noted that the arousal of aggression from early childhood interferes with the development of object relations. He also placed the impairments very early in life, although he, like Hartmann, believed that there might be organic components present in this illness. Bak believed that delusions of grandeur and mannerisms were desperate attempts to form a fixed, albeit bizarre and grandiose, identity in the face of a disintegration of the premorbid identity or sense of self.

Federn (1952) focused his attention on the disturbances in "ego feeling" that exist in schizophrenia. Noting that patients with schizophrenia frequently lose the feeling of cohesiveness of the "self" or the sense of the self's continuity over time, he believed that schizophrenia is primarily a disease of the ego. Expanding on Tausk's concept of ego boundaries, Federn wrote about an outer boundary of the ego interfacing with the external world and an inner boundary, or repression barrier. In schizophrenia, there is a loss of both boundaries. The loss of the outer boundary leads to a loss of the distinction between what is mental and what is external and real; the loss of the inner boundary leads to the failure of repression and the eruption into mental life of previously unconscious fantasies and the emergence of more primitive, archaic mental states.

Jacobson (1953, 1954a, 1954b), following Hartmann in the focus on the understanding of the development of self and object representations, noted that in early infancy the ego exists in an "undifferentiated" state in which there is no clear distinction between ego and id and, likewise, no clear demarcation of the self representation from the object representation. She believed that in states of ego regression in schizophrenia, the patient's ego returns to the state of "undifferentiation" of self and object representations, leading to their merging once again, and that this accounts for many of the delusions of transitivism.

Jacobson also outlined a progression in development of the process of identifications. Early in mental life the infant merely "imitates" the parents. This phase is followed by a period of "magical," or "total," identifications during which time the infant imagines in an unrealistic way that it shares various characteristics with the parents. During these two early phases there are fantasies of fusion, and the infant imagines itself to be "one" with the mother. There then is a gradual building up of "partial," or "selective," identifications whereby the child is actually beginning to realistically take on some of the parents' characteristics. This process leads finally to "mature" identifications, which are more lasting ego qualities that have been derived from the relations to the parents. Jacobson noted that in schizophrenia there is a breakdown of identifications and a regression to these more primitive modes of imitation and magical identifications. She also noted that there is a breakdown of superego identifications and functions, with very primitive, archaic ideas about guilt and responsibility emerging into consciousness.

While the ego psychologists in America were exploring the relationship between disturbances of the ego and the conflicts engendered by the aggressive and libidinal drives and placing them in a developmental perspective, across the Atlantic, in England, Klein (1946) was introducing the foundations of object relations theory, emphasizing the importance of conflicts involving the aggressive drive in the first year of life. She proposed a different timetable for a developmental progression in early life. Believing that the infant was capable of having fantasies at birth and throughout the first year of life, Klein formulated the idea that the infant goes through two crucial periods or positions within the first year that represent normal object relations configurations. The first, the *paranoid-schizoid position,* is present during the first 6 months of life, and the second, the *depressive position*, is present during the last 6 months of the first year. During the paranoid-schizoid phase, the normal infant must project aggression onto the mother in order to protect the "self," which has been experienced as good as a result of soothing experiences at the hands of the mother. The projection of aggression onto the object will then make the infant fear the hatred of the object, who is then regarded as persecutory. If the infant does not project the aggression, the infant is in danger of disintegration, losing not only ego functions but the mental representation of the self.

Klein introduced two new mechanisms of defense that, she believed, operate during the paranoid-schizoid position. They were *splitting* and *projective identification*. Klein believed that these two defenses are "normal" processes early on that must operate to build up the infant's internal world, that is, its internalized object relations. However, if the infant is endowed with too much aggressive drive or if there has been an excessive amount of frustration and tension, these defenses will persist and the infant may be unable to overcome the paranoid-schizoid position, leading to schizophrenia, paranoid psychosis, or schizoid personality (Segal 1973). Thus, for Klein and many of the object relations theorists who followed her, the dynamic issues in paranoid psychosis are related more to primitive fantasies dealing with destructive hatred toward the early caregiving person than to homosexual impulses derived from later stages of development.

Fairbairn (1954) is another British object relations theorist who studied the origins of schizophrenic illness. Klein had placed great emphasis on the innate, constitutional nature of the aggressive drive and the presence of infantile sadistic and envious fantasies derived from the aggressive drive. She even accepted Freud's belief in the death instinct, the presence of which made the projection of the aggression of the death instinct so imperative. Fairbairn, on the other hand, placed the major emphasis for the development of pathology on the inadequate caregiving of the mother. When there is considerable maternal withdrawal, there is profound deprivation. This withdrawal and consequent sense of deprivation lead the infant during the paranoid-schizoid position to regard its love as bad and destructive, leading to a withdrawal of emotional contact with the outer world and a disturbed sense of external reality. Thus, for Fairbairn and many other psychoanalytic theoreticians, the major determinant for the development of schizophrenia was thought to be the destructive effect of profoundly inadequate caregiving on the infant during the early months or first year of life.

Winnicott (1965) added to the existing views of the British object relations theorists by emphasizing that the infant exists in a mother-child dyad. He stressed that it is incorrect to conceptualize pathology as being derived from either innate, constitutional factors in the child or inadequacies of the caregiving person or mother. In anticipating later analysts who were to study the complex mother-child interaction by observing it in a real, live setting, Winnicott promoted the idea that normal development required an adequate fitting together of an individual infant's needs and the capacities of the mother to appropriately respond to its needs. Failures of the "good enough mother" to provide a facilitating environment for growth will, according to Winnicott, lead to a clinging to omnipotent fantasies and the development of a "false self" that compliantly goes along with the external world but increasingly turns inward toward autistic fantasy. Although he did not write a great deal about schizophrenia, Winnicott did state that failures in the facilitating environment result in the developmental faults that are found in that illness.

Sullivan (1953) introduced the interpersonal model to psychoanalysis. Like Winnicott, he believed that one cannot conceptualize the infant's development independent of the mother-child dyad. According to Sullivan, schizophrenic illness is caused by excessive anxiety in the mother being imparted to her child. This arouses three self states in the infant: a "good me" (low anxiety), a "bad me" (high anxiety), and a "not me" (intolerable anxiety). The latter self state is one of extreme dread or panic that leads to fears of disintegration such as are evident, later, during acute schizophrenic "end of the world" panic experiences. The profound anxiety also leads to the formation of defensive structures such as dissociation, sublimation, and projection. The function of the defenses is to maintain security in the face of fragmentation and panic.

The later years: 1960 to the present. Although Freud believed that schizophrenic patients are not amenable to psychotherapy or psychoanalysis because of their inability to form an adequate transference relationship to the physician, other analysts saw that these patients, despite their withdrawal, often can relate to their therapists. In addition, patients were found to vary greatly in their capacity to relate to others despite their illness. Most of the analysts described above who wrote during the "middle years" derived their understanding from the treatment of such patients.

This work has continued to the present time, even though the number of psychoanalysts treating schizophrenia has decreased as has the number of published psychoanalytic papers devoted to the subject. During the past 30 years there has been an increase in the use of neuroleptic medication in the treatment of schizophrenia, and some analysts have continued their work in conjunction with their patients' using medication.

A number of modern analysts continue to stress the importance of failures on the part of the early caregiver, usually the mother, in contributing to the development of the disorder. Fromm-Reichmann (1959) introduced the concept of the "schizophrenogenic mother." Searles (1959/1965) believed that the "schizophrenic patient did not experience, in his infancy, the establishment of, and later emergence from, a healthy symbiotic relatedness with his mother" (pp. 338–339). He also emphasized the importance of the therapist's countertransference reactions in understanding the experience of the schizophrenic patient and examined his countertransference feelings to help derive his conception of the early failures in development.

Giovacchini (1986), likewise, views schizophrenia as beginning with trauma in infancy, leading to fixations that produce profound deficits in structure formation. Later conflict, according to Giovacchini, causes a regression back to presymbiotic states of mental life characterized by lack of psychological content and fantasy.

Pao (1979) divided schizophrenia into subtypes: 1) the more acute cases, for whom early mother-child difficulties predispose the infant to experience organismic panic, and 2) chronic cases, in whom there may exist significant genetic-biological abnormalities.

In the former, and to a lesser degree in the latter, the mother fails to adequately respond to the cues of the needs of the infant, and this failure, combined at times with constitutional factors in the infant, leads to cumulative distress. This distress in turn leads to the use of primitive defenses, a heightened aggressive response to frustration, and an inadequate capacity for neutralization of the drives. There is a loss of the integrative capacity and a fragmentation of the sense of continuity of the self. Pao viewed the delusions of the schizophrenic patient as attempts to stabilize the fragmented sense of self and avoid the panic and sense of disintegration that would otherwise be present.

Robbins (1992), working within a psychoanalytically oriented framework in his treatment of schizophrenic patients, has noted that biological and hereditary factors are not sufficient to explain the etiology of the disturbance. He believes that good mothering and positive environmental experiences can protect a biologically vulnerable child and prevent him or her from developing schizophrenia.

Paranoid States

As previously mentioned, in this chapter we are using the term "paranoid states" to include a number of illnesses such as delusional disorder, paranoia, and paranoid personality disorder. It is well known that paranoid ideas and delusions can appear in a number of other illnesses such as delusional depression, mania, organic and toxic psychoses, and, of course, schizophrenia itself.

We have already noted that Freud specifically called Schreber's condition an example of paranoia rather than schizophrenia and emphasized the use of projection as a defense against latent homosexual impulses. He subsequently pointed out the mechanism of projection of impulses of unfaithfulness as well as homosexual impulses in delusions of jealousy (Freud 1922). With the growing awareness of the importance of the aggressive drive in psychopathology, the focus on the dynamics of paranoid ideation shifted to the role of hatred and aggression in the pathogenesis of such ideation. This was emphasized by Knight (1940) and by Bak (1946), the latter of whom formulated the idea that paranoia is a form of delusional masochism. Psychoanalysts no longer looked upon the difficulty in a man's accepting homosexual wishes as a problem of fears of being loved as a woman and thereby being feminine and castrated, but rather as a larger problem involving intense aggression toward the very person who is loved. It was now also understood that the arousal of aggression could begin very early in life and that it influences basic feelings of trust.

We have already outlined the contributions of the object relations theorists, beginning with Melanie Klein, to the study of schizophrenia. It is worth mentioning again in this subsection on paranoid states that these theorists emphasized that during the paranoid-schizoid position there occurs the intense arousal of oral sadism, either because of an excessive aggressive drive endowment or as a response to inadequate early nurturing. Oral sadism, especially oral envy, is projected onto the mother, who is then viewed as a persecutory figure. According to object relations theorists, objects are more likely to be seen as part-objects at this early time in development, resulting in the infant's fantasy that the persecutor is the hostile, devouring breast. The persecuting breast is introjected and becomes an internal persecutor. As summarized by Meissner (1978) in an extensive review of the paranoid process, "The ego struggles to defend itself against these internalized persecutors by processes of expulsion and projection. The resultant anxiety and the defense mechanisms associated with it form the basis of paranoia" (p. 11).

The object relations theorists conceive of the various paranoid disorders and schizophrenia as illnesses occuring along a continuum, with the basic mechanisms of paranoia outlined above operating as causative mechanisms in the development of these illnesses. With this in mind we now turn to an examination of the theories of the etiology and pathogenesis of schizophrenia and paranoid states.

Current Understanding: Questions and Controversies

Etiology, Pathogenesis, and Symptom Formation

Although Freud never made a definitive statement about the etiology and modes of pathogenesis of schizophrenia, he implicated the role of, on the one hand, intrapsychic conflict and, on the other, some primary deficit (see London 1973a, 1973b). Freud emphasized the impact of conflict in causing a regression to earlier, more primitive forms of psychic structure, fantasies, and thinking. For example, he felt that in response to severe conflict the schizophrenic person regresses to primary process thinking, an earlier form of childhood thinking involving displacement and condensation that is also evident in the formation of dreams. Primary process thinking is evident in delusions, loosened associations, and neologisms. On the other hand, when Freud described a different mechanism of repression, he seemed to be referring to a disturbance in thinking that has the quality of a deficit, perhaps brought on by an ego impairment that may exist independent of conflict.

However, Freud's concept of fixations at early stages of mental life and subsequent regression to these stages in the face of stress or intense conflict led those who followed him to formulate the view that the etiology of schizophrenia lies in impairments in development during the earliest months of life. The views of most of the psychoanalytic authors who have been cited in this chapter derive primarily from a study of the regressive manifestations during adult psychotic episodes and from the insight gained during psychoanalytic treatment of a schizophrenic adult over a long period of time.

From these two vantage points (i.e., the study of regressive manifestations and prolonged analytically oriented treatment), psychoanalysts have made reconstructions of development along two main lines. The first line follows Freud in attempting to reconstruct early normal phases of development from adult psychopathology. As we have noted, Freud reconstructed the early stages of normal psychosexual development from his analysis of the symptoms and character traits of his neurotic patients. He also derived his understanding of the normal primitive mental states of autoerotism and narcissism from the symptoms of psychosis. Continuing in this tradition, both Jacobson and Hartmann conceptualized a normal "undifferentiated" phase during which an infant cannot distinguish between its self representation and the object representation. When a person with schizophrenia demonstrates symptoms involving the loss of such distinctions (i.e., the loss of ego boundaries), this is taken to indicate a regression of the ego back to that time in life when such a lack of distinction is a typical component of a normal primitive phase of development. Similarly, when Klein observed the defenses she called splitting and projective identification in adult or childhood psychosis, she conceptualized a phase of infant mental life (during the first 6 months) during which such mechanisms are not only normal but the very means by which an internal mental representational life is built. The paranoid-schizoid position, then, is a normal configuration of mental life and internalized object relations. According to Klein, it is only when the infant cannot overcome the anxieties of this position that these defenses become pathological and the infant is left vulnerable to developing schizophrenia.

Freud had stated that if a person with schizophrenia regresses to such a primitive state of mental life, there had to have been severe fixations during this early period of life. Analysts who followed Freud, including most of those cited earlier in this chapter, took this concept a step further. They asserted that the cause of such fixations—we now are more likely to use the concept of a failure in development or arrested development—was due to failures on the part of the mother to provide the consistent and necessary nurturing to permit the proper development of adequate psychic structure and psychic differentiation. By and large, these analysts minimized or overlooked the importance of constitutional or biological factors, except to note that constitution must play some role in the etiology of every mental disorder.

Psychoanalytic concepts of the etiology and modes of pathogenesis of schizophrenia that rest so heavily on reconstructions of regressive symptoms, as do the concepts discussed in this section, present several serious problems. Undoubtedly, the disruption caused by profound mental illness leads to the eruption of regressive manifestations. These manifestations include primary process thinking, expression in words or behavior of infantile impulses, loss of ego controls, and disturbances in the sense of self and the integrity of ego boundaries, to name a few. However, the presence of a regressive symptom or behavior does not necessarily indicate a failure in early development. We are using the designation "regression" in a descriptive and not an etiological sense. Regressive phenomena can be brought about by a primary disturbance in brain functioning later in life, a disturbance that need not rest on earlier predispositions.

Another problem with this line of thought is that it is unclear whether regressive or primitive modes of mental functioning are replicas of actual functioning in infancy—that is, whether these manifestations really provide an accurate picture of the mental life of the infant. Although Freud (1900) believed that regressive experiences reveal early modes of psychic function—"what is older in time is more primitive in form" (p. 548)—it is likely that certain manifestations of psychotic states do not have counterparts in normal development. These manifestations may share some descriptive properties with, but are not necessarily similar to, those that actually occur in early development. For example, the common symptom of autism in schizophrenia described by Bleuler (1911/1950) to designate "detachment from reality, together with the relative and absolute predominance of the inner life" (p. 63) may be quite different from the infant's involvement with its own world during the first few months of life. In addition, more recent work on infant observation (see Stern 1985) has led to the conclusion that infants are hardly in an autistic state and are, quite early on, cued in and responsive to the caregiver's presence and ministrations.

A further problem with these etiological formulations has been that some of the symptoms of schizophrenia have been viewed as indicative of regression when actually they may be caused by biological abnormalities. It has been noted that Freud was influenced by the neurologist Hughlings Jackson (Freeman 1969; Solms and Saling 1986), who applied his concept of dissolution-evolution to mental illnesses as well as to neurological ones. Jackson proposed that the organic disease process causes dissolution of the highest cerebral centers, thereby producing the "negative" symptoms of both mental and neurological illnesses. The "positive" symptoms, such as delusions, "arise during activities" of what Jackson called "healthy nervous arrangements," evolution going on in what remains intact in the higher cerebral centers.

In schizophrenia, the negative, or deficit, symptoms include psychic withdrawal, loss of interest, inattention, thought blocking, poverty of speech, loss of will, and loss of feeling (anhedonia). These symptoms, which are present in the most serious forms of schizophrenia, are most likely caused by a primary biological disturbance and are not manifestations of regression to an infantile period of life, although they may sometimes have that appearance (Bilder et al. 1985; Crow 1985). They are correlated with structural and functional abnormalities in the brain as seen with computed tomography and magnetic resonance imaging. Cognitive deficiencies, similar to those found in persons with organic brain damage, show up on neuropsychological testing of schizophrenic patients with significant negative symptoms. However, other symptoms do appear to be a consequence of regression brought about by the illness's disrupting the mental organization. In addition, still other symptoms, such as delusions, may be derived from reactions to or attempts to deal with the trauma of the dimly perceived but poorly comprehended organic deficiencies, as well as having important dynamic meaning in themselves.

Regarding the distinctions between schizophrenia and paranoid states, we must note that there is still some uncertainty about what these illnesses share in common in terms of etiology and pathogenesis. Some forms of schizotypal personality and delusional (paranoid) disorder may have some primary biological determinants that contribute in part to disturbed thinking and paranoid ideation. Other types, including paranoid personality disorder, may be more rooted in traumas and conflicts of early ego development as outlined by object relations theorists. It is doubtful that all of these exist along an etiological continuum, however, because the biological underpinnings of schizophrenia now appear to be generally accepted by researchers and clinicians who are currently studying this illness.

An Integration of the Psychodynamic and the Biological Points of View

At the present time, much controversy exists concerning the origins of the schizophrenic disorders. We are using a term, schizophrenia, that designates what is most likely a group of disorders that show similar symptomatology but that may have different etiologies and pathogenesis. It is, of course, conceivable that profound impairments in early development induced by severe inadequacies in the caregiving person could lead to a psychosis such as schizophrenia as has been postulated by many of the authors cited earlier in this chapter. However, we do not as yet have the data from long-term longitudinal studies to demonstrate this mode of pathogenesis, which has been derived from reconstructions based on the manifestations of the adult illness. Prospective childhood studies that have been carried out thus far have shown no linear relationship between any type of impaired early mothering and the development of schizophrenia (see Kagan 1984; Murphy 1962; Murphy and Moriarity 1976; Thomas and Chess 1980).

Current psychiatric studies of schizophrenia show a renewed interest in Jackson's conception of negative and positive symptoms, although these symptoms are often not seen in pure form. It is still not altogether clear that the so-called positive symptoms may not also be directly attributable to organic deficits while some negative symptoms could also be a psychological reaction to these deficits. Nevertheless, patients with primarily negative symptoms have a poorer prognosis, are less likely to respond favorably to the currently available neuroleptic medications, show cognitive defects on neuropsychological tests similar to those shown by patients with known organic disease, and are more likely to show enlarged ventricles on computed tomography scans. These facts, along with the hereditary data (Rice and McGuffin 1986) and the partial effectiveness of neuroleptics, give every indication that most forms of adult schizophrenia are the consequence of as yet undiscovered biological processes (see Buchsbaum and Haier 1987; Meltzer 1987; Pardes et al. 1989 for reviews). Although exact historical data are hard to come by, it appears that in most cases symptoms were first manifested during adolescence. In contrast to the opinion of the many authors cited, many of these patients were frequently free from schizophrenic illness during childhood. Although there are also many cases in which behavior problems and schizoid traits were evident in childhood, the evidence that these early abnormalities in functioning are due to deficient early caretaking is not available.

However, the fact that there are major biological factors in the etiology of schizophrenia does not necessarily negate the role of deficient caregiving. It has been argued that the hereditary and biological factors are insufficient to cause the disease process. The concordance of schizophrenia in monozygotic twins seems to be about 50%. It may be that, for example, an individual has, as a result of a genetic factor, a predisposition for the illness but will develop the illness only when he or she experiences deficient caregiving or profound deprivation. We do not as yet know enough about the etiology to answer this question, but the data from adopted-away twins, as well as those from adopted-away offspring of schizophrenic parents, appear to confirm the conclusion that heredity far outweighs impaired nurturing. When biological psychiatrists propose an environmental factor in addition to heredity, they are just as likely to be referring to prenatal damage, birth injury, and later viral illness as they are to the nurturing environment.

Those analysts such as Bak, Hartmann, and Jacobson who believed that organic factors play an important role in the etiology of schizophrenia thought that these factors interfere with very early development. The fact that the gross manifestations are not clearly seen until adolescence does not necessarily argue against this point of view. The severe disturbance could have been masked or covered over, concealing the underlying defects. There are, however, no studies of child development that support such a conclusion. In addition, those psychoanalysts who believe that there is early impaired ego functioning are proposing that there is a profound disturbance in the differentiation of the ego during the first year of life and that, as a result of this disturbance, not only is object constancy not achieved, but there is a failure in the basic process of self and object differentiation. It is hard to imagine how such a basic disturbance in the formation of psychic structure often goes undetected during childhood and latency (see McGlashan 1989).

Such a biological view does not negate the importance of dynamic factors in the manifestations of the schizophrenic illness. Patients with this illness have dynamic conflicts that are similar to those in "normal" and neurotic persons. In persons with schizophrenia, however, these conflicts are occurring in an ego that is severely compromised in its functioning by virtue of the profound biological illness. The childhoods of schizophrenic patients may range from relatively normal to severely pathological, but we do not as yet know the influence of pathological rearing on the development of the schizophrenic process.

The adult manifestations of the illness are derived from an interaction among the basic biological abnormalities (cognitive deficits and positive and negative symptoms), the reaction of the patient to these abnormalities, dynamic issues related to the impact of these abnormalities, and dynamic conflicts that predate the outbreak of the illness and may influence its course and outcome.

A great deal remains to be understood about this profound illness from both a dynamic, developmental point of view and a neurobiological point of view. As psychoanalysts, we can still apply our knowledge of dynamic conflict to understand the particular stresses that will exacerbate the symptoms of schizophrenia and lead to poorer functioning. We do, however, have to revise the belief previously held by so many analysts that severe conflicts in infancy and even childhood play a primary role in the etiology and pathogenesis of most forms of schizophrenia.

References

Abraham K: The psycho-sexual differences between hysteria and dementia præcox (1908), in Selected Papers on Psycho-Analysis. Translated by Bryan D, Strachey A. New York, Basic Books 1960, pp 64–79

American Psychiatric Association: Diagnostic and Statistical Manual of Mental Disorders, 4th Edition. Washington, DC, American Psychiatric Association, 1994

Bak RC: Masochism in paranoia. Psychoanal Q 15:285–301, 1946

Bak RC: The schizophrenic defence against aggression. Int J Psychoanal 35:129–134, 1954

Bak RC: Object-relationships in schizophrenia and perversion. Int J Psychoanal 52:235–242, 1971

Bilder RM, Mukherjee S, Rieder RO, et al: Symptomatic and neuropsychological components of defect states. Schizophr Bull 11:409–419, 1985

Bleuler E: Dementia Praecox, or the Group of Schizophrenias (1911). Translated by Zinker J. New York, International Universities Press, 1950

Buchsbaum MS, Haier RJ: Functional and anatomical brain imaging: impact on schizophrenia research. Schizophr Bull 13:115–132, 1987

Crow TJ: The two-syndrome concept; origins and current status. Schizophr Bull 11:471–486, 1985

Fairbairn WRD: An Object Relations Theory of the Personality. New York, Basic Books, 1954

Federn P: Ego Psychology and the Psychoses. Edited by Weiss E. New York, Basic Books, 1952

Freeman T: Psychopathology of the Psychoses. New York, International Universities Press, 1969

Freud A: The Ego and Mechanisms of Defence (1936). New York, International Universities Press, 1946

Freud S: The neuro-psychoses of defence (1894), in Standard Edition of the Complete Psychological Works of Sigmund Freud, Vol 3. Translated and edited by Strachey J. London, Hogarth Press, 1962, pp 41–68

Freud S: Further remarks on the neuro-psychoses of defence (1896), in Standard Edition of the Complete Psychological Works of Sigmund Freud, Vol 3. Translated and edited by Strachey J. London, Hogarth Press, 1962, pp 157–185

Freud S: The interpretation of dreams (1900), in Standard Edition of the Complete Psychological Works of Sigmund Freud, Vols 4 and 5. Translated and edited by Strachey J. London, Hogarth Press, 1953

Freud S: Three essays on the theory of sexuality, I: the sexual aberrations (1905), in Standard Edition of the Complete Psychological Works of Sigmund Freud, Vol 7. Translated and edited by Strachey J. London, Hogarth Press, 1953, pp 135–172

Freud S: Psycho-analytic notes on an autobiographical account of a case of paranoia (dementia paranoides) (1911), in Standard Edition of the Complete Psychological Works of Sigmund Freud, Vol 12. Translated and edited by Strachey J. London, Hogarth Press, 1958, pp 1–82

Freud S: The disposition to obsessional neurosis: a contribution to the problem of choice of neurosis (1913), in Standard Edition of the Complete Psychological Works of Sigmund Freud, Vol 12. Translated and edited by Strachey J. London, Hogarth Press, 1958, pp 311–326

Freud S: On narcissism: an introduction (1914), in Standard Edition of the Complete Psychological Works of Sigmund Freud, Vol 14. Translated and edited by Strachey J. London, Hogarth Press, 1957, pp 67–102

Freud S: The unconscious (1915), in Standard Edition of the Complete Psychological Works of Sigmund Freud, Vol 14. Translated and edited by Strachey J. London, Hogarth Press, 1957, pp 159–215

Freud S: Some neurotic mechanisms in jealousy, paranoia and homosexuality (1922), in Standard Edition of the Complete Psychological Works of Sigmund Freud, Vol 18. Translated and edited by Strachey J. London, Hogarth Press, 1955, pp 221–232

Freud S: The ego and the id (1923), in Standard Edition of the Complete Psychological Works of Sigmund Freud, Vol 19. Translated and edited by Strachey J. London, Hogarth Press, 1961, pp 1–66

Freud S: Neurosis and psychosis (1924[1923]), in Standard Edition of the Complete Psychological Works of Sigmund Freud, Vol 19. Translated and edited by Strachey J. London, Hogarth Press, 1961, pp 147–153

Freud S: Inhibitions, symptoms and anxiety (1926), in Standard Edition of the Complete Psychological Works of Sigmund Freud, Vol 20. Translated and edited by Strachey J. London, Hogarth Press, 1959, pp 75–175

Freud S: An outline of psycho-analysis (1940[1938]), in Standard Edition of the Complete Psychological Works of Sigmund Freud, Vol 23. Translated and edited by Strachey J. London, Hogarth Press, 1964, pp 139–207

Fromm-Reichmann F: Psychoanalysis and Psychotherapy: Selected Papers of Frieda Fromm-Reichmann. Edited by Bullard DM. Chicago, IL, University of Chicago Press, 1959

Giovacchini P: Schizophrenia: structural and therapeutic considerations, in Towards a Comprehensive Model for Schizophrenic Disorders. Edited by Feinsilver D. Hillsdale, NJ, Analytic Press, 1986, pp 259–287

Hartmann H: Ego Psychology and the Problem of Adaptation (1939). Translated by Rapaport D. New York, International Universities Press, 1958

Hartmann H: Psychoanalysis and developmental psychology (1950), in Essays on Ego Psychology: Selected Problems in Psychoanalytic Theory. New York, International Universities Press, 1964, pp 99–112

Hartmann H: Contribution to the metapsychology of schizophrenia. Psychoanal Study Child 8:177–198, 1953

Jacobson E: Contribution to the metapsychology of cyclothymic depression, in Affective Disorders. Edited by Greenacre P. New York, International Universities Press, 1953, pp 49–83

Jacobson E: Contribution to the metapsychology of psychotic identifications. J Am Psychoanal Assoc 2:239–262, 1954a

Jacobson E: The self and the object world: vicissitudes of their infantile cathexes and their influence on ideational and affective development. Psychoanal Study Child 9:75–127, 1954b

Kagan J: The Nature of the Child. New York, Basic Books, 1984

Klein M: Notes on some schizoid mechanisms. Int J Psychoanal 27:99–110, 1946

Knight RP: The relationship of latent homosexuality to the mechanism of paranoid delusions. Bull Menninger Clin 4:149–159, 1940

London NJ: An essay on psychoanalytic theory: two theories of schizophrenia, Part I: review and critical assessment of the development of the two theories. Int J Psychoanal 54:169–178, 1973a

London NJ: An essay on psychoanalytic theory: two theories of schizophrenia, Part II: discussion and restatement of the specific theory of schizophrenia. Int J Psychoanal 54:179–193, 1973b

McGlashan TH: Schizophrenia: psychodynamic theories. in Comprehensive Textbook of Psychiatry/V, 5th Edition, Vol 1. Edited by Kaplan HI, Sadock BJ. Baltimore, MD, Williams & Wilkins, 1989, pp 745–756

Meissner W: The Paranoid Process. New York, Jason Aronson, 1978

Meltzer HY: Biological studies in schizophrenia. Schizophr Bull 13:77–111, 1987

Murphy LB: The Widening World of Childhood: Paths Toward Mastery. New York, Basic Books, 1962

Murphy LB, Moriarty AE: Vulnerability, Coping, and Growth: From Infancy to Adolescence. New Haven, CT, Yale University Press, 1976

Nunberg H: On the catatonic attack (1920), in Practice and Theory of Psychoanalysis, Vol 1. New York, International Universities Press, 1948, pp 3–23

Pao P-N: Schizophrenic Disorders: Theory and Treatment From a Psychodynamic Point of View. New York, International Universities Press, 1979

Pardes H, Kaufmann CA, Pincus HA, et al: Genetics and psychiatry: past discoveries, current dilemmas, and future directions. Am J Psychiatry 146:435–443, 1989

Rice JP, McGuffin P: Genetic etiology of schizophrenia and affective disorders, in Psychiatry, Vol 2: Psychoses, Affective Disorders and Dementia. Edited by Cavenar JO Jr, et al. New York, Basic Books, 1986, pp 147–170

Robbins M: Psychoanalytic and biological approaches to mental illness: schizophrenia. J Am Psychoanal Assoc 40:425–454, 1992

Searles HF: Integration and differentiation (1959), in Collected Papers on Schizophrenia and Related Subjects. New York, International Universities Press, 1965

Segal H: Introduction to the Work of Melanie Klein, New, Enlarged Edition. New York, Basic Books, 1973

Solms M, Saling M: On psychoanalysis and neuroscience: Freud's attitude to the localizationist tradition. Int J Psychoanal 67:397–416, 1986

Stern D: The Interpersonal World of the Infant. New York, Basic Books, 1985

Sullivan HS: The Interpersonal Theory of Psychiatry. Edited by Perry HS, Gawel ML. New York, WW Norton, 1953

Tausk V: On the origin of the "influencing machine" in schizophrenia (1919). Psychoanal Q 2:519–556, 1933

Thomas A, Chess S: The Dynamics of Psychological Development. New York, Brunner/Mazel, 1980

Winnicott DW: The Maturational Processes and the Facilitating Environment: Studies in the Theory of Emotional Development. New York, International Universities Press, 1965

11

Sexual Disorders

Stanley J. Coen, M.D.

Assessment of Sexual Psychopathology: A Clinical Portrait

Imagine a patient who, when he feels anxious, lonely, and insecure, leaves work to go to a pornographic movie theater. He becomes aroused watching pornographic movies, and then by putting coins in a slot, he opens a window through which he can fondle and kiss a woman's breasts. Sometimes he will ejaculate in a private booth at the pornographic movie parlor, and sometimes doing so will serve as a prelude to his seeking out a sexual masseuse. The masseuse will give him a regular relaxing massage and then, herself fully or partially nude, except for the ever-present latex gloves to protect herself from AIDS, will masturbate him to orgasm. Is this a sexual disorder? On the surface, it certainly sounds like one—like a perversion.

As psychoanalytic investigators, we want to know more. Although we certainly want to begin with details of the patient's behavior, we are not satisfied by phenomenological description. The patient is embarrassed and hesitant to disclose anything further of his shameful practices. He wants the analyst to help him to relinquish this behavior so that he can attend to his girlfriend. The analyst may feel repelled by the patient's sexual practices or titillated by the raunchy details. Either reaction may interfere with the analyst's making clear to the patient that for the sake of the treatment, much more detail is needed about behavior, fantasy, and history so that, together, analyst and patient can indeed understand this problem. The patient may protest that it is obvious that he has a perverse sexual disorder. But then we discover that the patient has no difficulty having intercourse with his girlfriend, provided that she is sufficiently warm and responsive with him. Further, he does not need to summon up any fantasies in order to have intercourse with her. This rules out the psychoanalytic definition of *obligatory perversion,* which requires specific fixed behavior for the patient to achieve orgasm. We learn that the patient tends to stay away from initiating sex with her. At first the patient's rationalizations seem convincing: that his girlfriend is too tired, irritable, and overwhelmed, from her very demanding job, to want anything other than to go to sleep.

The analyst encourages the patient to tell more, and the patient spontaneously reveals that when he feels most alone, he seeks out a pornographic movie theater or a sexual masseuse. At such times, he feels bereft, as if there were no one alive to comfort or help him. He does not consciously imagine anyone else being with him, certainly not his mother, father, girlfriend, mentors, or his newly acquired analyst. On the contrary, he is barely in touch with what he feels and what he wants other than this urgent pressure to get relief through his sexual activities. The analyst notes that pressured action seems to divert the patient from awareness of his feelings, wishes, and needs.

As we listen further, we keep open our hypotheses about the meanings and functions of the patient's sexual behavior, knowing all too well that premature conclusions foreclose psychoanalytic investigation and understanding. We certainly may have hypotheses in mind, but, like good detectives, we follow the clues, eager to discover more, constantly reformulating and refining our understandings. Soon the patient describes how comforted he feels by the masseuse, who massages him, allowing him to fondle and suck her breasts while she masturbates him. He lies there passively while she seems to do the work. He feels like a child, a baby; he remarks that most masseuses seem to encourage this by having pictures on their walls of a mother holding an infant in her arms. What does it mean that he wants so much to be held, to suck, and to be passive? Indeed, these are the fantasies he will use when masturbating, especially when he feels anxious and alone. We learn that when he travels or feels left on his own and he becomes anxious and depressed, he will either find a pornographic movie theater or sexual massage parlor or spend hours masturbating using fantasies of experiences with masseuses. In this patient, separation anxiety is being expressed in the form of a sexual disorder. But this connection, important as it is, is only one strand in our understanding of the patient's experience. We thus learn more about this patient's difficulties with functioning on his own—his tendency to become depressed and his difficulty working when he feels unsupported.

It becomes clear how much better he feels in the analyst's office and how much worse he feels when he and the analyst do not meet. We notice that the patient seeks out his sexual practices especially on days when he does not see the analyst. At first, the patient attempts to minimize his difficulty with being on his own by deliberately scheduling business trips to distant places that keep him from meeting with the analyst. And he tends not to think about the analysis and the analyst over weekends. The analyst points out to the patient the apparent contradiction that he seems to hunger for human contact and at the same time to run away from it, certainly in his relationship with the analyst. Then it also becomes clear how afraid the patient is to feel committed lovingly to his girlfriend, especially because of his fears that he will lose her.

Notice how the treatment process moves, how analytic interpretation of defense leads to new information, deepening and enriching what we have already learned.

The patient then remembers that he began his sexual practices after his mother's death. We learn about his feeling deprived of his mother's love, and his father's love too, in emotional and physical ways. He remembers little touching as a child, which is now what he craves so much. In the treatment, he begins to hunger for a mother and a father to love him, and wants the analyst to provide him with such care. He becomes afraid of how much he wants with the analyst, that he will overwhelm the analyst; he recalls fearing that neither parent could cope with his or her own needs, let alone with their son's. As his fears and hesitation to rely on the analyst are focused upon, he relaxes visibly, feels better and functions better, and wants to become part of the analyst's family. He becomes terrified of his homosexual dreams, in which he wants the analyst to fill him up with the analyst's seeming confidence and strength. In the analytic transference, in the patient's dreams and fantasies, the analyst becomes the masseuse—first female, then male—who will provide the patient with all he feels he has missed.

We seem to have moved from a presentation of a sexual disorder to a portrait of a needy, insecure, deprived man who craves attention and care. So much depends on the perspective from which we examine our clinical data. Here we certainly can amplify the nonsexual needs of the patient: how hungry he is for parenting, including encouragement, admiration, attention, touching, consistency, and love. We can consider preoedipal conflict, because these desires are indeed in conflict with the patient's ideals and standards as a capable adult. As he felt safer with the analyst, he disclosed much more about his anger when he felt frustrated and disappointed. We soon learned that the patient feared he was a destructive monster who would push everyone out of his way to get what he felt he needed so desperately.

So we have found sex and aggression. Sex in this patient included intense childlike hunger and need. And the aggression we have heard about so far involved feared destructiveness. But you might ask why we are placing hunger and need under the rubric of sex. Isn't connecting hunger and need with sex a psychoanalytic preconception that this compliant patient is content to satisfy? A thoughtful psychoanalyst would indeed welcome your question and even focus on this point as a line of inquiry with the patient. The analyst would ask the patient why he expresses wishes for closeness and caring in sexual terms rather than more openly and directly, without the diversion of sex. But then one might object that the analyst is disregarding the sexual meanings of this patient's behavior by seeking to reduce these meanings to preoedipal need.[1] That too, however, could become a useful line of inquiry with the patient, namely, about what he wants that is specifically sexual.

The reader may ask whether the explanations of perversion offered in the foregoing portrait are not redundant because similar conflicts appear in patients with borderline personality organization (see Chapter 8). Notice that the unsettling questions in the preceding paragraph can lead to new perspectives in our understanding of patients. In patients with similar conflicts, why do some express the conflicts in sexual ways, whereas most do not? In other words, what does it mean that some patients use a sexual mode for attempting to express and defend against conflicts that other patients manage without such sexual presentation? In certain respects, although psychoanalysis began with significant emphasis on sex and sensuality, psychoanalysts have, to some degree, come to take sex for granted—specifically, what is exciting in sex, and the defensive uses of a patient's sexuality. How and why do some patients learn to defend themselves by exploitation of sexual seductiveness? How does sex help to protect patients from psychological danger?

Sexual Addiction

The patient whose case was described in the preceding section could be regarded as having a sexual addiction. That is, he was addicted to certain sexual practices for relief from specific intense feelings, needs, and wishes. Because this behavior was not required

---

[1]By *preoedipal need*, we mean the patient's felt requirement for the provision of functions by another person that the patient feels unable to provide for himself. Such needs of others include maintenance of psychological balance; need satisfaction; protection against vulnerability and overstimulation; support for self-esteem and self-confidence; assistance with drive management and affect tolerance; and assistance with a variety of other ego functions, such as accurate perception and evaluation of oneself and others, judgment, memory, and thinking. We differentiate such dyadic needs from sexual and aggressive conflict involving three people, which we designate as *oedipal-phase conflict.*

for intercourse, it need not be regarded as a perversion.[2] We soon learned, through his feelings and reactions to the analyst in the analytic transference, that hungry wishes for contact were only part of the answer. Through attention to the patient's behavior, feelings, and fantasies, we observed that he sought to avoid intense need, disappointment, hurt, frustration, and violent rage when the analyst (or whoever the patient needed most) was not available to him. He avoided and denied all of this by his demonstration that the masseuse was always available to him and was willing to grant him his every wish, to let him do as he pleased with her. A masseuse's availability was so different from the limitations and frustrations with the analyst. But such hungry wishes led the patient to want much more with the analyst and to feel helpless, humiliated, and furious when he could not have what he wanted. Unlike with the analyst and with his mother before, with the masseuse he had the illusion that he could run the show and that he could endlessly get rid of and replace any one masseuse. In his childhood his mother had been seriously depressed and absorbed with her own needs; his father had been more available emotionally but had still sent the patient away rather than have to help him face the turmoil of their home. These experiences had all been too much for the patient to integrate, and he had identified with his father in turning to action to avoid feelings.

But what about the question of why he turned to a sexual addiction? For the patient described here, this question is difficult to answer satisfactorily. We learned that he craved the touching he felt he had missed with both parents as a child. From the author's earlier investigations with other patients, he expected to discover a background of sexual intimacies and sexual modes of defense that the patient had experienced with and learned from one or both parents. At most, this patient had some memories of watching mother dress up for parties, admiring her, and sharing in her plea-

---

[2]**Editors' note:** Dr. Coen is referring to a classical, more narrow definition of perversion. Some would view the described behavior as perversion, even if it did not involve intercourse.

sure in her attractiveness. But we did not recover memories of excessive seductiveness in the parent-child relationship (either parent); nor did we find evidence of a pattern of a parent's using sexualized seductiveness in an attempt to manage other conflicts.

Differing Aims and Meanings in Sexual Behavior

When we hear about sexual psychopathology in a patient, we want to determine which of the conflicts are sexual and which are not. Any patient may attempt to obscure more troublesome needs and conflicts by cloaking them in sexual guise. Think, for example, of a man or a woman who is hurt, disappointed, rejected, and angry when a love affair ends, and who then immediately "picks up" another person and has sex with him or her. The person in this situation is not *primarily* seeking sexual satisfaction, but rather is trying to ameliorate his or her injured self-esteem, helplessness, and perhaps difficulty with being left alone, by demonstrating the ability to seduce someone else. For some patients, sex becomes an ongoing, habitual attempt to protect against painful needs and feelings.

Sexualization

Sexualization (sometimes called *erotization* or *libidinization*) refers to the process by which sex is drawn upon not primarily for erotic pleasure but for the defensive meanings and functions it can render (see Coen 1981). As with the patient described above, sex can be especially helpful for calming rage, hurt, disappointment, aloneness, and need. Some patients who tend to rely extensively on sex for defense elaborate the fantasy of being an "omnipotent seducer," capable of arousing and engaging anyone; by elaborating such a fantasy, they protect themselves from feeling helpless, rejected, alone, and unable to influence a vitally needed person.

Typically, patients who draw upon sex in this manner have experienced a very uneven relationship with a parent, usually the opposite-sex parent. For example, another patient had a depressed, childlike mother who had become disfigured from an illness. Much of the time his mother had seemed unavailable, sleeping or lying in bed, with the patient wishing that she would overcome her depression and attend to him. He would try to make her feel better about herself by praising her or advising her on how to look more attractive. Sometimes his mother behaved very seductively with him, as, according to the patient, she walked around their apartment in a filmy nightgown, her fat buttocks clinging to the soft fabric. Or, she seemed to find ways to expose her body to him, so that he could see her genitals and breasts. She might leave the bathroom door unlocked or partially open so that the patient would not realize that she was in the bath. In the analysis, this bisexual man feared that his sexual desires for the analyst would lead them actually to have sex—that the analyst would want him sexually as much as he desired the analyst.

The patient dreamed of the analyst's sitting behind him in an open pink shirt, otherwise nude, writing on a notepad. When he turned to look at the analyst, the latter seemed demonic and no longer able to attend to the patient; the analyst was masturbating his exposed, erect penis to orgasm. The patient remembered how afraid he was that his mother would egg him on toward actual incest with her and that there would be nobody to stop it. This man was able to remember and to reexperience the many times he had felt sexually overstimulated as a child. Although he was terrified of incest, he was also afraid of other wishes and feelings, such as his desire to get so far inside of his mother (or analyst) that he would never have to fear being left alone again (merger wishes) or of feeling lonely, unwanted, neglected, rejected, and enraged. He would use the excited special feeling that he could arouse mother, analyst, or anyone else, man or woman, to counter his terrible feelings that he himself was worthless, unloved, and weak. Or, he would emphasize how weak and disabled he felt so as to reassure himself that he did not have the power to destroy or sexually vanquish anyone else.

Sexualization as the Path to Perversion

Thus, this patient drew upon early exciting experiences with his mother to protect against multiple other difficulties in his affects and self-esteem and in his relations with others. This patient developed bits of perversion. In contrast, *perversion* refers to a structured adult psychopathological formation without which adult sexual functioning cannot occur. That is, perversion is behavior that is *obligatory* for adult sexual performance; without engaging in his or her perversion,[3] the perverted person cannot function sexually.[4] The perverted person seeks to have his or her partner assist him or her with both sexual and nonsexual needs. Through his or her perverse behavior, the person is enabled not only to function sexually but to manage other, nonsexual needs. I regard perversion as a form of pathological dependency in which another person is sexually engaged so as to provide essential defensive reassurance against certain basic dangers that cannot be managed alone (see Coen 1992). A less rigorous approach to perversion considers *bits* of perverse behavior (as were evident in the patient here described) that serve important defensive requirements, whether or not they are *obligatory* for the patient's sexual functioning, to be the equivalent of perversion (e.g., see Novick 1990). Although I would not characterize the latter as perversion, the similarities between bits of perversion and perversion per se are worth stressing, especially in the study of pathological dependency.

As an adolescent, this patient would masturbate while looking in his father's mirror dressed in his father's underpants, imagining that he was becoming his father, who could then sexually enter his mother (mirror masturbation as a mirror or narcissistic perversion; see Bradlow and Coen 1984). Note that occasional masturbation in front of a mirror may be used by healthier patients to play out varied conflicts, especially to reassure them that they possess the parent's genitals rather than the child's. Indeed, a complex exhibi-

---

[3] Obligatory perversion is reported to occur far more often in men than in women.

[4] **Editors' note:** See Editors' note earlier in this chapter.

tionistic and voyeuristic drama involving multiple characters, the patient as child and as each parent, can be enacted in such sexual performances before a mirror.

With each of the two patients whose cases we have thus far discussed, as with all patients, we continually look in two directions: what does the patient run away from, and what does he run toward? There are dangers to be avoided and safety and reassurance to be sought in all human behavior. Thus, we recognize a sexual addiction in the first patient and bisexual aspects of perversion in the second patient. So far we have emphasized *primarily* the uses of sex for defense against nonsexual conflicts. Sexualization especially creates the illusion that rage and destructiveness in oneself and in the vitally needed other have been transformed into desire and love. For example, when each of the aforementioned patients masturbated, he imagined another person who desired him intensely and was willing to allow him to do as he pleased with the other. The more aroused the patient became, the less angry, destructive, rejected, and unloved he felt, as he now imagined the vitally needed person responding intensely to him.

Sexual arousal, with alteration of consciousness and changes in body feeling states, seems to make one's sexual fantasies almost real. This playacting seems to negate hatred and destructiveness in the patient and in his or her needed object. The patient pretends that he/she and the other, in their sexual excitement, now desire and love each other. Whatever bad, angry, destructive feelings each felt toward the other are imagined to have been transformed and disposed of during the exciting sexual act. This process, a kind of magical riddance, is used to reassure the patient that he or she will not actually destroy a vitally needed person through the power of his or her rage.

Psychoanalysts, including the present author, did not initially grasp and emphasize that there is no actual transformation of rage and destructiveness in sexualization. The "transformation" is illusory but sufficiently powerful for patients, especially dependent patients fearful of destroying a vitally needed person, to become addicted to such repetitive defensive enactments. That is, needy, dependent patients fear losing or destroying the other person through their rage. Hence, they need to keep reassuring themselves that they are no longer angry and in danger of destroying the very one they need. Because these patients believe that they are no longer dangerously angry when they are in the throes of their sexually excited illusion, they will need to repeat, again and again, these illusory defensive transformations of their anger. This pattern tends to become a way of life in which these patients crave and emphasize excitement so as to distract themselves from everything that is wrong within themselves and between themselves and their needed other. When confronted by patients who repetitively sexualize their anger, the clinician needs to maintain persistent interpretive focus on these patients' terror of facing and integrating their anger. Sexualized attempts to avoid one's own destructive forces preclude responsible management and integration of rage and destructiveness during psychotherapy or psychoanalysis.

Of course, psychoanalysts were not the first to discover how useful sexual excitement can be for avoiding psychic pain and danger. The Marquis de Sade, in *The 120 Days of Sodom,* recommended what we are now calling sexualization: "This thing, however frightful you wish to imagine it, ceases to be horrible for you immediately [as] it acquires the power to make you discharge. . . . Nothing's villainous if it causes an erection" (de Sade 1785/1966, p. 532).

Pathological Dependency as the Background for Sexualization and Perversion

We should emphasize even more clearly that such sexualized defenses in sexualization and perversion are forms of pathological dependency (see Coen 1992) in which patients avoid managing what is wrong within themselves by attempting to manipulate another person's responses to them. Patients who cannot assume responsibility for their own internal conflicts will tend to involve others in their attempts to defend against and to avoid such conflicts. Dependent patients feel that they cannot manage on their own without a vitally needed other, so no matter how loudly they talk about getting rid of or destroying the other, this is empty rhetoric aimed to minimize their need of the other. At some point, the dependent patient will have to abort his or her destructive impulses so as to preserve the one he or she needs so badly. And all these sexual games seem much more mature to the dependent patient than his or her more naked infantile need.

Conversely, patients will emphasize their infantile neediness, weakness, and disability to protect against more advanced conflicts. Remember that our first patient was initially content to be passive in his sexual behavior and fantasy. He feared active, aggressive, destructive impulses in himself. The second patient similarly emphasized his sense of defectiveness and weakness to protect against his destructive wishes. Dependent patients especially fear that their anger and destructiveness will somehow lead to the loss or destruction of their vitally needed other. Hence, dependent patients will keep retreating from facing and integrating their rage and destructiveness; they will move backward toward passivity, helplessness, weakness, and dependency. This is the regressive, defensive side of passive dependency. The progressive side involves these patients' working their way out of the childlike position in which they have become stuck. Thus, each of the two patients described earlier felt like a little boy in a man's world.

This feeling was most strikingly evident in the second patient's adolescent mirror masturbation and transference fantasies with the analyst in which the patient wanted to become the powerful father/analyst so as to possess the analyst's strength, especially his masculinity and phallus. The first patient also elaborated wishes to rob powerful men (and the analyst) of their strength, money, authority, and women. It became clear that the first patient was avoiding claiming his girlfriend sexually for himself—that he tended to avoid approaching her sexually when he was unsure what her response would be. He feared how angry he would become if she rebuffed him, but he also feared proclaiming himself a rival with other men for his girlfriend. With the masseuse, he masqueraded as a passive little boy who was no threat to other men. Later in treatment, he could feel how much he wanted to dominate the masseuse, to force her to do his bidding. And he could feel how much he did indeed want to compete with other men, to steal their valuable attributes and make them his own, while destroying these rivals. As he became more angry and felt more destructive with the analyst, wanting to become the authority himself at the analyst's expense, he would periodically retreat from this dangerous aggression back to passive dependency.

The second patient would emphasize his genital defect (which had been corrected surgically) as an entitled defense for his incestuous desires toward his mother and father and toward the analyst in the transference. That is, he seemed to be protesting to his own conscience that, because he was born with a genital defect, he need not be required to contain his incestuous desires in fantasy, as the ordinary person needs to, but could enact them with impunity. He pretended that he had already been punished with his congenital defect before he had even had the chance to imagine his crimes. On the one hand, his sense of genital defectiveness (and of being stuck feeling like an inadequate little boy) led him to want to rob and appropriate the analyst's strength and power. On the other hand, he defensively retreated to his sense of defectiveness when he feared the intensity of his envy and destructive wishes toward the analyst.

Sexual Defense and Sexual Conflict

Notice how we have moved from considering the *sexualized* disorders with which our patients presented to considering their *sexual* disorders. Both were present, as with all patients. Sex can serve defensive purposes, and, at the same time, there can be inhibition of adult sexual pleasure and functioning. Our perspective determines what we see. Thus, we have divided sexual disorders into two categories: one in which sex functions primarily for defense against more pressing dangers, and one that specifically involves conflicts over fantasied dangers associated with sexual behavior and sexual pleasure. The sequence of approaching these sides may vary in different patients' treatments. With the two patients described earlier, we began with analysis of the sexualized aspects of their disorder, emphasizing hunger, felt deprivation, neediness, hurt, loneliness, and the management of anger. Although initially we explored each patient's sense of inadequacy and deficiency to open up and to help motivate each patient to address what was wrong, later, sexual conflict became a more central focus of each treatment. When we refer to sexual conflict in these patients, we indicate not only fear of powerful sexual (incestuous) desires but also dangers of robbery, castration, and murder. Once more, sex and aggression come together.

For the child to work his or her way out of feeling deficient compared with the parent of the same sex requires an envious, hate-filled destructive rivalry. Of course, the child also loves and values the same-sex parent and needs this parent (and the other parent) to help the child mature further. For example, the child needs both parents to admire and enjoy the child's pleasure in displaying his or her body in order to feel valued and secure as a boy or girl. This so-called phallic exhibitionism is not confined to phallic display but includes the child's need for affirmation as he or she delights in the attractiveness and capabilities of his or her body. For the same-sex parent to provide this affirmation also requires that this parent (and later the analyst) be secure enough to be able to welcome the child into masculinity or femininity. Later, this parent (and, much later, the analyst) will need to tolerate the child's (and, much later, the patient's) envy, rivalry, and hatred without counterattack, rejection, or diversion of these feelings in the child (patient). The child's (patient's) persistent early needs, wishes, and angers will intensify and color his or her oedipal rivalry. In teasing apart the presentations in the clinical examples above, we have implicitly first addressed so-called preoedipal conflicts (sexualized disorder) before focusing on oedipal (sexual) conflicts. These phases of conflict will, of course, overlap and intersect, as we have seen. With other patients, the order of presentation of conflict and of what we address in treatment may vary.

Notes on the Development of Masculinity and Femininity

The sexual revolution, feminism, and the research of Masters and Johnson (1970) have influenced psychoanalysts to rethink their models of childhood sexual development. The bedrock of sexual conflict has been shifted from anatomy to gender identity. *Core gender identity* refers to one's biological self-designation as male or female, or, rarely, as hermaphrodite or as having ambiguous gender. Core gender is established before a person's psychological sense of maleness or femaleness can develop. After core gender identity and a sense of maleness or femaleness develop, sexuality then develops. Stoller (1976) has identified six factors that contribute to the formation of core gender identity: 1) sex assignment at birth; 2) the parents' attitudes toward the child's sex and the meanings the child attributes to these; 3) the neurophysiological organization of the fetal brain; 4) conditioning, imprinting, and other primitive forms of learning; 5) the developing body ego; and 6) intrapsychic development. Naming or labeling as boy or girl has been emphasized by many as the critical organizer of gender attitudes. Gender assignment and rearing are now regarded as more influential for the development of core gender identity than is anatomy, except when gender anatomy is distinctly deviant. Nevertheless, genital sensations and perceptions help to organize the body ego.

Psychoanalysis is far less phallocentric today than it was in the past. Most theorists stress parallel development for boys and girls, although the specific contents of fantasy and conflict differ between the genders. The girl is certainly not a deficient boy, lacking in the one thing, a phallus, that would make her valuable. Boys and girls each need to be valued, admired, and loved in their own right and gender. Boys and girls will each envy the parent of the opposite sex and of the same sex their adult body parts and valuable attributes. Penis envy is not limited to females! Indeed, as we indicated earlier in this chapter, it is a basic fact of every boy's development. Similarly, both boys and girls envy the mother her breasts and womb as nurturant, procreative, life-giving, and creative. Each child must struggle with his or her feelings of envy of the valued anatomical attributes and of the mind and psyche of each parent.

Similarly, we no longer believe that castration anxiety applies only to boys and not to girls. We may now call this punitive, retaliatory anxiety by other names—mutilation anxiety or anxiety about body damage—but we believe that both boys and girls fear their incestuous desires and wishes to rob and murder the rival, same-sex parent. To contain these dangerous wishes and to feel approved of by the internalized images of the parents, the child needs to build a restraining, punishing, and guiding agency (the superego) within his or her mind (see Chapter 2 for discussion of the superego). This punitive agency functions quite similarly in boys and girls, although the values and standards differ by gender. It is also true that in males mutilation anxiety is usually experienced as being more directly focused on the genitals than is the case in females, for whom fears of body damage may be more diffuse. But men, too, fear injury, damage, and illness to other parts of the body than just their prized penis and testicles. The more the genitals (and breasts and womb) become invested with pleasure and significance, and the more conflict there is about use and enjoyment of these body parts, the more afraid both male and female will be of punishment and damage to these valued body parts.

Sex and gender need to be understood in relation to all of childhood development, including individuation and autonomy. Some psychoanalytic thinking has tended to confuse issues of gender with issues of individuation. Most psychoanalysts do not believe simply that femininity in a man represents wishes to merge with a maternal introject. Nor do most psychoanalysts believe that a man must face the developmental task of differentiating himself from a primary sense of himself as feminine because of his early closeness with the mother. Men can have such merger wishes without feeling feminized. That is, there is a difference between wishing to be at one with the mother (so as to protect against loss and destruction) and wishing to become, thereby, the woman who is mother. This latter wish expresses the transsexual aim of becoming *transformed* into mother as woman, rather than merely seeking to cling to her. A man's feminine wishes can be viewed on a developmental spectrum from wishes to merge with mother, to preoedipal wishes for contact, dependency, protection, love, affirmation, and sexual gratification from father, to negative and positive triangular oedipal conflicts involving issues of dependency, power, aggression, lust, anxiety, and guilt. These other, nontranssexual, feminine wishes in men involve more limited, partial identifications with aspects of mother's femininity compared with the transsexual desire for full transformation into a woman.

Some psychoanalysts believed that wishes for merger in women promote or at least preserve femininity. Most of us, however, now believe that for a woman to become fully heterosexually feminine, she must achieve psychic independence. The woman must individuate and form selective partial identifications with the mother in the latter's role as heterosexual. The acquisition of sexual identity becomes a powerful motivator and vector to differentiate oneself from mother and to relinquish the omnipotentiality of infantile wishes (Jacobson 1964). Core gender plays an important role in the development of object choice and sexual fantasy. Some psychoanalysts have argued that preoedipal castration reactions in both boys and girls are significant organizing experiences for sexual identity and sexuality (Roiphe and Galenson 1981). However, these early experiences of anxiety also seem to be complicated by broader fears of object loss and body-image disorganization, making it difficult to determine the predominant danger. Psychoanalysts think in hierarchical terms, emphasizing that certain conflicts take center stage, with other issues playing a subsidiary role, during development as well as in adult psychopathology. Some psychoanalysts used to think that the girl's castration complex led her into the oedipal phase; others insisted that, as we now believe, there is a biological thrust to heterosexuality. Similarly, we now believe that the young girl's interest in babies derives *both* from preoedipal issues of self-object differentiation and from oedipal wishes to take mother's place in having father's baby.

Researchers with gay men and lesbian women now seek to differentiate inborn constitution from psychological disposition and to determine whether the latter is or is not involved in psychic conflict. Some argue that homosexual males had more difficulty with their masculine identity and self-esteem during childhood and adolescence than heterosexual males had. Although most adult homosexual men did not have marked gender identity disorder as children, we do not know whether many may have experienced gender identity disturbances representing a milder version of the disorder. Gender identity disorder in boys refers to ongoing distress about being a boy, with an intense desire to be a girl that is enacted in repetitive, obligatory play at female activities, including cross-dressing (Coates 1990, 1992; Coates and Wolfe 1995). Such boys want to be rid of their male genitalia. Most boys with gender identity disorder will develop homosexual object choice as adults (Coates and Person 1985). Gender identity disorder in boys is thought to involve significant interference with separation-individuation, leading to intense separation anxiety, together with multiple interferences by both parents with the development of the boy's masculinity, and the parental encouragement that he become, at least in part, female. Perhaps, as we suggested above, patients with profound separation anxiety who do not have aspects of gender identity disorder wish less strongly to be a woman than primarily to remain connected with mother.

Coates (1992; see also Coates and Wolfe 1995) describes a continuum in imitative behavior in boys with gender identity disorder from attempts to understand the mother's incomprehensible affects (depression, destructive rage toward the child) to the full wish to transform oneself into the mother as woman. By playing at becoming the mother as a woman, the child with gender identity disorder attempts to 1) understand the incomprehensible in his mother; 2) find ways to connect with his needy, vulnerable, depressed, hate-filled mother; 3) heal her by his becoming a female child; and 4) protect against need, change, loss, and attack by the mother through the illusion that he is now his mother.

Friedman's (1988) and Isay's (1985, 1986, 1987) critiques of traditional bias toward homosexual males have been helpful, especially in aiding us to grasp our own countertransference pressures to transform homosexual men into heterosexual men. We will need to determine through careful study and research which aspects of development in homosexuality derive from conflict and which do not. There is excessive closure in the models of both Friedman and

Isay. Even if we believed that the future homosexual boy desires only his father as his love object, we would still expect such desires to become contaminated by angry wishes related to frustration, deprivation, jealousy, and envy of the father's power and masculine attributes. And we would expect that feminine identifications derive not only from wishes to attract the father as the mother does, but also from the usual problems of separation-individuation and escape from masculine aggression. Certainly we can no longer regard homosexuality, in males or females, as a perversion, and can only speak of a perversion in this context when, as with heterosexual persons, we can indeed demonstrate that a perversion in any one person exists. Freud (1905) differentiated between, on the one hand, inversion as a deviation in the *object* of the sexual instinct and, on the other, perversion as a deviation in the *aim* of the sexual instinct. With any patient, homosexual or heterosexual, we need to assess collaboratively within an ongoing treatment what is conflictual, and thus potentially modifiable, in sexual orientation, as in any significant aspect of life.

A Schematic Approach to Neurotic Sexual Disorders

Neurotic sexual disorders in men include impotence, premature ejaculation, retarded ejaculation, diminished sexual desire, and, most common of all, psychanesthesia.[5] Common sexual problems in women include varying degrees of general bodily or sexual anesthesia, diminished sexual arousal and pleasure, vaginismus, and impaired ability to orgasm. Frigidity can, in a simple working definition, be referred to as marked inhibition of *responsiveness* during foreplay and intercourse. In this definition, reference to the inability to experience orgasm during intercourse is purposely avoided, and the definition is applicable to both heterosexuality and homosex-

---

[5] Freud (1912) described "psychanaesthetic" men as "men who never fail in the act but who carry it out without getting any particular pleasure from it" (p. 184).

uality. Notice that our attention has shifted to *inhibition,* away from the exploitation of excessive sexual feeling in *sexual addiction* or *perversion.* Remember, however, that we can also focus on what is inhibited in each of these other disorders.

Early psychoanalysts were surprised, given the universal persistence of oedipal conflict, guilt, and mutilation anxiety in both men and women, that most of us have no overt sexual impairment. Typically, our conflicts and inhibitions remain out of consciousness and do not affect our actual behavior. For example, patients with borderline personality disorder are usually capable of intact heterosexual functioning. Kernberg (1974) emphasizes that splitting mechanisms keep oedipal conflicts and pregenital needs separate, allowing the borderline patient to function sexually. Of course, in the patient whose case was presented at the beginning of this chapter, for example, if we focus more closely on the patient's avoidance of pursuing his girlfriend sexually, we may discover inhibition that is outside of the patient's awareness. A psychoanalytic approach emphasizes that any sample of sexual fantasy and behavior involves complex layering of sexual and aggressive drive needs and multiple defensive functions. Such sexual fantasy and behavior may simultaneously represent heterosexual, homosexual, and autoerotic pleasure, as well as multiple defensive needs in relation to aggression and sexuality, object relations, and narcissism, all in complex interrelationship. A psychoanalytic stance would regard such material as manifest content to be investigated for its latent meanings, in relation to drive and defense.

Level of Conflict and of Psychic Organization

Thus, preoedipal conflicts involving primitive narcissistic needs may be *condensed* into heterosexual functioning, or heterosexual functioning may be *adapted* to subserve earlier nonsexual needs. Conversely, the presence of a potency disorder or frigidity tells us nothing about the patient's *level of conflict.* It does not necessarily indicate *predominant* organization at the oedipal level, with oedipal guilt and mutilation (castration) anxiety. If a patient presents with a potency problem or frigidity, we need to assess the predominant level of organization of that patient's conflicts. The following is a highly schematic outline of how to approach such assessment in men and women.

At the *triangular oedipal level,* there is the danger stemming from persons of the same sex being *rivals* for *possession* of the love object of the opposite sex. The patient is capable of tolerating fantasy relationships that involve three people; he or she does not require exclusive symbiotic connection with one other person. Because patients at the dyadic level insist on exclusive connection to one other person, they cannot tolerate fantasy interrelations between and among three persons. Although the patient at the triangular oedipal level can imagine triangular fantasies, these fantasies do express conflicts. That is, these fantasies, like all fantasies, can be regarded as compromise formations that involve various wishes, defenses, and punishments. We imagine the adult patient as still struggling with versions of childlike conflicts viewed largely from within a child's mind. The patient experiences *guilt* over wishing to displace, rob, mutilate, and kill the parent of the same sex in order to possess sexually the parent of the opposite sex. We describe castration (mutilation) anxiety as the talion, or retaliation, punishment via bodily, especially genital, mutilation for incestuous longings and wishes to castrate, in the broad sense of removing the sexual attractiveness, power, and genitals of, the same-sex parent. This danger is similar for both men and women, although, as we have indicated, it is more common for women to experience the danger of bodily punishment and mutilation that is less specifically focused on the genitals. There may be elements of preoedipal fears condensed into the sexual symptoms.

It is useful to differentiate castration anxiety at the level of the *phallic-narcissistic phase,* which is regarded as a dyadic stage of object relations. During this stage the real or fantasied use of the body and genitals serves primarily exhibitionistic and narcissistic purposes, to gain the admiration of the object. The designation "phallic-narcissistic phase" unfortunately does not convey that little girls at this stage have similar exhibitionistic and narcissistic wishes involving their body and genitals. The child/patient is envious of the powerful body parts of the parent of the same sex and is anxiously aware that the parent of the opposite sex not only lacks these but has other powerful, desirable body attributes. The child/patient fantasizes stealing the powerful body parts of the same-sex parent and imagines already having stolen these from the parent of the opposite sex. He or she fears the same-sex parent's anger and the opposite-sex parent's envy as castration anxiety. For example, during this phase the boy experiences women as frighteningly envious and castrating objects. Only in the subsequent oedipal stage does mother become the desired sexual object whom the boy wishes to possess, impress, dominate, and care for in a masculine way. At this latter stage, male objects become rivals for possession of the female, not merely for possession of the penis. Fear of castration by the female becomes less intense usually at the oedipal stage. The reader should note that castration anxiety may include preoedipal issues of fears of object loss and of body-self dissolution that will resemble castration anxiety clinically and that are developmentally related in its formation. These latter fears are more profound, less focally delimited dangers than is castration per se; they threaten more global loss, of the object and of the self.

At the *dyadic preoedipal level* (the patient's having experienced either fixation at that level or regression from oedipal-level conflict), there is insistence on an exclusive relationship with one person. The patient fears loss of love from his or her internal objects[6] as a consequence of heterosexual functioning, especially because of the accompanying fantasies for which he or she feels deserving of punishment. Childhood experiences of being made to feel that genital pleasure is shameful and forbidden will tend to inhibit all persons but will especially restrict insecure, needy patients. Very

---

[6]*Internal object* refers to fantasy representations within the patient's mind of his or her relations with a parent. Internal objects are not veridical images of the parents but are images that depict the parent, to a large degree, according to the patient's needs, wishes, feelings, and fears. Such internal objects function psychodynamically within the patient's internal world to manage conflict and to lessen danger.

insecure patients who need a symbiotic relationship with another person viewed as a mother may fear loss of the object as a consequence of functioning heterosexually with his or her forbidden desires, separately from the imagined mother. Having a sexual partner is viewed as a betrayal of the exclusive, symbiotic relationship with the mother so that the patient feels terrified of losing this vitally needed fantasy connection with the mother. He or she fears that, in fantasy, during intercourse the object may be destroyed or may be incorporated orally or anally, or that the object may abandon the patient as punishment for heterosexual functioning with his or her forbidden fantasies. That is, the patient who functions at the dyadic preoedipal level is *primarily* concerned with acceptance and connection with the internal and external persons on whom he or she is dependent. Therefore, being separate and alone is more dangerous than are the sexual and aggressive desires. Punishment is imagined as global, extending to loss of love or abandonment rather than being focused in a more limited way on the genitals or on signals of guilt. Such angry, needy patients are especially afraid of destructiveness, which they imagine will occur in their aggressive sexual fantasies: somebody will be destroyed, the other or themselves. Similarly, they fear their insatiable hunger, greed, and envy, so that they imagine they will devour their fantasied sexual object or be devoured by it. These patients may fear that intense feelings (elation, arousal, greed, grandiose excitement, rage, etc.) may overwhelm them. Or, defensive wishes to regress, surrender, or fuse with the other may make closeness terrifying, as if self and other would *actually* become one. These patients may fear that the capacity for heterosexual functioning will help to move them out of a symbiotic maternal enmeshment.

Before we assume that such patients are indeed psychically fragile, we need to understand the conflicts and fantasies that terrify them and from which they wish to flee. Psychoanalysts need to consistently keep in mind the following organizing questions: What is the patient running toward, *and* what is he or she running away from? In other words, what are the more advanced conflicts that cannot be faced, and what are the regressive retreats to imagined safety?

In a more general, dynamic way, when confronted by *potency disorders* or *frigidity* (and specific fears of *orgasm*), we should also consider the following problems: the need for control of all emotions, especially forbidden passionate wishes (e.g., incestuous, insatiable, extractive); fearfulness of emotional vulnerability, need, and responsiveness to another person; intense mistrust; fear of one's own destructive aggression as well as of aggression that is projected onto others; and fears of taking too much during sex and thereby devouring the object or blurring the boundaries between self and other through surrender or merger. The ordinary patient, in contrast, is able to enjoy without terror the transitory blurring of boundaries that occurs during orgasm. One reason that *fears of orgasm* are more common in women than in men may be that men are usually better able to focus the excitement and the danger more specifically onto the genitals than are women, who usually experience sexual arousal in a more diffuse way throughout the entire body. The more intolerant and unaccepting of the girl's sensual development, and the more restrictive and punitive, mother, father, and culture have been, the more dangerous orgasm may seem to the woman.

To enjoy orgasm, a man or a woman cannot be terrified of passively yielding to the mounting sexual pleasure that he or she experiences and of yielding to the partner. People who are afraid of passive surrender to their own feelings and needs and to their partner go through the sexual experience focused on the partner's loss of control and on their own ability to seduce and manipulate the other's sexual feelings, with which they vicariously identify, without they themselves giving in to such feelings. Such fear of surrender is a crucial issue in retarded ejaculation and in sexual sadomasochism. It may occur in some persons during ordinary heterosexual intercourse as one aspect of detachment or the need for sexual conquest.

Because sexual functioning may be adapted to serve earlier (preoedipal, dependent, narcissistic) needs, the goal during intercourse then will not be mutually experienced sexual pleasure with a partner who is loved and regarded as a person in her or his own right. In addition, there is the danger of condensation of hostile aggression into sexuality, so that sexual functioning may be seen by the patient as potentially destructive. This destructiveness is not just based on phallic- and oedipal-phase dangers. When much rage and destructiveness are condensed into sexuality, the patient may imagine destroying the partner or being destroyed oneself during sexual contact. When there are excessive narcissistic needs and insufficiently felt valuation of oneself as an attractive, heterosexual person, heterosexual functioning may be difficult or impossible. "How can I, with my inadequate self, body, and genitals, function with a person of the opposite sex?" When there is significant narcissistic pathology, there will usually be condensation of humiliation at oedipal failure with more general preoedipal narcissistic injuries, so that one may feel unable to relate competently to another person of the opposite sex.

On the other hand, some persons may have impairment of general sensual pleasure. They may protect themselves against longings for tenderness, touching, and closeness, and rage at the relative absence of maternal physical tenderness by attempting to shut off such desires for physical closeness in themselves. Some persons go through the motions of heterosexual intercourse and are unable to masturbate or enjoy being touched. For example, a successful businessman was potent, but he barely touched his wife during lovemaking and he himself did not want to be touched. His wife said that he was always in a rush during sex. His mother had died when he was 4 years old and she probably had been depressed before that. This patient recalled little warmth and closeness with either mother or father. He could not remember ever having masturbated. He worked very hard to defend against wanting intense emotional and physical closeness with others. He just could not open up to the enjoyment of touching and being touched. This person's situation exemplifies one form of emotional detachment during sex.

The *goals* of sexual behavior with another person may include dependency, control, aggression, definition and enhancement of the self representation, defense against and mastery of object-related conflicts, and so forth. The sexual behavior with the other person can be used as a *vehicle* acceptable to the ego-ideal for expression of most other needs and conflicts. That is, we are again focusing on defensive uses of sex to manage nonsexual conflict. Indeed, we expect that sex will be enjoyable in its own right as sexual pleasure and simultaneously will express multiple associated meanings. A more mature behavior (adult sex) is used to substitute for infantile wishes and conflicts. There is adaptive value in being able to engage an object in mutually acceptable behavior that would be unacceptable if expressed more directly. Thus, most sexually *promiscuous* persons are infantile and needy, seeking dependent gratification, and are unable to tolerate frustration and delay; they have an imperative need for bodily contact to enhance self-esteem, calm aggression, assuage loneliness, and even, for some, to preserve psychic integrity.

Common Sexual Problems and Issues

The *common sexual disorders* have been regarded either as displaying a specific set of defenses and conflicts or as being the involuntary physiological consequence of intense anxiety in a sexual situation. For those investigators who emphasize the involuntary consequences of sexual anxiety, impotence and total frigidity represent the most severe anxiety in sexual situations and do not have psychodynamics that differentiate greater degree of sexual dysfunction from less incapacity (e.g., impotence from premature ejaculation). For these clinicians, the psychodynamics of impotence and premature ejaculation are no different; what differs is the level of anxiety. In this model, with lesser degrees of anxiety, the patient may be able to participate sexually *up to some point* before becoming incapacitated (impotence, premature ejaculation, or, for the woman, inability to have an orgasm). The alternative hypothesis is that there are specific psychodynamics for different forms of sexual dysfunction (e.g., impotence has different meanings than does premature ejaculation).

The reader should consider the psychodynamics discussed below as hypotheses to be considered with his or her patient rather than as templates for interpretation of sexual conflict. And the reader should attempt to integrate both the models of defense/conflict and of generalized anxiety during sexual functioning as leading to impaired functioning. Sometimes during an intensive treatment, sexual inhibition may disappear without specific interpretation of sexual conflict. On the other hand, many clinicians feel anxious and embarrassed by the task of working with the intimate details of their patients' sexual fantasies and behaviors and so tend to avoid asking about them.

Psychoanalysts have stressed sexual passivity in the sexual disorders of both men and women. By behaving passively during sex, patients can feel cared for by their partners and they can appease their conscience that they neither have initiated nor are responsible for sexual contact. When aggression is poorly tolerated, these persons can accept sex more readily if they can remain passive, because then they do not need to be responsible for the sadism and destructiveness that accompany their sexual desires. In effect, the patient hands over responsibility to the partner for his or her sexual wishes and the accompanying destructiveness. Hopefully, the aggression will have been integrated with and modulated by feelings of love and gratitude so that it merely adds spice to a mutually respectful, caring sexual union.

Feelings of inadequacy impair one's sense of attractiveness, desirability, effectiveness, and power, and so contribute to sexual disorders in both sexes. The sense of bodily defect may represent all that has gone wrong between child and parents, in reality as well as in fantasy. The child may focus concretely on the body part that is regarded as deficient or defective in order to externalize and contain multiple feelings and fantasies of what is wrong within himself or herself and what has been wrong between self and others. For example, one woman analysand reported that during late latency and early adolescence she had stuffed toilet paper into her panties so as to pretend she had a penis. She revealed during analysis her feeling that her breasts were not large enough. The analyst asked her, "Not large enough for what?" This question opened the door to her feeling that she lacked what was necessary to heal her mother's serious depression so that her mother could love her. If only she could have nurtured mother with large and full breasts, or as mother's lover with a generous penis, then perhaps she could have gained mother's love. Homosexual fantasies of her seducing and healing another woman continued into adulthood; she would be the man with the penis who could satisfy the other woman. Thus, she felt she lacked what she should have received from her mother (and from her father); she felt that she had too little good stuff inside or on her.

For both men and women, oedipal-level conflict indicates failure of resolution and integration of envy and rivalry with the opposite-sex parent. For example, the male patient continues to view himself as the little boy in relation to other men, who possess the phallus, which represents power, authority, and prestige, all of which he continues to envy. These patients feel too frightened of their hatred and destructiveness to be able to rob the envied rival (father) of his valued attributes and integrate this robbery. They may go through cycles of feeling some envy of and destructiveness toward the rival father, during which they wish to appropriate the father's attributes and destroy him. But, typically, this is quickly followed by a guilty undoing and repudiation of such destructive wishes, so that the patient again emphasizes (defensively) his sense of deficiency.

The Small Penis Syndrome

The *small penis syndrome* is common in men with sexual disorders as well as in other neurotic men who do not have an overt sexual disorder. A man with this syndrome, convinced that his penis is smaller than the ordinary man's, feels humiliated when others see his penis. He may be preoccupied with observing the large penises of other men, which he envies and wishes were his own. In terms of oedipal-level conflict, the small penis syndrome represents a disguise and submission because of oedipal guilt, castration anxiety, and whatever dependent needs for love and acceptance persist. By presenting himself as deficient, the patient aims to appease the feared rival, onto whom is projected the patient's hostile aggression and his wishes for punishment and containment. The patient aims to placate the rival by fantasied submission to him and by disguise of his own incestuous, castrative, and murderous wishes. The small penis syndrome is very common in neurotic men because of the difficulty many of these men experience in integrating their destructive envy of and rivalry with the father.

Like penis envy, the small penis syndrome should be regarded as an organizing metaphor, representative of feeling small, inadequate, envious of others, and unable to function instrumentally (i.e., with his penis) in the world. Phallic functioning may have come to represent most or all of the man's grandiose exhibitionistic needs. The more injured and impaired the man feels, the more he may attribute magical power to his penis for protection and for affirmation. Phallic narcissism may represent a regressive defense from oedipal dangers as well as the expression of earlier, unfulfilled needs and unresolved developmental tasks.

The Concept of Penis Envy

The concept of penis envy has given rise to much controversy in psychoanalysis. We take for granted that children, both boys and girls, will envy, *to some degree,* the valued attributes of the other gender. The controversy here has centered on the degree to which the girl's envy of the penis influences her feminine development. Grossman and Stewart (1976) described the reanalysis of two analytic patients whose first treatment had foundered over these women's concrete, paranoid, defensive construct of penis envy, which each prior analyst had, to a degree, colluded with rather than analyzed. These women fully believed that what was wrong with them was that they had been physically damaged (born without a penis) and were entitled to reparations because of it. What had to be analyzed was this attempt to externalize and localize profound feelings of deficiency onto the genitals as damaged. That is, the meanings and etiology of the sense of damage and deficiency had to be explored without the analyst's collusion with the patient that biology was at fault. Penis envy had to be regarded as a compromise formation, rather than a concretely crystallized factual representation of female defect, in order for it to be explored psychodynamically. Although most psychoanalysts had not regarded penis envy as an anatomical given, as the Grossman and Stewart (1976) article revealed, analysts, at times, could collude with their female patients in fixing blame on the woman's lack of a penis to justify her feelings of deficiency.

Penis envy is more of an issue for little boys than it is for little girls. All little boys envy the father's large phallus. Little girls vary in the importance they attribute to the phallus. To a degree, it is inevitable that each sex will envy the impressive attributes of the other. This will, however, be compounded by other pressures of envy, greed, dissatisfaction, rivalry, rage, and destructiveness, compounded by trauma and deprivation. Think of the "phallic" exhibitionistic phase as the last dyadic preoedipal phase during which exhibitionism and narcissism predominate. Then drive aims of sexual looking and exhibiting and narcissistic needs for admiration serve to firm, enhance, and integrate the little girl's self-representation. The little girl will bring to this stage her unresolved problems with narcissism and self-object differentiation. Prior impairment of the girl's developing self-esteem increases the likelihood that discovery of the genital differences between the sexes may be experienced as another traumatic deprivation. That is, the narcissistically impaired little girl adds to the ordinary meanings of the discovery of genital differences between the sexes her own added sense of feeling deficient and damaged. Now, she may feel, she has concrete proof that she is damaged, inferior, and unlovable. The primal scene can then also become traumatic as a narcissistic affront.[7] The narcissistically impaired child may be unable to manage the erotic stimulation of the primal scene without gratification because it repeats previous unbearable hurt, rejection, and deprivation. To feel left out of the parents' lovemaking, in fantasy and in reality, becomes unbearable because of feelings of rejection/abandonment, hurt, and rage. As noted earlier in this section, the sense of bodily defect may represent all that has gone wrong between child and parents, in

---

[7]By the primal scene, we refer to the child's fantasies of the parents' lovemaking. Of course, real experiences of seeing and hearing the parents involved with each other (in loving, hate-filled, or sexual ways) contribute to the child's fantasies about what transpires between the parents. However, as with any compromise formation, primal scene fantasies express and defend against various wishes, needs, fears, and punishments.

reality as well as in fantasy. That is, the child may focus concretely on the body part that is regarded as deficient or defective in order to externalize and contain multiple feelings and fantasies of what is wrong within himself or herself and what has been wrong between self and others.

Need, Wish, and Desire in Men and Women

It should be clear by now that boys and girls require love, acceptance, and admiration from both mother and father in order to value themselves as attractive and desirable. Both parents must be capable of managing and containing the varied, intense feelings and wishes they have toward the boy as masculine or toward the girl as feminine in order to facilitate each child's development of joy in his masculinity or in her femininity.

We need to order hierarchically a patient's intrapsychic conflicts when we are presented with clinical details of his or her sexual disorder. That is, some meanings, wishes, and needs will be more pressing than others and so will take precedence in the patient's psyche and, then, in our understanding of that patient's conflicts. For example, a woman who has not fully differentiated herself from her own mother, who feels she needs to cling dependently to her intrapsychic maternal imago, may be inhibited in taking over from mother full autonomous pleasure in her feminine functioning. She may be inclined to relinquish such feminine pleasure and adequacy in order to appease the fantasied envy of the vitally needed mother. A woman's fears of sexual attack by men may actually derive from early conflicts with the mother. That is, defense against rage at the pregenital mother and separation from her is maintained by displacement of the conflict onto men, thus preserving the mother as the intact primary object. This is the kind of analytic assessment that always needs to be made in order to clarify the predominant conflicts. What the woman feels she *needs* may turn out to be only what she *wishes for*, although she may want it strongly and want it for multiple reasons, involving both wish and defense. We would do exactly the same kind of assessment of needs, wishes, and desires with our male patients.

Childhood Abuse

Of course, actual attacks—emotional, physical, or sexual—may contribute to a patient's terror of allowing himself or herself to respond to uncontrolled sexual passion. For example, when there has been childhood sexual seduction, the child is usually overwhelmed by sexual arousal and by unbearable feelings of rage, hurt, disappointment, and betrayal by the adult who has taken advantage of his or her superior position, strength, and authority with the child. We always investigate the complex interdigitation of reality and fantasy because we believe that they cannot be fully separated. Most psychoanalysts believe that the impact of trauma differs from that of fantasy. However, we all assume that reality, *at some point*, is interpreted through subjective experience and fantasy. What really happened is vitally important, but so is how it is interpreted by the developing child and the effect the trauma and the persistent unintegrated traumatic affects have on the subsequent course of psychic development. Childhood sexual abuse may lead to repetitive attempts at mastery of the overwhelming feelings of sexual arousal, rage, hatred, hurt, and disappointment. To the degree that the sexually abused child needs his or her abusive parent, the child will need to deny, minimize, and distort clear perception of the trauma and processing of his or her feelings. A needy child cannot simply understand that a parent has exploited him or her and hate the parent for this abuse and betrayal. That would destroy the child's hopeful expectations for continued parental care and lead to unbearable despair. Wishes not to know, remember, and feel one's traumatic past need consistent attention together with the analyst's helping the patient to feel safe enough finally to be capable of integrating the unknowable.

Common Sexual Problems in Men

Premature Ejaculation

Certain specific psychodynamics have been suggested for particular sexual disorders. Thus, the man's rage and destructiveness toward women have been emphasized in *premature ejaculation*. The man who regularly experiences premature ejaculation may enact a hostile teasing and frustrating of his partner by first arousing her and then vengefully disappointing her; he offers his woman partner something good but refuses to actually give it to her. The patient may fear he will hurt or kill the woman by copulating with her, using his penis as a sadistic weapon. If the patient fears that forceful ejaculation will harm the woman, passive outflow of his semen reassures him. The patient may express his contempt at women by the equivalent of a defiant soiling or urinating on the woman. The patient angrily refuses to give his valuable semen to his woman partner. He hastens to finish the sexual act so as to escape from the dangers he fears in lingering and enjoying what he is doing. These dangers include destructiveness toward the woman and, in projection and retaliatory punishment, destructiveness toward himself. But taking his time and enjoying himself also involve dangers of needing another person, especially a woman.

Typically, the man who regularly experiences premature ejaculation cannot sit still; he wants to rid himself of his needs, close them off, and leave. The dangers from which he flees can include castration, aggressive destruction, depletion, engulfment, or, more generally, holding still with needing another person. Unable to tolerate the fact that he needs and must rely on his female partner, he runs away as quickly as he can from such acknowledgment. A man who feels bitterly deprived may resent having to wait patiently with concern until his partner is satisfied. Like a hungry and angry child, he may take his cookie and run before letting the woman have her turn. The phallic exhibitionism in a man who regularly experiences premature ejaculation has been stressed. The man wishes to have his penis admired, noticed, and touched by the woman who is to represent his mother. Premature ejaculation can be regarded as a compromise formation that allows some heterosexual pleasure with punishment. Persistent feminine identification may interfere with the man's feelings of potency and his ability to function competently during intercourse.

The haste and urgency of the patient who regularly experiences premature ejaculation may infiltrate his psychotherapy. He may want to finish everything quickly before he realizes his neediness and before he is "discovered" and "punished." A highly competent and successful executive complained of premature ejaculation with his wife but not usually with his mistress. He felt embarrassed and anxious about his intense passive longings toward women and men for admiration, recognition, love, touching, and support. When he was younger, he had been the passive partner in some homosexual behavior. This narcissistically needy man was very skilled at eliciting admiration from others. When he got it, he felt high. Left on his own, he would become depressed. He was very afraid of opening up and staying with his needs for his wife and for his analyst. He would keep trying to reject, close off, and move away from his neediness with both wife and analyst. He felt very embarrassed that he had "forgotten" a Valentine's Day card in the analyst's waiting room; he dreaded that the analyst might think this meant he wanted the analyst to love him. This man was terrified of his passive wishes to surrender as a female to the analyst so as to gain the father-analyst's love. He kept wishing to hurry up and finish the treatment, or not to see the analyst so often, even though he acknowledged that he used the analyst as an emotional "regulator." He continually kept an escape route planned with both wife and analyst. When he was left alone by his wife and analyst, he could not sit still. Intense loneliness, depression, and longings to be with someone else would lead him to use drugs, go to discotheques, seek out a woman, or at least fantasize about sex with a former mistress. He especially feared holding still with his intense passive longings, with wanting to submit and to be loved (homosexually) by the analyst. It was very difficult for him to work slowly, patiently, and persistently at a task. He would either avoid such situations or else rush through them in excitement, anxiety, and haste. His haste and urgency had a hungry, insistent quality that brooked no delay. Because of his envy and rivalry with powerful men and his wishes to steal from them and destroy them, he feared that the same would befall him during the sex act.

Impotence

Primary impotence, the situation in which a man has never been able to penetrate another person, is distinctly uncommon. In contrast, *occasional impotence* can affect any man. To understand occasional impotence, the clinician needs to assess the current situation that has produced sufficient conflict and anxiety so as to interfere with the patient's sexual functioning. For men with more sustained impotence, the clinician must assess the level of conflict, as I described earlier in this chapter. I would especially differentiate the patient's fears of women from his fears of men. That is, I would differentiate the patient's concerns about sexual intimacy with a woman, including his wishes to enter and be inside of her, from his concerns about masculine envy and rivalry. Fears of sexual contact with women may involve dangers of need and passivity, fears and wishes for merger with the woman, dangers of being harmed by the woman or of harming her, or, more generally, fears derived from varied levels of the mother/son relationship. To the degree that the woman is still regarded as the forbidden incestuous mother, the patient feels prohibited from sexual contact with her. Then his woman partner may feel like she belongs to another man (father, analyst) who will attack or destroy the patient if he presumes to have sexual contact with her. The man's entering a woman with his erect penis becomes a dangerous transgression that will be punished.

Retarded Ejaculation

Although any man may have occasional retarded ejaculation, sustained retarded ejaculation is distinctly uncommon. Occasional episodes of retarded ejaculation may occur when the patient feels a need to avoid full sexual relatedness with his partner, including giving his sperm to his partner. For example, a man who feels hesitant to impregnate his woman partner may suddenly develop retarded ejaculation. So too may a man who fears falling in love with his new partner. Note that the psychodynamics of impotence and retarded ejaculation may be similar for gay men, especially issues of fears of need, influence, loving, and destroying.

The man with sustained retarded ejaculation tends to be emotionally detached from his partner, content to remain erect without really being emotionally affected during sex as well as in an ongoing relationship. The patient may be a rather remote, self-contained, and self-absorbed man who seeks to have the other person respond to him rather than he have to feel excited by and desire the other person. I emphasize that the clinician needs to work with such defensive qualities in the patient with retarded ejaculation in order to help him become capable of warm human relatedness.

Fears of destructiveness during ejaculation are also common in patients with sustained retarded ejaculation. Very angry men may fear destroying their partners by the ferocity of their ejaculation or, by projection and retaliatory punishment, being destroyed themselves if they ejaculate. Such destructive fears need to be assessed in terms of the level of conflicted development that they represent, as we have done earlier in this chapter. Similarly, the clinician needs to determine how much of the conflict involves destructive fears between patient and partner and how much involves destructive dangers with imagined rivals over the power of phallic functioning.

Common Sexual Issues and Problems in Females

Research by Masters and Johnson (1970) clarified that female orgasm involves arousal of both the clitoris and the lower one-third of the vagina. Clitoral and vaginal orgasm cannot be clearly differentiated biologically. Female sexuality could be regarded as feminine and different from, but not inferior to, male sexuality. Some earlier psychoanalysts denied women their own feminine sexuality, regarding them as having to come to terms with their deficient version of male sexuality, in effect their penislessness. This view did not acknowledge that women have legitimate sexual pleasures of their own, different from and as valuable as men's desires. It is beyond the scope of this chapter to review recent advances in the psychology of women (see Schuker and Levinson 1991). But psychoanalysts have stressed similarities in the conflicts of men and women, although there are some differences in the contents of these conflicts. Contemporary psychoanalysts no longer believe that women begin feeling themselves to be deficient men, unless there is substantial psychopathology. That is, just as this chapter has stressed, the clinician attempts to understand the patient's surface presentation for its manifold meanings.

Women's Fears

Let us note certain themes that may be somewhat different for women than for men. Women probably experience greater, more diffuse bodily sexual arousal than do men. For women, therefore, arousal may pose a greater threat to preservation of body-self integration, boundaries, and the dangers of submission and merger. Most men can more easily focus arousal on their genitals without getting the rest of their body and their psyche involved in passionate excitement. The women undergoing treatment by the present author who have had marked inhibition of general bodily sensual response have been frigid. It appeared that they were not as able to make the division between genital sexual functioning and intimacy and sensuality that some men can make. The woman may control her partner by limiting her response to him, not allowing herself to value him fully and commit herself to him. This may represent a complex narcissistic protection in which the woman insists that the man is not that good in that he does not excite her. Abraham (1920/1968), in his classic paper on the "female castration complex," described one woman's defense against full acknowledgment of her need of her male partner by wanting to castrate and devalue him in fantasy.

"Open" and "closed" are metaphors frequently used by women to express sexual conflicts. Women may fear both opening themselves up to sexual pleasure and being closed off, physically and emotionally, and thus unable to respond pleasurably. Of course, the woman is "penetrated" by the man's penis during intercourse. This does not mean, as some once thought, that women need to be passive and masochistic, tolerating the man's aggression against their bodies. Women vary in how they elaborate the aggressive dangers of the penis's entrance into the vagina, dangers both from the man and from the woman. That is, women may picture the dangers of vaginal penetration as largely stemming from the man in entering her or from herself as she attacks the man's penis during intercourse. To the degree that the woman's hostile aggression is projected outward and/or she has been (physically or emotionally) traumatized by others, she will fear intrusion, invasion, attack, submission, being taken over, and harmed. The woman may also fear what she wishes to do to the man and to his penis, so that she does not feel safe enough to enjoy such fantasies, but must inhibit herself instead. The sexually active woman is ordinarily capable of enjoying varied hostile aggressive wishes toward the man without the terror that she will act on such desires. The woman can imagine that her genitals will extract the man's good supplies, that she will keep his penis forever or remove it so that it becomes her own possession, that she will dominate and mistreat him, and so forth.

In *vaginismus* (usually seen in unconsummated marriage), there is closure of the vaginal opening by muscle spasm. Injury, mutilation, invasion, and/or fusion are particularly feared, and the man's genital must be kept outside of the woman's body. The aggressive dangers, of course, may be attributed to the man as well as to herself. To allow the man's penis inside her may imply that the man and his penis are valuable to her, which the woman may experience as a humiliating submission and acknowledgment of dependent neediness. Some women with vaginismus seem similar to men with retarded ejaculation in their struggle to maintain rigid control over their body and their feelings; they may particularly fear letting themselves respond to stimuli not fully under their own control, introduced by someone else.

A Brief Introduction to Perversion

In persons with perversions, unlike in neurotic persons (who, in general, are healthier), resolution of conflict tends not to take place within their own mind. Hence, these persons feel the repetitive need to enact perverse dramas in which others are engaged so that they can authenticate themselves, their fantasies, and their defensive transformations. There are now two different approaches to perversion. In the traditional (rigorous) definition, to which, following Bak (1974), this chapter adheres, perversion is regarded as an adult psychopathological formation, consolidated through adolescent development, that is *obligatory* for the person with a perversion so that he or she can function sexually (see Coen 1985). In the looser attitude, *bits of perverse behavior* that serve important defensive requirements, whether or not they are *obligatory* for the patient's sexual functioning, are considered to be the equivalent of perversion (e.g., see Novick 1990). Although the author of this chapter would not call this perversion, the similarities are worth stressing, especially in the study of pathologically dependent patients.

Thus, we have noted bits of perversion earlier in this chapter when we investigated the functioning of sexualized defense in sexual addiction or mirror masturbation. Patients tend to identify with the action tendencies of their parents, so that they avoid feelings and needs through action. When these patients are unable to manage internal conflict within their own psyche, they may turn to others to spare them such conflict. One mode of engaging the other is sexual. The more that defense and object relations are sexualized, the greater is the likelihood of perverse enactment. Repetitive seeking of excitement is used to cover over all that is wrong in oneself, in the other, and in the relationship. Remember that sexualization is especially helpful in giving patients the illusion that they have tamed rage and hatred in self and other. When defense and object relations have been sexualized, patients seek, in sadomasochistic object relations or in bits of perversion, sexually exciting interactions with another that aim to reassure the patients against their fantasy terrors. These erotized repetitive enactments, because they provide only *temporary*, illusory reassurance, must be endlessly reenacted in sadomasochistic or perverse interactions. Such excited, sexualized interactions with another person that are used by the patient to defend against internal dangers link sadomasochistic object relations and perversion.

Obligatory perversions are stable defensive organizations that are highly resistant to change because of their central role in defense against destructiveness and preservation of the needed object. Although there are perversions (fetishism and transvestism performed alone) that do not require the presence of another person for their enactment, patients with such perversions intrapsychically still experience a need for the other. Persons with perversions usually emphasize their freedom from dependency, their ease of exchanging objects, while they idealize their excitement and pleasure, rather than their need of the other. By emphasizing their independence, they attempt to protect against the danger of intense need of the other, which exists in most of these persons, despite their vigorous and rage-filled protests to the contrary.

Levels of Perverse Functions

It is useful to schematically divide patients with perversions based on level of perverse functions. It should be kept in mind that this is a heuristic division and that actual patients may not fit neatly into such models.

The patient with higher-level perverse functions uses perverse behavior primarily to permit sexual functioning and orgasm, with the perverse behavior acting as a defense against castration anxiety and oedipal guilt. Applicable here is Bak's (1968) idea that the ubiquitous unconscious fantasy in perversion is the "phallic woman": the woman is imagined as having a penis. In conscious fantasy, the patient feels excited by her high heels, black garter belt, or even her whip, which unconsciously symbolize her phallus. The patient attempts by his act to validate such unconscious fantasy to defend against intense castration anxiety so as to be able to function sexually.

It is beyond the scope of this chapter to assess perversion in women except to note that bits of perversion tend to be reported as if they represented obligatory perversion. Bits of perversion and obligatory perversion are not the same. If a woman *occasionally* exhibited herself in a mirror or dressed up in black pantyhose, garter belt, and black spiked heel shoes, playing phallic dominatrix to her man, and thereby became sexually excited, these actions would be regarded as bits of perversion rather than as obligatory perversion. The exception would be if such behavior were *required* for her to function sexually. I have not treated a woman with an obligatory perversion. My patient who played at being a phallic dominatrix to her man did so in an attempt to repair her sense of herself as damaged, ugly, and monstrous. These feelings derived from a serious childhood illness that, she felt, had deformed her, from surgical interventions and restraints, and from her mother's critical rejection of her. I found my patient sexually attractive; I could barely see the hirsutism she hated. What seemed to me ugly in her were her angry, attacking qualities. My patient who as a child had stuffed toilet tissue in her panties did so as she pretended to have a generous penis with which to excite and cure her depressed mother.

For patients with *lower-level* perverse functions, the primary goal is no longer to permit *sexual functioning,* but to use sex for other, more pressing requirements. (However, as in patients with higher-level perverse functions, the perversion does allow sexual pleasure to occur.) This process, referred to as sexualization, as noted earlier in this chapter, involves the extensively elaborated defensive use of sexual behavior and fantasy, in which defense has greater urgency and significance in the patient's motivational hierarchy than does sexual drive gratification. Most patients with perversions present with more severe disturbance largely of the narcissistic and borderline types. These patients differ from other patients with lower-level character integration in their predominant reliance on sex for need satisfaction and closeness, defense, repair, adaptation, and preservation of equilibrium and psychic structure.

Etiology and Psychodynamics in Perversion

Even for higher-level perverse functions, we still need to ask why oedipal guilt and castration anxiety are defended against through perverse sexual behavior rather than in ordinary ways. All authors have connected the form of the perversion with infantile, usually traumatic, determinants. At times, however, perversion has been reduced only to the need to master childhood trauma, without sufficient consideration of how the perversion functions psychodynamically in the patient's current life. Even when we can demonstrate infantile trauma and seduction, we need to understand the intrapsychic consequences, constructions, and uses that have been made of such experiences. What is the importance and function of reenacting childhood seduction?

This author speculates that the magical quality of action may partly be determined by the fact that childhood seduction or "seduction-like experiences" have contributed to the illusion that magically the child's wishes, which the child knew were supposed to

remain at the level of fantasy, have been actualized. This may establish a precedent for "magical happenings," which the child may
draw upon when confronted with frustration and painful affects.
That is, in cases of childhood sexual seduction, the child's erotic
fantasies are, unfortunately, fulfilled and thus he or she comes to
believe that what is wished for will come true. Instead of using
ordinary intrapsychic defense, the child/patient turns to action,
which is now expected to magically transform what is wrong. For
example, masturbation or seducing others may be used to enhance
one's illusory omnipotent ability to turn what is wrong into something good and exciting. Confusion between reality and fantasy
usually results as to what has, and can, really happen. Such confusion serves defensive requirements against the negative affects and
dangerous perceptions associated with childhood sexual overstimulation (Blum 1973; Shengold 1963, 1967, 1971, 1974).

Denial or destruction of reality and its replacement by illusion
become predominant techniques of defense. Alternatively, a dual
reality is maintained, in which partial denial obscures painful reality, covering it with perverse illusion. Masturbation and seduction
of others then become vehicles for demonstrating one's magical
powers to affect oneself and others. This sense of one's illusory
power complements the concept that the patient desires repetition
of the seductive gratifications and at the same time attempts to
master and repair the associated traumatic affects of overstimulation, rage, and helplessness. The illusion of magical ability defends
against felt helplessness and inadequacy, as usually occurs with
childhood seduction experiences.

Development of sexualized defense as a predominant defensive
operation in the person with a perversion may draw upon abundant and intense sensual feelings early in life, the prominence of
sexualized defense in the mother-child relationship, and the usefulness of sexualized defense for mastering large quantities of hostile
aggression. One genetic model (see Coen 1985) proposes that
a sexualized mode of relating may develop when the mother seductively overstimulates the child and at the same time relatively neglects the child's emotional needs. Sexual drive pressure and the
ego's attempts to master such pressure are then available for further

use by the ego to express and master other conflicts. To compensate for mother's relative emotional unavailability, with the hope of reviving her flagging interest in him, the child turns to the predominantly available mode of relating to mother. When the mother's own predominant mode of defense has been sexual, the child may adapt, through identification, his mother's sexualization to meet his own more general needs for defense. Efforts to master sexual over-stimulation by active repetition and re-creation also serve multiple other defensive functions. The preponderant drive derivatives, affects, early defensive patterns, and identifications are drawn upon for vital defensive and adaptive needs.

Not only sexuality, but also unusually intense and abundant aggression must be confronted. This aggression results from early frustration, deprivation, and teasing overstimulation. When sexualized defense has been significantly involved in the mother's psychic organization and in the mother-child relationship, her psychopathology and maternal deficiency are additionally obscured for the mother and for the child. The typical mother under consideration is a depressed woman with substantial impairment of her ability to relate to her child as a unique person in his own right. Mother and child collude in their mutually shared pleasure in and defensive focus on the seductive bodily closeness, in lieu of other forms of relating. The depressed mother comes to life with seductive bodily stimulation, which she seeks from her child. She now feels temporarily invigorated rather than depressed.

Sexual seductiveness eventually becomes the child's predominant mode for relating to others and for expressing his intense object hunger. Masturbation and masturbation fantasy are the arena in which sexualized defense becomes elaborated in the childhood of the future patient with a perversion. In his masturbatory world, this child attempts to comfort and soothe himself, separate and apart from the insufficiently available and inappropriately responsive mother. He idealizes his masturbatory pleasures and his self-sufficiency and omnipotence in creating these pleasures on his own. Illusions of omnipotent ability for magical manipulation are enhanced by the masturbator's magical manipulation of his own genitals: he transforms them from a limp, dormant state into an excited, alive, gravity-defying one, all under his own control and direction. Defense is required against feelings of helplessness, over-stimulation, rage, and depression in relation to the unpredictable quality of the mother's empathic responsiveness to the child and of his feeling exploited and manipulated by mother for her own needs without significant recognition of himself as a unique, differentiated person.

The pathological object relationship is idealized and clung to, emphasizing how special, irresistible, and inseparable each person is from the other. Sexualized seduction, in fantasy and in perverse behavior, creates the illusion that destructiveness in self and other has been magically transformed into sexual desire and excitement. This illusory transformation becomes an addictive defensive need that must be endlessly enacted so as to preserve the magical transformation of bad into good.

References

Abraham K: Manifestations of the female castration complex (1920), in Selected Papers of Karl Abraham, M.D. Translated by Bryan D, Strachey A. London, Hogarth Press, 1968, pp 338–369

Bak RC: The phallic woman: the ubiquitous fantasy in perversions. Psychoanal Study Child 23:15–36, 1968

Bak RC: Distortions of the concept of fetishism. Psychoanal Study Child 29:191–214, 1974

Blum HP: The concept of erotized transference. J Am Psychoanal Assoc 21:61–76, 1973

Bradlow P, Coen SJ: Mirror masturbation. Psychoanal Q 53:267–285, 1984

Coates S: Ontogenesis of boyhood gender identity disorder. J Am Acad Psychoanal 18:414–438, 1990

Coates S: The etiology of boyhood gender identity disorder: an integrative model, in Interface of Psychoanalysis and Psychology. Edited by Barron JW, Eagle MN, Wolitzky DL. Washington, DC, American Psychological Association, 1992, pp 245–265

Coates S, Person ES: Extreme boyhood femininity: isolated behavior or pervasive disorder? Journal of the American Academy of Child Psychiatry 24:702–709, 1985

Coates S, Wolfe SM: Gender identity disorder in boys: the interface of constitution and early experience. Psychoanalytic Inquiry 15:6–38, 1995

Coen SJ: Sexualization as a predominant mode of defense. J Am Psychoanal Assoc 29:893–920, 1981

Coen SJ: Perversion as a solution to intrapsychic conflict. J Am Psychoanal Assoc 33(suppl):17–57, 1985

Coen SJ: The Misuse of Persons: Analyzing Pathological Dependency. Hillsdale, NJ, Analytic Press, 1992

de Sade A: The 120 days of Sodom (1785), in The Marquis de Sade: The 120 Days of Sodom and Other Writings. Compiled and translated by Wainhouse A, Seaver R. New York, Grove Press, 1966, pp 189–674

Freud S: Three essays on the theory of sexuality (1905), in Standard Edition of the Complete Psychological Works of Sigmund Freud, Vol 7. Translated and edited by Strachey J. London, Hogarth Press, 1953, pp 123–243

Freud S: On the universal tendency to debasement in the sphere of love (contributions to the psychology of love II) (1912), in Standard Edition of the Complete Psychological Works of Sigmund Freud, Vol 11. Translated and edited by Strachey J. London, Hogarth Press, 1957, pp 178–190

Friedman RC: Male Homosexuality: A Contemporary Psychoanalytic Perspective. New Haven, CT, Yale University Press, 1988

Grossman WI, Stewart W: Penis envy: from childhood wish to developmental metaphor. J Am Psychoanal Assoc 24(suppl):193–212, 1976

Isay R: On the analytic therapy of homosexual men. Psychoanal Study Child 40:235–254, 1985

Isay R: The development of sexual identity in homosexual men. Psychoanal Study Child 41:467–489, 1986

Isay R: Fathers and their homosexually inclined sons in childhood. Psychoanal Study Child 42:275–294, 1987

Jacobson E: The Self and the Object World. New York, International Universities Press, 1964

Kernberg OF: Barriers to falling and remaining in love. J Am Psychoanal Assoc 22:486–511, 1974

Masters WH, Johnson V: Human Sexual Inadequacy. Boston, MA, Little, Brown, 1970

Novick J: Discussion of the presentation "Sexual Addiction," by Coen S, Symposium on Perversion, Michigan Psychoanalytic Society, Dearborn, MI, November 1990

Roiphe H, Galenson E: Infantile Origins of Sexual Identity. New York, International Universities Press, 1981

Schuker E, Levinson N: Female Psychology: An Annotated Psychoanalytic Bibliography. Hillsdale, NJ, Analytic Press, 1991

Shengold L: The parent as sphinx. J Am Psychoanal Assoc 11:725–741, 1963

Shengold L: The effects of overstimulation: rat people. Int J Psychoanal 48:403–415, 1967

Shengold L: More about rats and rat people. Int J Psychoanal 52:277–288, 1971

Shengold L: The metaphor of the mirror. J Am Psychoanal Assoc 22:97–115, 1974

Stoller RJ: Sexual excitement. Arch Gen Psychiatry 33:899–909, 1976

12

Psychoanalytic Approach to the Psychosomatic Interface

Thomas Wolman, M.D.
Troy L. Thompson II, M.D.

S tudies of severe conditions at the psychosomatic interface, such as drug addiction (Krystal 1962; Rosenfeld 1960), survivor syndrome due to massive psychic trauma (Krystal 1968, 1978), eating disorders (Wilson 1971), and serious illness in the analyst (Schwartz 1987), bear witness to a renewal of psychoanalytic interest in the interrelationship of psyche and soma. After a lengthy detour into the primarily psychic realm, some psychoanalysts have begun to come full circle to a reconsideration of their roots in psychosomatic interactions. These roots can be found in Freud's earliest psychological contributions.

In this chapter we present a new paradigm of psychosomatic states, derived primarily from Freud's concept of the "actual neurosis," and then apply this model to a range of normal and psychopathological conditions. Although Freud's writings on actual neuroses had been dismissed by many as mere historical curiosities, they are now the subject of renewed interest for the light they may shed on present-day psychosomatic problems. We also discuss questions of psychosomatic pathogenesis, therapeusis, and some of the dilemmas that remain unsolved.

Historical Overview

The period 1890 to 1895 was a critical transition stage in Freud's evolution from neurologist to becoming the founder of psychoanalysis (see discussion by Leo Rangell in Chapter 1). By 1890, Freud was beginning to specialize in nervous disorders, a category that included a variety of somatic complaints as well as more clearly defined neuroses. For a time he treated some patients with "electrotherapy," and after his codiscovery of some of the medical actions of cocaine, he advocated the use of cocaine as pharmacotherapy for digestive disorders, fatigue, depression, and morphine addiction (Anzieu 1986). By 1895, Freud had left the soma behind, having staked out the psychical domain that was to occupy him for the rest of his life.

Only during this critical 5-year period would the psychic and the somatic be so intimately associated in Freud's mind. In 1890, Freud wrote that "a man's states of mind are manifested, almost without exception, in the tensions and relaxations of his facial muscles, in the adaptations of his eyes, in the amount of blood in the vessels of his skin, in the modifications in his vocal apparatus and in the movements of his limbs and in particular of his hands" (S. Freud 1905, p. 286). All psychical functions, Freud believed, have their somatic counterparts. This was so obvious in the case of affects that Freud noted that "some psychologists have even adopted the view that the essence of these affects consists only in their physical manifestations" (S. Freud 1905, p. 287). Not even a thought, he continued, is "without its physical manifestations or is incapable of modifying somatic processes" (S. Freud 1905, p. 288).

In this period, Freud was thinking as a psychosomaticist, shifting back and forth easily between a somatic and a psychical view of the same phenomenon (S. Freud 1905; Nadelman 1990). Freud's early correspondence with Wilhelm Fliess illustrates the partnership between the somatic and the psychical, with Freud trying out his psychological ideas and Fliess expressing his views on biological periodicity and hormonal influence (Anzieu 1986). The notion of a reciprocal relationship between mind and body was quite compatible with Freud's thinking at this time. He anticipated the modern psychosomatic concepts when he observed that "in some at least of these patients the signs of their illness originate from nothing other than a *change in the action of their minds upon their bodies*" (S. Freud 1905, p. 286). He cited as an example of this process the role that major affects might play in resisting or in increasing susceptibility to infectious illnesses, in bringing about "diseases of the nervous system accompanied by manifest anatomical changes and also diseases of other organs" (S. Freud 1905, p. 287), and in even possibly shortening life.

The step from psyche-soma to psyche made by Freud in 1895 (and cemented in 1900, with the publication of *The Interpretation of Dreams*) had major consequences for the future of psychoanalysis. Young psychoanalysts were attracted to the new psychical domain much as pioneers are attracted to virgin territory. And the psychoanalytic method proved to be an exquisitely sensitive instrument for the exploration of psychical processes, but a rather crude one for the investigation of the psyche-soma. Therefore, psychoanalysts have tended to concentrate on the psychical, somewhat to the exclusion of the somatic.

But whatever the causes of the relative neglect of the psychosomatic, the result has been a relative neglect of the psychosomatic field by psychoanalysts. True, many psychoanalysts, such as Alexander, Dunbar, and Engel, have made major contributions to psychosomatic medicine, but in so doing they were working largely as psychosomaticists rather than as psychoanalysts in the strict sense. It is interesting to note that those few analysts who continued to study this area, such as Winnicott, Schur, and Engel, maintained close ties with clinical medicine well into their careers. The resurgence of interest in psychosomatic phenomena may be considered an effect of the widening scope of psychoanalysis as it stretches the boundaries of the psychical (Stone 1954).

Freud's Conception of the Actual Neurosis

In the period 1893 to 1895, Freud introduced the term "actual neurosis" to describe the condition of patients who presented with symptoms other than those characteristic of well-defined hysterias, phobias, obsessions, compulsions, or paranoid ideas. In contrast to these latter symptoms, symptoms in patients with actual neuroses tended to be vague and nonspecific. In place of phobias, for example, these patients would complain of diffuse anxiety, unrelated to any psychical context—so called free-floating anxiety. The term "anxiety" in this context was mostly Freud's construction, because the patient with an actual neurosis would rarely refer to a *feeling* of anxiety, but instead would report its physiological effects (heart palpitations, dyspnea, etc.) (S. Freud 1895[1894]).

Freud was impressed with the dearth of ideational content associated with these symptoms. Ideas attached to these symptoms only after the fact, in the form of rationalizations. Thus, a sensation of tachycardia might be explained as a fear of heart attacks or vertigo as a fear of falling in the street. Freud argued that the anxiety is translated into so-called simple phobia as represented by literal statement. Thus, tachypnea is translated to "I am going to suffocate," and vertigo, to "I am going to lose my balance." What is missing is any metaphorical or symbolic subtext capable of supporting multiple interpretations.

These simple phobias are distinguished from actual neuroses proper by their inaccessibility to further interpretation. That is, the patient with a classically defined phobia will interpret the anxious feeling as a reaction to an imaginary danger situation. Similarly, the patient with a classical hysteria will interpret a sensory "hyperaesthesia" as a lesion within an imaginary anatomy. The patient with a classical obsession or compulsion will interpret the anxious feeling as the consequence of breaking a rule or of insufficiently performing a ritual. In each case, the specificity of the symptom depends on an unconscious psychical construction. Further elaborations and extensions may lead to the formation of a "symptom complex"—that is, an entire network of phobias, conversions, or compulsions (S. Freud 1909)—with an order of complexity well beyond any "actual" symptom.

Freud (1896) hypothesized that this lack of psychical partici-pation is the critical factor in the production of actual neurotic symptoms. In an actual neurosis, according to Freud, there is an inhibition of the patient's capacity to "psychically work-over" his or her subjective experience. In Freud's model of the psychosomatic interface, "psychical working-over"—that is, the activity of imagina-tive elaboration and symbolization—functions to unburden the psychic economy of organismic distress. In the absence of psychical working-over, this distress is transformed directly into the symp-toms of the actual neurosis (S. Freud 1898). The nature of these symptoms then depends largely on quantitative factors such as the additive effects of "noxae" (i.e., stress), the accumulation or the depletion of sexual energy, and the vulnerability of specific organ systems.

For this reason, psychotherapy often proved of little use in the resolution of the symptoms of the actual neurosis, which is in con-trast to the dramatic results evident with the hysterias (S. Freud 1895[1894]). Patients with actual neuroses were incapable of the hysteria patient's flights of fancy. Although the former appear to suffer from sexual frustration, they produce few sexual fantasies and in general show a decrease of "sexual libido or psychical desire" (S. Freud 1895[1894]). Moreover, their symptoms fail to reveal a con-vincing connection with the traumatic events of early childhood. Indeed, the very word "actual" in "actual neuroses" refers to the origin of these neuroses in current events as opposed to in infantile conflicts (Laplanche and Pontalis 1973).

Alexithymia

Contemporary psychoanalysts and psychiatrists refer to the com-plete or partial blockage of psychical working-over as *alexithymia*, or the inability to verbalize emotions. The study of alexithymia extends and elaborates Freud's model of the actual neurosis. According to Krystal (1982), the reactions of alexithymic patients are basically somatic, consisting of the "expressive," or physiological, aspects of affects, with minimal verbalization. The inadequate verbalization makes one feeling seem very much like another, and the lack of a personalized context conveys an impression of vagueness and undifferentiation. At times, however, alexithymic patients are subject to sudden, intense bursts of affects in the form of acute attacks (Nemiah et al. 1976). Afterward, they are unable to explain, or even acknowledge, the feelings of sadness or anger behind the tears and the raised voice. Some alexithymic patients apparently cannot localize affects in their bodies or identify the associated autonomic sensations (Nemiah et al. 1976). Therefore, they "often cannot tell whether they are sad, tired, hungry, or ill" (Krystal 1982, p. 355).

This difficulty in interpreting bodily cues causes alexithymic patients to feel alienated from their bodies. According to one observer, "They sit rigidly, move their bodies sparingly, use few gestures when they talk and maintain a near expressionless face" (Freyberger 1977, p. 433). To another, they look like robots trying to control their bodies as they would a machine (McDougall 1980). Still another compares their extreme stoicism to an inborn sensory anesthesia that puts them at risk for accidents (Bion 1962). The "robot" metaphor also implies a measure of autonomy from individual control. Thus, the body continues to express itself through facial movements, bodily gestures, sensorimotor manifestations, and physical pain (Marty and de M'Uzan 1963).

Alexithymic patients conceive of their body as a complex "thing," just as they conceive of their emotions as a physical event. Their style of thinking is pragmatic and utilitarian in the extreme. When interviewed, "they present a dull, mundane, unimaginative, utilitarian, and chronologically dominated recitation of concrete 'facts'" (de M'Uzan 1974, qtd. in Krystal 1982, p. 358; see also Krystal 1979). If, for example, an alexithymic patient is asked, "What kind of woman is your mother?," he will answer, "Well, she's tall and blonde" (Marty and de M'Uzan 1963). Winnicott (1949/1958) introduced the term "cataloguing" to describe such mental registration of events without elaboration of their emotional significance. Alexithymic patients' so-called *pensee operatoire* (Marty and de M'Uzan 1963) is completely lacking in any symbolic or metaphorical dimension. Thus, it is not surprising that these patients suffer from a paucity of an interior, emotional life. Krystal (1982) notes that they rarely report dreams other than an occasional one-sentence dream and are unable to associate to them or to other events. The same inability applies to daydreams, fantasies, reveries, and creative activities in general.

This curtailment of and deficiency in alexithymic patients' emotional and imaginative life rob their object relations of tone and color. Their relations with others are notably lacking in affect. Sexual relations may become pragmatic and compulsive, and the sexual experience itself may suffer from imaginative impoverishment (McDougall 1980). Alexithymic persons treat other people as a rough image of themselves—that is, "stripped of truly personal traits and indefinitely reproducible according to a stereotyped form" (de M'Uzan 1974, p. 106). This inhibits their capacity to form a self-object representation.

Krystal (1982) has analyzed the consequences of the above deficiencies as follows:

> [Patients with alexithymia] are particularly limited in their capacity for self-soothing, self-comforting and providing self-gratification. . . .
> *All vital and affect functions are experienced as part of the object representation.* Carrying out any "mothering," life-preserving, or soothing activities is reserved for the "external" mother or her substitute and proscribed for the subject. (p. 361)

Psychoanalysts have referred to the missing psychic dimension as a form of "psychic blindness," in which these patients are unaware of the psychical expression of their drives (Green 1975; Krystal 1982; McDougall 1980). Krystal (1982) observed that these patients "frequently behave like the color-blind patient who has learned to cover up his deficiency in perception by utilizing a variety of clues by which he inferred what he could not discern" (p. 356). These patients may, for example, acquire a "fantasy" by reading about it or borrowing it from a film. In this way, they learn to project an appearance of normality, compensating for their defect with a fine sensory acuity trained on external reality.

The Hidden Dimension:
The Psychosomatic Axis of the Mind

Freud used the dynamic interaction between "anxiety neurosis" and "hysteria" as the basis for a fundamental division between the "actual neuroses" and the "psychoneuroses." The category of actual neurosis came to include neurasthenia and hypochondriasis. Freud (1895[1894]) viewed anxiety neurosis and neurasthenia as an antithetical pair, characterized roughly by accumulation of excitation in the former and impoverishment of excitation in the latter. They were also the result, Freud postulated, of contrasting etiologies: sexual abstinence in the case of anxiety neurosis and excessive masturbation in the case of neurasthenia (S. Freud 1898). At a later date, Freud (1914) juxtaposed this pair to hypochondriasis, in which the patient "withdraws both interest and libido—the latter specially markedly—from the objects of the external world and concentrates both of them upon the organ that is engaging his attention" (p. 83).

Then Freud compared these three "actual neuroses" (neurasthenia, hypochondriasis, and anxiety neurosis) with their psychoneurotic counterparts, to make three more contrasting pairs: anxiety neurosis–anxiety hysteria, neurasthenia–conversion hysteria, and hypochondria–paraphrenia (psychosis). The elements of the pairs relate to their psychoneurotic counterparts in several ways. First, there is a similarity of the conversion mechanism in "the fact that in anxiety neurosis a kind of *conversion* takes place on to bodily sensations" (S. Freud 1895[1894], p. 98). Second, there is a similarity of presentation in the fact that "hysteria . . . which imitates so many organic affections, can easily assume the appearance of one of the 'actual neuroses' by elevating the latter's symptoms into hysterical ones" (S. Freud 1898, p. 270). Third, there is a contiguity between the elements such that every psychoneurosis rests on an "actual" foundation, and every actual neurosis develops a psychoneurotic "crust" or "shell."

Extrapolating from Freud's findings, the entire psychopathological field can be oriented around a psychosomatic, as well as a psychic, axis. Freud took a step in this direction when he remarked on the "actual" characteristics of the traumatic war neuroses

(S. Freud 1926). Freud never abandoned his theory of actual neurosis. In fact, he reaffirmed it in "Inhibitions, Symptoms and Anxiety" (S. Freud 1926), the paper to which we owe the essence of the structural theory. Some of his successors continued to make psychosomatic correlations to the major emotional disorders. For example, Sperling (1955) observed that psychotic and psychosomatic symptoms may alternate in the same patient. The somatic component of major depression (including somatic preoccupations and vegetative signs), particularly in the so-called nonmelancholic type, is, of course, well known.

Some analysts have grouped the psychosomatic disorders with the "action disorders," defining the latter according to their propensity to discharge tension through action and reaction rather than through mental elaboration and verbalization (McDougall 1980; Sperling 1968). In this formulation, acting out is the external counterpart to psychosomatic disturbance (Green 1975). Patients with addictive tendencies, often associated with psychosomatic disorders, show this preference for action in self-medicating behavior. Also, the elaborate rituals of some sexual perversions may compensate for a diminution of sexual arousal.

It is well known that physical illness interrupts the equilibrium between psyche and soma. In his discussion of narcissism, Freud (1914) wrote that the physically ill person "gives up his interest in the things of the external world, in so far as they do not concern his suffering. Closer observation teaches us that he also withdraws libidinal interest from his love-objects: so long as he suffers, he ceases to love" (p. 82). For our purposes, it is noteworthy that Freud made no distinction *economically* between organic disease and hypochondria (i.e., in terms of the demands made by these two conditions upon the mind). The hypochondriacal person is no more able to process normal sensory input than the person who suffers from organic disease. In each case—both the somatopsychic and the psychosomatic—the capacity for psychical working-over is overwhelmed by an influx of somatic excitation.

Some of the same conditions may apply to the so-called normal illnesses. Engel (1961) defined a "normal illness" as a condition that satisfies the criteria for an illness and that occurs inevitably during

the normal course of development. For him, bereavement constitutes the normal illness par excellence. Winnicott (1956/1958) characterized the primary maternal preoccupation of the new mother as
a normal illness. Other examples include puberty, pregnancy,
menopause/climacteric, and the normal diseases of aging (e.g., mild
osteoarthritis) (Wolman and Thompson 1990). These conditions
may be viewed either as illnesses or as developmental crises, depending on one's point of view (Jaques 1965). When viewed as
illnesses, they may be associated with some of the same difficulty in
psychic elaboration (i.e., the process of inwardly verbalizing, symbolizing, story telling, etc.) as are more typical psychosomatic
symptoms.

The Infantile Prototype of Psychosomatic States

The importance of the so-called psychosomatic reactions of infancy
has long been recognized. Anna Freud (1971) viewed these reactions as being physical with regard to their manifestations and
emotional with regard to their origin. She concluded,

> The affects engendered in the infant are discharged through the
> body; his physical experiences may find expression in his affective
> states. This easy access from mind to body and vice versa is known
> to be normal during the first year of life and becomes pathological
> only if it is maintained beyond this period after new pathways for
> discharge via thought, speech, and action have been opened up.
> (p. 83)

Winnicott (1949/1958) also conceived of the early psyche-soma
as a unity or intimate partnership. He observed that in early infancy
"the psyche and the soma are not to be distinguished except according to the direction from which one is looking" (p. 244). Experience
may be characterized as physical aliveness or as the imaginative
elaboration of somatic parts, feelings, and functions. Winnicott
drew the interesting conclusion that the earliest mental functions
work in such close partnership with the body, that "the mind does

not exist as an entity in the individual's scheme of things" (p. 244). Therefore, Winnicott's psyche-soma is a kind of "proto-mind"— a transitional state on the developmental path of the psyche.

The earliest mother-child relationship is also characterized by an easy access from mind to body and vice versa. Margaret Mahler (Mahler et al. 1975), among others, has pictured the immediately postnatal period as an extension of prenatal life, in which the aim is to promote homeostatic equilibrium primarily through physiological/somatopsychic processes. According to Winnicott (1960/1965), the mother "takes account of the infant's skin sensitivity, sensitivity to falling (action of gravity) and of the infant's lack of knowledge of the existence of anything other than the self" (p. 49). In Winnicott's writings, the mother's holding function is always conceived as a *joining* of the physical and the psychological; the mother holds her infant some of the time literally and all of the time metaphorically.

The mother's act of giving birth fuses the physical and the psychological into a single powerful experience. For the infant, birth represents the ultimate psychosomatic state. Freud always maintained the view that anxiety states preserve an echo of the birth trauma. For him, birth was prototypical of "the situation of non-satisfaction in which the amounts of stimulation rise to an unpleasurable height without its being possible for them to be mastered psychically or discharged" (S. Freud 1926, p. 137). Several authors have speculated on the influence of birth on preoedipal patterning and later personality development. On a less controversial plane, Anna Freud (1952) commented on the analogous redistributions of libido that occur during childhood illnesses and operative procedures.

Pathogenesis of Psychosomatic Symptoms

The consensus among most psychoanalysts is that a psychosomatic symptom is not symbolic (i.e., subject to multiple interpretations) in the same way as is a neurotic symptom. Instead, the former emerges whenever the threshold of psychosomatic equilibrium is exceeded. Such a position is in accord with Freud's (1895[1894], 1896, 1898,

1926) views. There is, however, much less agreement on the *origin* of nonsymbolization. A number of specific mechanisms and etiological configurations have been proposed.

For Winnicott, the critical event in the formation or origin of nonsymbolization is a dissociation or split between mind and body. The two halves of the psyche-soma begin to oppose each other in reaction to erratic mothering. According to Winnicott (1949/1958), "The thinking of the individual begins to take over and organize the caring for the psyche-soma, whereas in health it is the function of the environment to do this" (p. 246). In this way, Winnicott added, "the psyche of the individual gets 'seduced' away into this mind from the intimate relationship which the psyche originally had with the soma" (p. 247). This removes the possibility of a direct psychosomatic partnership and deprives the body of any psychic representation.

Other analysts have explained the dissociation in terms of primitive defense mechanisms. Winnicott (1949/1958) himself suggests a quasi-paranoid mechanism of localizing the mind inside the head so that the mind can be treated as an enemy. This unusual idea is not so far removed from McDougall's (1985) thesis of a violent repudiation or disavowal, in which whatever is denied representation in the mind eventually shows up in the body. Later, she conceded the possibility of preverbal mental representations, detached from any verbal links in preconscious functioning (McDougall 1985). Her growing clinical experience convinced her that psychosomatic states are not necessarily defects or do not necessarily indicate a lack of psychic capacity, but are massive defenses against narcissistic or psychotic fears.

Both Winnicott and McDougall invoke the idea of physiological regression. From this perspective, a given psychosomatic symptom is considered a revival of the infantile psychosomatic state. This position has been well described by Schur (1953):

> Of greater practical importance and more clearly evident is the physiological regression implied by the reappearance of discharge phenomena which were prevalent in infancy. The failure of desomatization represents physiological regression. We can now es-

tablish another relation: on the one hand, co-ordinated motor action, desomatization, and secondary processes; on the other, random response, involvement of basic vegetative processes[,] and primary processes. (p. 79)

The *extremity* of these mechanisms (i.e., primitive mental mechanisms, regression, etc.) may be a reaction to massive psychic trauma. Krystal (1968) has convincingly demonstrated high rates of psychosomatic symptoms in concentration camp survivors. McDougall (1985) notes that "psychosomatic vulnerablity is notably increased in patients who in childhood were exposed to traumatic events at the separation-individuation phase depicted by Mahler" (p. 115). Krystal (1982) singles out the presence of anhedonia as a very useful "marker" for those cases in which the alexithymia is posttraumatic. Constitutional factors presumably account for the other, non-trauma-induced cases, in his view.

McDougall (1980) has outlined two discrete patterns of disturbed mother-infant interaction, observed by the Paris psychosomaticians (Fain 1971). In the first pattern, the mother and baby are so symbiotically merged that the baby requires the mother herself to be the guardian of sleep in place of its own primitive reverie. In the second pattern, "the baby has created prematurely an autoerotic object that enables him to dispense with his mother" (McDougall 1980, p. 364). Both scenarios appear to inhibit the infant's nascent psychic activity.

McDougall's (1985) etiological formulations are thought-provoking but speculative. She believes that early preoedipal disturbances are incorporated into "a primitive oedipal organization in which the mother, while not repudiating the father, nevertheless is felt to have related to her child as a sexual complement or as a narcissistic extension of her own self, thereby establishing a specific form of relationship to her child's *bodily* self" (p. 117; emphasis added). Mothers of children who in the future will exhibit somatization may pay more attention to their children's bodily symptoms than to their children's emotions, almost as if mother and child shared the same body. The father, according to McDougall in her formulation, fails to penetrate the mother-child symbiosis but may serve as a model for a pseudonormal genitality in adulthood (McDougall 1985).

Psychoanalytic Treatment of Psychosomatic Symptoms

There is a basic dichotomy between psychosomatic and psychoneurotic states. Although defense plays a role in psychosomatic conditions, just what role it plays is controversial, and psychosomatic symptoms are not analogues of neurotic symptoms.[1] Psychical working-over through a dynamic process may change psychosomatic symptoms into psychoneurotic ones (Thompson 1991). Therefore, the psychoanalyst must address the apparent void of psychical working-over in his or her psychosomatic patients. Green (1975) believes the analyst must counter the relative meaninglessness of these patients' subjective experience with interpretive "images of elaboration," conveying the message that "this may mean that." The translation of this goal into analytic practice is illustrated by contrasting the techniques in two paradigmatic case examples in the work of Winnicott and McDougall, respectively.

Winnicott's Regressive Approach

Winnicott assumed that deep regression is necessary in the treatment of psychosomatic patients. He wanted the patient to reach back to the point before psychosomatic dissociation. From this new beginning, as Winnicott (1949/1958) noted, "progression would be possible" (p. 252). It is not clear exactly how Winnicott fostered this regression other than by curtailing his interpretive activity. He was implicitly inviting patients to cease the mental rumination that hindered their awareness of bodily cues. In at least one case, that of a 47-year-old woman, this

---

[1] See discussion by Martin Silverman in Chapter 6 of the differentiation of psychosomatic disorders from psychoneurotic disorders.

permissive attitude over a 2-year period precipitated a deep regression characterized by violent head banging.

To Winnicott, this behavior indicated the revival of an infantile psychosomatic disturbance in the raw state. The behavior may have originated in a childhood seizure or even during a traumatic birth. Winnicott understood the risks (suicide, for example) of this degree of regression. He trusted his own ability to contain the acting-out within the treatment setting until the patient was ready for the work of psychic elaboration. Meanwhile, he encouraged his patient to attend to her physical reactions—what he called her state of "aliveness"—without having to think about them. He still avoided the uncovering of unconscious meanings while these lay in a "potential state" (i.e., as if not completely registered in the mind as yet).

Only when the patient started to produce spontaneous verbal elaboration of her bodily states did Winnicott take up the task of interpretation. Only at this point could the various meanings of the head banging—the head signifying the bad mother, for example—be fully explored. This led, in time, to the appearance of a headache, which Winnicott accepted as the transformation of the psychosomatic state into a hysterical symptom. At this stage, he could say that she was telling him about an illness of her mind because psyche and soma were no longer dissociated.

McDougall's Nonregressive Approach

McDougall accepts Winnicott's implicit assumption that psychosomatic patients' symptoms will become accessible to interpretations only after the "hystericalization" of their psychosomatic symptom. The psychosomatic symptom must become the nidus for a new psychical creation. To accomplish this goal, McDougall adopts an approach opposite from that of Winnicott's. Instead of inviting regression, she actively stimulates the patient's sluggish and inhibited imagination.

At first, she simply encourages the patient to find words for somatic sensations. Once there is a verbal description such as "it feels like electric shocks are going through my arms," she makes this statement the basis of a primitive fantasy. If the patient does not produce a fantasy on his or her own, she suggests one from her stock based upon psychoanalytic knowledge. Together, she and the patient work out a lexicon of pregenital images, including penis-breast, mouth-vagina, and so forth. The analytic material may be "littered with themes of corporal damage, blood and body organs" that "appear violent, crude, or bizarre, as though the elements of which they are composed had waited long years in a larval state" (McDougall 1980, p. 398). At this stage, the purpose of McDougall's "interpretations" is not to uncover unconscious meaning but to facilitate the spontaneous *creation* of fantasy.

In the process of coming to birth, these new psychical formations run the risk of evolving in a psychotic or perverse direction. In the case of McDougall's patient "Paul," her approach succeeded in transforming his gastric ulcer into a quasi-hallucination of a breast covered with black craters. To encourage a more neurotic evolution, McDougall vigorously interpreted the projection as the patient's refusal to accept his wish to attack her with his eyes. This kind of transference interpretation and subsequent working-through helped transform the hallucination into a more hysterical "scotoma," or "blind spot." In McDougall's view, "the attack upon the external world is now turned back upon the self. The 'black craters' in the nipples have become black spots in his own eyes" (McDougal 1985, p. 204).

Thus, through the intermediary of a near psychotic state, McDougall's interpretive approach has transformed a psychosomatic state into a transference neurosis[2] of the hysterical type. Her assumption is that the patient's somatic disturbance can now be *channeled* into psychical pathways. Thus, Paul would now be more likely to express his "pain" as anxiety about bodily integrity. This process is illustrated by the following dream, typical of patients in whom these dynamics are at play, in which his castration anxiety is

---

[2]Laplanche and Pontalis (1973) define transference neurosis as "an artificial neurosis into which the manifestations of the transference tend to become organised" (p. 462). They further specify that the transference neurosis "is built around the relationship with the analyst and it is a new edition of the clinical neurosis; its elucidation leads to the uncovering of the infantile neurosis" (p. 462).

dramatized as his being pursued by the police. In this dream, Paul takes off his glasses so the police will not recognize him. Taking off his glasses signifies a gesture of surrender to the father and, moreover, reestablishes the scotoma. The fact that *his* face has changed indicates a new capacity to internalize the conflict. Thus, the dream reworks all the patient's psychosomatic conflicts in the psychical sphere.

A Contemporary Case of "Actual Neurosis"

Mark, a 21-year-old student, spoke of his anxiety as a kind of physical distress that, the therapist inferred, was devoid of any emotional ramifications or phobic elaboration. He seemed to place it in the same category as the chronic pain in the genitals he had experienced since puberty. This pain waxed and waned somewhat according to the rhythms of his sexual libido. It could become worse, for example, when he was sexually aroused or after he had ejaculated. It acted in general like a hyperesthesia of normal penile sensations and, thus, could be viewed as a symptom of an "actual neurosis" (S. Freud 1914, p. 84).

Interestingly, the pain did not interfere with the patient's sexual performance. Shortly after regular analytic sessions began, Mark had sexual intercourse for the first time, thus bringing to an end a long period of sexual frustration. Yet the loss of virginity seemed to lack any special significance to him. He would describe this and other sexual affairs as pragmatic encounters, lacking in both eroticism and emotional involvement. He experienced his sexuality as a physical need comparable to hunger or thirst.

In the first year of analysis, Mark treated his analyst with the same pragmatic indifference with which he had treated his partners in his recent sexual relationships. The analyst was just one of a long series of doctors who had failed to help him. The content of these early sessions consisted of long descriptions of his symptoms and activities, unaccompanied by free associations, fantasy, or dreams. It was his body language that proved more eloquent than his words: he sat slumped over in his chair like an inert "object" waiting to be acted upon. The transference was a crude doctor-patient interaction, in which he presented the analyst with a passive body. But attempts on the analyst's part to interpret Mark's lack of initiative were unheeded by Mark.

A first turning point in the analysis occurred when Mark began to generalize his "pain" into a global hyperesthesia to external stimuli. His eyes hurt from contact lenses; his head hurt from the music playing upstairs in his apartment building. He was most sensitive to noise in his apartment, cringing at the slightest creaking of a door. Already, the pain was beginning to concentrate in his head. And then, without preliminaries, he one day transferred the entire symptom complex to the analyst's office, which now became the source of noxious stimuli. He complained that the noise coming through the walls, the new thoughts generating in his mind, and even the analyst's bodily movements were tormenting him.

In this development he was displacing the pain from his penis to his head so that he could present it to his "head doctor." Mark's head was becoming the site of a new hysterical symptom *in statu nascendi*. He could now fantasize that the pain was caused by thoughts that were attacking his head from the inside. At times he felt able to rid himself of these thoughts by literally *pushing them out of his head*. Then he went a step further and expressed the idea that the evacuated thoughts were deposited inside the analyst's head. In fantasy, he was ejecting the analyst's interventions, which gave him a "pain in the head." This "head magic" represented a primitive negation of the analyst's interpretive activity.

In the fantasy, Mark and the analyst were connected through a series of "anatomical" relationships. At times, for example, Mark felt a wish to exercise control over the analyst's movements, as if Mark were the head and the analyst were the body. At other times, it was if Mark were the body and the analyst were the "head." The analyst was able to interpret the former as a wish to deprive the analyst of his interpretations, and the latter as a wish to deprive Mark of the means of thinking about the analyst's interpretations. "Why should I bother verbalizing my problems," Mark seemed to be saying, "when my bodily symptoms can get me anything I want?" This insight led Mark to understand his psychosomatic symptom as a conversion of the many forms of emotional distress into the single experience of physical pain.

In the last stages of the work, Mark began to incorporate features of the analyst's therapeutic stance into his "anatomical" fantasy. He now grew increasingly absorbed in the physical correlates of the analyst's "stance," such as his posture, emotional attitude, and level of activity. In this version of the fantasy, Mark would cast the analyst in the role of his own passive "body," and himself as the analyst's active "mind." On other occasions, he would provoke the analyst with ceaseless demands in a testing of the analyst's resolution to stand his ground. In this scenario, overflowing bodily impulsivity was pitted against a "mental barrier." Thus, Mark continued to explore the difference between himself and the analyst in terms of differences in bodily functions.

The aim of Mark's treatment was the attachment of a new psychoneurosis on the scaffolding of his "actual neurosis." The critical stages were as follows:

1. A pragmatic doctor-patient relationship
2. Transformation of the psychosomatic symptom into a hysterical symptom
3. Restructuring of the transference around an "anatomical" fantasy
4. Interpretation, linkage with childhood prototypes, and working-through of the new psychical formation

Much of the work with Mark could be described as a struggle against the resistance to verbalizing emotional states. "Cure" or "success" was based as much on the maturation of the patient's symbolizing capacity as it was on the amelioration of the original psychosomatic symptom. This "cure" must often be limited by the large, residual energic investment in the body ego that remains in patients like Mark.

Conundrums Related to the Treatment of Psychosomatic States[3]

Because Freud (1895[1894]) declared that the "actual neuroses" were not further reducible by psychological analysis nor amenable to psychotherapy, some analysts have questioned the effectiveness of psychoanalysis in the treatment of psychosomatic states. Their view is that "these patients simply do not respond to insights derived from psychotherapy" (Krystal 1982, p. 364; see also Nemiah 1978; Sifneos 1974). Krystal (1982) reports that "countless therapists have discovered the utter futility of saying to an alexithymic patient, 'You do not permit yourself to experience anger (or love) toward me.' They might as well have reproached a color-blind patient for not seeing them in technicolor" (p. 375). The patient, in short, is unable to "see" (i.e., understand and utilize) the interpretation.

Yet, Krystal is not pessimistic in his overall treatment strategy. He advocates a preparatory phase to analysis (Krystal 1982), with the goals of 1) explaining the nature of the problems to the patient, 2) enhancing affect tolerance, 3) dealing with the inhibition of self-care by attending to affects as signals, and 4) affect-naming and encouraging verbalization. Before a patient can become aware of the psychical nuances of an affect, he or she must learn to identify and verbalize his or her physiological responses. Other analysts, including those from whose work the case examples in this chapter were drawn, incorporate this preparatory phase into the analysis itself, waiting for a composite structure with a mixture of psychosomatic and psychoneurotic elements to appear in the transference, and then offering interpretations.

The question of the analyzability of psychosomatic states is more complicated than originally thought (Thompson 1988). Although in extreme cases patients often may be unanalyzable, many

---

[3] A "psychosomatic state" is defined structurally in terms of the parameters discussed in this chapter (e.g., difficulty symbolizing emotional distress). It would encompass classical psychosomatic disorders as well as somatoform disorder, included in DSM-IV (American Psychiatric Association 1994).

patients manifest a combination of neurotic, characterological, and psychosomatic symptoms in varying ratios. The pathology of the body ego also varies from quasi-autistic decathexis[4] to exaggerated overvaluation. Analysis may help initiate a truly psychical process in some of these patients. However, the undertaking is not without risk. McDougall's patient, who was discussed earlier, came near the edge of psychosis when the analyst succeeded in awakening the patient's dormant psyche. Other patients may develop a serious or even life-endangering exacerbation of their psychosomatic illnesses, instead of learning to experience strong emotion (Krystal 1982; Thompson 1991).

These types of difficulties reflect confusion over the complex interactions between psyche and soma and between cause and effect. In the past, analysts might have explained an ulcer as a vengeful "bite," which the patient was obliged to give himself as a punishment for his babyhood wishes to bite the mother's breast (Garma 1950). McDougall and others have pointed out that such explanations mistake the cause for the effect. In other words, they mistake the imaginative constructions that proliferate around a physical symptom *after the fact* for the cause of the symptom. Today, many psychoanalysts consider the possibility that somatic defenses are secondary phenomena, comparable to secondary revision or secondary gain. Analysts are now more likely to view these phenomena as complex synergistic interactions between somatopsychic and psychosomatic vectors.

These questions and conundrums raise the more basic question of the limits of psychoanalytic knowledge. Some of these limits are imposed by the psychoanalytic method itself. The power of psychoanalytic perception is based in part on its ability to *screen out* distracting somatic stimuli. The treatment is conducted in an atmosphere of mild sensory deprivation produced by the shared physical immobility, quietude, subdued lighting, reclining posture, neutral decor,

---

[4]*Cathexis* has been defined as "the fact that a certain amount of psychical energy is attached to an idea or to a group of ideas, to a part of the body, to an object, etc." (Laplanche and Pontalis 1973, p. 62).

and minimal eye contact that together constitute the usual psycho-analytic setting. Furthermore, the regression necessary for analytic work tends to bring the patient's interior imaginative life into the foreground. There are undoubtedly times in which the transference approximates a dream that disguises an organic stimulus in the interests of preserving sleep.

This blind spot concerning somatic phenomena may also be understood as a countertransference in the classical sense. McDougall (1980, p. 356) notes in this regard that a typical countertransference among analysts is to lose interest in the somatic sphere which is supposedly beyond the analyst's "sphere of influence." Overpsychologizing is another common reaction. In this instance, the analyst may interpret the patient's psychosomatic complaint in purely psychical terms, thus failing to recognize its somatic reality for the patient. The attitude of panpsychism (i.e., an extreme version of psychic determinism) plays the same role in the analyst as "color blindness" plays in the patient. Interestingly, Krystal (1982) attributes these problems to unsuspected alexithymia in the analyst.

Winnicott (1949/1958) formulated this issue as a false opposition between mind and psyche-soma. This false dichotomy tends to draw analysis into an excessive preoccupation with mental functioning as a thing in itself, far removed from bodily reality. Engel (1962) has drawn attention to the same mind-body dualism in medicine. He warns physicians against an excessive preoccupation with biology, just as Winnicott warns analysts against the possible seductions of mind. Neither the biological nor the psychical camp can afford to ignore the positive significance of the psychosomatic symptom insofar as it draws "the psyche from the mind back to the original association with the soma" (Winnicott 1949/1958, p. 254; see also Winnicott 1966). In essence, these analysts are calling for a return to the psychosomatic dimension of traditional analysis.

The most important conundrum may be the silent influence of the psyche-soma upon all psychoanalyses. There exists an "actual" component (or "somatic compliance," in Freud's later terminology) to most, if not all, neurotic symptoms, and individual psychosomatic symptoms may appear in any analysis. Somatopsychic events may also disturb the analytic process with traumatic impact

(Schwartz 1987). It is not known for certain, however, if either state represents an acting out, a failure to contain affects (at the peak of the transference neurosis, for example), or a reliving of a preverbal experience.

Finally, these considerations imply an expansion of the *goals* of analysis to include reconstruction of childhood psychosomatic states and effects of illness or surgical procedures; use of dreams to detect somatic stimuli; enhancement of awareness of physiological changes in moods and affects; and insight into early body schemas. Greater self-monitoring of somatic signals adds a psychosomatic component to self-analytic skills. By undermining the fantasy of bodily omnipotence, self-monitoring may expose unsuspected pockets of denial and thus contribute to enhanced reality testing. It may even detect early evidence of illness, thus enhancing physical as well as psychological health.

References

American Psychiatric Association: Diagnostic and Statistical Manual of Mental Disorders, 4th Edition. Washington, DC, American Psychiatric Association, 1994

Anzieu D: Freud's Self-Analysis. Madison, CT, International Universities Press, 1986

Bion W: Learning from experience, in Seven Servants. New York, Jason Aronson, 1962

Engel G: Is grief a disease? Psychosom Med 23:18–22, 1961

Engel G: Anxiety and depression withdrawal. Int J Psychoanal 45:84–96, 1962

Fain M: Prelude à la vie fantasmatique. Revue Francaise Psychanalyse 35:291–364, 1971

Freud A: The role of bodily illness in the mental life of children. Psychoanal Study Child 7:69–82, 1952

Freud A: The infantile neurosis: genetic and dynamic considerations. Psychoanal Study Child 26:79–90, 1971

Freud S: On the grounds for detaching a particular syndrome from neurasthenia under the description 'anxiety neurosis' (1895[1894]), in Standard Edition of the Complete Psychological Works of Sigmund Freud, Vol 3. Translated and edited by Strachey J. London, Hogarth Press, 1962, pp 85–117

Freud S: Heredity and the aetiology of the neuroses (1896), in Standard Edition of the Complete Psychological Works of Sigmund Freud, Vol 3. Translated and edited by Strachey J. London, Hogarth Press, 1962, pp 141–156

Freud S: Sexuality in the aetiology of the neuroses (1898), in Standard Edition of the Complete Psychological Works of Sigmund Freud, Vol 3. Translated and edited by Strachey J. London, Hogarth Press, 1962, pp 259–285

Freud S: The interpretation of dreams (1900), in Standard Edition of the Complete Psychological Works of Sigmund Freud, Vols 4 and 5. Translated and edited by Strachey J. London, Hogarth Press, 1953

Freud S: Psychical (or mental) treatment (1905), in Standard Edition of the Complete Psychological Works of Sigmund Freud, Vol 7. Translated and edited by Strachey J. London, Hogarth Press, 1953, pp 281–302

Freud S: Analysis of a phobia in a five-year-old boy (1909), in Standard Edition of the Complete Psychological Works of Sigmund Freud, Vol 10. Translated and edited by Strachey J. London, Hogarth Press, 1955, pp 1–149

Freud S: On narcissism: an introduction (1914), in Standard Edition of the Complete Psychological Works of Sigmund Freud, Vol 14. Translated and edited by Strachey J. London, Hogarth Press, 1957, pp 67–102

Freud S: Inhibitions, symptoms and anxiety (1926), in Standard Edition of the Complete Psychological Works of Sigmund Freud, Vol 20. Translated and edited by Strachey J. London, Hogarth Press, 1959, pp 75–175

Freyberger H: Supportive psychotherapeutic techniques in primary and secondary alexithymia. Psychother Psychosom 28:337–342, 1977

Garma A: On the pathogenesis of peptic ulcer. Int J Psychoanal 31:55–125, 1950

Green A: The analyst, symbolization and absence in the analytic setting, in On Private Madness. Madison, CT, International Universities Press, 1975, pp 30–60

Jaques E: Death and the mid-life crisis. Int J Psychoanal 46:502–514, 1965

Krystal H: The opiate withdrawal syndrome as a state of stress. Psychoanal Q 36(suppl):54–65, 1962

Krystal H: Massive Psychic Trauma. New York, International Universities Press, 1968

Krystal H: Trauma and affects. Psychoanal Study Child 36:81–116, 1978

Krystal H: Alexithymia and psychotherapy. Am J Psychother 33:17–31, 1979

Krystal H: Alexithymia and the effectiveness of psychoanalytic treatment. International Journal of Psychoanalytic Psychotherapy 9:353–378, 1982

Laplanche J, Pontalis J-B: The Language of Psycho-Analysis. Translated by Nicholson-Smith D. New York, WW Norton, 1973

Mahler MS, Pine F, Bergman A: The Psychological Birth of the Human Infant: Symbiosis and Individuation. New York, Basic Books, 1975

Marty P, M'Uzan M de: La pensée operatoire. Revue Francaise Psychanalyse 27:345–356, 1963

McDougall J: Plea for a Measure of Abnormality. New York, International Universities Press, 1980

McDougall J: Theaters of the Mind: Illusion and Truth on the Psychoanalytic Stage. New York, Basic Books, 1985

M'Uzan M de: Psychodynamic mechanisms in psychosomatic symptom formation. Psychother Psychosom 23:103–110, 1974

Nadelman M: Centennial of an overlooked Freud paper on psychosomatics. Psychoanal Q 59:444–450, 1990

Nemiah J: Alexithymia and psychosomatic illness. Journal of Continuing Education in Psychiatry 39:25–37, 1978

Nemiah J, Freyberger H, Sifneos PE: Alexithymia: a view of the psychosomatic process, in Modern Trends in Psychosomatic Medicine, Vol 3. Edited by Hill OW. London, Butterworth, 1976, pp 430–439

Rosenfeld H: On drug addiction. Int J Psychoanal 41:467–475, 1960

Schur M: The ego in anxiety, in Drives, Affects, Behavior. Edited by Loewenstein RM. New York, International Universities Press, 1953, pp 67–103

Schwartz HJ: Illness in the doctor: implications for the psychoanalytic processs. J Am Psychoanal Assoc 35:657–692, 1987

Sifneos P: Reconsideration of psychodynamic mechanisms in psychosomatic symptom formation. Psychother Psychosom 24:151–155, 1974

Sperling M: Psychosis and psychosomatic illness. Int J Psychoanal 36:320–327, 1955

Sperling M: Acting-out behaviour and psychosomatic symptoms. Int J Psychoanal 49:250–253, 1968

Stone L: The widening scope of indications for psychoanalysis. J Am Psychoanal Assoc 2:567–594, 1954

Thompson TL II: Psychosomatic disorders, in The American Psychiatric Press Textbook of Psychiatry. Edited by Talbott JA, Hales RE, Yudofsky SC. Washington, DC, American Psychiatric Press, 1988, pp 493–532

Thompson TL II: Psychosomatic phenomena, in Beyond the Symbiotic Orbit: Advances in Separation-Individuation Theory. Edited by Akhtar S, Parens H. New York, Analytic Press, 1991, pp 243–261

Wilson CP: On the limits of the effectiveness of psychoanalysis: early ego and somatic disturbances. J Am Psychoanal Assoc 19:552–564, 1971

Winnicott DW: Mind and its relation to the psyche-soma (1949), in Collected Papers: Through Paediatrics to Psycho-Analysis. New York, Basic Books, 1958

Winnicott DW: Primary maternal preoccupation (1956), in Collected Papers: Through Paediatrics to Psycho-Analysis. New York, Basic Books, 1958, pp 300–306

Winnicott DW: The theory of the parent-infant relationship (1960), in The Maturational Processes and the Facilitating Environment: Studies in the Theory of Emotional Development. New York, International Universities Press, 1965, pp 37–56

Winnicott DW: Psycho-somatic illness in the positive and negative aspects. Int J Psychoanal 47:510–516, 1966

Wolman T, Thompson TL II: Adult development, in Human Behavior: An Introduction for Medical Students. Edited by Stoudemire A. Philadelphia, PA, JB Lippincott, 1990, pp 178–205

Section III

Treatment

Introduction to Section III

Richard G. Kopff, Jr., M.D.
Edward Nersessian, M.D.

Psychoanalysis is a form of psychotherapy, or talking therapy, conducted under specific conditions established by Freud. The two principal conditions of this form of treatment are that 1) the patient (i.e., the analysand) is seen four or five times a week for 50 minutes each time, and 2) he or she lies on a couch, with the psychoanalyst sitting behind, out of the patient's view. Once on the couch, the patient is asked to "free-associate,"—that is, to say whatever comes to mind, no matter how irrelevant, unimportant, difficult, and/or embarrassing the thoughts may seem. While listening, the psychoanalyst detects certain patterns of thought, emotion, and behavior that are derivatives of underlying conflicts, and the resultant compromises. These patterns and compromises are gradually brought to the patient's attention by the analyst, which in turn leads the patient to provide new data in response.

Two characteristic things happen during this process: the development of resistance and the development of transference. *Resistance,* quite simply, means the patient cannot reveal his or her thoughts, or feels like not talking, or even feels like discontinuing the analysis. The analyst or often the patient himself or herself discovers the nature of the obstacle, a discovery that allows the analysis to resume. *Transference* refers to the appearance in the patient of thoughts and feelings toward the analyst that are derived (unconsciously) more from relationships with other important people in the patient's life than from the relationship with the analyst. These other important people are often parents or siblings, especially during earlier times and particularly in childhood.

The above discussion represents a simplified description of psychoanalysis, which is discussed more fully by Edward Weinshel and Owen Renik in Chapter 13. Analysis is often divided into three phases—beginning, middle, and end—with the end referring to the time when a date is set (often months before the end) for the analysis to come to a close. In Chapter 16, Phyllis Tyson discusses this phase (i.e., termination) and describes the issues that are especially important during this period.

Much of what has been said above is not universally accepted in all respects and is the subject of ongoing debate.[1] Some analysts feel that a couch, although it may be useful, is not essential and that psychoanalysis can be conducted face to face. Some analysts believe that although analysis is optimally effective when the frequency of sessions is four to five times a week, it can be effective when the frequency is three times a week. They argue that even at three times a week, sufficient intensity and momentum can develop. The American Psychoanalytic Association and the International Psychoanalytical Association continue to recommend, however, that psychoanalysis be conducted on the basis of meeting four to five times a week.

Similar differences of opinion exist regarding the 50-minute hour. This length of time has been agreed upon consensually, but there is no empirical evidence to show that 30 or 70 minutes would not be better. Clinical experience suggests that 50 minutes is optimal but that is all. The French psychoanalyst Jacques Lacan believed that the length of the session should not be a static given but, rather, should be tailored according to what is happening at the time; therefore, his sessions could be almost any length, even as brief as 30 minutes or even 5 minutes.

These issues might better be understood through comparative research, but, as Judy Kantrowitz stresses in her introduction to Section IV of this textbook, research in psychoanalysis is a very difficult undertaking.

---

[1] For a fuller discussion, see Brenner C: *Psychoanalytic Technique and Psychic Conflict.* New York, International Universities Press, 1976, Chapter 7, pp. 167–201.

As noted above, psychoanalysis is a form of psychotherapy. However, according to common usage, the term *psychotherapy*, or *psychoanalytic psychotherapy*, refers to a less intense treatment than psychoanalysis. In psychotherapy, the patient is usually seen one to three times a week, most often two times a week, and the therapy session is usually conducted face to face, without a couch being used. In Chapter 14, Paul Dewald describes the psychoanalytic psychotherapies in detail and shows how they differ from psychoanalysis proper. He outlines the indications and contraindications for the use of the various modalities and discusses in detail the techniques employed in the psychoanalytic psychotherapies.

A factor invoked more often in psychotherapy than in psychoanalysis is the concomitant use of other treatment modalities. The concept of combined treatment, discussed by John Oldham in Chapter 15, is a particularly timely and sometimes controversial issue as it relates to psychoanalysis. Some psychoanalysts feel that with careful selection of patients for analysis, there is no need to combine psychoanalysis with another modality, especially medication, and that it may even be better to avoid such combined treatment. On the other hand, others assert that the use of medication allows a group of patients to be psychoanalyzed who would otherwise be deprived of the benefits of a more intensive treatment. As with the other subjects of debate and controversy noted earlier in this introduction, it seems incumbent on psychoanalysts to move from expressions of opinion to review of data and, where possible, careful research on all these matters.

Even in a more straightforward area, that of termination, which Phyllis Tyson discusses in Chapter 16, many questions remain unanswered. For example, how much time should be allotted to this phase? Should there be occasional additional sessions (from time to time) after termination? Should there be systematic follow-up (not only as part of a research project)? What happens to the transference after termination? These are some of the exciting areas now being studied, and, hopefully, these explorations should lead to a more precise definition of the current technical issues being debated in the area of psychoanalysis as a treatment modality.

13

Psychoanalytic Technique

Edward M. Weinshel, M.D.
Owen Renik, M.D.

There is always a relationship between an analyst's theoretical orientation and his or her technique, but the precise nature of that relationship is not always clear. The techniques of analysts who belong to the same school of thought are frequently quite diverse, while analysts from different schools of thought say many of the same things. It is probably fair to say that the practice of psychoanalysis is a very personal endeavor. Although there are a number of general technical principles that hold for most analysts, we have not yet worked out a comprehensive, systematic theory of technique.

Every analyst's technique is related first and foremost to his or her conception of the goals of analysis. There are usually multiple goals: an analyst holds in mind certain general analytic tasks as well as specific objectives formulated for the individual analysand. Psychoanalytic techniques are the tools an analyst employs to work toward his or her goals. Any workman has a variety of tools at his or her disposal and chooses among them to carry out the particular task at hand.

Analytic Goals and Analytic Techniques

Freud began his 1937 paper "Analysis Terminable and Interminable" with what may be the briefest statement of the goals of psychoanalytic treatment: "Experience has taught us that psycho-analytic therapy—the *freeing of someone from his neurotic symptoms, inhibitions, and abnormalities of character*—is a time-consuming business" (Freud 1937, p. 216; emphasis added).

It is often noted that psychoanalysis is, on the one hand, a science that has its own research technique and produces its own body of theory and, on the other hand, a therapy in which theory is applied to relieve human suffering while clinical observations are made to provide further data for scientific examination. Therefore, when we speak of the goals of psychoanalysis, we inevitably refer, simultaneously, to scientific and to therapeutic goals. To some extent these goals can be distinguished, and in fact *must* be distinguished for ethical reasons, and yet to a significant extent they are inextricable. When Freud spoke in general terms of psychoanalytic treatment having as one of its aims freeing the patient from symptoms, he addressed an aspect of the goals of psychoanalysis that is also an aspect of the goals of many other human endeavors— namely, the therapeutic. However, as we try to be more specific about what we mean by "symptoms" and what we mean by "freedom from symptoms," we invariably become involved in science, and in doing so, we begin to formulate those aspects of the goals of psychoanalysis that help to distinguish it from other therapeutic modalities.

The evolution of the psychoanalytic theory of psychic functioning has entailed a parallel evolution of the psychoanalytic conceptualization of psychopathology and a corresponding evolution in the conceptualization of the goals of psychoanalytic therapy. A similar evolution takes place, microcosmically, within every successful clinical analysis. Commonly, analyst and analysand begin their work with somewhat different views about the latter's problems. Through the dialectical interaction between the two, a consensual understanding is forged. As the investigation proceeds, the patient's ideas about what constitutes his or her symptoms ("miseries") are likely to change a great deal, and the analyst's understanding will change as well.

This evolutionary process is observed by every clinical analyst and has been commented upon in a variety of ways. It can be described as an inevitable shift in focus from the analysis of symptoms, in the narrower sense, to the analysis of character. Initially, ego-dystonic components of the analysand's personality are likely to draw the analyst's critical attention; but in order for the analytic work to go forward, ego-syntonic traits must come under scrutiny as well (Abrams 1987).

The achievement of insight, in the sense of heightened self-awareness, probably remains a primary operational objective for most psychoanalysts in their daily clinical work. Effecting increased self-awareness for the analysand are any number of elements, the sum and substance of which constitute clinical analysis as we know it. A partial list would include investigating fantasies and dreams; gaining an understanding of the relevant traumatic past, whether on the basis of actual recovered memories or by reconstruction; establishing the role of drives and drive derivatives; clarifying both intersystemic and intrasystemic intrapsychic conflict; and carrying out an exposition of the content of anxieties and depressive affects (and other affects as well), together with gaining an understanding of the various ways in which these affects elicit defensive activity.

Whatever an analyst's particular theoretical orientation or emphasis, he or she is likely to understand analytic work as some sort of ongoing process in which the analysand, with the help of the analyst, enlarges and refines his or her capacity for self-observation. Therefore, in clinical psychoanalysis as it is generally understood (the diversity of individual approaches notwithstanding), when analysts' work proceeds, *insight and symptom relief merge into a single goal.* The analysand's resistances clarify themselves as the most immediately relevant symptoms to be studied, and no distinction can or need be made between investigation of the analysand's self-observational difficulties and investigation of his or her psychopathology. It becomes a matter of conviction, not based on faith but born of empirical evidence collected within analysis, that insight into the manner in which the analysand interferes with his or her self-examination is also insight into the causes of his or her pain. Increased self-awareness is accompanied by decreased subjective distress.

Interpretation of Resistance

A certain amount of difficulty with the term *resistance* has arisen because Freud used it in more than one way. Sometimes he spoke of resistance as a force—the force that prevents emergence of the repressed into consciousness, that perpetuates neurosis, that opposes analytic investigation. In the physical sciences, forces are never observed; a force is an inference based on observation, a concept used to bring order to observations. Similarly, in psychoanalysis, resistance as a force is a theoretical construct, a concept pertaining to the economic and dynamic metapsychological points of view. Freud also used the term resistance more descriptively—for example, to refer to a silence interrupting a patient's associations or to an irrational objection made by a patient to an analyst's interpretation. Resistance in this sense denotes a fact of clinical observation, and it is this usage that we find most relevant to our conceptualization of analytic work.

We have already suggested that there is an intimate relationship between analytic technique and the goals of analysis. A resistance is an observable phenomenon that indicates interference with an analysand's self-observation. Because a goal of analysis is expansion of the analysand's self-observation, the analyst's task is to address resistances, and his or her primary tool is interpretation.

Interpretation, too, is a term that has been defined in a number of ways. Our own usage is inclusive: we regard as an interpretation any remark an analyst makes that is designed to draw an analysand's attention to a resistance. There are myriad forms of resistance: an analysand may, for example, deny a fact, overlook a connection that seems obvious, explain away a feeling or a behavior, and so forth. Consequently, there are many forms of interpretation. However, whatever the specific form of resistance and form of interpretation, there is a characteristic relation between the two.

When an analyst identifies a resistance, he or she forms a *hypothesis* about an analysand's psychology—namely, that some aspect of the analysand's motivation that is outside his or her conscious awareness, at least for the moment, is interfering with his or her self-observation. Sometimes the hypothesis is quite specific—for example, that an analysand is bringing in dramatic dream material primarily to gain the analyst's admiration and approval. Sometimes the hypothesis is more open-ended—for example, that an analysand seems to be speaking more slowly and carefully than usual and that this must be for reasons that are not being articulated. Sometimes an analyst will feel very certain about his or her hypothesis, and other times he or she will feel tentative.

Interpretation of resistance is the technique an analyst uses to test hypotheses about motivations interfering with an analysand's self-observation. To function as a technique for hypothesis testing, an interpretation must deal exclusively with resistance in the descriptive sense (i.e., with facts of observation that are available to both analyst and analysand). Then the analysand's response to an interpretation, the further material he or she brings forth, constitutes data that either confirm or disconfirm the hypothesis. Of course, no one response to a single interpretation provides anything like conclusive evidence. In clinical analysis, experimental control, as it were, is poor, so that it is necessary to accumulate many instances, bearing on the same issue from a variety of angles and taking many interrelated possibilities into account, before a result begins to be established. Nonetheless, the process of hypothesis testing via interpretation of resistance, even if complex and roundabout, is an empirical one. Analysand and analyst both make observations and draw inferences based upon these observations. Hypotheses and evidence are presented by both participants in the analytic relationship and become the basis for an evolving mutual understanding that is the outcome of analytic work.

Authentic analytic investigation depends upon interpretation of resistance being carried out as a hypothesis-testing procedure in which inferences can be drawn by analyst and analysand together from facts of observation available to each. Freud alluded to this necessity when he spoke of the analyst's operating at the interface between conscious and preconscious thought.[1] *Preconscious thoughts* are thoughts that are available to a person's conscious awareness but remain outside conscious awareness until attention is focused upon them. When interpreting resistance, the analyst draws the analysand's attention to a preconscious thought—something that both analyst and analysand can observe but to which the latter has not paid attention. *Unconscious thoughts* are thoughts that are not in a form in which they can receive attention and become conscious. If the analyst interprets an unconscious thought to the analysand, he or she engages in "mind reading": the analyst claims to be able to know things about the analysand's mental life that the analysand himself or herself cannot know. Freud was aware that such comments are usually analytically useless, in that agreement or disagreement by the analysand is likely to be a function of his or her compliance or rebellion to the analyst's assumed authority; therefore, the analysand's response neither confirms nor disconfirms the analyst's suggestion. Analytic technique that departs from the interpretation of resistance is subject to the objection that has been voiced by critics of psychoanalytic methodology that analytic clinical work offers no opportunity for a formulation, once made, to be disproved.

Thus, for example, let us suppose that a patient is quite angry and critical of his analyst during an hour. The following day, he makes no reference to his anger or criticisms; moreover, he takes the opportunity several times to compliment the analyst on how nice he looks. The analyst forms the hypothesis that the patient is trying to undo his behavior of the previous hour. This hypothesis concerns a motivation on the patient's part that is not observable by the analyst. However, there are certain possibly relevant facts of observation, to which the analyst can direct the patient's attention: he can comment on the fact that the patient seems to be making quite a point of complimenting him, that the anger and criticisms of the

---

[1]We mean "conscious" and "preconscious" here as adjectives denoting degrees of availability to conscious awareness, rather than location among psychic systems in an obsolete topographical model of the mind.

previous day have been abruptly discontinued, and so forth. Comments of this kind constitute *interpretation of resistance,* as we understand it. The analyst addresses the facts of observation, leaving it to the patient to bring forward information about the patient's motivations. If eventually the patient volunteers that he feels ungrateful or regrets what he said the day before, the analyst's hypothesis receives some confirmation. If, on the other hand, the patient's associations go in a different direction, the analyst may have to revise his hypothesis.

As long as the analyst confines his or her remarks to the facts of observation, the analyst can be quite active without interfering with the analytic process. For example, should the aforementioned patient respond by saying that his compliments merely reflect the fact that the analyst is looking particularly well dressed, the analyst might pursue the matter by pointing out that his appearance does not explain why the patient has repeated his compliment so many times, or why he has not seemed to note the conspicuous contradiction of his compliments of today's hour with his recent criticisms of the analyst's appearance, and so forth. By contrast, were the analyst to begin by imposing his hypothesis upon the patient, suggesting to him that his compliments were intended to make up for his previous criticisms, it would be difficult to know what to conclude from the patient's reaction, whatever it might be.

Sometimes a patient will respond to an interpretation of resistance by articulating the analyst's hypothesis and accusing the analyst of being indirect (e.g., "You're saying that I'm complimenting you today because I want to make my hostile reactions to you of yesterday magically disappear. If that's what you think, why not just come out and say so?"). Such a response confirms that the facts of observation indicate the same conclusion to the patient as they did to the analyst. After all, when an analyst does not communicate his or her hypothesis, it is not to preserve a pseudo-Socratic posture; nor is it to get the patient to do something that the analyst could do himself or herself if he or she chose. The purpose of an interpretation is to draw the *patient's* attention to certain aspects of his or her mental life so that the patient can decide what he or she thinks about them. If the analyst sometimes puts two and two on the board, it is not the same thing as saying they add up to four! When a patient responds to an interpretation of resistance by insisting that the conclusion he or she draws has been implicitly suggested to him by the analyst, it is a kind of disavowal that needs to be addressed. This is not to say that there is never a place for an analyst's sharing his or her speculations with a patient; but when the analyst does so, it is best acknowledged explicitly, and agreement by the patient per se, or even the immediate production of material consistent with the speculation, cannot be equated with confirmation.

Transference

The term *transference* denotes an inference, namely, that someone's present experience is being influenced by assumptions based on his or her prior experience without his or her being aware that this is the case. The inference of transference is arrived at only after a considerable amount of analytic investigation has taken place. As the interpretation of resistance proceeds, it becomes evident that some particular attitude on the patient's part cannot be fully accounted for on the basis of present circumstances. Then patient and therapist must search for a relevant legacy from the past that will permit the patient's current attitude to be understood. Clinical analysis is not a historical exercise in which an analysand's childhood psychological development is a subject of interest for its own sake. Examination of the past takes place only to the extent necessary for the analysand and analyst to comprehend the present. When an analysand is all too glad to dwell upon the events of long ago without connecting them in any way to his or her current life, this is as formidable a resistance as if the analysand were to dismiss his or her childhood experience as ancient history with no relevance to his or her contemporary life.

Transference is an element of all relationships, and the contribution of transference gets identified in many contexts as analytic work unfolds. However, the arena in which the most definitive elucidation of transference takes place is the relationship between analyst and analysand. In this context, emotion is most fully experienced and, consequently, conflict is most immediate. As Freud put it, "[W]hen all is said and done, it is impossible to destroy anyone *in absentia* or *in effigie*" (Freud 1912a, p. 108). Colloquially, we tend to be a little sloppy in our usage and speak of the need to "pay attention to the transference" in clinical work. This phrasing is a kind of shorthand. What we mean is that it is important to pay attention to the patient's orientation toward the analyst because that orientation is determined in part by transference, and careful investigation of the treatment relationship itself is a crucial opportunity for the analysis of transference.

Because transference is inferred when an analysand's experience is not fully explained by his or her present situation, the first step in analyzing transference usually consists of establishing that such is the case, sometimes referred to as addressing the "reality resistance." For example, consider a young woman who suddenly begins to think seriously about discontinuing her analysis because it is too expensive. The expense and the inconvenience it causes her are very real; but this does not, in itself, entirely account for why just at this moment she should suddenly begin to feel intolerably pinched. The treatment has been costly all along, and her financial condition has not undergone any recent changes. There must be an additional reason for her discomfort. Now it emerges that she has begun to be aware of sexual feelings toward her analyst and that she regards these feelings to be inappropriate. Why inappropriate? Again, the reasons for this judgment are not self-evident on the basis of her actual current situation. Eventually, the patient's associations suggest that her distress and her urge to flee arise from a connection in her mind between her analyst and her father. Transference begins to be implicated.

To understand the unrealistic features of an analysand's experience of the treatment relationship, the analyst often is seemingly faced with making a choice between focusing on defensive maneuvers and focusing on transference of past into present. This choice is more apparent than real. Suppose the young woman we have been considering, for instance, experiences the anxiety generated by her sexual feelings as an anticipation that if she were to express her passion for her analyst, he would find her ridiculous. This anticipation is based on projection and externalization: the analyst is made agent of her own self-criticism, and her own capacity for contempt as a protective reaction against excitement is attributed to him. At one point in the patient's childhood, these same defensive maneuvers colored her perception of her father, so that identification of this transference and elucidation of her ways of dealing with conflict prove to be aspects of a single analytic enterprise. Perhaps at an earlier point in the patient's childhood she believed that her father reciprocated her passion, preferring her to her mother, a wishful fantasy of success that gave rise to guilty concern for the defeated rival. This perception, too, dominates her experience with her analyst during another phase of the treatment.

An analyst's sense of confidence that some aspect of transference has been demonstrated is the most reliable criterion available to him or her by which to judge that productive analytic work has taken place. We offer our patients the opportunity to become aware of, review, and alter obsolete conclusions that determine their contemporary approaches to their lives. Analytic work, when it is productive, unveils and examines compromise solutions that continue to be applied even though they were forged under conditions long past. Elucidation of transference is the point of analysis and the source of its therapeutic benefits. Essentially, clinical analysis is the analysis of transference, and therefore the joint conviction of analyst and analysand that a bit of transference has been brought into awareness is what definitely marks an instance of analytic success.

Transference Neurosis

We learn about transference piecemeal in analysis. Because we operate by isolating particular specimens of a patient's current experience for examination, and from studying these discover consequences of particular episodes in the patient's history, we tend to refer to our inferences in terms of particular transferences. And yet we know that all of a person's prior experience must bear in some way on every moment of his or her present life. If circumscribed events in a patient's past seem to be decisively responsible for ef-

fects in the here and now, it is because when we investigate determination, the limits of our insight necessitate that we let certain
parts stand for the whole. We say that particular transferences
"emerge" or "manifest" themselves at different times. This is a phenomenological way of depicting how our attention is successively
claimed by separate aspects of what is actually the unitary phenomenon of a patient's transference of past into present. Sometimes
circumstances show one or another facet of transference to advantage. However, that we tend to speak of the specific transferences
(plural) a patient makes, rather than his or her transference as
a whole, reflects the inevitably fragmented understanding we
achieve in any clinical analysis, no matter how thorough.

The fact that transference is a unitary phenomenon has consequences for our clinical method. In a given analysis, no piece of
analytic work stands alone; every inference of transference made
interrelates with others. The greater the extent to which a patient's
particular transferences can be fit together to form a coherent
whole, the greater our sense of conviction about the validity of what
has been inferred. Each successive analysis of an aspect of transference informs the next and is, in turn, retrospectively informed by it.
The reciprocal relations among the various separate inferences of
transference that we make during the course of an analysis influence our understanding of these inferences and contribute to our
sense of conviction about them.

It is because of the interdependence of particular inferences of
transference that the concept of a *transference neurosis* has utility.
A transference neurosis, as we conceptualize it, is a sequence of
interrelated transferences. Because what we do when we identify
transference is to construct an inference, a transference neurosis is
an inference about a series of inferences—that is, it is a "higher
order" inference. Clinical analysts constantly make inferences and,
subsequently, higher-order inferences. Our work with patients requires this.

Analysis of transference is a complex task having many steps.
The concept of transference neurosis pertains to an advanced stage
in the satisfactory analysis of transference, one that occurs only with
neurotic patients. Therefore, arrival at the stage of transference

neurosis has often been used as a criterion for judging when an analysis is reasonably "successful" or "complete." When we use the concept of transference neurosis in this way, it is crucial to avoid reification by keeping in mind that we are dealing not simply with facts of observation concerning the mental life of the analysand but with observations concerning the development of the analytic work, to which the analyst's functioning as well as the analysand's contributes. Also, because we make the assumption that analytic work can proceed farther with neurotic patients than with others, it is important that we try to specify what distinguishes the evolution of the analysis of transference in those cases.

In our view, a distinguishing component of a transference neurosis as opposed to other evolving sequences of interrelated transferences is that the transference neurosis culminates in exposure of the manifold conflicts of the oedipal phase of psychosexual development. We make this judgment on empirical grounds. Our clinical impression corresponds to the conventional wisdom that patients who have significantly engaged the essential dilemma of the oedipal phase of psychosexual development are distinguishable by the operations of their consciences. They have a capacity for guilt (i.e., autonomous moral judgments, as opposed to persecutory fears), a capacity for generally consistent reality testing, an ability to form and monitor affects of signal strength, and so forth. Their symptom formation tends more toward autoplastic compromise than alloplastic avoidance of conflict. All this is to say that a certain measure of effective superego functioning is crucial to the psychopathology we call *neurosis.*

The picture painted by early analytic theorists of an all-or-nothing formation of the superego through resolution of oedipal conflicts is a reductionistic one. It is widely appreciated now that all sorts of pregenital factors participate in the development of conscience and that, further, Freud's notions concerning the role of castration anxiety and the difference between male and female superego formation were in many ways misconceived. Nonetheless, there is reason to correlate superego development with the engagement of oedipal conflict. Sexual rivalry in the context of love is an important organizer, and, at least for the present, given the prevalence of nuclear families and the way relationships within them are structured, the oedipal struggle tends to be a primary occasion upon which an individual confronts the conflict between his or her narcissistic interests and his or her need to take a place within society. A number of analysts have felt that oedipal transference constitutes an important part, but not the entirety, of a transference neurosis (Blum 1971). Our conceptualization is in keeping with that view. Future social changes may alter the shape of normative psychosexual development, but for now it makes sense to us to stipulate transference of the core conflict of the oedipal phase as a feature of transference neurosis.

Working-Through

To speak of "an interpretation of resistance" might seem to imply that a single remark from the analyst, well phrased, will address, cleanly and decisively, a specific obstacle to self-awareness on the analysand's part. In fact, most often what occurs is an interpretive sequence, a series of interventions directed at identification and clarification of resistance. At the same time, resistance is a complex and plastic phenomenon, constantly altering in form in response to interpretation. Therefore, we are probably most faithful to the actual events of clinical analysis when we think of resistance and interpretation as evolving together, pari passu, as the investigation proceeds.

It is hardly surprising, then, that even in the most successful clinical analysis a considerable lag is noted time and again between the point at which a significant insight first appears and the point at which that insight bears fruit in the form of manifest behavioral change. This regularly observed interval is often referred to as the period of *working-through.*

Freud conceptualized working-through in metapsychological terms, first (Freud 1914) as reflecting the need for abreaction, and later (Freud 1926) as reflecting time needed for the rearrangement of libidinal cathexes. A more contemporary view of working-through is less exclusively theoretical and stays closer to phenomenology. As we analysts have gained more experience with the analysis of resistance, we have realized that an aggregate of related insights, rather than a single, definitive insight, is usually required to alter self-awareness sufficiently for adaptive behavioral change to occur.

Working-through in analysis can be compared to mourning. When a loved one is lost, for example, the bereaved person does not come to terms with loss all at once via the simple realization, "He is gone." Rather, there is a process of continual accretion in which many component losses, corresponding to various aspects of what can now no longer be, are identified and accommodated (e.g., We will never make love again. He will no longer be at the breakfast table. He is not there to share family news. He no longer arranges the annual summer vacation). Gradually, a comprehensive adaptation takes place, but this can only be arrived at over time, as each new truth makes itself felt; and it takes a long time before painful realizations no longer crop up with frequency.

Similarly, the analysis of resistance is a process in which fragmentary realizations accumulate over time to form a whole. Insight must be gained into the many and varied forms in which a particular motivation to avoid self-awareness can express itself before self-awareness expands to the point that behavioral change is produced.

Tact, Timing, and the Therapeutic Alliance

Although interpretation of resistance is the analyst's task and constitutes his or her analytic activity per se, a description of interpretation alone does not take into account much of what needs to occur if a clinical analysis is to progress. To begin with, there is the question of choice of interpretation. The most familiar dilemmas of everyday clinical analytic work generally consist of a kind of embarrassment of riches. Listening to a patient's associations, an analyst will feel able to identify a number of promising lines of inquiry, all of which are probably valid and deserving of attention. The question then becomes, Which would be best to pursue at the moment? Experience teaches us that although it may be possible for an analyst to communicate any number of accurate observations at a given point in analysis, only a minority of these observations will advance the work. Unfortunately, that an interpretation is a true statement about the analysand's mental life is only a necessary, not a sufficient, condition for an interpretation's efficacy.

Our technical rules of thumb tell us to work from the surface to address the resistance; but the problem remains how to determine where the surface lies and which is *the* resistance. The all-important matter of how to decide *what* to interpret and *when* is an aspect of analytic technique that is not easily spelled out. We tend to refer to the issues bearing on choice of interpretation under the headings of analytic *tact* and *timing*, meaning that we invite our analysands to observe themselves in ways that we judge they will be able to tolerate.

Analytic tact and timing take place within a two-person field. The contemporary view is very different from the one that prevailed more than 70 years ago when Freud wrote:

> In actual fact, indeed, the neurotic patient presents with a torn mind, divided by resistances. As we analyse it and remove the resistances, it grows together; the great unity which we call his ego fits into itself all the instinctual impulses which before had been split off and held apart from it. The psycho-synthesis is thus achieved during analytic treatment *without our intervention, automatically and inevitably*. We have created the conditions for it by . . . removing the resistances. It is not true that something in the patient has been divided into its components and is now quietly waiting for us to put it somehow together again. (Freud 1919[1918], p. 161; emphasis added)

Today, despite tremendous diversity among analysts with respect to theoretical orientation and technique, very few would subscribe to the idea that "psycho-synthesis" occurs "without our intervention, automatically and inevitably." We do not believe that the responsibility of the psychoanalyst is limited to dealing with resistances (nor do we think of resistances as being "removed"), and would not attribute to the patient entire responsibility for integration of the analytic work. We recognize that the analyst plays a continuous, appropriately active role throughout an analysis.

As appreciation of the ongoing participation of the analyst in the psychoanalytic process has increased, so also has attention to how and why the analyst participates as he or she does. The idealized and pseudo-objectified conception of a psychoanalytic process separate from the person of the analyst (described so well by Freud in the passage quoted above) has by now yielded to a searching curiosity and expanded view of the role of the analyst, including concentrated interest in the participation of the analyst's psychology in all phases of psychoanalytic understanding. Psychoanalysis, like every other systematic investigative discipline, has come to explicitly recognize the influence of the observing "instrument" (in this case, the mind of the analyst) on the thing observed and to make that influence a matter for study.

In the past, much consideration had been given to whether a narrow or a more expanded definition of *countertransference* would be most advantageous. This controversy has faded into the background lately, because most of us now assume that the entire array of an analyst's emotional responses—those specifically induced by an analysand's transferences, as well as those brought by the analyst a priori—must be taken into account in studying psychoanalytic technique and process. Increasingly candid—not needlessly exhibitionistic but appropriately self-revelatory—descriptions of how an analyst uses his or her own emotional responses in analytic work have begun to make their appearance in the last 10 years.

Quite a wide angle of view is now being taken in looking at the analyst's self-inquiry as part of his or her ongoing work. Detailed studies are made of the resistances encountered in self-analysis. A number of reports have addressed the way in which countertransference responses can be masked by the ordinary procedures of clinical analysis, unnoticed because they are coincident with attitudes regarded as part of proper technique. Attention is being given more and more to the details of self-analytic technique: the use made by the analyst of his or her own dreams, apparently irrelevant thoughts during an hour, doodling, note taking, and other grist for the self-analytic mill. For example, the role of case reports as an aid to self-analysis, in training and afterward, has been studied, and a link between resistance to writing up cases and resistance to self-analysis has been proposed.

The whole topic of *countertransference enactment* has come up for review. At the very least, we think of countertransference enactments as inevitable in clinical analysis. There is widespread acceptance of the idea that an optimal analytic stance, free from such enactments, may be an ideal to strive toward, but it is one that is never achieved in practice. Above and beyond the inevitability of countertransference enactments is the question of the role of these enactments in the psychoanalytic process. Is it simply that analysts manage to learn from the errors that, due to human limitations, they are bound to make? Or are countertransference enactments by the analyst, as are transference enactments by the analysand, in some way a necessary component of the analytic process?

In the analytic encounter, as has been frequently noted, the interactions between analyst and analysand are such that the latter is able to re-create and master crucial pathogenic experiences. This observation brings up the vexing problem of the concept of *corrective emotional experience*. Is clinical psychoanalysis a corrective emotional experience? And if so, how is this taken into account in our theory of technique?

One of the most important shaping trends of the last 40 years has been a reaction against the technical innovations introduced by Alexander and French (1949). At the same time there has been an awareness on the part of many that if we do not continue to try to take account of the interactive aspect of the psychoanalytic process—the ways in which the particulars of analytic work are negotiated between analyst and analysand—we will have thrown out the baby with the bath water. Thus, some theories of the analytic process suggest that the analyst is a new object, providing new experiences that permit development to go forward; others emphasize the mutative role of empathic responsiveness; still others conceptualize the analyst as passing tests so as to disconfirm the patient's pathogenic beliefs.

A difficulty comes when we try to reconcile these ideas with our formulations concerning the interpretation of resistance. If psychoanalysis is a corrective emotional experience, then a systematic theory of analytic technique should direct the analyst in determining how best to provide a corrective emotional experience for the analysand. We immediately come up against, in one form or another, the problems raised by the recommendations of Alexander and French. It is presumptuous for an analyst to take it upon himself or herself to decide when a patient's psychological development went astray and how the defect can be remedied. Furthermore, contrived role playing within the treatment relationship is hypocritical. Such presumption and hypocrisy contradict what most of us understand to be the essence of the psychoanalytic clinical collaboration.

One effort to resolve this dilemma has been through the claim that ordinary psychoanalytic procedure, the neutrality of the analyst and his or her commitment to the investigative task, in itself provides the required corrective emotional experience. By interpreting resistances, the analyst engenders a corrective emotional experience. Our clinical concepts, properly applied, guide us toward providing optimal frustration-gratification sequences for our analysands.

Some theorists sequester all purposeful interactive aspects of the analytic relationship under the separate heading of the "treatment alliance" or "therapeutic alliance," maintenance of which by the analyst is distinguished from psychoanalytic technique per se. This theoretical isolation keeps the concept of psychoanalytic process free from contamination by the concept of a corrective emotional experience. However, regardless of the categories we establish, we are left with clinical reality: the observation that "relationship" factors are of crucial importance in clinical analysis and that effective management of them is part of effective analytic technique.

Free Association

For most psychoanalysts, the method of free association lies at the heart of clinical technique. The so-called *fundamental rule* of psychoanalysis asks the analysand to let thoughts come into mind as best he or she can, and to verbalize these thoughts as completely as possible in the presence of the analyst—even if they should seem embarrassing, silly, trivial, or offensive. A patient who accepts this request engages in the effort to *free-associate.*

As an analysand free-associates, he or she provides valuable and necessary data about his or her life, past and present. Completely free association is, of course, an ideal never achieved in practice. Interferences with the process of free association (i.e., *resistances*) are indications of the influence of internal mental conflict and provide an opportunity to investigate the unconscious source and the composition of such conflict.

Free association was not Freud's original investigative technique. "Remembering, Repeating and Working-Through" (Freud 1914, pp. 147–151) provides an excellent synopsis of some of the important early changes in Freud's technique. A principal shift was from the emphasis on catharsis through memory retrieval to an emphasis on discovering how and why the patient fails to remember. In this new conception resistances were to be dealt with by interpretation rather than by exhortation. Abreaction as a concept was replaced by the idea of work performed by the patient in striving to examine his or her reluctance to freely associate in accordance with the fundamental rule. Instead of focusing on a specific topic, the analyst "contents himself [or herself] with studying whatever is present for the time being on the *surface* of the patient's mind [his or her associations], and he [or she] employs the art of interpretation mainly for the purpose of recognizing the resistances which appear there, and making them conscious to the patient" (Freud 1914, p. 147; emphasis added). To the extent that the patient was no longer encouraged to associate to a specific preselected subject, but was invited to say whatever came to mind, a greater degree of freedom of thought became possible.

From this point of view, which now prevails, an analysand is asked to participate in a process in which he or she plays an active role, discovering and sharing with the analyst an increasing knowledge of his or her own mental functioning. Most of the time, the analyst does not select the topic of the ongoing analytic work; the patient makes that decision.

The basis of the analyst-analysand partnership is investigation of the latter's mental life. The way in which the analyst participates will play a significant part in the establishment of the *psychoanalytic situation*. It is often recommended that an analyst's mind operate during analytic work in a state of "evenly-suspended attention," which "consists simply in not directing one's notice to anything in particular" (Freud 1912b, p. 111). *Neutrality* is a concept related to the analyst's appropriate stance that has received a great deal of discussion. Although there is no one formula for how the analyst should behave in his or her psychoanalytic relationship, it is expected that he or she will be genuine, aware of and able to tolerate his or her affective reactions, and capable of avoiding the use of the patient for his or her own narcissistic needs. Clearly, this means the analyst is not merely a mirror in which the patient can view himself or herself; nor is the analyst a psychic surgeon who operates without emotion; nor must the analyst be perfect, without areas of unanalyzed conflict, in order to do his or her work.

Although the contemporary psychoanalyst is prepared for interaction with his or her analysands, interaction is not to be equated with a *laissez aller* relationship in which professional values and technical objectives are disregarded. Every analyst is aware of his or her limitations—his or her transferences to the patient and countertransferences to the patient's transferences. Today we are more concerned than in the past with understanding the ways in which the analyst's personality, including his or her limitations, plays a part in the psychoanalytic process.

When patient and analyst can work together in a reasonably productive way, then, as Arlow (1985) notes,

> [w]ithin the psychoanalytic situation, free associations offer a living record of the moment to moment functioning of the patient's mind. It is not a placid, continuous scroll of recollections. It is a dynamic record, reflecting a relatively unstable equilibrium of forces in conflict. The phenomenology of this instability is rich and varied, and its dynamism and significance can be grasped in their fullness during the psychoanalytic situation, as one observes and studies the moment to moment variation in the patient's communications. The patient's productions reflect the changing contribution emanating from the several psychic agencies, and they encompass the well-recognized phenomena ordinarily described

under the heading of resistance and defense as well as intrusive fantasies, impulses, thoughts, affective states, parapraxes, and so forth.

The interplay of forces in conflict determines the form and sequence in which the elements of communication appear in the course of free association. Accordingly, from the patterns that the elements communicated assume, meanings beyond those conveyed in the literal, expository prose can be inferred. Such inferences articulate motives and wishes quite unknown to the analysand, as well as the methods and reasons for disowning and denying such wishes and impulses. (pp. 22–23)

The method of free associations provides analyst and patient with a text to be examined as they pursue knowledge of the unconscious determinants of the patient's mental life. Kris (1982), for example, describes how he looks for the evolution of insight into two types of conflict as evidence that associations are becoming freer from unconscious obstacles. Kris articulates systematically, carefully, and explicitly his particular conception of the method of free association, a method that every clinical analyst uses, in one form or another, to guide his or her work.

The Analysis of Dreams

Initially, psychoanalytic technique and dream technique were virtually synonymous. Freud analyzed himself primarily through an investigation of his dreams. Perhaps the most quoted of psychoanalytic aphorisms is Freud's remark that *"the interpretation of dreams is the royal road to a knowledge of the unconscious activities of the mind"* (Freud 1900, p. 608). What Freud discovered, at first through the analysis of dreams, was how to understand and work with unconscious activities of the mind.

For some analysts, the dream and the deciphering of dreams still constitute the royal road to a knowledge of the unconscious activities of the mind. However, others feel that as we have accumulated more and more clinical experience, it has become evident that analytic work with transference and resistance, with fantasies, and with almost any material introduced into the analytic session by the analysand can be as fruitful as analytic work with dream material. Early psychoanalysts were most eager to get a grasp of the content of the unconscious and to transmit that information to their patients as quickly as possible. The analysis of dreams was ideal for this particular purpose. However, as time went on, analysts learned that telling patients what their unconscious thoughts are is not a reliable means of investigating unconscious mental life and making it conscious. Much more effective is to invite consideration of the obstacles to self-awareness (i.e., resistances). Only gradually did analysts learn to deal with resistances by understanding rather than by forceful exhortation. Blum (1976) points out that "with the advance of psychoanalytic theory and technique it was understood that there was no royal road into the unconscious *without* resistance" (p. 316; emphasis added).

The separate term *dream analysis* is somewhat misleading. A slight modification to "analysis of dreams" would probably be more appropriate. There is no special technique for working analytically with dream material; the techniques used are the same as those used to understand symptoms, waking fantasies, or transferences. In other words, the analysis of dreams is an integral part of any psychoanalysis and cannot be treated as a discrete operation separate from the rest of the work. Freud (1911) warned that "it is scarcely ever right to sacrifice this therapeutic aim to an interest in dream-interpretation" (Freud 1911, p. 92). Although there have been many alterations made in the psychoanalytic theory of dreams and the manner in which dreams are commonly approached clinically, the majority of these changes have been consequent to general changes in psychoanalytic thinking. The psychoanalytic theory of dreams or of the analysis of dreams in particular has not changed in relation to the theory as a whole.

Not all analysts are equally interested in or adept at the analysis of dreams, and not all patients are equally prolific in their production of dreams. Such variation determines the way in which dreams figure in any given clinical psychoanalysis. Nevertheless, there are common elements among the various ways in which analysts and analysands work with dreams: the patient reports a dream (often, but not necessarily, at the beginning of the analytic session) and may or may not offer associations to it. The analyst may or may not respond immediately. He or she is concerned not only with the content of the dream but also with the context in which the dream appears, the way it is recounted, and how the whole might reflect what is taking place currently within the treatment relationship. The analyst pays attention to the affects that formed part of the dream experience, as well as to the patient's affective responses to having dreamed.

Focus on transference elements in the dream content and the dream presentation (and on countertransference responses to them) often reveals how those elements are serving as resistances. For instance, a patient may offer the analyst a bouquet of dreams as a present in the hope of receiving approval or attention; or the patient may report a highly erotic dream, with the unconscious hope of exciting and seducing the analyst; or the patient may overwhelm the analyst with a plethora of dreams that defy understanding.

Dreams constitute nocturnal continuations of daytime waking thoughts and are therefore often triggered by events and experiences of the previous day. The traces of this instigation in the manifest dream report are termed the *day residue.* At the same time, current experiences mobilize archaic impulses and ideas from early life. One of the goals of an ideally thorough analysis of a dream is the identification of both sets of factors. Consider the following example:

> A graduate student was having trouble writing her dissertation. This conscientious young woman was plagued by an unjustified fear that she would be accused of plagiarism. She would have to copy work already done, she felt, because she was incapable of being sufficiently original. In the midst of this struggle she had a dream in which she stole a bicycle and was caught and humiliated for having stolen it. In her associations she had no difficulty connecting the bicycle with her dissertation, which she also felt she could obtain only through theft. The preceding day she had been thinking how much time she wasted riding her bicycle instead of working on her dissertation.

From their preceding work the analyst and the patient had a great deal to draw upon in understanding the dream. For example, successful completion of her dissertation meant following in the footsteps of her academically prominent father, an act that the young woman equated with theft because of its connection with her fantasies of oedipal triumph and competition with her younger brother. Also, much attention had been given to the significance of producing something and to originality. Bicycle riding was, no doubt, an overdetermined metaphor, referring in part to sexual impulses about which she was concerned. These and similar ideas marked well-traveled interpretive paths that were no less valid for their being familiar but that seemed stale and yielded little of value in connection with this dream.

During the course of the hour, the analyst happened to ask the patient for her associations to the particular bicycle portrayed in the dream. She began to relate what few details she could recall— a headlight, a dented fender, a wire basket on the back—and realized that she was describing the bicycle she currently owned.

Thus, the patient's actual bicycle had appeared in the manifest content of her dream, and the discovery of this piece of reality necessitated that the dream be understood in an entirely new way. Instead of simply expressing a confession of guilt and a need for punishment, the dream now appeared to contain a complaint of being unjustly accused and attacked for a blameless activity: taking possession of her own bicycle. Following the patient's association of the bicycle with her dissertation, the dream expressed her objection that she had a right to complete her degree and go on in her career without feeling guilty of theft.

The patient's dream contained a fantasy of getting what she wanted and feeling innocent in doing so, but this aspect of the dream was kept out of awareness by what might be termed an error of omission. Knowledge that the bicycle she "stole" in the dream was in reality her own was disavowed and excluded from the dream report.

Because dreams are nocturnal continuations of preconscious waking thoughts from the preceding day, the aptness of a dream interpretation can be confirmed if it permits these thoughts to be recalled. This young woman had already mentioned having wondered the day before why she spent time riding her bicycle instead of working on her dissertation. After the aspect of her dream that was a complaint and a protest of innocence had been unveiled, she remembered a fleeting idea from the day before, something like "I ought to be able to feel as free and enthusiastic working on my dissertation as I feel now riding my bicycle."

The analysis of a dream can be used to identify psychodynamic mechanisms that occur in waking life. For instance, the particular way in which reality was falsified to disguise a pleasurable wish in this young woman's dream exemplified a defensive maneuver of the greatest significance for her. At another point in her analysis, she developed serious physical symptoms that proved to have no organic basis. The analyst suspected a hysterical identification and found a way to ask her if what she was experiencing might not be similar to something she had observed in the past. She was puzzled by the question. She felt certain she had told the analyst of her father's illness (she had not), to which her symptoms obviously corresponded closely. This was the same mechanism as in her dream: she had disavowed knowledge of a critical piece of reality— her father's illness—and excluded it from what she reported in analysis.

The piece of reality that made its way into this patient's dream was a particular perception—the image of her bicycle. Because of the associations it elicited, the memory of this perception both gave pleasure and aroused anxiety. Because it gave pleasure it was repeated in her dream, and because it raised anxiety it was defensively falsified. The specific method used to defensively falsify a stimulating conflict-producing perception was characteristic for her. It also had traceable historical roots.

She had been cared for in childhood by a warm and kindly maid, whose attentions the little girl had sometimes interpreted as openly seductive. When her parents went away, she pretended to herself that the maid was her mother. This game would be conveniently put out of the child's mind when the parents returned. It was one childhood version of the disavowal and omission of a feeling of righteous possessiveness that occurred in her dream.

Analysis of a dream can allow the focus of the analytic work to alter. In this instance something was added to the patient's awareness of her guilty need to fail and to criticize herself. Her covert feeling of entitlement and her need to disguise it could be demonstrated and thus could come under investigation.

The analysis of a dream can sometimes point the way to a line of interpretation that helps elucidate the current state of the treatment relationship and its transference determinants, as in the following case:

> A young man in analysis was exquisitely sensitive to any feelings of attachment to his analyst. His foremost method of denying them was to experience the treatment relationship entirely in terms of rivalry and struggle. If the analyst canceled an hour, he did the same in short order. If he had fantasies of the analyst enjoying himself over a weekend—something he would never disclose but that could sometimes be inferred—he began the week by regaling the analyst with tales of his recent adventures. Any suggestion that his competitive view of the analytic relationship might have a defensive function he dismissed as a hackneyed theory of the analyst's intended to brainwash him into becoming a typical dependent analytic patient.
>
> Not long after the analyst announced the dates of his impending summer vacation, the patient had a dream in which he was back in college, meeting in the auditorium with a group of students. It was fall, and the professor was reading aloud from a list of names. Those students who were mentioned would not be allowed to enroll again because they had received "incompletes" in certain necessary courses. The patient knew that his name was to be called. He could remember no more about the dream except a vague feeling of discomfort.
>
> Undoubtedly, the dream had something to do with the upcoming vacation and with the question of whether the patient would continue his analysis in the fall, although he volunteered no concern about the analyst's discontinuing. As a matter of fact, he made it very clear that he was looking forward to the break and that he was nonchalant about beginning again the following month. He had no associations to his feeling of discomfort and was skeptical that this aspect of the dream had anything to do with the analyst or his vacation. The patient expected the analyst to assume that the patient was upset because they were not going to be meeting.
>
> In his associations to the dream, it emerged that being readmitted in the fall had once been a concern for the patient during his college years. In order to devote a good part of their time to working on the school newspaper, he and a group of his friends had

reduced their loads during the regular academic season, making up for it by scheduling courses in the summer session. When summer came, the temptation to play was too strong for some of his friends, who had received incompletes and, as a result, had not been allowed to continue the next year. The patient himself had been sufficiently disciplined, but just barely, to get by.

The patient's getting by even though his friends did not was a success that could easily be understood in terms of the transference relationship and the analyst's vacation. The patient's dream indicated his feeling that he had obligations he must mind over the summer if he wished to ensure the continuation of his analysis in the fall. He was afraid that the temptation to play might be too strong for him this time.

The parallel between the patient's college experience and what could be concerning him about the approaching summer interval in the analysis was interpreted to the patient. The analyst reminded him of the glee he usually felt about "one-upping," and suggested to the patient that he might be afraid that he would do things over the summer he would not be able to talk to the analyst about when they met again. This brought a rueful chuckle. The patient admitted he expected the analyst to think of him as pining away, whereas he had no such intention. Furthermore, he could not be sure how the analyst would regard some of the things the patient liked to do. The wishful idea, also expressed by his memory, that he would be the sole survivor in the analyst's caseload did not come to light until much later. At this point, it came to light that for some time in his treatment this patient consciously avoided disclosure of his past homosexual activity, as well as his frank homosexual fantasies about the analyst.

In the early days of psychoanalysis it was not uncommon for the analyst to conduct a very systematic study of every dream the analysand presented. Each detail of the dream report was carefully explored through the patient's associations. This kind of exhaustive examination of a dream has become less common. One disadvantage of comprehensively studying every dream is that the analyst determines how dream elements receive attention. In a sense, when the analysand is left to decide whether or not to associate, and to which elements of the dream, his or her associations are "freer" than when those decisions are made by the analyst.

Nonetheless, some acquaintance with the technique of detailed analysis of a dream is important. There is no better example than Freud's classic report of his "Irma dream" (Freud 1900, pp. 106–121). A thoughtful discussion of the pros and cons of abandoning exhaustive analysis of dreams for a more "modern" approach can be found in Erikson's inspired paper "The Dream Specimen of Psychoanalysis" (Erikson 1954).

Selection of Patients for Analysis

Who should be in analysis? The most familiar, and in some ways the simplest, answer to the question is everyone who needs it and can make use of it. People who *need* analysis are those who have psychological symptoms that cause enough distress to warrant the time, effort, and expense that are likely to be required by analytic treatment. Not everyone who thinks he or she has psychological symptoms actually has psychological symptoms, or his or her symptoms may not be the ones he or she thinks are present. For example, a patient seeks analysis because he feels his personal difficulties are ruining his marriage. He realizes as he begins to look into his situation that his marital difficulties are being caused to a very great extent by the severe emotional disorder of his spouse and that he has hoped unrealistically to remedy the situation by altering himself, because he is afraid that his spouse is unwilling to be treated, and is possibly untreatable. The patient's denial of his spouse's disorder, his pessimism about it, his reasons for picking such a spouse in the first place, and so forth are all important problems. They may be problems that indicate that analysis would be appropriate; but on the other hand, it often develops, after obtaining consultation, that a person in this situation faces and decides to deal realistically with his or her spouse's condition and has no need for further treatment himself or herself.

It is not at all unusual for a person to seek psychoanalytic treatment out of a misguided effort to change an external (nonpsychological) circumstance. Some patients with chronic organic illness entertain unrealistic hopes for amelioration through analysis. Some patients feel that they should be more successful in their careers than they are and seek analysis on the assumption that they are being held back by neurotic constraints, because they are unable to consider that they may have simply reached the limits of their talents. Sometimes a patient's unrealistic approach to his or her situation is something that can benefit from analytic investigation; but sometimes, too, it is simply necessary for the patient to face facts, avoidance of which would be facilitated by embarking upon a psychoanalytic self-investigation. There are cases in which important psychological symptoms can be effectively addressed by a more limited inquiry than is involved in clinical psychoanalysis. There are also persons who, even if they need clinical psychoanalysis, are prohibited from obtaining it for logistical reasons. These situations are ones in which psychotherapy, rather than psychoanalysis, may be indicated. The similarities and differences between psychoanalysis and psychotherapy, and the indications for one as opposed to the other, constitute a complex subject for discussion.[2]

The question of who can *make use* of analysis brings up the whole issue of "analyzability," which has been approached from many points of view. Ego strength, capacity to tolerate regression, psychological mindedness, and a host of related concepts have been invoked—and elaborate psychometric systems developed to measure them—in the effort to predict what sort of patient will be able to carry out the work of clinical analysis. Because our own conception of psychoanalytic work centers around the analysis of resistance, we would emphasize a patient's manner of dealing with resistance—and especially with interpretation of resistance—as an important indicator of his or her analyzability. In evaluating a patient for analysis, we look for evidence that the patient is able to consider new ways of looking at himself or herself, particularly when the shift in view is not altogether gratifying for him or her. Such evidence bespeaks a capacity to identify obstacles to self-awareness and to address the motivations for them, which is at the

---

[2]See Paul Dewald's discussion of psychoanalysis and psychotherapy in Chapter 14.

heart of the patient's task, as we see it. Some analysts view the initial evaluation as exclusively an information-gathering, diagnostic enterprise, quite separate from the analytic work that may be begun later, and therefore recommend against making interpretations while evaluation for analysis is still under way. For us, information gathering includes the effort to determine how a patient responds to interpretation of resistance, so that the line between initial evaluation and the beginning of analytic work—if analytic work can occur—is not easily drawn. By the same token, we might say that the evaluation of a patient's analyzability continues even after the analytic work has been under way for some time, and it is often not until termination that the evaluation is completed!

Exact criteria for analyzability are difficult to spell out in detail. It is easier in some ways to be definitive about what are *not* criteria for analyzability, in our view. Neither the details of a patient's history nor his or her presenting symptoms, in themselves, are very reliable indicators of capacity for analytic work. Certainly, manifest symptomatology and historical data are factors to be considered within a total picture; but the same symptom can arise from very different underlying psychologies, and what appears narratively as the same historical event can constitute a different experience with very different consequences for one individual than for another. Thus, every analyst has found it impossible to get anywhere with a patient whose symptoms seemed relatively mild and whose history seemed relatively atraumatic, and has undertaken analysis with someone whose history was grim and whose symptoms were severe and found that the work went swimmingly.

> An analyst received a referral from a colleague in another city of a patient who had to relocate because of his job. The referring analyst considered psychotherapy the treatment of choice. The patient was a severely depressed man whose mother had died before his second birthday. The history of early object loss coupled with the depressive symptom picture, the referring analyst thought, indicated that the patient was unanalyzable. The analyst who received the referral had the impression that the patient was interested in and capable of self-investigation, and therefore suggested analysis, to which the patient agreed. It developed that the

patient had lost his mother when he was just over a year old, but his father had remarried almost immediately in order to give the boy a new mother. The woman the father married loved children, and she was very successful in helping the infant boy transfer his affections to herself. She remained very devoted to the patient throughout his childhood. At the same time, the marriage between the patient's father and his new wife—who had been selected primarily for her maternal qualities—was less than passionate. The combination of his mother's absorption in him and the troubled marriage between his parents contributed to the development of a powerful conviction of oedipal triumph on the patient's part, with commensurately intense unconscious guilt. Analysis of this conviction proved quite possible and relieved what had seemed to the referring analyst an intransigent anaclitic depression.

Some analysts think of the initial phase of treatment as a "trial analysis." In our view, the best way to determine analyzability is through trial analysis, which we believe can begin in the initial consultative interview. Every analysis is, in a certain sense, a trial analysis until termination is reached.

References

Abrams S: The psychoanalytic process: a schematic model. Int J Psychoanal 68:441–452, 1987

Alexander F, French T: Psychoanalytic Psychotherapy. New York, Ronald Press, 1949

Arlow J: The structural model, in Models of the Mind. Edited by Rothstein A. New York, International Universities Press, 1985

Blum H: The conception and development of the transference neurosis. J Am Psychoanal Assoc 19:41–53, 1971

Blum H: The changing use of dreams in psychoanalytic practice. Int J Psychoanal 57:315–324, 1976

Erikson E: The dream specimen of psychoanalysis. J Am Psychoanal Assoc 2:5–56, 1954

Freud S: The interpretation of dreams (1900), in Standard Edition of the Complete Psychological Works of Sigmund Freud, Vols 4 and 5. Translated and edited by Strachey J. London, Hogarth Press, 1953

Freud S: The handling of dream-interpretation in psycho-analysis (1911), in Standard Edition of the Complete Psychological Works of Sigmund Freud, Vol 12. Translated and edited by Strachey J. London, Hogarth Press, 1958, pp 89–96

Freud S: The dynamics of transference (1912a), in Standard Edition of the Complete Psychological Works of Sigmund Freud, Vol 12. Translated and edited by Strachey J. London, Hogarth Press, 1958, pp 97–108

Freud S: Recommendations to physicians practising psycho-analysis (1912b), in Standard Edition of the Complete Psychological Works of Sigmund Freud, Vol 12. Translated and edited by Strachey J. London, Hogarth Press, 1958, pp 109–120

Freud S: Remembering, repeating and working-through (further recommendations on the technique of psycho-analysis II) (1914), in Standard Edition of the Complete Psychological Works of Sigmund Freud, Vol 12. Translated and edited by Strachey J. London, Hogarth Press, 1958, pp 145–156

Freud S: Lines of advance in psycho-analytic therapy (1919[1918]), in Standard Edition of the Complete Psychological Works of Sigmund Freud, Vol 17. Translated and edited by Strachey J. London, Hogarth Press, 1955, pp 157–168

Freud S: Inhibitions, symptoms and anxiety (1926), in Standard Edition of the Complete Psychological Works of Sigmund Freud, Vol 20. Translated and edited by Strachey J. London, Hogarth Press, 1959, pp 75–175

Freud S: Analysis terminable and interminable (1937), in Standard Edition of the Complete Psychological Works of Sigmund Freud, Vol 23. Translated and edited by Strachey J. London, Hogarth Press, 1964, pp 209–253

Kris A: Free Association: Method and Process. New Haven, CT, Yale University Press, 1982

14

The Psychoanalytic Psychotherapies

Paul A. Dewald, M.D.

The term *psychotherapy* is applied to a large number of psychological treatments in which the attempt is to modify a patient's
symptoms or behavior through psychological interaction and influence. In that sense, psychotherapy is the generic term, and *psychoanalysis* is one form of psychotherapy applicable to a relatively small
number of individual patients. However, as a general psychological
theory of mental functioning, psychoanalysis can be used to conceptualize and understand a variety of different forms of psychotherapy, and
the techniques developed by psychoanalysis can be modified and used
in a variety of other forms of psychological treatment.

Psychoanalysis was probably the first systematically conceptualized theoretically based effort at providing psychotherapy to
psychologically ill patients. Other scientifically based forms of psychiatric treatment have evolved in a variety of directions, attempting to achieve a variety of different goals. The psychoanalytic
psychotherapies are those that have specifically and conceptually
evolved from modifications of psychoanalysis, and the application
of psychoanalytic and psychodynamic theory and process to a vari-

ety of therapeutic situations. As such, the therapies to be discussed in this chapter are considered psychoanalytic only if the therapist's conscious rationale and conceptual understanding and techniques explicitly evolved from those originally developed for psychoanalysis proper.

The various forms of psychoanalytic psychotherapy therefore represent examples of applied psychoanalysis. The general psychoanalytic theory of mental function and psychopathology, extensively described and documented in the chapters in Sections I and II of this textbook, forms the basis of understanding the patient and the patient's problems. However, the following elements of basic theoretical understanding are particularly emphasized in relationship to the psychotherapeutic situation (Frosch 1990; Gabbard 1994).

1. It is necessary to distinguish core from derivative psychic structure and compromise formations (Dewald 1978). The basic core of personality has evolved and developed in the first 5 or 6 years of life and is usually largely unconscious and inaccessible to the individual. This core is an active stimulus for subsequently developing states and behavior patterns known as *derivative structures and compromises.* Although mainly unconscious, the childhood wishes, thoughts, fantasies, memories, relationships, fears, and beginning defensive structures all remain dynamically active and, in that sense, have a continuing impact on motivation in subsequent development. However, the subsequent manifestations of these infantile and early childhood core phenomena are expressed through behavior patterns appropriate to the continued development of the individual. As such, these developing states and behavior patterns are known as derivative structures and compromises. These derivative levels of mental life and organization are increasingly influenced by and dependent upon the later developmental unfolding of genetically and biologically determined capacities, as well as experiential and environmental stimulation, models for identification, experiences, traumas, support systems, and family and sociocultural factors, all of which significantly affect the form that these various derivative structures and functions achieve. The effects, dynami-

cally and psychologically, are interpersonal as well as intrapsychic, and environmental feedback to the individual's responses further molds and influences behavior, particularly in terms of conscious and preconscious adaptation and understanding. It is at these levels of conceptual understanding that the psychoanalytic psychotherapies focus their primary attention.

2. The psychoanalytic psychotherapies emphasize particularly the importance of postoedipal personality development and conflict, along with typical adult developmental stages of function and interaction.

3. The psychotherapist focuses on the dynamic role and importance of the various environmental vicissitudes of opportunity, including social and cultural setting with family and community responsiveness, and also including the various traumatic vicissitudes of life that confront the individual as he or she matures.

4. In adapting the genetic point of view of the importance of earlier states of conflict or trauma in the understanding of current human behavior, the psychoanalytic psychotherapies particularly emphasize the typical events, conflicts, relationships, and traumata that occur in adolescence and latency. These forms of therapy generally leave the deep core unconscious processes of infancy and early childhood unexplored.

The following significant technical modifications in the theory and practice of psychoanalysis have been specifically adapted to the psychotherapy situation:

1. The structure of the therapeutic situation is a significant factor in the initiation and evolution of the treatment process. The traditional intensive two-person situation of classical psychoanalysis is modified in terms of the frequency and duration of sessions, the face-to-face setting, treatment in individual or group experience, contact with others in the patient's life (spouse, parent, work supervisor, teachers, friends), and so forth. The therapy may also take place on an outpatient or an inpatient basis, during a weekend marathon, with a time-limited or time-unlimited agreement, and so forth.

2. The role and management of transference and its various manifestations are also subject to a variety of adaptations depending on the psychotherapeutic goals and strategy.

3. The management of defense, resistance, and regression also is modified in accordance with the form and strategy of the particular psychotherapy chosen.

4. The mobilization or suppression of previously preconscious or unconscious conflict likewise is a function of the therapeutic strategy and the goals of the treatment process. In psychoanalysis proper the strategy is to mobilize as many and as deep level conflicts as is possible given the therapy situation and the nature of the patient's capacity to participate in it. In the psychoanalytic psychotherapies the process of mobilization or the suppression of conflict is a matter of choice by the therapist and is a selective decision.

5. The therapist's level of activity is often considerably greater and more varied than in psychoanalysis. Therapist activity may range from quiet listening and neutrality, to active interaction, direction, and advising, to, in an inpatient setting, full control of the patient's behavior and privileges. The therapist's decision about which level of activity is appropriate depends upon the particular therapeutic strategy and technique of psychotherapy being used.

6. The use of psychotropic medication as part of the therapeutic procedure is more frequent and appropriate in psychotherapy than in psychoanalysis (Ostow 1979).

7. The approach to the termination of treatment is more variable than in psychoanalysis, and the nature of the termination process is determined by the overall strategy of the treatment. Some forms of psychoanalytic psychotherapy involve a planned and definitive termination of the treatment and of the relationship to the therapist. Other forms of treatment occur on an intermittent basis, with the patient returning at times of symptom exacerbation for further focal therapeutic attention and work. In some forms of supportive treatment, patient and therapist meet regularly or irregularly but on a continuing basis.

Varieties of Psychoanalytic Psychotherapy

The different forms of psychoanalytic psychotherapy can be grouped along several different spectrums based on some of their essential qualities:

+ Psychoanalytic psychotherapy may involve *expressive* (also called insight-directed, definitive, conflict-resolving, conflict-activating, etc.) forms of treatment or *supportive* (also called suppressive, symptom-oriented, behavior-oriented, superficial, etc.). None of the psychoanalytic psychotherapies are purely expressive or supportive, but understanding the differences between these therapeutic approaches can permit a more clear conceptualization of the treatment process and more accurate prediction of response to various types of intervention (Dewald 1969; Karasu 1989; Meissner 1988; Rockland 1989; Werman 1984).

+ Psychoanalytic psychotherapy may be *time-unlimited, long-term, or time-indeterminate,* or be *time-limited, brief, or specifically focused on issues of separation, loss, and the time limits of therapy.*

+ Psychoanalytic psychotherapy may be *focal and directed toward particular symptoms, behavior patterns, or specifically determined forms of conflict,* or *more diffuse, unfocused, and aimed at characterological modification and change.*

+ Psychoanalytic psychotherapy may occur with *one patient at a time,* or with *more than one patient* at a time, such as in marital or family therapy and group therapy (Grotjahn 1977).

It is also possible to apply psychodynamic principles and concepts to the understanding of the therapeutic process that occurs in a variety of therapy situations labeled nonpsychoanalytic, and even to some situations that are specifically conceptualized by their participants as nonpsychotherapeutic (i.e., Alcoholics Anonymous, weight-loss groups, the doctor-patient relationship in medical practice, etc.).

Indications and Selection of Goals

The choice of which form of psychoanalytic psychotherapy to recommend is a function of what treatment goals have been selected by the therapist and established by the patient and the therapist together. A number of factors contribute to that selection process, including the following:

1. *The patient's conscious and (as far as it can be inferred) unconscious motivation for treatment and his or her personal goals.* Some patients are already aware of the internal nature of their difficulties and recognize a need to resolve their own inner conflicts; some other patients can relatively easily become aware of their own contribution to their difficulties; other patients may externalize their problems and blame family, friends, or reality situations for the symptoms they have; still other patients may be seeking only relief from symptoms and have no interest or curiosity about what causes the distress.

2. *The patient's ego capacities to participate in a therapeutic process.* These capacities include ability to form object relationships; capacity for basic trust; psychological awareness and introspection; reality testing; capacity for affective experience; willingness to work toward long-range goals; and tolerance of anxiety and/or depression.

3. *Reality factors.* These factors include the ability to schedule regular appointments; the ability to pay the fees involved; the nature of the patient's support system; the degree of stability in the patient's life situation; and reality stressors.

4. *Nature, severity, duration, and degree of disability associated with the patient's illness or characterological problems.*

5. *The patient's experience of and responsiveness to any previous therapeutic efforts.*

6. *The nature and intensity of the therapist's personal and emotional response to the patient and the illness.* The therapist may have a variety of conscious or unconscious countertransference responses to the patient, which may influence his or her recommendations for the treatment of choice.

There are no specific or single issues or factors that serve as absolute indications for or contraindications to any particular form of psychoanalytic psychotherapy. The setting of goals should be a mutual decision by patient and therapist after assessing and balancing positive strengths and indications versus negative weaknesses or limitations against the anticipated demands of the treatment process, and thus the likelihood that the selected goals will be met (Kernberg et al. 1989; Volkan 1987).

Studies of the predictability of therapeutic results in the psychoanalytic psychotherapies have shown outcome to be extremely unpredictable in any single case. Luborsky (1988), in an extensive study, demonstrated that the ability of the patient to form a therapeutic alliance is the most reliable predictor of treatment outcome. Treatment goals, once selected, must be open to revision as the therapeutic situation unfolds. The goals of an expressive psychotherapy may require revision toward more supportive and less ambitious achievements; or the patient originally deemed appropriate for supportive therapy may prove more apt to the therapeutic process, and a more ambitious expressive therapy may be undertaken. However, treatment works best if patient and therapist are seeking common goals within an appropriately chosen therapeutic method and plan.

Strategy of the Treatment Process

When the goal is to effect definitive change in an individual's personality or resolution of internal psychological conflicts, forms of psychoanalytic psychotherapy that require a mobilization and activation in the therapeutic situation of the issues and conflicts in question are indicated. In these psychotherapies the goal is to reduce the patient's resistances and defenses against awareness of inner conflicts and/or distressing thought content, as well as to make conscious the patient's methods of adaptation. The strategy is to bring these mental processes to the awareness and recognition of the patient. The rationale for this procedure is based on the fact that at the time of life when these various conflicts occurred, the person was less equipped to cope with or to find effective resolutions for them. The latency-age or young adolescent child who is still dependent upon the family caretakers has fewer options for independent choice and action to deal with and adapt to the variety of conflicts that confront him or her. The expectation is that with further maturation and the increased potential for conflict resolution or adaptation available to the adult, and with the aid of the therapeutic process, the person should be capable of more effective conflict resolution and compromise formations than he or she was able to develop while trying to settle the issues on his or her own.

When the goal is more narrowly focused—resolution of a specific psychological conflict, symptom, or inhibition—the same principle of activating that conflict in the person's awareness obtains, but the range of issues to be activated tends to be significantly narrower. The therapist (and the patient) pays selectively more attention to material targeted as related to the therapeutic strategy and goals decided upon with the patient and essentially avoids or ignores components of psychological function not specifically related to these goals.

When the goal of the treatment process is to reestablish a prior level of adjustment or adaptation, to prevent deeper distress or decompensation, or predominantly to provide symptom relief, behavioral change, or reduction of disability, more supportive forms of psychotherapy are indicated. In this context the basic strategy involves suppressing and reducing emerging conflict, actively assisting the patient in establishing more effective defensive operations, and strengthening the more useful adaptive and/or defensive functions that the patient already has been able to develop. In such situations the therapist allows the patient's transference responses to remain unconscious, but instead uses them (i.e., the patient's wish to please the therapist, the patient's dependency on the therapist, the patient's needs for praise and feedback, etc.) to manage the patient's symptoms and behavior in keeping with the chosen goals. In that way management of the transference (in contrast to working-through and resolution) is used to achieve symptomatic or behavioral goals; already conscious issues and feelings are discussed, but the nature of the patient's unconcious conflicts and his or her awareness of them are not actively explored. This is in contrast to expressive forms of therapy, in which the transference is consciously mobilized and then conflict used as a paradigm of the patient's problems occurring in the therapeutic relationship.

The following case example may help to clarify the differences in dynamic strategies between expressive and supportive therapy:

> A 38-year-old school teacher came to discuss a family situation in which his wife was spending more and more time with a male psychotherapist working out some of her major childhood conflicts and traumata. The patient was increasingly concerned that she was withdrawing from him and their two children, was inappropriately angry and abusive toward them, and was neglecting her family responsibilities. He feared she was having a sexual affair with the therapist.
>
> The patient was anxious, depressed, and preoccupied to the point that his work was being interfered with. He also had initiation insomnia. He was undecided as to how to confront and deal with the problems in his relationship with his wife.
>
> The history revealed that his mother had died of heart disease when he was 7, that his father had been chronically depressed and unavailable to him, and that the family had deteriorated socially and financially. The father remarried, but the patient and his sister did not get along with the stepmother. The patient suppressed his unhappiness, loneliness, and fears behind an externally successful record of school and athletic performance. He felt deep guilt and shame regarding adolescent and early adult sexual feeling and experience, and married because he felt obligated to his wife after having had sexual relations and fearing she was pregnant. The marriage was chronically unhappy and overtly stormy from the beginning. The wife complained that the patient was inadequate as a husband, a man, and a sexual partner. The patient felt constantly inferior and tried to submissively appease and placate her. He was warm and supportive of his children. He was limited in his friendships and outside activities, but occasionally he sought solace in brief, casual sexual encounters with other women.

If the treatment strategy was to provide supportive therapy, emphasis might be placed on the patient's immediate response to the wife's behavior as understandable; reduction of the acute anxiety, depression, and sleeplessness might be effected by medication; efforts to improve communication between the patient and his wife might be initiated; the patient's reaction formation defenses against dependency and need regarding the wife might be encouraged; his sense of himself as a competent person might be actively supported; and different ways of understanding and confronting the wife's relationship with her therapist might actively be suggested. Once the acute situation subsided, the therapist might suggest and/or conduct marital therapy.

If the treatment strategy was to provide focal therapy, emphasis might be placed on the threat of loss of the marriage, its connection to the loss of the patient's mother when he was a child, and his fears that confronting various situations might further alienate his wife. It might also include completion of the mourning process regarding the death of his mother.

If the treatment strategy was to achieve more definitive and characterological change, it might require helping the patient recognize and modify his needs to appease; his sexual guilt and inhibitions and the ways he had allowed his wife's contempt to undermine his own self-esteem; his fears of abandonment and loss that had led him to neurotically tolerate an unhappy and disruptive marriage; his pattern to deny his own needs and maintain the defensive facade of caring for others at his own expense; his unresolved attachment to his mother and his various defenses against full mourning; and his inhibition of his own aggressively competitive and angry feelings.

As described earlier, the therapeutic process ranges along a spectrum from a suppressive, symptom-oriented, behavior-directing focus on already conscious psychic contents to significant conflict-activating reduction of defenses and resistance, with emergence of a paradigm of psychological conflict in the therapeutic relationship. In this latter process, the transference issues activated and experienced in the therapeutic relationship parallel the patient's current extra-therapeutic situations and relationships and ultimately permit an understanding of how earlier levels of psychic organization, conflict, and conflict solution have been re-created or continued into the present.

Although rigidity of therapeutic technique is inappropriate and the pursuit of purity in the therapeutic process should not become an end in itself, nevertheless, a general consistency in the therapeutic approach can enhance the likelihood that the goals that had been set will be achieved. In expressive psychotherapies certain elements of the treatment process can be conceptualized as supportive, and in supportive forms of psychotherapy there may be explanations offered that provide new information to the patient and increase his or her awareness.

Unless the therapist understands which interventions or attitudes will foster activation of conflict and which will suppress the awareness of unconscious conflictual forces, he or she may inadvertently behave in ways contrary to fulfilling the overall goal. For example, if when the patient is functioning well in an expressive treatment, or when interventions tend to be conflict activating or transference abstinent the therapist becomes less active, the patient may experience this change as disappointing, distressing, or anxiety provoking. On the other hand, if when the same patient experiences distress, intensification of conflict, or behavioral disruption the therapist responds more actively, offering reassurance, advice, or other interventions to reduce the conflict, the patient will consciously or unconsciously experience the therapist as "more giving" during states of distress and regressive symptomatic experience than during times of progress and movement toward maturation. The therapist may thus inadvertently introduce an iatrogenic form of reward for regression and symptom upheaval, which can then interfere with the therapeutic strategy.

Another element of general strategy is that once the goals of treatment are being approached or have been achieved, it is time to consider the appropriateness of termination of treatment, even if the patient has other neurotic or characterological problems. Treatment should not be unduly prolonged unless, after specific evaluation, both therapist and patient agree to modify or extend the goals of treatment. Such an agreement should consider how effectively the patient has been able to use the therapeutic experience. If there is reason to believe that the patient can achieve further effective levels of benefit from therapy, the new goals and their implications should be explicitly understood and renegotiated between the two participants. However, if the therapist wants to prolong treatment but the patient no longer wants to (or vice versa), the two participants will be working at cross purposes. It is also not unusual for therapists to impose their own therapeutic zeal and ambition onto the patient, who may be willing to participate for unconscious transference reasons.

Techniques and Tactics

The specific individual techniques and tactics of psychotherapy are a function of the goal(s) of therapy and of the strategy chosen to fulfill this goal. The strategy is carried out through a variety of specific elements and components of the treatment process (Dewald 1972).

The Therapeutic Situation

The structure of the therapeutic situation in regard to frequency of appointments, duration of sessions, setting in which the participants meet, and arrangements regarding payment, missed sessions, vacations, and so forth, should be consistent with the therapeutic strategy. If the strategy involves mobilization of conflict and experience and expression of the conflict as a manifestation of transference in the therapeutic situation, the sessions must be sufficiently frequent and of long enough duration to permit the patient to establish and develop significant emotional reactions to the therapist. Other things being equal, the more frequently and regularly the patient and therapist meet, the more likely is it that the patient's transference experiences will be intensified and ultimately become consciously manifest. In the expressive psychoanalytic psychotherapies, multiple sessions per week (two or three) often are required, with each session lasting 45 or 50 minutes. This structure offers enough time and contact for the patient to move from conscious reporting of events and relationships to more intrapsychic elaboration of subjective psychological processes. However, the needs of the patient and the clinical judgment of the therapist may make it necessary for the patient and therapist to meet more frequently. At other times the limitations imposed by the patient's life circumstances may make it necessary to schedule fewer or less regular sessions. In the case of "marathon" therapy, arrangements include prolonging the duration of sessions. The therapist must be aware that how the therapeutic situation is structured will have a significant effect on the type of therapeutic process that unfolds.

If the strategy is more supportive and is to maintain a focus on already conscious behavior and thought processes, the sessions may be briefer (15 to 30 minutes) and at less frequent or regular intervals. When the patient is experiencing intense disruption or regression, more frequent sessions may be necessary to modify the patient's distress; as the patient improves, however, the frequency is usually reduced again.

When the patient is experiencing severe and persistent regression or disorganization of behavior, it may be necessary to hospitalize the patient for a brief, or at times extended, period. This may require reassessment of the treatment goals, but in general the therapeutic tactics in the hospital should remain consistent with the treatment strategy (Fromm-Reichmann 1950).

The Therapeutic Relationship and Transference

In the expressive range of psychotherapy, the strategy is to activate an appropriate level of conscious awareness of direct transference experience toward the therapist as part of the treatment relationship. At times, multiple transferences may be activated, simultaneously or sequentially. Therapist's techniques that intensify the patient's experience and recognition of transferences (and thus increase his or her awareness of how earlier conflicts and behaviors are being reenacted in the present) include, but are not limited to, the following:

1. Maintaining consistent neutrality
2. Maintaining personal ambiguity and anonymity
3. Encouraging the elaboration of transference responses

4. Interpreting resistances and defenses against experience and/or expression of transferences
5. Not correcting the patient's transference reactions by reality explanations until the patient has had an opportunity to explore and elaborate on them
6. Comfortably accepting transference distortions and affective responses without personal need to interrupt them
7. Demonstrating to the patient the therapeutic usefulness of working out transference responses

In supportive therapeutic situations, in which the strategy is to use, but not consciously activate and analyze, transference responses, the therapist's techniques include the following:

1. Providing symbolic gratification of appropriate transference wishes
2. Presenting active positive or negative responses to the patient's material or behavior, including thoughts, feelings, and verbal interactions
3. Prompting reality feedback and correcting potentially disruptive transference reactions
4. Maintaining support for defenses against conscious awareness of transferences
5. Providing the patient an active model for identification regarding ego and superego functions
6. Seeking to maintain positive transference responses while avoiding or actively dispelling negative transferences
7. Revealing appropriate personal information

If in spite of the supportive therapeutic strategy the patient becomes consciously aware of and troubled by transference feelings and fantasies, the therapist must offer active explanations and reassurance of their transient nature. The therapist must try to prevent and protect the patient from self-damaging acting out of transference reactions.

Management of Regression

Expressive forms of psychotherapy and the emergence of transference experience involve a form of partial reversal of development, and the expression of earlier (as far back as adolescence and latency) levels of psychological organization, conflict, and emotional function in a person of the patient's current status. To that end, regression in the service of the ego and of the therapeutic task is encouraged and supported by the therapist. The therapist assists the patient's capacity to permit this kind of "as if" regressive experience during the treatment sessions and encourages reversal of and the patient's recovery from the regression after the patient has left the session. For example, with the patient whose case was reported near the beginning of this chapter, the therapist might encourage the patient to feel again the sadness of his mother's death, the anger and disappointment at his father's behavior, his inability at that time to express his feelings, and his loneliness and need to deny his emotions through outwardly successful performance. The patient could then be able to recognize how he repeated those feelings and conflicts in his marriage.

In symptom-oriented and supportive forms of psychotherapy, regression is actively discouraged, and elements of reality testing and progressive problem solving are emphasized instead. With the patient whose case was just alluded to, the emphasis might be on his need to confront the wife's behavior directly, to accept the responsibility of being a husband and father, and to explore new ways of making his marriage more fulfilling for his wife and for himself.

Management of Resistance

In expressive forms of psychotherapy, the tactics are for the therapist systematically to point out various defenses and resistances used by the patient. The aim is to encourage in the patient reduction in the use or intensity of these psychic operations so that those conflicts protected by these functions can become more consciously available for scrutiny. Interpretations of resistances are also directed to the patient's experiences in the transference, as well as other forms of psychological defensiveness. In these interventions the therapist's tact, timing, and intensity are particularly important so that the patient not feel "nagged" or "blamed."

When the situation is supportive and the strategy is to suppress or more effectively control conflict, the therapist helps the patient maintain those resistances that are most useful or effective. The therapist may actively encourage the strengthening of such functions or the substitution of new and more effective defenses and resistances, both in the therapy situation and in everyday life. If a particular defense proves to be significantly disruptive or self-defeating, or if it jeopardizes the continuation of treatment, the therapist should actively intervene to discourage its use and suggest a more effective alternative.

Management of Conflict

In expressive forms of psychotherapy, conflict is deliberately activated, with the anticipation that the patient, in the experimental and controlled setting of the therapeutic situation and relationship, will have an opportunity to develop and practice new modes of conflict containment or resolution. The therapist does not artificially manipulate the situation, but by calling attention to manifestations of conflict and by interpreting defenses against awareness of it, as well as by interpreting and pointing out various transference manifestations, the therapist actively seeks to undermine the patient's characteristic modes of avoiding conflict and bring such feelings and difficulties into conscious awareness. Frequently such awareness occurs first in the treatment setting and in the phenomenology of the transference relationship. It may then be generalized to other settings or situations outside of the treatment relationship as the patient gains confidence and success in new modes of adaptation. To the extent that such new forms of behavior provide mastery, pleasure, or more effective interaction with others, a further consolidation of the new patterns can occur.

In more supportive forms of psychotherapy, the therapist seeks to suppress and/or minimize the conflicts experienced by the patient. At times the therapist functions as an alter-ego in the approach to problem solving, actively modeling and making recommendations for more effective conflict containment or adjustment, or, in some cases, even intervening for the patient in situations of distress or conflict with other people.

The Role of Identification

In the expressive forms of psychotherapy, the patient comes to identify with the therapist's exploratory attitude and curiosity and his or her tolerance for awareness of previously unconscious psychic events and behavior. This form of identification strengthens the therapeutic alliance. However, other forms of identification with the therapist's behavior, values, interests, or activities are seen as resistances to individual and personal development. Sooner or later, these forms of identification are dealt with as defenses by the patient against independence and emancipation.

In supportive forms of psychotherapy, the presumption is that the therapist will be a more effective model for overall psychic function, value systems, and behavior patterns than those with whom the patient had previously identified. The therapist therefore uses himself or herself actively as a model for both ego and superego functions. The rationale for this approach is based on the important role of parental models and value systems in every individual's basic personality development. Internalization of the therapist's balanced superego model can be significant in reducing various forms of neurotic guilt and shame, and identifications in the realm of ego functions can be helpful in the patient's developing more effective forms of adaptive behavior.

The Role of Reinforcement

Direct suggestion and reward for appropriate behavior tend to be minimized in the expressive forms of psychotherapy (although a component of reinforcement through verbal and/or nonverbal responsiveness is unavoidable). The tactical aim is to encourage the patient's self-determination and enhance the patient's emotional independence from external authoritarian rewards or punishments. Therefore, the therapist remains relatively neutral and constant in reaction to the patient's progress or successes.

However, in the supportive forms of psychotherapy, the therapist uses the existing unconscious transferences and the patient's desires for a complementary response from the authoritarian parental figure to mold behavior in keeping with learning theory methods. The therapist responds actively in transference-gratifying ways to those patient behaviors deemed appropriate, thus enhancing the likelihood of those behaviors becoming more solidly established in the patient. This approach is taken even at the cost, for the patient, of continuing his or her dependence on and need for external authoritarian judgment and decision making.

Levels of Therapist Feedback and Activity

In all forms of psychoanalytic psychotherapy, the extent to which the therapist provides feedback to the patient is significantly greater than in psychoanalysis, if only by virtue of the fact that the patient has the opportunity for continuous monitoring of the therapist's appearance, facial expressions, and other nonverbal behaviors. This monitoring frequently provides the patient with correction of transference fantasies or distortions and thus tends to limit the depth and intensity of the transference reactions that occur.

In expressive forms of psychotherapy, the therapist's level of activity tends to be relatively constant within reasonably defined limits. The therapist avoids, when possible, actively intervening in the events or relationships in the patient's life so as to enhance the individual's independence and capacity for self-determination. Because there is a generalized relative paucity of feedback from the therapist, those cues and clues that are available to the patient take on added significance and suggestive power. In this way the things a therapist responds to with interest, the things he or she does not react to, the tone of voice or words chosen, or any of the other observable behaviors he or she manifests—all are scanned by the patient and come to exert significant suggestive influence (even if unintended by the therapist).

In supportive forms of psychotherapy, the therapist offers significantly more direct verbal as well as nonverbal feedback as part of therapeutic strategy and tactics to mold and influence the patient's overt behavior through active intervention. By correcting an anxiety-provoking transference experience, by actively encouraging reality testing, or by providing a model for more effective adaptation through the feedback being offered, the therapist seeks to maintain the patient's defenses against regression and more primitive levels of organization, as well as to maintain a primarily positive and nonconflicted transference relationship and experience with the patient. The therapist may provide many different levels of activity and intervention, even to the extent of hospitalizing the patient, contacting others in the patient's personal or occupational environment, prescribing (or referring the patient to someone who will prescribe) medication, and recommending other adjuncts to promote more adaptive behavior and/or to reduce stress. The continuing and overtly active feedback results in the patient's experiencing less unconscious transference stimulation based on subtle and uncorrected cues gleaned by scanning the therapist.

The Importance of Therapeutic Consistency

Throughout this section I have been deliberately using the pedagogic device of viewing the ends of a spectrum of psychotherapies in order to develop conceptualizations of the nature and effects of the therapist's activity and interventions. The more these strategies and tactics can be maintained at reasonably consistent levels (independent of the specific individual interventions that the therapist may be called upon to make), the more effectively can therapist and patient continue to work toward the therapeutic goals that have been set. The framework described here allows the therapist to make rough predictions of the probable effects of an intervention or, subsequently, to understand why the interventions that were made produced the effects they did.

If major shifts from one perspective to the other or significant inconsistencies in the therapist's behavior, attitude, or interventions occur, the treatment may become confusing or actually disruptive for the patient, as well as discouraging and unfulfilling for the therapist.

Countertransference Issues

For the most part, in the psychoanalytic psychotherapies the patient's transference experience does not reach the intensity of a transference neurosis that occurs in psychoanalysis (see Chapter 13). However, the pressures experienced by the patient toward reenactment in the therapeutic situation of earlier forms or manifestations of psychic conflict and developmental processes remain high, and the patient unconsciously attempts to elicit from the therapist a countertransference response that is complementary to the patient's transferences. In some respects the possibilities for acting out of transference-countertransference issues are more intense in the psychoanalytic psychotherapies than in the more contained, controlled, and relatively interactionally limited setting of psychoanalysis.

In addition to the usual stimuli for countertransference experience that would occur in psychoanalysis, there are specific issues related to the psychotherapeutic situation to which the therapist must be alert.

In the face-to-face arrangement of most psychotherapy situations, the patient can constantly assess the therapist's nonverbal responses. This situation may create a problem in terms of, on the one hand, disclosure of personal reactions or, on the other hand, an artificial stiffness and attempt at maintaining "a poker face." Because the patient and therapist meet less frequently than in psychoanalysis, the therapist will have less detailed access and understanding of the patient's internal and intrapsychic life and experience. At the same time, the needs and pressures for active response and/or intervention by the therapist tend to be greater in the psychotherapies, and the possibility of the patient's acting out in relationships outside of the therapeutic setting is enhanced by the relative infrequency of the therapeutic sessions.

It is far more difficult for the therapist to maintain comfortable silence in a face-to-face situation than when he or she can "hide" behind the couch, and some therapists may experience discomfort in being intently scrutinized.

If the psychoanalytic psychotherapy is being undertaken with a patient with more intense and severe psychopathology for whom full psychoanalysis is considered unsuitable, it may at times be more difficult to engage the patient in a stable and sustained therapeutic relationship, and the already existing level of regression resulting from the illness may enhance tendencies toward reenactment. Depending upon the nature of such reenactments, the therapist may then be tempted to intervene in ways that become too actively directing or controlling, or the therapist may be provoked into various affectively charged responses to the patient.

Psychotherapy demands a greater degree of flexibility, responsiveness, interaction, and activity on the part of the therapist than does the usual psychoanalysis. In psychoanalysis a temptation to modify the usual psychoanalytic situation or technique may be used by the therapist as an alerting signal to question whether disruptive countertransference elements are intruding into the therapeutic setting. This alerting signal is not as available in the psychoanalytic psychotherapies because there are greater reasons for modifying therapeutic technique, and such responses (behavioral as well as verbal) may be more readily rationalized and escape self-analytic scrutiny by the therapist. Optimally, however, the therapist will be comfortable in the psychotherapeutic situation and will continue to monitor the transference-countertransference interactional processes as they occur.

The methods of the psychoanalytic psychotherapies usually involve certain built-in limitations in regard to the intensity of the treatment process and the amount of change and modification in the patient's basic personality that can occur. For the therapist who finds it difficult to accept more limited goals in the treatment of his or her patients, these limitations can lead to the therapist's experiencing a significant sense of disappointment in the method, or may stimulate an attempt by the therapist to push the results of the method beyond reasonably appropriate goals. A not infrequent countertransference-inspired temptation is to go deeper and more extensively into genetic material than the method will reasonably allow for a meaningful change to occur, or to try to achieve the goals of an analysis in the setting of psychotherapy.

Conversely, an attitude of disappointment in the methods may foster feelings of contempt or dissatisfaction at "merely" doing psychotherapy, or a sense that supportive psychotherapy is "too superficial to be meaningful." Such reactions would represent a disruptive form of countertransference that would probably impair therapeutic effectiveness.

Special Issues of Brief Psychotherapy

In the last 30 years extensive attempts have been made to modify the therapeutic situation by applying psychoanalytic understanding and techniques to forms of brief psychotherapy. In this country these efforts were initially stimulated by some of the dramatic successes of psychoanalytically informed psychotherapy during World War II. The work of Alexander and French (1946) involved applying concepts derived from psychoanalysis to focal psychotherapy and activation of "the corrective emotional experience." Other workers have expanded upon those early experiences, and there now exist a number of different forms of brief psychoanalytic or dynamic psychotherapy (Balint et al. 1972; Davenloo 1980; Luborsky 1984; Malan 1976; Mann 1973; Sifneos 1979; Small 1971; Strupp and Binder 1984). Each of these models has specific characteristics relating to the techniques being recommended and to such issues as the frequency of sessions, the total number of sessions, indications for treatment, appropriate goals, and so forth.

However, some general principles seem common to most of these forms of brief psychodynamic psychotherapy. The patients selected should have the capacity to promptly establish a reasonably trusting relationship and to be able to sustain adaptive behavior and performance in the face of modest levels of anxiety or depression. They should be capable of relating to the therapist in a way that allows the outlining of a specific focal conflict or problem that then becomes the major focus of therapeutic interest and attention. These patients should also have the capacity for psychological mindedness and introspection as well as for affective responsiveness.

Patients with chronic, rigid characterological disturbances, or those with basic mistrust of and remoteness from interpersonal interaction, and those with difficulty in reality testing or with major forms of acting out are considered poor candidates for brief therapy. Brief therapy is considered inappropriate for most patients with major suicidal preoccupation or potential and for patients for whom object losses have precipitated major and severe decompensation.

Most of the brief psychodynamic therapeutic methods recommend continuous active focus on and interpretation of the transference and repeated linking of it to the patient's other current interpersonal relationships and to earlier parental interactions. The therapist actively interprets to the patient how these three areas of experience are linked together within the particular dynamic conflict previously identified as the chief concern. There is a conscious and deliberate avoidance of the emergence of unrelated areas of disturbance or conflict. The therapist exerts a highly selective influence by directing his or her attention toward or away from material that the patient uncovers in association with the focal conflict.

In these brief forms of therapy the therapist uses active confrontational and interpretative techniques and keeps the originally determined goals of treatment actively in mind. The therapist introduces the anticipation of termination promptly when the original goals are near being reached. When the number of therapeutic sessions is fixed from the beginning (i.e., Mann 1973), issues of termination are actively focused on from the outset and the needs to achieve mastery and to consider separation and loss as a continuing theme throughout life are emphasized. The loss of the therapeutic relationship is used as a paradigmatic version of separation and loss in the patient's life.

Group Processes

Another variation of psychodynamic psychotherapy is its application to therapeutic groups and the process of group psychotherapy.

The group setting involves significant variations from the individual two-person field of therapy.

First, multiple transferences—not only to the therapist(s) serving as group leader but also to individual members of the group—are activated in the group experience. In addition, the group serves as a symbolic representation of a family, and transferences are also activated in individual members toward the group as a whole. In expressive group therapies, there is a focus on these multiple transference interactions, either by the group as a whole or by the individual group members experiencing them. This focus can provide an emotionally immediate and intense situation of conflict activation or of adaptation and control. Other group members who are not immediately involved in the particular interaction have an opportunity to observe varieties of conflict activation and resolution and to participate vicariously.

Simultaneously, the group provides a "real life experience" inasmuch as the usual "tilt" in the two-person psychotherapy field is not present and the group members are not trained therapists whose role is to manifest empathy and understanding of the individual pathology of the other participants. As a result, positive or negative reactions to individual members reflect a sense of real-life authenticity.

The group also provides a model for ego as well as superego functions: the group can foster the development of certain problem-solving techniques, adaptations to conflicts, new modes of integration and defense, new values, and new models for identification in the ways of problem solving and living. Additionally, the group develops its own value system to which the individual members are expected to subscribe. Acceptance by the group frequently requires that the individual accept new values and attitudes considered appropriate by the group members. The group may at times actively interpret or confront individual members in regard to resistances, and acceptance by the group may involve the member's willingness to attempt the challenge of reducing his or her defensiveness.

These issues become particularly important in the treatment of delinquent adolescents, as well as in the treatment of specific patient populations such as drug- and alcohol-abusing patients, patients who are survivors of incest or other childhood abuse, or patients who are too inhibited to interact alone with a therapist. Part of the process is also the group's directly manifest and expressed pleasures or praise when the individual group member responds in a way considered appropriate by the group. This support provides direct group transference reinforcement and reward for modifications of behavior and can enhance the self-esteem of the individual. The sharing with members of the group of certain specific painful experiences, and acceptance by the group in spite of previous transference expectations of rejection or guilt, can permit the group member to feel a sense of relief from the isolation that had previously been part of his or her defensive armor. In this way individuals can expose deeper levels of feelings and thought processes that he or she had previously considered unacceptable. Such disclosure may facilitate the gradual shift toward a more true sense of self and authenticity.

Termination of Therapy

The management of the termination of psychoanalytic psychotherapy should be in keeping with the overall strategy and tactics used to guide the treatment from the beginning.

The termination phase, the importance of which in psychoanalysis is discussed by Phyllis Tyson in Chapter 16, is also significant in the various forms of psychoanalytic psychotherapy, and if it is not effectively carried through, some of the earlier treatment success may be jeopardized (Dewald 1982; Hollender and Ford 1990; Kernberg et al. 1989; Luborsky 1984; Rockland 1989; Strupp and Binder 1984; Werman 1984).

The more intensely the transference has been the conscious vehicle for therapeutic change in the expressive form, the more affectively meaningful will be the process by which patient and therapist bid each other goodbye. The anticipation of loss of the relationship may reactivate feelings related to other, earlier losses in the patient's life, as well as a sense of anxiety about whether the patient is ready to "go out on his or her own." There may be disappointment about less-than-optimal therapeutic results, as well as the symbolic meaning of letting go of past hopes and wishes embodied in the relationship to the therapist. The patient or the therapist, or both, may experience such feelings. The patient may experience sadness at the loss of the therapist as an empathic and helpful new person in the patient's life, as well as anticipate missing the opportunity to feel and speak openly about the private responses and thoughts characteristic of the therapy situation. The patient may also experience positively the anticipation of being out of therapy while at the same time feel a sense of guilt for seeming disloyal to the therapist.

To activate and partially work through some of these responses, the therapist and patient preparing for termination must allow enough time for the process to occur. The therapist should focus on, among other issues, awareness of the patient's multiple possible resistances to experience of the conflicts and affects that are evoked by the anticipation of termination. To this end, the structure of the therapeutic situation is maintained until termination is complete, and "weaning" or quick forms of termination are understood to be resistances. The therapist must also be aware of possible countertransference reactions to the termination.

In supportive therapies the same techniques used throughout to manage the unconscious transferences for conflict-reducing or behavior-influencing tactics may be applied to the termination process. The effort is directed at minimizing the stress of the ending of treatment and at maintaining for the patient a continuing positive and supportive relationship to the therapist. To this end techniques are used to "wean" the patient by gradually reducing the frequency of therapeutic sessions while actively supporting and reinforcing the patient's independence and actively indicating the therapist's continuing interest and availability. For some patients the emphasis may be on interruption of regular or continuous therapeutic contacts in favor of intermittent return for brief periods as the need arises.

Expressive psychotherapy seeks to activate unpleasurable feelings, memories, or associations related to the stress of termination of the treatment process and to the loss of the relationship to the therapist. In supportive psychotherapy, the very techniques that are seen as resistance in the previous model are used to minimize the stress in the supportive treatment end of the spectrum. This is done in keeping with the basic strategy of seeking to reduce the intensity of conflict, seeking to gratify the patient's acceptable transference wishes, and seeking to minimize stress so that symptomatic exacerbations do not occur. As an illustration, the process of "weaning" would be seen as a form of resistance against grief and mourning in expressive therapy, whereas it is seen as a justifiable reduction of stress and attempt to minimize painful affect in supportive therapeutic techniques.

Conclusions

In this brief overview I have attempted to describe the considerable range of variability in the applications of psychoanalytic theoretical understanding and clinical technique in the field of psychotherapy. For a variety of reasons, the number of patients for whom full or classical psychoanalysis is the treatment of choice is distinctly limited. The applications of psychoanalytic theory and elements of technique allow the powerful influence that psychoanalysis can provide to be applicable, at least in partial form, to the broader and larger number of patients for whom various forms of psychoanalytic psychotherapy are indicated. These benefits of applied psychoanalysis thus become available to patients for whom such a treatment setting would be more appropriate to their own individual needs.

References

Alexander F, French T: Psychoanalytic Therapy: Principles and Applications. New York, Ronald Press, 1946

Balint M, Ornstein PH, Balint E: Focal Psychotherapy. Philadelphia, PA, JB Lippincott, 1972

Davenloo H (ed): Short-Term Dynamic Psychotherapy. New York, Jason Aronson, 1980

Dewald PA: Psychotherapy: Dynamic Approach. Oxford, UK, Blackwell Scientific, 1969

Dewald PA: Toward a general concept of the therapeutic process. International Journal of Psychoanalytic Psychotherapy 5:283–299, 1972

Dewald PA: The process of change in psychoanalytic psychotherapy. Arch Gen Psychiatry 35:535–542, 1978

Dewald PA: The clinical importance of the termination phase. Psychoanalytic Inquiry 2:441–461, 1982

Fromm-Reichmann F: Principles of Intensive Psychotherapy. Chicago, IL, University of Chicago Press, 1950

Frosch J: Psychodynamic Psychiatry: Theory and Practice. Madison, CT, International Universities Press, 1990

Gabbard GO: Psychodynamic Psychiatry in Clinical Practice: The DSM-IV Edition. Washington, DC, American Psychiatric Press, 1994

Grotjahn M. The Art and Technique of Analytic Group Therapy. New York, Jason Aronson, 1977

Hollender MH, Ford CV: Dynamic Psychotherapy: An Introductory Approach. Washington, DC, American Psychiatric Press, 1990

Karasu TB: Psychoanalysis and psychoanalytic psychotherapy, in Comprehensive Textbook of Psychiatry/V, 5th Edition, Vol 2. Edited by Kaplan HI, Sadock BJ. Baltimore, MD, Williams & Wilkins, 1989, pp 1442–1461

Kernberg OF, Selzer MA, Koenigsberg HW, et al: Psychodynamic Psychotherapy of Borderline Patients. New York, Basic Books, 1989

Luborsky L: Principles of Psychoanalytic Psychotherapy: A Manual for Supportive Expressive Treatment. New York, Basic Books, 1984

Luborsky L: Who Will Benefit From Psychotherapy? New York, Basic Books, 1988

Malan DH: The Frontier of Brief Psychotherapy. New York, Plenum, 1976

Mann J: Time-Limited Psychotherapy. Cambridge, MA, Harvard University Press, 1973

Meissner WW: The psychotherapies: individual, family, and group, in The New Harvard Guide to Psychiatry. Edited by Nicholi AM. Cambridge, MA, Belknap Press/Harvard University Press, 1988, pp 449–480

Ostow M: The Psychodynamic Approach to Drug Therapy. New York, Psychoanalytic Research and Development Fund, 1979

Rockland LH: Supportive Therapy: A Psychodynamic Approach. New York, Basic Books, 1989

Sifneos PE: Short-Term Dynamic Psychotherapy. New York, Plenum, 1979

Small L: The Briefer Psychotherapies. New York, Brunner/Mazel, 1971

Strupp HH, Binder J: Psychotherapy in a New Key: Time-Limited Dynamic Psychotherapy. New York, Basic Books, 1984

Volkan VD: Six Steps in the Treatment of Borderline Personality Organization. Northvale, NJ, Jason Aronson, 1987

Werman DS: The Practice of Supportive Psychodynamic Approach to Psychotherapy. New York, Brunner/Mazel, 1984

15

Combining Treatment Modalities

John M. Oldham, M.D.

The "broadening scope of psychoanalysis" is a phrase that refers to, among other things, the application of psychoanalysis to a widening array of patients. In addition, greater attention is being given to combinations of psychoanalysis and other types of treatment, such as pharmacotherapy, couples therapy, family therapy, and group therapy. Recent interest in combined treatment emerges from clinical experience (e.g., work with borderline patients) and from research findings in general psychiatry (e.g., the National Institute of Mental Health [NIMH]–sponsored Treatment of Depression Collaborative Research Program [Elkin et al. 1989]). Published reports of psychoanalysis used concurrently with other interventions, however, remain scarce, although the concept is by no means a new one. As early as the 1940s, advocates recommended combined psychoanalysis and marital therapy, and in the 1960s, shortly after great strides were made in psychopharmacology, the use of medication as an adjunct to facilitate the therapeutic effect of psychoanalysis in certain cases was proposed.

Until recently, however, the subject has remained underemphasized, exemplified by the paucity of attention to these clinical practices in the standard psychoanalytic journals. As outcome and pro-cess research increases in psychoanalysis, and as outdated carica-tures of the psychoanalyst (e.g., as a totally opaque "mirror") recede, this reluctance of many psychoanalytic clinicians to write about these variations of treatment may abate.

Psychoanalysis and Pharmacotherapy

In 1962, Ostow, in his book entitled *Drugs in Psychoanalysis and Psychotherapy*, advocated the use of medication in selected cases for patients in psychoanalysis, and he has continued to stress the im-portance of this option (Ostow 1983). His position in his early writ-ings on the subject was that psychoanalysis is the primary, potentially "curative" ingredient of the treatment, but that its effi-cacy can be enhanced in some cases by the adjunctive use of medi-cation. Ostow's steady insistence on the usefulness of this approach has been an important influence, although some have argued that it reflects a bias that underestimates the biological component of many illnesses treated by psychoanalysts today. These critics would contend that Ostow views psychoanalysis as the only curative inter-vention, inappropriately relegating psychopharmacology to a merely palliative role (Brockman 1990; Roose 1990).

In 1983, Lipton reported a letter he had received in 1971 from Anna Freud indicating her views on the subject, which were similar to those of Ostow. Freud wrote, "As far as I am concerned I have had great help from medical colleagues used to the administering of the modern drugs, with three patients in severe states of depression. In all of these cases the therapeutic use of drugs did not in any way interfere with the progress of the analysis, quite on the contrary it helped the analysis to maintain itself during phases when otherwise the patient might have had to be hospitalised" (Lipton 1983, p. 1583). Other than this brief communication, and Ostow's 1983 paper, there have been only spo-radic reports in the literature on this subject.

Cooper, in 1985, presented a persuasive case for an affirmative answer to his question "Will neurobiology influence psychoanaly-sis?" He noted that most analytic treatment carries with it a strong implication that it is a major analytic task of the patient to accept responsibility for his actions. In the psychoanalytic view, this responsibility is nearly total. . . . However, it now seems likely that there are patients with depressive, anxious, and dysphoric states for whom the usual psychodynamic view of responsibility seems inappropriate and who should not be held accountable for their difficulty in accepting separation from dependency objects, or at least they should not be held fully accountable. (Cooper 1985, p. 1399)

He went on to argue that for some chronically depressed or anxious patients, antidepressant medication produces greatly beneficial mood stabilization, tending to normalize the way they see the world. Cooper added, "It may be that we have been coconspirators with these patients in their need to construct a rational-seeming world in which they hold themselves unconsciously responsible for events" (p. 1399).

This type of process is illustrated in a case, which I reported on, of a patient who had been in treatment for over a decade (Oldham 1989). Although not psychoanalysis, the initial approach was a psychoanalytic one, and choice of this approach was based on a conviction that this borderline patient's anxieties, moods, and chaotic interpersonal relationships were products of intrapsychic conflict that could be resolved by analytically oriented treatment. Only much later in the treatment did it become clear that the patient had a "hysteroid dysphoric" (Liebowitz and Klein 1979) type of mood disorder and needed medication. The addition of antidepressant medication greatly stabilized the patient's mood and brought with it enormous relief for the patient, who had become convinced that her inability to respond sufficiently to therapy represented her own failure and weakness of character. The psychodynamic formulations worked on over many years were not invalidated by the recognition of a "biological" mood disorder, but a more appropriate treatment approach was subsequently devised.

In 1986, Normand and Bluestone reviewed the use of pharmacotherapy in psychoanalysis, raising important ethical concerns such as the right of a patient to swifter relief of certain symptoms than might be produced by psychoanalysis alone (e.g., depression or anxiety that might be relieved by medication). The authors pointed out, as well, that the use of medication may make the benefits of analysis available to some patients, such as borderline patients, who otherwise might not be treatable analytically. The authors presented as an illustration a case of a patient in analysis for severe character pathology whose analysis was facilitated by periodic limited courses of antianxiety medication.

Other case reports have appeared that support the efficacy of medication, when indicated, in the course of psychoanalysis. Cooper (1985) reported a patient in analysis whose treatment, Cooper believed, benefited from the addition of imipramine; he described another patient, whom he saw in consultation, who had developed bipolar disorder in the course of analysis. Though the patient's analyst would not consider medication, the patient arranged on his own to obtain lithium, which greatly helped him and enhanced his motivation for further analytic work. Wylie and Wylie (1987) reported a case of "modified analysis," that is, modified by the addition of phenelzine after 18 months of analysis alone. In the authors' opinion, the medication ameliorated the patient's anxiety in a way that made acknowledgment of and attention to the transference possible and enhanced the continued analytic work, with a positive outcome being attained. A somewhat different case was described by Glen (1988), of a patient in analysis who needed prescriptions for withdrawal from dependency on antianxiety drugs. The analyst, with admitted trepidation, provided the prescriptions to help the patient complete the withdrawal. A successful outcome for the drug dependence problem was attained, and the analysis continued to completion with a highly therapeutic outcome.

Kris (1989) contended that "a variety of combinations of drugs with psychoanalytic psychotherapy are standard treatments at present. . . . From the view point of psychoanalytic therapy, where medication makes it possible for the patient to participate in the free association process, the combination is useful and sometimes essential" (p. 12). Viederman (1989) reviewed the subject of psychoanalysis and the use of psychoactive drugs, emphasizing the importance of appreciating the special meaning that combined approaches impose on the psychoanalytic situation. In his opinion, "one of the tasks in analytic work is to titrate the degree of anxiety or depression in order to permit the examination of intrapsychic conflict. Severe symptomatic impairment that limits the possibility of efficient work is an indication for the use of antidepressants" (p. 85). He went on to add, however, that "there is no simple answer concerning whether the analyst should administer and regulate these drugs or a consultant should do so" (p. 85), a problem also discussed by Normand and Bluestone (1986), Roose (1990), and others.

Not only must the analyst be comfortable with his or her level of knowledge and expertise to prescribe medications himself or herself, but he or she must have an understanding of the often-times quite complex way such a development can affect the roles of and interaction between analyst and patient. Roose (1990), in describing the intensive activity called for on the part of the analyst for effective medication monitoring, concluded that "in order to be an effective pharmacologist, the analyst would necessarily have to abandon repeatedly technical neutrality and disrupt the analytic process" (p. 6). However, it is not clear that by actively inquiring about side effects, dosage regulation, and so forth, the analyst would necessarily deviate from technical neutrality. Certainly, Kernberg (1975) has argued that neutrality is not measured by the degree of verbal activity on the analyst's part. Also, the concept of neutrality does not imply that the analyst lacks an overall attitude of therapeutic concern that may lead him or her to actively question the patient about numerous other aspects of the patient's life besides the patient's response to medication. Silber (1989), for example, described a case in which panic attacks occurred during sessions, requiring the analyst to actively "define verbally and clarify" the patient's affect state and its links to the transference and the past. This sporadic high degree of verbal activity on the part of the analyst was seen as entirely appropriate and within the bounds of "a classically conducted analysis." In this case, the patient periodically abandoned the use of the couch when experiencing panic attacks, representing another variable that need not necessarily detract from the analyst's continued neutrality.

There is a common tendency to equate neutrality with being "nondirective" and to assume that psychoanalysis is nondirective.

There is a difference, however, between behaving appropriately as an expert professional and being "directive" in a judgmental or non-neutral way. The psychoanalyst is always directive in some ways (e.g., by recommending the "fundamental rule" of free association, the importance of dreams, the use of the couch, etc.). These directives are "prescriptions" based on education and experience, just as prescribing of medications is based on expert knowledge and clincial experience, and in both cases the patient's feelings about these recommendations can be explored. Even if, however, one views this type of activity as potentially within the bounds of technical neutrality, in all cases the meaning of the interaction must be carefully analyzed. For example, as Kernberg (1975) noted regarding borderline patients, "the unconscious meanings of taking medications as part of the psychotherapeutic relationship have to be focused upon and consistently brought into the psychotherapeutic process because the primitive defensive operations of patients with borderline personality organization may be masked by a symbolic utilization of medication" (p. 132). Kernberg gave as an example the situation in which a borderline patient's "need for omnipotent control of an object may be expressed in the patient's unconscious feeling that when he possesses medication, he has control over the therapist" (p. 132).

These issues are, as many have implied, complex. Careful outcome research of these questions has not been done, and the methodology to do outcome research for long-term psychotherapy and psychoanalysis is sharply limited by the many variables introduced inevitably over the course of lengthy treatment. Precautions have been proposed about the introduction of medication as an addition to psychoanalysis, such as the concern about loss of neutrality (Roose 1990). Normand and Bluestone (1986) warn that another risk might be the premature termination of analysis because of beneficial effects from medication that result in an erroneous illusion that no further analytic work is indicated. The case reports cited earlier in this section (Cooper 1985; Glen 1988; Oldham 1989; Wylie and Wylie 1987) involve positive outcomes, but there may well be others without such felicitous results.

Increasingly, however, the case is being made for the appropriateness of combining psychoanalysis with the use of medication when indicated. For example, in the task force report of the American Psychiatric Association on treatments of psychiatric disorders, it is argued that in the case of mood disorders,

> remission of a severe depression—and, in particular, of the melancholic symptoms that are so unbearable—will reduce the patient's obsession with his misery and make him more available for productive therapeutic work. Experienced analysts . . . who successfully used psychoanalytic psychotherapy with severely depressed individuals for many decades strongly recommend the use of antidepressants and report no impedance to the process of therapy. (Bemporad 1989, p. 1826)

When medications are administered, it is important to attend to the dynamics of this treatment component, whether it is being provided by the treating psychoanalyst or by a separate consultant. The transference meaning of directly providing the medication (e.g., gratification) should be explored, just as the transference meaning of referring the analysand to a consultant (e.g., rejection) should be addressed.

The following case, in which the decision was made not to prescribe an antidepressant, illustrates some of the complex aspects of this issue and reminds us that each analyst must make a carefully judged individual decision on a case-by-case basis.

> The patient, a 30-year-old, childless, divorced researcher, was referred for psychoanalysis to an analytic candidate in training. The patient had obtained her doctorate with honors several years previously and worked in a nontenured academic setting. She worried excessively about job security, but her chief reason for wanting analysis was a pattern of unsatisfying relationships with men. Several brief prior therapy experiences for anxiety and depression had been of only slight benefit.
>
> The patient was an only child whose mother was a bitter, unhappy woman who was intensively intrusive in the patient's life and was frequently depressed, was repeatedly institutionalized, and had been given several courses of ECT. The father was a laborer, a source of contempt for the patient's mother, and a grandiose but ineffectual dreamer who was highly seductive with the patient.

Early in analysis, the patient became anxious about a rapidly developing intense transference attachment to the analyst, which she defended against by impulsively acting out and moving in with a man with whom she was involved. Nonetheless, an erotic transference developed, but she was intelligent and psychologically insightful, and she responded to the analyst's interventions and interpretations appropriately and made progress in the analysis. After about 3 years, the man she lived with left her, plunging her into a stormy depressive episode.

Although it was clear to the therapist that the intensity of her depressive reaction to this loss was accentuated by a transference element, reflecting her rage and disappointment in the analyst's unavailability as a romantic object in her life, her depression persisted and deepened. She developed insomnia and weight loss, and desperately pleaded with the analyst to give her medication or to hospitalize her. The analyst was extremely distressed by the situation, feeling that the patient might well benefit from medication, but aware as well of her unconscious masochistic wish to defeat the analyst, dismantle her analysis, and follow her mother's footsteps and label herself chronically mentally ill. The analyst consulted his supervisor, who strongly advised that he vigorously interpret these and other meanings in the situation and not respond by providing medication. With great trepidation, he proceeded accordingly. Eventually, the patient's depression abated, she understood these meanings of her reaction, and the analysis proceeded to a highly successful termination.

The irony here is that, in retrospect, it was clear that this patient developed a DSM-III-R-diagnosable major depressive disorder in the course of analysis. The treating analyst in this case, now a training analyst, indicated that if this patient were in treatment with him now, he would not be able *not* to arrange for her to obtain appropriate medication for the depressive episode. It is impossible to know how such a response, if at all, would have changed the course of the analysis and/or the outcome. Although the patient's biological, familial depressive illness was clearly present and could have led to a crisis or to a tragic result, as it turned out the patient did not force herself to have the same destiny as her mother's, and her self-esteem was, it is persuasive to believe, strengthened as a result.

It is always important to carefully and systematically diagnose all comorbid conditions in patients in treatment. When a patient in psychoanalysis is diagnosed with a condition clearly known to be responsive to medication, then it is clinically and ethically indicated to make such a recommendation to the patient. Not all situations are entirely clear, however, especially when intense transference reactions develop in the course of an analysis. Either way, there may be some uncertainty as to whether the decisions made were the best ones, because one can only judge the effectiveness of the chosen path by the results obtained. In all cases, it is crucial to maintain an active, interpretive stance, even when concurrent psychopharmacology and psychoanalysis are being administered.

Psychoanalysis and Couples or Family Therapy

A second type of combined treatment is the concurrent process of psychoanalysis and couples therapy or family therapy. There are many versions of this option, including brief interviews of family members by the treating psychoanalyst, a period of concurrent couples or family treatment by the analyst during the course of the analysis of one of the family members, referral to an outside couples or family therapist for such work during the course of analysis, or sequential treatment planning, involving family intervention, followed by individual psychoanalysis of any or all family members.

As early as 1938, Oberndorf addressed the special problems of couples whose motivation that led them to marry stemmed at least in part from unresolved neurotic conflicts in both marital partners. He reported nine cases from his practice in which he personally psychoanalyzed, independently, both marital partners. Although he addressed the unique technical complexities of this arrangement, he concluded, "The danger of each patient utilizing the analyst as a source of resistance to an extraordinary extent can be avoided if the latter maintains his position of neutrality with the utmost inviolability" (p. 474).

Mittelmann, in 1948, reported a similar point of view, describing the concurrent analyses by the same analyst of both partners in a marriage. He argued that such work "makes more concrete both the realities and the neurotic interactions between the mates" (p. 196). He described special transference problems in this type of situation, and he agreed with Oberndorf on the importance of a neutral stance. Mittelmann reported successful outcome in 11 of 12 instances of simultaneous treatment of married couples. However, in only 4 of these cases were simultaneous analyses per se conducted; in the other 8 cases, analysis of one spouse and "briefer psychotherapy" with the other spouse were carried out. Extensive information was provided about only one couple, and it is unclear what criteria were used to classify the treatment outcomes as successful (in two instances, the couples divorced).

In my experience, significant questions exist about the advisability of such simultaneous treatment, in which it is extremely difficult to prevent distortion and to maintain confidentiality and neutrality. For example, a patient was seen recently in consultation who had severe marital troubles. She had been in analysis for 10 years with the same analyst who was psychoanalyzing her husband, whose treatment had been going on for 15 years. The patient had quit in anger because of a conviction that her analyst gave her bad advice, advice based on his work with the husband. The marriage seemed doomed, and neither analysis was successful.

Attention has shifted from concurrent psychoanalysis of both marital partners to concurrent couples or family therapy and psychoanalysis of at least one member of the couple or family. Ackerman (1958) emphasized that if the analyst were "to observe the two-way emotional interchange of patient and family, he would then be in a position to match his perception of the patient and his [the patient's] family relationships not only against the patient's perceptions, but also against the family members' perception of the patient" (pp. 31–32). More recently, Szalita (1972) strongly advocated "family interviewing" in the course of psychoanalytic work, especially early in treatment, that "as an adjunct to individual psychoanalysis may serve to shorten the lengthy process of analysis and correct the distorted impressions one may get from the biased individual account" (p. 35).

In my experience, it is often useful, when possible, to meet with a spouse or with significant family members for a more complete clinical evaluation. This is particularly useful in the initial phase of treatment and has the advantage of serving as a reference point for the analyst when neurotic distortions emerge later. However, the benefit of this approach is limited, because in-depth knowledge of family dynamics is not possible from brief interviews.

Others have emphasized not just the informative value of direct observation of marital partners or family members by the psychoanalyst, but the therapeutic value of a course of marital or family therapy occurring concurrently with ongoing psychoanalysis (Finkelstein 1988; Nadelson 1978). The marital or family work can be done by the psychoanalyst who is treating the family member or by an independent therapist. Graller (1981, p. 176) described the "hopeless position of facing the failure of an analysis because of an 'unmanageable spouse' or important other," and he recommended as one possible solution "adjunctive marital therapy" in such situations. He reported his experience of seven cases in which he provided marital therapy and one partner or both were in analysis with another analyst, an arrangement that he felt successfully resolved impasses in the analytic work. In most cases, the indication for this type of concurrent arrangement is a specific predominance of a marital or family problem that has a "here and now" immediacy and becomes a major preoccupation of the individual in psychoanalysis. In marital situations, as Nadelson (1978) pointed out, this arrangement is more often indicated when the problem is relatively acute and both spouses seem reasonably motivated to work on their relationship and express desire to preserve the marriage.

At times, in my experience, brief work with a couples therapist while one spouse is in analysis can be quite beneficial directly and can have a secondary benefit in cases in which the spouse not in analysis may have been frightened to seek treatment because of his or her unfamiliarity with therapy and the unknowable consequences of the issues that may arise. The couples therapy experience may feel sufficiently nonthreatening, because its focus is on "the relationship," and yet may lead to much needed individual treatment for the spouse.

Psychoanalysis and Group Therapy

In many ways, interest in concurrent psychoanalysis and group therapy has paralleled the growing interest in the other forms of combined treatment described in this chapter, and some of the principles and problems are similar. Sager (1960), in a comprehensive review of this version of combined treatment, outlined prior objections to this type of work. He cited two important questions: "1) . . . Is concurrent therapy, as an integrated tool, possible, or does the analyst use the group as an adjunct to individual therapy when he is prejudiced in favor of the latter, and vice-versa? 2) What is the operational usefulness of concurrent psychotherapy compared with individual analysis or group therapy alone?" (p. 227). He described with candor his own anxieties as he began to experiment with putting his own analytic patients in concurrent group therapy that he led, and he itemized some of the problems of the arrangement. His experience, however, was that the combination proved beneficial. In his view, the concurrent work provides "the patient with a means of understanding and working through his problems which is not readily available in either type of therapy alone" (p. 232), a conclusion presumably based on his view of the importance of highly variable social contexts in patients' lives. His answers to the two questions posed were affirmative. Similar views were held by Spotnitz (1961), who also described his personal experience of expanding his work from psychoanalysis to include group therapy, and his growing conviction that some patients "need both experiences—combined therapy" (p. 4).

Stein (1964) described two ways in which transference is different in group therapy than in psychoanalysis or in individual analytic treatment: "(1) the intensity of the transference directed toward the therapist is lessened . . ., and (2) the transference is split . . . since it is directed toward the other patients in the group as well as toward the therapist" (p. 416). He proposed that these special features of the group setting represent advantages in treating some patients with severe character disorders who may develop insurmountable resistance in psychoanalysis, so that concurrent group and analytic treatment can prove more effective. He cautioned, however, that concurrent therapy should be carefully evaluated in each case, because "in many instances it confuses and complicates the transference in both forms of treatment, leading to increased resistance and therapeutic difficulties . . ." (p. 423). In his view, the borderline patient with ego defects and narcissistic traits is most likely to incrementally benefit from this arrangement. Similar views have been expressed more recently by Scheidlinger (1982) and by Schachter (1988), who stated that "concurrent group and individual psychoanalytic psychotherapy constitutes a contribution to the widening scope of application of psychoanalytic treatment" (p. 456).

Conclusions

As new knowledge emerges concerning the biopsychosocial nature of mental illness, new applications of traditional treatments and new combinations of treatments should be considered. Psychoanalysis alone remains the treatment of choice for some patients, just as any one of a number of other forms of treatment will be recommended as the treatment of choice for other patients. Combined treatment—that is, the combination of psychoanalysis and pharmacotherapy, couples or family therapy, or group therapy—should be recommended, as well, as the treatment of choice, when indicated. No treatment recommendation is foolproof, and the patient should have an informed opportunity to consider alternative treatments and make his or her own decision. Therapists should remain flexible—able to recommend changes, add new combinations, or discontinue unworkable ones—as treatment progresses.

References

Ackerman NW: The Psychodynamics of Family Life: Diagnosis and Treatment of Family Relationships. New York, Basic Books, 1958

Bemporad JR: Intensive psychotherapy and psychoanalysis, in Treatments of Psychiatric Disorders, Vol 3. Washington, DC, American Psychiatric Association, 1989, pp 1824–1833

Brockman R: Medication and transference in psychoanalytically oriented psychotherapy of the borderline patient. Psychiatr Clin North Am 13:287–295, 1990

Cooper AM: Will neurobiology influence psychoanalysis? Am J Psychiatry 142:1395–1402, 1985

Elkin I, Shea MT, Watkins JT, et al: National Institute of Mental Health Treatment of Depression Collaborative Research Program: general effectiveness of treatments. Arch Gen Psychiatry 46:971–982, 1989

Finkelstein L: Psychoanalysis, marital therapy, and object-relations theory. J Am Psychoanal Assoc 36:905–931, 1988

Glen J: A parameter. Annual of Psychoanalysis 16:217–230, 1988

Graller JL: Adjunctive marital therapy: a possible solution to the split-transference problem. Annual of Psychoanalysis 9:175–187, 1981

Kernberg OF: Borderline Conditions and Pathological Narcissism. New York, Jason Aronson, 1975

Kris AO: Psychoanalysis and psychoanalytic psychotherapy (Chapter 8), in Psychiatry. Edited by Michels R, Cavenar JO Jr, et al. Philadelphia, PA, JB Lippincott, 1989

Liebowitz MD, Klein DF: Hysteroid dysphoria. Psychiatr Clin North Am 2:555–575, 1979

Lipton MA: Editorial: a letter from Anna Freud. Am J Psychiatry 140:1583–1584, 1983

Mittelmann B: The concurrent analysis of married couples. Psychoanal Q 17:182–197, 1948

Nadelson CC: Marital therapy from a psychoanalytic perspective, in Marriage and Marital Therapy. Edited by Paolino TJ Jr, McCrady BS. New York, Brunner/Mazel, 1978, pp 89–164

Normand WC, Bluestone H: The use of pharmacotherapy in psychoanalytic treatment. Contemporary Psychoanalysis 22:218–233, 1986

Oberndorf CP: Psychoanalysis of married couples. Psychoanal Rev 25:453–475, 1938

Oldham JM: Treatment of a hysteroid-dysphoric patient. Journal of Personality Disorders 3:354–358, 1989

Ostow M: Drugs in Psychoanalysis and Psychotherapy. New York, Basic Books, 1962

Ostow M: The influence of psychiatric drug therapy on the future of psychoanalysis, in Psychopharmacology and Psychotherapy. Edited by Greenhill MH, Gralnick A. New York, Free Press, 1983, pp 79–96

Roose S: The use of medication in combination with psychoanalytic psychotherapy or psychoanalysis (Chapter 13), in Psychiatry. Edited by Michels R, Cavenar JO Jr, et al. New York, JB Lippincott, 1990

Sager CJ: Combined individual and group psychoanalysis, 2: concurrent individual and group analytic psychotherapy. Am J Orthopsychiatry 30:225–241, 1960

Schachter J: Concurrent individual and individual-in-a-group psychoanalytic psychotherapy. J Am Psychoanal Assoc 36:455–480, 1988

Scheidlinger S: Focus on Group Psychotherapy. New York, International Universities Press, 1982

Silber A: Panic attacks facilitating recall and mastery: implications for psychoanalytic technique. J Am Psychoanal Assoc 37:337–364, 1989

Spotnitz H: The Couch and the Circle. New York, Alfred A Knopf, 1961

Stein A: The nature of transference in combined therapy. Int J Group Psychother 14:413–424, 1964

Szalita AB: The relevance of family interviewing for psychoanalysis. Contemporary Psychoanalysis 8:31–44, 1972

Viederman M: Psychoanalysis and the use of psychoactive drugs. Bulletin of the Association for Psychoanalytic Medicine 28:83–88, 1989

Wylie HW Jr, Wylie ML: An effect of pharmacotherapy on the psychoanalytic process: case report of a modified analysis. Am J Psychiatry 144:489–492, 1987

16

Termination of Psychoanalysis and Psychotherapy

Phyllis Tyson, Ph.D.

ermination is that phase of the psychoanalytic or psychothera-peutic process during which patient and therapist consider when and how to conclude their collaboration, and then effect this conclusion. It is a two-way process, and although the tasks for patient and analyst differ, the process involves patient and analyst anticipating bringing their work to a close and working through the effects of this change in their relationship. Because becoming involved in a dynamically oriented psychotherapy or psychoanalysis is usually such an intense and meaningful experience for both patient and therapist, the ways in which the patient and therapist anticipate feeling about the loss of their relationship, and the meanings that this loss comes to represent, can be a critical area of exploration throughout the entire psychotherapeutic process. Failure to work through difficulties encountered during termination, or a failure to complete the termination process, therefore renders an essential aspect of the analytic work incomplete (Glover 1955; Rangell 1966) and may impact the final resolution and outcome of treatment, be it psychoanalysis or psychotherapy.

Although it is perhaps impossible to separate the tasks of the patient from those of the analyst in the termination process, in this chapter I examine these topics separately. I also consider the tasks of the patient in terms of the development level of conflicts, the affects and defenses that typically emerge, and the transference neurosis. Our knowledge of the dynamics of the termination process, although based mostly on in-depth studies of the clinical situation of psychoanalysis, can also inform our work in varieties of other psychotherapeutic situations, which will be briefly considered.

Termination in Psychoanalysis

Tasks for the Patient

From the very beginning of any treatment, psychoanalysis or psychotherapy, the issue of termination is present, as the patient wonders how long the treatment will take and how the patient or analyst will know when it is time to consider stopping. Before an agreed-upon date is set to terminate the analytic relationship, there is a period during which the idea of termination germinates, grows, and reaches fruition. The process of termination can therefore be said to begin when both patient and analyst recognize that the major goals of therapy have been reached. Some would prefer that this judgment be based on relatively objective goals having been met, and a variety of suggestions about possible criteria have been made. These include symptomatic relief (Nunberg 1954; Shane and Shane 1984); the resolution of the transference neurosis (Bridger 1950; Buxbaum 1950; Ferenczi 1927/1955; Firestein 1978; Greenacre 1954/1971, 1966/1971; Held 1955; Kramer 1967; Kubie 1968; Macalpine 1950; Novick 1976, 1982; Panel 1969; Rangell 1966; Stone 1961; G. R. Ticho 1967); the patient's taking responsibility for insight (Rangell 1982); the patient's establishment of psychological mindedness and a capacity for self-analysis (Panel 1969; Siegel 1982; Shane and Shane 1984); and structural change and greater efficiency of ego functioning (Freud 1937).

Psychoanalysis, as a science and as an art, involves a fluid mixture of objectivity and subjectivity. Freud (1913) acknowledged the subjective nature of the treatment process in his observation that the analyst "cannot determine beforehand exactly what results he will effect. He sets in motion a process . . . He can supervise this process, further it, remove obstacles in its way, and he can undoubtedly vitiate much of it. But on the whole, once begun, it goes its own way . . ." (p. 130). Because of the subjective nature of the psychoanalytic process, we recognize that when not forced by external circumstances or by countertransference pressures, most patients and analysts, mostly through intuition, come to an awareness that the conclusion of the treatment is a definite and imminent reality.

Tasks Relevant to Resolving Developmental Conflict

Termination stands apart from other aspects of the psychotherapeutic process in that it involves doing the work of mourning—experiencing and working through the various affective reactions that are stimulated by the anticipation of separation from and loss of the relationship with the analyst. Because the analyst becomes a central figure around which derivatives of childhood wishes, fantasies, and yearnings are revived during treatment, anticipating a final separation from the analyst may arouse in the patient unresolved conflicts and associated affective responses from all developmental levels.

Separation-individuation wishes and conflicts.   With some patients on some occasions the analyst's attention and devotion lead to the emergence of an early mother-infant transference, in which the patient's desire for a perfect, omnipotent, all-giving, and perfectly understanding mother-analyst becomes evident. If such regressive dependence has been a theme at times during the analysis, the thought of loss of the analyst may arouse considerable anxiety. Separation anxiety is one of the earliest potentially traumatic affective experiences an individual may have; it is often experienced as a sense of helplessness in the face of passively feeling a loss of the object. Although separation anxiety is a common theme in every analysis, stimulated particularly by the analyst's vacations, the reality of termination may especially evoke these archaic concerns, which now emerge in their full intensity and undisguised form.

At times, intense negative transference reactions develop as the patient recognizes the final frustration implied by termination (Dewald 1982). That is, sometimes a patient may withhold the full intensity of rage associated with infantile loss of omnipotence and helplessness in order to preserve the relationship with the analyst, maintaining unconscious hopes of ultimate fulfillment of grandiose infantile wishes. When the patient finally recognizes the futility of such hopes, he or she may feel there is nothing in the relationship with the analyst to preserve. Intense rage may follow, and the associated anxiety and helplessness may reveal certain limitations in the degree to which psychoanalysis can repair structural deficits. If a severe regression ensues and the patient appears to lose the gains of the analysis, such as the capacity to maintain self and object constancy,[1] the analyst and patient may have to rethink the matter of termination, even if a date has been set.

For example, one patient, a high-functioning 33-year-old, unmarried professional woman, had throughout her analysis main-

---

[1]*Object constancy* is a concept first introduced by Hartmann (1952/1964) to refer to a stage in object relations wherein the relationship is not destroyed or disrupted by sexual or aggressive impulses. Although used variously throughout the literature (see Tyson and Tyson 1990 for discussion), the term has become particularly associated with Mahler's theory of the separation-individuation process (Mahler et al. 1975). Mahler thought that with some resolution of loving and hating feelings, the mental representation of the mother comes to be for the most part a loving one whose function is to provide comfort and support in the mother's absence. By identification with his or her comforting mother, the child is better able to comfort himself or herself and therefore to function separately. The concept is especially important because of the ego functioning implied. Now, the child, instead of being overwhelmed by the intensity of his or her affects, is better able to regulate himself or herself. *Self constancy* implies the capacity to sustain a unified self representation that is basically positive but encompasses all the different, affectively toned ideas about one's self. This capacity is reinforced and stabilized by increasing ego capacities for impulse control and pleasurable feelings of mastery that make one feel one is lovable. It is the ego functioning associated with object and self constancy that is so important to evaluate in terms of termination. When termination stimulates intense negative transference reactions such that the patient's capacity to regulate affects is undermined, his or her capacity to maintain a basically positive feeling about himself or herself may also be severely stressed and, consequently, the gains of analysis may be compromised.

tained a fantasy of symbiotic "oneness" with her female analyst. With a sense of her loved analyst always with her, she had come to feel increasingly confident in herself, and her symptoms of depression abated. However, the full extent of this fantasy and its function only became apparent as she began to consider terminating her analysis. On recognizing that she would never have this fantasy fulfilled by her analyst, she became extremely angry and depressed, feeling painfully alone, helpless, and unlovable. She remembered that such a feeling had dominated her childhood, but she had always had the sense that her mother could make it better if she would only try. She remembered having had a repetitive childhood fantasy of having a hole in her pocket. She had fantasized going into the forest where the fairies would dance for her and they would give her a dime. But on returning home she would discover that her dime had slipped through the hole in her pocket. She had always been angry that her mother would not sew up the hole. She would have been rich had she been able to hold on to her dimes. The prospect of termination unleashed such anger toward her idealized analyst that once again, as in her childhood, she felt like a lonely, cheated, powerless child.

Without the challenge of an acknowledged termination period, during which patient and analyst anticipate the impending loss, the existence of unconscious separation-individuation wishes and conflicts and the function of associated magical fantasies may mask the extent of certain structural weaknesses. Although unmasking such weaknesses may not necessarily extend the analysis, their exposure may facilitate a more complete analysis. It may be because of such factors that Glover (1955) maintained that no analysis is complete without "the touchstone" of the termination phase.

Oedipal conflict.   The process of termination may stimulate unresolved oedipal wishes, conflicts, and associated guilt. Although analysis of these would undoubtedly have been a part of the treatment throughout, they often arise in a new, different, and more intense way during termination. That is, recognizing the impending loss of the analyst and the analytic relationship forces the patient to acknowledge that the derivatives of oedipal libidinal wishes that were revived in the transference will never be satisfied. Intense anger, envy and jealousy, longing and sadness—that is, the painful affects associated with early childhood oedipal wishes and disappointments—may arise. These may be directed toward other patients, toward the analyst's spouse and family, or directly toward the analyst. The analyst's technique is now challenged with balancing the patient's need to express and work through these affects and the frequent result—that the guilt and anxiety associated with these affects tend to undermine the patient's self-esteem. Titrating the associated anxiety becomes an imperative, yet delicate and difficult task.

A session during the termination phase of the patient whose case was mentioned in the previous subsection illustrates the intermingling of preoedipal and oedipal themes and the vulnerabilities in self-esteem that accompany their expression. She began a session by expressing the painful feelings that the thought of ending her analysis had stimulated:

> All these feelings, they're about control, anger, and being left. I hate you, I want something different from you. You always say I can express my anger, but what good does it do? Whenever I do I just feel alone, disconnected; I still don't get what I want—I don't get to go home with you, be a part of your life, be important to you. You have your husband, your family, I'm just another patient in your life. Now I feel bad, you'll probably hate me for saying that; I feel alone and afraid. I hate the part of me that wants to cling to you, wants to be important to you. I'm tired of jumping on myself; the worst part is how ready I am to jump on myself. When I get into hating you, I'm convinced I'm bad. I know that's not true, but an earlier part of me says that it is. I wish I didn't get so depressed thinking about not coming here anymore . . . [long pause] I just had a fantasy, you are very, very sick, you didn't send me away, you let me take care of you. Your hands are cold, I wasn't sure if you could hear me—I told you to hang on, I needed you. But you died. Your husband was outside. I comforted him, and then—I couldn't believe this part—we started dating! I was able to take your place for him! I lost you, yet someone that belonged to someone as great as you could choose me, so I could be as great as you—that felt so good! It was a way of having you when I couldn't have you. I wish I could gobble you up.

At times the patient may attempt to actualize some kind of oedipal fulfillment in a disguised manner, for example, by engaging the analyst in sadomasochistic interactions. These provide still different challenges to the analyst's technique as well as to his or her countertransference awareness and management. For example, the patient in the above example came to a recent session with the fantasy that after she finished her analysis, rather than lose the analyst, she might use the analyst as a mentor. Maybe she would write a novel and ask the analyst to review the manuscript. But then she worried that the analyst might steal her ideas. Remembering the patient's wish to steal her husband, the analyst suggested it was she, the patient, who was envious and jealous of the analyst. The patient responded with memories of previous affairs and thoughts about how it had always been easier to fall in love with a man who was already married. The patient and analyst reconstructed the displacement of the patient's oedipal envy of her mother and her wish to steal what her mother owned, and recognized that that wish was now part of the transference as both patient and analyst faced termination.

To progress in development, the child must renounce gratification of the libidinal and aggressive impulses associated with preoedipal and oedipal wishes and come to terms with the differences in sexes and differences in generations. This process involves the child's beginning to accept responsibility and a sense of his or her own guilt. Termination involves a similar task. The patient must give up the possibility of gratifying, via the analyst, whatever preoedipal and oedipal fantasies were stimulated during the course of treatment, give up the quest for fulfillment of the impossible, and come to terms with the recognition that the analyst has a real life outside the analysis from which the patient is and will be excluded.

Unresolved adolescent conflict. There is one developmental phase in which separation is a normal developmental task: adolescence. Indeed, because separation is a normal part of adolescence, many analysts discuss termination especially in terms of adolescence (Dewald 1964; Gitelson 1967; Miller 1965; Panel 1969; Rangell 1966). For adolescence to be complete, the adolescent must actively engage in a process of emotionally and physically moving away from his or her parental objects. So it is with the patient in analysis. The patient passively experiences many losses of the analyst during the course of the analysis, dictated particularly by the analyst's vacations. These losses evoke affective responses associated to passively experienced separations in early development. However, the termination process demands that the patient actively leave the analyst, not passively experience the loss. It is the activity on the part of the patient that makes the process similar to adolescence.

Blos (1967) maintains that in order for the adolescent to become psychologically autonomous and free of the parents, he or she must accomplish the tasks of the "second individuation." One of the crucial tasks in this process is the de-idealization of parental object representations. The child's thought processes are egocentric during the time the object representations are formed in early childhood, so he or she tends to view the parents as ideal because of the central position they hold in his or her life. The adolescent tends to cling to these ideal images of all-loving, all-fulfilling ideal objects while at the same time he or she harshly criticizes the parents whom he or she now sees as inadequate and disappointing. The resulting interpersonal strife causes the adolescent to feel a loss of internal support and a sense of emptiness, accompanied by a sense of painful alienation and object hunger.

Often these are the painful affects that are aroused during the termination phase as the patient asks, "Is this all there is? Why am I no better?" The patient often anticipates that a sense of emptiness will accompany the loss of the analyst, and he or she experiences fears, anxieties, and uncertainties about his or her future and about his or her capacity to deal effectively with future conflicts without the help of the analyst. These fears recapitulate the adolescent's painful affects as he or she struggled toward psychological independence.

Just as the adolescent must de-idealize his or her parents and internalize new ego ideals as part of the process of adolescent individuation (see Tyson and Tyson 1990 for an explanation of these adolescent processes), so, too, the patient must struggle with his or her disappointments and disillusionments concerning the analyst and the analytic process. The patient must recognize that the analysis cannot protect him or her from the pain of current intrapsychic conflict or ensure against the pain of future conflicts that may appear at any time in life. The patient must acknowledge that the outcome of analysis has its limitations—that there is no such thing as a perfect analyst, a perfect analysis, or a perfectly analyzed individual (Gaskill 1980; Loewald 1978; Rangell 1966). Indeed, Freud (1937) commented on this myth of perfectibility when he emphasized that "our aim will not be to rub off every peculiarity of human character for the sake of a schematic 'normality,' nor yet to demand that the person who has been 'thoroughly analysed' shall feel no passions and develop no internal conflicts. The business of the analysis is to secure the best possible psychological conditions for the functions of the ego; with that it has discharged its task" (p. 250). If these disappointments can be addressed during the termination phase, the patient may have less difficulty with postanalytic disappointment (G. R. Ticho 1967).

Affect and Defense in the Termination Process

There are important psychological tasks for the patient to confront as he or she begins the termination process. Previously gained insights must be reworked and synthesized (Ekstein 1965) and turned into effective and lasting change (Greenson 1965). The termination process typically arouses intense affects as various conflicts and possibly related insights are rearoused and reworked. Often, formerly abandoned symptoms reoccur temporarily. Such resurgence may discourage patient and analyst, yet generally these affects and symptoms are of short duration, for the regressive intensification of the transference is balanced by the treatment alliance being at its maximum efficiency (E. E. Ticho 1972). Now new and more mature patterns of adaptation and hopeful anticipations of the future oscillate with retreat and regression.

In this regard, Kanzer (see Panel 1975) points out that not all of the affects encountered during the termination phase are unpleasant. There also can be "relief, joy, and a hunger for new experiences for which money, time, and psychological preparedness are now available" (reported in Panel 1975, p. 172). These positive affects can often mitigate the anxiety aroused by the anticipated separation and loss. Loewald (1962) notes that although termination may be experienced as deprivation and loss, it can equally signify emancipation and mastery. If a more stable sense of self and object constancy can be internalized as part of the termination process, then termination can effect a greater capacity for intimacy as well as a greater sense of autonomy and mastery. If a greater capacity to bear guilt and self-responsibility can be internalized as a part of reworking the oedipal transference, then termination can also open up new possibilities for mature love relationships. This effect was evident with the woman whose case was presented earlier. As the patient's idealization of her analyst and her harsh self-criticisms that led her to feel inadequate and worthless whenever she felt intense hostility toward her analyst were interpreted, she came to see that it was her hostility that interfered with her experiencing her analyst as constant. Before the analysis she had been mostly unaware of her hostility, only of the resulting depression. By recognizing that depression, for her, signaled underlying rage, she came to recognize that it was her anger, associated with holding on to impossible infantile demands, that had interfered with her experiencing the intimacy that might have been available in her relationship with her mother. As she came to accept responsibility for her own anger and to give up blaming her mother and her analyst for their shortcomings, she came to recognize that it was her infantile demands and her associated anger that made her feel distant and separate. Feeling separate, she felt sad, lonely, and inadequate. As the work progressed, she reported that when she did not feel angry, she felt better about herself, more connected to her analyst, yet more confident in her ability to function without her analyst. She recognized that she then also felt more open to relationships with men.

Because the termination process often arouses intense anxiety, a variety of defenses often are employed. Some patients, for example, attempt to deny the importance of the analyst as a transference object and, instead, experience a hunger for new or substitute objects (Reich 1950). By finding a new love object, having a baby, or choosing a new occupation, a patient may attempt to displace transference wishes and affects by seeking gratification elsewhere. Although on the surface these may appear to be simple attempts to deny loss and avoid the mourning of the loss of the analyst, such displacements betray complex compromise formations involving the expression of derivatives from the preoedipal, oedipal, and adolescent conflicts discussed earlier.

Some patients attempt to defend against the anxiety associated with termination by denying the irrevocability and inevitability of the loss of the analyst; that is, they deny the existence of the termination. Although patient and analyst have together concurred that the treatment should come to an end, the patient forestalls the concrete act of selecting a date for the final session. Other patients deny the intensity of underlying affects and attempt to select a date that gives inadequate time for the full exploration of separation themes and related affects. Dewald (1982) points out, however, that such denial serves an unconscious magical attempt to hold onto the object and to pretend that the loss is not occurring.

Some patients attempt to defend against the separation and implied final relinquishing of infantile wishes by maintaining fantasies of having a different kind of relationship with the analyst following the termination. Indeed, fantasies of achieving some kind of libidinal gratification may persist up to the very last session. Often patients have specifically organized fantasies about the last session that involve a major departure from the previously maintained analytic situation and relationship.

The patient's intense feelings of disappointment are occasionally accompanied by a wish to frustrate the analyst. Wishes for revenge may motivate a patient to sacrifice the therapeutic gains of a termination process and to terminate prematurely. Such a foreshortening of the analysis is a manipulative effort to disappoint and arouse guilt in the analyst for the perceived failure of the treatment process.

Some patients, in unconscious attempts to avoid the painful process of termination, express wishes to terminate immediately when the subject of termination first arises. Novick (1982) reports that a tendency toward premature termination is typical of resistances to the positive transference in the analysis of adolescents (see Reich 1950; Spiegel 1951; Adatto 1958; A. Freud 1970/1971; Panel 1970).

Indeed, adolescents often begin treatment with a plan for unilateral termination. Novick maintains that the persistence of this adolescent phenomenon can often be found in the adult's fantasies and expectations about treatment, particularly about how and when it will end. If these fantasies and expectations are not made the subject of analytic investigation early in the analysis, they may provide a powerful resistance to the patient's becoming fully engaged in the analytic process (see also Calef and Weinshel 1983) and also to his or her becoming fully involved in the termination process.

Resolution of the Transference Neurosis

Blos (1968, 1976) has explored the question of when and how adolescence ends. There are pitfalls in comparing the termination process with the normal adolescent process, because there are significant affective, cognitive, and intellectual differences between adolescents and adults. Nevertheless, Blos comments on one aspect of adolescent development that has an important analogous counterpart in the termination process: the need to come to terms with and to give up grudges about irredeemable childhood events or traumas, and the need to establish a sense of historical continuity with the past. Giving up the hope for and mourning the loss of the wished-for preoedipal omnipotent, all-perfect mother-analyst, or giving up the quest for oedipal victory and the resentment of oedipal failure, makes it possible for the patient to establish a continuity with his or her past.

These conflicts are typically embodied in the *transference neurosis*. Consequently, the need to resolve the transference neurosis has always been emphasized as a crucial task for the termination process (e.g., Rangell 1966). It is widely believed that the transference neurosis, understood as both a repetition of the infantile neurosis and an opportunity for providing new forms of object relations, is the hallmark of psychoanalysis. That is, when the patient originally comes to treatment, wishes, conflicts, associated affects, and the compromises and adaptations made by the patient in trying to cope with the conflicts from his or her past are often fixed and walled off and function independently, outside of the patient's awareness. As the treatment progresses, old wishes are revived, and the analyst becomes increasingly central to those wishes and associated conflicts. In this way, the encapsulated constituents are brought back into the mainstream of the patient's mental functioning (Bird 1972). Establishing the transference neurosis thus allows analyst and patient together to scrutinize the whole of the complex fabric of the patient's inner world. Allowing the patient to know who he or she is and where he or she came from, as part of the gains of the analysis of the transference neurosis, then eventually makes the disengagement from the analyst more possible without disorganizing disruption occurring. One of the essential aspects of the termination process would then include coming to terms with the shared meaning of what has been experienced as these transference themes evolved, were elaborated, and were eventually resolved throughout treatment (Emde 1990; Shane and Shane 1984).

For most patients, the work of termination will not be completed by the time of the final session. The process must be continued by the patient alone during the weeks or months following the discontinuation of treatment. Indeed, Macalpine (1950) described analytic termination as involving a tracing back of the path to adulthood and noted that only part of this way back falls within the time limit of analytic termination; the full adaptation to adulthood is most often completed by the analysand after termination. During the postanalytic stage, according to Macalpine, great improvements often occur. Firestein (1978) has reviewed a number of authors who also observe continued improvement and symptom relief following analytic termination. We might conclude that to the extent that the treatment has been successful and some capacity for self-analysis has been established, the patient will be able independently to work through the affects and conflicts evoked, although some patients may find that planned follow-up visits with the analyst are also helpful in consolidating treatment gains.

Tasks for the Analyst

Maintaining the analytic situation, continuing transference abstinence, working with the specific resistances, and interpreting the dynamics and processes of termination are the most important tasks for the analyst during the termination phase.

Most analysts agree that it is essential that there should be no modification of the usual analytic technique during the termination phase. Most analysts also agree that there is greater proclivity for countertransference interference during the termination process (Firestein 1978) and that the analyst must possess and exercise finely tuned self-analyzing functions to maintain abstinence and thereby ensure the success of the termination process.

Termination involves a loss for the analyst as well as for the patient. The analyst must give up whatever emotional attachments with the patient were formed over the course of the analysis and mourn the loss of the relationship. An inability to do so because of countertransference interference may lead to an unnecessary prolongation of the treatment process. In this regard, the setting of the date for the final session frequently becomes a pivotal issue for both patient and analyst in coming to terms with the reality of the termination.

Because a date makes termination an unavoidable reality, there is much discussion about the technique involved in setting the date for termination. Although it is essential to allow sufficient time for the termination process to unfold, be worked through, and be resolved, there are no hard-and-fast rules about the length of time between setting a date and the final session. Many analysts maintain that the actual setting of the date is a task for the patient, although most would agree that the analyst should be actively involved in the process (for exceptions, see Brenner 1976; Glover 1955; Rangell 1966). Patients may attempt to defend against the mourning process by denying the finality of the terminal date. This denial is reflected in the patient's tendency to select a time when a break in the treatment would normally occur. It is incumbent on the analyst to advise the patient of the importance of a final date and to suggest that the patient select a date that can stand on its own and not become embedded in external, extraneous factors such as the analyst's vacation.

Just as patients have fantasies of a perfect analysis, so, too, analysts often wish to turn out a perfectly analyzed patient. There is, however, no such thing as a perfect analysis; in fact, some patients can achieve only modest gains toward mental health. Therefore, another important termination-related task for the analyst is to come to a comfortable recognition of the limitations of what the analytic technique and process can accomplish. In other words, the analyst must master his or her therapeutic ambition (Rangell 1966; E. E. Ticho 1972) and prepare to face the end of the analytic work with the patient. A related pitfall is the frequent confusion of analytic goals and life goals (E. E. Ticho 1972). Often the analyst is unaware of the extent to which he or she has colluded with the patient's wish to prolong the analysis until a particular life goal has been accomplished.

As was commented on earlier, the termination process often arouses an intense negative transference to a degree not evident earlier in the analysis. It is essential that the analyst be able to tolerate the patient's negativism and aggression, as well as his or her pain and distress over the regression and a return of symptoms, if such occurs. Although rethinking the date is sometimes necessary if the regression is severe, the analyst must otherwise maintain the analytic situation and work with the resistances as they arise. Doing so may be difficult in the face of these evoked negative affects, and the analyst may be tempted to abandon the analytic position, to become "more real" to the patient, to encourage a more social or reality-oriented form of relationship, or to favor a more active, symptom-oriented, or supportive stance. Avoidance of resistance by such provisions of transference or countertransference gratifications interferes with the termination process and neglects the fact that the analytic process continues after the analysis is terminated (Hurn 1971; Lipton 1961). Such modifications imply either that the patient is not fully analyzable or that there has been some degree of failure in completing the analysis (Dewald 1982).

Separation and loss are ubiquitous life experiences. The capacity to recognize the loss, to experience and express appropriate affects, to grieve and mourn the lost object, and eventually to be available for new meaningful relationships is a sign of emotional maturity. Successful integration and mastery of the affects and conflicts associated with the termination process of psychoanalysis offers both patient and analyst an opportunity to establish those capacities in an immediate and meaningful way. Therefore, one of the most important tasks for the analyst involved in the psychoanalytic process is interpreting the dynamics and processes of termination. There is much to be gained by the analyst in his or her appreciating and empathetically sharing the patient's process as the patient gives up the relationship with the analyst.

Applications to Psychotherapy

Because experiences of separation and loss are ubiquitous in human experience, and because any experience of separation can potentially tap into the affects associated with a previously experienced separation originating at any developmental level, the underlying principles of the termination process are similar in psychotherapy and psychoanalysis (as are the underlying principles of conducting psychotherapy and psychoanalysis, discussed by Paul Dewald in Chapter 14 of this textbook). Although the technical handling of the situations may vary, much of the discussion about termination in psychoanalysis may be helpful in understanding the psychotherapy patient's reaction to the anticipated termination.

In comparison with the psychoanalytic situation, responses to termination in psychotherapy are likely to be less intense and less prolonged. However, depending on the form of psychotherapy and on what has occurred during the course of the treatment—particularly the nature, intensity, and degree of awareness the patient has achieved of the dynamics of the transference—recognizable affective reactions do occur. The therapist should therefore be alert to the possibility that anticipating termination may set off in the patient reactions appropriate to separation experiences earlier in the patient's life and that the patient may respond with a variety of the regressive responses or utilize some of the typical defenses described earlier in this chapter.

Only a few general comments about the technical handling of these responses are possible because there are so many different types of psychotherapies. Indeed, some therapies involve expressive psychoanalytic processes; others place more emphasis on symptom relief by active, manipulative, or supportive interventions; and still others utilize interpretive and anxiety-provoking methods that are time-limited and in which active anticipation of termination is a factor from the beginning. If the therapy has been of a dynamic nature, it is usually helpful to interpret the patient's reactions, at least at a derivative level, and to facilitate working-through of the affective responses much as was described for the psychoanalytic situation, depending on the intensity of the transference relationship. On the other hand, if little interpretive work has been undertaken before termination, and if the transference has been relatively diluted and unconscious in the patient's mind and has been experienced in a displaced form with persons outside the therapeutic situation, little interpretive work may be necessary about termination. A patient may terminate such treatment without the marked reactions that have been described as being typical of psychoanalysis.

It should be emphasized, however, that the strategy of the termination phase should be consistent with the basic strategy of the therapy as it was determined at the outset. Patients in psychotherapy, just like patients in psychoanalysis, have varieties of wishful fantasies and yearnings. The intensification of these wishes with the prospect of termination often leads these patients to more diligently seek gratification during the last sessions of their treatment. As in psychoanalysis, it is important that the therapist keep in mind the transference nature of these reactions and be able to tolerate the patient's negative and hostile feelings, as well as the patient's positive, loving feelings and his or her demands for gratification. Major departures from the previously maintained situation and relationship, by providing various forms of gratification, are usually stimulated by a countertransference wish to avoid the patient's negative transference. However, such departures are likely to undermine the therapeutic gains that have been made over the course of the treatment and deprive the patient of the opportunity to work through the termination and consolidate treatment gains following the actual termination.

Forced Terminations

Optimally, termination is a mutually agreed-upon decision. Both patient and therapist come to the conclusion that the therapeutic goals have been more or less achieved, within the limitations of the technique and the patient's personality. However, there are a variety of situations, most characteristically in training programs, social agencies, clinics, and hospital settings, in which, for administrative, educational, financial, personal, or other reasons, the therapist must terminate the treatment before therapist and patient come to a mutually agreed-upon ending point. Termination under these circumstances may not follow the general principles outlined earlier in this chapter.

Under ideal circumstances, the patient actively decides when and how to leave the therapist, thereby achieving some mastery over passively endured separations. Forced termination, however, involves a decision made by someone else that does not take into account the patient's needs or the patient's progress in the psychotherapeutic process. A forced termination is therefore likely to be experienced as a repeat of earlier, passively experienced separations, and a variety of transference reactions relevant to earlier experiences of helplessness may be evoked. Although the patient may have a realistic appreciation of the reasons for the termination and may have even engaged in treatment knowing that a forced termination was a possibility (since clinics are often staffed by therapists at various stages of training), angry feelings of betrayal or abandonment still may arise.

A particular difficulty for both patient and therapist is to balance those affective responses derived from unresolved past experiences and those evoked by the current situation. A major difficulty arises in that the situation does create realistic stress and disruption for the patient, and feelings of betrayal, abandonment, anger, loss, and anxiety are sometimes justified. Nevertheless, it is helpful for the therapist to keep in mind that the patient's affective responses will be in keeping with reactions to similar previous imagined or experienced situations. Although some of the affective responses can be attributed to current reality, a forced termination can still be used as an opportunity for the patient to more fully understand, work through, and achieve greater mastery over past emotional responses to inevitable traumas. For this reason, it is important that the termination be anticipated and the affective responses be recognized and dealt with as early as possible so that some working-through can occur before the actual termination comes about. In this regard, if the termination is necessary because the therapist is moving or leaving the particular setting, the decision to transfer the patient to a new therapist, rather than automatically being made, should be based on the observation of how effectively the patient works through and masters the reactions to the forced termination.

Forced termination, particularly when the termination is forced on both therapist and patient, also stimulates countertransference responses. Although the therapist may know from the outset of treatment that a forced termination is inevitable, he or she, manifestly or tacitly, nevertheless encourages the patient's trust. Because of this, the therapist often feels guilty at "betraying" the patient. However, as with any other countertransference response, it is important that this guilt not lead the therapist to delay informing the patient of the impending termination. Too often the patient is notified only shortly before the forced termination must occur, and this deprives both patient and therapist the opportunity to explore and master whatever inevitable responses arise. As in any form of psychotherapy, ample time should be set aside for the termination process. It is also important that the therapist's own guilt about a forced termination not interfere with his or her tolerating and interpreting the negative transference. Working through these affects not only results in significant therapeutic gains but also provides both patient and therapist an opportunity to recognize that negative reactions may derive from the importance that the therapist has assumed for the patient. In this case the negative feelings may be less an angry reaction to the termination and more a defensive avoidance of experiencing the sadness and grief over the loss. When such termination reactions are not acknowledged and dealt with by therapist and patient, a significant portion of the work remains incomplete. Even if other issues have been resolved, this "unfinished business" may lead the patient to seek further psychotherapy, immediately or at a later date. When such therapy commences, the patient may transfer to the new therapist inappropriate expectations regarding the eventual termination of that therapy. Although the new therapist would, in any case, be the recipient of a variety of transferences, the new therapy may carry an extra burden of the unexpressed old negative transference. Unless skillfully handled, this added burden of unexpressed old negative transference may interfere with or disrupt further therapeutic progress.

Conclusions

The process of termination in psychoanalysis or in psychotherapy involves complementary tasks for patient and therapist. The ability of each to complete his or her tasks will contribute significantly to the overall success of the treatment. Fear, uncertainty, sadness, and grief, as well as sometimes anger, disappointment, and resentment but also a sense of mastery and hopeful anticipation, are among the affects aroused in the patient by the anticipation of the ending of therapeutic collaboration. Reasons why these affects occur have been discussed as well as some frequently seen defenses used to ward off the most painful of these affects. What is needed in order for the patient to work through these affects to complete the termination process has also been discussed. Among the tasks the therapist must confront is overcoming a sense of sadness, loss, disappointment of therapeutic ambitions, guilt about errors or countertransference enactments, and temptations to change treatment strategy or to give up prior attitudes of abstinence in order to ward off the patient's negative affects. Together, patient and therapist struggle with these separate tasks as they share in the process of giving up their therapeutic collaboration. Successful integration and mastery of the affects and conflicts associated with these tasks offers the patient the opportunity to be emotionally available for new meaningful relationships. Empathically sharing the patient's process while mastering countertransference responses offers the therapist the opportunity to be available for new meaningful therapeutic endeavors.

References

Adatto CP: Ego reintegration observed in the analysis of a late adolescent. Int J Psychoanal 39:172–177, 1958

Bird B: Notes on transference: universal phenomenon and hardest part of analysis. J Am Psychoanal Assoc 20:267–301, 1972

Blos P: The second individuation process of adolescence. Psychoanal Study Child 22:162–186, 1967

Blos P: Character formation in adolescence. Psychoanal Study Child 23:245–263, 1968

Blos P: How and when does adolescence end? Adolesc Psychiatry 5:5–17, 1976

Brenner C: Psychoanalytic Technique and Psychic Conflict. New York, International Universities Press, 1976

Bridger H: Criteria for the termination of analysis. Int J Psychoanal 31:202–203, 1950

Buxbaum E: Technique of terminating analysis. Int J Psychoanal 31:184–190, 1950

Calef V, Weinshel EM: A note on consumation and termination. J Am Psychoanal Assoc 31:643–650, 1983

Dewald PA: Psychotherapy: A Dynamic Approach. New York, Basic Books, 1964

Dewald PA: Serious illness in the analyst: transference, countertransference, and reality responses. J Am Psychoanal Assoc 30:347–363, 1982

Ekstein R: Working through and termination of analysis. J Am Psychoanal Assoc 13:57–78, 1965

Emde R: Mobilizing fundamental modes of development: empathic availability and therapeutic action. J Am Psychoanal Assoc 38:881–913, 1990

Ferenczi S: The problem of the termination of the analysis (1927), in Final Contributions to the Problems and Methods of Psycho-Analysis. Edited by Balint M. Translated by Mosbacher E. New York, Basic Books, 1955, pp 77–86

Firestein SK: Termination in Psychoanalysis. New York, International Universities Press, 1978

Freud A: Problems of termination in child analysis (1970), in The Writings of Anna Freud, Vol 7: Problems of Psychoanalytic Training, Diagnosis, and the Technique of Therapy, 1966–1970. New York, International Universities Press, 1971, pp 3–21

Freud S: On beginning the treatment (further recommendations on the technique of psycho-analysis I) (1913), in Standard Edition of the Complete Psychological Works of Sigmund Freud, Vol 12. Translated and edited by Strachey J. London, Hogarth Press, 1958, pp 121–144

Freud S: Analysis terminable and interminable (1937), in Standard Edition of the Complete Psychological Works of Sigmund Freud, Vol 23. Translated and edited by Strachey J. London, Hogarth Press, 1964, pp 209–253

Gaskill HS: The closing phase of the psychoanalytic treatment of adults and the goals of psychoanalysis: "the myth of perfectibility." Int J Psychoanal 61:11–23, 1980

Gitelson M: Analytic aphorisms. Psychoanal Q 36:250–270, 1967

Glover E: The Technique of Psychoanalysis. New York, International Universities Press, 1955

Greenacre P: Problems of infantile neurosis: contribution to a discussion (1954), in Emotional Growth: Psychoanalytic Studies of the Gifted and a Great Variety of Other Individuals, Vol 1. New York, International Universities Press, 1971, pp 50–57

Greenacre P: Problems of overidealization of the analyst and of analysis: their manifestations in the transference and countertransference relationship (1966), in Emotional Growth: Psychoanalytic Studies of the Gifted and a Great Variety of Other Individuals, Vol 2. New York, International Universities Press, 1971, pp 743–761

Greenson RR: The problem of working through, in Drives, Affects, Behavior, Vol 2. Edited by Schur M. New York, International Universities Press, 1965, pp 277–314

Hartmann H: The mutual influences in the development of ego and id (1952), in Essays on Ego Psychology: Selected Problems in Psychoanalytic Theory. New York, International Universities Press, 1964, pp 155–182

Held R: Les criteres de la fin du traitement psychanalytique. Revue Française Psychanalyse 19:603–614, 1955

Hurn HT: Toward a paradigm of the terminal phase: the current status of the terminal phase. J Am Psychoanal Assoc 19:332–348, 1971

Kramer C: Maxwell Gitelson: analytic aphorisms. Psychoanal Q 36:260–270, 1967

Kubie LS: Unsolved problems in the resolution of the transference. Psychoanal Q 37:331–352, 1968

Lipton S: The last hour. J Am Psychoanal Assoc 9:325–330, 1961

Loewald HL: Internalization, separation, mourning, and the superego. Psychoanal Q 31:483–504, 1962

Loewald HL: Psychoanalysis and the History of the Individual. New Haven, CT, Yale University Press, 1978

Macalpine I: The development of transference. Psychoanal Q 19:501–593, 1950

Mahler MS, Pine F, Bergman A: The Psychological Birth of the Human Infant: Symbiosis and Individuation. New York, Basic Books, 1975

Miller I: On the return of symptoms in the terminal phase of psychoanalysis. Int J Psychoanal 45:487–501, 1965

Novick J: Termination of treatment in adolescence. Psychoanal Study Child 31:389–414, 1976

Novick J: Transference varieties in the analysis of an adolescent. Int J Psychoanal 63:139–148, 1982

Nunberg H: Evaluation of the results of psychoanalytic treatment. Int J Psychoanal 35:2–7, 1954

Panel: Problems of termination in the analysis of adults. Reported by Firestein SK. J Am Psychoanal Assoc 17:222–237, 1969

Panel (Landauer EL, reporter): Problems of technique in the analysis of adolescents (mimeo), Proceedings of the 5th Annual Meeting of the Association for Child Psychoanalysis, 1970

Panel: Termination: problems and techniques. Reported by Robbins WS. J Am Psychoanal Assoc 23:166–176, 1975

Rangell L: An overview of the ending of an analysis, in Psychoanalysis in the Americas. Edited by Litman RE. New York, International Universities Press, 1966, pp 141–173 [Reprinted in Rangell L: The Human Core: The Intrapsychic Base of Behavior, Vol 2. Madison, CT, International Universities Press, 1990, pp 703–725]

Rangell L: The self in psychoanalytic theory. J Am Psychoanal Assoc 30:863–891, 1982

Reich A: On the termination of analysis. Int J Psychoanal 30:179–183, 1950

Shane M, Shane E: The end phase of analysis: indicators, functions, and tasks of termination. J Am Psychoanal Assoc 32:739–772, 1984

Siegel BL: Some thoughts on "Some Thoughts on Termination" by Leo Rangell. Psychoanalytic Inquiry 2:393–398, 1982

Spiegel LA: A review of contributions to a psychoanalytic theory of adolescence. Psychoanal Study Child 6:375–393, 1951

Stone L: The Psychoanalytic Situation: An Examination of Its Development and Essential Nature. New York, International Universities Press, 1961

Ticho EE: Termination of psychoanalysis: treatment goals, life goals. Psychoanal Q 41:315–333, 1972

Ticho GR: On self-analysis. Int J Psychoanal 48:308–318, 1967

Tyson P, Tyson RL: Psychoanalytic Theories of Development: An Integration. New Haven, CT, Yale University Press, 1990

Section IV

Research

Introduction to Section IV

Judy L. Kantrowitz, Ph.D.

Psychoanalytic theory does not lend itself to research easily. There are many reasons for this. Psychoanalytic concepts are complex, and it is difficult to establish reliability in their evaluation. It is often hard to develop criteria that reflect the original ideas sufficiently to test their validity. Metapsychological theory (a description of psychological process, comprising its dynamic, topographic, and economic aspects as defined by Freud, that refers to theoretical constructs) is too distant from observable behavior. Clinical theory offers greater potential for study, but the difficulties remain. The questions must be, on the one hand, defined discretely enough to allow for reliable and replicable observations and, on the other hand, complex enough that the findings contribute to knowledge in the field. To undertake meaningful research, we must be certain that the concept(s) studied reflects the current state of knowledge. Consistency in defining terms and observations linked to clinical concepts is essential; abstract and metapsychological language is to be avoided. The criteria that confirm or disprove our hypotheses need to be specified. All concepts require operational definitions to ensure comparability of meaning.

The psychoanalytic researcher who tries to study the clinical situation encounters difficulties at every step of the investigation: the influence of the observer, whose presence changes the field observed; the special characteristics of the volunteer, whose unknown motives lead to questions about representativeness and limit the generalizations that can be made from the findings; and the limitations of the data due to both the selected area of observation and the methods chosen to make those observations. Investigators who try to find data to support pivotal psychoanalytic concepts are limited to a technology that, although ever increasing in its sophistication, still lacks the complexity for investigating these multilayered constructs. Researchers who draw on related disciplines to illuminate and support psychoanalytic concepts must take into account the limitations in comparing one field with another.

In this section of this textbook, three areas of psychoanalytic research are reviewed: outcome studies of psychoanalysis and psychotherapy, empirical evidence for psychoanalytic assumptions, and the relationship of psychoanalysis to neuroscience. The authors present both the history of investigations and the state of knowledge in their areas of research. They each address the limitations of the research and the problems encountered because of the state of knowledge or the present level of technology.

Robert Wallerstein, in Chapter 17, reviews the conceptual, definitional, and methodological issues in investigations of psychoanalytic treatment outcomes. He traces the evolution of changing methods, definitions, and concepts over almost seven decades. The historical sweep of his comprehensive review of outcome studies allows the reader to see the interplay between theory and research findings. Psychoanalytic assumptions—such as the resolution and dissolution of the transference neurosis at termination, the primacy of interpretations as the curative element in treatment, and the interchangeability of analysts—are modified and reformulated as data from the outcome studies call these earlier conceptualizations into question. The new conceptualizations in turn lead to new studies. One trend in current research on psychoanalytic treatment attempts to relate empirical evidence from process and outcome studies. Another contemporary area of investigation focuses on the stability of the analytic outcome. The proposal to employ systematic follow-ups after the termination of psychoanalysis could address both research and clinical concerns about stability of outcome.

Howard Shevrin, in Chapter 18, presents the empirical data relevant to assumptions underlying the psychoanalytic method. Independent evidential support is offered to confirm the presence of a psychological causative unconscious revealed by a process of free association that is facilitated by a psychoanalyst's interventions. Shevrin reviews the independent evidence for the assumption that underlying causes have a history in the individual's past. He outlines the history of research studies that use the subliminal perception method that has become progressively more complex and sophisticated. Although studies conducted outside of the psychoanalytic treatment setting offer general support for the presence of a causative unconscious, Shevrin can find little independent evidence from research that free association facilitated by outside intervention reveals unconscious causation. A one-to-one relationship between childhood experience and unconscious conflict has not so far been demonstrated by cognate methods of investigation. Shevrin notes some of the limitations both of these studies and of the assumptions psychoanalysts have made about causation. He emphasizes that data from independent studies are not comparable to the data from psychoanalysis: one cannot extrapolate from observations of behavior to introspective descriptions of experience. Psychoanalysis has taught us, as Shevrin points out, "that the same behavior can 'mean' different things and that the inner experience of the same behavior—its causes—can differ greatly from time to time."

Morton Reiser, in Chapter 19, also considers the problems of the lack of comparability of data in his review of mind/brain research. Reiser concludes, as does Shevrin, that the introspective data from psychoanalysis are not comparable to and cannot meaningfully be correlated with objective quantitative data from neurobiological experimental studies. However, objectivity, reliability, and quantification in psychoanalytic data are more attainable now than previously because of the development and use of electronic sound and video recording techniques. These newer methods of investigation and the combined experimental methods of cognitive psychology and neural science may provide a bridge for studying the relationship between concepts and findings in both domains. Using the concept of memory, Reiser brings together two bodies of research. From cognitive neuroscience studies, he reports data showing that the same circuits and structures of the brain that carry out perception and memory also process affect, creating associational links between new and old perceptual data in the corticolimbic neural networks. From sleep and dream research studies, Reiser compiles parallel evidential support for the role of memory and affect in clinical material. Dreams produce nodal images that become linked in an extended network based on common affective themes. When one works with an individual patient over time, patterns of affective themes emerge that contain perceptual memory traces from earlier times that lead to core conflicts. These affect-laden memory traces linked with conflict are revived in dream images. Reiser makes clear that these two sets of data are from different domains. He sees the implication of these parallel findings as leading to reformulations of theory and investigations in other clinical situations in which the role of memory is central.

Although the areas and methods of investigation differ, these three authors share an appreciation of the complexity of undertaking psychoanalytic research. They document the difficulties but continue the generation of new hypotheses and methods based on previous studies. The implications of their findings have relevance for both theory and clinical practice. Their commitment to and excitement about systematic investigation of psychoanalytic theory and technique assure that the field will not stagnate. Their work serves as a springboard for the next generation of psychoanalytic researchers.

17

Outcomes of Psychoanalysis and Psychotherapy at Termination and at Follow-Up

Robert S. Wallerstein, M.D.

I n any discussion of the efficacy (i.e., the outcome) of psychoanaly-sis and of the linked psychoanalytic psychotherapies as treatment modalities, as discernible upon treatment termination and/or at fol-low-up, one must necessarily address a host of interrelated defini-tional, conceptual, methodological, and practical considerations that cover all the major theoretical and technical issues of the psychoana-lytic therapies as treatment procedures. These considerations in-clude the following:

1. The goals of these treatment modalities, both ideal and practical (i.e., realizable).
2. The issue of suitability or treatability as opposed to analyzability, the two being distinct, although often conflated.
3. The indications and contraindications for these treatments as these have evolved over time with increasing experience and expanding theoretical and technical knowledge. Consideration

of indications and contraindications for these treatments includes the issues of the widening or narrowing scope for analytic treatment and of so-called heroic indications for analysis.

4. The role of the initial diagnostic and evaluation procedures in proper (differential) treatment planning (as opposed to the view that only a trial of analysis or a trial of therapy can lead to proper formulation and prognostication).

5. The role of prediction (including the question of predictability) in relation to issues of outcome of expectable reach and limitation.

6. The theory of technique and of how treatment works, including a consideration of the procedures by which the goals of treatment are achieved—that is, a statement of the relationship of means to ends.

7. The similarities and differences between psychoanalysis and the dynamic psychotherapies based on the different therapeutic goals projected for patients with differing illness pictures and distinct character organizations. Through consideration of these similarities and differences, the appropriate specific technical approaches from within the available range of psychoanalytically based psychotherapies may be determined.

8. The criteria for "satisfactory" treatment termination.

9. Evaluation of results. This is a conceptual as well as technical issue involving assessment of therapeutic benefit versus analytic completeness in terms of resolution of intrapsychic conflict and structural changes in the ego.

10. Assessment of what theoretically constitutes the ideal state of mental health, and the unavoidable impingement on efforts to empirically make such an assessment by value judgments as well as by the vantage point and the partisan interests of the judge.

11. Determination of whether follow-up assessment, for clinical and/or research purposes, is a desirable, feasible, and appropriate activity in relation to psychoanalytic therapies.

12. The place of the continuing accretion of experience and knowledge concerning the aforementioned areas by the traditional case study method innovated by Freud versus the desirability or necessity for more formal systematic clinical research into these

issues by methods, of course, that are responsive to the subtlety and the complexity of the subjectivistic clinical phenomena and, at the same time, remain loyal to the canons of empirical science.

There is a considerable, and in some cases vast, literature, mostly based on clinical experience but in some instances based on research protocols, related to each of these areas of inquiry. To maintain a delimited and manageable focus on the central questions of the chapter, I do not specifically address any of this literature in detail, except for those reports momentarily germane to the central argument. I wish to focus instead on the issue of *outcomes in psychoanalysis* (with reference, where relevant, to the psychoanalytic psychotherapies) as assessed primarily at treatment termination, but also, especially in recent years, during planned follow-up. My primary emphasis in this chapter is on formal and systematic research study rather than the far larger and much antecedent clinical and theoretical literature on these issues out of which, of course, have grown the questions that research studies have addressed.[1]

First-Generation Research: Early Statistical Studies

As early as 1917, within the first decade of the introduction of psychoanalysis in America, Coriat reported on the therapeutic results achieved in 93 cases based on his own "personal investigations and experience" (Coriat 1917, p. 209). Of the 93 patients, 73% were declared either recovered or much improved, and these rates were nearly equal across all of the diagnostic categories used by Coriat, although those patients with more severe illness required longer

---

[1]This same focus frames a comprehensive, 45-page report (including tables and a nearly exhaustive bibliography) entitled "On the Efficacy of Psychoanalysis" (Bachrach et al. 1991) prepared by the Subcommittee on Outcome Research of the Committee on Scientific Activities of the American Psychoanalytic Association. Reference is made to that report for a more detailed and inclusive discussion of the issues covered in this chapter as well as for strategic and tactical recommendations for future research directions.

duration of treatment. As with all of the early statistical studies to be noted here, the judgments of improvement were made by the treating clinician based on (usually) unspecified criteria, and no individual clinical detail or supporting evidence was presented to enable the reader either to see the basis of the judgment or to arrive at an alternative conception.

In the decade of the 1930s several comparable (but larger scale) reports emerged from the collective experiences of the psychoanalytic clinic treatment centers of some of the pioneering psychoanalytic training institutes. Fenichel (1930) reported from the first decade of experience of the Berlin Psychoanalytic Institute, the first formally organized psychoanalytic training institute in the world. During that first decade, 1,955 consultations were conducted and 721 patients were accepted for analysis. Sixty percent of the "psychoneurotic" patients, but only 23% of the "psychotic" patients, were judged to have received substantial therapeutic benefits.[2] However, essentially the same proportion of patients were declared to be unchanged or worse in the two diagnostic categories (22% and 24%, respectively). Six years later, Jones (1936) reported on 738 applicants to the London Psychoanalytic Clinic, of whom 74 were taken into psychoanalysis. Forty-seven percent of the neurotic patients were judged to have benefited substantially, with only 10% judged to be unimproved or worse. Of the 15 so-called psychotic patients, 14 were considered "treatment failures." A year after Jones's report, Alexander (1937) reported on 157 cases from the Chicago Psychoanalytic Clinic; 63% of the neurotic patients, 40% of the psychotic patients, and 77% of patients whose symptoms were designated as "psychosomatic" were judged to have received substantial therapeutic benefit, with no more than 10% in any category judged to be unchanged or worse. During this same period, Kessel and Hyman (1933), two internists who followed up 29 cases referred for psychoanalysis, reported that the neurotic patients (all but two)

---

[2]Psychotic, in the context of the reports discussed in this paragraph, is to be taken as ambulatory and in some sense functioning in the community; the patient is considered "psychotic" from the standpoint of the quality of his or her mental life.

had benefited and that the psychotic patients' condition had remained unchanged or had worsened.

In a 1941 review article evaluating the results of psychoanalysis,
Knight combined the findings of the Berlin Psychoanalytic Institute
study, the London and Chicago Psychoanalytic Clinic studies, and
the Kessel and Hyman study and added 100 cases treated at The
Menninger Clinic between 1932 and 1941, where the overall results
were judged to be completely comparable to those in the other
studies in the observed outcomes with neurotic and psychotic patients. In the overall composite tabulation, comprising 952 cases,
patients were classified into neurotic, psychotic, psychosomatic,
and "other" categories based on whatever (unspecified) criteria governed the original judgments. The combined substantial therapeutic
benefit rate was approximately 60% for the neurotic patients, close
to 80% for the psychosomatic patients, and only 25% for the psychotic patients, with about 20% unchanged or worse among both
the neurotic and the psychotic patients. Knight made particular
reference to all the pitfalls of these simple statistical summaries, the
absence of consensually agreed-upon definitions and specified criteria, the crudity of nomenclature and case classification, and the
failure to address issues of the experience and skill of the therapists
in relation to cases of varying degrees of severity.

The most ambitious study of this first-generation genre was the
report of the Ad Hoc Committee on Central Fact Gathering Data of
the American Psychoanalytic Association (Hamburg et al. 1967).[3]
This committee, originally established in 1952, collected data over
a 5-year span and produced a report to the membership (unpublished) in 1958. The data consisted of 10,000 initial responses to
detailed questionnaires submitted by the 350 then members and the
450 then candidates-in-training in the American Psychoanalytic

---

[3]Although the span from Coriat (1917) to this study (1967) is a half-century, I refer
to all of these studies as "first generation" in terms of their degree of conceptual
and methodological sophistication—the state of the art that they represent—rather
than in temporal terms (although, of course, each "generation" of studies either
was initiated at a later point in time than its predecessor or spanned a later period
of time).

Association, plus responses to just over 3,000 termination question-naires submitted upon completion of treatment. The criteria for both diagnosis and improvement were, as with all the previous studies, unspecified, and numerous flaws in the original question-naire construction led to many unintended confusions, ambiguities, and omissions in the responses, leading to the original decision against scientific publication of the findings. In the early 1960s, however, a successor committee to the first was charged with re-viewing the data to try to salvage what was still scientifically useful and publishable. The Hamburg committee ultimately produced an "experience survey" (American psychoanalysis, circa the 1950s) comprising three areas: 1) facts about the demographics and the sociology of analytic practice, 2) analysts' opinions on their patients' diagnoses, and 3) analysts' opinions on the therapeutic results achieved. Judgments were made about changes in symptoms, in the patients' feeling states, in their character structures, and in their total functioning. Not unexpectedly, the great majority were de-clared substantially improved.

And in the last of this kind of study to be reviewed here, in the very next year, Feldman (1968) reported on the results of psycho-analysis in clinic case assignments based on the 11-year history of the clinic of the Southern California Psychoanalytic Institute. The group whose outcomes were under study consisted of 120 analytic patients selected from 960 evaluations and represented a total sam-ple, consecutive and unselected. The patients seemed more compre-hensively evaluated and studied than those in the earlier reports, having been chosen after 4 to 5 hours of group interview and com-mittee discussion and a careful review of the detailed semiannual Institute reports, which were gathered during the entire time the individuals were patients at the clinic and their analysts had not yet graduated. (Some of the patients could be followed into private practice status after their analysts graduated from the Institute.) Efforts were made to specify improvement criteria in the poor, fair, good, and very good categories. Difficulties were experienced for the research because of lack of clear and agreed-upon criteria, con-cepts, and language for diagnostic assessment, analyzability, and analytic results. Improvement rates reported were again completely comparable to those of all the preceding studies, with two-thirds of the patients being in the good or very good improvement categories.

Taken together, these so-called first-generation outcome and efficacy studies of psychoanalysis, the sequence of which actually spanned the half-century from 1917 to 1968, were scientifically simplistic and failed to command the interest of the psychoanalytic clinical world. Most analysts would, to some extent, agree with Glover (1954) in his ironic and dour assessment in the latter part of this time span:

> [L]ike most psycho-therapeutists, the psycho-analyst is a reluctant and inexpert statistician. No accurate records or after-histories of psycho-analytical treatment exist: such rough figures as can be obtained do not suggest that psycho-analysis is notably more successful than other forms of therapy: and in any case none of the figures is corrected for spontaneous remission or resolution of symptoms. (p. 393)

Glover further pointed out that "in the case of adults . . ., an after-history of at least 5 years is essential. Unfortunately it has to be admitted that satisfactory after-histories are seldom forthcoming: consequently our knowledge of the therapeutic range of psychoanalysis is vitiated by unchecked surmise which too often errs on the side of complacency" (p. 398). Glover also noted that "the success of a child analysis cannot be satisfactorily checked until an after-history of 15 years has been secured" (p. 398).

It is a polemic such as this that spurred what I call the second-generation studies: the efforts at more formal and systematic outcome research geared toward overcoming the glaring methodological simplicity that marked each of the studies described to this point.

Second-Generation Research: Formal and Systematic Outcome Studies

The methodological flaws in the first-generation–type statistical enumerations of psychoanalytic outcomes, which span the full half-century from 1917 to 1968, have already been indicated. I have discussed the lack of consensually agreed-upon criteria at almost every step—from initial diagnosis and assessments of analyzability to outcome judgments of therapeutic benefit and analytic result— and the use of these judgments by unspecified, and even unformulated, criteria by the (necessarily biased) therapist as, in most cases, the sole evidential primary database. Another methodological difficulty is that these studies have all been retrospective, with all the potential therein for bias; confounding and contamination of judgments; post hoc, ergo propter hoc reasoning and justification; and so forth.

Efforts to address these issues, including the introduction of methods of prospective inquiry and even of fashioning predictions to be validated or refuted by subsequent assessment, began in earnest in the decades of the 1950s and 1960s. Three major projects based on studies of clinic cases from the Boston, Columbia, and New York Psychoanalytic Institutes, respectively, stand out as the major representatives of this second-generation research approach.

Boston Psychoanalytic Institute Studies

In 1960, Knapp et al. reported on 100 supervised psychoanalytic cases from the Boston Psychoanalytic Institute clinic, in which the patients were rated initially (prospectively) for suitability for analysis. Twenty-seven of these patients were followed up just a year later by questionnaires addressed to the treating analysts to ascertain how suitable for psychoanalysis each patient indeed had turned out to be—to the extent that suitability was discernible and could be judged at that relatively early treatment point. To avoid the dangers of post hoc reasoning and reconstructive rationalization, the evaluation procedures (initial committee judgments on suitability and subsequent judgments of the treating analysts' questionnaire responses) were "blind" and were carried out by different judges in almost all instances. Considering the variable quality of the initial clinic records, written by many different persons, that constituted the data on which prediction was based, there was fair but limited success in assessing suitability for analysis at the initial evaluation. However, two significant limitations of this study should be remarked. First, the testing of the predictions took place only at the 1-year mark in treatment rather than more suitably upon termination of the therapy; clearly much can change in this regard—in both directions—at later points in the analysis, as clinical experience amply attests to. Second, and this is an issue in all research on this model, the cases selected by psychoanalytic institute clinic committees for student analyses were already carefully screened, with obviously unsuitable cases having already been rejected. The range of variability in the accepted cases was thus considerably narrowed, making differential prediction within that group inherently less reliable.

Sashin et al. (1975), inspired by Knapp et al.'s work, subsequently studied 183 patients treated at the Boston Psychoanalytic Institute clinic during the years 1959 to 1966. Final data were collected for 130 patients (72%) after an average of 675 treatment hours and at a point averaging 6 years after treatment termination. The effort was aimed at what the authors called a "quantitative, systematic study" of the "patient factor predictability of outcome" (p. 345). Predictor variables were assessed by use of a 103-item evaluation rating questionnaire and based on six major outcome criteria that first had been elaborated by Knight (1941) (i.e., restriction of life functioning by symptoms, subjective discomfort, work productivity, sexual adjustment, interpersonal relationships, availability of insight). Each criterion was assessed by a 5-point rating scale. Many predictor items were not rated by the judges (having been left unanswered too frequently, showed insufficient variation, or showed poor reliability). Of the 46 items finally retained, only 10 had any usefulness or predictive value in relation to assessed outcomes, and for these items only modest (albeit statistically significant) correlations were found. These few relationships, which might have appeared on the basis of chance alone, were studied to determine if they could be meaningfully understood in clinical terms, but the groupings "made little clinical sense" (Bachrach et al. 1991, p. 894, quoting personal communication from J. I. Sashin). In overall conclusion of these two Boston Psychoanalytic Institute studies, there was only fair prediction to judgments of analyzability as assessed at the 1-year mark in treatment, and there was no effective prediction of treatment outcomes from the patients' characteristics as judged at initial evaluation. Nor was any effort made to distinguish therapeutic benefit from the successful navigation of an analytic process over the treatment course. Further Boston Psychoanalytic Institute studies, by Kantrowitz and her co-workers, will be described later in this chapter as representative of the third generation of psychoanalytic outcome research studies.

Columbia Psychoanalytic Center Project

The findings from the Columbia Psychoanalytic Center Project, a study contemporaneous with the Boston Psychoanalytic Institute studies, were written up in a final accounting in a sequence of publications in 1985 (Bachrach et al. 1985; Weber et al. 1985a, 1985b, 1985c). The authors reported in sequence the characteristics of the patients, findings from the outcome study from sample 1 (1,348 patients treated between 1945 and 1962), findings from the outcome study (by somewhat altered and improved criteria) from sample 2 (237 patients treated between 1962 and 1971), and, finally, a clinical and methodological review with recommendations for future directions.

The project was designed to consist of prospective studies of large numbers of patients, with data collected from multiple perspectives over time (initially and upon treatment completion). This approach would provide opportunities to compare findings in psychoanalysis (about 40% of the total sample) with those in psychoanalytic psychotherapy (the other 60%), with patients all treated by the same body of therapists. The authors stated that all previous studies had been limited in at least one of the following ways: small sample size, inadequate range of information about outcomes, data not based on terminated cases, or findings based only on retrospective data. And no other study had permitted comparison of large numbers of terminated analyses and psychotherapies, conducted by the same analysts, in which all of the pertinent information was not based on retrospective assessment. Also, in the Columbia project the criteria for therapeutic benefit were established distinct from the criteria for analyzability (i.e., the judgment about the success of development of an analytic process). The criteria of *therapeutic benefit* comprised 1) the circumstances of treatment termination, 2) clinical judgments of overall improvement, and 3) change scores on various indices of improvement. The criteria of an evolved *analytic process* represented judgments about 1) patterns of handling psychological data, 2) more flexible use of ego resources, and 3) transference manifestations during treatment.

A most striking finding from this project was that, uniformly and across every category of patient, the therapeutic benefit measures always substantially exceeded what were referred to as the *analyzability measures* (presumably, measures of an evolved analytic process). For example, only 40% of those patients who completed analyses with good therapeutic benefit were characterized as having been "analyzed," as defined by the project criteria.[4] An equally striking finding is that the outcome of these treatments, both in terms of therapeutic benefit and in terms of analyzability, was only marginally predictable from the perspective of the initial evaluation, whether the direct predictions by the clinic's admissions service chief or the various scales of the presumed predictor variables were considered. This finding is, of course, fully in keeping with those from previous known studies—for example, the Boston Psychoanalytic Institute studies cited earlier—and of course is linked to the fact that the various analytic clinic populations in these studies were all carefully screened, with those individuals presumed to be overtly unsuitable for psychoanalysis having already been eliminated from consideration. As Weber et al. (1985a) cautiously state, "The prudent conclusion from these findings is not that therapeutic benefit or analysability are per se unpredictable, but that once a case has been carefully selected as suitable for analysis by a candidate, its eventual fate remains relatively indeterminate" (p. 135).

---

[4]The elucidation of the meaning of this startling kind of finding turned out to be a major focus of the findings and conclusions of The Psychotherapy Research Project of The Menninger Foundation (Wallerstein 1986, 1988), to be described later in this chapter.

Another significant finding of interest was that "retrospective assessments of patient qualities by the treating analyst show a more substantial relationship to outcome than assessments made at the beginning of treatment" (Weber et al. 1985a, p. 136). This difference in the relationship of assessments to outcome could clearly be based on either the greater accuracy of retrospective judgments at termination, the greater contamination of such judgments, or some undetermined admixture of both. More expected were the findings that those individuals selected for psychoanalysis were assessed initially as functioning at higher levels compared with those individuals selected for psychotherapy and that those in psychoanalysis achieved greater therapeutic benefit than did those in psychotherapy, especially when the analyses continued longer, beyond the candidates' graduations and into their private practices. This positive correlation between therapeutic benefit and treatment length did not hold for the psychotherapies in the same way, which caused the authors to suggest "that treatment length and therapeutic benefit are related for psychoanalysis, but perhaps not necessarily for other psychotherapies where progression does not pivot upon a natural process requiring years to evolve" (Weber et al. 1985a, pp. 136–137). This is, of course, a conclusion to which many might take exception.

In their overall conclusion, the authors stated that their sample (sample 1) was three times larger than any previously reported in the literature, that it was the first to have a psychotherapy comparison group, and that it was one of the first (along with the New York Psychoanalytic Institute study, to be described next) to make the conceptual distinction between analyzability and therapeutic benefit. The authors noted a major limitation—"We do not feel that the circumstances of this investigation provide more than the most rudimentary exploration of the contribution of the analyst's qualities to the treatment process" (Weber et al. 1985a, p. 138)—and this omission, of course, could have been a major contributor to the poor level of predictability of treatment outcomes. They stated in this regard that "not only may it be that a fundamental assessment of analytic potentials may only be possible in the course of analysis . . . but there are also matters of changing life circumstances and the *analyst-analysand match* to be considered" (p. 138; emphasis added).

Sample 2 was a smaller sample, gathered a decade after sample 1, and introduced some refinements in methods of data collection and involved some differences in observational vantage points. Regardless, in almost every particular, all of the findings of sample 1 were replicated. These confirmations were all reinforced from a data source that had not been tapped in sample 1, namely, patient accounts elicited from patient questionnaire responses before and after treatment. Again, the authors cited as of particular interest that "the evidence so far suggests that less than half the cases taken into analysis by candidates develop an analytic process and that the figure is not substantially higher for more experienced analysts" (Weber et al. 1985b, p. 261), and here they cited from the New York Psychoanalytic Institute studies, to be described in the next subsection.

Overall, Weber, Bachrach, and Solomon (1985b) concluded from both samples, which encompassed a more than 25-year span, that

> our findings in both studies and those of Erle (1979) and Erle & Goldberg (1984) [the New York Psychoanalytic Institute investigators] show that a substantially greater proportion of analysands derive therapeutic benefit than develop an analytic process, and that the development of an analytic process is associated with the highest levels of therapeutic benefit. Yet, what we do not yet know precisely is the nature and quality of therapeutic benefit associated with the development of an analytic process and without its development. (p. 261)

This last question of course, as already mentioned, was the central focus of The Psychotherapy Research Project of The Menninger Foundation, being carried out over this same time span, to be described later in this chapter in the section on third-generation research studies.

The final article by these authors in their series of four (Bachrach et al. 1985) was devoted to a review of clinical and methodological considerations. The authors stressed the advantages of their project over other comparable studies: 1) the sample size was very large; 2) the design was prospective, with prearranged schedules and hypotheses and predictive evaluations having been done before outcomes were known; 3) many (clinically meaningful) scales were incorporated; 4) independent judges were used, in addition to evaluations by patients and therapists; and 5) psychoanalysis and psychotherapy were comparatively assessed. Nonetheless, the authors acknowledged that theirs was essentially an opinion poll: "What we did was to have analysts assess cases in their customary ways and to have them express their judgments on quantitative dimensions" (Bachrach et al. 1985, p. 381). In other words, the investigators tried to make the opinions reliable (i.e., analysts would make similar judgments given the same set of data) and comparable through the use of standardized quantitative rating scales. This method, however, also made their work clinically relevant: "It is precisely because our methodology pivoted upon a clinical survey of psychoanalysts about their own cases and the cases of candidates, and was consistently framed according to standard clinical precepts, that we believe our findings bear correspondence to the findings of psychoanalytic research proper [i.e., the findings from the traditional psychoanalytic case study method]" (Bachrach et al. 1985, p. 381).

The most important substantive conclusion from the Columbia project had to do with the relationship of therapeutic benefit achieved to the development of a properly psychoanalytic process:

> [T]he observation is that some patients treated by psychoanalysis develop an analytic process and achieve therapeutic benefit, while others achieve therapeutic benefit while not apparently developing an analytic process. By analytic process we refer essentially to a collaborative endeavor between analyst and analysand in which increasingly intense and cyclic analysis of resistance and transference in free association evolves into the development of a transference neurosis and transference phenomena, and where continued analysis leads towards enhanced awareness and mastery of intrapsychic conflict which we conceptualize as structural change. . . . By therapeutic benefit we refer to the non-specific amelioration of symptoms and the general improvement in the mental economy of patients. (Bachrach et al. 1985, p. 382)

However, the linked and almost equally important finding was that the predictability of these developments "remains relatively indeterminate among carefully selected cases" (p. 381), or, stated alternatively, "that most suitably selected patients treated by psychoanalysis achieved substantial gains; though the level of these gains is no more than marginally predictable from the perspective of initial evaluation" (p. 386).

New York Psychoanalytic Institute Studies

The New York Psychoanalytic Institute studies (Erle 1979; Erle and Goldberg 1979, 1984) were designed similarly to the Columbia Psychoanalytic Institute Project, though with more of a focus on treatments carried out by more experienced analysts. The investigators began (Erle and Goldberg 1979) with a comprehensive and sophisticated treatment of the conceptual and methodological issues involved in proper outcome research (together with an excellent review of the literature on these issues), which they subsequently summarized as follows:

> In a review and discussion of the problems in the assessment of analyzability . . ., we noted: (a) a lack of consistency in the definition of terms; (b) difficulty developing and validating criteria for patient selection; (c) the assumption that prediction of analyzability is, or might be, reliably made at the outset of treatment; (d) failure to differentiate between analyzability and therapeutic benefit; (e) the need for a prospective study which would assess all phases of an analysis: selection, prediction, analytic process, and outcome. (Erle and Goldberg 1984, p. 715)

The first of the New York Psychoanalytic Institute studies (Erle 1979) consisted of a sample of 40 supervised analytic cases selected from 870 applicants to the Treatment Center of the New York Psychoanalytic Institute over a 2½-year span in the late 1960s. The results were completely comparable to those of the Boston and Columbia Psychoanalytic Institute studies. Twenty-five of the patients terminated satisfactorily (i.e., by mutual consent), but only 11 of these patients were considered to be completely analyzed; 24 of the patients were judged to have benefited substantially, but only 17 were judged to have been involved in a proper psychoanalytic process. Those who stayed in treatment for longer periods were judged to be more suitable and had better outcomes. However, 3 of the 9 who were in treatment more than 6 years were declared to have benefited substantially in an intensive psychotherapeutic sense but were judged to be not analyzed or analyzable. In a sample of 42 private patients from 7 analyst colleagues of Erle who started treatment in the same calendar period and were assessed in the same manner as the Treatment Center patients, substantially comparable results were obtained.

The second study (Erle and Goldberg 1984), extending the work of the earlier study, involved a sample of 160 private patients gathered over a subsequent 5-year time span from 16 cooperating experienced analysts. The sample, as evaluated by the treating analysts, ranged from those patients "made for analysis" to those taken into analysis on the basis of "heroic" indications (p. 722). The outcomes from these experienced analysts were completely comparable to results of their own (and those of others) earlier studies of clinic patients treated by candidates.

Pfeffer Studies (New York) and San Francisco and Chicago Replications

Over a time span parallel to these relatively large sample outcome studies of psychoanalytic clinic patient populations (as well as some comparison private patient groups), in which patients were assessed by pre- and/or post-treatment rating scales and grouped statistically, Pfeffer, also at the New York Psychoanalytic Institute Treatment Center, initiated a wholly other kind of outcome and follow-up study of terminated psychoanalyses by intensive individual case studies of a research-procured population (Pfeffer 1959, 1961, 1963). His first report was of nine patients who had completed analyses under the auspices of the New York Treatment Center and who agreed to a series of follow-up interviews by a "follow-up analyst" who had not conducted the treatment. The interviews were open-ended, once a week, and were considered "analytic" in the sense that they were "structured around the issue of results, but remain[ed] unstructured within this framework in that the patient . . . [took] the lead in introducing and elaborating various themes relating to results" (Pfeffer 1959, p. 420). The interviews ranged from two to seven in number before each participant agreed on a natural close. The chief finding, in all instances, consisted of the rapid reactivation of characteristic analytic transferences, including even acute and transitory symptom flare-ups, as if in relation to the original treating analyst, with subsequent rapid subsidence, at times aided by pertinent interpretations, and in a manner that indicated the new ways of neurotic conflict management achieved in the analysis. Of course "those aspects of the transference neurosis that are unanalyzed remain organized as transference residues which are available for neurotic reactions in certain life situations" (Pfeffer 1959, p. 437).

Pfeffer (1963), in the last of his series of reports, essayed a further description of, as well as a metapsychological explanation of, these "follow-up study transference phenomena" (p. 230): "The recurrence in the follow-up study of the major preanalytic symptomatology in the context of a revived transference neurosis as well as the quick subsidence of symptoms appear to support the idea that conflicts underlying symptoms are not actually shattered or obliterated by analysis but rather are only better mastered with new and more adequate solutions" (p. 234). The neurotic conflicts thus "lose their poignancy" (p. 237). The metapsychological explanation is that

> in the regression of the analytic process the person of the analyst initially becomes the present-day representative of the oedipal father of the past. Then with the resolution of the transference the analyst becomes, in addition, the father in relation to whom the oedipus complex is resolved. In the course of the analysis, the person of the analyst becomes, and after the analysis remains, it is here suggested, a permanent intrapsychic image intimately connected with both the regressively experienced conflicts and the resolution of these conflicts in the progression achieved. (p. 238)

Two other research groups, one in San Francisco (Oremland et al. 1975; Norman et al. 1976) and one in Chicago (Schlessinger and Robbins 1974, 1975, 1983), replicated the Pfeffer studies, with some slight alterations in method, and confirmed what has come to be called "the Pfeffer phenomenon." In the San Francisco studies the subjects were chosen from among individuals who, it was agreed, had been very successfully analyzed and yet with whom "specific areas of incompleteness were discovered when 'successful' cases were called back for restudy" (Oremland et al. 1975, p. 820). And in their further study the authors concluded that "the transference neurosis is not obliterated during analysis. Rather, the patient experiences, understands, and senses varying degrees of control over it—i.e., it becomes a structure that comes under the control of the unconscious ego" (Norman et al. 1976, p. 491). They further noted that the "infantile neurosis had not disappeared. What had changed was the degree to which it affected his [the individual whose case was under follow-up study] everyday life" (Norman et al. 1976, p. 492). The Chicago studies, with a more developmental focus, more specified and focused change criteria, and larger samples, likewise confirmed the Pfeffer findings. As Schlessinger and Robbins (1983) summarized,

> Psychic conflicts were not eliminated in the analytic process. The clinical material of the follow-ups demonstrated a repetitive pattern of conflicts. Accretions of insight were evident but the more significant outcome of the analysis appeared to be the development of a preconsciously active self-analytic function, in identification with the analyzing function of the analyst, as a learned mode of coping with conflicts. . . . The resources gained in the analytic process persisted, and their vitality was evident in response to renewed stress. (p. 9)

This focus on the development of the self-analytic function as (at least to some degree) a proper and expectable outcome in successful analyses has been highlighted as well by Kramer (1959) and Ticho (1967). The overall finding from all three groups—that even in analyses considered highly successful, neurotic conflicts are not obliterated or shattered, as was once felt to happen, but are tamed, muted, lose their poignancy, and so forth—is echoed in the well-known analytic quip that we all still recognize our good friends after their analyses.

Overview of Second-Generation Studies

Characteristic of these second-generation studies—whether group-aggregated broad statistical accountings (the Boston [Knapp et al. 1960; Sashin et al. 1975], Columbia [Bachrach et al. 1985; Weber et al. 1985a, 1985b, 1985c], and New York [Erle 1979; Erle and Goldberg 1979, 1984] studies) or individually focused, in-depth research studies (the New York [Pfeffer 1959, 1961, 1963), San Francisco [Norman et al. 1976; Oremland et al. 1975], and Chicago [Schlessinger and Robbins 1974, 1975, 1983] studies)—was the failure to conceptually or practically separate out outcome results discerned at treatment termination from the issue of the degree of stability of these results as revealed at some established follow-up point subsequent to the termination. There was, therefore, no way to determine whether there had been consolidation and further enhancement of treatment gains, simple maintenance of treatment achievements, or actual regression back toward the pretreatment state.

Conceptually these studies failed to accord specific theoretical status to what Rangell has called the "postanalytic phase" (see Rangell 1966/1990, pp. 718–725). A variety of possible courses characterize this phase. Some analyses are finished and the former patient does not return. In other cases the door is clearly left open for any returns that might be indicated. For example, as Rangell points out, "it is frequently the case that a patient with an optimum ending will call again, even years later, for a specific and localized need to which he is immediately accessible. The path between the analyst and the patient's unconscious can remain surprisingly open, so that a 'deep interpretation' may be made almost at once [in a single interview] with convincing receptivity and effective results" (p. 719). If this is not possible—if there is too rigid an avoidance of further contact—it is more likely that there has been a flaw and a major incompleteness in the termination. In still other cases the analytic relationship can be succeeded by a social or interprofessional relationship of greater or lesser constancy and intensity. Again, this can be rendered problematic in two opposite directions:

> At one extreme there is an undue retention of "the analytic attitude" when it is not only no longer indicated, but is actually inhibitory

and harmful.... At the other extreme, however, in an effort to avoid or undo such an outcome, there is sometimes a gratification or stimulation of the patient by a premature and excessive social intimacy which is reacted to as a threatened seduction.... In contrast to both of these, the desired goal should be a transition to a normal interchange in which the analyst can be seen and reacted to as a normal figure and no longer as an object for continued transference displacement. (Rangell 1966/1990, p. 722)

In the third-generation studies, to be described in the next section, the distinction between results at the termination point of the study and those at a subsequent prearranged follow-up point (from 2 to 5 years after the termination point of the study) becomes a clearly demarcated research focus. In the third-generation research, one advance over the second-generation studies is that many more varying forms of post-termination therapist-patient contact or interaction are delineated.

Third-Generation Research: Combined Process and Outcome Studies

What I refer to as "the third-generation studies" of the results of psychoanalysis have actually been carried out contemporaneously with the (conceptually) second-generation studies that have just been described. The third-generation research comprises systematic and formal psychoanalytic therapy research projects that have essayed both to assess psychoanalytic outcomes across a significant array of cases and to examine, via the intensive longitudinal individual study of each of the cases, the processes through which these outcomes were reached. These studies have combined the methodological approaches of the group-aggregated studies (the Boston, Columbia, and New York Psychoanalytic Institute studies) with those of the individually focused studies (the New York [Pfeffer], San Francisco, and Chicago studies). Like the best of these second-generation studies, the third-generation studies have carefully delineated definitions of terms, constructed rating scales, and tried to operationalize their criteria at each assessment point. The third-generation research consists of prospective studies, starting with initial pretreatment assessment of the patients. Unlike the second-generation studies, the third-generation studies have carefully separated outcomes at termination from functioning at a specified subsequent follow-up point in an effort to account for further changes, in either direction, that took place during this "postanalytic phase."

Bachrach and colleagues (1991), in their comprehensive survey of research on the efficacy of psychoanalysis, singled out the more recent Boston Psychoanalytic Society and Institute studies (Kantrowitz 1986; Kantrowitz et al. 1986, 1987a, 1987b, 1989, 1990a, 1990b, 1990c) and The Psychotherapy Research Project of The Menninger Foundation (Wallerstein 1986, 1988) as the only ones that met the array of specifications.

More Recent Boston Psychoanalytic Institute Studies

The more recent Boston Psychoanalytic Institute studies were undertaken in the 1970s, and the findings were published in the following decade. Twenty-two supervised psychoanalytic patients at the Boston Psychoanalytic Institute clinic were selected for prospective study. The initial assessment was based on a psychological projective test battery, with measures then being constructed of variables salient to therapeutic change: 1) affect availability, tolerance, complexity, and modulation; 2) level and quality of object relations; 3) adequacy of reality testing; and 4) the nature and level of motivation for change. Seven-point rating scales were constructed for each variable. The analyses were all conducted at a frequency of four or five times weekly and lasted from $2\frac{1}{2}$ to 9 years. Approximately a year after termination the initial projective test battery was repeated and both the patient and the treating analyst were interviewed.

Kantrowitz and colleagues described the findings from these studies in a series of papers (Kantrowitz et al. 1986, 1987a, 1987b). Nine of the 22 patients (41%) were felt to have had a successful analytic result, 5 (23%) were felt to have had a modified (limited) analytic result, and 8 (36%) were felt to be unanalyzed. Nonetheless, the greater number of patients achieved therapeutic benefits along each of the change and outcome dimensions, affect management, level and quality of object relationships, and adequacy of reality testing. Along each dimension the therapeutic benefit achieved exceeded the analytic result in terms of the degree of successfully completed analytic work. Of course, as Kantrowitz and colleagues (1986) pointed out, "there is support for the idea that the better the analytic result, the greater the improvement in the capacity to modulate affect [for example]" (p. 546). However, as the authors later noted, "the improvement [in level and quality of object relations] occurred even though approximately one third of these patients were in treatment which their analysts perceived as having failed to even partially resolve the transference neurosis" (Kantrowitz et al. 1987a, p. 35). The authors summarized that, "in support of the Menninger findings [to be discussed later in this section], the Boston study found that change in affect management (availability and tolerance), as measured in projective test data[,] is associated with at least partial resolution of the transference neurosis; such change can and does occur, however, without a transference neurosis being established or resolved" (Kantrowitz et al. 1986, p. 551). That is, a consistent and important finding was that therapeutic benefit was achieved by the majority of the patients and regularly in excess of what could be accounted for by the evocation and the interpretive resolution of the transference neurosis. This will be further elaborated in the discussion of the Menninger project, in which a major focus was on the effort to explicate the mechanisms of change on bases other than interpretive resolution of intrapsychic conflict.

Although most patients in the Kantrowitz et al. studies derived significant therapeutic benefit from their analytic experience, successful outcome could not be predicted from any of the predictor variables. This led Kantrowitz et al. (1989) to speculate "that a particularly important omission [from the predictor variables] might have been consideration of the effect of the [therapist-patient] match in shaping the two-person psychoanalytic interaction" (p. 899). By "match" the authors intend "an interactional concept" that refers to "a spectrum of compatibility and incompatibility of the patient and analyst which is relevant to the analytic work. . . . The

interaction may facilitate or impede the engagement in, and the resolution of, the analytic process" (p. 894). They further elaborated that
"match ... covers a broader field of phenomena in which countertransference is included as one of many types of match" (p. 895).
Match, the authors noted, "can also refer to observable styles, attitudes,
and personal characteristics" (p. 895), which are not necessarily rooted
in conflict. And, as Kantrowitz (1986) earlier noted, although "this
mesh of the analyst's personal qualities with those of the patient has
rarely been a special focus of attention ... most analysts when making
referrals do consider it; few assume that equally well-trained analysts
are completely interchangeable" (p. 273).

   This same team of investigators then conducted follow-up interviews with this same patient cohort in 1987, 5 to 10 years after the
treatment terminations. The interviews included the retrospective
assessment of the goodness of the analyst-patient match as one of
the variables considered to assess patient outcomes (Kantrowitz et
al. 1990a, 1990b, 1990c). Nineteen of the 22 individuals in the patient
cohort were located, and 18 agreed to the 2-hour semistructured
interview and open-ended treatment review (audiotaped and later
transcribed). Four data sets were now available: the pre- and post-
treatment projective tests, the interviews with the analysts at the
termination point, the interviews with the patients at the same
point, and the 1987 follow-up interviews with the patients. A variety
of change measures were used in the follow-up interviews; global
improvement ratings, affect tolerance and management, level and
quality of object relations, adequacy of reality testing, work satisfaction and accomplishment, and overall self-esteem. Overall results at
the follow-up point were as follows: 3 individuals had consolidated
and further improved, 4 had remained stable, 6 had deteriorated
somewhat but the gains from the original treatment had been restored upon additional treatment, and 4 had deteriorated and remained so despite additional treatment. One individual had
returned to the original analyst and was still in treatment and therefore was not counted.

   The most striking finding, however, was that, again, the stability
of achieved gains in the follow-up period could not be predicted
from the assessments at termination: "The stability of psychological

change five to ten years after termination of psychoanalysis could not be predicted by the analysts' assessment of the development and at least partial resolution of the transference neurosis during the analysis" (Kantrowitz et al. 1990a, p. 484). Or, put alternatively, "psychological changes were no more stable over time for the group of patients assessed as having achieved a successful analytic outcome concomitant with considerable therapeutic benefit than for the other group of patients assessed as having achieved therapeutic benefit alone" (Kantrowitz et al. 1990a, p. 493).

The authors also focused on the assessment of the development of the self-analytic function, presumably both a goal of treatment and a criterion for termination.[5] Again, although 13 of the 18 individuals described a variety of self-analytic processes, there was no direct relationship between the attainment of the self-analytic function and the maintenance of the therapeutic gains. As the authors pointed out,

> The present study suggests ... that some patients are able to acquire what we have traditionally considered an important analytic result, the development of a self-analytic function, without working through the transference neurosis, if we accept their analysts' assessments. (Kantrowitz et al. 1990b, p. 652)

The authors, in assessing the analyst-patient match, felt that with 12 of the 17 individuals, the kind of match (impeding or facilitating) did play a role in the outcome achieved (Kantrowitz et al. 1990c). They gave examples of what they considered facilitating matches with good ultimate outcomes, impeding matches with poor outcomes, and more complex situations in which the kind of match seemed at first to be facilitating to the unfolding of the analytic process but seemed later in the treatment to have an influence in preventing the completion of the analytic work.

---

[5]The authors defined "self-analysis" as "the capacity to observe and reflect upon one's own behaviors, feelings, or fantasy life in a manner that leads to understanding the meaning of that phenomenon in a new light" (Kantrowitz et al. 1990b, pp. 639–640).

The Menninger Foundation Studies

The other so-called third-generation psychoanalytic therapy research study to be described here is The Psychotherapy Research
Project of The Menninger Foundation, the most comprehensive and
ambitious research program of its type ever carried out (Wallerstein
1986, 1988; Wallerstein et al. 1956). The intent of The Psychotherapy
Research Project was to follow the treatment careers, and insofar as
possible the subsequent life careers, of a cohort of patients (ultimately 42 in number), half in psychoanalysis and half in other
psychoanalytic psychotherapies, with each patient receiving the
treatment deemed clinically indicated for him or her. It was intended that patients be followed, beginning with the period of their
initial pretreatment, 2-week-long comprehensive psychiatric evaluation, throughout the whole natural span of their treatment, however many years this might take. There was then to be planned,
formal follow-up for at least several years after the patients' treatment terminations and their (usual) return to their home communi-
ties, and then open-ended follow-up thereafter as circumstance
might make possible and as the span of interested observation
might last.

In actuality, the whole cohort of patients entered into their
treatment over the span of the mid-1950s (contemporaneous with
and even preceding many of the second-generation studies); their
periods of treatment ranged from as short as 6 months, in the case of
unanticipated treatment disruptions, to a full 12 years. All individuals in the sample were reached for formal follow-up information at
the designated 2- to 3-year mark, and over a third of the patients
were followed for periods ranging from 12 to 24 years beyond their
treatment terminations. Four of these patients were actually still in
ongoing treatment, with total observation spans of 30 years, at the
time of the writing of the final clinical accounting from this project
in 1981–1982 (Wallerstein 1986).

The aim of The Psychotherapy Research Project was to learn as
much as possible about 1) what changes actually take place in psychoanalysis and other psychoanalytically based psychotherapies
(*the outcome question*), and 2) how those changes come about or are

brought about, through the interactions over time of what variables in the patient, in the therapy and the therapist, and in the evolving life situation, that together co-determine those changes (*the process question*). How the project created and carried out a research program geared to try to answer those questions maximally has been described in detail over the 30-year span of this research enterprise in some 7 published books and monographs and approximately 70 articles. None of that will (or could) be repeated here.[6] At this point, it should just be iterated that three overall treatment groups were set up—psychoanalysis, expressive psychotherapy, and supportive psychotherapy—based on the then consensus in the psychoanalytic therapy literature on defining characteristics of these (discrete) therapeutic modes, together with differential indications derived from the dynamic formulations of the nature of the patients' lives, developmental history, character structure, and presenting-illness picture.

The project expectations within this framework were twofold: 1) the relatively modest expectation of giving a firmer empirical evidential base to this received conceptual wisdom, and 2) the more ambitious expectation of discerning and specifying in more detail both the particular reach and limitation of the therapeutic outcome for each patient appropriately treated within each of the proffered therapeutic approaches. There was an especial interest in the more empirical elaboration of the psychological change mechanisms operative within both the uncovering (i.e., expressive) and the "ego-strengthening" (i.e., supportive) therapeutic modes. Given this overall intent, what can be said about the actual therapeutic processes and outcomes as assessed some 30 years after the project start after the fullest possible study of the patient cohort across their treatments and their lives over this time span?

The book *Forty-Two Lives in Treatment* (Wallerstein 1986) represents the full statement of the findings and conclusions of The Psychotherapy Research Project. The main highlights can best be

---

[6]For a complete bibliography of The Psychotherapy Research Project publications, write to Robert S. Wallerstein, M.D., 290 Beach Road, Belvedere, California 94920.

presented through a lengthy quotation from the concluding part of an earlier summarizing paper (Wallerstein 1988).[7]

> I will bring our overall conclusions together as a series of sequential propositions regarding the appropriateness, the efficacy, the reach and the limitations of psychoanalysis (varyingly "classical" and modified) and of psychoanalytic psychotherapy or psychotherapies (varyingly expressive and supportive)—always of course with the caveat, as this was discerned within this segment of the overall patient population, that . . . data apply to . . . those (usually sicker) individuals who have been brought to or have sought their intensive analytically guided treatment within a psychoanalytic sanatorium setting.
>
> 1. The first proposition has to do with the distinctions so regularly made in the psychodynamic literature between "structural change" (gratuitously called "real" change), presumably based on the interpretive resolution of unconscious intrapsychic conflicts, and "behavioral change" or change in "manifest behavior patterns" that are (invidiously considered) "just altered techniques of adjustment" and presumably are all that can come out of the other, nonexpressive, noninterpretive, non-insight-aiming change mechanisms, i.e., the varieties of supportive psychotherapeutic techniques and implementations that I have presented in this paper. Intrinsic to this way of dichotomizing between kinds of change has always been the easy assumption that only structural change or real change as brought about through conflict resolution marked by appropriately achieved insight can have some guaran-

---

[7] A note is in order in regard to the relationship between the outcomes, to be described at this point, achieved in psychoanalyses and psychoanalytic psychotherapies as discerned in The Psychotherapy Research Project, and the outcomes described in the literature achieved in nonanalytic psychotherapies and in pharmacological treatments of mental and emotional disorders. The results (outcomes) are not strictly comparable for a variety of reasons. A most critical reason has to do with the difference in outcome criteria. In the pharmacological treatment of depression or the behavior modification treatment of phobias, for example, the outcome criterion employed is the amelioration of the specific target symptom. In psychoanalytic therapies, whether psychoanalysis proper or the range of psychoanalytic psychotherapies, the outcome criterion has to do with overall change in personality functioning in all relevant areas, with specific symptom abatement part of and subordinate to the overall change in behaviors, attitudes, and propensities (i.e., character and personality change).

tee of inherent stability, durability, and capacity to weather at least ordinary future environmental vicissitudes. It goes without saying that the commonplace value distinction automatically follows: that change brought about by expressive-analytic means is invariably "better," and this is, of course, the basis for the widely believed clinical operating maxim, "Be as expressive as you can be, and as supportive as you have to be." It is clear from the experiences documented from our PRP [The Psychotherapy Research Project] study that I question strongly the continued usefulness of this effort to link so tightly the *kind* of change achieved (real change, better change) with the intervention modes, expressive or supportive, by which it is brought about. If we accept the observations made from the study of our PRP cases that the changes reached in our more supportive therapies and via intrinsically supportive modes seemed often enough to be just as much structural change, to be just as stable and enduring, just as able to help the patient cope with life's subsequent happenstances, as the changes reached in our most expressive-analytic cases, then we must accept that the one way (the interpretive-uncovering way) does not have such an exclusive corner on inducing true structural change.

2. The second proposition has to do with the conventional proportionality argument, that therapeutic change will be at least proportional to the degree of achieved conflict resolution. Put this way, this proposition is almost unexceptionable, since it is clear that there can be significantly more change than there is true intrapsychic conflict resolution, on all the varying (supportive) bases through which change can be brought about, as well as properly proportionate change where the change is all or "purely" on the basis of conflict resolution with accompanying insight—if such an ideal type ever actually exists in practice—but it would be hard to imagine real conflict resolution (and accompanying insight) without at least proportional concomitant change in behaviors, dispositions, attitudes, symptoms, etc. However, in the closely related arena of the proportionality of therapeutic change to the degree of attained insight (as distinct from conflict resolution), I have already indicated in passing that we had three instances within our PRP population of achieved "insight" seemingly in excess of induced change. This, of course, is a common enough problem and a frequent enough complaint, both within and about psychoanalytic treatment, and has been the subject of considerable discussion in the psychoanalytic literature. In our own three instances such concepts as undigested intellectual insights or of insights within an

ego-weakened or psychotic transference state were invoked. What is meant here, of course, is insights that for varying reasons are not consequent to true conflict resolution and do not reflect it.

3. The third proposition, often linked to the proportionality argument, but in the light of our findings much more debatable and clearly separated from it, has to do with the necessity argument that effective conflict resolution is a necessary condition for at least certain kinds of change. It is certainly clear that an overall finding from our project—and almost an overriding one—has been the repeated demonstration that a substantial range of changes, in symptoms, in character traits, in personality functioning, and in life-style rooted in lifelong and repressed intrapsychic conflicts, have been brought about via the more supportive psychotherapeutic modes and techniques, cutting across the gamut of declared supportive *and* expressive (even analytic) therapies, and that in terms of the usual criteria—stability, durability, and capacity to withstand external or internal disruptive pressures—these changes can be (in many instances) quite indistinguishable from the changes brought about by typically expressive-analytic (interpretive, insight-producing) means.

4. A counterpart to the proposition based on the tendency to overestimate the necessity of the expressive (analytic) treatment mode and of its operation via conflict resolution in order to effect therapeutically desired change has been the other proposition, based on the happy finding that the supportive psychotherapeutic approaches, mechanisms, and techniques so often achieved far more than were expected of them—in fact often enough reached the kinds and degrees of change expected to depend on more expressive and insightful conflict resolutions—and did so in ways that represented indistinguishably "structural" changes, in terms of the usual indicators of that state. In fact, proportionately, each within its own category, the designated psychotherapy cases did as well as the designated psychoanalytic ones. More to the point, the (good) results in the one modality were not overall less stable or less enduring or less proof against subsequent environmental vicissitude than in the other. And more important still, within the psychotherapy group (of 20), the changes predicted, though more often predicated on the more expressive mechanisms and techniques, in fact were more often actually achieved—often the same changes—on the basis of the more supportive mechanisms and techniques.

And even more, within the psychoanalysis group (of 22), in almost every case there were modifications, parameters, etc., some analytically resolved but mostly not, and all of them in the direction of more supportive modes and aspects, so that even by our liberal PRP criteria, there were only 10 (not quite half) of the psychoanalytic cases who were in overall retrospect viewed as having been in essentially unaltered analyses, 6 who were in substantially modified (in supportive directions) analyses, and 6 who were considered really converted to varyingly supportive-expressive psychotherapies. By the usual stricter criteria of customary outpatient psychoanalytic and psychotherapy practice, just about every single one of our PRP psychoanalytic cases would be considered substantially altered in varyingly supportive directions. Put into overall perspective, more of the patients (psychotherapeutic and psychoanalytic alike) changed on the basis of designedly supportive interventions and mechanisms than had been expected or predicted beforehand, on the basis of either our clinical experience or our theoretical positions.

5. Considering these PRP treatment courses from the point of view of psychoanalysis as a treatment modality, just as more was accomplished than expected, and more stably, and more enduringly with psychotherapy, especially in its more supportive modes, so psychoanalysis, as the quintessentially expressive therapeutic mode, was more limited—at least with these patients—than had been anticipated or predicted. This has been, of course, a function of a variety of factors. In part it has reflected the whole ethos of the psychoanalytic sanatorium and the psychoanalytic treatment opportunities that it is intended to make possible. The dominant theme here has been the concept that the psychoanalytically guided sanatorium, with its possibilities for protection, care, and life management of the (temporarily) behaviorally disorganized and incompetent individual, could make possible the intensive psychoanalytic treatment of patients who could not be helped to resolve their deep-seated personality difficulties satisfactorily enough with any other or lesser treatment approach than psychoanalysis, but who also could not tolerate the rigors of the regressive psychoanalytic treatment process within the usual outpatient private practice setting.

This, of course, is what has led to the concept of psychoanalysis on the basis of so-called heroic indications, which by the nature of the kinds of patients brought to The Menninger Foundation, necessarily comprised such a substantial segment of our PRP psychoanalytic population. In our PRP experience, however, the central tenets of this proposition were found wanting; these particular patients characteristically did very poorly with the psychoanalytic treatment method, however it was modified by parameters, and however buttressed with concomitant hospitalization, and they in fact comprised the great bulk of the failed psychoanalytic treatment cases. On the other hand, there were certainly enough instances of very good outcomes among the very ill and disordered in support-ive-expressive psychotherapies that we can feel that the whole broad spectrum of "sicker" patients who are being talked about here can indeed do much better in an appropriately arranged and modulated supportive-expressive psychotherapy, if the ingredi-ents are put together skillfully and imaginatively enough, and if one can ensure truly sufficient concomitant life management. That last stipulation, concerning the need for adequate enough life management, is of course one of the central keys to the success of the treatment recommendations being proposed here, and, by that token, reaffirms a proper role either for the psychoanalytic sanato-rium or for some less controlled life regimen made more possible by modern-day, psychoactive-drug management. The big differ-ence is in the departure from the effort at psychoanalysis per se (even modified psychoanalysis) as the treatment of choice for these "sicker" patients in that setting. On this basis, I have spoken of the failing of the so-called heroic indications for *psychoanalysis,* and am instead inviting a repositioning of the pendulum in its swings over time around this issue, more in the direction of "narrowing indica-tions" for (proper) psychoanalysis along the lines marked out by Anna Freud.

6. The predictions made for prospective therapeutic courses and outcomes tended to be for more substantial change and for more permanent change (i.e., more "structural change") where the treatment plan and implementation were to be more expressive-analytic, and where these changes were expected to be more based on thoroughgoing intrapsychic conflict resolution through pro-cesses of interpretation, insight, and working through. And pari passu, and again in terms of the conventional psychodynamic wisdom, the more supportive the treatment was intended to be (had to be), the more limited and inherently unstable the antici-pated changes were predicted to be. What our research study has revealed in great detail is that all of this was (again, overall) consis-tently tempered and altered in the actual implementation in the treatment courses. The psychoanalyses, as a whole, as well as the expressive psychotherapies as a whole, were systematically modi-fied in the direction of introducing more supportive components

in widely varying ways, and by and large accomplished more limited outcomes than promised (hoped), and, as indicated, with a varying but often substantial amount of that accomplished by noninterpretive, i.e., supportive, means. The psychotherapies, on the other hand, often accomplished a fair amount more, and in several of the more spectacular cases a great deal more, than initially expected and promised, and again, however the admixture of intervention techniques was originally projected, with much of the change on the basis of more supportive modes than originally specified. (Wallerstein 1988, pp. 144–149)

Which brings us to the question, What did all this labor in The Psychotherapy Research Project add up to in relation to the issue of results and efficacy in psychoanalysis and in psychoanalytic psychotherapy? Again, I refer the reader to the same 1988 paper just quoted:

It can be most broadly generalized as follows: (1) The treatment results, with patients selected either as suitable for trials at psychoanalysis, or as appropriate for varying mixes of expressive-supportive psychotherapeutic approaches, tended—with this population sample—to converge, rather than diverge, in outcome. (2) Across the whole spectrum of treatment courses in the 42 patients, ranging from the most analytic-expressive, through the inextricably blended, onto the most single-mindedly supportive, in almost every instance—the psychoanalyses included—the treatment carried more supportive elements than originally intended, and these supportive elements accounted for substantially more of the changes achieved than had been originally anticipated. (3) The nature of supportive therapy, or better the supportive aspects of all psychotherapy, as conceptualized within a psychoanalytic theoretical framework, and as deployed by psychoanalytically knowledgeable therapists, bears far more respectful specification in all its form variants than has usually been accorded it in the psychodynamic literature. And (4) from the study of the kinds of changes reached by this cohort of patients, partly on an uncovering insight-aiming basis, and partly on the basis of the opposed covering-up varieties of supportive techniques, the changes themselves—divorced from how they were brought about—often seemed quite indistinguishable from each other, in terms of being so-called real or structural changes in personality functioning.

In the light of the conceptual and predictive framework within which the Psychotherapy Research Project of The Menninger Foundation was planned and implemented three decades earlier, there is of course considerable real surprise in the overall project findings: that these distinctive therapeutic modalities of psychoanalysis, expressive psychotherapy, supportive psychotherapy, etc., hardly exist in anywhere near ideal or pure form in the real world of actual practice; that real treatments in actual practice are inextricably intermingled blends of more or less expressive-interpretive and more-or-less supportive-stabilizing elements; that almost all treatments (including even presumably pure psychoanalyses) carry many more supportive components than are usually credited to them; that the overall outcomes achieved by those treatments that are more "analytic" as against those that are more "supportive" are less apart than our usual expectations for those differing modalities would portend; and that the kinds of changes achieved in treatments from the two ends of this spectrum are less different in nature and in permanence than again is usually expected, and indeed can often not be easily distinguished. None of this is where, three decades ago, we expected to be today. From another perspective, in terms of the corridor comments made by practitioners in informal interchanges about the conditions and nature of professional practice, which reflect what they regularly find that they do in actual practice as against how technique is conceptualized for formal presentation in professional meetings, our PRP research conclusions are far less surprising. (Wallerstein 1988, pp. 149–150)

Present Status of Outcome Research and Future Directions

Convergence of Empirical Process and Outcome Studies

Two major directions dominate contemporary investigation of psychoanalytic treatment processes and outcomes: 1) the convergence of empirical psychoanalytic process studies with the outcome studies described in the accounting of the several generations of outcome research, and 2) a more clinical concern with the values, both clinical and research, that would accrue from the more systematic

building of routine follow-up inquiry into regular clinical psychoanalytic practice.

The elaboration of empirical psychoanalytic process studies is
exemplified in the contents of a 1988 book, *Psychoanalytic Process
Research Strategies,* edited by Dahl, Kaechele, and Thomae. For approximately two decades now, a variety of psychoanalytic researchers, almost all in the United States and the former Federal
Republic of Germany, have been studying microscopically moment-
by-moment psychoanalytic interactional processes, in single hours
or in small segments of hours, using audiotaped and transcribed
psychoanalytic treatment hours. Many of the most significant of
these studies are represented by chapters in the aforementioned
book. Each group has developed its own concepts of the basic units
of the psychoanalytic situation and psychoanalytic process and its
own instruments to measure these, and has utilized these units in
relation to its own available database, though there has been some
sharing of sample hours from a particular psychoanalytic patient
(Mrs. C.) across a number of these groups. The book edited by Dahl
and colleagues represents an effort to compare findings from these
disparate studies in a search for principles of convergence. In the
introduction to that book, by Dahl, the hope is expressed that this
convergence will be found in the principle enunciated by Strupp,
Schacht, and Henry in the initial chapter: "that the description and
representation, theoretically *and* operationally, of a *patient's conflicts,*
of the *patient's treatment,* and of the *assessment of the outcome,* must be
congruent, which is to say, must be represented in comparable,
if not identical[,] terms" (Dahl et al. 1988, p. ix). This proposed
fundamental integrative principle is called the *principle of problem-
treatment-outcome congruence* ("P-T-O congruence" for short) (Strupp
et al. 1988, p. 7).

An effort is currently under way to put the principle of P-T-O
congruence to systematic empirical test. Wallerstein is currently
organizing, under the auspices of the American Psychoanalytic Association, the Collaborative Multi-Site Program of Psychoanalytic
Therapy Research, bringing together a total of 16 ongoing psychoanalytic therapy research groups studying psychoanalytic treatment processes and/or outcomes. To be included in this program are

all of the United States groups represented in the book edited by Dahl et al. and the current outcome study groups from the third-generation outcome studies (the group of Kantrowitz et al. in Boston and Wallerstein's current successor group to the The Menninger Foundation studies in San Francisco). The program is designed to accommodate all of the groups' using their own concepts and instruments upon a common, agreed-upon database from available audiotaped and transcribed psychoanalytic hours from already completed psychoanalytic treatments, as well as upon such hours from new psychoanalytic cases, so that appropriate before-and-after studies (as well as planned follow-ups) can be prospectively built in. A comparison of findings by all of these process and outcome study groups will enable us, finally, to determine the degrees of convergence of the concepts and instruments elaborated to this point by the different groups and, also, the degree and the nature of the imbrication of process and outcome studies (i.e., the degree to which the principle of P-T-O congruence holds).

This is one direction that what I call fourth-generation studies are taking—one that, if successful, promises not only to integrate the various psychoanalytic process studies carried out more or less independently over the past two decades, but also to integrate process studies with outcome studies, in a more complete fulfillment of an aim articulated as early as 1958 by The Psychotherapy Research Project (Wallerstein and Robbins 1958). At that time, Wallerstein and Robbins (1958) reported the following:

> We believe that in theory process and outcome are necessarily interlocked and that the hypotheses that will yield the answers sought can only come from . . . [a] study paying equal attention to both components. Any study of outcome, even if it only counts a percentage of cases "improved," must establish some criteria for "improvement," and these in turn derive from some conceptualization of the nature of the course of illness and the process of change, whether or not this is explicitly formulated. Similarly any study of process, in delineating patterns of change among variables, makes at varying points in time cross-sectional assessments which, if compared with one another, provide measures of treatment outcome. (p. 118)

This statement was a forerunner of the much later articulated principle of P-T-O congruence.

Enhanced Clinical Concern With Assessment of Outcome at Follow-Up

The second current direction of outcome and efficacy studies stems from more directly clinical considerations. This effort was spearheaded by a panel discussion chaired by Joseph Schachter at the December 1987 meeting of the American Psychoanalytic Association, "Evaluation of Outcome of Psychoanalytic Treatment," the participants of which addressed the question, "Should follow-up by the analyst be part of the post-termination phase of analytic treatment?" (Panel 1989). Schachter, in his opening presentation on that panel, posed the issue of the value of regular and systematic follow-up for a different—and more valid—perspective on psychoanalytic outcomes. He referred to a questionnaire on this subject that he had distributed to analysts in five institutes to which he had secured a 52% return. It was clear from these questionnaire results that conventional practice characteristically applies a double standard to follow-up contact. It is not expected with our patients, and when it does occur it is usually regarded as an expression of unfinished business or something untoward in the prior treatment or treatment termination. However, we take for granted the expectation of post-termination contact with our own training analysts.

Luborsky talked, based on a review of his research studies, of the positive effects of follow-up contact in maintaining treatment gains, especially useful for patients with some deficiency in the capacity for internalization of a secure representation of the analyst. He also said that it provided a useful opportunity to assess the need for further therapy, but cautioned that it could hinder the completion of the work of termination and separation. Martin indicated, from a clinical context and based on an experience survey, that two-thirds of successfully terminated analytic patients nonetheless contacted (mostly by letter or phone) their former analyst at some time within the first 3 years after termination. And, as reported by Johan (Panel 1989), "Martin pointed out that since we now accept the idea of adult developmental tasks, the door should be more than open for the analysand to return if and when he encounters new developmental tasks which bring him once again into unconscious conflict" (p. 817). Schlessinger pursued, from the perspective of his research studies, this same developmental theme, stating that every analysis is necessarily incomplete, that the post-termination phase is a period of consolidation of internalizations that constitute the developing self-analytic function, and that this process is consistently facilitated by planned follow-up interviews.

Wallerstein, on the same panel, began with the historical statement that

> psychoanalysis has never developed a tradition of systematic followup study to evaluate outcome and to improve technique and theory for a variety of reasons, partly theoretical, stemming from the conception of the unfolding transference neurosis and its analytical resolution as the precondition for cure [and that planned postanalytic contact between analyst and analysand would play into the perpetuation of transference fantasies and would represent a collusion reflecting some unanalyzed transference-countertransference residues], and partly historical, having to do with the happenstance of its development as a private practice–based discipline and training outside of the academic setting [where followup on treatment would more logically and naturally be built into the clinical operation]. (Wallerstein 1989, p. 921)

Then, drawing on The Psychotherapy Research Project experience, Wallerstein focused specifically on the consideration of the impact of follow-up qua follow-up on the issues of treatment termination and resolution and on the nature of the post-treatment period from three perspectives: 1) the range of conscious reactions to, and degrees of cooperation with, the planned follow-up studies with these research patients; 2) the reverberating meanings of the follow-up experience, including the potential for attenuating or delaying the psychological treatment closure or for, oppositely, facilitating the treatment resolution; and 3) the varieties of continuing contacts with the treating analyst during the follow-up period, including returns to treatment, as assessed by an experience survey.

Wallerstein concluded, overall, that "we can be reasonably reassured that the impact of *planned* follow-up study on the termination and outcome of psychoanalytic therapies, while not always inconsequential, does not seem to be detrimental and can, in fact, prove helpful and providential to the patient's and the therapist's therapeutic purposes" (Wallerstein 1989, p. 939). He also noted that "both our individual patients and our field as a science will profit thereby" (p. 940)—that is, by systematic, planned follow-up built into our regular clinical as well as research activities.

On the same panel, several speakers from the floor offered cautionary statements. Calder warned that "gains would be bought at a price" in terms of the "possibility of transference and countertransference acting out" (reported by Johan in Panel 1989), and Firestein pointed out that the evidence was still unclear in regard to which way is best to consolidate treatment gains, follow-up or no follow-up.

Schachter (1990a, 1990b) pursued a number of studies in follow-up to the aforementioned panel. Based on results from a questionnaire distributed to those who attended the panel, he found that the audience's attitude toward follow-up had indeed shifted toward the attitude of many of the panel participants, in that many in the audience stated that they now either hoped to hear from the patient or would like the patient to return to see them at some specified period after treatment termination (Schachter 1990a). Then, by reexamining Wallerstein's data from *Forty-Two Lives in Treatment*, Schachter stated his belief that Wallerstein's claim that in 6 of the 42 cases the follow-up seemed in some way to attenuate or delay processes that would otherwise have led to earlier psychological closure of the treatment course was not supported by Wallerstein's detailed data.

The most recent chapter in this story was a successor panel discussion, "Stability of Gain Achieved During Analytic Treatment From a Followup Perspective," also chaired by Schachter, at the December 1990 meeting of the American Psychoanalytic Association. For this panel, representatives of the two third-generation outcome studies, Kantrowitz and Wallerstein, were invited to give presentations in which each presented clinical data from two research-studied psychoanalytic cases—one in which treatment gains were consolidated, and even enhanced, during the post-termination follow-up period, and one in which there was regression toward the pretreatment status—in order to attempt to elucidate the determinants of an individual's course after treatment (i.e., why the individual tends toward consolidation or regression). Bachrach and Rangell were the invited discussants.

Wallerstein (1992), in his write-up for this panel, compared two treatment courses, two women with quite similar illness pictures (difficulties in being a mother, and unresolved hostile identifications with malevolent preoedipal mother imagoes), who had come to comparably seemingly satisfactory therapeutic results at treatment termination but who diverged sharply in their postanalytic courses. One was able to consolidate and extend her treatment gains, and this seemed related to the supportive family context, as well as to the availability and utilization of surrounding professional help, her family physician, the social worker in an adoption agency, and her parish priest. The other patient, who suffered a symptom regression and ultimately returned for reanalysis with the original analyst, ended her analysis alone and lonely, shouldering the responsibility for two children, both in therapy, and then entered an unhappy second marriage in which the ambivalent dependent relationship with the mother was reenacted, very different from the more secure dependency she had experienced with her first husband, who had died. In the report of the whole panel, Martin (Panel 1993) summarized the two contrasting cases presented by Wallerstein, as well as the two presented by Kantrowitz, and then distilled from the formal discussions by Bachrach and Rangell the overall feeling that the factors shaping these differing post-treatment courses were indeed very complex, often ambiguous, and, at this stage of our development, still largely to be elucidated. It is itself a very wide-open research arena.

It is clear, overall, that currently psychoanalytic therapy research—which has already yielded significant knowledge about the nature of treatment outcomes and efficacy as discerned at the termination and follow-up points through the first three generations of studies, from 1917 to the present—is now poised at a new level. This new level holds the possibility for truly accelerating breakthroughs, both methodological and substantive, as the current fourth generation of studies are carried out through their planned natural cycle.

References

Alexander F: Five Year Report of the Chicago Institute for Psychoanalysis: 1932–1937. Chicago, IL, Chicago Institute for Psychoanalysis, 1937

Bachrach HM, Weber JJ, Solomon M: Factors associated with the outcome of psychoanalysis (clinical and methodological considerations): report of the Columbia Psychoanalytic Center Research Project (IV). International Review of Psycho-Analysis 12:379–388, 1985

Bachrach HM, Galatzer-Levy R, Skolnikoff A, et al: On the efficacy of psychoanalysis. J Am Psychoanal Assoc 39:871–916, 1991

Coriat IH: Some statistical results of the psychoanalytic treatment of the psychoneuroses. Psychoanal Rev 4:209–216, 1917

Dahl H, Kaechele H, Thomae H: Psychoanalytic Process Research Strategies. New York, Springer-Verlag, 1988

Erle JB: An approach to the study of analyzability and analysis: the course of forty consecutive cases selected for supervised analysis. Psychoanal Q 48:198–228, 1979

Erle JB, Goldberg DA: Problems in the assessment of analyzability. Psychoanal Q 48:48–84, 1979

Erle JB, Goldberg DA: Observations on assessment of analyzability by experienced analysts. J Am Psychoanal Assoc 32:715–737, 1984

Feldman F: Results of psychoanalysis in clinic case assignments. J Am Psychoanal Assoc 16:274–300, 1968

Fenichel O: Statistischer bericht uber die therapeutische tatigkeit 1920–1930. Zehn Jahre Berliner Psychoanalytisches Institut Int Psychoanal Verlag, 1930, pp 13–19

Glover E: The indications for psycho-analysis. Journal of Mental Science 100:393–401, 1954

Hamburg DA, Bibring GL, Fisher C, et al: Report of Ad Hoc Committee on Central Fact-Gathering Data of the American Psychoanalytic Association. J Am Psychoanal Assoc 15:841–861, 1967

Jones E: Decannual report of the London Clinic of Psychoanalysis, 1926–1936. London, London Clinic of Psychoanalysis, 1936

Kantrowitz JL: The role of the patient-analyst "match" in the outcome of psychoanalysis. Annual of Psychoanalysis 14:273–297, 1986

Kantrowitz JL, Paolitto F, Sashin J, et al: Affect availability, tolerance, complexity, and modulation in psychoanalysis: followup of a longitudinal, prospective study. J Am Psychoanal Assoc 34:529–559, 1986

Kantrowitz JL, Katz AL, Paolitto F, et al: Changes in the level and quality of object relations in psychoanalysis: followup of a longitudinal, prospective study. J Am Psychoanal Assoc 35:23–46, 1987a

Kantrowitz JL, Katz AL, Paolitto F, et al: The role of reality testing in psychoanalysis: followup of 22 cases. J Am Psychoanal Assoc 35:367–385, 1987b

Kantrowitz JL, Katz AL, Greenman DA, et al: The patient-analyst match and the outcome of psychoanalysis: a pilot study. J Am Psychoanal Assoc 37:893–919, 1989

Kantrowitz JL, Katz AL, Paolitto F: Followup of psychoanalysis five to ten years after termination, I: stability of change. J Am Psychoanal Assoc 38:471–496, 1990a

Kantrowitz JL, Katz AL, Paolitto F: Followup of psychoanalysis five to ten years after termination, II: development of the self-analytic function. J Am Psychoanal Assoc 38:637–654, 1990b

Kantrowitz JL, Katz AL, Paolitto F: Followup of psychoanalysis five to ten years later after termination, III: the relation between resolution of the transference and the patient-analyst match. J Am Psychoanal Assoc 38:655–678, 1990c

Kessel L, Hyman H: The value of psychoanalysis as a therapeutic procedure. JAMA 101:1612–1615, 1933

Knapp PH, Levin S, McCarter RH, et al: Suitability for psychoanalysis: a review of one hundred supervised analytic cases. Psychoanal Q 29:459–477, 1960

Knight RP: Evaluation of the results of psychoanalytic therapy. Am J Psychiatry 98:434–446, 1941

Kramer MK: On the continuation of the analytic process after psychoanalysis (a self-observation). Int J Psychoanal 40:17–25, 1959

Norman HF, Blacker KH, Oremland JD, et al: The fate of the transference neurosis after termination of a satisfactory analysis. J Am Psychoanal Assoc 24:471–498, 1976

Oremland JD, Blacker KH, Norman HF: Incompleteness in "successful" psychoanalyses: a followup study. J Am Psychoanal Assoc 23:819–844, 1975

Panel: Evaluation of outcome of psychoanalytic treatment: should followup by the analyst be part of the post-termination phase of analytic treatment? Reported by Johan M. J Am Psychoanal Assoc 37:813–822, 1989

Panel: Stability of gains achieved during analytic treatment from a followup perspective. Reported by Martin G. J Am Psychoanal Assoc 41:209–217, 1993

Pfeffer AZ: A procedure for evaluating the results of psychoanalysis: a preliminary report. J Am Psychoanal Assoc 7:418–444, 1959

Pfeffer AZ: Followup study of a satisfactory analysis. J Am Psychoanal Assoc 9:698–718, 1961

Pfeffer AZ: The meaning of the analyst after analysis: a contribution to the theory of therapeutic results. J Am Psychoanal Assoc 11:229–244, 1963

Rangell L: An overview of the ending of an analysis (1966), in The Human Core: The Intrapsychic Base of Behavior. Vol 2. Madison, CT, International Universities Press, 1990, pp 703–725 [Originally published in Psychoanalysis in the Americas. Edited by Litman RE. New York, International Universities Press, 1966, pp 141–165]

Sashin JI, Eldred SH, van Amerongen ST: A search for predictive factors in institute supervised cases: a retrospective study of 183 cases from 1959–1966 at the Boston Psychoanalytic Society and Institute. Int J Psychoanal 56:343–359, 1975

Schachter J: Does a panel discussion on analytic technique have any effect on an audience of analysts? J Am Psychoanal Assoc 38:733–741, 1990a

Schachter J: Post-termination patient-analyst contact, I: analyst's attitudes and experience, II: impact on patients. Int J Psychoanal 71:475–486, 1990b

Schlessinger N, Robbins FP: Assessment and followup in psychoanalysis. J Am Psychoanal Assoc 22:542–567, 1974

Schlessinger N, Robbins FP: The psychoanalytic process: recurrent patterns of conflict and changes in ego functions. J Am Psychoanal Assoc 23:761–782, 1975

Schlessinger N, Robbins FP: A Developmental View of the Psychoanalytic Process: Follow-up Studies and Their Consequences. New York, International Universities Press, 1983

Strupp HH, Schacht TE, Henry WP: Problem-treatment-outcome congruence: a principle whose time has come, in Psychoanalytic Process Research Strategies. Edited by Dahl H, Kaechele H, Thomae H. New York, Springer-Verlag, 1988, pp 1–14

Ticho G: On self-analysis. Int J Psychoanal 48:308–318, 1967

Wallerstein RS: Forty-Two Lives in Treatment: A Study of Psychoanalysis and Psychotherapy. New York, Guilford, 1986

Wallerstein RS: Psychoanalysis and psychotherapy: relative roles reconsidered. Annual of Psychoanalysis 16:129–151, 1988

Wallerstein RS: Followup in psychoanalysis: clinical and research values. J Am Psychoanal Assoc 37:921–941, 1989

Wallerstein RS: Followup in psychoanalysis: what happens to treatment gains? J Am Psychoanal Assoc 40:665–690, 1992

Wallerstein RS, Robbins LL: Further notes on design and concepts [from The Psychotherapy Research Project of The Menninger Foundation: Second Report]. Bull Menninger Clin 22:117–125, 1958

Wallerstein RS, Robbins LL, Sargent HD, et al: The Psychotherapy Research Project of The Menninger Foundation: rationale, method and sample use. Bull Menninger Clin 20:221–278, 1956

Weber JJ, Bachrach HM, Solomon M: Factors associated with the outcome of psychoanalysis: Report of the Columbia Psychoanalytic Center Research Project (II). International Review of Psycho-Analysis 12:127–141, 1985a

Weber JJ, Bachrach HM, Solomon M: Factors associated with the outcome of psychoanalysis: Report of the Columbia Psychoanalytic Center Research Project (III). International Review of Psycho-Analysis 12:251–262, 1985b

Weber JJ, Solomon M, Bachrach HM: Characteristics of psychoanalytic clinic patients: Report of the Columbia Psychoanalytic Center Research Project (I). International Review of Psycho-Analysis 12:13–26, 1985c

18

Psychoanalytic Research: Experimental Evidence in Support of Basic Psychoanalytic Assumptions

Howard Shevrin, Ph.D.

Rare among sciences, psychoanalysis is both an applied and a basic science. From the outset, Freud conceived of psychoanalysis as a new kind of investigative method, a treatment of mental disorders, and a theory of mind. He believed that it was through the psychoanalytic investigative method practiced as a treatment that we would learn about facts of the mind, in particular the extent and nature of its unconscious aspect, that would yield a unique and comprehensive theory of mental functioning.

In 1895, early in his nascent career as the first psychoanalyst, Freud attempted to formulate a comprehensive theory of this kind, entitled "Project for a Scientific Psychology" (Freud 1950[1895]). In this daring undertaking, Freud drew upon his early clinical findings obtained with an as yet not fully formed psychoanalytic method and attempted to explain these observations on the basis of highly speculative neurophysiological theories. He decided that this early ambitious effort was premature and did not complete or publish this theory. The original manuscript was found among his papers, and an edited version was finally published in 1954 (Bonaparte et al. 1954). Pribram and Gill (1976), in a careful assessment of the "Project" from the standpoint of modern cognitive theory, pointed out that Freud anticipated several important discoveries, such as the notions of a "neuron" as the functional unit of the nervous system and the synapses connecting these neurons (Freud called them "contact barriers"). More recently, Erdelyi (1984) has also drawn upon the "Project" to show that embedded in it are quite modern ideas about cognition. Psychoanalysis was thus conceived from the outset as providing the basis for a comprehensive psychological theory linked closely to the brain.

Freud nevertheless believed that the main, if not exclusive, source of observations for this comprehensive theory was to be found in the clinical application of the method as a psychological treatment. Only in this way, he believed, could the phenomena necessary for the theory be obtained. Brenner (1982) and Edelson (1988) have in different ways supported this view of Freud's. Others (Grunbaum 1989; Holzman 1985) have criticized this position as too narrowly restricting psychoanalysis.

The position that will be developed in this chapter is in agreement with both of these seemingly contradictory views. It will be my main aim in this chapter to show that, properly understood, the psychoanalytic method has a significant range of application and, as do all methods, significant limitations. By first examining the nature of the method, I undertake to demonstrate how the body of psychoanalytic data proper and related bodies of data in psychology together constitute substantial evidence in support of at least several fundamental tenets of psychoanalysis. Insofar as the psychoanalytic method has been, from Freud's time to the present, at the core of psychoanalysis as both a treatment and a science, it is essential at the beginning of our inquiry to describe and assess this method. In my analysis I pay particular attention to the assumptions of the method and what is required for their independent evidential support. I then try to show how evidence in several important areas of independent investigation does, in fact, lend credence to these assumptions undergirding the psychoanalytic method.

Basic Assumptions of the Psychoanalytic Method

Every method must start with certain assumptions, and the psychoanalytic method is no exception. At the same time, we must not confuse our analysis of the assumptions underlying the method with the actual way in which the method developed historically. Scientific methods develop by fits and starts, are changed with the experience of their practitioners, or are shaped, as in the case of psychoanalysis, by one powerful intellect. Nevertheless, one can stand back and examine the method and, logically but not historically, inquire as to its inherent organization as a scientific instrument of investigation. In so doing, we should not confuse the method itself with how the method is used (i.e., its technical application) or with the explanatory theories developed to make sense of the findings brought to light by the method. We will in this section be talking about the method itself and ignoring its technical applications in treatment and the explanatory theories (see Shevrin 1984 for an extended discussion of these issues).

Psychoanalytic method is based on four essential assumptions:

1. There is a psychological causative unconscious.
2. Free associations can lead to discovering these unconscious psychological causes.
3. The psychoanalyst's interventions serve to "free up" the free association process so that the discovery of underlying unconscious causes can be facilitated.
4. These underlying causes have a history in the individual's past.

If you are ready to "buy" these assumptions, then in principle you are ready to apply the psychoanalytic method. It is in the nature of any assumption, however, that the assumption is taken for granted without proof being necessary. Ultimately, however, methods stand or fall on the truth of their assumptions.

To take one historical example, in the 18th century, the practice of mesmerism assumed the existence of "animal magnetism" that passed from the mesmeric therapist to the patient and cured the patient's largely psychological disorder. When a royal French commission, including such scientific luminaries of the time as Lavoisier and Franklin, concluded that there was no scientific support for the existence of "animal magnetism," mesmerism was dealt a fatal blow, although it persisted for many years, and gradually fell into disrepute. Along with its demise, unfortunately, many important observations and phenomena related to what later would be called hypnosis also disappeared for over half a century (Ellenberger 1970).

Another historical example is provided by the 19th-century practice of phrenology, in which the method of examining a person's cranium for tell-tale bumps that would reveal underlying mental faculties and personal propensities was based on the assumption that there was a close relationship between the contours of the cranium and underlying brain regions and functions. When this did not, in fact, turn out to be the case, phrenology was finished as a science, although some of its generative ideas about brain localization live on, but in more complex forms and tied to assumptions more fully validated by more elaborate methods, such as positron-emission tomography.

The assumption of a psychological, causative unconscious. As noted by Edelson (1984), that a psychological causative unconscious exists is a fundamental presupposition of psychoanalysis (see also Shevrin 1984). Citing Freud in this respect from *The Interpretation of Dreams* (Freud 1900, p. 531)—that "when conscious purposive ideas are abandoned, *concealed* [i.e., unconscious] purposive ideas assume control of the current of ideas" (emphasis and interpolation added by present author)—Edelson correctly points out that the same method based on its presuppositions "cannot . . . be used to provide evidential support for them" (p. 135). Evidential support for the presuppositions of the psychoanalytic method must be provided by methods *independent* of the psychoanalytic method. It follows, then, that independent evidence must be found for the psychological causative nature of unconscious mental processes.[1]

The assumption that free associations can reveal unconscious psychological causes. The deceptively simple instruction to the analytic patient is to "say whatever comes to mind" and not to censor any thoughts or feelings. To the extent that the patient follows this instruction, it is assumed that these free associations will lead to and reveal the nature of the unconscious causes. As an important corollary of this assumption, it is also the case that these unconscious causes may not be revealed *directly* but through various disguises. Freud, in the same passage cited earlier by Edelson (1984), noted that one of the theorems of the psychoanalysis of neuroses was that "superficial associations are only substitutes by displacement for suppressed deeper ones" (Freud 1900, p. 531). But what are the rules or laws governing these indirect manifestations?

As Rapaport (1944/1967) pointed out, we lack a canon of psychoanalytic inferences. The method *assumes* that there must be such a canon, but working it out is another matter. The absence of such a canon is reflected in the question, often asked halfjokingly, How do we judge from the pattern of free associations when the patient is talking about a cigar and when he is really talking about a phallus? Although often treated as something of a joke, making this distinction in all its various manifestations is at the heart of psychoanalytic understanding. Yet, in effect, it is *assumed* that we can infer from so-called displacements and substitute formations the underlying "meaning," that is, the unconscious cause.

The assumption that the psychoanalyst's interventions can "free up" the free association process. In its simplest form, the assumption that the psychoanalyst's interventions can "free up" the free association process requires that it be possible for the analyst to

---

[1]By *psychological*, psychoanalysts refer to ordinary elements of experience: perceptions, memories, thoughts, feelings, motivations, and so forth.

assist the patient to overcome obstacles and difficulties in the free association process by appropriate interventions. These interventions can be directed at any impediment to the free association process, from the patient's silence to complex intellectualizations. Interventions can take a variety of forms, from questions, to clarifications, to confrontations, to propositional statements of cause-and-effect relationships referred to as *interpretations* (Ramzy and Shevrin 1976). These interventions all have the same aim: to overcome "resistance" (i.e., impediments to free associations) and to free the process to uncover unconscious causes.

The assumption that the underlying psychological causes have a personal history. The assumption that the underlying psychological causes have a personal history is self-evident in its meaning. What needs to be stressed so as not to misapprehend the scope of the assumption is that the assumption posits nothing about *how far back in time* these essential underlying causes go. The effective causes might be quite recent, or the explanation of the phenomenon might not be complete unless we were to trace it back to childhood. How far back one needs to go is an empirical, and not a methodological, issue.

Evidence in Support of the Basic Assumptions of the Psychoanalytic Method

The Assumption of a Psychological, Causative Unconscious

Freud was aware of the need for independent evidence for his assumption of a psychological causative unconscious. He thought that substantial independent evidence was already available, mainly provided by the phenomenon of posthypnotic suggestion. However, the truly unconscious status of posthypnotic suggestion has been challenged by investigators who have explained hypnosis on the basis of social role rather than on the basis of an altered state of consciousness (Sarbin and Coe 1972). From the "social role" standpoint, the posthypnotic suggestion is not "repressed" or "dissociated," but, rather, response bias induced by the hypnotic subject's appreciation of what is expected of him or her by the hypnotist accounts for the outcome.

There were, however, a number of early hypnotic studies that attempted to demonstrate not only the role of posthypnotic suggestion but also the way suggestion was transformed or disguised when it was finally acted upon posthypnotically (Schroetter 1911/1951; Roffenstein 1924/1951; Nachmansohn 1925/1951). Setting aside the social role explanation of hypnosis for the moment, and accepting the view that hypnosis involves an altered state of consciousness resulting subsequently in an absence of awareness, investigators in these early studies undertook not only to show the operation of an unconscious cause affecting behavior but also to provide evidence to support the other "pillar" of Freud's presuppositional base for free associations: that the unconscious purposive influence is often evident through various displacements and substitutions. In these early studies an effort was made to find out if these unconscious causes reveal themselves in consciousness through various transformations. If such support could have been found, it would indeed have been important because it would have provided independent evidence for perhaps the most difficult presupposition of all. Always, the psychoanalyst is in the position of inferring from indirect evidence the presence of the psychological unconscious cause. From the outset, psychoanalysis has been challenged exactly on this score because there did not appear to be any clear objective set of rules on the basis of which these inferences could be ordered. Difficulties in establishing reliability in psychoanalytic judgments may also be the result of this same problem, because different analysts may be following different rules of inference with respect to the same psychoanalytic material. These early hypnotic studies were the first to attempt to establish the nature of these transformations on the basis of which psychoanalysts make their inferences about what is going on unconsciously. Unfortunately, these studies were, on the whole, poorly executed and, more important, relied on the same kind of intuitive inferences that psychoanalysts rely on in the clinical situation. Nevertheless, these early studies were suggestive of a direction in which research could develop and, by the very efforts, indicate that these early investigators understood the importance of providing independent evidence for significant psychoanalytic presuppositions. We will encounter later in this chapter other efforts to deal with this same problem.

About the same time as these early hypnotist-investigators were conducting their experiments, a Viennese sensory physiologist, Otto Poetzl (1917/1960), was developing a new method for exploring independently of the psychoanalytic clinical situation the role of unconscious psychological causes and their transformations in conscious experience. Deriving from his experience as a neurologist attending to brain-injured soldiers during World War I, Poetzl's method involved the brief exposure of complex visual scenes, only part of which could be consciously glimpsed by the subject at the time of exposure. He was then able to demonstrate that the elements of the picture not noted consciously at the time of exposure would reappear in dreams that the subjects had that night and reported to the experimenter the following day. So began the remarkable history of the use of subliminal perception, which was in time to be fruitfully exploited by a number of psychoanalytic investigators.

Poetzl (1917/1960) had a remarkable speculative gift and, for his time, an unusual empirical, if not experimental, turn of mind. Experience with brain-injured patients in World War I, particularly patients with occipital lesions in the brain, led Poetzl to hypothesize that normally functioning visual perception is based on an "abstracting" process that inhibits a variety of more primitive processes, such as diplopia (double vision).[2] However, injury to the visual cortex impairs this abstracting process and frees primitive processes, such as diplopia, from inhibition. One important consequence is that simultaneously perceived aspects of the stimulus in normal perception are experienced sequentially. Poetzl further believed

---

[2]Recent research on stereoscopic vision would tend to support Poetzl's earlier notion insofar as we know that in stereoscopic vision either a blend of the two images coming from the separate eyes or a suppression of one of the images occurs.

that this view of the perceptual process paralleled what Freud was describing as condensation and displacement, in particular as they occurred in dreaming.[3] He hypothesized that this abstracting process impaired by brain injury could be functionally impaired in non-brain-injured individuals by brief presentations of visual stimuli. Poetzl was, as noted above, able to show for the first time that previously unseen parts of a briefly flashed picture appeared to emerge in dreams reported the following day.

In a series of empirical studies of individual subjects, Poetzl identified many instances of apparent symbolic transformation in dreams of unreported pictorial elements, as well as various spatial rotations, fragmentations, and reversals of figure ground that he likened to Freud's primary process mechanisms reflected in superficial associations and various substitute formations.

The subliminal perception method invented by Poetzl made it possible to study under controlled conditions the influence of an unconscious psychological cause on consciousness. At the very least, Poetzl's work demonstrated that much more registers in the perceptual apparatus than is consciously available at the time and that these registrations out of awareness can then have an effect on subsequent experiences such as dreams. Poetzl also tried to demonstrate that the mechanisms of condensation, displacement, and symbol formation were at work in the manner in which these subliminal perceptions were processed. However, as with findings from the early posthypnotic suggestion experiments, these findings were often the result of the same kind of inferences from manifest content that the analyst employed with clinical data and thus could not be considered as independent evidence for the nature of these transformations. It would also need to be said that these early experiments were by modern experimental standards poorly controlled, anecdotal, and interpreted in a highly speculative manner. Nevertheless, it is of some importance to take note of the fact that Freud referred to Poetzl's groundbreaking work in a footnote,

---

[3] The reader is referred to Chapter 1, in which Leo Rangell discusses the role of condensation and displacement as incidences of the primary process.

added in 1919, in *The Interpretation of Dreams* (1900, p. 181), citing the Poetzl research as a significant addition to Freud's dream theory and believing that the method held great promise.

With this early work on subliminal perception, a significant question emerged that has by no means been settled. Poetzl believed that the "primitive" perceptions that emerge with the disinhibition of the visual "abstracting" process because of either organic damage or brief exposures are inherent in perception itself and thus are not necessarily the result of dynamic defensive processes. Rather, these defensive processes "use" these by-products of perceptual disinhibition but do not cause them. In short, they are not the *by-product*, but rather the convenient *targets* of such displacements and substitute formations. In more recent language, the question can be phrased as follows: Is the "primary process" a mode of early thought that persists as an undercurrent in adult life and that is put to defensive use, or is it always the outcome of defensive processes? The answer to this question is not only of purely scientific interest but also of clinical relevance. If a patient is in a regressed, or even psychotic, state, can we still interpret the appearance of primary process ideation as mainly the outcome of displacements and substitute formations subject to psychoanalytic interpretation, or is this simply the only mode of thinking available, in which case its contents may or may not be subject to psychoanalytic inference?[4]

In a series of pioneering experiments, Fisher repeated and extended the Poetzl procedure (Fisher 1956, 1957, 1960; Fisher and Paul 1959; Paul and Fisher 1959). Although his early experiments were empirical rather than experimental in nature in keeping with what Poetzl originally did, Fisher's later experiments were well controlled. The same peculiar "primitive" perceptions emerged in Fisher's research as emerged in Poetzl's. Seemingly, fragments of the subliminal visual stimulus would appear in dreams and images (e.g., a portion of a star appearing as a number 4), or there would be figure-ground reversals atypical of waking perception. It is of inter-

---

[4]See Holt 1967 for an extended discussion of this issue.

est to note that these "primitive" part-perceptions resembled the way in which perceptions are "broken down" in the course of their processing, as described by Reiser (1990) based on the work of Mishkin (1982). Poetzl may have been more correct than he realized. The fragmentary percepts emerging as a result of subliminal registration may indeed be the pieces of the perception-in-formation that are initially disassembled and then reassembled, as described by Mishkin. In this case, then, displacements and substitute formations may initially be perceptual givens that are then put to defensive use. At this point, an important caveat must be mentioned: The potential displacements and substitute formations thus far addressed have been dealt with mainly on a *perceptual level* and not on a conceptual and symbolic level, although the two tend to merge.

The method of subliminal perception begun by Poetzl and advanced by Fisher is the first method—independent of the psychoanalytic method—to provide the opportunity for investigating, on the one hand, unconscious psychological causes and, on the other, the way in which these causes affect conscious processes. This method therefore allows one to address both the first assumption having to do with unconscious psychological causes and a corollary of the free association assumption having to do with displacements and substitute formations. A body of research of such rich relevance is of particular importance to psychoanalysis and the foundations of its method. To the extent that these findings stand up, then, it cannot be said, as it was said of phrenology and mesmerism, that whatever phenomena psychoanalysis may bring to light, its fundamentional understanding is based on unsubstantiated assumptions, as some continue to say (Crick and Mitchison 1983; Hobson and McCarley 1977).

Subsequent to the work of Poetzl and Fisher, considerable research began to appear. By 1971 so much had been accomplished that it was possible for Dixon (1971) to publish a book-length review and assessment of subliminal research. This book was followed 10 years later by another book (Dixon 1981), bringing matters up to date on the intervening decade, during which research on subliminal perception had been taken up by cognitive psychologists. In that same vein, Shevrin and Dickman (1980) reviewed research on selective attention and subliminal perception, demonstrating how the two are closely related, theoretically and empirically. By 1980, on a purely theoretical and methodological basis, Shevrin and Dickman could say with some confidence that the psychoanalytic assumption of a psychological causative unconscious had received ample independent support. Two further reviews have appeared, one dealing with research on subliminal perception and dreaming (Shevrin 1986) and the other with subliminal perception and repression (Shevrin 1990).

However, it could be argued that the assumption of a psychological causative unconscious had, to that time, received only the most *general* support. The research did not support any concept of drive or motive as unconscious psychological causes, nor did it provide strong evidence for the way in which unconscious causes affect consciousness. With respect to the latter, it could be said that the early subliminal evidence strongly suggested that the transformations undergone by unconscious causes are more a function of cognitive than a function of motivational dynamic factors. Several lines of later research have attempted to go beyond the purely cognitive to include drive and motive as they bear on dynamic considerations.

Silverman's large body of research on subliminal psychodynamic activation might be considered an effort in this general direction (Silverman 1983). One particular paradigm might serve to illustrate Silverman's approach. In several experiments he attempted to show that a subliminal stimulus ("Beating Dad") would enhance dart-throwing ability in males and that the opposite message would diminish this ability. The subliminal stimulus drew directly on oedipal dynamics. Dart-throwing success might be seen as a substitute formation replacing more direct unconscious competitive strivings with father. Results have been mixed, with some experiments yielding positive results and others failing to replicate those results (see Balay and Shevrin 1988 for a review and evaluation of Silverman's research).

In a series of experiments Shevrin and co-workers introduced a novel stimulus that was designed to tap certain characteristics of primary process substitute formations and displacements (see

Shevrin 1973 for a review of this research). It was intended to demonstrate that a subliminal stimulus registering unconsciously would affect consciousness in predictably different ways consistent with clinical experience and in particular with Freud's theory of dream formation. The stimulus most often used was a picture of a pen and knee, an instance of a commonplace puzzle called a *rebus* (the pictorial representation of a word, in this case the word "penny").

Freud had discussed in some detail, in particular in *The Interpretation of Dreams,* the ways in which words are often treated as sounds in dreams and recombined in novel ways unrelated to their original meanings. In effect, words are treated as concrete sound patterns detached from their denotation, much as a contour in a picture can be recombined and rearranged in a new manner (e.g., a contour depicting a hill can be incorporated as a contour depicting a breast). Using a rebus stimulus allows one to identify two predictable transformations with some precision and reliability: 1) the *rebus combination* (i.e., the picture of the pen and knee) constituting a pictorial representation of a word (i.e., "penny"), with its associations such as money, nickel, and so forth; and 2) *clang associations* to the words pen and knee (e.g., words such as "pennant," containing the clang sound "pen," and words such as "any," containing the clang sound "knee"). Finally, conceptual associations of the pen and knee could also be identified (i.e., words such as "ink," "paper," "leg" or "foot," etc.). Scoring reliability would pose no problem because the judges' task was essentially clerical once adequate normative lists of associations were obtained. Shevrin and Luborsky (1961) indeed found that both rebus and clang effects could be demonstrated subliminally by using a priming list of words containing the rebus word and clang associates.

In a series of three studies employing the rebus stimulus, Stross and Shevrin (1962, 1965, 1968) explored the nature of subliminal transformations in hypnosis and the waking state. The rebus stimulus was flashed once at 1 msec under moderate illumination. Subjects were asked to describe, either in a hypnotic or a waking state, whatever they could see of the stimulus. It was determined that the stimuli were subliminal in both states and, indeed, that repeated recalls of the stimulus did not enhance recovery in either state.

Following their unsuccessful attempts to describe the briefly flashed stimuli, the subjects were asked to produce a number of other responses: 1) consciously visualized images, 2) free association words, and 3) dream recalls. Stross and Shevrin found that hypnosis enhanced subliminal *conceptual* effects (i.e., associations like leg to knee) but did not enhance the clang and rebus effects. For rebus effects to appear, a nighttime dream was necessary. The consciously visualized images contained aspects of the stimulus but mainly on the conceptual level. Hypnosis could enhance conceptual recovery, although a nighttime dream was apparently necessary for rebus effects to appear. Of further interest was the enhancing effect of hypnosis upon a subsequent waking state in which subjects continued to show the hypermnesic properties (enhanced recovery of subliminal contents) of the previous hypnotic state, whereas subjects in the waking state preceding hypnosis did not. On the whole, the findings did not support the earlier Fisher results that primary process transformations begin almost immediately following the exposure of the picture. A dream did appear to be necessary for recovering primary process transformations. It could still be argued, however, that the primary process transformations investigated with the rebus technique were verbal, whereas those studied by Fisher were visual, and that visual primary process transformations are more likely to occur without dreaming, perhaps because of their close kinship to the nature of perceptual processing itself (Mishkin 1982), whereas verbal transformations may be closer to the symbolic level.

Shevrin and Fisher (1967) conducted a sleep/dream study, with 10 female subjects, wherein the penny was compared with a blank stimulus. Responses were obtained following Stage 1 rapid eye movement (REM) sleep and Stage 2 non-REM (NREM) sleep. The main hypothesis of the study was that rebus effects would appear following Stage 1 REM sleep and that conceptual effects would appear following Stage 2 NREM sleep. Dreaming mainly occurs in REM sleep and nondream experience in NREM sleep. The findings clearly supported the hypothesis for associations obtained following awakenings from these two different sleep stages. It was as if the sleeping state, whether REM or NREM, persisted in its effects in the immediately following waking state, a finding parallel to an earlier finding (Stross and Shevrin 1968) that the hypnotic state influenced the subsequent waking state. Moreover, it appeared that the two sleep stages enhanced their respective subliminal recoveries (rebus level for REM, conceptual level for NREM) when compared with associations obtained in the waking state following the subliminal presentation. Subliminal effects, either primary process or secondary process, were greater in their respective states of consciousness during sleep than in the waking state preceding sleep. When it is borne in mind that in this study during sleep the subject was awakened alternately following REM and NREM states, it would appear that subliminal effects change as a function of state (dreaming vs. nondreaming) within the same person for the same stimulus.

Although these rebus studies demonstrated that a subliminal stimulus undergoes different transformations depending on whether the subject is awake or asleep, in dreaming or in nondreaming sleep, these findings were still unrelated to motivational dynamics, as a particular class of unconscious psychological causes. The positive outcome of the rebus research was to show how, as a function of state, unconscious factors could affect consciousness differently than conscious factors. If it could be argued that lying on the couch and free-associating helps the patient achieve such a changed state of consciousness, then the rebus studies could provide independent evidence as to how unconscious causes affect the free association process. We will take up this point later in this chapter.

By way of another subliminal research paradigm, Shevrin and co-workers attempted to investigate unconscious conflict and motivational dynamics (Shevrin 1988; Shevrin et al. 1992, in press). Patients suffering from phobic and pathological grief reactions were carefully assessed in a series of audio-recorded interviews and psychological tests. A team of four psychoanalysts studied the protocols and arrived at a formulation of the unconscious conflict causing the symptoms. The judges then selected words used by each patient that captured the nature of the conscious symptomatic experience and the purported unconscious conflict. These words and suitable control words were then presented to the patients subliminally and supraliminally. Brain responses in the form of event-related potentials were obtained, drawing upon an innovation already used in several previous rebus studies (Shevrin 1973). It was possible to show that on the basis of certain frequency features of the brain response, the unconscious conflict words were classified correctly only when presented subliminally, and not supraliminally. The reverse appeared to be true for the conscious symptom words. It was as if the brain could "recognize" the unconscious conflict words as belonging together only when they were presented out of awareness. When the words were presented in awareness, the brain responded as if it did not "recognize" that these same words went together. It was tempting to hypothesize that some defensive, inhibitory process supervened when the words were presented supraliminally.

These findings can be illustrated by the following case:

> The patient, a young man of 20, suffered from a public eating phobia. Whenever he attempted to eat at a cafeteria, restaurant, or any public place, he would experience severe difficulties in swallowing, he would become extremely anxious and short of breath, his heart would beat rapidly, and he would develop a severe and instantaneous headache, nausea, and generalized tension. As soon as he would leave the public eating place, all of his symptoms would immediately disappear.
>
> Following a careful analysis of the patient's interview and test protocols, the clinical research group decided that the most likely unconscious conflict accounting for the patient's symptom involved an intense struggle over oedipal wishes. In particular, there was a dream the patient reported in the first interview that he continued to elaborate in one way or another throughout the evaluation. In this dream, a figure appeared behind the chimney in a room in which the patient was sleeping, emerged threateningly, and in the final version of the dream thrust a sword under the bed in which the patient was sleeping that emerged through the patient's throat. The figure behind the chimney was eventually identified as one of his closest friends, John, from whom at one time he had succeeded in winning a girl, only to give her up shortly thereafter, a pattern repeated many times with other male friends—a clear oedipal scenario. Once when the patient was describing the dream in the interview, he was surprised by a sensation

he suddenly experienced. This sensation traveled from his temple to the neck and was something like a tension in his muscle that was not altogether unpleasant. He related this sensation to his experience of having difficulty swallowing in a public eating place, but indicated that the effect of the sensation during his recounting of the dream was the opposite, pleasant rather than anxiety arousing.

Despite the violence of the dream, throughout the evaluation the patient was compliant and forthcoming and described all of his relationships in this manner. On the basis of evidence such as that provided by the dream, the clinical team concluded that the patient was attempting to defend himself against intense oedipal competitive and rivalrous feelings by taking on the role of a compliant, submissive young man, in particular in his relationships with other men.

Some of the words selected to capture the patient's conscious experience of his symptom were "swallowing," "cafeteria," and "short of breath." Some of the words or phrases selected to capture the patient's hypothesized unconscious conflicts were "stab me," "John," "ripped apart," and "men hugging." The violent words were selected to capture the patient's anxiety over being attacked for his competitive strivings as appeared in his revealing dream, while a phrase like "men hugging," used by the patient elsewhere in the protocols, was selected to characterize something of the friendly, compliant position toward men.

The results of this investigation demonstrated that an unconscious conflict identified for a particular patient and reflected in the patient's own words (as in treatment) was correlated with different brain events consciously and unconsciously. However, only indirectly did the research bear upon the way in which an unconscious conflict affects consciousness. The previous rebus research and this last described investigation, when taken in combination, show that unconscious psychological causes affect consciousness in a qualitatively different way—by way of what Freud referred to as "superficial associations" (rebus effects)—and that unconscious conflict has an existence independent of the psychoanalyst's inferences from conscious manifestations, an *independence* supported by the brain correlates. However, these studies do not demonstrate these two principles—a causative unconscious revealed through superficial associations—at work on the same data, a task that remains for the future.

The Assumption That Free Associations Can Reveal Unconscious Psychological Causes

Although there has been much written on the free association process based on clinical experience (Kris 1982), there has unfortunately been very little research on the free association process independent of the clinical situation. In addition, the few studies for which findings have been reported were preliminary approaches. The first such study was conducted by Colby (1960), who created a quasi-experimental analytic situation in which male subjects were paid for lying down on a couch and following the free association rule while being audio-recorded. The main variable of interest was the presence of the experimenter sitting behind the subject but not saying anything, or his absence.

Colby wished to find out what influence the presence of the experimenter would have on the subject's free associations. He determined that the experimenter's presence resulted in the subject's free associations becoming more characterized by references to people, including references to males (the same sex as the experimenter). Colby interpreted his results as indicating that the mere presence of the psychoanalyst was sufficient to cathect or activate object relations patterns, in particular those bearing on the same sex as that of the analyst.

Bordin (1966) investigated the relationship between various personality characteristics and properties of the free association process, such as 1) *involvement,* or the degree to which feeling and thought were present simultaneously; 2) *spontaneity,* or the degree to which experiences were related free of ordered, sequential control; and 3) *freedom,* or the degree to which blocking and circumlocutions were absent. Free associations were collected in experimental circumstances similar to those in Colby's (1960) study. Ratings along the dimensions of involvement, spontaneity, and freedom for 40 subjects were tested for correlation with these subjects' scores on a variety of personality tests, including the Rorschach. Among a number of significant correlations, two Rorschach indices are of special interest in defining the personality attributes conducive to the free association process: 1) number of sex-related responses and

2) number of form-differentiated responses. The increased number of sex-related responses pointed to a greater freedom of access to material ordinarily not communicated, while the increased number of form-differentiated responses indicated a capacity to remain in good touch with reality. The subject who free-associates success-fully has the kind of personality that can allow access to conflictual material, quite often sexual, while maintaining good contact with reality. Although perhaps of greater interest from a clinical perspec-tive than from a methodological standpoint, the study shows that in a nonclinical setting, free associations can lead in the direction of significant unconscious content and that the more freely the subject can associate, the more likely this is to be the case.

Clearly a need exists for more independent research on the nature of the free association process as it bears on the significant psychoanalytic assumption that free associations can reveal uncon-scious causes.

The Assumption That the Psychoanalyst's Interventions Can "Free Up" the Free Association Process

The research on how the free association process can reveal uncon-scious psychological causes is fragmentary, but the research on the effects of interventions on free associations, outside the clinical set-ting, is even more limited. Colby (1961), in another study, demon-strated that an intervention stated in terms of cause and effect by the experimenter resulted in more forthcoming associations than an intervention in the form of a question. Colby's experiment is of interest not only because studies such as Colby's are rare but also because this experiment is an attempt to examine experimentally the effectiveness of interpretations.

The subjects in Colby's study were four young men who partici-pated in a situation similar to that in Colby's earlier study described in the previous subsection. This time, however, the experimenter, after waiting for some 10 to 25 minutes after the start of a session, would either ask a question appropriate to the subject's associa-tions or make what Colby referred to as a "causal-correlative" state-ment. The measure used was the amount of "amplification" of free associations that followed. By "amplification," Colby referred to utterances as "proceedant" (i.e., amplifying upon the persons or topics involved in the intervention) or, on the contrary, "avoidant." The main finding was that causal-correlative statements resulted in significantly more proceedant associations, as well as more associations in general. An illustration of a causal-correlative interpretation and its effects is offered by Colby (1961, p. 234) and presented in shortened form here:

> S.: Frank borrows his uncle's car. . . . He doesn't care about his appearance. He gets mad at people that dress up. . . . I feel like I'm shaking. As if . . . is the room shaking? Feels like its shaking.
>
> E.: You feel the room is shaking because this guy shakes you up more than you realize.
>
> S.: Well . . . Yeah. I figure he actually has that kind of effect on me. . . . I guess subconsciously . . . Well, I can't remember when I've thought about it outside. . . . I'd be actually scared to go and talk to him because the guy would really be offended. . . . I'm mad. What can I say? Keep away from my girl? You know, this sounds like presumptuousness, possessive. . . .

Note how the intervention hinges on the double meaning of the word "shake," an example of the indirect way in which unconscious causes affect free associations. Limiting the findings from Colby's study is the fact that we do not know how correct or incorrect the interpretation was and whether he had in fact identified the unconscious cause for the subject's shaking. The evidence is circumstantial and persuasive but not beyond challenge.

The way in which free associations are assumed to reveal unconscious causes has as much to do with the particular state of mind the individual achieves as with the operation of specific inhibitory defenses. In fact, the two may be closely related. The individual's lying on the couch, not seeing the analyst, and attempting to be as open as possible may induce a change in state, or mind-set, toward a more passive, receptive position. There are a number of subliminal studies showing that this kind of mind-set is conducive to the recovery of subliminal stimuli (Fisher and Paul 1959; Fiss 1966; Fiss et al. 1963; Murch 1969). In a recent study, M. Snodgrass, H. Shevrin, and M. Kopka showed that when the subject was told to guess the subliminal stimulus by letting a word pop into his mind, the subject did better if, paradoxically, he did not try hard to do it. This result suggests that to intend or to exert effort to recover unconscious contents does not work; rather, one must let "it" happen.

The Assumption That the Underlying Psychological Causes Have a Personal History

Here we venture into an extremely complex set of problems that have only in recent years been explored, mainly, the relationship between, on the one hand, the data obtained from the application of the psychoanalytic method and the explanatory theories these data have elicited and, on the other, the observations of children and the theories these observations have necessitated. Our interest is not in the empirical issues as such, but in their methodological implications. In the genetic assumption underlying the psychoanalytic method, it is simply asserted that the psychological unconscious causes go back in time, that is, have a history in the individual's past. Implicit in this assumption is nothing about how far back in the individual's history the causative experiences lie. But no matter how far back one can trace these experiences, it must be shown that they have a determining effect on the pathology treated in the psychoanalysis. It is the latter requirement that causes the greatest empirical and logical difficulty. Let us illustrate the achievement and the problem with two fairly widely known psychoanalytic ideas: infantile sexuality and the Oedipus complex.

Infantile sexuality.   It was apparently the case that Freud—a proper Victorian gentleman, albeit a physician of worldy experience—was surprised by his patients' revelations that their sexual experiences were not restricted to adulthood or even adolescence, but went back to early childhood as well. Moreover, these early sexual experiences appeared to be causally related to their later difficulties. The patient known as the Wolf Man reported that at 18 months he saw his parents having intercourse, with his father behind his mother, on three separate occasions (Freud 1918[1914]). This early experience, as reported by the patient, appeared to have greatly affected the patient and played a significant role in his later difficulties. Apparently the psychoanalytic method unearthed a quite early childhood cause of later adult pathology.

First, it is important, as indicated earlier, to distinguish between the data as such and the posited cause-and-effect relationships in the data. The Wolf Man's telling Freud of a childhood primal scene memory is, in its own right, a datum. A particular power of the psychoanalytic method is that it elicits from patients many childhood memories, a significant number of them sexual in content, and that these memories seem, from the context of recall in the treatment process, related to their adult experiences. These considerations are all relevant to the psychoanalytic task; in this important respect, they have a prima facie validity. It is the patient's own experience that results in the emergence of these early memories of a sexual nature; this emergence is not determined or biased by the psychoanalytic method. The psychoanalyst is free to form the hypothesis that current difficulties appear to have earlier childhood causes. On the other hand, to establish the validity of this hypothesis is a totally different matter. Can a child of 18 months be capable of such perceptions and form discrete memories of them? Even if these conditions were met, how does one establish that they were in fact causative, given that so much has happened between 18 months and the time of the adult treatment? Meissner (1989), in an excellent critical evaluation of the role of infant research in psychoanalysis, cites the results of a study by Kohlberg, Ricks, and Snarey (1984) devoted to assessing the role of childhood development as predictive of adult adjustment. The study concluded that there was little support for the idea that emotionally disturbed children necessarily become disturbed adults. Moreover, emotional deprivation, trauma, or conflict in early childhood need not lead to adult pathology. At best, psychoanalysts can take the position that early pathology may be a *necessary*, but not *sufficient*, condition for adult pathology. Neurotic adults all may show early childhood pathology, but not all individuals with early pathology develop into neurotic adults.

However, even this formulation leaves unanswered the question as to *whether* and in *what way* early pathology causes adult pathology. As Meissner points out, the fact that some early memories recalled in psychoanalysis are consonant with adult pathology does not in itself establish that these early experiences were causes of the adult pathology. Edelson (1984) has argued pursuasively that *enumerative inductionism*—that is, simply finding and adding up positive instances—does not constitute proof unless we can also demonstrate that in the absence of these experiences the phenomenon would not have occurred.

Oedipus complex.   Let us next turn our attention to the Oedipus complex, the discussion of which may perhaps suggest a way out of this difficulty. On the basis of his own self-analysis and the subsequent analysis of many patients, Freud hypothesized that each individual passes through a certain period of emotional development between the ages of roughly 3 and 6 years in which the child desires and loves the parent of the opposite sex and rejects and hates the parent of the same sex. How and to what extent this developmental crisis is resolved leaves its mark, largely unconscious, on all of us.

First, we can see that Freud's hypothesis posits that certain significant unconscious psychological causes begin their work at about age 3 years. The genetic assumption is thus given a quite early beginning. Second, the hypothesis claims universality—that all children go through this stage. It would seem that this particular claim is subject to empirical validation by cross-cultural observation. Third, the hypothesis claims that the oedipal crisis and how it is resolved persist as unconscious psychological causes and significantly influence the course of later adult neurosis. It is with respect to this claim that Meissner's analysis and the outcome of Kohlberg et al.'s study prove so fatal to those who would insist that the causal links are established by infant research.

It is possible to imagine, as Freud himself did, that analysis can *post*dict but that synthesis—going back the other way—cannot *pre*dict. In other words, from psychoanalytic material we can arrive at a construction of the past that reflects what may in fact have happened, but from a knowledge beforehand of the past we cannot predict the adult outcome. The sheer number of potential causes at the outset and their complex interactions may be so great, and the intervention of accidental events so unpredictable and yet important, that prediction is risky at best. A knowledge of outcome is by its very nature selective from among all possible causes and their interactions. Perhaps what is called for is a superordinate theory explaining how complex organizations shift, change, and evolve over time, rather than a reductionist theory linking individual causes and their specific effects.

Another difficulty in coordinating early childhood events and later adult outcome is that the infant and child investigator is presented with *observations of behavior,* not *introspective reports of experience.* We learn from analysis that outward behavior and inner experience are far from perfectly correlated; indeed, we have learned from psychoanalysis that the same behavior can "mean" different things and that the inner experience of the same behavior—its causes—can differ greatly from time to time. Thus, to extrapolate from a child's behavior to an adult's inner experience would appear to be comparing apples and oranges.

Perhaps, however, we can turn to child analysis as a less discrepant source of data insofar as the child analyst through play therapy can arrive more directly at the child's inner experience and is not simply observing behavior. The problem with this approach is that the child analyst is essentially using the same method as is the adult analyst, treating children's play experiences as if they were free associations, and thus cannot provide independent evidence for any cause-and-effect relationships between childhood experience and adult pathology. At best, the child analyst would be gathering information consistent with the psychoanalytic method and various explanatory theories.

In summary, it can be said that the genetic assumption of the psychoanalytic method is correct as it stands insofar as it points to the past as causative and thereby supports the hypothesis that childhood experiences may play some role in adult neurosis. But beyond that, the field is open for further research and theorizing.

Summary and Conclusions

Our review of the four basic assumptions of the psychoanalytic method has been encouraging in several important respects and sobering in other respects. Our review has highlighted what has in fact been achieved and underscores what more needs to be done. What is most heartening is that perhaps the single most important presupposition of the psychoanalytic method—the assumption of unconscious psychological causes—has received the most substantial support from research based on methods entirely independent of the psychoanalytic clinical method. This body of experimental research does not as yet provide substantial evidence for the various indirect ways in which unconscious psychological causes affect consciousness, but there are promising methods being developed in the field.

Only a few studies have addressed the power of free associations to uncover psychological causes. Findings from the few that have done so are encouraging, but much more needs to be undertaken. The effect of different interventions on the ability of free associations to lead to the discovery of unconscious causes is another area of research that requires much more work than has heretofore been accomplished. Finally, the genetic assumption concerning the role of past history in determining adult pathology is perhaps the most complex and replete with the most pitfalls of both a methodological and a logical nature. It is possible that a new way of theorizing about these historical cause-and-effect relationships might be required based not on a reductionistic consideration of individual causes and their effects, but on levels of organization and their evolution and modification over time.

References

Balay J, Shevrin H: The subliminal psychodynamic activation method: a critical review. Am Psychol 43:161–174, 1988

Bonaparte M, Freud A, Kris E: The Origins of Psychoanalysis. New York, Basic Books, 1954

Bordin ES: Personality and free association. Journal of Consulting Psychology 30:30–38, 1966

Brenner C: The Mind in Conflict. New York, International Universities Press, 1982

Colby KM: Experiment on the effects of an observer's presence on the image system during psychoanalytic free association. Behavioral Science 5:216–232, 1960

Colby KM: On the greater amplifying power of causal-correlative over interrogative inputs on free association in an experimental psychoanalytic situation. J Nerv Ment Dis 133:233–239, 1961

Crick F, Mitchison G: The function of dream sleep. Nature 304:111–114, 1983

Dixon NF: Subliminal Perception: The Nature of a Controversy. London, McGraw-Hill, 1971

Dixon NF: Preconscious Processing. New York, Wiley, 1981

Edelson M: Hypothesis and Evidence in Psychoanalysis. Chicago, IL, University of Chicago Press, 1984

Edelson M: Psychoanalysis: A Theory in Crisis. Chicago, IL, University of Chicago Press, 1988

Ellenberger HF: The Discovery of the Unconscious: The History and Evolution of Dynamic Psychiatry. New York, Basic Books, 1970

Erdelyi MH: Psychoanalysis: Freud's Cognitive Psychology. San Francisco, CA, WH Freeman, 1984

Fisher C: Dreams, images and perception: a study of unconscious-preconscious relationships. J Am Psychoanal Assoc 4:5–48, 1956

Fisher C: A study of the preliminary stages of the construction of dreams and images. J Am Psychoanal Assoc 5:5–60, 1957

Fisher C: Subliminal and supraliminal influences on dreams. Am J Psychiatry 116:1009–1017, 1960

Fisher C, Paul IH: The effect of subliminal visual stimulation on images and dreams: a validation study. J Am Psychoanal Assoc 7:35–83, 1959

Fiss H: The effects of experimentally induced changes in alertness on response to subliminal stimulation. J Pers 34:577–595, 1966

Fiss H, Goldberg F, Klein GS: Effects of subliminal stimulation on imagery and discrimination. Percept Mot Skills 17:31–44, 1963

Freud S: The interpretation of dreams (1900), in Standard Edition of the Complete Psychological Works of Sigmund Freud, Vols 4 and 5. Translated and edited by Strachey J. London, Hogarth Press, 1953

Freud S: From the history of an infantile neurosis (1918[1914]), in Standard Edition of the Complete Psychological Works of Sigmund Freud, Vol 17. Translated and edited by Strachey J. London, Hogarth Press, 1955, pp 1–123

Freud S: Project for a scientific psychology (1950[1895]), in Standard Edition of the Complete Psychological Works of Sigmund Freud, Vol 1. Translated and edited by Strachey J. London, Hogarth Press, 1966, pp 281–397

Grunbaum A: The Foundations of Psychoanalysis: A Philosophical Critique. Los Angeles, University of California Press, 1989

Hobson JA, McCarley RW: The brain as a dream state generator: an activation-synthesis hypothesis of the dream process. Am J Psychiatry 134:1335–1348, 1977

Holt RR: The development of the primary process: a structural view, in Motives and Thought: Psychoanalytic Essays in Honor of David Rapaport (Psychological Issues Monogr 18/19). Edited by Holt RH. New York, International Universities Press, 1967, pp 345–383

Holzman PS: Psychoanalysis: is the therapy destroying the science? J Am Psychoanal Assoc 33:725–770, 1985

Kohlberg L, Ricks D, Snarey J: Childhood development as a predictor of adaptation in adulthood. Genetic Psychology Monographs 110:91–172, 1984

Kris AO: Free Association: Method and Process. New Haven, CT, Yale University Press, 1982

Meissner WA: The viewpoint of a devil's advocate, in The Significance of Infant Observational Research for Clinical Work with Children, Adolescents and Adults (Workshop Series for the American Psychoanalytic Association, Monograph 5). Edited by Dowling S, Rothstein A. Madison, CT, International Universities Press, 1989, pp 175–194

Mishkin M: A memory system in the monkey. Philos Trans R Soc Lond B Biol Sci 298:85–95, 1982

Murch GN: Responses to incidental stimuli as a function of feedback contingency. Perception and Psychophysics 5:10–20, 1969

Nachmansohn M: Concerning experimentally induced dreams (1925), in Organization and Pathology of Thought. Edited by Rapaport D. New York, Columbia University Press, 1951, pp 257–287

Paul IH, Fisher C: Subliminal visual stimulation: a study of its influence on subsequent images and dreams. J Nerv Ment Dis 29:315–340, 1959

Poetzl O: The relationship between experimentally induced dream images and indirect vision (1917), in Preconscious Stimulation and Dreams, Associations and Images: Classical Studies (Psychological Issues Monogr 7). Edited by Fisher C. New York, International Universities Press, 1960, pp 41–120

Pribram KH, Gill MM: Freud's "Project" Re-assessed. New York, Basic Books, 1976

Ramzy I, Shevrin H: The nature of the inference process in psychoanalytic interpretation: a critical review of the literature. Int J Psychoanal 57:151–159, 1976

Rapaport D: The scientific methodology of psychoanalysis (1944), in The Collected Papers of David Rapaport. Edited by Gill MM. New York, Basic Books, 1967, pp 165–220

Reiser MF: Mind, Brain, Body: Toward a Convergence of Psychoanalysis and Neurobiology. New York, Basic Books, 1990

Roffenstein G: Experiments on symbolization in dreams (1924), in Organization and Pathology of Thought. Edited by Rapaport D. New York, Columbia University Press, 1951, pp 249–256

Sarbin TR, Coe WC: Hypnosis: A Social Psychological Analysis of Influence Communication. New York, Holt, Rinehart, & Winston, 1972

Schroetter K: Experimental dreams (1911), in Organization and Pathology of Thought. Edited by Rapaport D. New York, Columbia University Press, 1951, pp 234–248

Shevrin H: Brain wave correlates of subliminal stimulation, unconscious attention, primary- and secondary-process thinking, and repressiveness, in Psychoanalytic Research: Three Approaches to the Experimental Study of Subliminal Perception (Psychological Issues Monogr 30). Edited by Mayman M. New York, International Universities Press, 1973, pp 56–87

Shevrin H: The fate of the five metapsychological principles. Psychoanalytic Inquiry 4:33–58, 1984

Shevrin H: Subliminal perception and dreaming. Journal of Mind and Behavior 7:379–395, 1986

Shevrin H: Unconscious conflict: a convergent psychodynamic and electrophysiological approach, in Psychodynamics and Cognition. Edited by Horowitz MJ. Chicago, IL, University of Chicago Press, 1988, pp 117–167

Shevrin H: Subliminal perception and repression, in Repression and Dissociation: Implications for Personality Theory, Psychopathology, and Health. Edited by Singer JL. Chicago, IL, University of Chicago Press, 1990, pp 103–119

Shevrin H, Dickman S: The psychological unconscious: a necessary assumption for all psychological theory? Am Psychol 35:421–434, 1980

Shevrin H, Fisher C: Changes in the effects of a waking subliminal stimulus as a function of dreaming and nondreaming sleep. J Abnorm Psychol 72:362–368, 1967

Shevrin H, Luborsky L: The rebus technique: a method for studying primary-process transformations of briefly exposed pictures. J Nerv Ment Dis 133:479–488, 1961

Shevrin H, Williams WJ, Marshall RE, et al: Event-related potential indicators of the dynamic unconscious. Consciousness and Cognition 1:340–360, 1992

Shevrin H, Bond JA, Brakel LA, et al: Conscious and Unconscious Processes: An Experimental Investigation Based on Convergent Psychodynamic, Cognitive, and Neurophysiological Methods. New York, Guilford (in press)

Silverman LH: The subliminal psychodynamic activation method: overview and comprehensive listing of studies, in Empirical Studies of Psychoanalytic Theories, Vol 1. Edited by Masling J. Hillsboro, NJ, Lawrence Erlbaum, 1983, pp 69–100

Stross L, Shevrin H: Differences in thought organization between hypnosis and the waking state: an experimental approach. Bull Menninger Clin 26:237–247, 1962

Stross L, Shevrin H: A comparison of dream recall in wakefulness and hypnosis. Int J Clin Exp Hypn 15:63–71, 1965

Stross L, Shevrin H: Thought organization in hypnosis and the waking state: the effects of subliminal stimulation in different states of consciousness. J Nerv Ment Dis 147:272–288, 1968

Relationship of Psychoanalysis to Neuroscience

Morton F. Reiser, M.D.

Do our Spirit/Minds occupy our bodies temporarily—as part of an unknowable eternal journey? If so, while so "entrapped," are we limited in our mental lives to functions that lie within the biological repertoire of brain-body mechanisms? Can Spirit/Mind exert influence on body functions? Can it be affected by them?

OR

Are we our bodies—single organisms experienced as dual because unitary mind–brain/body functions are manifested in two domains, separately detected, described, and conceptualized by the different methods and in the different "languages" of mind and body?

These are not new questions, nor are they likely to find satisfactory answers in the near future—perhaps ever. All the same, psychoanalysis, even though it works primarily with mental phenomena, needs to be aware of broader background issues, because it deals with whole people—minds in bodies—that are in social interaction with other whole people.

Historical Background

Freud believed that a theory of mind should ultimately take into account and be in conformity with known facts about the biology of the brain. In 1895 he abandoned his "Project for a Scientific Psychology" (Freud 1950[1895]) because the known biology of the brain at that time (end of the 19th century) was incomplete and incommensurate with the richness and complex detail of the psychological observational data he was collecting. This is not the case now (end of the 20th century). In abandoning the "Project" for a purely psychological theory, however, he did not give up the hope (and belief) that mental life would—when enough was known—be understood in terms of its underlying biology. In 1920 Freud declared that

> this [confusion] is merely due to our being obliged to operate with the scientific terms, that is to say with the figurative language, peculiar to psychology (or, more precisely, to depth psychology). We could not otherwise describe the processes in question at all, and indeed we could not have become aware of them. The deficiencies in our description would probably vanish if we were already in a position to replace the psychological terms by physiological or chemical ones. . . .
>
> . . . *Biology is truly a land of unlimited possibilities. We may expect it to give us the most surprising information and we cannot guess what answers it will return in a few dozen years to the questions we have put to it.* (Freud 1920, p. 60; emphasis added)

As will be clear from what follows in this chapter, the asymmetry between the two data sets—psychoanalytic and neurobiologic—is not the same as it was when Freud abandoned "The Project." The dazzlingly rich and rapid advances in physiology and neuroscience that occurred following Freud's time have uncovered many new facts about brain/body functions that have potentially important implications for understanding phenomena that are of central concern to psychoanalysis—for example, the nature of, and interrelationships between, perception, memory, and affect, and their roles in generating dream imagery and psychosomatic responses to stress. During this same epoch, new clinical psychoanalytic observations on patients with psychiatric and psychosomatic disorders and recent experimental behavioral and psychophysiological observations of infants and young children have led to suggested revisions of psychoanalytic concepts concerning cognitive and personality development.[1] All of this new information has rekindled interest in exploring the interface between the psychoanalytic and neurobiologic domains.

Early Explorations: "Psychosomatic Medicine"

Following World War II, alerted by their experience in treating soldiers under stress, clinicians in all branches of medicine became impressed by the frequency with which they could in civilian practice observe associations between "life stress" and onset and exacerbation of illness, and by the influence of the doctor-patient relationship on the course of disease and response to treatment (Wolff 1950). This awareness occurred at a time when American medicine was very much influenced by the following:

1. Hans Selye's fundamental research on the role of the adrenals (Selye 1950) and the general adaptation syndrome and the diseases of adaptation (Selye 1946).
2. The discovery and pharmaceutical development of ACTH (adrenocorticotropic hormone) and cortisone and demonstration of

---

[1]Leigh and Reiser (1992, p. 362–363) have summarized these revisions as follows: "The newer perspectives assign less exclusive or primary importance to the libidinal line of development, and place more emphasis on evolving relationships with important people during infancy and childhood. It is the combined influence of these relationships along with/and upon intrinsic biological maturation that is now considered to shape development of (1) cognitive ego structures, mechanisms of defense and coping (Ego Psychology); (2) mechanisms for modulating affective and empathic communication (Interpersonal Psychology); (3) enduring internal psychic representations of the influential people (objects) of infancy and childhood, and the effects of those internalized object representations on patterning of relationships in real life (Object Relations); and (4) developing a sense of self as an integrated, dependably competent and strong person (Self Psychology)."

their therapeutic effects in rheumatoid arthritis and conditions involving allergic and immune responses such as bronchial asthma, neurodermatitis, and various other diseases involving the immune system (Mote 1951a, 1951b).

3. An academic clinical tradition that reflected Walter Cannon's basic discoveries on the physiology of emotion and the derivative clinical approach of Soma Weiss and the leading academic clinical teachers and scientists he trained (including, among others, Eugene Stead, Eugene Ferris, John Romano, and George Engel). This tradition was characterized by its emphasis on the principle of homeostasis and systems physiology, and the role of autonomic and neuroendocrine systems (which are closely tuned to and influenced by emotional meanings) in the pathogenesis of disease.

Little wonder that psychoanalysts played major roles in generating significant research data and in developing important theoretical formulations concerning the participation of putative psychological factors and emotional stress in the etiology and pathogenesis of some chronic medical ("psychosomatic") disorders. The period from, roughly, the late 1940s to the mid-1960s was a richly productive era. During this period an extensive and complex literature was generated encompassing unresolved questions regarding both medical and psychiatric pathogenesis that extend beyond the scope of this chapter. These issues have been extensively reviewed and discussed elsewhere (Alexander 1950; Knapp et al. 1966, 1970; McEwen and Brinton 1987; Reiser 1975, 1984; Weiner 1977, 1989; Wolff 1950). However, one (somewhat ironic) feature deserves special attention here. Although the brain is part of the body, much of the early psychosomatic work had to treat the brain as a "black box" and to omit consideration of its role in constructing theories that assigned a major role to emotion. Observed correlations between (often unconscious) emotional meanings of life experiences and patterns of peripheral autonomic innervation and peripheral endocrine profiles had to be interpreted in the absence of information about brain mechanisms that mediate cognitive-emotional interactions in the brain.

By contrast (and to introduce the next section), consider the fact that in 1989 Joseph E. LeDoux, a neuroscientist, was able to write as follows:

> Emotion and cognition are mediated by separate but interacting systems of the brain. The core of the emotional system is a network that evaluates (computes) the biological significance of stimuli, including stimuli from the external or internal environment or from within the brain (thoughts, images, memories). The computation of stimulus significance takes place prior to and independent of conscious awareness, with only the computational products reaching awareness, and only in some instances. The amygdala may be a focal structure in the affective network. By way of neural interactions between the amygdala and brain areas involved in cognition (particularly the neocortex and hippocampus) affect can influence cognition and cognition can influence affect. Emotional experiences, it is proposed, result when stimulus representations, affect representations, and self representations coincide in working memory. (LeDoux 1989, p. 267)

LeDoux's paper lists 91 references, only 10 of which antedate 1952; *most are from the 1980s!*

The yield produced by the revolution in brain science that for a time distracted attention from psychosomatic phenomena can now facilitate redirection of research interest back to unresolved issues in that field—now with more definitive techniques and information at hand for uncovering previously inaccessible intervening brain structures and mechanisms. For example, the limbic structures and circuits referred to above (mainly the amygdala and hippocampus) that are so intimately involved in cognitive-emotional interactions through connections to the neocortex also connect to and stimulate the hypothalamic centers that govern autonomic, neuroendocrine, and immunologic output from the brain (see Reiser 1984, Chapters 12 and 13).

Development of Contemporary Neuroscience

Acceleration of the rate of advance in neurobiology and neuroscience can be roughly dated to the 1950s. In many ways this acceleration that enabled subsequent developments in neurobiology and cognitive neuroscience began with the development of the microelectrode and related electronic technology for recording from single neurons as well as from populations of contiguous neurons, the development of the electron microscope, and the development and maturation of computer science and statistics. The field then advanced along with the progress in the above related fields and the life sciences in general, and with the development of increasingly sophisticated technologies that could be applied to study of the nervous system: general and stereotaxic neurosurgery, neuroanatomy, neuropsychopharmacology, molecular and cell biology and genetics, tissue culture, neurochemistry, enzyme and protein chemistry, and noninvasive methods for brain imaging in waking subjects during varying mental states and during performance of mental tasks.[2] These noninvasive techniques have made it possible to correlate specific cognitive operations with levels of neural activity (Farah et al. 1989; Shevrin 1988; Shevrin and Fritzler 1968), metabolic activity, and blood flow in specified regions of the brain (Reiman et al. 1989).

Cognitive psychology, building on technological advances, on information theory, and on computer science, expanded into the field of artificial intelligence, which entails the design of computer circuits and programs that are capable of carrying out computations involved in cognitive functions of the brain. In this way models of how the brain might do these computations are developed and studied. With these models one can demonstrate how the brain could do these computations but is not able to know how it actually does do them. More recent models that employ circuits and programs (e.g., parallel distributed processing [Rumelhart et al. 1986]) organized to resemble known patterns of cognitive brain circuitry attempt to come closer to modeling actual brain operations (Mountcastle 1978).

---

[2]Positron-emission tomography (PET), single-photon emission computed tomography (SPECT), magnetic resonance imaging (MRI), special forms of electroencephalography (such as power spectrum electroencephalography and evoked potential technology), and magnetoencephalography.

The research strategy of combining cognitive psychological knowledge and techniques with neurobiologic knowledge and techniques has eventuated in the emergence of the new field of cognitive neuroscience. Toward the goal of mapping mind onto brain, cognitive neuroscience investigates the neural mechanisms and structures involved in advanced cognitive functions such as learning, perception, memory, and affect. (Illustrative examples will be reviewed below.) The circle is closing. One can easily see how research interests in the two domains of mind and brain may be converging on issues of common concern to both.

Conceptual Problems That Complicate Interpretation of Covariant Mental and Biological Data

Is there a role for psychoanalysis in the search for information that can contribute to the task of mapping mind onto brain? Clearly the answer is yes—at least in principle there should be. The psychological data that the psychoanalytic process generates about mental aspects of cognitive and affective functions should complement the data generated by neuroscience about the neurobiologic aspects. But practical definition and implementation of that role in actual practice are far from easy. There are a number of complicating factors to consider in reviewing gains already achieved and in identifying promising areas of opportunity for future study.

Crossing Domains

The domain of mind deals with meanings and motives that are devoid of any material physical quality. The domain of brain deals with physical phenomena—matter and energy. These two domains use different languages, methods, and concepts; units are not interchangeable between them, nor can covariant changes be interpreted as being due to cross-domain cause-effect sequences in either direction (Edelson 1984). Ideas are not molecules, even though changes in the former surely must somehow be synchronously coupled with changes in the latter as cognitive mind/brain functions occur.

Emergent Functions in Ascending Levels of Complexity in Biological Systems

As one ascends from one level of complexity to the next, new functional capacities appear (emerge)—"emergent" functions that were not contained in or explained by functions of the lower level (Blois 1988; Gould 1985, 1986). For example, molecular biology of single neurons does not adequately account for the new functional capacities that emerge when a few regional neurons synapse and function as a simple circuit using the connectivity of the synaptic junctions to communicate. Similarly, properties of the simple circuit synapses do not explain the added functional capacities that emerge when many widely dispersed neurons are interconnected in complex networks. When domains and levels are both crossed, the problems are compounded. For example, ascending excitation originating in the pons can induce a dreaming *state of the brain* (rapid eye movement [REM] sleep), but not a *dream experience* (higher level, different domain; see Reiser 1990). Such considerations limit the explanatory scope and relevance of progressively reductionistic neurobiologic data in relation to progressively higher cognitive functions such as language and symbolic meanings.

These problems and possible ways of avoiding or minimizing the interpretive problems they pose have been discussed in detail elsewhere (Reiser 1984, 1990). The *dual track approach,* which provides one possible (and promising) way of solving these interpretive problems, involves parallel separate tracking of data pertaining to the same phenomenon in each of the two realms (mind and brain); derivation of functional principles that seem to obtain in each of the domains; and then examination of the separately derived principles for pattern resemblances and isomorphisms. Those pattern resemblances and isomorphisms detected would suggest convergence of—not identity among—the principles derived from data observed by the methods of the different disciplines.

Asymmetry of Data Sets in the Domains of Mind and Brain

Because the nature of the data produced during the clinical intro-spective psychoanalytic process is subjective and impressionistic, these data are not directly comparable or amenable to correlative study with objective quantitative data produced by experimental neurobiologic studies. This incomparability places very real and relatively great, *but not absolute,* limitations on the possibilities for progress in mapping mental onto neural phenomena. Two factors are operating to address this problem:

1. Considerable progress has been made in rendering the clinical data more objective, quantitative, and reliable through the use of electronic sound- and video-recording techniques (sometimes in conjunction with synchronized physiological measurements of autonomically innervated functions such as heart rate, electrical skin resistance, etc.) (Dahl et al. 1978; Gill and Hoffman 1981; Horowitz 1979, 1988; Knapp et al. 1966, 1970).

2. Because cognitive psychology is conceptually closer to neurobi-ology than is psychoanalysis, the combination of its experimental methods with those of neural science (cognitive neuroscience) furnishes a promising bridge for the study of the relationship between the findings and concepts of psychoanalysis and those of the biological neural sciences.[3]

Information bearing on this latter question is accumulating at an extremely rapid rate. A comprehensive review would entail far more than can be covered in a single chapter.[4] Instead, in the text that follows I will focus on a selected sector of cognitive function to illustrate how converging psychoanalytic and neurobiologic data can lead toward enhanced understanding of mind/brain relation-ships. I first describe a central adaptive challenge to mind/brain—

---

[3]Even this bridge, though more promising, is not perfect; see discussion of this matter by Tulving and Gazzaniga (Gazzaniga 1991).

[4]For an excellent comprehensive review, see Levin 1991.

a challenge requiring memory function for survival. Memory is an appropriate issue to discuss because, after all, it has been of central concern to psychoanalysis from the very beginnings of that field. After discussing the adaptive challenge, I then present in summary form two parallel overviews of the cognitive-emotional memory interactions involved in meeting that challenge: the first according to brain principles inferred from cognitive neuroscience data, and the second according to mind principles inferred from clinical psychoanalytic data. I then endeavor to demonstrate how recognition and analysis of similarities between the two sets of principles can be applied toward developing a fuller understanding of how mind/brain meets that adaptive challenge.

The Adaptive Challenge

Mind/brain receives information from both internal and external sources through stimulation of the sensory apparatus, including special sense organs for taste, smell, hearing, and vision. The latter two bring information from distant as well as proximal sources in the external world. This information, experienced subjectively as sensations and perceptions, is important for survival. To plan and execute appropriate behavior, the cognitive apparatus must provide ways to evaluate the significance of currently perceived data. Highly developed cognitive systems are needed to process information—that is, to register, recognize, evaluate, store, and retrieve information when needed, and to evaluate new information by matching it to information retrieved from perceptual and affective memory of past experiences.

How Does the Brain Process Information?— Answers From Cognitive Neuroscience

Cognitive neuroscientists, using anatomical tracer studies and other anatomical techniques, have identified the circuits involved in some specified cognitive mind/brain functions. Using techniques that monitor electrical and metabolic activity in the brain, they have been able to determine which cells and regions of the brain are most active during performance of specified cognitive tasks such as recognition of and discrimination between complex sensory stimuli. The actual functional importance of individual circuits and structures so identified can then be determined by administering specified cognitive tasks to animals after the designated brain regions or pathways have been removed surgically or modified by drugs with known central pharmacological effects (Mishkin and Appenzeller 1987; Squire 1987; Zola-Morgan et al. 1989a, 1989b).

These processes have been worked out in most detail for the visual system. Information registered on the retina by light-wave energy is transduced there into electrophysiological energy, which can then be conducted and processed by the brain via conduction along nerve pathways and across synaptic clefts. Extensive and complex processing in the lateral geniculate bodies, primary visual cortex, and many thousands of synapses in the prestriate cortex separates various part-aspects of the image (color, size, shape, texture),[5] to be processed in separate pathways and subsystems (Livingstone and Hubel 1988). Finally, the part-aspects are reassembled part by part in area TE of the inferior temporal cortex (Mishkin 1982). From there the reassembled image is routed via the entorrhinal cortex to a complex system of subcortical limbic lobe structures (including the hippocampus and amygdala), where it is extensively processed both for perception and for forwarding into memory systems. Not until the information collected in area TE has made connection (through the amygdala and hippocampus)[6] to the prefrontal cortex and association cortex can it be meaningfully evalu-

---

[5] Position is processed along a separate path to the parietal cortex, but that information is also directed to the inferior temporal cortex and reassembled with the other aspects.

[6] Emotions and memory are intimately intertwined because of extensive reciprocal connections between the amygdala, hippocampus, and neocortex. There is, however, some dissociation or separation between emotion and memory at lower levels of neural systems within the medial temporal lobe. It has been shown recently that declarative memory is related to function of the hippocampus and adjacent anatomically related cortex (Zola-Morgan et al. 1989a, 1989b). The amygdala is important in acquiring connections between emotions and stimuli as in conditioned emotional learning (Clugnet and LeDoux 1990; Davis et al. 1987; LeDoux 1989; LeDoux et al. 1989).

ated in relation to previous experience (Mishkin 1982; Mishkin and Appenzeller 1987).

This complex processing system, called the *corticolimbic system,* in addition to providing the structures and connections required for perceptual and memory functions, also contains structures and circuits that generate and regulate affect. *These perceptual and memory functions are carried out by the very same circuits and structures that process affect. In this way, associative links are established between new percepts and older perceptual information that has been stored in the association cortex.* It should be added that the comparative evaluative functions are influenced by brain-stem centers (e.g., the locus coeruleus) that regulate arousal and alertness (Aston-Jones and Bloom 1981; Aston-Jones et al. 1984). These corticolimbic connections are schematically depicted in Figure 19–1.

A Special Kind of Circuitry

The reciprocally interconnected cortical and subcortical systems that make up the corticolimbic circuits are composed of complex neural nets containing multiple reentry paths, feedback, and loops within loops, arranged in overlapping progressions. The computations required are amazingly complex. The anatomical and physiological circuitries interconnecting these neural nets have been compared to circuitry patterns employed in "parallel and distributed" computer processing systems (Mountcastle 1978; Rumelhart et al. 1986). These systems distribute parts of computations to a number of small computer circuits that carry out the assigned computations simultaneously (in parallel), and the results are then combined for computation in higher-order circuits. Wiring arrangements in the brain are strikingly similar. Individual cortical neurons are arranged in columns and modules in such a way that individual cells are connected with many widely distributed modules and therefore with individual neurons in many circuits other than their own.[7]

---

[7]It is probably worth noting that such an arrangement would be quite compatible with the mental mechanisms of "condensation" and "displacement" that Freud described in studying the formation of dream images.

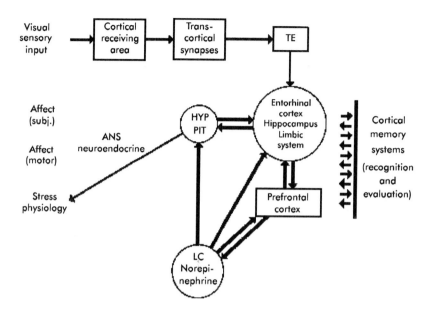

Figure 19–1. Schematic diagram of the corticolimbic brain circuits involved in the cognitive processing of visual information and in linking this system with bodily affect and stress mechanisms (see text for details). TE = area TE, located in inferior temporal lobe; HYP = hypothalamus; PIT = anterior pituitary; ANS = autonomic nervous system; LC = locus coeruleus.

Images are not stored in memory as focal engrams (like images in photographic film). Rather, widely distributed neurons are considered to constitute patterned processing circuits that correspond to previously registered percepts. Both perception and recall of an image probably involve some degree of "re-creation" or "re-perception" of it. As Edelman (1987) notes, "It would not be surprising if, to some extent, every perception were to be considered an act of creation and every memory an act of imagination" (p. 329).

The stability and the threshold for reactivation of such stored perceptual patterns would be expected to be related to strength of synaptic transmission across the junctions involved, and this would in turn relate to the number of times these synapses had been so traversed (Kandel 1979; Kandel and Schwartz 1982), reflecting the influence of experience on formation of cognitive circuits (i.e., neural Darwinism) (Edelman 1987). Strength and stability of stored perceptions also are enhanced by the degree of emotional arousal at the time of registration (McEwen and Brinton 1987; Shors et al. 1989), and, quite possibly, the threshold for revival or reactivation is influenced by emotional arousal as well, via effects of hypothalamic neurohumors on synaptic transmission in brain circuits.

Inferred Brain Principles

The following are principles concerning affect and the brain:

1. Affect serves as the organizing agent whereby residual records of perceptual images are associatively linked in corticolimbic *neuronal networks*. The affect generated by an experience connects the perceptual content of that experience to stored perceptual residues that were registered during earlier meaningful life experiences that involved the same or highly similar affects.
2. Emotional arousal influences strength of registration and selective reactivation of stored perceptual residues.

How Does the Mind Process Information?— Answers From Psychoanalysis

"Dream of the Botanical Monograph"

Psychoanalytic process, using the method of free association, provides an opportunity to observe mental manifestations of memory as displayed in the imagery of dreams. In discussing the "Dream of the Botanical Monograph" (see Freud 1900, pp. 282–284), Freud first described the presence of what he termed "nodal" images in the dream. He observed that the words "botanical" and "monograph" were associatively connected to multiple underlying dream thoughts that converged on, and imparted multiple meanings to, each word: "Each of the elements of the dream's content turns out to have been 'overdetermined'—to have been represented in the dream-thoughts many times over" (Freud 1900, p. 283). It was in this way that Freud described his *observations* on the relationship between the manifest and latent contents of the dream. He formulated hypothetical mental mechanisms (i.e., condensation and displacement) to account for the observed phenomena.

Starting with these observations, and after detailed restudy of the "Dream of the Botanical Monograph" and detailed analysis of many other dreams (from analyses of patients in my own clinical practice), it was possible for me to formulate the concept of the *nodal memory network*—an hypothesized extended and enduring network of mental representations (Reiser 1990). The psychoanalytic observations upon which that concept is based are detailed elsewhere (Reiser 1990) and can be briefly summarized as follows.

Dream collages appear to be put together from parts of sensory percepts registered during different developmental stages of the individual's life. The perceptual residues are primarily visual, but they may also be in auditory, tactile, proprioceptive, and sometimes olfactory and taste modalities. The dream images are associatively connected by virtue of shared emotional meanings and arranged accordingly in nodal memory networks. Remembering of percepts and establishment of associative links between them appear to be based on the circumstance of their having been registered during situations or events when similarly strong (often conflictual) feelings had been aroused. For example, Freud's "Dream of the Botanical Monograph" occurred at a time in his life when he was troubled by conflict between, on the one hand, a compelling need to pursue his favorite interests in research activities that would further his ambitious strivings and, on the other hand, a feeling of obligation to spend more time and devote more attention to his family's needs.

DREAM OF THE BOTANICAL MONOGRAPH

I had written a monograph on a certain plant. The book lay before me and I was at the moment turning over a folded coloured plate. Bound up in each copy there was *a dried specimen of the plant, as though it had been taken from a herbarium.*

(Freud 1900, p. 169; emphasis added)

Freud described his associations to the dream as being organized in six trains of thought. Each of the trains has been discussed and schematically diagrammed in detail elsewhere (Reiser 1990). One of the diagrams (that of train 4) is reproduced in Figure 19–2.

Study of the text and schematic diagrams indicates that images in Freud's dream were drawn from images that had been registered during recent and past situations involving the same set of conflicting motives and feelings. The discussion that follows immediately below uses one of the dream images as an illustrative instance of the

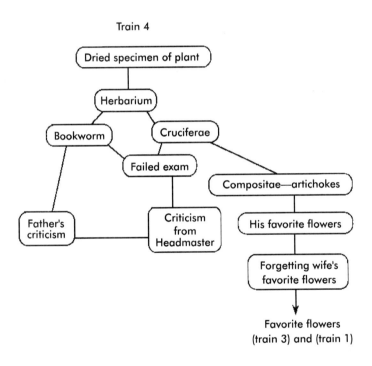

Figure 19–2. Train 4 of Freud's free associative trains of thoughts to the "Dream of the Botanical Monograph" (Freud 1900, p. 169). A nodal point (e.g., his wife's favorite flower, the cyclamen) is an idea or image that connects with several other trains of thoughts. Arrows at the lower right indicate where this train of thought connects to trains 1 and 3 via this node. Reprinted from Reiser MF: *Memory in Mind and Brain: What Dream Imagery Reveals.* New York, Basic Books, 1990. Copyright 1990, Morton F. Reiser. All rights reserved.

functional principle involved: an image, the dried specimen of a plant, is hypothesized to have been saved and later revived in the dream. It begins with Freud's statement of the relation of the "nodal points" to the affective context of the dream. (On the afternoon preceding the dream, the conflict described above had been stirred up during a conversation Freud had had with a senior colleague, Dr. Königstein.) Freud noted, "Thus 'botanical' was a regular nodal point in the dream. Numerous trains of thought converged upon it, which, as I can guarantee, had appropriately entered into the context of the conversation with Dr. Königstein. . . . So, too, 'monograph' in the dream touches upon two subjects: the one-sidedness of my studies and the costliness of my favourite hobbies" (Freud 1900, p. 283).

The dream image—"a dried specimen of the plant, as if it had been taken from a herbarium"—alluded to an incident in secondary school when Freud had failed to identify a plant from an herbarium. He had felt criticized by the headmaster and guilty and ashamed for having neglected his botanical studies to pursue other interests. The dried specimen in the dream is hypothesized to be a revival (i.e., reactivated perceptual processing pattern) corresponding to the actual visual image originally perceived during that emotionally painful incident. The putative role of affect in organizing the mnemic perceptual image of train 4 and the network of associated ideas is schematically depicted in Figure 19–3.

Study of this and many other dreams indicates that the network of a single dream can become part of an extended network when a nodal image from that dream becomes associatively linked to nodal images of other dreams by virtue of the fact that the experiences during which the various nodal images were registered share common affective themes. When a sufficient number of connections can be traced by *longitudinal* study of an individual patient, an overall pattern emerges of affective themes carrying perceptual memory traces from progressively earlier and earlier life experiences and converging on core unresolved conflictual issues in that person's life. For example, the "Dream of the Botanical Monograph" links to the Irma dream (Freud 1900, p. 107) and the Count Thur dream (Freud 1900, p. 209) by virtue of Freud's conflicted feelings connected with the idea of cocaine, which is represented by nodal images in each of these dreams. The perceptual memory traces that were revived as images in the dream allude to thoughts and feelings associated with those conflictual experiences. To illustrate, the entire nodal network revealed by analysis of all six trains of thought evolved in Freud's associations to the "Dream of the Botanical Monograph" is schematically depicted in Figure 19–4. Also depicted are the connections of this dream to the Irma dream and the Count Thur dream.

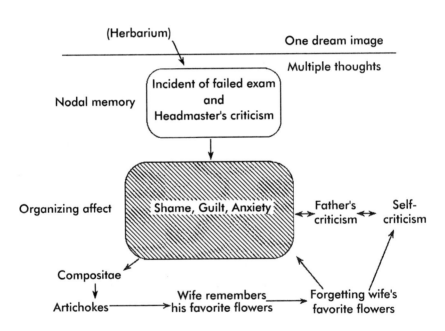

Figure 19–3.   The putative role of the affect cluster, evoked by the idea of failure, in organizing perceptual images and ideas as a network. Depicted are a single dream image (dried specimen of a plant) and the multiple ideas represented in the associations to it in train 4 of Freud's "Dream of the Botanical Monograph." Reprinted from Reiser MF: *Memory in Mind and Brain: What Dream Imagery Reveals.* New York, Basic Books, 1990. Copyright 1990, Morton F. Reiser. All right reserved.

This concept of the nodal memory network is consistent with findings of a number of psychoanalytic clinicians who have conducted psychophysiological laboratory studies of REM sleep and dreaming, including Fisher (1954, 1956, 1957, 1959), Palombo (1978), and Greenberg and Pearlman (1974, 1975, 1980), among others. It is in agreement also with concepts developed by two extensive long-standing programs of sleep laboratory research—one headed by Howard Roffwarg (Roffwarg et al. 1962, 1966, 1975, 1978, 1983), the other by Rosalind Cartwright (1983; Cartwright et al. 1987), who in a review of her group's work and that of others particularly emphasizes the concept of memory networks (Cartwright 1990).

Inferred Mind Principles of Memory Organization

From the detailed observations described in the preceding subsection, the following functional principles[8] are inferred to underlie the storage and arrangement of memories in the mind:

1. Memories are stored and arranged in the mind according to (encoded by) sensory percepts registered during the remembered experiences.
2. Sensory percepts registered during states of emotional arousal are stored in nodal memory networks according to the principle that percepts with the capacity to evoke the same affects (i.e., percepts with shared affective potential) are associatively linked.
3. The affective potential of a percept derives from the affect generated by the experience during which the percept was originally registered.[9]
4. A single percept with affective potential is associatively linked with other percepts (belonging to different experiences) that have the same affective potential. Such a percept constitutes

---

[8] The description of the five functional principles is reprinted from Reiser MF: *Memory in Mind and Brain: What Dream Imagery Reveals.* New York, Basic Books, 1990, pp. 91–92.

[9] The "strength" of the stored residue seems proportional to the intensity of the emotion connected with the experience.

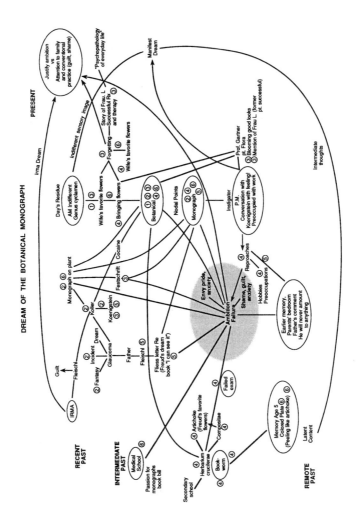

Figure 19–4. The nodal memory network underlying Freud's "Dream of the Botanical Monograph." The circled numbers refer to the trains of thought in which the thoughts were expressed. Historical location of memories is depicted by a counterclockwise scheme starting with the present in the upper right hand corner. The reference to the early memory in the parents' bedroom (bottom center) is from the Count Thur dream and indicates the connection of this network to that dream, as the reference to the Irma dream indicates the connection of this network to that other dream (see text for details). The shaded area locates the organizing affects. Reprinted, with modifications, from Reiser MF: *Memory in Mind and Brain: What Dream Imagery Reveals.* New York, Basic Books, 1990. Copyright 1990, Morton F. Reiser. All rights reserved.

a node in the network, in the sense that percepts belonging to several experiences may be associatively linked to it (condensation).

5. As life experiences accumulate, the nodal network expands, branches out, and becomes more complex. Percepts belonging to very early traumatic experiences constitute highly condensed nodes; later experiences are encoded by less dense perceptual nodes at greater distance temporally from the earlier registered central percepts.

The overall mind principle can be stated in summary form: *Sensory residues in the mind are organized by affect and arranged accordingly as nodal memory networks.*

Mind and Brain Functional Principles: A Comparison

1. The mind principle of affective linkage, which I propose to call the *affective organization of memory* (AOM), can be regarded as analogous to the brain principle of connection via limbic system linkage. This is a quite reasonable assumption when it is remembered that affect is a phenomenon that has both psychological *and* physiological manifestations. Because it is expressed in both mind and brain/body, the functional principles mediating the role of affect in the shaping of apparently separate aspects of memory phenomena in the two domains can nevertheless be expected to reflect the influence of a common source.

2. The mind principle of nodal memory networks that allows for condensation and displacement in mental cognitive process is analogous to the brain principle of neural networks arranged so as to allow for parallel and distributed processing in computational information processing.

Implications

Although these mind-brain analogies suggest convergences rather than identity of findings, they do strongly support the idea that data from the two realms are *complementary* (Holton 1970) rather than antithetical. They also suggest that better balanced psychobiological models of mind–brain/body can be constructed, taking data from both domains, rather than from one, into account. For example, the premise that affective linkage—the principle governing establishment and maintenance of associative links in nodal memory networks in the mind—is *analogous* to the principle by which limbic system linkage to cortical neural networks governs development of associative links in the brain has a number of potentially interesting implications:

1. This premise made it possible for me to suggest revision of Freud's model of image formation in dream process that brings it into conformity with available information from both cognitive neuroscience and psychoanalysis (Reiser 1990). Briefly stated, the postulate holds that the first step in dream formation takes place during the day. Emotions associated with attempting to deal with unresolved (current) life problems "recruit" (i.e., lower synaptic thresholds in) perceptual circuits that embody processing patterns conforming to sensory residues stored from earlier experiences that involved similar affects. These "sensitized" circuits await activation during REM sleep, when ascending excitatory PGO (pontine-geniculate-occipital) waves could stimulate them to "light up" and appear in the dream (step 2). This hypothesis would better explain 1) the relation between meaningful content of the dream and current life problems (Cartwright 1990), and 2) the occurrence of repetitive dreams in posttraumatic syndromes such as posttraumatic stress disorder (PTSD), than would the activation synthesis model proposed by Hobson and McCarley (1977) and Hobson (1988).
2. Similarly, this premise suggests that the same mind-brain principle could be applied in investigating the mechanism of repetitive waking hallucinatory imagery in the flashbacks of patients with PTSD (Figure 19–5).
3. This premise may suggest potentially promising leads for investigation of the role of traumatic memories in precipitating panic attacks in patients whose panic disorder began following emotionally stressful events (Roy-Byrne et al. 1986).

4. The premise would suggest a rationale for combining psychotherapy with pharmacotherapy in appropriately studied and
   selected patients with PTSD or another anxiety disorder (Figure
   19–5).

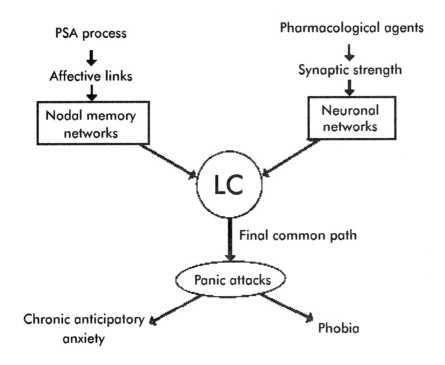

Figure 19–5. Schematic depiction of the locus coeruleus and related
aminergic systems involved (collectively designated as LC) as a final
common path accessible to parallel activation by revived conflictual
memories (nodal memory networks) and/or by stimuli from activated
neuronal networks. This figure is intended to illustrate the hypothesis that
this final common pathway can be influenced (stimulated or inhibited) via
either parallel path or by both acting together. This idea provides a rationale
for combining pharmacological agents (which influence strength of
synaptic transmission in neural nets) with psychotherapeutic techniques
(which influence affective linkages in nodal memory networks) in
management of patients with panic attacks, PTSD, or another, related
anxiety disorder.

5. Careful analysis of clinical psychoanalytic data (see Reiser 1990, Chapter 5) suggests that encoding of data—from the patient's memory network into the analyst's memory—occurs as the analytic interchange between patient and analyst proceeds. This phenomenon may account for the analyst's ability to recall relevant material from the patient's history at appropriate moments and to time and phrase interpretations effectively. This process may constitute an important aspect of empathy.

Conclusions

The challenges are clear. All of the material reviewed in this chapter is suggestive and promising, but at the same time the prospects are not compellingly strong regarding the potential for a future role for psychoanalysis in the advances taking place in mental and behavioral life sciences—so much of it without psychoanalytic participation or interest. Both within and without the psychoanalytic profession there is insufficient appreciation of the power of the psychoanalytic process to contribute data that could complement what is being accomplished in neighboring psychological, social, and biological sciences.

For this situation to change it will be necessary for psychoanalysis to make a significant investment in research and research training in scientific method. There is a need to develop a cadre of psychoanalysts whose careers will be devoted primarily to research, some in psychoanalysis itself and some in collaboration with investigators in neighboring disciplines. Clearly the potential for articulation with social and psychological disciplines is, at present, greater than with neuroscience. Largely this is because of the asymmetry referred to earlier in this chapter between psychoanalytic data and those of neuroscience. But this situation can be improved by making progress in clarifying the nature of the psychoanalytic process and by continuing to develop new research methods that will further improve the objectivity and reliability of psychoanalytic data and, at the same time, capture the real essence of the psychoanalytic process. Such progress and development of research methodology will require a new generation of research analysts. If that can be realized, there should be hope for increased interest in what psychoanalysis can contribute to the further development of mental and behavioral life sciences.

References

Alexander F: Psychosomatic Medicine. New York, WW Norton, 1950

Aston-Jones G, Bloom FE: Norepinephrine-containing locus coeruleus neurons in behaving rats exhibit pronounced responses to non-noxious environmental stimuli. J Neurosci 1:887–900, 1981

Aston-Jones G, Foote FL, Bloom FE: Anatomy and physiology of locus coeruleus neurons: functional implications, in Norepinephrine. Edited by Ziegler MG, Lake CR. Baltimore, MD, Williams & Wilkins, 1984, pp 92–116

Blois MS: Medicine and the nature of vertical reasoning. N Engl J Med 318:847–851, 1988

Cartwright RD: Rapid eye movement sleep characteristics during and after mood-disturbing events. Arch Gen Psychiatry 40:197–201, 1983

Cartwright RD: A network model of dreams, in Sleep and Cognition. Edited by Bootzin RR, Kihlstrom JF, Schacter DL. Washington, DC, American Psychological Association, 1990, pp 179–189

Cartwright RD, Stephenson K, Kravitz H, et al: Life events effects on REM sleep. Sleep Research 16:267, 1987

Clugnet M-C, LeDoux JE: Synaptic plasticity in fear conditioning circuits: induction of LTP in the lateral nucleus of the amygdala by stimulation of the medial geniculate body. J Neurosci 10:2818–2824, 1990

Dahl H, Teller V, Moss D, et al: Counter-transference examples of syntactic expression of warded-off contents. Psychoanal Q 47:339–363, 1978

Davis M, Hitchcock JM, Rosen JB: Anxiety and the amygdala: pharmacological and anatomical analysis of the fear-potentiated startle paradigm. Psychology of Learning and Motivation: Advances in Research and Theory 21:263–305, 1987

Edelman GM: Neural Darwinism: The Theory of Neuronal Group Selection. New York, Basic Books, 1987

Edelson M: Hypothesis and Evidence in Psychoanalysis. Chicago, IL, University of Chicago Press, 1984

Farah MJ, Weisberg LL, Monheit M, et al: Brain activity underlying mental imagery: event-related potentials during mental image generation. Journal of Cognitive Neuroscience 1:303–316, 1989

Fisher C: Dreams and perception: the role of preconscious and primary modes of perception in dream formation. J Am Psychoanal Assoc 2:389–445, 1954

Fisher C: Dreams, images and perception: a study of unconscious-preconscious relationships. J Am Psychoanal Assoc 4:5–48, 1956

Fisher C: A study of the preliminary stages of the construction of dreams and images. J Am Psychoanal Assoc 5:5–60, 1957

Fisher C: The effect of subliminal visual stimulation on images and dreams: a validation study. J Am Psychoanal Assoc 7:35–83, 1959

Freud S: The interpretation of dreams (1900), in Standard Edition of the Complete Psychological Works of Sigmund Freud, Vols 4 and 5. Translated and edited by Strachey J. London, Hogarth Press, 1953

Freud S: Beyond the pleasure principle (1920), in Standard Edition of the Complete Psychological Works of Sigmund Freud, Vol 18. Translated and edited by Strachey J. London, Hogarth Press, 1955, pp 1–64

Freud S: Project for a scientific psychology (1950[1895]), in Standard Edition of the Complete Psychological Works of Sigmund Freud, Vol 1. Translated and edited by Strachey J. London, Hogarth Press, 1966, pp 281–397

Gazzaniga MS: Interview with Endel Tulving. Journal of Cognitive Neuroscience 3:89–94, 1991

Gill M, Hoffman I: Analysis of Transference, Vol 2: Studies of Seven Audio-Recorded Psychoanalytic Sessions (Psychol Issues Monogr 54). New York, International Universities Press, 1981

Gould SJ: The Flamingo's Smile: Reflections in Natural History. New York, WW Norton, 1985

Gould SJ: Evolution and the triumph of homology, or why history matters. American Scientist 74:60–69, 1986

Greenberg R, Pearlman C: Cutting the REM nerve: an approach to the adaptive role of REM sleep. Perspect Biol Med 17:513–521, 1974

Greenberg R, Pearlman C: REM sleep and the analytic process: a psychophysiologic bridge. Psychoanal Q 44:392–402, 1975

Greenberg R, Pearlman C: The private language of the dream, in The Dream in Clinical Practice. Edited by Natterson JM. New York, Jason Aronson, 1980, pp 85–96

Hobson JA: The Dreaming Brain. New York, Basic Books, 1988

Hobson JA, McCarley RW: The brain as a dream state generator: an activation-synthesis hypothesis of the dream process. Am J Psychiatry 134:1335–1348, 1977

Holton G: The roots of complementarity. Daedalus 99:1015–1055, 1970

Horowitz MJ: States of Mind: Analysis of Change in Psychotherapy. New York, Plenum, 1979

Horowitz MJ (ed): Psychodynamics and Cognition. Chicago, IL, University of Chicago Press, 1988

Kandel ER: Psychotherapy and the single synapse: the impact of psychiatric thought on neurobiologic research. N Engl J Med 301:1028–1037, 1979

Kandel ER, Schwartz JH: Molecular biology of learning: modulation of transmitter release. Science 218:433–443, 1982

Knapp PH, Mushatt C, Nemetz SJ: Asthma, melancholia, and death, I: psychoanalytic considerations. Psychosom Med 28:114–133, 1966

Knapp PH, Mushatt C, Nemetz SJ, et al: The context of reported asthma during psychoanalysis. Psychosom Med 32:167–188, 1970

LeDoux JE: Cognitive-emotional interactions in the brain. Cognition and Emotion 3:267–289, 1989

LeDoux JE, Romanski L, Xagoraris A: Indelibility of subcortical emotional memories. Journal of Cognitive Neuroscience 1:238–243, 1989

Leigh H, Reiser MF: The Patient: Biological, Psychological, and Social Dimensions of Medical Practice, 3rd Edition. New York, Plenum, 1992

Levin FM: Mapping the Mind: The Intersection of Psychoanalysis and Neuroscience. Hillsdale, NJ, Analytic Press, 1991

Livingstone M, Hubel D: Segregation of form, color, movement and depth: anatomy, physiology, and perception. Science 240:740–749, 1988

McEwen BS, Brinton RE: Neuroendocrine aspects of adaptation. Prog Brain Res 72:11–26, 1987

Mishkin M: A memory system in the monkey. Philos Trans R Soc Lond B Biol Sci 298:85–95, 1982

Mishkin M, Appenzeller T: The anatomy of memory. Sci Am 256(6):80–89, 1987

Mote JR (ed): Proceedings of the Second Clinical ACTH Conference, Vol 1: Research. New York, The Blakiston Company, 1951a

Mote JR (ed): Proceedings of the Second Clinical ACTH Conference, Vol 2: Therapeutics. New York, The Blakiston Company, 1951b

Mountcastle VB: An organizing principle for cerebral function: the unit module and the distributed system, in The Mindful Brain: Cortical Organization and the Group-Selective Theory of Higher Brain Function. Edited by Edelman GM, Mountcastle VB. Cambridge, MA, MIT Press, 1978, pp 7–50

Palombo SR: Dreaming and Memory: A New Information Processing Model. New York, Basic Books, 1978

Reiman EM, Fusselman MJ, Fox PT, et al: Neuroanatomical correlates of anticipatory anxiety. Science 243:1071–1074, 1989

Reiser MF: Changing theoretical concepts in psychosomatic medicine, in American Handbook of Psychiatry (Arieti S, Editor-in-Chief), Vol 4: Organic Disorders and Psychosomatic Medicine. Edited by Reiser MF. New York, Basic Books, 1975, pp 477–500

Reiser MF: Mind, Brain, Body: Toward a Convergence of Psychoanalysis and Neurobiology. New York, Basic Books, 1984

Reiser MF: Memory in Mind and Brain: What Dream Imagery Reveals. New York, Basic Books, 1990

Roffwarg HP, Dement WC, Muzio JN, et al: Dream imagery: relationship to rapid eye movements of sleep. Arch Gen Psychiatry 7:235–258, 1962

Roffwarg HP, Muzio JN, Dement WC: Ontogenetic development of the human sleep-dream cycle. Science 152:604–619, 1966

Roffwarg HP, Herman JH, Lamstein S: The middle ear muscles: predictability of their phasic activity in REM sleep from dream material. Sleep Research 4:165, 1975

Roffwarg HP, Herman JH, Bowe-Anders C, et al: The effects of sustained alterations of waking visual input on dream content, in The Mind in Sleep: Psychology and Psychophysiology. Edited by Arkin AM, Antrobus JS, Ellman SJ. Hillsdale, NJ, Lawrence Erlbaum, 1978, pp 295–349

Roffwarg HP, Gatz P, Farber J: Temporal organization of PGO wave transmission during REM sleep in the auditory and visual systems in the cat. Sleep Research 12:51, 1983

Roy-Byrne PP, Geraci M, Uhde TW: Life events and the onset of panic disorder. Am J Psychiatry 143:1424–1427, 1986

Rumelhart DE, McClelland JL, The PDP Research Group: Parallel Distributed Processing: Explorations in the Microstructure of Cognition. Cambridge, MA, MIT Press, 1986

Selye H: The general adaptation syndrome and the diseases of adaptation. J Clin Endocrinol 6:117–230, 1946

Selye H: Stress. Montreal, Acta Medical Publishers, 1950

Shevrin H: Unconscious conflict: a convergent psychodynamic and electro-physiological approach, in Psychodynamics and Cognition. Edited by Horowitz MJ. Chicago, IL, University of Chicago Press, 1988, pp 117–167

Shevrin H, Fritzler D: Visual evoked response correlates of unconscious mental processes. Science 161:295–298, 1968

Shors TJ, Seib TB, Levine S, et al: Inescapable versus escapable shock modulates long-term potentiation in the rat hippocampus. Science 244:224–226, 1989

Squire LR: Memory and Brain. New York, Oxford University Press, 1987

Weiner HM: Psychobiology and Human Disease. New York, Elsevier, 1977

Weiner HM: Dynamics of the organism: implications of recent biological thought for psychosomatic theory and research. Psychosom Med 51:608–635, 1989

Wolff HG: Life stress and bodily disease—a formulation, in Life Stress and Bodily Disease. Edited by Wolff HG, Wolf S, Hare C. Baltimore, MD, Williams & Wilkins, 1950, pp 1059–1094

Zola-Morgan S, Squire LR, Amaral DG: Lesions of the amygdala that spare adjacent cortical regions do not impair memory or exacerbate the impairment following lesions of the hippocampal formation. J Neurosci 9:1922–1936, 1989a

Zola-Morgan S, Squire LR, Amaral DG, et al: Lesions of perirhinal and parahippocampal cortex that spare the amygdala and hippocampal formation produce severe memory impairment. J Neurosci 9:4355–4370, 1989b

Section V

Current Topics of Special Interest to Psychoanalysts

Introduction to Section V

Richard G. Kopff, Jr., M.D.
Edward Nersessian, M.D.

The final section of this textbook is the shortest, comprising only two chapters. However, it is the section that will be assuming an increasingly larger part of the textbook in the future. The reason is that these chapters deal with areas of ongoing reevaluation and reassessment of theory. Many of the subjects tackled here are controversial, but increasing attention is being directed toward them, and this will lead to new discoveries and will extend the boundaries of psychoanalytic theory.

This is not to imply that this section could not have been much larger. In fact, many more chapters could have been included. Concerns regarding the final size of this volume dictated limiting the size of this section. Because we felt that in this first edition our goal should be to present to the interested reader a general exposé of basic psychoanalytic theory, we placed more emphasis on subjects that we considered to be the most informative for learning and evaluating psychoanalytic ideas. Nevertheless, there is no question that these two chapters point the direction for future advancement.

20

The "Construction" of Femininity: Its Influence Throughout the Life Cycle

Ethel Spector Person, M.D.

> Once a parent or doctor has identified a child, always by
> the anatomic conformation of his genitals (perhaps this is
> the meaning of "anatomy becomes destiny," anatomy in
> conjunction with social attribution) as male or female,
> there are released the separate cultural syndromes that
> are related to the rearing of male or female children.
>
> Gagnon and Simon (1973)

The course of life dictates that all of us will face certain universal developmental dilemmas and will, in the course of resolving them, take our places in the cycle of generations. Though the tools we bring to the task are shared by all of our species, the specific strategies employed will be shaped by gender. In fact, gender role

Reprinted from *The Course of Life*, Vol. 5. Edited by Greenspan SI, Pollock G. New York, International Universities Press, 1993, pp. 15–42. Used with permission. Because this paper was originally written in 1988, though only published in 1993 because of a publishing delay, I have made a few changes to take into account new research over the past years.

identity, one's sense of one's femininity or masculinity, gives rise to differences in adaptive strategies that begin in the first year of life and last throughout life.

The recent psychoanalytic focus on the psychology of women qua women is a welcome corrective to a badly skewed perspective dating from Freud's time. In essence, Freud had postulated that masculinity was the natural state from which the girl retreated into femininity upon the fateful discovery that she had no penis (Freud 1924a, 1925, 1931, 1933). Subsequent to Freud, insofar as the specifics of female development and adaptive potential were considered at all—and generally they were given short shrift—they were presented as deficiencies. Obviously this perspective was not only skewed theoretically but at times injurious to the psychotherapy of women. From a clinical point of view it was therefore essential that those aspects of development relating specifically to femininity be given their due.

But the new focus on the development of women has not just benefited the work done in the consulting room; it has also led to a major theoretical reformulation regarding the nature and origin of gender. As both Chodorow (1978) and Mitchell (1974) have pointed out, Freud's theory that man is born while woman is made is both sexist and inconsistent. We now know that masculinity and femininity (as distinct from maleness and femaleness) are parallel constructs, not ordained by nature, but irreversibly patterned in the earliest years of life. The old paradigm that sexuality organizes gender is no longer accepted; today it appears that gender organization precedes the phallic-oedipal phase and to a large degree orders the fantasies that become attached to sexuality. All of these new developments, which I will expand upon shortly, redound to the benefit of psychoanalytic theory and practice. Moreover, they confirm and extend the earliest psychoanalytic position on gender—that it is a central organizing schema in personality development.[1]

---

[1]Although personality theories differ in their understanding and description of the dynamic through which gender asserts itself, all share an implicit and unvarying assumption regarding its importance.

I would agree with Gagnon and Simon's (1973) apt formulation that there are two "cultural syndromes" that are universal: masculinity and femininity. And I will try to demonstrate some of the ways in which the constructs of gender shape even that which we tend to think of as fundamentally biological: sexuality.

Having applauded these new developments in psychoanalytic theory, I would also urge that we understand that the emphasis on women's psychology poses problems of its own. One problem is that although female psychology has been accorded the status of a separate area for study, there is not yet any comparable emphasis on *male* psychology, because male psychology is, implicitly, the basis for our understanding of all psychological development—that is, we identify human psychology with male psychology. Inadvertently, then, although the new emphasis is intended to redress an imbalance—to pay attention to what has previously been ignored— the corrective in fact perpetuates the erroneous belief that male psychology is the norm and female psychology a variant.

A second and more fundamental problem has to do with the notion of the polarization of the sexes. Because Freud focused so much on sexual (libidinal) development and body ego as the primary forces in personality differentiation and maturation, psychoanalytic theory sometimes appeared to emphasize differences between the sexes at the expense of recognizing their similarities. The more recent literature, perhaps in overreaction to the earlier exclusion of specifically female developmental issues, has focused so much on differences as to suggest that there is, in the words of Marie de Gournay, Montaigne's "adoptive" daughter, "not one human race but two" (qtd. in Barry 1987, p. 63). Such a view may deflect us from a full valuation and theorization of problems that are fundamentally human, rooted in humankind's nature and condition, with developmental consequences for all. I refer to some general issues of adaptation, among them the consolidation of a separate self, the relationship between self and other, the quest for meaning, and the necessity of coming to terms with one's place in the cycle of generations, including the fact of one's mortality. Solutions to life tasks may vary, but the underlying dilemmas are well-nigh universal.

To recapitulate: There are indeed valuable new contributions to the clinical and theoretical approach to female psychology. These contributions have led to a reconceptualization of the construction not just of femininity but of masculinity as well. Nonetheless, our knowledge is far from complete, and our frequent overemphasis on gender differences tends to obscure what is fundamental to all human development.

Reformulating Femininity

Freud relied essentially on a single concept—that of penis envy, which he believed was the girl's inevitable response to her discovery of the anatomical difference between the sexes—to explain female psychology, including the development of sexuality, normal gender development (the acquisition of femininity), and neurotic conflict. Believing masculinity to be the natural state and femininity to be no more than the outcome of thwarted masculinity, Freud naturally assumed that the feminine state was somehow deformed and diminished and that women would display lifelong infantilism and immaturity as compared with men. Contemporary psychoanalysis, by contrast, takes a multidimensional point of view. In consequence, theories of the acquisition of femininity (gender identity) have been revised and are no longer prejudicial to women.

Freud (1925, 1931, 1933) believed that psychological development, essentially the same for both sexes up until the phallic phase, diverged only with the child's discovery of the anatomical differences between them—the fact that boys have penises whereas girls do not. Freud derived his theory of masculinity and femininity, what we now call *gender role identity*, from what he believed were contrasts between the behavior (and mental content) of the two sexes after that discovery. In Freud's psychology, penis envy, or the masculinity complex, was at the center of the female psyche, whereas castration anxiety was central in the male. Freud thus postulated that femininity grew out of frustrated masculinity—the female's desire to be something she is not—and masculinity from the male's drive to preserve and enhance what he already is. Freud suggested that on discovering the sexual distinction, the little girl is overcome by a sense of clitoral inferiority and the penis envy that must inevitably follow, and hence she develops the compensatory characteristics of passivity, masochism, narcissism, and dependency. These characteristics, in Freud's view, represent an attempted adaptation to (and restitution for) a profound narcissistic wound. In this view, femininity is no more than a retreat from an inadequate capacity to be male. Because Freud believed that his female patients' problems were derivative of penis envy, he also believed that women's treatment was inherently limited, the cause of their problems—genital inferiority—being irreversible.

With the benefit of hindsight, we now find it puzzling that such a theory had any adherents at all, because it is evident to mothers, nursemaids, and anyone with even moderate exposure to young children that girls and boys begin to diverge in behavior, mannerisms, and interests by 12 to 18 months of age, much earlier than Freud theorized, and prior to the time when children first conceptualize the difference between the sexes in terms of a genital difference. Freud's formulation underscores the danger of deriving developmental theories from adult analyses without validating the theories by observations conducted throughout the course of infancy and childhood.

Even early on in the history of psychoanalysis, there were alternative formulations distinct from Freud's, among them proposals by Horney (1924, 1926, 1932, 1933) and Jones (1927, 1933, 1935), both of whom observed an early divergence between masculine and feminine behavior before the age when children were able to conceptualize the anatomical distinction.[2] Both Horney and Jones—in stark contrast to Freud—proposed that femininity was primary, not derivative, that it antedated the phallic phase, and that it was essentially biological, grounded in awareness of the vagina rather than in disappointment over the lack of a penis. As Jones (1935) put it, "The ultimate question is whether a woman is born or made" (p. 273).

---

[2]Some have credited Horney's insights, in part, to her being the mother of daughters and thus able to make observations at first hand.

He—and Horney—opted for the view that *both* women and men are "born."

These two theorists differed from Freud in still another, though related, way. Whereas Freud saw the girl's libidinal turn to the father as defensive, following her defeat in not being able to possess the mother sexually, Jones and Horney, in contrast, believed that heterosexuality was instinctive for females as well as males. Consequently, the girl was motivated by lust rather than envy, desiring the penis libidinally rather than narcissistically. The claim for innate femininity was grounded in a biological assumption (erroneous, as it turns out) of innate heterosexuality—a position that surely has its ironies, as Horney has come to be best known for her insights as a culturalist.

Over time, theorists have attempted to integrate information garnered in direct observation of children with more purely psychoanalytic data. Direct observation has confirmed Horney's and Jones's contention of an early divergence between feminine and masculine development. But their explanations, grounded solely in assumptions about biology and genital awareness, have proved incorrect. Restricting ourselves to their explanations, we would be unable to account for the fact that boys with congenital absence of the penis and girls with congenital absence of the vagina are both observed to develop gender roles appropriate to their genetic sex (Stoller 1968). Moreover, the preponderance of current research suggests that sexual object choice is acquired, not innate (Baker 1981). This evidence suggests that Horney and Jones, like Freud, gave too much priority to anatomy, to perceptions of genitals and of genital sensations as solely determinative of gender development. Although they were right in giving the same weight to "primary" femininity as to masculinity, correctly perceiving them as parallel constructs, to designate them as completely innate or biological is to obscure the complexity of gender development. We must look beyond Freud, and even Horney and Jones, for a fuller understanding of the sources of gender differentiation.

Some of our crucial information has come from gender studies of intersexed children. Through such studies, Money, Hampson, and Hampson (1955a, 1955b, 1956) demonstrated that the initial and indispensable step in gender differentiation is the child's self-designation as male or female. This self-designation (core gender identity) evolves according to the sex of assignment; core gender is the child's resulting sense, unconscious as well as conscious, of belonging to one or the other sex. Because core gender identity is primarily related to sex of assignment, it need not always correspond to biological sex. For example, a genetic male—perhaps a male child with a severe hypospadia—mistakenly assessed as female, and labeled as such at birth, will develop along feminine lines.[3] Evolving from the sex of assignment, core gender is consolidated well before the phallic phase and the child's knowledge of the anatomical distinction between the sexes: the external genitals will later confirm and symbolize core gender identity, but only after the fact.

It seems that core gender identity is for the most part cognitively and socially constructed, deriving from nonconflictual learning experience, and that it is immutable by the third year of life.[4] Once established, core gender locates the "appropriate" object for imitation and identification, thereby leading to the development of gender role identity (masculinity or femininity), manifestations of which are observable to some extent by the end of the first year of life. These findings do not mean, however, that biological factors such as hormones play no role in the development of masculinity and femininity. For example, in boys, a high level of assertive aggressive play is seen cross culturally. This is also true in other mammalian species. The consensus of scientific opinion has it that this assertion/aggression may well be due to prenatal exposure to the male hormones known as androgens (Friedman and Downey 1995).

As behaviorally expressed, gender role identity refers to such culturally and institutionally determined attributes as predominant interests, mannerisms, and emotional responsiveness. In addition to

---

[3] Because gender and biology generally correspond, it had not always been clear that core gender identity is related more closely to sex of assignment than to any other single factor.

[4] For an exception to the general rule, see a study by Imperato-McGinley and associates (1979).

such outward manifestations of role, the feminine-masculine polarity also organizes the individual's self-image, the belief that "I am feminine," or "I am masculine," as measured against the cultural norm; consequently, gender role identity is an important aspect of self-identity. Although its roots are laid down in the first years of life, gender role identity is not a static self representation; it continues to develop and fluctuate well into adulthood. It is a dynamic (or functional) self representation, modified by sexual (qua sexual) development, conflict, and the self-evaluation of gender performance, which varies with the motivation and capacity to behave in accordance with the prescribed gender role at any given time (Ovesey and Person 1973; Person and Ovesey 1983).

There is a growing psychoanalytic consensus, then, that classical formulations failed to theorize the acquisition of core gender identity ("I am female/male") and gender role identity ("I am feminine/masculine") in accordance with the actual chronological facts of development. The child's relatively late discovery of the anatomical differences, although important, is no longer seen as determinative per se. It has been said that it "is the study of gender identity that has offered the most important correction to Freud's theory of feminine development" (Howell 1981, p. 16).

Gender role identity now appears to be more fundamental to personality development than sexual identity is. The beginnings of gender role identity are intertwined with the development of self-identity, and consequently gender role identity is integral to any well-articulated concept of self. In fact, self-identity and gender role identity appear to develop coterminously, to be inextricable from each other. In this sense, one can say that gender precedes sexuality in development and organizes sexuality, not the reverse (Person 1980).

Only by learning (in the unconscious sense) their gender and identifying with one or the other parent are children launched into the oedipal period. Freud's contention that the resolution of the Oedipus complex is crucial to the divergent development of gender is still considered valid. But, in fact, in his account he tacitly assumes that the child has already consolidated core gender identity and that the construction of gender role identity is well under way.

However, despite recent changes in our understanding of what constitutes femininity, psychoanalysts have not rejected those factors previously considered determinative for gender identity; they have simply reassessed them. Genital sensations, genital self-stimulation, the discovery of the sexual distinction, castration anxiety, penis envy, and the Oedipus complex are all still viewed as important factors, but it is now recognized that chronologically they do not come first, nor do they completely account either for the fact of gender divergence or for the *content* of either femininity or masculinity.

Moreover, other factors are now weighed in for their influence on the shape of gender.[5] Early object relations are different in the two sexes and appear to influence certain attributes of femininity and masculinity. Object relations are now considered to be operative in the preoedipal identifications and fantasies that emerge as soon as the child has differentiated self from object. Investigators from different disciplines have focused on those differences in infantile object relations implicit in the almost exclusive female monopoly of child care—the fact that girls are raised by the same-sex parent, boys by the opposite-sex parent. Stoller (1968), following a lead by Greenson, emphasizes the need for the boy, unlike the girl, to disidentify from the mother. Basing his conclusions on his work with male transsexuals, he suggests a normal state of proto-femininity for both sexes. Consequently, he assumes a greater fragility in the male sense of gender and a tendency to overcompensate by a kind of masculine protest. Feminist theorists, such as Nancy Chodorow (1978), also emphasize the male's defensive posture revealed in the male's hypertrophied sense of boundaries, but focus more on the vulnerabilities implicit in female individuation. Thus, Stoller and the feminists, both proponents of asymmetrical parenting as critical to the development of gender, come to opposite conclusions about its impact, with Stoller focusing on the fragility of male gender identity, and Chodorow on the impairment of female individuation and the sense of a separate self. Despite their

---

[5] I am focusing here on *psychological* factors; but one must be aware also of the influence of hormones, particularly at critical junctures in the life cycle.

disagreement as to the precise impact of the asymmetric preoedipal situation, most contemporary theorists recognize that this time frame presents different potential threats and conflicts (as well as strengths) to the two sexes. In sum, then, theorists posit learning, identification, asymmetric preoedipal situations, and still other factors—in addition to the genital difference—as the important building blocks of gender identity.

What, then, of the content of femininity in our culture, of its directives and prescriptions? Many commentators have noted the female tendency to communion as contrasted to the male tendency to autonomy, to connectedness over separation, to caregiving over instrumentality, and so forth. And they have assumed that the commitment to relationships—perhaps even specifically to motherhood—may ultimately organize femininity. Yet this formulation, too, seems oversimplistic; even if descriptively true, it does not adequately theorize the origins of these central commitments. Are the causal events to be located solely in discrepancies in object relations, as is so often assumed?[6] One must be especially cautious here, because the content of gender role identity is so culturally variable.

Naturally, the concept of "normalcy" or appropriate femininity colors how clinicians regard women and how women regard themselves. Our changing conceptualizations of the origins of gender (and the content of gender role) have had many implications for theories of normative femininity and major consequences for clinical work, particularly in two ways. First, our evaluation of many "feminine" characteristics has been upgraded; take, for example, Gilligan's (1982) work on the differences between men and women in the hierarchy of values informing their moral judgments—a difference that she refuses to reduce to any simplistic notion of better or worse, higher or lower. Second, the range of "acceptable" behavior for women has been enormously expanded. In a classic paper, Broverman and associates (1970) convincingly argued that mental health professionals restricted to Freud's theoretical formulations

---

[6]Of course, similar questions must be raised about the origins of the masculine commitment to agency, instrumentality, and so forth.

were in the unhappy position of reinforcing popular biases about women rather than challenging them, sanctioning dependency and passivity as normal female qualities and independence and assertiveness as normal male qualities. Accordingly, until recently, mental health professionals sometimes attributed any dissatisfaction women expressed concerning their traditional role to penis envy and psychopathology and naturally enough encouraged their women patients to cleave to paths tried and true.

With the current reformulations, "femininity" has been freed from its stereotypical description as necessarily passive, masochistic, dependent, and narcissistic in content. The content of femininity is now regarded as multidetermined, with major input from cultural prescriptions as well as early object relations. Given that the content of femininity is now seen as shaped by so many external sources, with that portion of it viewed as innate correspondingly reduced, there are no longer any compelling theoretical reasons for seeing any inherent restrictions on women's creativity and autonomy. Consequently, modern theory does not view female prospects (in life or in therapy) as intrinsically limited, as Freud's theory explicitly posited. Nor is femininity any longer viewed as a kind of deficient masculinity. Instead, femininity and masculinity are now seen as parallel constructs. And now, for the first time, we can scrutinize more dispassionately the creative and the constricting aspects of both feminine traits and masculine ones.[7]

Female Sexuality

Theories of female sexuality have been just as radically revised as those of gender. And here, too, as in the case of gender, these changes in theory have operated in tandem with changing social attitudes about sexuality. And these changes have had important practical results in women's lives.

---

[7]We are still only beginning to explore the special problems men face by virtue of those traits characteristic of masculine gender role identity.

Freud hypothesized that female sexuality, compared with male sexuality, must necessarily be weak or hyposexual, given the girl's need to switch both object (from mother to father) and organ (from clitoris to vagina), and her disparagement of her own genitals as compared with the boy's genitals. According to Freud, penis envy was decisive not only in the development of femininity but in normal sexual development too. Penis envy was responsible for the girl's turn away from her mother (renouncing the clitoris as inadequate and blaming the mother for her inadequate endowment) and toward her father (to get a penis from him). Such a double switch was believed to result necessarily in diminished libido, in essence, a weak sex drive. This theory appeared to be substantiated by the inability of so many women patients to achieve orgasm. But even in the early years of psychoanalysis, Clara Thompson (1950/1964) was able to identify a more pervasive problem for women in obtaining sexual gratification. She believed that a woman's major sexual dilemma was not caused by penis envy but by the selectively restrictive culture. Following Thompson's lead, more and more theoretical attention has been paid to the pervasive cultural prohibitions against female sexuality.

Simultaneously with the exposé of the cultural prejudices against female sexuality, theorists and researchers have reformulated their concepts in this area. The crucial role of clitoral eroticism in adult women, as demonstrated by Masters and Johnson (1966) and others, has led to a repudiation of Freud's theory of clitoral-vaginal transfer. Today, very few continue to hold to the view that true femininity depends on achieving vaginal orgasm. Nor is female sexuality any longer viewed as necessarily debilitated.

There is much more recognition that maximum sexual pleasure often depends on adequate clitoral stimulation and that such stimulation is not always (or even most often) an automatic outcome of heterosexual coitus. Together with significant changes in sexual attitudes and behavior, this knowledge has permitted more women to find sexual fulfillment than ever before, a major benefit of the scientific studies of sex.

In addition, sexuality has been freed from the constraints of a stereotypical 19th-century view of femininity, with its emphasis on female submissiveness to male preferences.[8] Female sexual inhibition was often based on intimidation by the male and deference to him. Inhibitions were manifested in a repertoire of related behaviors and attitudes such as the lack of insistence on adequate stimulation, the practice of faking orgasm, the assumption that the male orgasm terminated the sexual encounter, and the excessive attention paid to pleasing rather than being pleasured (Dinnerstein 1977; Person 1980). As it has turned out, many so-called frigid women have no major unconscious conflicts that inhibit either sexual arousal or orgasm. They suffer instead from ignorance about what constitutes appropriate stimulation (often matched by their lovers' ignorance of female sexuality) or from interpersonal intimidation. Apparent sexual inhibitions often begin to resolve themselves when these women achieve a sense of personal autonomy and, as a result, greater self-assertiveness. The result of such an achievement is not simply greater sexual pleasure for women, but a significant redefinition of the female-male bond.

Surprisingly enough, some psychiatrists persist in minimizing the benefits of the sexual revolution for women. They suggest that what we see are merely behavioral changes, while the underlying wishes and conflicts remain unchanged. Such an argument denies the importance of orgasm per se, its power to reaffirm the "incontrovertible truth" of the reality of personal existence (Lichtenstein 1961/1977; see also Eissler 1958; Person 1980). Liberated sexual behavior among women provides both sexual pleasure and a foundation for increased self-esteem. The potential released by changes in sexuality may thus result in a transformation transcending the sexual.

But what have we learned of the basic "nature" of female sexuality? Just as femininity was once viewed as the result of thwarted masculinity, so, too, was female sexuality seen as a kind of inhibited male sexuality. Insofar as female sexuality is now "liberated," we can better address the question of the degree to which unfettered female

---

[8] This submissiveness has been plausible only because of the female commitment to bonding, to relationship, and to identity construed as the self-in-relationship.

sexuality resembles male sexuality or, rather, obeys its own laws.

Feminists themselves are not in consensus about the answers. Some favor the presumably egalitarian view that the sexualities are essentially identical; others contend that they are necessarily disparate. According to Simone de Beauvoir (qtd. in Fuchs 1980, p. 311), there is more to eroticism than any mere collection of genital facts: "there will always be certain differences between man and woman; her eroticism, and therefore her sexual world, have a special form of their own and therefore cannot fail to engender a sensuality, a sensitivity, of a special nature. This means that her relations to her own body, to that of the male, to the child, will never be identical with those [of] the male." Fuchs suggests that Beauvoir was on the verge of making a necessary connection between woman's body and form and her eroticism, a task Fuchs sees as essential to a female erotic. This feminist position comes very close to the psychoanalytic focus on the importance of the body ego in psychological development.

In contrast, the egalitarian view finds support in the discovery by Masters and Johnson that female and male sexual response cycles are similar, even down to the timing of orgasmic contractions, and derives further plausibility from the evidence that androgen is the "libidinal" hormone in both sexes. This latter view is, however, only manifestly egalitarian. In truth, in this view, sexuality is seen as basically masculine; that is, male sexuality is believed to come closer to expressing human sexuality uncorrupted by cultural or psychological constraints.[9]

In fact, although there are some strong resemblances between the two sexualities, there are also major differences. Some of these differences are biological, but, as contemporary sex theorists know, sexuality is not so completely defined by biology as was once imagined. Although obviously having a biology and biological limits, sex, like gender, is subject to cultural and historical variability. As

---

[9]Such a view tends to obscure the fact that certain aspects of male sexuality, which long were believed to reflect a biological or instinctual imperative—just as masculinity was believed to be innate—are, in fact, actively shaped by society's prevailing definitions of masculinity. The assumption that the expression of sexuality—by either sex—is culture-free is naive.

Foucault (1978) has demonstrated, the individual's experience of sexuality has a historical component (over and beyond one's personal history). Some of the current changes in the theory and practice of sex permit us a closer look at the way gender shapes the expression of sexuality within the limits that biology imposes.

Viable theories of female and male sexualities must recognize and give proper weight to differences that appear to be the result of a biological imperative, but they must also acknowledge differences set into motion by gender identity and by the prescriptions of a particular culture. Overall, these differences are so great, at present, as to suggest that there are not only two separate sexual biologies but two separate sexual "cultures," as well. To some degree, females and males inhabit two separate sexual worlds. In this chapter I can only allude briefly to some of these differences and to the ways in which they appear to be shaped by both biology and the prescriptions of gender.

It is useful, in this regard, to distinguish among the various components of sexuality. The sexes differ in sexual behavior, eroticism, and primacy of sexuality. *Sexual behavior* refers to those formal characteristics that are observable, sometimes measurable, and relatively "objective." (It is in this area that one sees the greatest impress of biology.) *Eroticism* has to do with the realm of the subjective and psychological, of desire and excitement as experienced. According to Beauvoir, it is that dimension of human experience that has to do with the sexual, but in conjunction with a lived experience, not a collection of genital facts (Fuchs 1980). (And, of course, it is here that one sees the greatest impress from gender identity and cultural variability.) The *primacy of sexuality* refers to how central sexuality is to the personality, how closely related it is to identity. (And this appears to be heavily influenced by both biology and the psychological aspects of gender.)

Formal Aspects of Sexual Behavior

Certain formal similarities between men's and women's sexual response cycle and the orgasm have been demonstrated: these similarities have been most emphasized by Masters and Johnson (1966). Yet this is not the only dimension of sexual behavior. As Symons

(1979) puts it, "Men and women differ far less in their potential physiological and psychological responses during sexual activities per se than they do in how they negotiate sexual activities and in the kinds of sexual relationships and interactions they are motivated to seek" (p. 179).

Specifically, the sexes differ in what is commonly called *drive behavior*. Female sexuality, often considered less robust than that of the male, is sometimes designated hyposexual. This means that females are thought to display low "drive" or appetitive behavior compared with males or, in another frame of reference, that the male threshold for sexual release is lower. In recent years, however, it has been recognized that the trajectories of "drive" are different in the sexes, the male peak occurring in the teen years, the female in middle life. Females may end up with as much sexual interest or "drive" as males, or even more. But for many this is consolidated later and remains tied to relational preoccupations.

It is during the adolescent years, particularly in the induction into genital sexuality, that the most striking differences in "drive" behavior are manifested.[10] In males, adolescence is characterized by the beginning of overt sexual activity. The hormonal shifts of puberty cause bodily changes that focus attention on emerging sexuality and frequently result in spontaneous arousal and orgasm. The frequency of spontaneous ejaculation in adolescent males almost ensures the integration of genital sexuality into male psychosexual development and fantasy life. Thus, the male sex drive does seem tied to a biological imperative.

But the situation appears different for girls. Spontaneous orgasm is relatively rare in female adolescents. For them the most explicit manifestation of their developing sexuality is menstruation, and menstruation often tends to inhibit, not enhance, sexual exploration, both for symbolic reasons and because of the threat of pregnancy. Masturbation is not practiced by many adolescent girls prior to their introduction to interpersonal sexuality; whether this is be-

---

[10]Although genital activity may begin prior to adolescence, according to Kinsey, only one-fifth of males and one-tenth of females experience orgasm prior to age 12.

cause of cultural inhibitions or biological differences is not clear.[11] The study of female masturbation in future generations may help to clarify this issue, particularly the study of women who came of age after the advent of the women's movement.[12]

Low female drive is thought to be demonstrated by the relatively low rates of adolescent masturbation, the tendency for sexuality to be first awakened in the context of an interpersonal relationship and to remain tied to intimacy, the ability to tolerate inorgasmia, and the chronologically late achievement of first orgasm in many women. Further, female sexuality appears relatively fragile because it is so often variable or erratic, and because orgasm may be completely suppressed in such a wide variety of historical and personal circumstances. By these criteria, the female sex drive appears less a biological imperative than that of males, and more a learned dynamic grounded in psychological motivation.

However, drive behavior is not the only measure of sexuality.

---

[11]Typically, males achieve arousal and orgasm earlier. In males over 80% have masturbated to orgasm by age 15, whereas only 20% of females have done so (Kinsey's data, as reported by Gagnon and Simon [1973]). This discrepancy is still apparent in data collected 20 years later (Gagnon and Simon 1973). According to these data, the pattern of masturbation in females is less predictable than it is in males; in females only about two-thirds ever masturbate to orgasm, and, of those, half discover masturbation after having been introduced to orgasm in an interpersonal context.

There may be a trend in recent years toward more and earlier reporting of masturbation, but most studies reveal more males masturbating. Sorenson (1973) found that 58% of boys and 39% of girls of all ages had masturbated at least once and that boys masturbated more frequently. Arafat and Cotton (1979) concluded that "the percentages of both males and females who masturbate appear to approximate the figures given by Kinsey . . ." (p. 113). Hunt (1979) suggests that his figures approximate Kinsey's but that there may be a small overall increase. In contrast, the sexual difference in coital behavior (age and incidence) has tended to disappear.

[12]Ford and Beach (1951) claim that in all human societies that have been studied, "males are more likely than females to stimulate their own sexual organs" (p. 199). Further, in both lower mammals and primates there is relatively little female masturbation. Consequently, Ford and Beach support an "evolutionary," or biological, component. With the same data available, Gagnon and Simon (1973) formed a cultural interpretation. Psychological interpretations abound as well.

The capacity for responsiveness and orgasmic discharge, usually referred to as *consummatory behavior*, is greater in women: only women are capable of multiple orgasms, for example. Are we then to conclude that our scientific (and psychoanalytic) bias accords greater weight to drive than to consummatory behavior? It is otherwise difficult to understand how women's sexuality could be considered deficient, or hyposexual, relative to men's.

Hormonal Differences

Insofar as hormonal differences account for sexual differences, they are probably most influential in affecting the formal characteristics of sexuality. In humans, this conclusion is largely based on studies of patients with some characteristics of intersex conditions—for example, the follow-up of girls born with the andrenogenital syndrome (AGS). In girls with AGS, the adrenal cortex does not synthesize cortisol but releases too much androgen, which is the hormone believed to account for masculine sexuality. These girls are born with genital masculinization. Even when operated on at birth (surgically feminized), these girls are different from matched control subjects in quite specific ways: they display higher physical energy, prefer rough play, live as tomboys, and show low maternal rehearsals (doll play). In other words, there seems to be a hormonal component to some of the behaviors that constitute gender identity.

As regards the biologically influenced aspects of sexuality per se, the sexuality of late-treated AGS women is of interest. These women tend toward a sexuality more typically masculine than feminine in its formal characteristics: they have more erotic dreams resulting in orgasm than control females, they are more responsive to visual stimuli, and they display what investigators have portrayed as high sex drive (for a good summary statement, see Symons 1979). However, they do not view themselves as masculine in either gender or sexuality. Their erotic fantasy preoccupations correspond more to feminine than to masculine ones, and, in fact, they were disturbed by, and glad to be rid of, those manifestations of typically masculine sexuality that they themselves viewed as masculine—their clitoral hypersensitivity and tendency toward initiating eroticism (Money

1961). In their ultimate consolidation of gender identity, they adapt to "feminine" norms. According to Money (1965), "the imagery of the erotic thoughts and desires is all suitably feminine in keeping with the sex of rearing and the psychosexual identity" (p. 9). These studies seem to demonstrate considerable override of socialization on hormonal predisposition, at least as regards eroticism. But, in some of his later studies, John Money and his colleagues have suggested that there may be a hormonal influence in object choice (see, e.g., Money et al. 1984). This, too, is the tentative hypothesis of some people studying the mechanism of homosexual object choice.

Thus, while some of the studies on pseudohermaphroditic or intersexed patients establish the primacy of endocrines in shaping certain formal characteristics of sexuality (and of personality traits as well), they also establish the primacy of socialization (in its widest sense) in shaping the overall content and direction of gender identity and eroticism.

Eroticism

When we explore eroticism, particularly fantasy life, we have less rigorous information, but here we are more clearly in the realm of the psychological—the arena in which sexuality is most obviously influenced by gender and personal history.[13] Both sexes fantasize

---

[13] Part of the patterning in sexuality clearly comes from gender socialization and prescriptions of role. Women and men vary along gender lines in cognitive and perceptual styles, predominant defenses, and goals. According to Lewis (1971), women are field-dependent and more prone to feelings of shame (i.e., of not living up to internalized ideals) and to depression, whereas men are field-independent and more likely to transgress and to react with guilt. Women tend to hysterical defenses, men to obsessive and paranoid ones. Women are affiliative, men oriented to status and power. According to Bakan (1966), women are trained to communion, men to agency. These basic differences in thinking and adaptive modalities are reflected in typical sex fantasies and in the meanings that attach to sexual behavior.

Nonetheless, there are differences that may have a biological predisposition. The only major statistical analysis of fantasies was done by Kinsey and associates (1948, 1953). They discovered that not only the content but also the formal attributes of sexual fantasies vary with gender. So, for example, most males both fantasized during masturbation and had nocturnal sex dreams. By contrast, over

predominantly about their erotic preferences, be these heterosexual or homosexual, or sadomasochistic. Because male erotic preferences are more varied (e.g., perversions occur in more abundance and diversity among men), so too are their fantasies, and men appear to generate more sexual fantasies than do women.

Male erotic fantasies are usually explicitly sexual. They are often impersonal; autonomy, mastery, and physical prowess are central concerns. Many men's erotic fantasies portray domination. In one questionnaire study done by the Fantas Project at the Columbia Psychoanalytic Center, 44% of the male subjects reported domination fantasies (Person et al. 1989). However, male fantasies may also portray submissiveness or masochism. In fact, Freud (1924b) first described "feminine" masochism as it occurred in men. A common theme in male sexual fantasies is that of sex with two women; a lesbian scene is almost a prerequisite in heterosexual pornographic films. (For an object relations interpretation of this phenomenon, see Person 1986.)

Barclay (1973), in a study on the sexual fantasies of men and women at Michigan State University, noted that "male fantasies sounded like features of Playboy Magazine or pornographic books, and included elaborate descriptions of the imagined sexual partner. . . . They were stereotyped . . . without personal involvement. Women [in men's fantasies] are always seductive and forward, ready to have intercourse at any time . . . [with a] major emphasis on highly visual imagery" (p. 209).

Female erotic fantasies are not always explicitly sexual. Among women, affiliative and romantic fantasies, with or without any manifestly sexual content, are just as common as more obviously and explicitly sexual ones and are often evoked as sexual fantasies.

---

one-third of the females did not fantasize during masturbation; fantasy occurred more frequently in older females. Perhaps this correlates with the finding that females tend to fantasize about what actually has occurred, whereas males more frequently fantasize about unfulfilled desires. Although fewer women than men have sexual dreams accompanied by orgasm, more can reach orgasm by fantasy alone. Both sexes may use fantasy to control levels of excitement during intercourse.

Thus, many fantasies that do not on the surface appear to be sexual—for example, the not uncommon nurse fantasies (taking care of injured or debilitated men)—may be experienced as erotic. Pregnancy and breast-feeding fantasies are other examples. As noted by Barclay (1973), "Caring for someone was probably the most common of all themes. Our original hypothesis was that caring or nurturant fantasies were not sexual, but so many of our female subjects reported them with masturbatory activity or coupled with intercourse that we were compelled to accept them as having the same degree of sexual connotation as the more explicit sexual fantasies reported by men" (pp. 211–212).

Barclay (1973), in the aforementioned study, found that the women in the study, in contrast to the men, all reported "that the imaginary person in the sexual fantasy was a man whose face resembled someone they knew or were close to" (p. 210). But female sexual fantasies generally are more varied than is usually acknowledged. Femme fatale fantasies, for example, often reveal a wish to dominate.

Female fantasies are often thought to be masochistic. The database to which the label "feminine" masochism is attached has never been fully elucidated, but the term is used loosely to apply to the frequency of slave, prostitute, rape, beating, and humiliation fantasies elicited during analyses (Person 1974). However, in the data reported by Person et al. (1989), about 10% of both sexes reported masochistic erotic fantasies.

Not only are there differences between the sexes as regards conscious erotic fantasies. Unconscious fantasies reveal the impact of the specific female (or male) oedipal configuration. Women and men present manifestations of different unconscious desires and, thus, different conflicts, rivalries, and longings. These differences in unconscious fantasy are too well known to require further elaboration.

Overall, it is in the area of eroticism, in the content of the conscious and unconscious fantasies that elicit and accompany desire, that we see the greatest impact of gender identity on sexuality. This is particularly apparent in the male tendency to domination fantasies, a product of both gender socialization and the male developmental experience (Person 1986, 1995).

The influence of gender identity on eroticism has been demonstrated by pseudohermaphrodite studies, some of which have already been discussed. It has been observed that the few genetic males who are misdiagnosed and raised as females grow up dreaming the dreams of women; similarly, misdiagnosed women dream the dreams of men. Gender identity launches the individual onto a particular psychosexual pathway; it is decisive for the shape of the oedipal configuration, which is the crucial event in acculturation and provides the content for much of fantasy life (the specific wishes and fears, rivalries, and longings of unconscious life). Biology (genetic sex), as it turns out, is not necessarily determinative for core gender, gender identity, or certain aspects of sexuality.

It seems, then, that in the area of eroticism, the psychological development of gender identity overrides the biological component of gender identity and may have more to do with organizing sexuality than does biology (Person 1980; Person and Ovesey 1983). Only by learning their gender and primarily identifying with one or the other parent can children proceed into the oedipal period. To say that gender orders sexuality is not to detract from the autonomous qualities of sexuality (some of which are clearly biologically mandated) or from interactions between sexuality and gender. This formulation emphasizes that gender, itself the result of postnatal events, organizes object choice and sexual fantasies, which then become linked to the experience of genital pleasure.

Primacy of Sexuality

Another major distinction between the sexes is in the primacy of sexuality, the way in which sexuality is tied to perceptions of the self. The male more frequently views sexuality as self-enhancing and self-defining, whereas the female views it as affiliative and imbued with interpersonal meaning. This difference is reflected in the male appetite for pornography, the female one for Harlequin and Silhouette romances. The difference is not between domination and submission, but between the desire for control (for men) and for bonding (for women); between sex first experienced as an autonomous act and sex first experienced as interpersonally meaningful. This difference in the subjective significance of sex may help to explain the common observation that men generally are more promiscuous and display a greater interest in partner variation. Although this particular pattern is shifting, with more women adopting the so-called male pattern, the differential still exists. Certain authors have taken this difference as fundamental to the sexes; Symons (1979) goes so far as to claim that it reflects a genetic difference, and there surely may be a biological component. But it is also plausible to relate differences on the promiscuity-monogamy continuum to sexual meaning, and to investigate the developmental process by which sexuality comes to represent autonomy for males and attachment for females, without resorting to an exclusively biological explanation. Sexuality constitutes but one of the numerous forums in which the female gender prescription toward affiliation asserts itself; and the male interest in "variety" likewise seems to have some psychological roots (Person 1986).

A wealth of clinical evidence suggests that in this culture, genital sexual activity is a prominent feature in the maintenance of a sense of masculinity, while it is a variable one as regards femininity (Person 1980). Thus, an impotent man always feels that his masculinity, and not just his sexuality, is threatened. In men, gender role identity appears to "lean" on sexuality. It is almost impossible to locate a man who has never achieved orgasm, by any route whatsoever, who does not have significant psychopathology. In many males, the value accorded sexual performance is so great that performance anxiety is the leading cause of secondary impotence. However, for a woman, the issue of whether or not she is orgasmic—or sexually active—although extremely important, may have fewer implications for her personality organization. Put another way, there is a difference between men and women in the primacy they accord sexuality, at least in this culture. In men, one can say that active sexuality is a mainstay of gender and of self-worth. In women, gender identity and self-worth can more easily be consolidated by other means. This difference in the relationship between genital sexuality and gender may be the single most telling distinction between female and male sexuality and may be another manifestation of the masculine emphasis on performance and the female emphasis on bonding as confirmations of gender role identity.

Cultural dictates regarding femininity and masculinity can shape the expression or inhibition of sexuality, as exemplified by the suppression of female sexuality in Victorian culture. The ultimate consolidation of sexual identity (as distinct from gender role identity) rests on the attainment of an actualized sex life, characterized by both the assumption of a sociosexual role and the achievement of sexual gratification. Sexual identity generally incorporates a component of one's sociosexual role, assumed by the individual to indicate that she or he is following sexual expectations appropriate to the surrounding society or culture (or subculture). As culturally shaped and reinforced by gender identity, sexual identity is extremely significant, sometimes even taking priority over subjective desire when the two are in conflict.

The fact that in sex one is both the desiring subject and someone else's desired object makes the attainment of sexual identity necessarily complicated and elusive. And here the difference between the sexes is striking. Although being the loving subject and the desired object play a role in sexual identity for both sexes, one or the other facet is often more exaggerated, to the impoverishment of the other—the male more often overidentifying as subject, the female as object (Person 1985). Both males and females are diminished by these distortions, for extreme self-typing as subject or object leads to a marred or incomplete sexual identity. But for women in many historical periods, our own by no means excluded, the overemphasis on being a desired object, together with culturally selective restrictions, has affected sexual identity so much that the very ability to experience sexual pleasures has often been inhibited. This phenomenon of inhibited sexuality has in turn come to be perceived as peculiarly—and innately—feminine. The result is that an unfortunate misperception is even more unfortunately perpetuated.

Conceptual Limitations of a Gendered Psychology

Thus far I have described the ways in which the study of women as separate from men has profited us, both clinically and theoretically. We have seen that biological sex (the male/female polarity) does not invariably translate out into specific characteristics of gender role identity (the masculinity/femininity polarity). This is borne out by the fact that though there is always, in every culture, a dichotomy between what is considered masculine and what feminine, the *content* of what is masculine or feminine is culturally variable. Moreover, even within a given culture each individual will display a mixture of traits generally considered either masculine or feminine.

What is still needed, however, is a theory of gender that integrates object relations, the symbolic investment of the genitals, and sexual differences, along with the cultural perspective. We have made some progress. Though we do not yet have a coherent theory of gender, we have recognized the importance of factors as diverse as biological differences, learning, power relations, scripting, socialization, sex-discrepant expectations that shape fantasies, and cultural myths in the formation of gender role, in addition to what we have already learned from the standard psychoanalytic formulation about the importance of body awareness, sexual distinction, and the vagaries of the Oedipus complex.

But there are issues even more fundamental than how gender is formed and how its specific contents are shaped within a given culture. The fact that the dichotomy of gender is universal, though its contents are not, raises complex developmental and psychoanalytic questions that cannot be reduced to a simple cultural perspective. What is not truly understood is the habit of mind by which most cultures, perhaps all, acknowledge *two* genders. The question, then, is why only these two gender possibilities exist. Modern biology has broken down the components that together constitute "sexuality," and it is clear that a number of intersexes exist; essentially, however, we still regard sex as either male or female. Similarly, we come to identify ourselves as *either* and *only* masculine or feminine (though not always adequately so, as revealed, for example, in the statement "I think I'm not man enough"). Even though, in fact, traits associated with gender show different patterning in each individual, we still think in terms of masculine and feminine as somehow being opposites. Given that gender is profoundly related to, if not determined by, one's sex, perhaps the question should be not why there are only two genders, but why we are so insistent on choosing between them. It is the *rigidity* of the gender division that is most disquieting, the degree to which we are invested in making black-and-white distinctions as to gender, the insistence within any given culture on maintaining these distinctions (even though the *content* of gender role identity varies greatly from culture to culture). The problem of gender, then, is a question not only of two-ness but of either/or-ness.

Be that as it may, the two most important categories by which young children appear to self-identify are age and sex. Age is mutable (though the young hardly think so), but sex (except for transsexual persons) is not. Around the sexual difference we construct rules of fairly strict conformity to our culture's designation of what constitutes appropriate masculinity and femininity (the more so the younger we are). Seeing how sexually determined the range of narratives allowed to people in all cultures is—however much those narratives differ from culture to culture—we are all the more forcibly reminded of the rigidity of gender division. We seem to suffer a cognitive limitation that affords room for two categories only—same and different, male and female, masculine and feminine, either/or.

This dichotomy in the way we view ourselves (and the world) translates into an unfortunate judgmental tendency when we compare the different trajectories in the development of male and female. First one theory, then the other, wants to give the advantage—or disadvantage—to one sex or the other. (Hence, for Freud, the girl suffers because she must switch her libidinal object; for Stoller, the boy suffers because he must disidentify; and so on.) When this happens, too great a focus on gender can come to interfere with our sense of the essential unity of humankind. Our fundamental dilemmas are more alike than different. Each of us is bounded (trapped) by our own subjective experience, yet in need of congress with an other. We all suffer from conflicts, unfulfilled yearnings, embittered defeats, and we all share envy, jealousy, fear, and rage as part of our emotional heritage—along with our capacities for love, altruism, happiness, and sympathy. The battle of the sexes is often no more than a skirmish in a much larger struggle— the universalized love-hate relationship between the self and the other (of whatever age and gender). The problems of the separate self (and the need for relationship), of autonomy and communion, of the need for meaning, and of the threat of oblivion ultimately transcend the fact of gender. But gender becomes a scaffolding for self-identity and predisposes to specific adaptive strategies consonant with our "appropriate gender." When such strategies conflict with the fullest expression of our humanity—as they sometimes do—then we are diminished, not simply defined, by gender.

References

Arafat IS, Cotton WL: Masturbation practices of college males and females, in Human Autoerotic Practices. Edited by DeMartino MF. New York, Human Sciences Press, 1979, pp 104–115

Bakan D: The Duality of Human Existence: Isolation and Communion in Western Man. Boston, MA, Beacon Press, 1966

Baker S: Biological influences on human sex and gender, in Women: Sex and Sexuality. Edited by Stimpson CR, Person ES. Chicago, IL, University of Chicago Press, 1981, pp 175–191

Barclay AM: Sexual fantasies in men and women. Medical Aspects of Human Sexuality 7(5):205–216, 1973

Barry J: French Lovers: From Heloise and Abeland to Beauvoir and Sartre. New York, Arbor House, 1987

Beach FA: Cross-species comparisons and the human heritage, in Human Sexuality in Four Perspectives. Edited by Beach FA. Baltimore, MD, Johns Hopkins University Press, 1976, pp 296–316

Broverman IK, Broverman DM, Clarkson FE, et al: Sex-role stereotypes and clinical judgments of mental health. J Consult Clin Psychol 34:1–7, 1970

Chodorow N: The Reproduction of Mothering: Psychoanalysis and the Sociology of Gender. Berkeley, University of California Press, 1978

Dinnerstein D: The Mermaid and the Minotaur: Sexual Arrangements and Human Malaise. New York, Harper Colophon, 1977

Eissler K: Problems of identity. J Am Psychoanal Assoc 6:131–142, 1958

Ford CS, Beach FA: Patterns of Sexual Behavior. New York, Harper, 1951

Foucault M: The History of Sexuality, Vol 1: An Introduction. New York, Random House, 1978

Freud S: The dissolution of the Oedipus complex (1924a), in Standard Edition of the Complete Psychological Works of Sigmund Freud, Vol 19. Translated and edited by Strachey J. London, Hogarth Press, 1961, pp 173–179

Freud S: On the economic problem of masochism (1924b), in Standard Edition of the Complete Psychological Works of Sigmund Freud, Vol 19. Translated and edited by Strachey J. London, Hogarth Press, 1961, pp 155–170

Freud S: Some psychical consequences of the anatomical distinction between the sexes (1925), in Standard Edition of the Complete Psychological Works of Sigmund Freud, Vol 19. Translated and edited by Strachey J. London, Hogarth Press, 1961, pp 241–258

Freud S: Female sexuality (1931), in Standard Edition of the Complete Psychological Works of Sigmund Freud, Vol 21. Translated and edited by Strachey J. London, Hogarth Press, 1961, pp 223–243

Freud S: Femininity (1933), in Standard Edition of the Complete Psychological Works of Sigmund Freud, Vol 22. Translated and edited by Strachey J. London, Hogarth Press, 1961, pp 112–135

Friedman RC, Downey J: Biology and the Oedipus complex. Psychoanal Q 64:234–264, 1995

Fuchs JP: Female eroticism. The Second Sex: Feminist Studies 6:307–313, 1980

Gagnon JH, Simon W: Sexual Conduct: Social Sources of Human Sexuality. Chicago, IL, Aldine, 1973

Gilligan C: In a Different Voice: Psychological Theory and Women's Development. Cambridge, MA, Harvard University Press, 1982

Horney K: On the genesis of the castration complex in women. Int J Psychoanal 5:50–65, 1924

Horney K: The flight from womanhood: the masculinity-complex in women, as viewed by men and women. Int J Psychoanal 7:324–339, 1926

Horney K: The dread of women: observations on a specific difference in the dread felt by men and by women respectively for the opposite sex. Int J Psychoanal 13:348–360, 1932

Horney K: The denial of the vagina: a contribution to the problem of the genital anxieties specific to women. Int J Psychoanal 14:57–70, 1933

Howell E: Women: from Freud to the present, in Women and Mental Health. Edited by Howell E, Bayes M. New York, Basic Books, 1981, pp 3–25

Hunt M: Changes in masturbatory attitudes and behavior, in Human Autoerotic Practices. Edited by DeMartino MF. New York, Human Sciences Press, 1979, pp 231–248

Imperato-McGinley J, Peterson RE, Gauthier T, et al: Androgens and the evolution of male gender identity among male pseudohermaphrodites with 5a-reductase deficiency. N Engl J Med 300:1233–1237, 1979

Jones E: The early development of female sexuality. Int J Psychoanal 8:459–472, 1927

Jones E: The phallic phase. Int J Psychoanal 14:1–33, 1933

Jones E: Early female sexuality. Int J Psychoanal 16:263–275, 1935

Kinsey AC, Pomeroy WR, Martin CE: Sexual Behavior in the Human Male. Philadelphia, PA, WB Saunders, 1948

Kinsey AC, Pomeroy WR, Martin CE, et al: Sexual Behavior in the Human Female. Philadelphia, PA, WB Saunders, 1953

Lewis H: Shame and Guilt in Neurosis. New York, International Universities Press, 1971

Lichtenstein H: Identity and sexuality (1961), in The Dilemma of Human Identity. New York, Jason Aronson, 1977, pp 49–126

Masters WH, Johnson VE: Human Sexual Response. Boston, MA, Little, Brown, 1966

Mitchell J: Psychoanalysis and Feminism. New York, Pantheon Books, 1974

Money J: Sex hormones and other variables in human eroticism, in Sex and Internal Secrets, Vol 2. Edited by Young WC, Corner GW. Baltimore, MD, Williams & Wilkins, 1961, pp 1383–1400

Money J (ed): Sex Research: New Developments. New York, Holt, Rinehart & Winston, 1965

Money J, Hampson JG, Hampson JL: An examination of some basic sexual concepts: the evidence of human hermaphroditism. Bulletin of the Johns Hopkins Hospital 97:301–310, 1955a

Money J, Hampson JG, Hampson JL: Hermaphroditism: recommendations concerning assignment of sex, change of sex, and psychologic management. Bulletin of the Johns Hopkins Hospital 97:284–290, 1955b

Money J, Hampson JG, Hampson JL: Sexual incongruities and psychopathology: the evidence of human hermaphroditism. Bulletin of the Johns Hopkins Hospital 98:43–57, 1956

Money J, Schwartz M, Davis VG: Adult erotosexual status and fetal hormonal masculinization and de-masculinization: 46,XX congenital viralizing adrenal hyperplasia and 46,XY androgen-insensitive syndrome compared. Psychoneuroendocrinology 9:405–414, 1984

Ovesey L, Person ES: Gender identity and sexual psychopathology in men: a psychodynamic analysis of homosexual, transsexualism and transvestism. J Am Acad Psychoanal 1:53–72, 1973

Person ES: Some new observations on the origins of femininity, in Women and Analysis. Edited by Strouse J. New York, Grossman, 1974, pp 250–261

Person ES: Sexuality as the mainstay of identity: psychoanalytic perspectives, in Women: Sex and Sexuality. Edited by Stimpson CR, Person ES. Chicago, IL, University of Chicago Press, 1980, pp 36–61

Person ES: Female sexual identity: the impact of the adolescent experience, in Sexuality: New Perspectives. Edited by DeFries Z, Friedman RC, Corn R. Westport, CT, Greenwood Press, 1985, pp 71–88

Person ES: The omni-available woman and lesbian sex: two fantasy themes and their relationship to the male developmental experience, in The Psychology of Men: New Psychoanalytic Perspectives. Edited by Fogel G, Lane FM, Liebert RS. New York, Basic Books, 1986, pp 236–259

Person ES: By Force of Fantasy: How We Make Our Lives. New York, Basic Books, 1995

Person ES, Ovesey L: Psychoanalytic theories of gender identity. J Am Acad Psychoanal 11:203–227, 1983

Person ES, Terestman N, Myers W, et al: Gender differences in sexual behaviors and fantasies in a college population. J Sex Marital Ther 15:187–198, 1989

Sorenson RC: Adolescent Sexuality in Contemporary America. New York, World, 1973

Stoller RJ: Sex and Gender. New York, Science House, 1968

Symons D: The Evolution of Human Sexuality. New York, Oxford University Press, 1979

Thompson CM: Some effects of the derogatory attitude toward female sexuality (1950), in On Women. Edited by Green MR. New York, Mentor & Plume Books, 1964, pp 142–152

21

Vulnerability and Response to Trauma in Women: Developmental Issues

Carol C. Nadelson, M.D.

> None of us can help the things that Life has done to us . . .
> They're done before you realize it, and once they're done
> they make you do other things until at last everything
> comes between you and what you would like to be, and
> you've lost your true self forever.
>
> > A Long Day's Journey Into Night
> > *Eugene O'Neill*

Abuse and victimization, like all traumatic life events, can have long-term repercussions and test an individual's intrapsychic resources. In this chapter I focus on the experience of abuse, beginning with a brief theoretical conceptualization of the responses to traumatic life events. I relate this discussion to aspects of women's development and psychology to further elucidate some of the determinants of women's vulnerability and response.

A Historical View of Traumatic Events

Historically, psychoanalysts paid relatively little attention to the psychological impact of trauma or of "real" life events until the extensive investigations of "war neuroses" in the 1940s brought the impact of these experiences into focus (Grinker and Spiegel 1945; Kardiner and Spiegel 1941; Rado 1942). Before that time psychoanalytic theorists had focused more on a concept of neurotic anxiety that was intrapsychically constructed, and they had been less specifically concerned with the psychological impact of external trauma.[1]

In attempting to ascertain who is vulnerable to posttraumatic symptoms, Freud had stated that powerful external factors can arouse, in anyone, the weak and helpless child who is ordinarily hidden by the mask of conventional adult behavior (Freud 1920). To explain regression as a response to trauma, Furst (1967) proposed that stresses that involve a threat of bodily damage could reactivate early memories of physical danger that had previously been repressed and could evoke past feelings of helplessness or lack of control.

As interest in stress and trauma grew, other investigators expanded earlier concepts through their studies on the repercussions of illness and surgery on patients. One counterintuitive observation that proved important in galvanizing interest and expanding our psychodynamic understanding was that some patients expressed more concern about the disruption of their daily patterns of living than about their illnesses, disabilities, or deformities (Deutsch 1942; Sutherland and Orbach 1953). These reactions began to be understood as aspects of normal adaptation under fear-provoking circumstances rather than as evidence of pathological denial or symptoms of neurosis.

Work with disaster survivors presented evidence that symptomatic reactions to catastrophes are "not those of individuals with

---

[1] Freud (1920) had earlier suggested that there might be a difference in the impact of real trauma as opposed to fantasied trauma, when he observed that the dreams of those who had experienced early trauma were attempts at mastery of these events rather than wish fulfillments (Freud 1920).

weak egos," but, rather, that disaster may reawaken anxieties in most people, so that "all of us are susceptible to traumatic neurosis" (Titchener and Kapp 1976, p. 299). Researchers also found that therapeutic effectiveness was enhanced by helping victims link past and "previously worked-through childhood anxieties with the overwhelming anxieties aroused by the . . . disaster" (Titchener and Kapp 1976, p. 299).

Engel (1963), extending the discussion to consider the role of threat of loss or injury as well as the actual loss or injury, when he stated that a traumatic reaction could occur if an individual experienced 1) the loss or threat of loss of an object, body part, status, plan, ideal, way of life, and so forth; 2) injury or threat of injury with infliction of pain or mutilation that is actual or threatened; and 3) frustration of drives. Engel emphasized that actual experience was not necessary and that threat was sufficient to cause a traumatic response. This view has particular salience for abuse and victimization because threats alone are often perceived as traumatic and responses to them may be very similar to those that occur with actual trauma, especially if the threats are persistent and repetitive. Care providers working with hostages, detainees, battered women, and kidnap victims are cognizant of this factor. In these situations, an emotional bond, evolving out of the victim's fear and his or her dependency on the perpetrator for his or her life and even bodily functions, may be forged by persistent threat rather than by actual violence (Herman 1992). This bond also controls the expression of anger as well as other affects.

Attempts to understand the process of mastery of traumatic experience led to the elucidation of the defense mechanisms utilized. These included denial, symptom formation, repetition of aspects of the events, dissociation, and identification with the aggressor (Greenson 1949). Furst (1967) also noted that some mechanisms used by individuals that were protective against further exposure to trauma could be psychologically costly, leading to intensified reliance on more ego-alien or regressive defense mechanisms and resulting in loss of self-esteem. It is also possible that defense mechanisms such as projection or denial are incorporated into the developing ego structure.

Psychological Response to Trauma

Guilt, fear of retaliation, the reactivation of separation anxiety, and threats to narcissistic integrity are some of the psychological determinants of responses to abuse that also contribute to subsequent responses to trauma (Strain and Grossman 1975). Janis (1954) suggested that the guilt that is often seen after trauma might be related to the emergence of unacceptable unconscious aggressive impulses. The mobilization of these aggressive impulses could be related to the decrease in self-esteem that is often observed, because these impulses might be experienced as violations of superego expectations (Deutsch 1942; Grinker and Spiegel 1945; Strain and Grossman 1975).

The preservation or loss of self-esteem is an important component of a person's response to trauma. As we know, self-esteem evolves through a complex interweaving of intrapsychic, developmental processes and life events that are experienced as successes or failures. The judgment of success or failure is associated with internalized goals and standards of the individual's ego ideal (Glover 1941; Jacobson 1975; Schmideberg 1942). A positive or negative perception of one's ability to cope with a trauma may change the course of the resolution of that trauma, and it may also alter self-esteem and future capacity to respond to trauma. A successful response may enhance self-esteem, whereas an ineffective one may be damaging.

Some traumatic experiences are thought to evoke unacceptable fantasies and impulses, many of which involve sexuality and aggression. The presence of these fantasies may evoke shame and guilt, especially because a traumatic experience can threaten the ego's ability to distinguish reality from fantasy. Even the presence of these fantasies has been seen as potentially enhancing behavior on the part of a potential perpetrator to incite an action such as rape (Nadelson and Notman 1979). Deutsch (1944, 1945) believed that masochistic sexual fantasies reduce the guilt evoked by "forbidden" sexual pleasure because, in fantasy, the woman surrenders passively and is thus freed from being responsibile for her sexual wishes. The presence of unconscious rape fantasies does not imply that women will act in a way that will provoke rape, just as the presence of aggressive and murderous fantasies does not imply that persons will act out their aggression or be murderous. Rape fantasies do not depict the reality of the violence, humiliation, fear, helplessness, and powerlessness of the situation, nor is the rapist the object of the fantasy (Nadelson and Notman 1979).

The fact that abuse victims are so often blamed for provoking the abuse, or criticized for not responding in a way that is seen as more "appropriate" or "optimal," may be a factor contributing to damaged self-esteem and impaired capacity for future response, thus increasing future vulnerability (Nadelson and Notman 1979).

Janis (1958) suggested that threats that could not be influenced by the individual's own behavior were unconsciously perceived in the same way as were parental threats of punishment for "bad" behavior experienced in childhood. Such threats in childhood resulted in attempts to control anger and aggression to ensure that there was no further provocation that could justify punishment (Janis 1958). For some individuals, self-blame and low self-esteem may be understood as effects of past victimization more than as causes of subsequent victimization (Nadelson and Notman 1979).

Young children normally attenuate even their "ordinary" anxieties, such as fear of the dark or unfamiliar places, with optimistic fantasies about compensatory satisfaction and rewards in the future if they "behave." These fantasies serve as effective reassurances in threatening situations. Children who are abused use similar mechanisms, imagining loving relationships and future happiness. They may also dissociate or distort reality and come to believe that some of the events did not occur; that another person was the abuser, and not the person whom they had trusted who was actually perpetrating the abuse; or perhaps that the experiences were not so painful. An exacerbation of past anxiety symptoms and diminished use of fantasy have also been observed in many persons who have experienced major stress or trauma (Janis 1958).

When there is a history of early victimization, it is likely that the trauma itself, and the betrayal by parental figures or those in authority, might make the usual protective fantasies more rigid or less available, and might even inhibit aspects of the process of ego maturation that evolves through the use of fantasy in childhood. Such disruption in the process of ego maturation may result in the failure to integrate a cohesive self-image and can have profound implications for future development and vulnerability. These early traumatic experiences can also shape responses to later victimization experiences and may account, at least in part, for the clinical observation that survivors of childhood abuse are more likely to be victimized as adults (Herman 1992).

Hartman and Burgess (1986) described an "encapsulation process" in abuse victims. The offender requires silence, and the child complies out of fear. As a result, the child's psychic energy is depleted and maturation is disrupted. This process can have significant effects on superego development, on the child's sense of self, on his or her capacity for arousal and inhibition, and on his or her awareness of body state, sense of personal power, and self-comforting, self-preserving, and self-protective behaviors.

Children are also more likely than adults to blame themselves. Shengold (1989) described "mind fragmenting operations" used by abused children to preserve "the delusion of good parents" (p. 26). It has been suggested that "only the mental image of a good parent can help the child deal with the terrifying intensity of fear and rage which is the effect of the tormenting experiences" (Shengold 1979, p. 579, qtd. in Rieker and Carmen 1986, p. 365). This can lead to anger against the self or others throughout life. Several studies report profoundly self-destructive behaviors emerging after victimization (see Lystad 1986). Green (1978) concluded that "the abused child's sense of worthlessness, badness, and self-hatred as a consequence of parental assault, rejection, and scapegoating formed the nucleus for subsequent self-destructive behavior" (p. 581).

Girls in incestuous relationships with their fathers fear losing them if they do not comply or if they report. Mothers often deny that incest took place, or blame their daughters, and even reject them. Reporting can bring the mother's wrath and rejection and can precipitate the loss of the father. Thus, if the girl reports, she may lose her mother and her family as well, in which case she will again be victimized; she will find herself alone and abandoned, with no recourse and no control, and her worst fear will have been realized.

The preoedipal tie, with early closeness and caretaking, may also help to explain why so many fewer mothers than fathers are sexually abusive. A number of studies suggest that the close contact and bonding that occur during this life stage are a determinant of later incest avoidance and that disruption of this early relationship leads to an increase in incest (Erickson 1993). In one study, which looked at the antecedents of father-daughter incest, it was reported that fathers' involvement in the early socialization of their daughters constituted a major differentiating variable in predicting sexual abuse (Parker and Parker 1986). The authors reported that 36% of abusing fathers, as contrasted with 6% of nonabusing fathers, were not in the home at all during the first 3 years of their daughters' lives. Likewise, abusing fathers were less involved in nurturant activities with their daughters. Only about 5% of abusing fathers, but 37% of nonabusing fathers, were frequently involved in performing the nurturant tasks of child care. Nonbiological fathers constituted 46% of the abusers and 17% of the nonabusers. The authors suggested that it is not biological status as much as the nature of the relationship that is the risk factor for incest. Stepfathers were most often absent during the early years of their stepdaughters' lives. The authors hypothesized that the level of attachment that normally occurs with early sustained parent-child bonding is not reached with stepfathers or those who are not in the home. The female child under these conditions may be more likely to be a stimulus to sexual arousal.

Gender and the Developmental Aspects of Abuse

Women are more frequently the victims of trauma and abuse than are men, within their families as well as in the outside world. As I indicated above, they are frequently suspected of playing a role in "precipitating" these abuses. Their responses also appear to differ from men's responses to being abused. There are some data suggesting that abused men tend to identify with the aggressor and are more likely to later victimize others, whereas women are more likely to establish relationships with abusive men, in which they and their children are victimized (Carmen et al. 1984; Jaffe et al. 1986; van der Kolk 1989). Among the etiological factors in vulnerability to abuse may be differences in the meaning of relationships for men and women and the importance of relationships for the development and maintenance of self-esteem, as well as the differences we find between men and women in the perception and expression of aggression and dependency (Chodorow 1978; Gilligan 1982; Miller et al. 1981).

In attempting to enhance our understanding of these gender differences and their implications for women who have been abused, I briefly review some relevant psychoanalytically based hypotheses, acknowledging that it is only possible, in this chapter, to touch on a few of the many issues that have been addressed in the recent literature.

Before beginning, one caveat is necessary: that men and women are not polar opposites with very different traits. They are, in fact, more alike than different. Those gender differences in behavior that are reported are small and are primarily in the expression of aggression (Maccoby and Jacklin 1974).

There are, however, more subtle affective and attitudinal differences that are often specific to a particular historical period or cultural group, that may not be measurable by standard means but that influence our thinking and behavior. For example, our assumptions about the relational orientation of women as opposed to men are often discussed as if it were a "hard wired" trait. In reality, we draw inferences from clinical cohorts in particular contexts. Moreover, even those traits with a primarily biological etiology change over time and are influenced by their environment, even at subcellular levels. Thus, differences between men and women must be placed in perspective.

Gender Differences in Preoedipal Development

Gender role expectations are important variables that are often ignored. Men, for example, may have even more difficulty disclosing sexual abuse because of its potential to damage the "masculine" image that others have of them, as well as their own internalized self-image. For women, the more passive, helpless, and dependent image may be more intrapsychically and societally acceptable at this time in history.

Among the areas of psychoanalytic theory that contribute most to this discussion is the growing appreciation of the importance of gender differences in preoedipal development. This area of study includes gender identity, separation-individuation, and superego development. Some of the ideas and hypotheses that have been proposed have salience for our discussion.

Chodorow (1978) suggested that, contrary to classic psycho-analytic developmental theory, a woman's early and primary identification with her mother substantially influences her development in a way that makes her developmental experience different from the developmental experience of a man. Chodorow indicated that, for example, in the process of separation-individuation, girls do not experience the same pressure to separate as do boys. Girls can establish their feminine identity because of the close and already present tie to their primary identification figure, their mother.

In the process of identification, a mother perceives and relates to her infant daughter as a reflection of her own self-image, her internalized relationship with her own mother, and her identification with this daughter (Bernstein 1983). These early identifications and attachments are not experienced the same way for boys because both mother and son experience each other not as "same" but as "different," and the boy must separate from his mother and turn to a figure who is often not as available or present for his masculine identification (Chodorow 1978; Schafer 1968a, 1968b). Thus, in women, identity and self-definition can be said to evolve more through "connectedness" rather than "separateness," as opposed to the process in men (Nadelson 1989a). For women, the capacity for intimacy may accompany the process of identity formation and may thus occur in a developmental phase different from that in which Erikson proposed it to occur when he elaborated his developmental theory using the male as his generic developmental model (Gilligan 1979).

Relational Factors in Self-Esteem and Identity

The difference in developmental experience of women and men can lead to differences in the place of relationships in women's and men's lives. Women have been said to derive an important aspect of their early identity from their relationships with others, whereas men may derive their identity largely from seeing themselves as separate and autonomous (Peck 1986). Women continue to identify and to be identified in the world more through their relationships than do men. These relational ties are a major component of women's self-esteem. In fact, Person (1982) has suggested that women's fears of loss of love in relationships are founded, in part, on their closeness to and fear of abandonment by their mothers. Girls develop a heightened sensitivity to approval and disapproval, especially their mothers' approval and disapproval, and the threat of loss of love continues to be a source of anxiety to women throughout their lives. Because of this primacy of relational ties, women also may see themselves as more vulnerable to loss throughout their lives.

Relationships and Incest

Understanding the nature of the relationships in incest adds another dimension to our understanding of vulnerability. The significance of betrayal by someone who is emotionally close may have special implications for girls, who are more often incest victims because of their developmental relational orientation. When the perpetrator is a relative or friend, the fear of rejection or abandonment may be profound. The reluctance of many incest victims to disclose either the acts or the identity of their perpetrator may be related to these concerns. Many women who have had early histories of abuse may continue to fail to act in their own best interests because of their desire to preserve relationships, even if these relationships are abusive. For some women this can result in behavior that may continue to put them at risk for victimization. The threat of loss, then, may support behavior that has been interpreted as masochistic but that does not really fit a more contemporary interpretation of the concept of masochism.

"Masochism" and Vulnerability to Abuse: A Reconceptualization

One of the often-cited experiences that have been used to support a traditional understanding that "masochism" plays a role in vulnerability to sexual abuse is that victims sometimes report having experienced sexual arousal during abusive experiences. Arousal in this situation occurs infrequently and is not the immediate, or even a relevant, concern of most victims, who fear for their lives and whose primary concern is therefore survival; for many victims, however, having been aroused may, later, evoke feelings of shame or guilt. The occurrence of sexual excitation does not prove the point, unless one fails to understand the abuse experience and the nature of sexual response.

The use of the psychoanalytic construct "masochism," as it is traditionally applied, can be misleading because it fails to capture the complexity of the interaction between victim and victimizer in abusive situations. Person (1974), in her reconsideration of "feminine masochism," pointed out that contemporary theory would support the view that masochism in women derives more from adaptive, interpersonal, and social role factors than from intrinsic libidinal endowment, anatomical sexual distinctions, or the view of coitus as aggressive. This is not to say that masochism, as a "neurotic" problem related to unconscious pathology, does not exist.

Social Factors in Women's Expression of Aggression

Another aspect of women's psychology that has implications for our understanding of the behavior of victims of abuse is the significance of the internalization of societal ambivalence about aggression in women and the prohibition against its expression. Women internalize this restriction in expressing aggression based, to a considerable extent, on what is repeatedly reinforced as acceptable "feminine" behavior. Thus, many women have difficulty acknowledging and accepting their own aggressive or competitive feelings or responding actively to those who are hostile or attacking (Nadelson et al. 1982). If they do express aggression, not only are they threatened with possible loss of relationships, but the aggressive feelings themselves may be experienced as violations of an internalized concept of feminine identity, thus threatening their self-esteem.

This situation is further reinforced by the tendency, as I noted earlier in this chapter, for abuse victims to be blamed. They are considered provocative, insufficiently cautious, or in other ways responsible for abuse. The terrifying and traumatic nature of abuse may not be acknowledged, and the woman's worst fear may be realized—abandonment by the society as well as by her family or those close to her. This abandonment may be interpreted by a woman as resulting from her own actions, and she may come to feel that what she did was wrong. This may in part explain the observation that women who have been abused often do not express overt anger, at least initially, or else displace their anger onto others, including their caregivers (Notman and Nadelson 1976). Because the presence of anger or retaliatory feelings that are ego-alien may further diminish their self-esteem, abused women may feel prohibited from acting self-protectively, such as leaving a repetitively abusing living situation, or from even reporting abuse.

Factors Determining Response to Trauma

As traumatic life events, abuse and victimization call upon an individual's capacity for mastery in unique and specific ways. The nature, meaning, and timing of an event (whether it is expected or a surprise, whether it occurs as an isolated experience or is repetitive), past history of trauma and response, the threat to life or body integrity, the individual's perception of having control over the events, the relationship of the trauma to other life stresses, individual personality and situational factors (including life stage), and the environmental supports and resources that are available—all are important in understanding the individual experience of trauma (Nadelson and Notman 1979; Notman and Nadelson 1976). In addition, there is evidence that genetic factors play a role in the response to trauma (True et al. 1993). There is no accurate way to predict a given individual's response or to prepare for it, although those variables noted above are influences in future response.

Life Stage and Specific Situational Factors

Consideration of age, life stage, and specific situational factors can add another dimension to our understanding. When, for example, abuse occurs in a young woman, her evolving autonomy can be threatened, particularly if she is blamed for being careless or provocative. Being victimized can also imply to a woman that she may not be able to care for herself. It is difficult to walk the line between dependence and independence when there is external validation that one is indeed vulnerable. Families may respond with overprotectiveness, which may serve to further undermine the evolution of a sense of autonomy. It is not uncommon for parents to take over and want their daughter to come home to live or to seek a situation in which there is more protection (Notman and Nadelson 1976). Although this response is realistic when immediate safety is at issue, the potential developmental repercussions must also be appreciated. Young women struggling with conflicts around autonomy may react by capitulating and compromising their autonomy. On the other hand, they may rebel and become less cautious than is optimal.

The Consequences of Victimization

The aftermath of abuse, particularly if the abuse is repeated, is often a residual sense of helplessness and loss of autonomy that may intensify conflicts about dependency and stimulate self-criticism, shame, and guilt in many areas of life (Nadelson and Notman 1979; Notman and Nadelson 1976). Difficulty in handling anger and aggression, and persistent feelings of vulnerability, are also common repercussions.

"Learned helplessness," a phenomenon described primarily in women, appears to be a salient feature of vulnerability to abuse (Seligman 1975; Walker 1979). Learned helplessness is manifested by the adoption of a helpless, powerless stance in order to establish and maintain a relationship. Adopting such a stance requires that angry and aggressive affects be dealt with, usually by the defense mechanisms characteristic for that individual. For those women who are chronically traumatized, the price of a relationship may be the acceptance of this posture, because any insubordination could result in dire consequences. The perception of an inability to effect change or the perception that a situation will be made worse by taking action may keep individuals in abusive situations. Even the positive reaction of hostages toward their captors, the so-called Stockholm syndrome,[2] seems to be based on a combination of terror, dependence, and gratitude. This is similar to the picture seen in many other abusive situations. A variant of this phenomenon can be characterized as "learned hopefulness," whereby the person believes that he or she can effect positive change by trying to stay in an abusive situation, despite evidence to the contrary, because he or she denies, dissociates, or responds to omnipotent fantasies.

In her description of the impact of the traumatic experience, Herman (1992) notes that

> the survivor's intimate relationships are driven by the hunger for protection and care and are haunted by the fear of abandonment or exploitation. In a quest for rescue, she may seek out powerful authority figures who seem to offer the promise of a special care-taking relationship. By idealizing the person to whom she becomes attached, she attempts to keep at bay the constant fear of being either dominated or betrayed. (Herman 1992, p. 111)

Herman then points out that a pattern of intense, disappointing relationships can result. The survivor desperately longs for nurturance but has difficulty establishing safe boundaries. She is self-denigrating and overly attuned to the needs of others at her own expense, thus leading to the risk for repeated victimization.

Abuse victims generally do not view themselves as having control or choice. Their ability to dissociate intensifies the potential for danger in future situations because they may not consciously expe-

---

[2]The Stockholm syndrome has been described as when "a kidnapping or terrorist hostage identifies with and has sympathy for his or her captors on whom he or she is dependent for survival" (Edgerton and Campbell 1994, p. 128).

rience clues to danger (Herman 1992). Revictimization, then, is frequently an outcome (van der Kolk 1989).

There is evidence that people generally seek increased attachment in the face of external danger (van der Kolk 1989). The bond between batterer and battered spouse in abusive marriages resembles the bond between captors and hostages, or cult leaders and followers (Dutton and Painter 1981; Walker 1979). Walker (1979) described a concept of "traumatic bonding," suggesting that intermittent negative reinforcement—especially in the form of isolation or prohibition of contact with others, as often occurs in battering families—can consolidate the attachment between victim and victimizer. The victim dissociates emotionally during the abuse, even disbelieving that it is taking place, and remains "connected" to the abuser. A posttraumatic response follows and typically includes numbing and constriction of affect, which results in inactivity, depression, self-blame, and feelings of helplessness.

It is important to underscore that lifelong psychic scars follow abuse. There is a burgeoning literature connecting abuse with a number of psychiatric illnesses, including depression; borderline personality disorder; multiple personality disorder (dissociative identity disorder) and other dissociative disorders; anxiety disorders, including posttraumatic stress disorder and phobias; substance abuse, including alcoholism; sleep disorders; eating disorders; and sexual disorders (Chu and Dill 1990; Kluft 1985, 1990; Nadelson 1989b; Terr 1991; van der Kolk 1987; Winfield et al. 1990). Long-standing symptoms, in addition to diagnosed disorders, may include persistent suspiciousness, restriction in going out, fear of being alone, terror, anxiety, and depressive symptoms, as well as changed sexual attitudes (Nadelson et al. 1982). Whereas some have suggested that a history of previous "mental" disorder may increase vulnerability to abuse, others suggest that abuse, especially if it is repeated, is more likely to cause "mental" disorder (Stark and Flitcraft 1988).

The loss of a sense of self and the profound disturbances in identity formation seen in patients with multiple and borderline personality disorders are striking. That these disorders are more often diagnosed in women may relate to the greater incidence of early victimization of female children.

As I indicated earlier, studies also suggest that those who were abused in childhood are at risk for being abused later in their lives or for becoming abusers themselves (Herman 1992). This is especially likely to occur when the abuse started early and was long lasting, when the perpetrator had a close relationship with the victim, when the child perceived the sexual interaction as harmful, and when the abuse occurred within a family atmosphere that was experienced as cold and rejecting.

Many women grow up perpetually fearful, especially when threats of abandonment and rejection and abuse begin early in life. Among the long-term consequences that we see clinically, although not specifically categorized as psychiatric disorders, is inhibition of even appropriate risk-taking behavior and independent action. As I indicated earlier, in their subsequent relationships, patients with early abuse histories may continue to fear abandonment and, because of this, remain in abusive relationships, unable to risk leaving. An interesting recent report indicated that for many women posttraumatic symptoms increase over time (Frank et al. 1979). They often delay reporting abuse and seeking treatment, in part because they are more likely to have known their assailants and to fear abandonment and retribution. Because of these fears they may also take longer to specifically define and acknowledge the events that transpired as sexual assault.

Thus, from the intrapsychic perspective there are important developmental repercussions, some of which may not be manifested in specific syndromes but are nevertheless responsible for psychic pain, symptoms, and compromised functioning. For children and adolescents who have been victims of abuse, the picture of the adult world, as well as their own self-concept, changes. They are deceived by those they trusted and cared about, and they are helpless to understand and deal with these frightening and confusing experiences.

It may be difficult for many men who do not face the same risk or fear of sexual abuse to empathize with womens' lifelong concern about their vulnerability. The expectation in childhood and adolescence that one is vulnerable to abuse is internalized as part of the self concept. Many aspects of one's life are guided by fear and the necessity to be self-protective. Men have a different experience; they may expect that violence can occur, but they also expect to fight, and win. They do not expect that they are likely to be victimized, unless there is a specific reason, such as living in a dangerous neighborhood. The reinforcement of passivity in women related to societal prohibitions on the expression of aggression, as I suggested earlier, can intensify the sense of helplessness and lack of control. It is also paradoxical that women are, on the one hand, often seen as provoking assault and, on the other hand, admonished for being fearful and dependent.

Therapeutic Implications

Some of the responses and behaviors of those who are victimized evoke profound countertransference reactions in those professionals treating them. It may be difficult to work with battered and abused women, who often evoke frustration and anger because of their tendency to displace anger, as noted above, and their passivity, their failure to follow through on suggestions, and the frequency with which they return to the abusive situation. Some therapists overidentify with these patients and may also project their own feelings, fantasies, or experiences, which may include judgment about the appropriateness of the response. These countertransference problems can compromise the therapeutic relationship.

The mistrust and low self-esteem of many of these women also may make it difficult for them to establish trusting relationships, including with a therapist. Because of their early experiences of abandonment and betrayal, they expect deception and have no basis for trust. Thus, they may be slow to develop a therapeutic alliance and may repeatedly test the therapeutic relationship. Rejection on the part of the therapist because of his or her not believing that the abuse has taken place can be another revictimization. These patients are often unaware of the rage they harbor because they have repressed these feelings; they fear loss of control and defend against the damage to their self-esteem that would ensue if they were to acknowledge these "unacceptable" feelings.

Initial treatment approaches must support these patients' self-esteem and promote their regaining of a sense of control and mastery. From the short-term, acute perspective, a number of therapeutic approaches have been valuable. To understand the dynamics and formulate a treatment plan, however, it is important to attend to the many complex variables that have been described in this chapter. For example, group therapy has often been recommended, with the expectation that the shared experience can facilitate more successful resolution. For many women, particularly soon after abusive experiences, sharing with strangers can be overwhelming and impersonal and may violate their fragile sense of self, and such sharing may only be possible in time. For incest victims, sharing with "strangers" may feel like a betrayal, and they, too, may do better with individual therapy, especially in the immediate aftermath of the event or just after they have revealed what happened to them.

It has also been suggested that the conceptualization of oneself as a survivor rather than as a victim facilitates more successful coping (McCarthy 1986). When the individual experiences herself as a victim, she often experiences self-negation and guilt. Survivors, on the other hand, are seen as having a validated trauma (i.e., all agree the experience was traumatic) and as having succeeded in mastering it. The self-concept of victim as opposed to survivor represents passive rather than active modes of adaptation.

A long-term therapeutic approach must address self-esteem problems and long-standing deficits brought on by repeated abuse. For many abused women, who have difficulty experiencing a sense of self, this is a difficult task. Some authors have suggested that therapists have overemphasized the severity of the long-term problems because cases reported in the literature are drawn from a more disturbed patient population, and that many women do not evidence low self-esteem or self-blame and do not typically evidence severe symptoms (Walker 1983). For any treatment approach to be successful, however, there is a need for emphasis on attaining autonomy for the abused individual. Overemphasis on victimization can be countertherapeutic.

References

Bernstein D: The female superego: a different perspective. Int J Psychoanal 64:187–201, 1983

Carmen E, Rieker P, Mills T: Victims of violence and psychiatric illness. Am J Psychiatry 141:378–379, 1984

Chodorow N: The Reproduction of Mothering: Psychoanalysis and the Sociology of Gender. Berkeley, University of California Press, 1978

Chu JA, Dill DL: Dissociative symptoms in relation to childhood physical and sexual abuse. Am J Psychiatry 147:887–892, 1990

Deutsch H: Some psychoanalytic observations in surgery. Psychosom Med 4:105–115, 1942

Deutsch H: The Psychology of Women: A Psychoanalytic Interpretation, Vol 1. New York, Grune & Stratton, 1944

Deutsch H: The Psychology of Women: A Psychoanalytic Interpretation, Vol 2: Motherhood. New York, Grune & Stratton, 1945

Dutton D, Painter S: Traumatic bonding: the development of emotional attachments in battered women and other relationships of intermittent abuse. Victimology 6:139–155, 1981

Edgerton JE, Campbell RJ (eds): American Psychiatric Glossary, 7th Edition. Washington, DC, American Psychiatric Press, 1994

Engel G: Psychological Development in Health and Disease. Philadelphia, PA, WB Saunders, 1963

Erickson MT: Rethinking Oedipus: an evolutionary perspective of incest avoidance. Am J Psychiatry 150:411–416, 1993

Frank E, Turner SM, Duffy B: Depressive symptoms in rape victims. J Affect Disord 1:269–277, 1979

Freud S: Beyond the pleasure principle (1920), in Standard Edition of the Complete Psychological Works of Sigmund Freud, Vol 18. Translated and edited by Strachey J. London, Hogarth Press, 1955, pp 1–64

Furst SS: Psychic trauma: a survey, in Psychic Trauma. Edited by Furst S. New York, Basic Books, 1967, pp 3–50

Gilligan C: Woman's place in man's life cycle. Harvard Education Review 49:431–446, 1979

Gilligan C: In a Different Voice: Psychological Theory and Women's Development. Cambridge, MA, Harvard University Press, 1982

Glover E: Notes on the psychological effects of war conditions on the civilian population. Int J Psychoanal 22:132–146, 1941

Green AH: Self-destructive behavior in battered children. Am J Psychiatry 135:579–582, 1978

Greenson R: The psychology of apathy. Psychoanal Q 18:290–303, 1949

Grinker R, Spiegel J: Men Under Stress. Philadelphia, PA, The Blakiston Company, 1945

Hartman CR, Burgess AW: Child sexual abuse: generic roots of the victim experience. Journal of Psychotherapy and the Family 2(2):77–87, 1986

Herman JL: Trauma and Recovery. New York, Basic Books, 1992

Jacobson E: The regulation of self-esteem, in Depression and Human Existence. Edited by Anthony EJBT. Boston, MA, Little, Brown, 1975

Jaffe P, Wolfe D, Wilson S, et al: Family violence and child adjustment: a comparative analysis of girls' and boys' behavioral symptoms. Am J Psychiatry 143:74–77, 1986

Janis IL: Problems of theory in the analysis of stress behavior. Journal of Social Issues 10:12–25, 1954

Janis IL: Psychological Stress. New York, Wiley, 1958

Kardiner A, Spiegel H: War Stress and Neurotic Illness. New York, P B Hocher, 1941

Kluft RP (ed): Childhood Antecedents of Multiple Personality. Washington, DC, American Psychiatric Press, 1985

Kluft RP: Incest-Related Syndromes of Adult Psychopathology. Washington, DC, American Psychiatric Press, 1990

Lystad M (ed): Violence in the Home: Interdisciplinary Perspectives. New York, Brunner/Mazel, 1986

Maccoby E, Jacklin C: The Psychology of Sex Differences. Stanford, CA, Stanford University Press, 1974

McCarthy B: A cognitive behavioral approach to understanding and treating sexual trauma. J Sex Marital Ther 12:322–329, 1986

Miller JB, Nadelson CC, Notman MT, et al: Aggression in women: a reexamination, in Changing Concepts in Psychoanalysis. Edited by Klebanow S. New York, Gardner Press, 1981, pp 157–167

Nadelson CC: Issues in the analysis of single women in their thirties and forties, in The Middle Years. Edited by Liebert R, Oldham J. New Haven, CT, Yale University Press, 1989a, pp 105–122

Nadelson CC: Sexual abuse, in The Free Woman: Women's Health in the 1990s. Edited by Hall E, van Everaerd W. Carnforth, UK, Parthenon Publishing Group, 1989b, pp 710–725

Nadelson CC, Notman MT: Psychoanalytic considerations of the response to rape. International Review of Psycho-Analysis 6:97–103, 1979

Nadelson CC, Notman MT, Miller JB, et al: Aggression in women: conceptual issues and clinical implications, in The Woman Patient, Vol 3: Aggression, Adaptations, and Psychotherapy. Edited by Notman MT, Nadelson CC. New York, Plenum, 1982, pp 17–28

Notman MT, Nadelson CC: The rape victim: psychodynamic considerations. Am J Psychiatry 133:408–413, 1976

Parker H, Parker S: Father-daughter sexual abuse: an emerging perspective. Am J Orthopsychiatry 56:531–549, 1986

Peck T: Women's self-definition in adulthood: from a different model. Psychology of Women Quarterly 10:274–284, 1986

Person ES: Some new observations on the origins of femininity, in Women & Analysis: Dialogues on Psychoanalytic Views of Femininity. Edited by Strouse J. New York, Viking Press, 1974, pp 289–302

Person E: Women working: fears of failure, deviance and success. J Am Acad Psychoanal 10:193–204, 1982

Rado S: Pathodynamics—treatment of traumatic war neurosis (traumatophobia). Psychosom Med 4:362–369, 1942

Rieker PP, Carmen E: The victim-to-patient process: the disconfirmation and transformation of abuse. Am J Orthopsychiatry 56:360–370, 1986

Schafer R: Aspects of Internalization. New York, International Universities Press, 1968a

Schafer R: On the theoretical and technical conceptualization of activity and passivity. Psychoanal Q 37:173–198, 1968b

Schmideberg M: Some observations on individual reactions to air raids. Int J Psychoanal 23:146–176, 1942

Seligman M: Helplessness. San Francisco, CA, WH Freeman, 1975

Shengold LL: Child abuse and deprivation: soul murder. J Am Psychoanal Assoc 27:533–559, 1979

Shengold L: Soul Murder. New Haven, CT, Yale University Press, 1989

Stark E, Flitcraft A: Personal power and institutional victimization: treating the dual trauma of woman battering, in Post-traumatic Therapy and Victims of Violence. Edited by Ochberg FM. New York, Brunner/Mazel, 1988, pp 115–151

Strain J, Grossman S: Psychological Care of the Medically Ill: A Primer in Liaison Psychiatry. New York, Appleton-Century-Crofts, 1975

Sutherland A, Orbach C: Psychological impact of cancer and cancer surgery: depressive reactions associated with surgery for cancer. Cancer 6:958–962, 1953

Terr LC: Childhood traumas: an outline and overview. Am J Psychiatry 148:10–20, 1991

Titchener JL, Kapp FT: Family and character change at Buffalo Creek. Am J Psychiatry 133:295–299, 1976

True WR, Rice J, Eisen S, et al: A twin study of genetic and environmental contributions to liability for posttraumatic stress symptoms. Arch Gen Psychiatry 50:257–264, 1993

van der Kolk BA: Psychological Trauma. Washington, DC, American Psychiatric Press, 1987

van der Kolk BA: The compulsion to repeat the trauma: re-enactment, revictimization, and masochism. Psychiatr Clin North Am 12:389–411, 1989

Walker L: The Battered Woman. New York, Harper & Row, 1979

Walker L: The battered woman syndrome study, in The Dark Side of Families. Edited by Finkelhor D, Gelles G, Hotaling G, et al. Beverly Hills, CA, Sage, 1983, pp 31–49

Winfield I, George L, Swartz M, et al: Sexual assault and psychiatric disorders among a community sample of women. Am J Psychiatry 147:335–341, 1990

Index

Abend, S. M., 286, 295
Abraham, Karl
  aggression and hostility in depression, 303–304
  character concept, 243
  depression as oral issue, 302–303
  mania theories, 312
  object relations contributions, 93–94
  pathological disappointment in love and depression, 303
  as pioneer, 8
  preambivalent and ambivalent phases of the oral stage, 94
  schizophrenia and hysteria distinction, 325–326
Abuse and victimization. *See also* Posttraumatic stress disorder
  aggression expression and, 679–680
  blaming the victim, 673, 680
  children and, 673–675
  consequences of, 669, 681–685
  differences between men's and women's responses to, 675–681
  encapsulation process in abuse victims, 674
  factors determining response to, 680
  gender and developmental aspects, 675–681
  group therapy and, 478
  historical view of traumatic events, 670–671
  incest, 674–675, 678, 686
  initial treatment approaches, 686
  learned helplessness, 681–682
  learned hopefulness, 682
  life stage and, 681
  long-term therapy, 686
  "masochism" and vulnerability to, 679
  preoedipal development and, 676–677
  psychological response to trauma, 672–675
  self-concept of survivor rather than victim, 686
  self-esteem and identity and, 672, 673, 676, 678, 685
  sexual disorders and, 376
  situational factors, 681
  Stockholm syndrome, 682
  therapeutic implications, 685–686
  traumatic bonding, 683
  victims' view of not having control or choice, 682–683
  vulnerability and response of women to, 669–686
  women as more frequent victims, 675
Ackerman, N. W.
  couples therapy combined with psychoanalysis, 494
ACTH. *See* Adrenocorticotropic hormone
Action disorders, psychosomatic disorders and, 399

691

Cohesion
  self psychology concept, 143
Colby, K. M.
  free association study, 592
  intervention study, 593–594
Coltart, Nina, 111
Columbia Psychoanalytic Center
  Fantas Project, 658
  second-generation research,
    540–545, 549–550
Combination therapy
  couples or family therapy and
    psychoanalysis, 493–495
  early recommendations for,
    485
  group therapy and psycho-
    analysis, 496–497
  pharmacotherapy and psycho-
    analysis, 486–493
Compromise formation, 176–187
Compulsive character, 252–253,
  259, 263
Condensation
  dreams and, 26
Conscious thought
  topographical theory compo-
    nent, 4, 27
"Contributions to the
    Metapsychology of Psychotic
    Identifications" (Jacobson), 277
Conversion neurosis
  case examples, 222–223
  coexistence with other psycho-
    logical symptoms, 221–222
Cooper, A. M.
  use of medication for patients
    in psychoanalysis, 486–
    487, 488
Copernicus, 9–10
Core gender identity, 359, 361, 645

Coriat, I. H.
  early statistical research, 533–
    534
Corrective emotional experience,
  439–440
Corticolimbic system, 616–618
Countertransference
  Anna O. case, 14–15, 17–18
  countertransference enact-
    ment, 439
  definition, 438
  forced termination of therapy
    and, 519
  psychoanalytic psychothera-
    pies, 474–476
"Count Thur" dream, 621–622
Couples therapy
  combined with psychoanalysis,
    493–495
Cramer, Bertrand, 117–118
Cyclic character, 259

Dahl, H., 564
Darwin, Charles, 9–10, 57
Day residue, 24, 445–446
Death
  role of in psychic life, 47–48
de Beauvoir, Simone
  female sexuality, 652, 653
Defense component of psychic
  conflict, 175
Defense mechanisms
  borderline patients and, 293–
    294
  childhood abuse and, 673–674
  disavowal, 273
  Freud's concept, 271–272, 273,
    293
  Kris Study Group conclusions,
    293–294

Neuroses (*continued*)
depressive neurosis, 223–228
early investigations into hysteria, 190–194
Freud's contrasting pairs of,
398
Freud's observations, 189–190
more serious psychological disturbances and, 199–200
obsessional neurosis, 213–221
phobic neurosis, 207–213
psychological understanding
of, 195–201
reasons people seek treatment,
200–201
variation of, 228
"war neuroses," 670
Newman, Kenneth, 98
New York Psychoanalytic Institute
second-generation studies, 545–
547, 549–550
Normand, W. C.
pharmacotherapy combined
with psychoanalysis, 487–
488, 489, 490
Novick, J.
termination of therapy, 511–512
Nunberg, Herman
character concept, 259–262

Obendorf, C. P.
couples therapy combined
with psychoanalysis, 493,
494
Object constancy
termination of therapy and,
504–505
Object libido, 44
Object love stage of libidinal
development, 323

Object relations
alexithymia and, 397
borderline patients and, 290
borderline personality disorder
and, 285
femininity and masculinity
and, 647–648
paranoia and, 333
Object relations theory
Abraham's contributions, 93–94
American School
British Schools comparison,
97–98, 112–113
focus of, 111–112
Hartmann's theories, 113–114
Jacobson's theories, 114–115
Kernberg's theories, 115–117
Mahler's theories, 115
object representation
development, 112–113
British Schools
American School comparison,
97–98, 112–113
Bion's theories, 103–106
Independent School, 106–111
Kleinian school of internal
objects, 98–103
nonmedical psychoanalysts,
97
persons with psychotic,
borderline, and other
primitive mental
disorders and, 97–98
shift in focus of
psychoanalysis, 96–97
definitions, 89–90
Freud's contributions, 90–93
Hungarian School, 94–96
internal world of objects presupposition, 90

Sexual disorders *(continued)*
  similarities of conflicts in men
      and women, 380
  small penis syndrome, 372–373
  vaginismus, 382
  in women, 363
  women's fears, 381–382
Sexuality. *See also* Female
      sexuality; Femininity;
      Masculinity; *Three Essays on
      the Theory of Sexuality*
  aims of sexual instinct, 30–31
  as basic concept, 4
  developmental view of, 31
  deviations as function of nor-
      mal life, 31–32
  early observational data, 16
  primacy of, 660–662
  self-typing as subject or object
      and, 662
Sexualization
  bisexual man example, 352–
      354, 357
  definition, 351
  dependency role, 355–357
  perversion and, 353–354
  transformation of rage and de-
      structiveness and, 354–355
Shengold, L. L.
  defense mechanisms of abused
      children, 674
Shevrin, H.
  rebus stimulus studies, 587–591
  subliminal perception study
      review, 585–586
Signal anxiety, 59–60
Silber, A.
  pharmacotherapy combined
      with psychoanalysis,
      489

Silverman, L. H.
  subliminal perception studies,
      586
Simon, W.
  gender identity, 641
Sleep
  sleep/dream studies, 588–589,
      623
Small penis syndrome, 372–373
Smith, Bruce, 98
Snarney, J.
  role of childhood development
      as predictive of adult ad-
      justment, 596, 597
Solomon, M.
  second-generation research, 543
"Some Character-Types Met With
      in Psychoanalytic Work"
      (Freud), 242
"Some Forms of Emotional
      Disturbance and Their
      Relation to Schizophrenia"
      (Deutsch), 275
Southern California
      Psychoanalytic Institute
  early statistical research, 536–537
"Splitting of the Ego in the
      Process of Defence" (Kohut),
      273
Spotnitz, H.
  group therapy combined with
      psychoanalysis, 496
Stein, A.
  group therapy combined with
      psychoanalysis, 496–497
Stern, A., 275–276
Stewart, Harold, 111
Stewart, W.
  penis envy, 373–374
Stierlin, Helm, 117